Renaissance War Studies

Renaissance War Studies

J.R. Hale

THE HAMBLEDON PRESS

Published by The Hambledon Press
35 Gloucester Avenue, London NW1 7AX

ISBN
0 907628 02 8 (cased)
0 907628 17 6 (paper)

History series Volume 11

© J. R. HALE 1983

British Library Cataloguing in Publication Data

Hale, John Rigby
   Renaissance war studies. – (History series; v. 11)
   1. Military art and science – History
   2. War – History
   I. Title
   355'. 02' 09   U27

Conditions of Sale – This book shall not without the written consent of the Publishers first given be lent, re-sold, hired out or otherwise disposed of by way of trade in any form of binding or cover other than that in which it is published.

Printed and bound in Great Britain by
Robert Hartnoll Ltd. Bodmin, Cornwall

CONTENTS

Acknowledgements vii
Preface ix

I. FORTIFICATIONS

1 The Early Development of the Bastion: an Italian Chronology *c.* 1450– *c.* 1534 — 1
2 The End of Florentine Liberty: the Fortezza da Basso — 31
3 Tudor Fortifications, 1485–1558 — 63
4 Francesco Tensini and the Fortification of Vicenza — 99
5 The First Fifty Years of a Venetian Magistracy: the *Provveditori alle Fortezze* — 159
6 To Fortify or Not to Fortify? Machiavelli's Contribution to a Renaissance Debate — 189
7 The Argument of Some Military Title Pages of the Renaissance — 211

II. TRAINING AND RECRUITMENT

8 The Military Education of the Officer Class in Early Modern Europe — 225
9 On A Tudor Parade Ground: the Captain's Handbook of Henry Barrett, 1562 — 247
10 Military Academies on the Venetian *Terraferma* in the Early Seventeenth Century — 285
11 Men and Weapons: the Fighting Potential of Sixteenth Century Venetian Galleys — 309

III. CONTEMPORARY REACTIONS TO WAR

12 Sixteenth-Century Explanations of War and Violence — 335
13 War and Public Opinion in Renaissance Italy — 359
14 Gunpowder and the Renaissance: an Essay in the History of Ideas — 389
15 The True Shakespearean Blank — 421
16 Printing and the Military Culture of Renaissance Venice — 429
17 Andrea Palladio, Polybius and Julius Caesar — 471
18 Incitement to Violence? English Divines on the Theme of War, 1578 to 1631 — 487

Index — 519

ACKNOWLEDGEMENTS

The articles collected here first appeared in the following places and are reprinted by the kind permission of the original publishers.

1   *Europe in the Late Middle Ages*, ed. J.R.Hale, J.R.L.Highfield and B.Smalley (Faber, London, 1965), 466-494.

2   *Florentine Studies: Politics and Society in Renaissance Florence*, ed. Nicolai Rubinstein (Faber, London, 1968), 501-532.

3   *History of the King's Works*, Vol. 4, ed. Howard Colvin (H.M.S.O., London, 1982), 367-401.

4   *Studi Veneziani*, X (1968), 231-289.

5   *Renaissance Studies in Honor of Hans Baron*, ed. Anthony Molho and John A. Tedeschi (Dekalb, Illinois, 1971), 501-529.

6   *Essays in Honour of John Humphreys Whitfield*, ed. H.C.Davis, J.M.Hatwell, D.G.Rees and G.W.Slowey (St. George's Press, London, for the Department of Italian, University of Birmingham, 1975), 99-119.

7   *Newberry Library Bulletin* VI, No. 4 (1964), 91-102.

8   *Cultural Aspects of the Italian Renaissance: Essays in Honour of Paul Oskar Kristeller*, ed. Cecil H. Clough (Manchester University Press, 1976), 440-461.

9   The Society for Renaissance Studies. Occasional Papers No. 5.

10 *Studi Veneziani*, XV (1973), 273-295.

11 *War and Society: a Yearbook of Military History*, ed. Brian Bond and Ian Roy (Croom Helm, London, 1975), 1-23.

12 World Copyright: The Past and Present Society, Corpus Christi College, Oxford, England. This article first appeared in *Past and Present: a journal of historical studies*, no. 51 (May 1971), 3-26.

13 *Italian Renaissance Studies*, ed. E.F.Jacob (Faber, London, 1960), 94-122.

14 *From the Renaissance to the Counter-Reformation: Essays in Honor of Garrett Mattingley*, ed. Charles H. Carter (Random House, New York, 1965), 113-144.

15   *Shakespeare Quarterly*, XIX, No. 1 (1968), 33-40.
16   *Medievalia et Humanistica*, New Series, 8 (1977), 21-62.
17   *Journal of the Warburg and Courtauld Institutes, XL (1977), 240-255.*
18   *Florilegium Historiale: Essays Presented to Wallace K. Ferguson*, ed. J.G.Rowe and W.H.Stockdale (University of Toronto, 1971), 369-399.

The illustrations of Chapter 3 are H.M.S.O. copyright and appeared originally in Vols. 3 and 4 of *History of the King's Works*, ed. Howard Colvin.

PREFACE

Like a Renaissance army, this book is recruited from many sources, and I must first thank those owners of copyright who make its array possible. I have omitted articles part of whose substance will appear in forthcoming books and the readily available chapters in the *New Cambridge Modern History*. It was, however, the writing of these which first opened my eyes to the fascination of tracing the ways in which war affected material, emotional and intellectual life in Renaissance Europe and I would like to record my gratitude to those bold editors, Professors G.R.Potter, G.R.Elton and R.B.Wernham, who guessed at the very enthusiasm they helped to create.

J.R.H.
University College
London

ARTICLES NOT INCLUDED IN THE PRESENT VOLUME

1. A Newberry Library Supplement to the Foreign Books in M.J.D.Cockle's *A Bibliography of ... Military Books up to 1642. Papers of the Bibliographical Society of America* (1961), 137-139.

2. War and Public Opinion in the Fifteenth and Sixteenth Centuries, *Past and Present* (1962), 18-35.

3. Violence in the late Middle Ages: a Background, in *Violence and Disorder in Italian Cities, 1200-1500*, ed. Lauro Martines (University of California, 1972), 19-37.

4. From Peacetime Establishment to Fighting Machine: the Venetian Army and the War of Cyprus and Lepanto, *Il Mediterraneo nella Seconda Metà del '500 alla Luce di Lepanto* (Florence, 1974), 163-184.

5. Renaissance Armies and Political Control: the Venetian Provveditorial System 1509-1529, *The Journal of Italian History (1979), 11-31*.

6   [Venetian] Terra Ferma Fortifications in the Cinquecento, *Florence and Venice: Comparisons and Relations*, vol. 2, ed. Sergio Bertelli, Nicolai Rubinstein and Craig Hugh Smyth (Florence, 1980), 169-187.

7   Industria del Libro e Cultura a Venezia nel Rinascimento, *Storia della Cultura Veneta: dal Primo Quattrocento al Concilio di Trento*, vol. 3, part 2 (Vicenza, 1980), 245-288. An expanded version of Chapter 16 in this volume.

8   Castiglione's Military Career, *Italian Studies*, (1981), 41-57.

9   *New Cambridge Modern History*, Vol. 1 (1957): International Relations in the West: Diplomacy and War 1493-1520; Vol. 2 (1958): Armies, Navies and the Art of War 1520-1559; Vol. 3 (1968): Armies, Navies and the Art of War 1559-1610.

FORTHCOMING BOOKS

Venice: the Military Organization of a Renaissance State (with M.R.Mallett)

War and Society in Renaissance Europe

1

THE EARLY DEVELOPMENT OF THE BASTION: AN ITALIAN CHRONOLOGY
c. 1450–c. 1534

The most significant of all architectural forms evolved during the Renaissance was the angle bastion. By resisting the new artillery and providing platforms for heavy guns it revolutionized the defensive-offensive pattern of warfare, and its speedy adoption by state after state during the sixteenth century dramatically affected the appearance of cities throughout Europe—and further afield: the application of the angle bastion to forts and town walls led to a homogeneity of style wherever Europeans settled overseas; from Havana and San Juan in the Caribbean to Mombasa and Mozambique in East Africa and on to Diu and Goa across the Indian Ocean, visitors saw the outlines that characterized townscapes from the Baltic to the north African coast. The international style *par excellence* of the Renaissance was that of military architecture, and its module was the angle bastion. It did not only extend in space, it endured in time. The next period of intensive development in the art of fortification, associated with the career of Vauban (1633–1707), elaborated and re-deployed the basic Renaissance forms, and on sites where attack from the heaviest forms of siege guns was not anticipated, fortifications continued to be built in the manner of the mid-sixteenth century. Neither the star forts built to guard the mouth of the Mississippi in the war of 1812 nor the walls of Fort McHenry as they appeared to the author of *The Star-Spangled Banner* would have appeared strange to

Antonio da San Gallo the younger, the Florentine architect who died in 1546.

Not surprisingly, there has been strong competition among architectural and military historians to establish what nation, or what individual, invented the most radically effective architectural element since the arch. This controversy, which was waged most strongly at the turn of the last century, has not yet provided a solution. It has been dogged by chauvinism and obscured by the unfamiliarity of its protagonists with monuments outside their own countries.[1] It has been diverted from methodical fieldwork by the romantic notion that a great breakthrough must be the work of a great man. It has been confirmed by vague terminology and a misunderstanding of the technical terms used by contemporary writers.[2] This essay does not offer a solution: that can only follow from a detailed comparative chronology of military architecture in France, Germany, Italy and the Iberian peninsula from the middle of the fifteenth to the middle of the sixteenth centuries.[3] There can be no doubt, however, that in the first generation of the sixteenth century it was the Italians who experimented most freely, and that it was they who, in the second generation, became the acknowledged leaders, and the most prolific exporters of the new bastioned fortification. A survey which charts the way in which they reached this position is, therefore, of special interest even if it cannot settle, absolutely, the question of precedence.

A glance at the historiography of the subject in Italy will show how necessary it is to take an extensive look at the

[1] Even the opposition of Viollet-le-Duc to the Italians' claims as innovators in the new fortification was not based on a knowledge of the relevant buildings. See his *Dictionnaire raisoné de l'architecture français du XIe au XVIe siècle* (1854–68), under *bastion* and *boulevard*. The same ignorance of fortifications south of the Alps led Cosseron de Villenoisy to claim in his *Essai historique sur la fortification* (Paris, 1869) that the systematized bastioned front was a development of the north, and of the second half of the sixteenth century. A. von Cohausen's assertion that 'der Ausgangspunkt der neueren Befestigungsweise Deutschland war' (*Die Befestigungsweisen der Vorzeit und des Mittelalters*, Wiesbaden, 1898, 331) led him to exaggerate the importance of certain sites (Menzberg, Neckarbischofsheim) in an attempt to combat Italian claims to priority.

[2] The word 'bastion' (*bastione*) first appears in Italian documents of the late fourteenth century and has been the source of much confusion. See P. Pieri in *Archivio Storico per le Provincie Napoletane* (1933), 154.

[3] The suggestion of Turkish precedence, raised from time to time since A. de Zastrow's *Histoire de la fortification permanente* (Paris, 1866, trans. E. de la Barre Duparcq) has been effectively rebutted by L. A. Maggiorotti, 'Le origini della fortificazione bastionata e la guerra d'Otranto', *Rivista d'Artiglieria e Genio* (1931), 93–110, and by Kevin Andrews, *Castles of the Morea* (Princeton, 1953), especially 231–2.

monuments themselves. Contemporary writers are not helpful. Machiavelli's scorn for Italian military prowess led him to ascribe innovations in the art of fortification to the example of the French invaders—though he does not mention bastions in this connexion—in a passage in the *Art of War* (1522) which was echoed almost verbatim in 1562 by the military amateur Girolamo Maggi.[1] The same contempt for his own countrymen led Guicciardini, in his *History of Italy* (written 1536–40) to make the easy conquests of the French the motive for changes in every aspect of warfare, including fortification, though he suggested that a glimpse of new methods was offered by the Turks when they dug themselves in after the Otranto raid of 1480. By the middle of the century writers were prepared to name the inventor of the angle bastion. To Gian Giacomo Leonardi (d. 1562) it was Alfonso I of Ferrara (1505–34),[2] to Vasari it was Michele Sanmicheli (d. 1558); 'before his time they were made of a circular form, by which the difficulty of defending them was much increased'.[3] All these statements can be proved wrong by buildings known to their authors.

Vasari's assertion was repeated in Scipione Maffei's influential *Verona Illustrata* (vol. 3, 1732) and was not seriously challenged until the publication in 1841 of an edition of Francesco di Giorgio's treatise on civil and military architecture.[4] In a series of appendices Carlo Promis made the first critical investigation into the origin of the new fortification. He dismissed the claims of the Turks to be innovators, he destroyed the legend that bastions had been invented in the Hussite wars and subsequently introduced into north Italy by Bohemian engineers; by pointing to works at Florence, Urbino, Bari, Pisa and the island of Rhodes he showed that Sanmicheli could not have been the inventor of the angle bastion, and he began the tradition which gave this distinction to Francesco di Giorgio, who died in 1502. This thesis was taken up and discussed in a brisk but inconclusive manner in technical military journals in France, Germany and Italy, but it was not until 1880 that there

---

[1] Machiavelli, *Arte della Guerra*, ed. Sergio Bertelli (Milan, 1961), 498–9; Maggi, *De gli ingegni militare*, MS. Biblioteca Nazionale Fiorentina (subsequently referred to as B.N.F.), Palat. 464, 326.
[2] *Trattato delle fortification di nostri tempi*, MS. in Oliveriana Library, Pesaro, no. 220, quoted by L. Serra, 'Architettura militare del Rinascimento nelle Marche', *Rassegna Marchigiana* (1933), 455.
[3] *Vite*, ed. G. Milanesi, 9 vols., (Florence, 1878–85) vi, 353.
[4] *Trattato di architettura civile e militari*, ed. Cesare Saluzzo (Turin, 1841).

was a serious attempt to tackle the subject afresh. In that year, the Dominican father Alberto Guglielmotti produced a history of late fifteenth and sixteenth-century fortification in the present province of Lazio.[1] The first attempt to apply scientific archaeological standards to military works of the Renaissance, his studies of the structure and building history of such forts as the *rocca* at Ostia Antica, Castel S Angelo, and the forts at Civitacastellana, Nettuno and Civitavecchia are still of value, but in a preliminary discussion he made Tàccola (Mariano di Jacopo, d.1458) the inventor of the angle bastion, and used a medal of Pope Calixtus III (1455–8) to show that it was already thought of as an element in a symmetrical-bastioned front. These early dates were greeted with incredulity: the medal was pronounced a forgery, and it was shown that what he had taken to be bastions in the Marciana (Venice) MS. were the attempts of Tàccola to represent juts in the sea-coast on which he drew his quite conventional forts.[2] Since then the claims of other artists and architectural theorists to be the crucial innovators have been put forward, among them Brunelleschi,[3] Filarete, Leonardo da Vinci, Fra Giocondo and Michelangelo. None is convincing, because none has been discussed against the background of the fortifications already in existence when each claimant expressed his ideas.[4] The art historian has not been tempted to do fieldwork, and the architectural historian has not helped him by attempting a study which would perforce include many buildings which cannot be attributed to a great name.[5] These claims are looked at in the chronological study which forms the centre of this essay.

It would be disingenuous not to point out the limitations on the accuracy of such a survey, quite apart from my own errors

---

[1] *Storia delle fortificazioni nella Spiaggia Romana* (Rome, 1880).

[2] General Schröder, 'Martini e la fronte bastionata', *Archiv für die Artillerie-und-Ingenieur-Offiziere des deutschen Reichsheeres* (August and September, 1891) and E. Rocchi, *Le origini della fortificazione moderna* (Rome, 1894), 3–4, 17–45.

[3] For literature, see below. I do not discuss the claims of Brunelleschi, the latest contender, as the case urged by Piero Sanpaolesi [*Brunelleschi* (Milan, 1962), 100] is based on one section of the wall of Pisa, the building history of which is not entirely clear.

[4] Ignazio Calvi makes such an attempt in the introductory chapter to his *L'architettura militare di Leonardo da Vinci* (Milan, 1943) but it is neither full nor accurate enough to be convincing.

[5] The last attempt to write a general account of gunpowder fortifications was E. Rocchi, *Le fonti storiche dell'architettura militare* (Rome, 1908). In spite of confused arrangement, and a grave shortage of references, it remains the best introduction to the subject.

of judgment and knowledge. Many forts and town walls of the transition period (*c.* 1450–*c.* 1530) have been destroyed or altered beyond recognition. Fortifications were often built over a period of years and though the ground plan may still reflect the ideas of their planners, important details, especially gunports, parapets and platforms may represent an important divergence from them; such details are, besides, vulnerable to decay and later modification. Details of many forts, especially the angle where the flank of a bastion joins the curtain, are choked with vegetation and cannot be properly seen. Gun chambers and internal passages are frequently blocked by internal collapse, refuse or rebuilding. Among vanished monuments are field fortifications of earth, a medium in which experiment could be especially free. Documentary evidence for the fifteenth century is extremely sparse. Drawings become more copious as the sixteenth century advances, partly because of an increased emphasis on the accurate relationship of the various components of a fort or town wall, partly because of the growing prestige of military architects and the interest in their plans as works of art. Even by the middle of the sixteenth century, however, it is seldom easy to say (where the monument does not exist) whether a plan represents the building itself or a project for it. Very few plans are dated. Models were constantly used, but in contrast with the many models of secular buildings which remain from this period, I know of none of a fort. This may be due to the hazards of travelling to and fro between the architect, the agency responsible for the commission and the masons on the site, it may be due to a lack of interest in military architecture among later collectors, or it may be the result of a desire for secrecy, a reason, possibly, for the destruction of plans as well. Written descriptions are rare. Usually a government record will say 'as in the plan', or 'according to the model' or 'as the architect himself will explain'. This possibly reflects the lack among officials of a technical vocabulary adequate to describe increasingly complex works.

Non-technical drawings, paintings and engravings are all suspect. Artists thought of forts in terms of symbols—like a city in the hand of a patron saint, or the generalized town view in a chronicle chapter heading—and there was a considerable time-lag before a new style of building was generalized into a new type of symbol. Medals were struck to commemorate the building of an important work, but, as with plans, they can be used only with great caution. They may be accurate but represent a plan subsequently changed. They may be symbolic rather than descriptive.[1] These hazards, and the shortage of detailed monographs on individual buildings must blur our vision. Such lacunae led an early student of the subject to give up the search for the origin of the bastion in despair.[2]

Radical changes in fortification only take place when there is a radical change in offensive weapons. It was long thought that the amazement expressed by such writers as Guicciardini and the explosives expert and gun-founder Vanuccio Biringuccio[3] at the superior weapons of the French meant that changes in military architecture must be looked for, first and foremost, in France. It has been shown, however, that, granted the general superiority of French artillery, especially field artillery, Italian siege guns developed steadily from their first recorded employment in the thirteenth century, and that with the increasing use of iron balls in the fifteenth their power was amply sufficient to stimulate innovations in defence. In Italy, moreover, conditions were especially favourable to experiment. The peninsula was divided into many independent and mutually hostile territories. There were many frontiers to defend; recent conquests needed the manacle of a fort, insecure princes needed citadels in which they would be safe from a revolt of their own people. Enterprise was not fettered by a uniform system of licences for castle building. Even after the Peace of Lodi in 1454 there were enough pin-prick wars, especially in central Italy, in the Romagna, the Marche and the heartlands of the papal states, to necessitate a constant vigilance; overseas, and not far overseas, was the growing menace of the Turks. Nowhere else in Europe, moreover, was

[1] On the custom of placing special medals under the foundation stones of fortresses in this period, see R. Weiss, *Un umanista veneziano, Papa Paolo II* (Venice, 1958), chap. 4. Good examples of misleading medals are the two struck to celebrate the connection of Sixtus IV and of Giuliano della Rovere (later Pope Julius II) with the fortress of Ostia. In both instances the fort is made to look more traditional than it was. P. Verdier, 'La Rocca d'Ostia dans l'architecture militaire du Quattrocento'. *Mélanges d'archéologie et d'histoire* (1939), 303. They are reproduced in R. Weiss, *The Medals of Sixtus IV* (Rome, 1961), figs. 37–9.

[2] Luigi Marini, *Saggio istorico ed algebraico su i bastioni* (Rome, 1801). He comes to the same conclusion in the second dissertation in his valuable edition of the *Della architettura militare* of Francesco de Marchi, 2 vols., (Rome, 1810) i, 7.

[3] *De la pirotechnia* (Venice, 1540). This exaggeration of French superiority was challenged by Rocchi (*Origini . . .*, 83 ff.) and by P. Pieri, *Il Rinascimento e la crisi militare italiana* (Milan, 1952), sections ii and iii of part two.

the prestige of the architect so high or so articulate, and the military engineer was not yet isolated from the kudos attached to the liberal arts. Alberti pointed out in the middle of the fifteenth century that 'if you were to examine into the expeditions that have been undertaken, you would go near to find that most of the victories were gained more by the art and the skill of the architects than by the conduct or fortune of the generals; and that the enemy was oftener overcome and conquered by the architect's wit without the captain's arms, than by the captain's arms without the architect's wit'.[1] Castiglione commended drawing to the courtier not only as a thing excellent in itself but of the greatest use in planning military operations and designing fortifications.[2] According to Francesco de Hollanda, Michelangelo celebrated the artist's role in war 'especially in designing the form and proportions of citadel and defensive work, and of bastions, ditches, mines, counter-mines, trenches, gun-ports, blockhouses', etc.[3] The close connexion between the arts and fortification hardly needs emphasizing. To restrict ourselves to Florentines: according to Vasari, Arnolfo was not only the designer of the Florentine cathedral and of S Maria Novella but of the city walls; he said that some held the impregnable fortress of the Giusta at S Frediano at Lucca to be the work of Giotto; Brunelleschi designed fortifications at Pisa, Pesaro and elsewhere; Leonardo inspected forts for Cesare Borgia; Michelangelo was put in charge of the fortifications of Florence during the great imperialist siege of 1529–30, and when Cosimo I wished to strengthen the city's fortifications still further he distributed the works among a number of artists, including Benvenuto Cellini.[4] Michelangelo's fame in the liberal arts was mentioned in his appointment as one of the reasons for putting him in charge of the fortifications, but it is from an unfavourable comment on his defences that we have the first hint of an opinion that fortification was, in part at least, a job for soldiers.[5]

[1] Preface, *Ten Books on Architecture*, trans. J. Leoni (London, 1955), x.
[2] *Il libro del Cortegiano*, ed. V. Cian (Florence, 1947), 123.
[3] *Da pintura antiga*, ed. E. Radius (Milan, n.d.), 97.
[4] In his *Autobiography* Cellini says that *c.* 1544 he was also asked by Francis I to advise him how to fortify Paris.
[5] The terms of his appointment are quoted in Paola Barocchi's edition of Vasari's life of Michelangelo, 5 vols., (Milan, 1962) iii, 915. On 918 she quotes from the *Breve istorietta dell'assedio di Firenze*: 'E 'perchè l'uffizio del buono architettore è di levar ben la pianta e formare il modello de' ripari secondo la natura del

During the transition period not only was there no distinction between 'art' and military engineering, but the mathematical interests of art theorists were particularly suited to the development of a type of fortification based on geometrical principles. The cult of harmony, proportion and symmetry among artists fitted the need for precisely angled fire and regular, coherent planning, and if the age produced plans which show more concern for ideal geometrical forms than military practicability, this interest, which was shared by humanist princes, helped the integration of the angle bastion within an ordered system of defence.[1] Such an interest in the new fortification—which, from its dependence on aesthetic theory, its connexion with town planning and its interest in the writings of the ancients, can be called 'humanist' with as much justification as the ecclesiastical architecture of the period—was not restricted to such princes as Sigismondo Malatesta, Lorenzo de' Medici, Federigo di Montefeltro or Francesco Maria della Rovere, it was common to the educated classes, not excluding the clergy: Roberto Valturio was a papal abbreviator, the fortifications of Padua and Treviso were re-cast by the Dominican Fra Giovanni Giocondo. And if the political state of Italy led to an amount of building and remodelling that cannot be matched elsewhere, the movement of innovating military architects up and down the peninsula meant that, with varying degrees of success, their ideas were presented to more conservative administrations and that they learned from one another's work. In 1487 Giuliano and Antonio da San Gallo the elder, who had recently been in the papal states tried, vainly, to persuade the Florentine government not to proceed with the traditional fortress they were building at Sarzana.[2] Francesco di Giorgio, Giuliano da Maiano, Giuliano da San Gallo, Fra Giocondo, Benedetto da Maiano and Antonio Marchesi da Settignano were all in Naples at some period between 1485 and 1495. Francesco di Giorgio met Leonardo in

---

luogo; questo, come di tutti li altri valentissimo, mirabilmente fece. Mail cognoscer da che banda possin esser i ripari offesi, o come difesi, e che effetto fachino in quelli i fianchi e le cannoniere, non uffizio è d'architettore, ma di pratico, valente e buon soldato, che delle fortezza sia stato non solamente speculatore, ma difensore'.

[1] The relationship between geometry and fortifications is discussed in J. R. Hale, 'Some military title pages of the Renaissance', *The Newberry Library Bulletin* (1964), 91–102. See below, 211–22.

[2] Rocchi, *Fonti* . . ., 136–7.

Milan and Pavia, a fact which complicates attempts to determine the priority of their ideas. Francesco also knew Fra Giocondo and Baccio Pontelli, who designed fortifications across central Italy from Ostia to Recanati and Loreto. Architects who had worked for different states met in conference, as at Civitavecchia in 1515 or were sent on tours of inspection, as when Antonio da San Gallo the younger, Michele Sanmicheli and Pierfrancesco Fiorenzuoli da Viterbo went round the Romagna in 1526 for Clement VII.[1]

Before looking at individual buildings it might be helpful to state the principle ways in which guns affected the art of fortification. The thickness of medieval walls was determined by their height and the need to provide a walk from which marksmen could shoot, protected by crenellations. The main danger the defenders faced was at the moment of assault, and towers, taller than the walls, and unscaleable, were built at intervals so that attacking parties armed with rams or ladders could be shot at from the flanks. Walls were machicolated so that such parties could also be subjected to a curtain of missiles dropped vertically on their heads. The slung fire of siege engines was not so accurate that they could land repeated blows on the same place: their main role, like the mortars which succeeded them (some of the earliest guns which have survived are of this form) was to harass the inhabitants, particularly by hurling incendiary materials over the wall. Neither the ram nor the mine affected the thickness or height of the wall: this was determined by the need to prevent scaling and maintain an effective vertical defence from the machicolation. The gun provided for the first time a hard-hitting long-range horizontal blow and by the fifteenth century a reasonably accurate one. To counter this, walls were made thicker (not necessarily lower, where time and money allowed) and were scarped, sometimes very emphatically, on the outside for some two-thirds of their heights; in this way it was hoped to deflect some of the impact of the cannon balls. Scarping was accepted the more readily

[1] Their report was printed by L. Beltrami, *Relazione sullo stato delle rocche di Romagna* . . . (Nozze Emanuele Greppi, Bice Belgioioso, n.p., 1902). It deals with Imola, Faenza, Forlì, Cesena, Rimini, Cervia and Ravenna. Except for Cesena, where a more thorough modernization is recommended—lowering of walls, addition of bastions of some sort (neither text nor drawing is very clear on this point)—the report is mainly concerned with strengthening the existing works and clearing ditches. Interesting as it is, this rare work throws no light on contemporary ideas.

because it weakened siege ladders by increasing the angle at which they were set to the wall.[1] Strong scarping was a first reaction, and is rarely found after the fifteenth century, but it had the effect of so seriously reducing the effectiveness of vertical fire that there was little point in having machicolation: in compensation, greater attention was paid to flanking fire.

The importance of flanking fire from towers had always been recognized, and at first the reaction to gunpowder was to build gun towers on the model of the old round or pentagonal towers but thicker, and provided with key-hole or letter-box-shaped loops for hand guns or small cannon instead of arrow slits; for the gun, from the point of view of defence, was first seen as a weapon to be used against assault parties rather than as a long-range deterrent. Gradually, however, it was realized that guns could be used to break up the besiegers' concentrations and dismount their artillery. Heavy guns were no use inside towers: they made too much smoke and their arc of fire was too restricted by loops in immensely thick masonry, so they were placed on platforms on top of the towers. From this moment we are in sight of the bastion, which is not a gun tower but a solid platform thrust forward to obtain as wide a field of fire as possible while retaining the tower's role of providing flank cover to the adjacent parts of a fortification.[2] The tower was basically a defensive, the bastion an aggressive form. When the tower became a platform it had to be still more massive, and for reasons of cost, as well as the convenience of running guns from one platform to another along the wall walks, was dropped to the level of the wall. An object of fortification became to present as few projections to be knocked off as possible: crenellations were replaced by pierced parapets, bastions and walls were designed to present an even silhouette. A scraped platform which had to bear the weight of heavy guns at its edge had no place for machicolation: this absence of vertical defence meant that methodically devised flanking fire now became the only protection against assault. This problem, and the masking of flank batteries (*traditori*—traitors, the Italians called them) from fire from the field became a major point of discussion among early sixteenth-century engineers.

[1] A point made by Alberti and Francesco di Giorgio.
[2] Reluctance to make this distinction has led many a searcher for the origin of the bastion on a wild goose chase back into the fourteenth century.

The bastion developed from the tower,[1] and existing towers suggested two favourable shapes: round or pointed-pentagonal. Medieval Italy provided examples of both in plenty, and the first bastions were built in both forms. The round was probably easier to build (it needed less squared masonry), it provided some deflection to a ball at every point, and it had no vulnerable sharp points; on the other hand it left dead ground at its head which could not be covered by flanking fire, and with the absence of vertical protection from machicolation together with the use of gunpowder in mining, the danger of dead ground became so great that the angle bastion gradually became the norm.[2] Like the exaggeratedly scarped wall, the round bastion taught a useful lesson before it lost favour. Where a scarped round bastion met such a wall a withdrawn flank was created. This evidently suggested the location of the concealed battery. A high proportion of angle bastions were built in the sixteenth century with round protective shoulders, though the future lay with batteries cut back in a straight flank at its meeting with the wall.

A traditional feature which lingered on in transitional fortresses was the *mastio* or keep. Too high to be an effective gun platform it was retained on grounds of prestige, to provide suitably splendid apartments for the prince or castellan, and as a place of refuge. Political instability within a state led to an emphasis on points of retreat within the walls, a preoccupation which reached an extreme in the labyrinthine fantasies of Filarete and Leonardo.[3] Mature gunpowder fortifications laid

[1] The most direct link between the two were the massive corner towers of fortresses which, though at the same level as the walls, were taller than normal bastions in order to retain the prestige and beauty which was considered due to a lofty princely residence. I use the term tower bastion for this short-lived type. As an example see plate 8.

[2] This involved a breach with the advice of the ancients. One school of thought tried to believe, by an optimistic reading of ancient siege tactics, that the Greeks and Romans had known about gunpowder, an attitude sardonically rebutted by Francesco di Giorgio: why don't we find traces of gun loops in these walls, he asks; why did they go on using catapults? (*Trattato* ed. cit., 249). Defending the angle bastion, an anonymous writer of the mid-sixteenth century comments: 'Si come adunque sappiamo, che gli antichi hanno fuggiti gli angoli, ancor che in molte altre cose errassero: così noi non potrendo fuggirli per nō lasciar alcuno spatio del recinto indifeso...', *Discorsi delle fortificationi*, MS. B.N.F., XIX, 2, fol. 7.

[3] Machiavelli, in the *Art of War* (ed. cit., 496), points out the bad effect on morale of having a place to which to retreat. Sanmicheli made the same point when the Venetians were contemplating building a citadel in Padua in 1544 and asked his advice: 'a mio giuditio è una mala cosa quando quelli che stanno a guardia de una città habbiano speranza de potersi ritirar in uno castello'. C. Semenzato in *Michele Sanmicheli 1484–1559. Studi raccolti dall'accademia di agricoltura scienze e lettere di Verona* (Verona, 1960), 87.

all their emphasis on the *enceinte*, treating it as a continuous gun platform. This function was recognized by the Spanish military engineer Pedro Navarro, when he inspected the walls of Florence with Machiavelli in 1526. 'A city can expect to have more guns than an army can carry with it; whenever you can present more guns to the enemy than he can range against you, it is impossible for him to defeat you.'[1] This is the concept that underlay the changes planned for these walls in the following years by Michelangelo. It was the concept that changed a fort from an inert defensive object to an attacking agent reaching far out against an enemy by means of mutually supporting outworks, the half-moons, crown-works, horn-works and the rest so beloved of Sterne's Uncle Toby.

The theory and practice of gunpowder fortification in the middle of the sixteenth century can be explained by a group of buildings in the Romagna and Marche, and the writings of Leon Battista Alberti and Filarete. In his *De re aedificatoria* (written between 1440 and 1450), Alberti makes no reference to the special nature of guns, as opposed to earlier siege engines, but he emphasizes the superiority of flanking fire to vertical defence, he recommends strong scarping and that 'those parts which are exposed to battery should be made semi-circular, or rather with a sharp angle like the head of a ship'. He also mentions the advantage of having triangular projections from the wall and adds that 'some think no wall is so safe against battery as those which are built in uneven lines, like the teeth of a saw'. He is entirely concerned with defensive strength. There is no suggestion that large guns can be used by the defenders to attack. He is primarily interested in fortifications as giving protection to a city, and, within the city, to the prince: they are necessary to preserve the urban scene, the physical environment of civic life which fascinates him, and he was not moved to rethink them in a way which would take serious account of the new weapon. The same is true of Filarete's *Trattato di architettura* (written *c.* 1460). Like Alberti he is more preoccupied by the ideas of classical writers than by the developments in fire power and their consequences in his own day, and though he provides for gun-loops in the towers and walls of his ideal city—the towers were to be considerably higher than the walls—and

---

[1] Quoted by Machiavelli in his 'Relazione di una visita fatta per fortificare Firenze', printed in Bartelli, ed. cit., 297.

points out that walls now have to be thicker than formerly, his concern with fortifications is to contrive a dignified and solid cladding to the urban environment and the labyrinth-guarded citadel which are the main subject of his treatise. He has been regarded as an innovator because Sforzinda was planned in the form of an eight-point star (Alberti had suggested that a star might be a good shape for a fortress) and because the city's main gate was to be defended by a triangular ravelin, but there is no suggestion that either of these ideas was connected with artillery, offensive or defensive.[1]

In contrast to this basic indifference to the new problems of defence, we have a document[2] which shows the town of Foligno's plans for rebuilding its walls in 1441, after they had been severely damaged by the artillery fire of Cardinal Vitelleschi's siege train in 1439. Among the measures proposed were: scarping of curtain walls; angled scarping on the outer face of round towers; the building of new tower bastions (*torrono*) of angle (*a spigolo*) form, presumably pentagonal, projecting well forward from the walls; pointed ravelins; a *glacis* sloping away from the town 'so that it can all be commanded by anyone standing on the battlements (*merli*)'; on either side of one angle ravelin, gun-loops were to be cut in the curtain wall to cover (*che rade*) its faces.

Drastic rebuilding in Foligno has left no trace of these works, if they were ever carried out. But some of them can be illustrated from analogous works which still survive. The tower bastions must have looked like those at Corinaldo (plate 1) and Morro d'Alba (plate 2). Similar towers and strongly scarped walls can be seen at Ostra and S Arcangelo di Roma (*c.* 1447). The ravelins were probably similar to the one at Corinaldo (plate 3), which is mentioned in an inventory of *c.* 1455.[3] The word *rivellino* or *revellino* does not necessarily refer (as it came to in the sixteenth century) to a small outwork standing at some distance from the wall; it was used to describe works which could be round (like the other ravelin at Corinaldo) or square

---

[1] Parts of Filarete's treatise have been printed (from the B.N.F. MS., Palat. 372, by W. von Oettingen, *Antonio Averlino Filaretes Tractat ueber die Baukunst* (Vienna) 1890), but the reader should be warned that the editor's interpretive drawings sometimes read progressive points into the text which are not there.
[2] Printed by A. Angelucci in 'Spigolature militare dell'archivio communale di Foligno', *Archivio Storico per le Marche e per l'Umbria* (1886), pp. 477–9.
[3] Printed in the same journal in the same year, 126, by D. Gaspari, 'Fortezze marchigiane e umbre del secolo XV'.

(as at Castel d'Emilio or Certaldo) or, as in this case, presenting an angled face to the field.[1] The importance of the ravelin in the development of the bastion is that it was never conceived as a tower, and its position beside a gate, where the main rush of an assault might be expected, helped its builders to see it in terms of breaking up the attack at a distance as well as harassing it with flanking fire at the gate itself. By the 1360s the tower bastion is in some instances beginning to look like the mature angle bastion. Matteo Nuti's polygonal work in the town wall (1464–9) at Fano, though it has no flanks to speak of, serves the function of a platform (plate 4), and when he placed a tower bastion beside the gate at Cesena[2] (plate 5) in *c.* 1466 it took on an added purposefulness from its ravelin-like position.[3]

The progress towards the angle bastion made between the 1440s and 1460s was restricted in area and carried out, for the most part, in obscure hill towns. It was halted for a while by the adoption of round forms in a series of splendid and conspicuous palace-fortresses: in Naples (Castel Nuovo, 1443–58), near Rome (Tivoli, 1458–64 and Bracciano, 1470–85), in Tuscany (Volterra, from 1472), and in the Romagna itself in a succession of square strongholds with round tower bastions at the corners: Forlimpopoli (1471–80), Imola (1472–3), Pesaro (1474–1505), Senigallia (*c.* 1480) and Forlì (1481–3). In general these buildings are conservative, relying on mass, and accepting large areas of dead ground at the faces of their tower bastions. Gunports are few and small, providing inadequate flanking fire; considerable importance still attaches to vertical defence. Tower bastions and walls are level, and the tops of all the tower bastions provide solid platforms, but their parapet

---

[1] Though no documents have been produced to date the fortifications of Morro d'Alba, Ostra, and Castel d'Emilio, are so similar in style and detail (especially the round brick gun-loops) that they must belong to the mid-century programme of Corinaldo. The ravelin at Certaldo is probably rather later. It, too, is undocumented.

[2] On Cesena, see F. Mancini and W. Vichi, *Castelli, rocche e torri di Romagna* (Bologna, 1959), 221.

[3] It is tempting to follow the dating of L. Serra which puts the three square corner bastions of the *rocca* at Fano at 1452, and as Nuti's work. All are level with the curtain walls and the faces of the south-eastern one are considerably longer than the flanks, but the evidence for their date is too slight to establish the *rocca* as a remarkable anticipation of the form the mature angle bastion was to take. Detailed work on this fortress, which is at present used, as are so many of its kind, as a prison, is of prime importance in charting the development of fortification in this area. 'Architettura militare del Rinascimento nelle Marche', *Rassegna Marchigiana* (1934), 1–2 and *L'Arte nelle Marche. Il periodo del Rinascimento*, (Rome, 1934), 116–17 and (town wall), 107.

embrasures remain too small for the use of heavy guns. They were the last great fortified residences, paying lip-service to the existence of guns, but relying in the main on their magnificent burliness.[1] It is in the Romagna, once again, that progress is most noticeable, with the girth of the tower bastion swelling at the expense of its height, from its slim form at Forlimpopoli (plate 6) to the thicker form at Imola (plate 7) and to the most magnificent round tower bastions of all, at Senigallia (plate 8).[2] Scarcely less important in emphasizing the role of the bastion as a routine element in gunpowder fortification, were the new walls surrounding the town of Colle Val d'Elsa (1479), the abbey of Grottaferrata (1484), the castle at Nepi (*c.* 1484) and the town wall of Bracciano, which, though undocumented, is closely analogous to the wall at Nepi.[3] The moderate height of the town wall at Colle enabled the tower bastions flanking the Volterra gate[4] to be low in relation to their girth, so that the tower element almost disappears. When Baccio Pontelli (possibly the architect of Senigallia) surrounded the abbey of Grottaferrata with a low wall and round corner bastions at the same level, only their bracketed and vulnerable battlements suggest that he was thinking in terms of a shrunken tower, rather than of a straightforward gun platform. The bastions in

---

[1] When building operations were recommenced on the Castel Nuovo after the earthquake of 1456, a low terrace, a sort of shrunken outer ward, was built out from its base which could serve as a continuous platform for artillery, but the state of the parapet today makes it impossible to judge whether it was in fact used for anything other than small arms fire. See R. Filangieri, *Castel Nuovo Reggia Angoina ed Aragonese di Napoli* (Naples, 1934), 51–72. Similar action was taken at Gaeta. The tower bastions of the fortified residence were too high to permit of accurate fire from their platforms and the establishment of a gun terrace was a logical compensation for this. A terraced outer ward with round bastions at the same level extends in front of the Orsini castle of Bracciano as well.

[2] On these *rocche*, see Serra, opera cit. and Mancini, op. cit. The *rocca* at Pesaro was the work of Luciano Laurana, architect of the ducal palace of Urbino. Its form is similar to the others, but its state of preservation (including much restoration) worse. The corner tower bastions at Forlì are more tower-like and are above the level of the curtain.

[3] This *enceinte* was designed by Antonio da San Gallo the elder, according to G. Giovannoni, *Antonio da Sangallo il Giovane*, 2 vols., (Rome, 1959) i, 343. It surrounds an ordinary high-towered mid-fifteenth century castle, and was in turn protected by a massive angle-bastioned front designed in 1540 by Antonio da San Gallo the younger. These three layers of fortification give Nepi a special interest which has not yet been properly investigated. Cf. G. Silvestrelli, *Città castelli e terre della regione romana*, 2 vols., (Rome, 1940) ii, 559. The town wall at Bracciano likewise lacks a historian, but see L. Borsari, *Il castello di Bracciano* (Roma, 1895).

[4] All that remains, apart from a circular detached blockhouse with two tiers of letter-box gun slits outside the wall on the earth. Giuliano da San Gallo was concerned with the works at Colle, along with Francione and others. G. Marchini, *Giuliano da Sangallo* (Florence, 1942), 83.

the castle *enceinte* at Nepi (plate 9) look more businesslike and though their state of preservation makes it impossible to be sure of this, they were probably thought of as platforms for guns of some weight, as were those of Bracciano, where bastions of a similar shape and size have two tiers of letter-box slits in the flanks, giving a wider traverse than was possible for the round loops at Nepi.

In the evolution of the bastion, the most crucial period was the decade preceding the French invasion of September 1494. In this period a few fortifications mark time: the massive fort of Sarzana,[1] begun by the Florentines in 1487, though its loopholes provide four tiers of flanking fire, still relies on vertical defence from machicolations: the stone cannon balls embedded in its walls as a decoration come from guns larger than any it could fire itself (plate 10); the similar but slighter Orsini castle at Avezzano (1490) has tower bastions that rise well above the curtain walls. But by the time the French arrive the decision of military architects has been made to reduce the 'tower' aspect of the tower bastion still further, to augment its firepower, to rationalize the support given by one bastion to another, and to make increasing use of the angled shape.

The *rocca* outside Ostia was built between 1482-6. Triangular in form, it has two great drum bastions and a pentagonal one, all level with the curtains (plates 11 and 12). In some ways this fortress, too, marks time, with its keyhole loops, its bracketed machicolation, its tall central watch-tower and its fragile battlements (the massive parapet on the pentagonal bastion is due to restoration), but for the first time the flanking fire is well rationalized so that no surface, apart from the heads of the round bastions, is left uncovered; there are embrasures for large guns near the bottom of the outer faces of the pentagonal bastion; the lower gun chambers are connected by a passage running in the thickness of the wall, the lengths of which can be enfiladed from screens pierced with gun-loops in case an enemy should break in. The work of Baccio Pontelli, Ostia is the only transition fort to have received detailed modern attention, and for its beauty as well as its science, it well deserves it.[2] In his works of the late 'eighties, at Osimo and Offida

---

[1] E. Rocchi, 'La citadella di Sarzana ed il forte di Sarzanello', *Rivista d'Artiglieria e Genio*, (1904) ii, 137–54. Reliable only for Sarzana. Idem., *Fonti* . . ., 136–7.

[2] Verdier, op. cit.

1 Corinaldo, tower in town wall

2 Morro d'Alba, tower in town wall

3 Corinaldo, gate in town wall

4 Fano, Nuti's bastion in town wall

5 Cesena, tower bastion in *enceinte* of the Rocca Malatestiana

6 Forlimpopoli, Rocca

7 Imola, Rocca

8 Senigallia, Rocca

9 Nepi, *enceinte* of Rocca

10 Sarzana, Rocca

11 Ostia Antica, Castello

12 Ostia Antica, Castello

13 Offida, town wall

14 Brolio

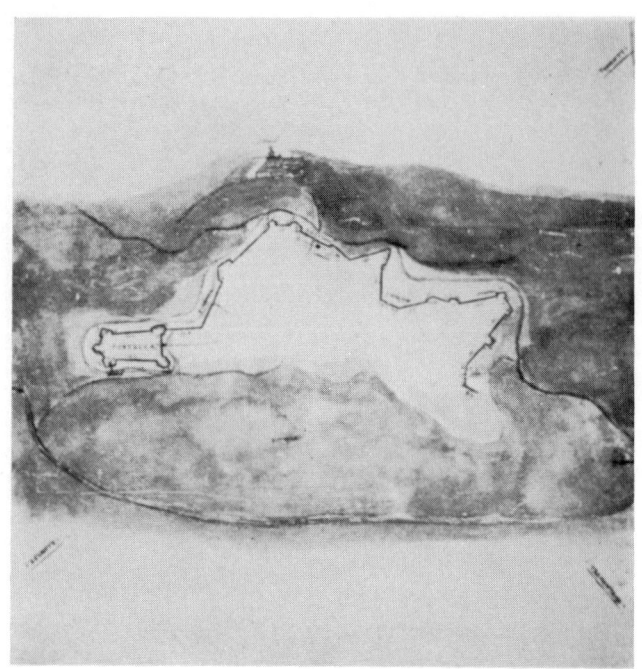

15 Poggio Imperiale, from Francesco de Marchi, *Trattato d'architettura militare*, Florence, Biblioteca Nazionale, II.I.280, f. 19^r

16 Poggio Imperiale, Rocca

17 Poggio Imperiale, Rocca

18 Poggio Imperiale, town wall

19 Rome, Castel S. Angelo

20 Civita Castellana, Rocca

21 Sarzanello

22 Sarzanello

23 San Leo, Rocca

24 Sassocorvaro, Rocca

25 Sassocorvaro, Rocca

26 Cagli, Francesco di Giorgio's tower

27 Mondavio, Rocca

28 Mondavio, Rocca

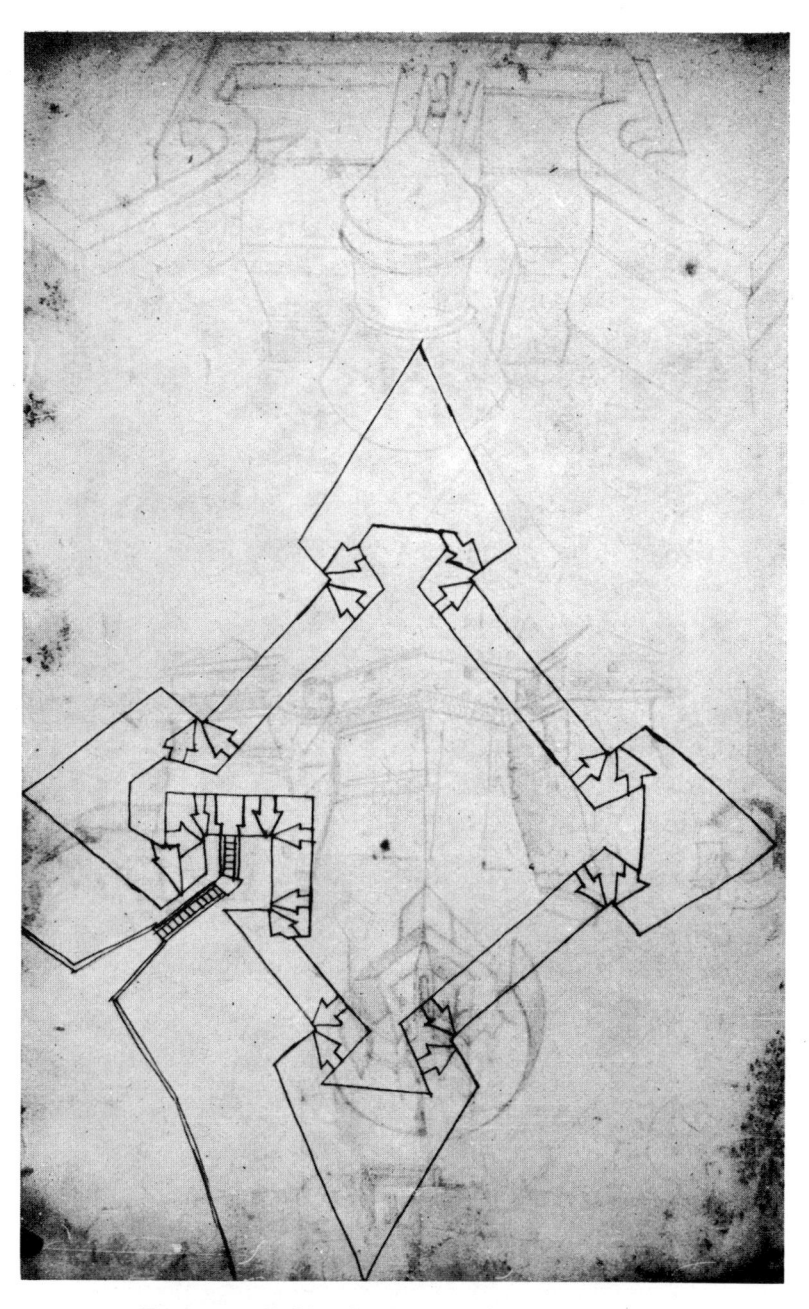

29 Francesco di Giorgio, fortress plan, ms. cit. f. 240ᵛ

30 San Sepolcro, Rocca

31 Nettuno, Rocca

32 Arezzo, Fortezza Medicea

33 Civitavecchia, Rocca

34 Civitavecchia, Rocca

35 Pisa, Francesco de Marchi, ms. cit. f. 8ʳ

36 Livorno, Fortezza Vecchia

37 L'Aquila, Castello

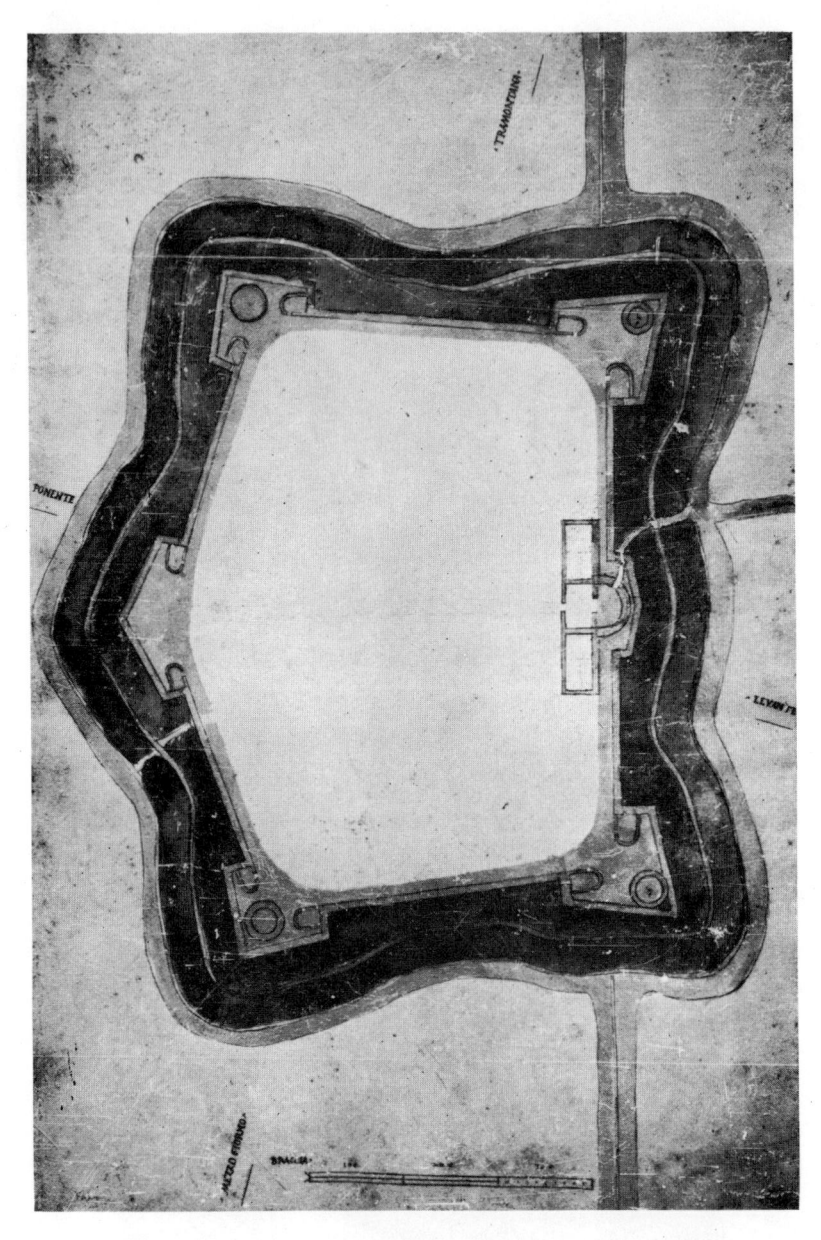

38 Florence, Fortezza da Basso, Francesco de Marchi,
ms. cit. f. 3ʳ

39 Urbino, town wall

40 Loreto, town wall

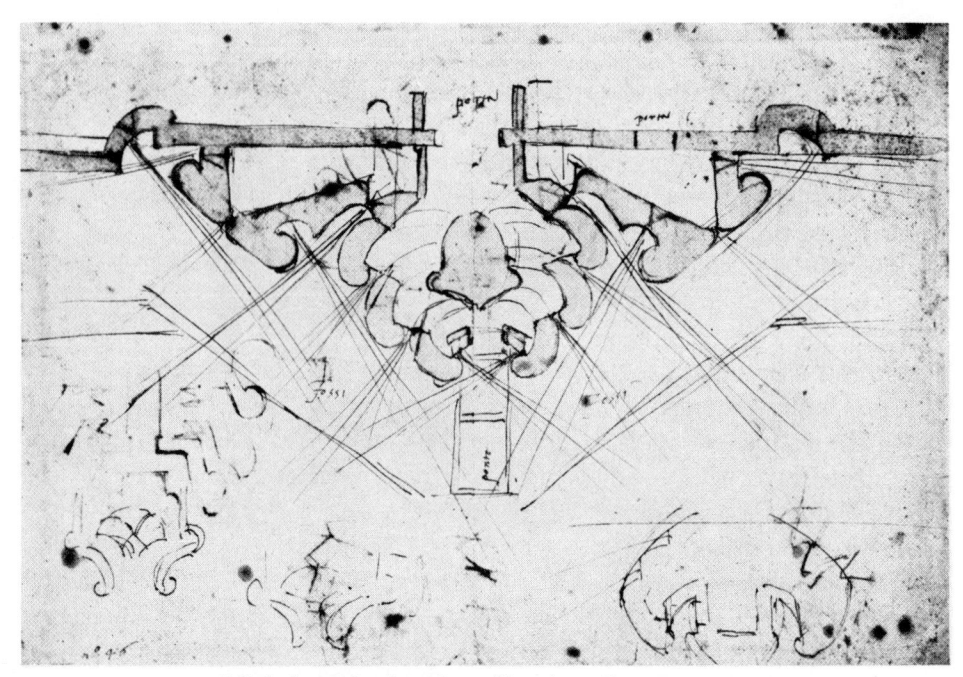

41 Michelangelo, drawing of bastion, Casa Buonarroti, 22A

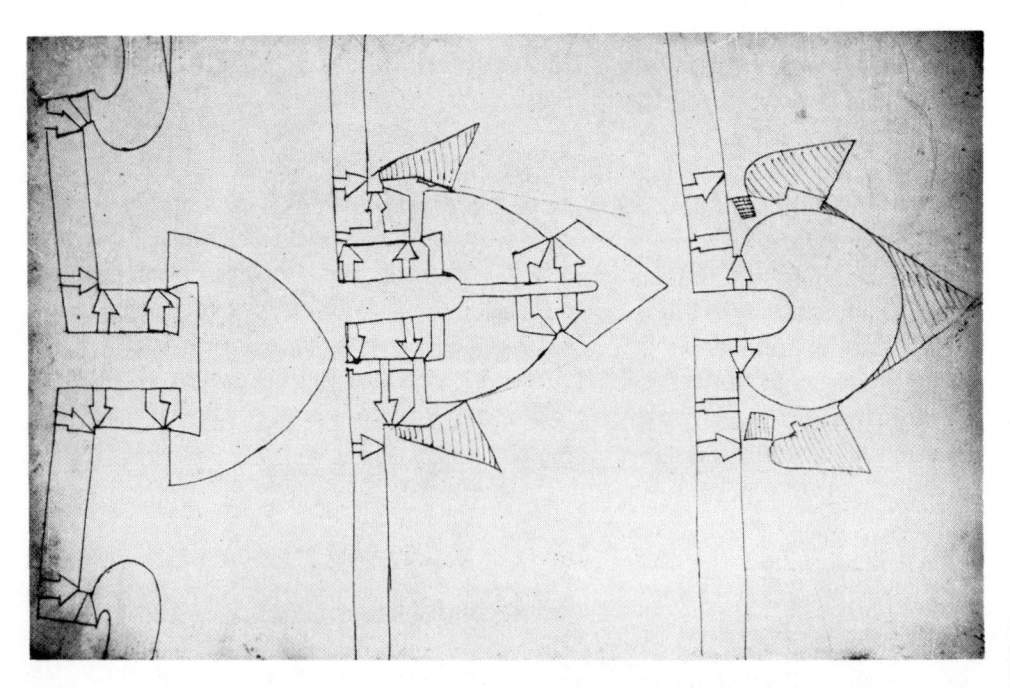

42 Francesco di Giorgio, drawings of bastions, ms. cit.
f. 140r

(plate 13) Pontelli gave up round forms and reverted to more tower-like, lightly defended bastions.

If Ostia was the most advanced fortress of its time, the most advanced *enceinte* was certainly that of Brolio,[1] the castle which controlled the approaches to Tuscany from Siena. Ruined in the war with Naples and the papacy in 1478-9, the castle's *enceinte* was completely rebuilt by the Florentines from 1484. At each of the five corners is a square bastion (plate 14). Not all are symmetrical. The four tiers of small keyholes below the cordon in the flanks of most of them are suitable only for small-arms, and the restricted fields of fire are not arranged to provide an accurate coverage of the adjacent curtains or bastion faces, but here is a bastioned front that would be recognizable as such to the engineers of Peschiera, perhaps the most superbly accomplished *enceinte* of the mid-sixteenth century.

Even more instantly recognizable would have been the defences of Poggio Imperiale, commanding another of the valley approaches into Tuscany from Siena. It was the first site in Italy—and no contender has been advanced from elsewhere —to combine a bastioned fortress with a bastioned town wall; planned in 1487, it never attracted settlement from nearby Poggibonsi and remains incomplete, as can be seen from Francesco de Marchi's mid-sixteenth century plan (plate 15). Little is known about its building history;[2] in spite of its unique importance it has been ignored by students of fortification. The works there are mentioned in a document of 1488 with Giuliano da San Gallo as the architect in charge. Another shows them going forward in 1490, a third names Antonio da San Gallo the elder as their superintendent in 1495. Further work is mentioned in 1511, and it is likely that some reconstruction was carried out by Cosimo I during the Sienese war of 1552-7. There seems little reason to doubt that what can be seen today represents the plan devised by Giuliano for Lorenzo the Magnificent, who is known to have supported his criticism of the Sarzana fortifications. There are no inscriptions, but the sculptured emblems of

[1] A. Casabianca, *Le mura di Brolio in Chianti* (Siena, 1900), with plan. The plan in B. Ebhardt, *Die Burgen Italiens*, 6 vols. (Berlin, 1910-27), fig. 434, is misleadingly symmetrical. It is a failing, indeed, of several of his plans. Other relevant plans in Ebhardt are: S Leo (fig. 18), Cesena (fig. 60), Sarzanello (fig. 108), Senigallia (figs. 411-13), Bracciano (figs. 445-50).
[2] E. Repetti, *Dizionario geografico fisico storico della Toscana*, 6 vols. (Florence, 1834-46) *sub*. Poggio Imperiale. It is mentioned briefly in Marchini, op. cit., p. 88 and G. Claussess, *Les San Gallo*, 3 vols., (Paris, 1900) i, 105-6.

the people and commune of Florence, the cross and lily, which are set above the inner gate of the entrance on the south-west, suggest a date before 1512. If any construction, rather than restoration, was carried out under Cosimo I, it was probably the tufa cladding of part of the south-east front of the citadel, though it is difficult to believe that the elegant but vulnerable sally port in the middle bastion (plate 16) can be as late. The bastions of the citadel (plate 17) are solid; the embrasures above the cordon and, where they occur, low down in the flanks or face, are for guns of large calibre. The flanking fire accurately covers the adjacent curtains and faces. The bastions of the town wall are evenly scarped from top to bottom, with no trace of cordon. They vary in size and are provided with keyhole loops in flank and face (plate 18); internal passages connect the chambers in a bastion with others in the length of the wall.[1] Owing to the small aperture of the loops, the flanking fire is not accurate at all points, and the distance between some of the bastions makes it unlikely that small-arms fire would have reached across with any accuracy. There is much tantalizing uncertainty about Poggio Imperiale, but it is reasonably certain that it entitles Giuliano to be considered as the first architect to explore the possibilities of the angle bastion in a large scale and diversified defensive system.

Two further works, one a reconstruction, one a new building, completes the story of Italian gunpowder fortification on the eve of the French wars. In 1492 Alexander VI employed Antonio da San Gallo the elder to modernize the round towers which Nicholas V had erected at the corners of Castel S Angelo[2] in Rome, and Antonio surrounded them with seven-sided bastions. Further additions under Pius IV have obscured much of this work, but the S Matteo bastion, in spite of a conjectural reconstruction of the upper works, shows the nature of Antonio's approach to the bastion (plate 19). Antonio was also the principal architect of Cesare Borgia's palace fort at Civitacastellana,[3] begun in 1494. Pentagonal in shape, the fort retains the conventional central *mastio*; its keyhole and letter-box slits are small and do not provide a perfectly systematized flanking

---

[1] This system of internal works has not been properly unblocked and restored. The second main entrance to the *enceinte* is also blocked: this may well contain an inscription or emblem that would help date it.

[2] M. Borgatti, *Castel Sant'Angelo in Roma* (Rome, 1931), 234–6.

[3] Guglielmotti, op. cit., 139 ff.

fire, but it does away not only with machicolation but with the conventional bracketing that lingered on, as, for instance, at Sarzanello, and of its five bastions, only one is round (plate 20). Sarzanello,[1] a hill-top fort, was designed in 1493 as an equilateral triangle with round corner bastions, conventional in shape and in the provision of keyhole loops for fire towards the field, but possessing flanking embrasures for large guns above the cordon and unusually massive parapets—if these are, indeed, part of the original structure (plate 21). In 1497 the Genoese, into whose hands the fort had come, began the remarkable triangular detached ravelin which juts hugely out towards the edge of the plateau most vulnerable to fire from a nearby hill (plate 22). Without forbears or progeny similar in size, this immense platform completes one of the most strikingly situated and well preserved of transition forts.[2]

We are now in a position to judge the claims made on behalf of Francesco di Giorgio, whose treatise dates from c. 1495.[3] From Saluzzo's edition of 1841 he has persistently been seen as the pioneer of the transition from medieval to modern fortification. In the words of one recent authority: 'Fully comprehending the novel challenge offered to defensive works by artillery, he laid down new principles of construction ... his work represents the transition from Renaissance fortification, which adapted medieval principles to new needs, to the modern bastioned front'.[4] And in those of another: 'Francesco di Giorgio worked out the new style in fortification ... he asserted, before anyone else, with the marvellous foresight with which all competent students now credit him, the theory and practice of the bastion, the origin of modern fortification'.[5]

That Francesco was highly conscious of the effect of guns and believed that new methods, relying not on mass but intelligently disposed units, were needed to counter them, there is no doubt.

---

[1] A. Neri, 'Il forte di Sarzanello', *Archivio Storico Italiano* (1885), 345–53.

[2] It is surrounded by a covered way, complete with *places d'armes*. The fort itself shows no trace of later reconstruction and this may mean that the covered way itself is of the early sixteenth century. If this is true it is the earliest of covered ways to have survived. But this would make it an astonishingly sophisticated achievement.

[3] There is no internal evidence, but it is generally accepted as dating from the last years of his life.

[4] L. Serra, 'Le rocche di Mondavio e di Cagli e le altre fortezze di Francesco di Giorgio Martini nella Marca', *Miscellenea di storia d'arte in onore di Igino Benvenuto Supino* (Florence, 1933), 435.

[5] R. Papini, *Francesco di Giorgio Architetto*, 3 vols. (Florence, 1946), 168.

There is also no doubt that he looked upon himself as a pioneer: 'he who can discover the answer to this manner of attack deserves to be called divinely, rather than humanly gifted'.[1] But before turning to his theoretical writings, it would be as well to look at the fortifications he actually built. Only few remain, and one of these, S Leo (plate 23) is attributed to him with some uncertainty. The others are Sassocorvaro (plates 24 and 25), built some time in the 1480s, Cagli (plate 26), built *c.* 1484 and of which only one detached tower from the wall leading up to the hill fort remains, and Mondavio (plates 27 and 28) of 1490–2. These works are fascinatingly idiosyncratic, but when they are compared with the works we have been discussing they appear quite irrelevant to the answers already proposed to the problem of fortifying against artillery. Towering and under-armed, they represent the massive doodling of a genius who is not prepared to sacrifice fantasy to logic, and it is not surprising that the least eccentric design, that of S Leo, is least certainly his.

The treatise lays down basic principles with firmness: the need to present glancing surfaces by means of scarping and of angled walls; the importance of flanking fire and the enfilading of ditches; the usefulness of outworks: ravelin and blockhouse (*capannato*) to break the force of an assault; the need to sink defences as much as possible from the attacker's fire. The drawings show many forms of bastion, but several of these are not solid and provide walks for small-arms rather than platforms for guns. The drawings, moreover, show a marked divergence from the principles of the text. They abound in impractical geometrical fantasies in which he rings elaborate changes on Alberti's suggestions of star and zigzag shapes: his designs abound in superfluous elements which could easily be knocked off, which get in the way of each other's fire, or are so placed as to be too high (as in some examples of *capannati* on towers, or too sunken to be of much use). He is still primarily concerned with the moment of assault rather than with long-range bombardment; he litters his ditches with booby-traps and harassing spurs, *tenailles* and blockhouses. Also, like Filarete, he is concerned with the political security of the prince or castellan within the city and devises complicated routes to the *mastio*. Though aware of the danger of mining, a strong liking for round or very obtuse forms, unprotected by flanking

---

[1] *Trattato*, ed. Saluzzo, 251.

fire, produces large areas of dead ground. His gun-ports are designed for small-arms, and even those that look suited to heavy cannon in plan reveal his preoccupation with short-range arms when he re-draws them in elevation.[1] One of the only two plans[2] that appears to be abreast of progressive contemporary buildings (plate 29), is matched on the facing page by a bird's-eye view that makes a very similar ground plan look remarkably old-fashioned: the angle bastions are scarped to two-thirds of their height, and continue up to a roofed storey projecting on bracket-corbels until their height is considerably greater than the ground area they cover. In short: while a case can be made from his text that he was abreast of current practice, he was not ahead of it, and his drawings and actual buildings show that he was diverted from dealing with simple, mutually dependent low-lying forms by a scholar's exuberant interest in ideal geometrical patterns, and by the relish for vertical mass he derived from church and palace, the staple of his architectural work.

Claims similar to those made for Francesco di Giorgio have been advanced on Leonardo da Vinci's behalf since J. B. Venturi declared in 1797 that he was 'fort supérieur aux ingénieurs de son temps',[3] but they have usually been made more guardedly because no trace of a bastion (as opposed to ravelin-like approximations to it) appears among his drawings. Leonardo designed no forts himself. The only finished drawing of a fort[4] is of an elaborate Francesco di Giorgio-like structure probably based on buildings he saw when working for Cesare Borgia as inspector of fortifications[5] in 1502. His own ideas are often difficult to interpret: the drawings are frequently so small that details are indistinguishable; lines of fire can be confused with measuring or composition lines; it is not easy to discern levels of building in plans that are not accompanied by elevations or bird's-eye views. But some conclusions can be

---

[1] Most of his drawings of guns (except for the page of drawings of existing types on fol. 48r) are concerned with short-range 'shrapnel' of various sorts: mortars, shooting baskets or frames full of stones, etc. He suggests, too, giant machines for scorching attackers off the walls by means of catherine wheels (MS. B.N.F. II, i, 141 ff., 198r,v, 215v).

[2] The other (MS. cit., fol. 82r) is for a triangular bastioned fort. There are irregularities in the drawing that suggest that his imagination was more concerned for the triangle shape than for the lines of fire from the bastions.

[3] *Essai sur les ouvrages physico-mathématiques de Léonard da Vinci*, reprinted in G. B. de Toni, *Giambattista Venturi e la sua opera Vinciana* (Rome, 1924), 189.

[4] Reproduced in Calvi, op. cit., fig. 88.

[5] His title was 'architecto et ingegnero generale'.

drawn from the numerous sketches made from the 1480s into the early years of the next century and preserved, for the most part, in MS.B., the Leicester MS. and the Codex Atlanticus.

In the earlier drawings he clings to round towers, strongly scarped at the base, and provided with small and secretive gun-loops right up against the curtain for flanking fire. Pointed shapes he reserves for ravelins. These are often very large, covering an entire curtain, and set in a wide wet ditch. They are open on the inner face, so that they can be covered by fire from the curtain and its towers; the only plan of such a system that has a clearly marked fire pattern[1] emphasizes the mutual defensibility of curtain and ravelin rather than the co-operation of the fire of both out to the field. He does not favour a *glacis*, seeing it as a lodgement in which an enemy can establish himself rather than as an advanced firing position—the true function of *glacis* and covered way. Like earlier theoretical writers, he is mainly concerned with what happens at the moment of assault and when the enemy actually breaks in. He provides round tower bastions with parapet embrasures in the flanks which have double openings: one to sweep the outer face of the curtain and another to enfilade its wall-walk. His project for strengthening the Sforza castle of Milan includes an outer *enceinte*—square, with round tower bastions at the corners—which has a firing gallery on its inner side, so that if the enemy gets through he will come under fire from the defence he has just penetrated. In the later drawings he becomes more concerned than ever with intricate systems of retreat—the medieval principal of outer ward, inner ward and keep from which contemporary practice was escaping—with *capannati*, concentric walls and underwater and underground passages: he is preoccupied with the anatomy, rather than the striking power of a fortress, pays little heed to providing the outer *enceinte* of his labyrinths with flanking fire and increasingly favours a curved surface for parapet, curtain and ravelin. He experiments with various forms of embrasure, but from the point of view of protection, not from that of mounting an effective firepower. Taking his drawings together with those in other contemporary treatises,[2] the conclusion seems inescapable: the revolution in

---

[1] Calvi, fig. 25.
[2] B.N.F. MS. Palat. 767 (Anon); Buonaccorso Ghiberti, B.N.F. MS. Magl. N. XVII. D.2. Both *c.* 1500. Neither has a title.

gunpowder fortification was carried through, not by theorists, even theorists of genius, but by working architects and masons.

This does not exclude the importance of architects of genius in exploiting more fully the measures of lesser men—Baccio Pontelli was possibly, Giuliano da San Gallo certainly, an architect of genius; but men whose genius was as much, or more, speculative than practical were lured from essentials by other considerations: politics, geometry, town planning; the tough outer shell which the new fortification required left a central void which their imaginations longed to fill. While Leonardo was working for Cesare Borgia, and sketching ideal fortress towns, Giuliano was designing or building three actual structures which established the angle bastion—in these instances with round shoulders protecting flank batteries—as the principal and normal element of a fortress: at Borgo San Sepolcro (plate 30), planned in 1500 and built between 1502 and *c.* 1505; at Nettuno (plate 31), built 1501–3; and at Arezzo (plate 32), planned in 1502, built from 1503.[1]

The story of the bastion in the next thirty years can be quickly told, first in terms of the fort, then of the town wall. Only in the next fort to be built, Bramante's *rocca* at Civitavecchia,[2] begun in 1508, was the round form of bastion still used. The fort is rectangular with four corner bastions, one of which (plate 33) is entirely solid, the others have gun-ports low in the flank, opening from chambers common to both flanks. The great hexagonal tower (plate 34) in the middle of the curtain on the harbour side serves both as bastion and *mastio*; it was completed, after Bramante's death, by Michelangelo. In the following year, 1509, Giuliano da San Gallo designed a fort to hold down Pisa after its capture by the Florentines. In poor condition, and too overgrown to allow details of the bastions to be seen clearly in photographs, its plan (modified in the course of construction[3]) can be grasped from de Marchi's drawing[4]

---

[1] See Marchini, op. cit., for dates. The project for incorporating the *rocca* at Borgo San Sepolcro with a new overall defence for the town (fols. 28r–28(a)r in Ferrante Vitelli's untitled MS. in the library of the Museo del Genio in Rome) was not carried out. One bastion was, instead, greatly extended, *c.* 1540, on the model of a similar addition made to the *rocca* at Arezzo, ordered by Cosimo I (see de Marchi's plan, B.N.F. II, i, 280, fol. 13r). Unknown to the literature of fortification, the *rocca* at San Sepolcro cries for detailed investigation.

[2] Rocchi, *Fonti* . . ., 145–6. Guglielmotti, op. cit., 189–240.

[3] Cf. Giuliano's original plan in his Sienese sketchbook, ed. Falb (Siena, 1902).

[4] MS. cit., fol. 8r.

(plate 38). The date, (probably 1518 for the design) and the author (probably one of the San Gallo) of the *rocca* which guards the harbour of Livorno (plate 36) are both in doubt.[1] This powerful fortress, unusual for the height of its bastions and the strength of the armament in its concealed flanks, shares with so many of its contemporaries the distinction of being ignored by architectural historians and by a government otherwise so zealous in the protection of the great monuments of the Renaissance. Similar obscurity surrounds the angle-bastioned *rocca* at Bari (probably *c.* 1520);[2] neither it nor the similar *rocca* at Barletta (1532–7) are as advanced as the Tuscan fortresses and cannot compare in strength, firepower or the rational combination of parts with the Fortezza da Basso at Florence,[3] designed in 1533 by Antonio da San Gallo the younger and illustrated here from de Marchi's plan[4] (plate 38). Begun in 1534 and brought rapidly to completion as it can be seen today (except for later masonry in the flank batteries) this fortress, hailed by Vasari as 'untakeable' and by Francesco de Hollanda as 'the finest fort in Europe' is a symbol both of the new Medici domination of Florence and Italian domination of the new fortification.

The use of the angle bastion in town walls was more hesitant than in fortresses. Biagio Rossetti used round bastions in the stretches of the Ferrara wall he built for Ercole I between *c.* 1500 and *c.* 1506.[5] The first walls to be re-built on a large scale were those of Padua and Treviso in face of the threat presented to them by the League of Cambrai, whose armies invaded the Veneto in 1509. On the strength of an assertion by Marin Sanudo that their engineer, Fra Giocondo, 'wanted to make angles in the walls' it has been claimed that Fra Giocondo was the inventor of the angle bastion.[6] It is by no means clear, however, that Sanudo was referring to bastions, and all the indications

---

[1] See Clausses and Giovannoni, opera cit., and G. Nudi, *Storia urbanistica di Livorno* (Venezia, 1959), 82.
[2] G. Bacile di Castiglione, *Castelli Pugliesi* (Rome, 1927), 48–64 (with plan).
[3] MS., cit., fol. 3r.
[4] L. Dami, 'La fortezza da Basso', *Arte e Storia* (1915), 162–4. Also M. Borgatti, 'Le mura e le torri di Firenze', *Rivista d'Artiglieria e Genio*, (1900) iv, 273–322. Originally called the fort of S Giovanni, it was called 'da basso' after the erection of the fort of S Giorgio (the Belvedere) on the heights above the Boboli gardens.
[5] U. Malagù, *Le mura di Ferrara* (Ferrara, 1960), 10.
[6] G. Fiocco in his edition of Vasari's *Vita di Fra Giocondo*, 2 vols., (Florence, 1915) i, 45. The claim is repeated in R. Brenzoni, *Fra Giovanni Giocondo Veronese* (Florence, 1960), 69.

are that Padua (like Treviso) was strengthened with round bastions, first built in a hurry of earth and timber. None of Fra Giocondo's works remains in its original form, but when the fortifications of Padua were consolidated from 1513 under the direction of Bartolomeo d'Alviano, he continued to use round bastions, facing Fra Giocondo's with stone and constructing others. The first angle bastions at Padua date from 1526–30.[1] There are no angle bastions at Treviso. Three angle bastions were added to the wall of Ferrara by Alfonso I between 1512 and 1518,[2] and the town wall of Civitavecchia, planned in 1515 but now destroyed (if indeed it was built according to this plan[3]) was for a regular angle-bastioned front. This design was determined on after those of Antonio da San Gallo the younger had been approved by a group of practising soldiers, including Pedro Navarro and Giovan Paolo Baglioni, and their endorsement of the angle shape led Antonio Fiorentino, who had been present at the conference, to change from the round to the angle shape for the bastions he was constructing for the new *enceinte* of the Castel Nuovo.[4] The town walls of Urbino (plate 39), Pesaro and Senigallia, which were probably begun *c.* 1515[5] used angle bastions, but when Loreto was refortified after the Turkish raid on the nearby Porto Recanati in 1518, the main works consisted of two great round bastions (plate 41), finished in 1521.[6] And when Verona was strengthened from 1520 after its walls had fallen into grave disrepair during the sieges of 1509 and 1516, the new bastions were round, with one exception: Michele dei Leoni's bastion dalla Maddalena of 1527. It was subsequently altered by Michele Sanmicheli, whose own works, employing angle bastions, did not begin there until *c.* 1530.[7]

It is not altogether surprising, then, that among the bastions suggested by Machiavelli and Navarro in 1526 for the walls of

[1] G. Rusconi, *Le mura di Padova*, 2nd edn. (Bassano, 1921), 58 ff.
[2] Malagù, op. cit., 21 and A. Frizzi, *Memorie per la storia di Ferrara*, 2nd edn., (Ferrara, 1848) iv, 266, 283.
[3] On the dating controversy (which has not been resolved), see L. Celli, 'Le fortificazioni militari di Urbino, Pesaro e Senigallia del secolo XVI', *Nuova Rivista Misena* (1895), 74 ff.
[4] R. Filangieri, op. cit., 282.
[5] Serra and Celli, opera cit.
[6] Serra, *L'arte nella Marche*, 109–12. I have not been able to find a copy of P. del Monte, *Il santuario di Loreto e le sue difese militari* (Loreto, 1929).
[7] E. Langenskiöld, *Michele Sanmicheli the architect of Verona* (Uppsala, 1938), *passim*.

Florence, the only two whose shape is specifically mentioned were to be round,[1] or that their plans were altered when Michelangelo was put in charge of the fortifications in 1529.[2] None of his work survives as he designed it; what we see is due to Antonio da San Gallo the younger who consolidated the defences after 1534; as only angle bastions can be seen today, it is most likely that Michelangelo's bastions were in that form. In August 1529, moreover, he had been sent to look at the fortifications of Ferrara, where the latest bastions were angled, and in none of his many drawings of the time of the siege is there anything but various forms of angle bastion. These drawings have been studied by Charles de Tolnay, who concluded that 'from the point of view of military effectiveness, the projects of Michelangelo seem to be the most perfect fortification plans of the sixteenth century. In fact, the possibility of a successful enemy attack was reduced to a minimum and at the same time a maximum of active defence was assured'.[3] This is to go too far. In the series of crustacea-like bastions (plate 41) which recall some of the designs of Francesco di Giorgio (plate 42) Michelangelo shows a far greater concern than any previous theorist with the dynamic, attacking role of the bastion, but by clinging to elaborately protected embrasures of small traverse he produced bastions which would be difficult to build, full of vulnerable projections and requiring a numerous armament. The future lay not with these opulent fantasies, but with platforms of simple plan, and wide embrasures or a low parapet over which guns could fire in any direction. That Michelangelo did actually build bastions at Florence is clear from contemporary criticisms[4] that they had too many flanks and too many embrasures, but it is probable that drawings like the one illustrated here are indeed fantasies: doodlings prompted by the actual needs of Florence but following a

[1] 'Baluardo tondo'. It may be that the shape is specified on these occasions because the pentagonal shape is taken for granted elsewhere.
[2] 'Governatore e procuratore generale delle fortificazioni della città'. This was on 6th April. From 10th January he had been a member of the *nove della milizia*. Barocchi, op. cit., i, 128.
[3] 'Michelangelo studies', *Art Bulletin* (1940), 136.
[4] De Tolnay, ibid., p. 136, footnote. The fact that these works were hastily made of temporary materials—earth and straw faced with unbaked bricks—rather than San Gallo's disapproval of them may account for their disappearance before Vasari painted the city's southern walls in his fresco in the Palazzo della Signoria.

purely aesthetic impulse towards a more open architectural style.[1]

It was in 1534, the year in which the Fortezza da Basso was begun in Florence, that the angle bastion may be said to have become the norm in town defences. In August of that year Turkish raids on the Lazio coast and at the mouth of the Tiber caused Clement VII to fear for the safety of the capital itself, and after a conference of soldiers and architects, Antonio da San Gallo's plan for an angle-bastioned *enceinte* for the Borgo (the present Vatican city) was approved and begun. These fortifications, and those that were begun soon after on the south of the city[2] between Porta S Paolo and Porta S Sebastiano, became the subject of intense publicity, and not only because they were seen by every visitor to Rome: their progress was attended by much, and often acrimonious debate among the architects, including Michelangelo, who were consulted as each new section was planned. These debates, however, were concerned with the siting of the defences and the length of curtain between bastions: there was never any doubt that the angle bastion was the only form to be used.

The life of the round bastion still flickered on here and there. Paul III himself—he had succeeded Clement VIII just before the Borgo defences were begun—had a round bastion built to defend the entrance to the *rocca maggiore* at Assisi in 1535-8;[3] far in the south, round tower bastions were constructed at Lecce and Cotrone in the 'forties. But these were remote and unimportant exceptions. Controversy remained lively, but it was restricted to various forms of the angle bastion, particularly as to how batteries at various levels were to be so housed in its flanks that their field of fire could be as wide as possible—in order that, in Galileo's terminology,[4] the flanking *tiro che*

---

[1] With reference to the treatment of space in the Laurentian library and the Capitoline Hill, etc., J. S. Ackerman comments in *The Architecture of Michelangelo*, 2 vols., (London, 1961) i, 53: 'The necessity to find an architectural solution for projectiles in constant radial motion along infinitely varied paths must have helped to remove from his mind the last vestiges of the static figures and proportions of the Quattrocento'.

[2] M. Borgatti, 'Le mura di Roma', *Rivista d'Artiglieria e Genio*, (1890) ii, 325-403, with plans, and 'Il bastione ardeatino a Roma', ibid., (1916) ii, 207-23, with plans.

[3] A. Brizi, *Della rocca di Assisi* (Assisi, 1898), 439-40. Plans.

[4] For Galileo's perfect bastion, which had a large gun chamber (protected by a round shoulder) housing four guns firing (a) out to the adjacent covered way and some distance into the field, (b) along the opposite bastion face, (c) into the opposite bastion face, to dislodge mining parties, etc., (d) into the adjacent curtain and along it, see the diagram in the Florence, 1932 edition of his *Trattato di Fortificazione*, p. 123.

Verona
Treviso
Padua
Ferrara
Sarzanello
Sarzana
Imola
Pisa
Livorno
Florence
Forli
Forlimpopoli
Cesena
Volterra
Certaldo
Poggio Imperiale
S. Arcangelo di Roma
Colle di val d'Elsa
Brolio
S. Leo
Sassocorvaro
Pesaro
Arezzo
Fano
Borgo S. Sepolcro
Urbino
Mondavio
Cagli
Senigallia
Corinaldo
Ostra
Castel d'Emilio
Morro d'Alba
Osimo
Loretto
Assisi
Civitavecchia
Civita Castellana
Bracciano
Nepi
Offida
Rome
L'Aquila
Ostia Antica
Tivoli
Grottaferrata
Avezzano
Nettuno
N
Naples
Barletta
Bari

striscia could be combined with *tiro che ficca* directed along the covered way and into the field—or whether there should be any batteries at all below the platform. The experiment at L'Aquila (plate 42) in 1535 was an isolated one. Elsewhere, practice did no more than refine upon the round-shouldered models of Giuliano, and the square-shouldered ones of Antonio da San Gallo.

Looking back, then, we see that the core of the development we have been describing lay in central Italy. In the parts of the country most open to northern influence, fortifications remained conservative; nothing new from Lombardy or the Trentino; Venice herself remained reactionary until she employed an architect, Sanmicheli, who had formed his ideas south of the Veneto. From the Spanish-influenced kingdom of Naples we have only the abortive experiment of the gun terrace. Other countries had to adapt fortification to the challenge of gunpowder: the *enceinte* of Mont S Michel (1426–45) is a practical, Dürer's *Etliche underricht, zu befestigung der Stett, Schloss, und Flecken* (Nüremberg, 1527) a theoretical example. Certain specially vulnerable sites were forced to produce defence methods which were possibly independent of Italian example, such as the barbican-bastion in late fifteenth-century Rhodes.[1] The purpose of this essay is no more ambitious than to suggest that the bastioned front, in the treatment of which the Italians were universally acknowledged to be the leaders by the middle of the sixteenth century,[2] was the product of an indigenous and consistent development from the middle of the *quattrocento*.

---

[1] But this does not justify B. M. St J. O'Neil's 'If, therefore, one asks the question, "Who invented the bastion?" The present writer suggests that the answer should be "Pierre d'Aubusson at Rhodes in 1496" '—with reference to the Boulevard d'Auvergne, in *The Antiquaries Journal* (1954), 52. This fine article suffers by ignoring contemporary Italian work and the writings of Italian scholars, especially those of G. Gerola, e.g. 'Il contributo dell'Italia alle opere d'arte militare rodiesi', *Atti del R. Istituto Veneto di scienze, lettere ed arte* (1930), especially 1019 and 1027.

[2] The most thorough survey is provided by L. A. Maggiorotti, *L'opera del genio italiano all'estero*, 3 vols. (Rome, 1936–9). It is, however, a work of propaganda, is inadequately documented, and, in Europe, only covers Spain, Portugal and Hungary.

2

THE END OF FLORENTINE LIBERTY: THE FORTEZZA DA BASSO[1]

Covering an area of some 118,884 square metres, the Fortezza da Basso[2] is the largest historical monument in Florence. But quite apart from its size, it deserves study on two accounts: it is the first mature statement of the new principles of fortress design that were to provide a norm for the next three centuries,[3] and it became a symbol of despotism as powerful in the eyes of sixteenth-century Florentines as was the Bastille to eighteenth-century Frenchmen.

The Florentines had always been touchy on the subject of fortresses within the city. As their sister republic, Venice, relied for defence on the lagoon, so the Florentines relied upon their walls. With a constitution designed to prevent the accumulation of power in the hands of one family, and with a mood that made Cosimo de' Medici reject the original plans for his palace as too ostentatious, Florence — unlike Milan, or Ferrara, or the petty despotisms of the Marche and Romagna — was not the place for a political leader to try to fortify himself. The Duke of Athens had found this to his cost,[4] and with Florentine

---

[1] I wish to acknowledge that Professor Guido Morozzi, Soprintendente ai Monumenti per le Provincie di Firenze, Arezzo e Pistoia, took a generous interest in my work. I am also indebted to Dr Randolph Starn, who read this essay in MS. (and is in no way responsible for any errors that remain), and to the hospitality of Professor Myron Gilmore, Director of the Harvard Centre for Renaissance Studies at I Tatti.
[2] On the name Fortezza da Basso, v. Appendix below, pp. 61–2.
[3] J. R. Hale, 'The Early development of the Bastion: an Italian chronology c. 1450–c. 1534,' in *Europe in the Late Middle Ages*, ed. J. R. Hale, J. R. L. Highfield and B. Smalley (London, 1965), pp. 466–94. See above, pp. 1–29.
[4] For his treating the Palazzo della Signoria as a personal stronghold, creating a personal guard and attempting to disarm the citizens — two more parallels to Alessandro de' Medici's policy — v. Marchionne Stefani, *Cronaca Fiorentina*, R.I.S., vol. XXX, pt. I, esp. pp. 199–200. And Vasari: 'il duca aveva in animo di fare una fortezza sopra la costa di S. Giorgio', i.e. where the Belvedere was eventually built. For this,

republicanism becoming more self-conscious during the century and a half that followed his expulsion, it seemed less and less likely that Florence would permit a citadel to be built athwart its walls. Machiavelli, addressing himself to a tyro prince, declared that even if a ruler wished to build a fortress in order to bridle a restless people, it would not work: it would only enrage them the more and bring about his ruin. And he cited the Castello Sforzesco to prove his case.[1] Yet in 1534 work began on a building that was to test his thesis more intimately, the Fortezza da Basso.

The outcry that went up when this bridle was slipped in place owes something to the tradition: citadels for tyrants, walls for a free people; but it owes something, too, to the peculiar nature of Florentine republicanism. The city's sense of freedom had persisted throughout periods of undoubted oligarchical rule, it had swallowed rigged elections and partisan foreign policies, it had survived, between 1512 and 1527, the piecemeal dismantling of republican institutions. Something of it stubbornly lived on after the Republic's defeat in arms in 1530 and the establishment of Alessandro de' Medici as 'duca'. Then, in 1534, for the first time in Florentine history, appeared the concrete, visible evidence that freedom was in fetters. It was this even more than the constitutional changes of 1532[2] that made it clear that the word republic was about to become meaningless.

In 1533 Alessandro tactlessly had his own arms carved over the newly enlarged fort at the Porta alla Giustizia.[3] Giannotti, writing the first chapter of his *Della Republica Fiorentina* in the next year while the Fortezza da Basso was being built, referred to such works as evidence that a republic was being challenged by a tyranny,[4] and when the first garrison was installed in 1535, that apolitical but keen Medicean, Giorgio Vasari, echoed his party's glee that they had acquired a 'yoke for their critics'.[5] He reaffirmed this opinion in his portrait of Alessandro

---

and for the Duke's aim of transforming the Palazzo della Signoria into 'a strong fortress', see the Life of Andrea Pisano, *Lives* . . . , tr. Mrs. J. Foster, vol. I (London, 1845), pp. 151–2.

[1] *Discorsi*, II, 24.

[2] On which see A. Anzilotti, *La costituzione interna dello stato fiorentino sotto il duca Cosimo de' Medici* (Florence, 1910), pp. 29–30.

[3] 'A Giovanni di Lorenzo detto Bicci scarpellino £84 sono per havere intagliato l'arme dell'Ilustrissimo Signore Duca in pietra per la porta della Iustitia', A.S.F., Capitani di Parte, 14 rosso, fol. 335r. On this fort, see below.

[4] *Opere politiche e letterarie*, ed. F.-I. Polidori (Florence, 1850), vol. I, p. 66.

[5] 'Si vedevano sù per le mura, circondandole attorno, un pieno di soldati, facendo corona al giogo de mal contenti', K. Frey, *Der literarische Nachlass Giorgio Vasaris* (Munich, 1923), p. 42. Letter of 11 December 1535 to Pietro Aretino. Description of

(plate 1). The picture was painted in Alessandro's lifetime, and Vasari explained its iconography in a letter to Ottaviano de'Medici who was concerned, if glancingly, with the construction of the Fortezza. The artist's opinion, therefore, is not likely to be at variance with that of the Medici themselves. He explains that the human figures who decorate the legs of the stool ('round, to show his unending dominion') represent the Florentine people, who need neither arms nor legs, for they are made to obey, not to act of their own volition. Underneath the stool is the shadowy figure of Volubility, from whose bridled mouth run bonds which wrap round the term-like extremities of the 'Florentines'. 'This', Vasari wrote, 'is to show that this unstable people are bound and steadied by the fortress that has been built, and' — he adds — 'by the love that his subjects bear towards His Excellency.' The garrison took over in December.

In the spring of the same year the critics had already registered their alarm with the Emperor. In April both Cardinal Ipolito de' Medici (who was hoping to replace Alessandro) and the Florentine exiles sent embassies to Charles V in Barcelona. The cardinal warned Charles that among other misdeeds, Alessandro 'was at the moment building a fortress at great expense as the sole guarantee of his safety', while the exiles put it more strongly, saying that every condition of tyranny was present in Florence now that 'a great fortress was being built with the blood of that unhappy people, as a prison and slaughter-house for the distressed citizens.'[1]

It is not surprising that at the formal confrontation next year between the exiles and Alessandro with his representatives before the Emperor in Naples, the Fortezza should figure among the exiles' gravamina. Not only had Alessandro disarmed the citizens — even going so far as to impound the weapons hung as votive offerings in the churches — but he had built a fortress, 'a thing totally inappropriate to a free city, as the examples of Venice, Siena, Lucca and Genoa clearly show.'[2] To which the answer was that the very presence of the exiles was a sufficient explanation; with such malcontents to take advantage of the disturbed state of Italy, every means had to be taken to preserve the government which had been planned for the benefit of Florence

---

the portrait in G. Bottari, *Raccolta di Lettere sulla Pittura, Scultura ed Architettura* (Milan, 1822), vol. III, pp. 22–3.

[1] Francesco Settimanni, *Memorie Fiorentine*, A.S.F., Manoscritti, 125, fols. 190r and 184r.

[2] From the debate printed in F. Guicciardini, *Opere Inedite*, ed. G. Canestrini, vol. IX (Florence, 1867), p. 336.

[3] Ibid., 369.

both by pope and emperor. Not a very satisfactory answer, but a sufficient one, for, as we shall see, Charles V himself was convinced that the Fortezza was a necessity.

Henceforward, the connection between the Fortezza and Medicean tyranny became a liberal dogma. Lorenzino's *Apologia* for assassinating Alessandro, though generalized and rhetorical, associated the building of fortresses with the evils of tyranny,[1] and the historians perpetuated this sinister view. According to Segni, for example, it was built because the Medici determined 'to place on the necks of the Florentines a yoke of a kind never experienced before: a citadel, whereby the citizens lost all hope of ever living in freedom again'.[2]

This has remained the standard view,[3] but before accepting it in its black and white republican form, we must see if there was a military, as distinct from any private political motive behind the construction of the Fortezza. As always when dealing with the first half of the century, there is a danger of following too readily the opinions of the most diligent and the most eloquent historians, who were republican almost to a man.

The principle that fortresses were useful in subduing subject peoples as well as defending the towns of the *dominio* from outside enemies was well established in Tuscany. Volterra was gripped by its *rocca* in 1472. Citadels were begun in Borgo San Sepolcro in 1500, in Arezzo (after the revolt in Val di Chiana) in 1502, in Pisa after its defeat in 1509; the project for the Fortezza Vecchia in Leghorn dates from 1518. Nothing like a citadel was projected for Florence itself, however, even when the city expelled the Medici once more in 1527 and prepared its defences to withstand a siege.

Though Florence fell in 1530 as a result of blockade and treachery rather than by direct assault, considerable thought had been given to strengthening its walls. As Busini explained to Varchi, the fortifications had been improved before the siege, but these improvements had fallen far short of what should have been done. Partly this was because republics always take a long time to make up their minds and grasp at any argument that may delay drastic action, and partly it was because the Florentines thought that their hills amounted to an outer line of defences, that the besieging armies would retire to winter

---

[1] See the version printed in L. Lazzarini, *Lorenzino de' Medici* (Milan, 1935), p. 217.
[2] *Storie fiorentine* (Leghorn, 1830), vol. II, p. 400.
[3] It cropped up again in the Risorgimento, e.g. '*Delenda Carthago.*' *Le fortezze erette dai tiranni per mitragliare i popoli. La fortezza di Perugia, e i forti di S. Giovanni e di S. Giorgio [the Belvedere] in Firenze* (Florence, 1859).

quarters, and that the Pope could not afford to keep them for long in the field. All these expectations had proved illusory.[1]

That this attitude was shared by others is shown by the creation, on 18 April 1531, of a new body, the *Cinque Uomini Provveditori delle Fortezze della Città et Dominio Fiorentino*.[2] Though this was a party measure, it was to enable all citizens and subjects to feel safe in any emergency that might arise in the future.[3] The magistrates, four of whom were to be chosen from the greater and one from the lesser gilds, were to adopt as their seal, 'S. Giovanni, advocate and protector of our city'. They were to conduct their affairs — this was four months before the arrival of Alessandro in Florence — as with the full authority of the whole Florentine people, and were to restore, modify or extend[4] the city's fortifications as seemed best to them.

Their first extant order — and the fragmentary nature of the sources for the entire period covered by this study must be borne in mind — was a proclamation to ensure such effectiveness as the existing walls possessed.[5] It was acknowledged that many houses had been demolished in order to make room for the new bastions built on the eve of the siege and to ensure a clear field of fire from the walls, but the *provveditori* considered that as it was in the city's interest to maintain and extend its fortifications, no rebuilding or new building was to be allowed within 500 *braccia*[6] of the walls (interpreted as a line drawn from point to point of adjacent towers or bastions) on three sides of the city, and 300 on the hilly side of the Oltrarno. Beyond that, only small agricultural buildings would be licensed, up to a limit of 1000 *braccia*. There was to be no tampering with the existing walls or bastions (which had been built very hastily), no removal of building materials, no animals were to work or stray within 25 *braccia* on pain of a fine of twenty-five florins plus two jerks of the rope for their owner. And the records show a steady expenditure on walls and gates in the next two

---

[1] *Lettere di Giovambattista Busini a Benedetto Varchi sopra l'assedio di Firenze*, ed. G. Milanesi (Florence, 1860), pp. 128–9.

[2] The *provvisione* setting up this magistracy survives in a copy in A.S.F., Capitani di Parte, 10 rosso, fol. 77v ff. They are also called 'procuratori'.

[3] '... accioche e loro ciptadini et qualunche altro habitante in quelli viva sicuro sanza avere alcuno sospecto da tucto li accidenti che potessino nascere', ibid., fol. 77v.

[4] 'affare di nuovo', 'nuova hedifichatione', ibid., fol. 78v.

[5] Undated, but in full, A.S.F., Carte Strozz., Ser. I, XCVIII, fols. 112r–113v; recorded and dated A.S.F., Capitani di Parte, 10 rosso, fols. 80r–80v.

[6] The Florentine *braccio* at this time was $23\frac{1}{3}$ inches according to a line drawn by the military engineer Giambattista Bellucci, Florence, Bibl. Riccardiana, MS. 2587, fol. 27v.

years, strengthening them and adapting them further to the use of artillery.[1]

These works can fairly be considered as in the general interest of Florence; they affected the walls. The first hint of a citadel appears in February 1532 when, in connection with the government's scheme to confiscate arms in order to emasculate any tendency to revolt, Francesco Vettori wrote to Filippo Strozzi saying 'I should like to see them in a secure place; a fortress would be suitable, either where the *capitani* have already started work, or somewhere else'.[2] Where the *capitani* di Parte Guelfa, who were in charge of building operations, had been at work was outside the Porta alla Giustizia, where the eastern wall met the north bank of the Arno (plate 2). This corner had been rapidly reinforced before the siege by a bastion which covered any attempt to come downstream (flat-bottomed boats could have got across the fish-weir at this point) into the city (plate 3), and by an earthwork[3] which was later rationalized into the Baluardo di Mongibello on the lines of a design by Antonio da Sangallo (plate 4). The bastion was designed by Michelangelo, and according to Giannotti,[4] it was one of his most important works for the siege, the others being the encircling of S. Miniato and the bastion near Porta S. Giorgio. Its incorporation into the Baluardo di Mongibello made up a complex important enough to be called 'Citadella Vecchia' on de Marchi's mid-century plan (plates 5 and 6); 'vecchia' in contrast to the Fortezza da Basso.

When work began at the Porta alla Giustizia after the siege the *provveditori* (and from 1532 the *Capitani di Parte Guelfa*, into which magistracy they became absorbed) must have looked on it as a civic, rather than a Medicean, enterprise. The Arno had damaged the riverside section of the defences, and the attacks that had been launched on this side of the city during the siege made their consolidation logically part of a programme of repair. During the siege the works had not been extensive. In a list of troops needed to man the city's strong points, the Porta alla Giustizia was allocated two hundred men, while other gates-with-bastions were given more: three hundred for S. Gallo, five hundred for S. Giorgio.[5] No accounts survive for the first, the 'civic',

---

[1] E.g. for the western length, where the Fortezza was soon to be built, A.S.F., Capitani di Parte, 14 rosso, fols. 325v and 340r.
[2] L. A. Ferrai, *Lorenzino de' Medici e la Società Cortigiana del Cinquecento* (Milan, 1891), p. 452.
[3] Varchi, *Storia fiorentina* (Florence, 1838–41), vol. II, p. 198.
[4] Op. cit., vol. I, p. 258.
[5] A.S.F., Carte Strozz., Ser. I, XIV, fol. 33r.

rebuilding, but by the early summer of 1533 the *capitani* are spending large sums to provide an *enceinte* large enough to store the city's artillery and the confiscated arms of the Florentines, and possibly to turn Michelangelo's bastion into a keep or *mastio*.[1] By December of that year Alessandro's arms were in place, but it could still be argued that it was a work designed to protect the city as a whole. Even when Antonio da Sangallo submitted a plan (probably in 1534) (plate 7) that would have provided it with an ingeniously intricate entrance, which meant that everyone entering the gate would have to twist and turn under constant fire, his bastion, though more complex than most, could not possibly be interpreted as anti-city; it is directed against enemies from outside. Well before this, however, it had been decided, as we shall see, to build another strong point. 'Judging that the fortress at the Porta alla Giustizia was inadequate, [Alessandro] ordered the building of a really strong citadel at the Porta a Faenza.' Thus Scipione Ammirato.[2] But was the Citadella Vecchia thought inadequate to protect Alessandro, or the city as a whole?

The 'Spanish Peace' which seems in retrospect to have damped down the fires of war in Italy during the 1530s did not appear in this friendly guise to contemporaries. Relations between Charles V and Francis I remained uneasy; Italy might at any moment become once more their battlefield. Savoy, Milan: these remained danger spots. Towed in the wake of papal foreign policies, Florence could not expect to avoid involvement if these led to war; the rebuilding of the city walls after the siege was not merely in the interest of appearance or amenity. The early thirties, moreover, were full of scares of Turkish landings, and these culminated in 1534 with a series of new Italian fortifications, of which the Fortezza da Basso was only one. The corsairs had been striking further and further north. Clement VII, startled by landings at the mouth of the Tiber, called a conference of soldiers and military architects at Rome and began work on the city's walls; Antonio da Sangallo was already re-fortifying Ancona. In May the Pope imposed a tax throughout his states for defences against the Turks;[3] and, according to

---

[1] The accounts are in A.S.F., Capitani di Parte, 14 rosso, fol. 318r ff. 'A spese della muraglia della porta alla giustizia per tener in conservo le artillerie et munitione della citta.' The difference seen in the form of the river bastion between the fresco of Vasari and the Buonsignori engraving may be explained by the item (ibid., fol. 325r) 'per fattura di uno castello con tutti i suo fornimenti', but the development of the Citadella Vecchia — all traces of which disappeared in the middle of the nineteenth century — will probably always remain obscure. I know of no study devoted to it.

[2] *Opuscoli* (Florence, 1642), p. 154.

[3] C. Guasti, *I Manoscritti Torrigiani donati al R. Archivio di Stato di Firenze* (Florence, 1878), pp. 473–4.

Varchi, when Alessandro called on the Florentines to pay an *accatto* for the Fortezza, one of the reasons he gave was the Turkish menace.[1] With the Citadella Vecchia finished, it was not inappropriate to concentrate on the opposite side of the city, with its level ground facing Prato and the main route to the sea.[2] Moreover, the Fortezza was only one part, if the most sensational, in a defence programme inaugurated after the siege and carried on throughout Cosimo's reign. In 1534 other defences in the *dominio* were strengthened, Pontassieve,[3] for instance, and Arezzo, where Luigi Guicciardini, its commissary, was eager to finish the citadel begun early in the century by Giuliano da Sangallo; the Fortezza Vecchia at Leghorn was completed in this year. In 1539 Cosimo ordered a survey of all the forts in the *dominio*.[4] This was followed by heavy expenditure on the walls of Pistoia in 1544-45,[5] and in the latter year by the commencement of the bastioned trace that formed a hypotenuse inside the south-west triangle of the old city wall of Florence and was the work of (among others) Baccio Bandinelli and Benvenuto Cellini (plate 8).[6] Arezzo may be a special case; its record during the siege makes it likely that a citadel there was as much a political as a military necessity, but elsewhere the Medicean fortifications can be interpreted as in the strategic interests of Florence and Tuscany as a whole.

This, I think, is as strong a case as can be put, without disingenuousness, for the building of the Fortezza on military rather than on partisan grounds. It is tempting to see it as a good case; posterity has — at least since the nineteenth century — been so absorbed with republican Florence that the quality of Medici rule and the solid advantages it gave to the city and *dominio* have been examined with comparatively little care, and less sympathy. But if we look more closely at the motives for building the Fortezza we shall find that, while a military objective may have added a gloss to the decision, it was constructed mainly to support an unpopular régime.

There is, indeed, a second issue here: how far can the building of the Fortezza be represented as the precaution taken by a responsible body

---

[1] Op. cit., vol. III, p. 77.
[2] As plate 38 shows ('bastion' da farsi') the *Capitani* were still concerned to strengthen this approach to the city in the following century. 'Bastione del Serpe' is the consolidation of the bastion built there in preparation for the siege of 1529.
[3] A.S.F., Otto di Pratica, Copialettere, 31, fol. 75v.
[4] A.S.F., Mediceo del Principato, Carteggio Universale, 624.
[5] Giambattista Bellucci, *Trattato delle Fortificazioni di Terra*, Bibl. Riccardiana, MS. 2587, fol. 34r ff.
[6] M. Borgatti, 'Le mura e le torri di Firenze', *Rivista d'Artiglieria e Genio* (1900), vol. iv, pp. 319-20, and his excellent map.

of *grandi* — as distinct from the personal aims of Alessandro, Clement and Charles — to protect what they saw as the true political interests of Florence? But the analysis of the political temper of Florence after the siege is not yet sufficiently far advanced to permit an answer to this: such an answer would depend on a judgment of how far the pro-Medicean *grandi* were merely using the Medici rather than self-interestedly identifying themselves with the family. All we can do is emphasize that there was nothing in the popular or aristocratic traditions of the city that prepared the way for controlling it by force.

The terms of the Republic's capitulation in 1530 were that while the city's institutions should remain, Alessandro should be received as head (*capo*) of the government. In the interest of reaching an agreement without much delay the terms were vague and turned out to be unsatisfactory to both parties; the guarantees were too weak for the republicans, the definition of their status too unclear for Alessandro and his supporters. Behind the negotiations loomed the authority of Clement and Charles V, and Clement negotiated the betrothal of Charles's daughter Margaret to Alessandro as a means of increasing the Emperor's concern for the new government, but by the end of 1531 Alessandro and the Pope saw their position weakening both within the city and outside it, as an ever-growing band of exiles plotted a violent return.

In the winter of 1531–32 Clement asked for advice from the most prominent citizens whom he considered trustworthy either because they were devoted to the Medici family, or because they saw it as the only hope of lasting peace. During the previous period of Medici control, from 1512 to 1527, the Medici popes, Leo X and Clement himself, had also asked for advice, and what emerges as something quite new is a note of desperation, a reliance on force, that was lacking in the counsel given before 1527.

The idea of a Medicean fortress — suggested possibly by the works proceeding at the Porta alla Giustizia and the growing conviction that Alessandro needed a large personal guard with secure barracks — was discussed during that winter in Rome. The information comes from Nerli, but he was there, and reports that while Filippo Strozzi urged Clement to build a citadel, another spokesman, Iacopo Salviati, countered with the Machiavellian argument that the strongest fortresses that can be built are the benevolence of rulers and the content of subjects.[1] Segni says that Luigi Guicciardini also pleaded for a citadel,

---

[1] R. von Albertini, *Das Florentinische Staatsbewusstsein im Übergang von der Republik zum Prinzipat* (Bern, 1955), p. 192. This provides by far the best commentary on the political and institutional events of Alessandro's rule, short as the relevant section is.

not so much for Alessandro himself as for the defence of the whole inner group of Medici partisans.[1]

That the historians can be trusted at this point is suggested by the written proposals directed to Clement VII or his agent the Archbishop of Capua. Francesco Guicciardini, while not mentioning a fortress, emphasized the degree to which the régime was on the defensive: 'we have a whole people opposed to us, and the young more than the old.'[2] For Francesco Vettori the situation was such that 'we must think in terms of maintaining our rule by force . . . we are constrained to govern by fear',[3] and in the letter to Filippo Strozzi of 2 February 1532 he summed up by saying that besides increasing Medici control over the city's administration, they should 'finish the Fortezza alla Giustizia'.[4] Luigi Guicciardini, in his written advice, contented himself with suggesting a strengthening of Alessandro's bodyguard,[5] and it is Vettori who emerges — from the sources that survive — as the most persistent advocate of a citadel. In October, writing to Bartolomeo Lanfredini, he went a step further than his letter of February: 'having made a trifling fortress which cannot be taken without artillery, it would be still better to build another which could be defended by artillery.'[6]

The situation in Florence was meanwhile deteriorating still further. Alessandro gave his enemies fresh fuel for resentment when he confiscated pikes and guns and forbad the carrying of any weapons other than sword and dagger within an eight mile radius of the city,[7] and still more when he enlarged his guard and made an outsider, Alessandro Vitelli, its commander. The government's growing sense of panic is shown in the at times almost daily toll of finings, bannings and executions on political grounds. By 1535 a charge of un-Medicean activities could be tagged on as a matter of course to an accusation of homosexuality.[8]

---

[1] Op. cit., vol. II, p. 341.
[2] *A.S.I.*, vol. I (1842), p. 455.
[3] Ibid., pp. 438 and 440.
[4] Ferrai, op. cit., p. 454.
[5] *A.S.I.*, vol. I (1842), p. 465.
[6] Printed in von Albertini, op. cit., p. 450. For the *pareri* in general see the important article by Felix Gilbert, 'Alcuni discorsi di uomini politici fiorentini . . .', *A.S.I.*, vol. XCIII, ii (1935), pp. 3–24.
[7] Giovambattista Adriani, *Istoria de' Suoi Tempi* (Prato, 1822), vol. I, p. 10.
[8] For condemnations see Settimanni's margins (MS. cit.) *passim*. 'Addì XXIII di Dicembre 1535. Maso di Carlo Strozzi cittadino fiorentino per avere usato il vizio di sodomia con più fanciulli, aver date pugnalate a più persone, e parlato malamente del presente governo di Firenze fu condannato in pena della forca colla confiscazione de' suoi beni.' Fol. 223v.

In such an atmosphere the idea of a large safe citadel became increasingly reassuring. Luigi Guicciardini mentioned the idea as being in the air in a letter to Francesco on 26 April 1533, implying that unless the régime could be strengthened they would have to submit to more interference from France or Spain,[1] and in May he added that everything depended on Alessandro remaining in control, 'nothing else can preserve the independence (*salute*) of the city, our enemies being more determined and venemous than ever, and only waiting their chance'.[2]

Against this background, then, we may accept Nerli's account of the genesis of the Fortezza with some confidence: 'In 1533, as it seemed neither to the Pope nor to him [Alessandro] that the fortress which had been modified (*mutata*) at the Porta alla Giustizia would be sufficient or appropriate for what they had in mind, there began a series of discussions between Alessandro Vitelli, captain of the duke's guard, and others skilled in the art of war, together with engineers and architects sent by the Pope, as to where they should build, and they decided on the Porta a Faenza. But matters were delayed until the Pope should return from France, where he went in September.'[3]

After the event, it was generally agreed that the idea of the Fortezza came from Clement himself. Segni — crediting Clement with a prevision of Filippo Stozzi's later rebellion — thought so, so did Vasari;[4] this was the common opinion in Florence.[5] Guicciardini stated it without equivocation. When Clement returned from France, he wrote in the *History of Italy*, knowing that he was in danger of dying, he 'urged on the building of a powerful citadel in Florence for the greater security, as he saw it, of his house, for he was not sure how much longer his nephew's good fortune might last'.[6] But when Marchetto, in Iacopo Pitti's dialogue the *Apologia de' Capucci*, read this passage aloud he was pounced on by Publio, who commented: 'He tries to put all the responsibility on the shoulders of the Pope. The author of the Fortezza was Filippo Strozzi, who suggested it at a conference of various citizens in the presence of the Pope.'[7] This view was supported by Varchi, and Segni also portrays Strozzi as urging Alessandro to proceed with its construction. It is unlikely that we shall ever know who planted the idea in Clement's mind — Strozzi's claim is only more appealing than

---

[1] *Op. ined.*, vol. IX, pp. 259 and 262.
[2] Ibid., p. 270.
[3] Filippo de' Nerli, *Commentari*... (Augusta, 1728), p. 270.
[4] Quo., G. Giovannoni, *Antonio da Sangallo il Giovane* (Rome, 1959), vol. I, p. 108.
[5] Anon., *Diario o cronica di Firenze*, B.N.F., II, I, 313, fol. 152v.
[6] Ed. C. Panigada (Bari, 1929), vol. V, p. 316.
[7] *A.S.I.*, vol. IV, 2(1853), p. 376.

Vettori's through the irony of his later imprisonment and death in the Fortezza[1] — but without Clement so radical a break with Florentine convention could never have been embarked upon. That the initiative came from outside Florence, and from Clement himself, possibly in consultation with Charles V, is not unlikely. On Clement's death, Alessandro sent an embassy to the Emperor in Madrid, asking him to continue his protection and to hasten his marriage to Margaret. The princess had already visited Florence in April 1533,[2] but the marriage was postponed while Alessandro's fate, it seemed, still hung in the balance. In the reply to his request dated 1 March 1535, Charles was still hesitant. 'It is important that the fortress should be so far completed that when the princess arrives in the city she should be able to find safety by taking refuge in it, and be secure in case of any uprising.' Alessandro was urged to hurry on the building as quickly as he could.[3] The Fortezza was the concern not only of Alessandro's immediate *entourage* but of his mighty sponsors.

It is therefore appropriate that the first two architects we hear of in connection with planning the Fortezza were already working for Clement. Both Vasari and Condivi say that Alessandro asked, via Alessandro Vitelli, for the services of Michelangelo, but that he refused to leave Rome.[4] On 10 March 1534 Alessandro wrote to Antonio da Sangallo the younger in the guarded tone which at this troubled time came naturally to him.[5] 'As I want you to come to Florence in order to take advantage of your advice and service in connection with a certain project of mine, which I will tell you about myself, I would be grateful if you could come here as soon as possible. Having nothing more to say, I conclude.'[6] On 15 March, when Sangallo could have only just arrived, Luigi Guicciardini wrote from Florence to his brother in Bologna to say that a fortress was definitely going to be built, and that while there was still the question of finding the money, it had appeared that it would not be too expensive at least to get its strongest point (*cassero*) into

---

[1] And because historians were still, in the sixteenth century, prone to find a refreshing moral in the humbling of the mighty. As von Albertini points out (op. cit., p. 219), 'Sein Palast in Florenz, an dem er weiterbaute, hatte mehr den Charakter eines fürstlichen Sitzes als den eines Privatpalastes.' Having run both with the hare and the hounds, Strozzi was a natural suspect.
[2] Settimanni, fol. 321r.
[3] Ibid., fols. 174v and 176v.
[4] Paola Barocchi ed., Giorgio Vasari, *La Vita di Michelangelo* (Milan, 1962), vol. III, pp. 1175–6. Both say that Michelangelo was afraid of Alessandro, Condivi puzzlingly adds that he gave the excuse 'che non aveva tal commissione da papa Clemente'.
[5] As when he changed commanders at Volterra.
[6] A.S.F., Manoscritti, 65, fols. 16v–17r. Printed in G. Gaye, *Carteggio inedito d'artisti*... (Florence, 1840), vol. II, pp. 252–3.

1. Vasari, Alessandro de' Medici
(Photo: Alinari)

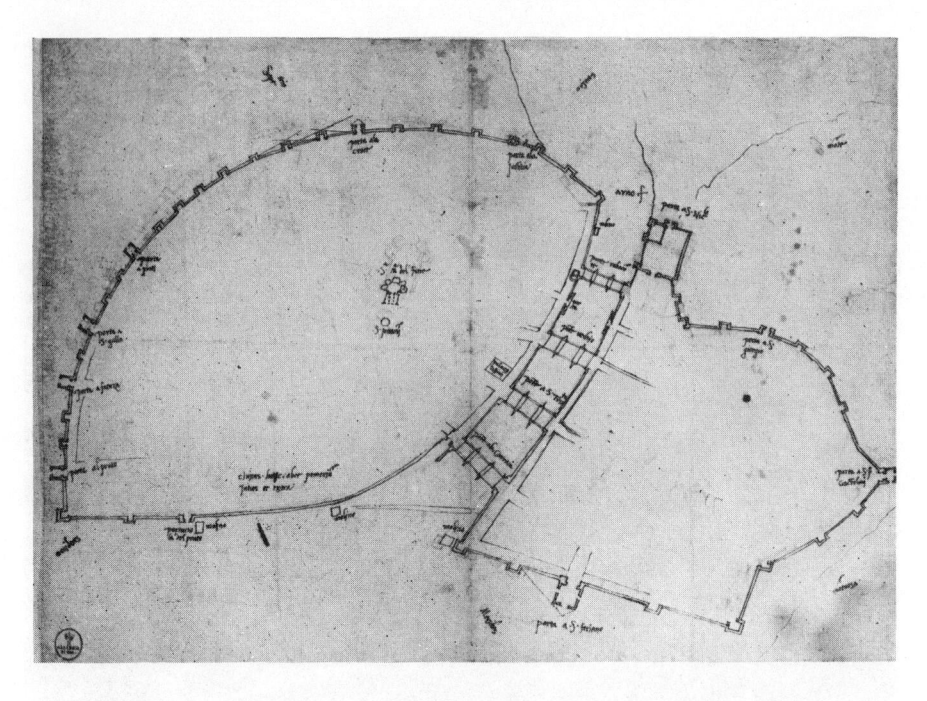

2. Baldassare Peruzzi, The Walls of Florence (*c.* 1520). Uffizi, 360 A.

3. Vasari, The Siege of Florence. Detail from the fresco in the Palazzo Vecchio, Florence

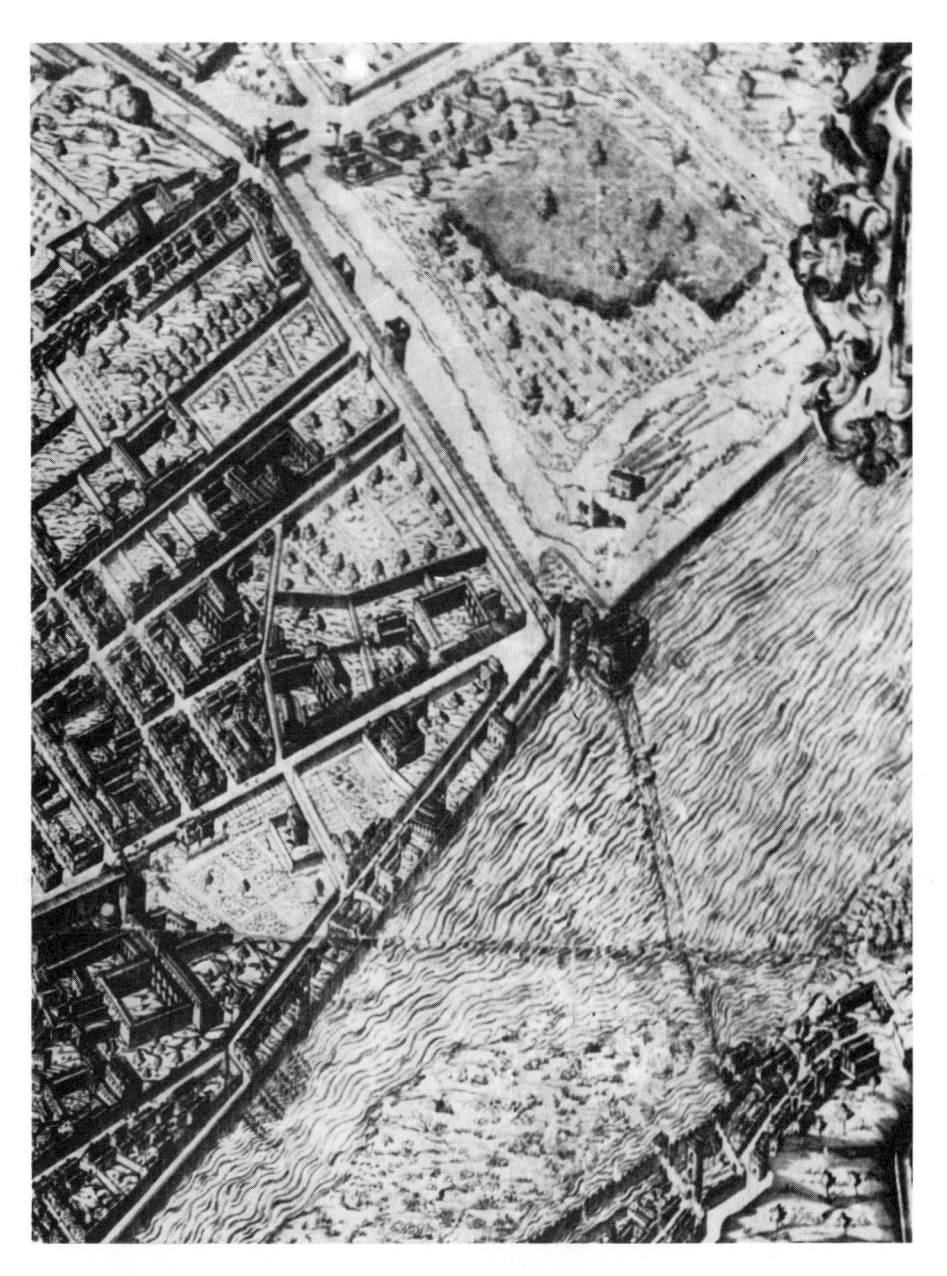

4. Citadella Vecchia. Detail from no. 8

5. Francesco de Marchi, The Walls of Florence. From
Trattato d'Architettura Militare, B.N.F., 11,1,280, fol. 2r

6. Detail from no. 5

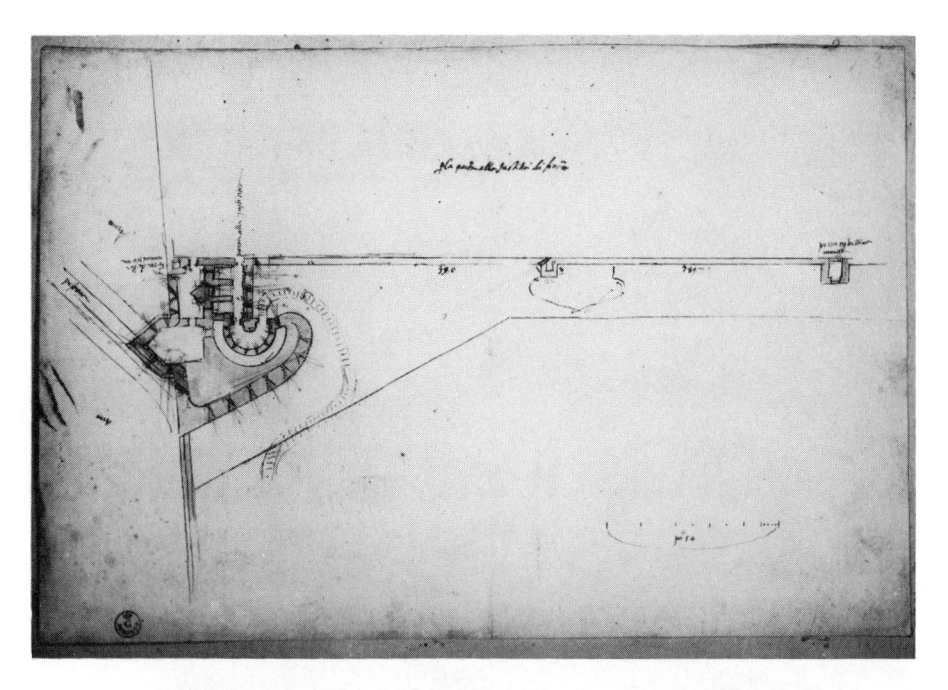

7. Antonio da Sangallo the younger, project for improving the Citadella Vecchia at Porta alla Giustizia. Uffizi, 761 A.

8. Stefano Buonsignori, Plan of Florence (1584)

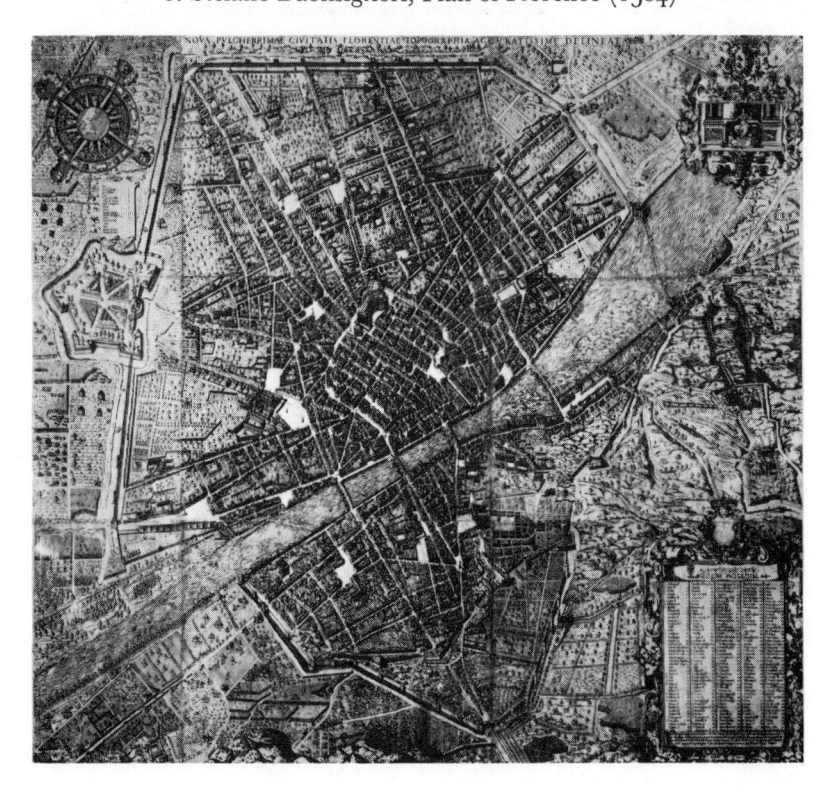

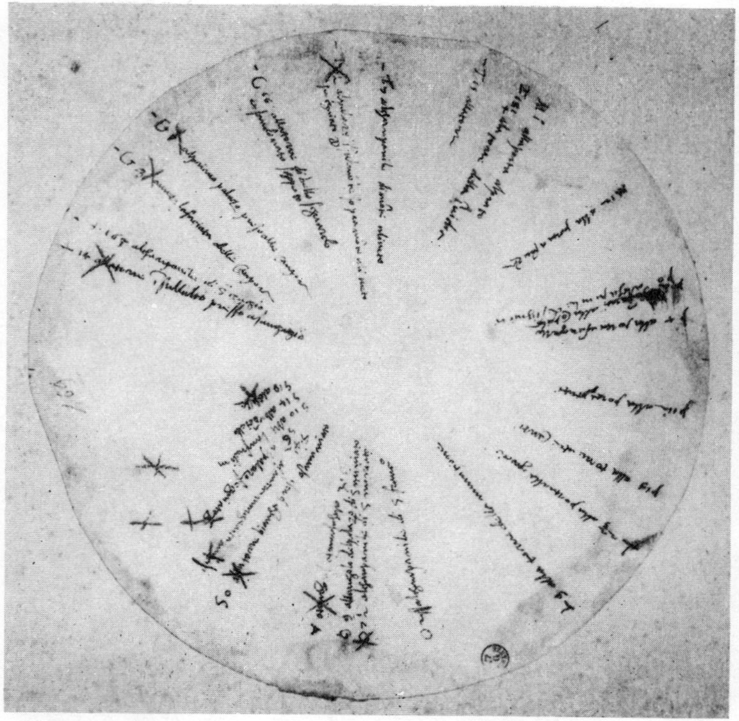

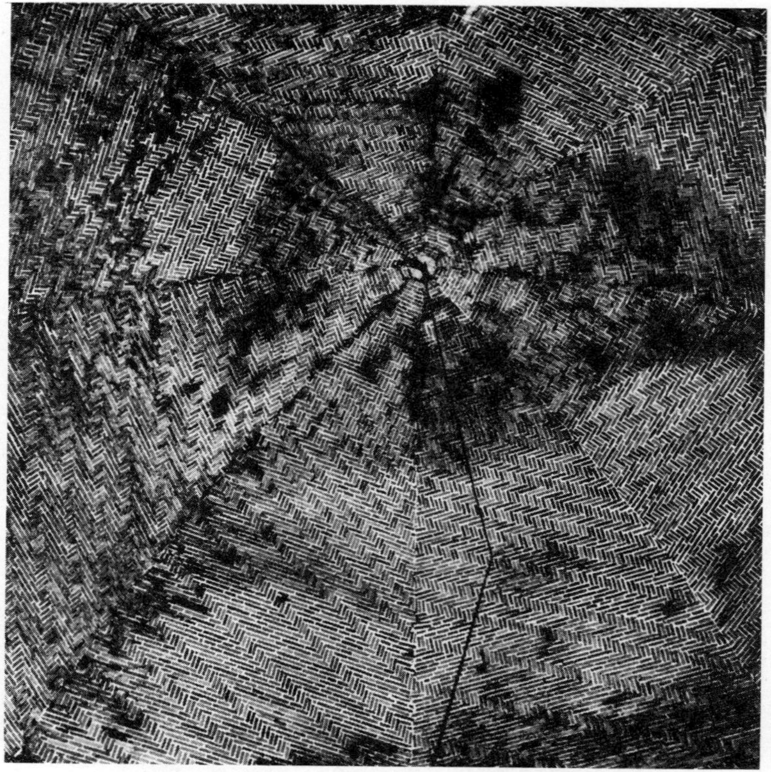

10. Fortezza da Basso, dome of central hall

9. Antonio da Sangallo, distance rose, Florence. Uffizi, 773 A.

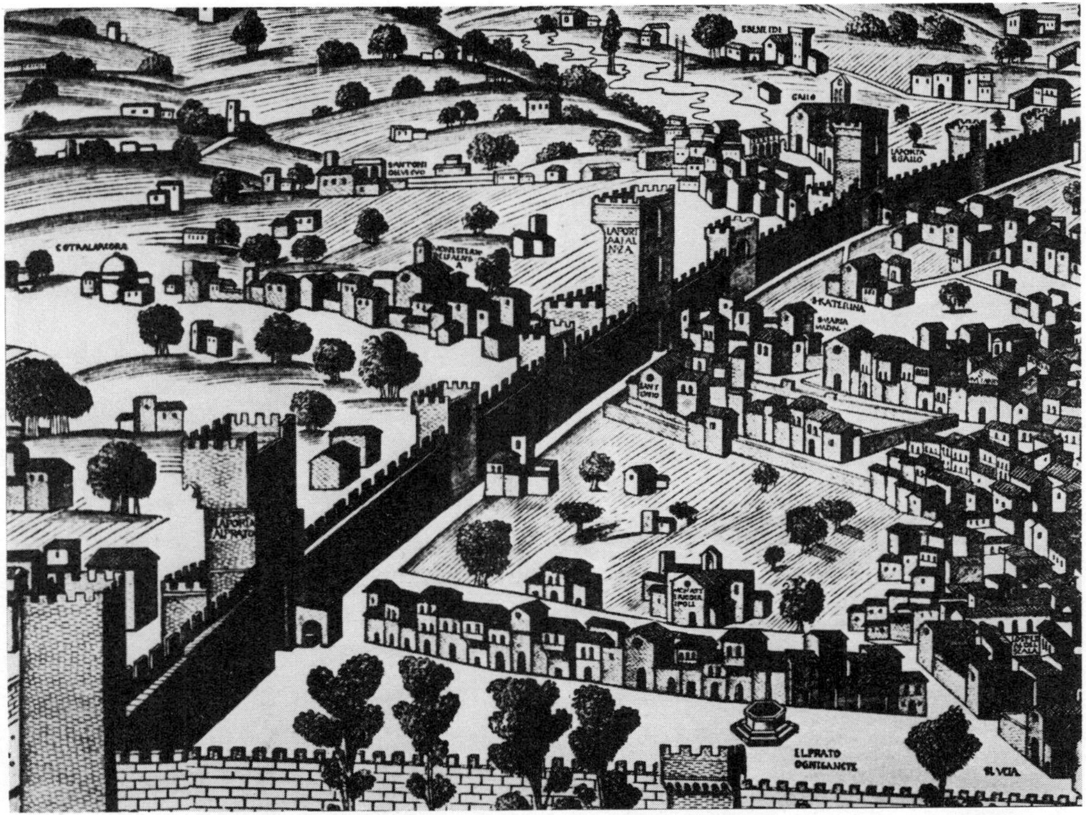

11. Detail from the 'Berlin' woodcut view of Florence (c. 1470)

12. Fortezza da Basso. Detail from no. 8

13. (*opposite, above*) Astrological diagram for the foundation time of the 'Arx Florentina'. A.S.F., Carte Strozziane, Ser. 1, 129, fol. 196r

14. (*opposite, below*) Antonio da Sangallo. Sketches for a fortress at Porta S. Gallo. Uffizi, 758 A.

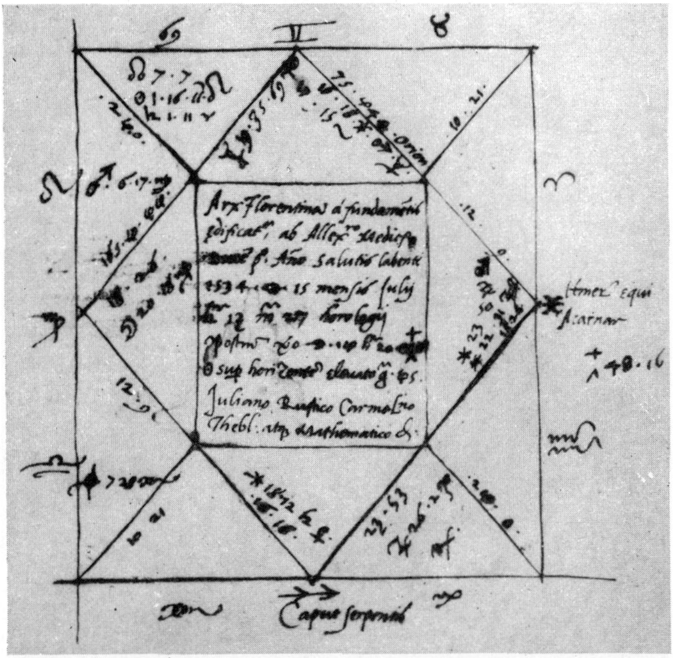

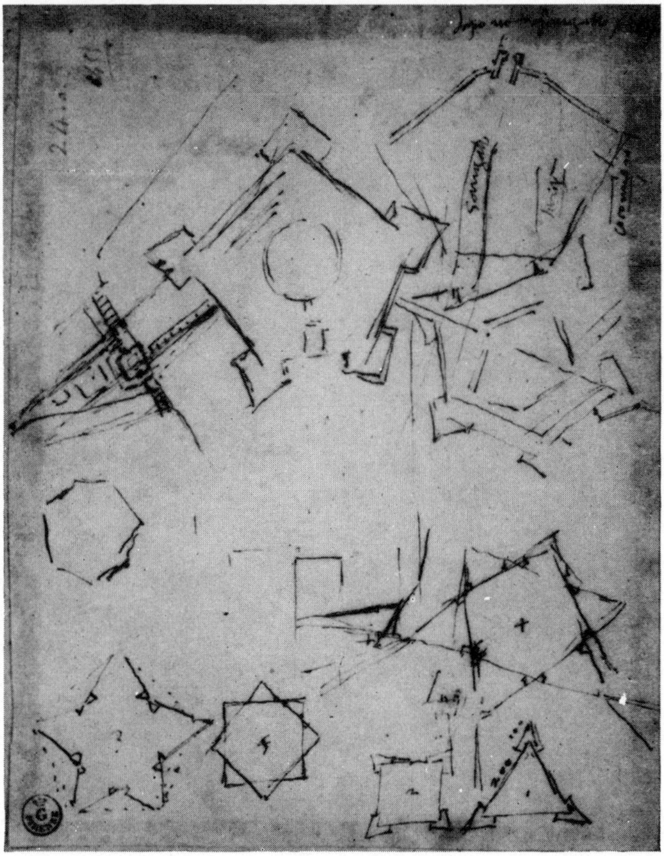

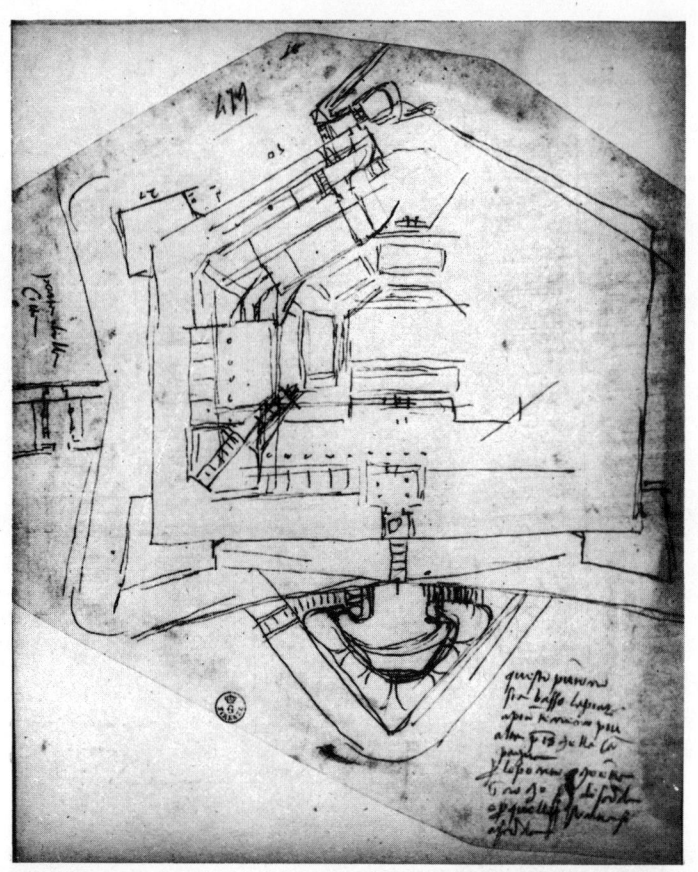

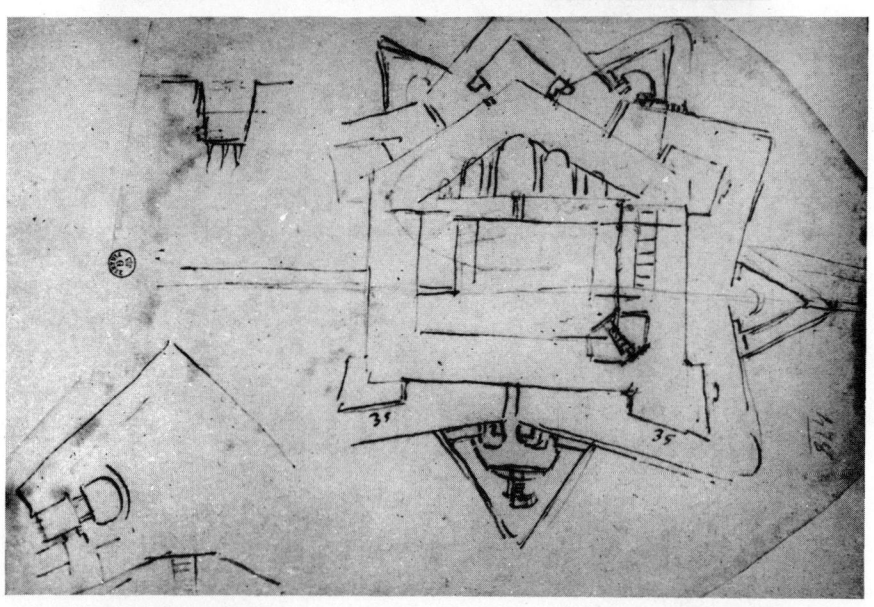

15 and 16. Antonio da Sangallo, preliminary drawings for Fortezza.
Uffizi, 783 A. (*above*), 782 A. (*below*)

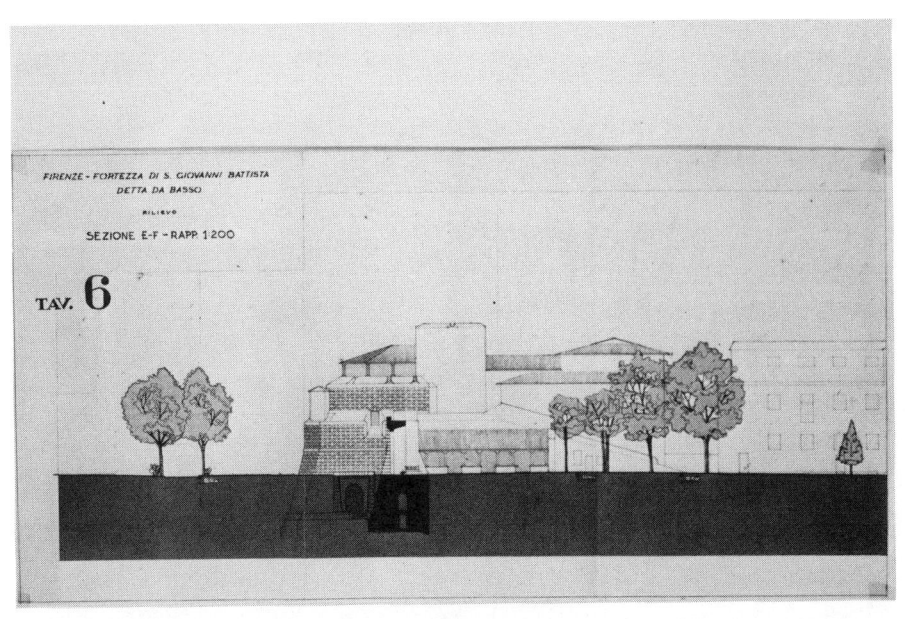

17. Fortezza da Basso. Section showing *mastio* and Porta a Faenza

18. Fortezza da Basso. *Mastio* from rampart

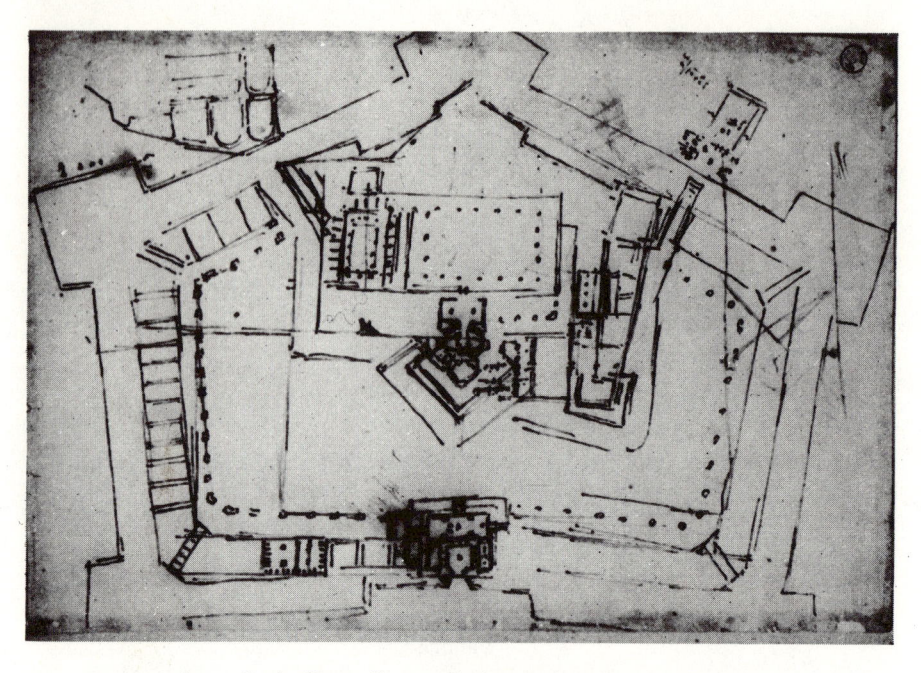

19. Antonio da Sangallo, preliminary drawing for Fortezza, Uffizi, 760 A.

20. Bastiano da Sangallo, Fortezza, plan. Uffizi, 315 A. The back is endorsed to Antonio, and this plan was probably sent to him in Rome from Florence

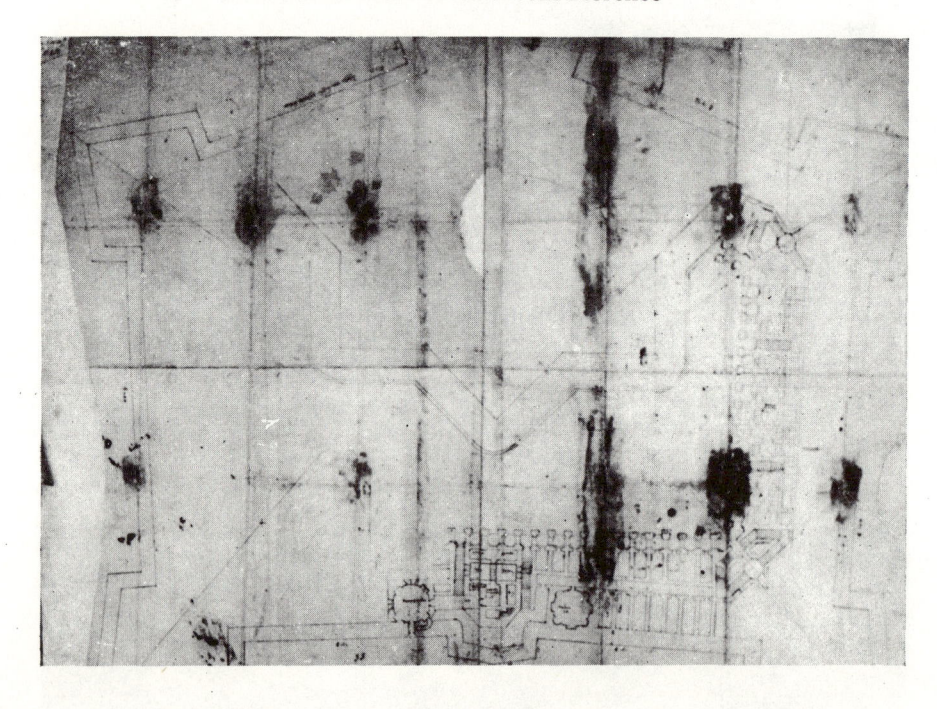

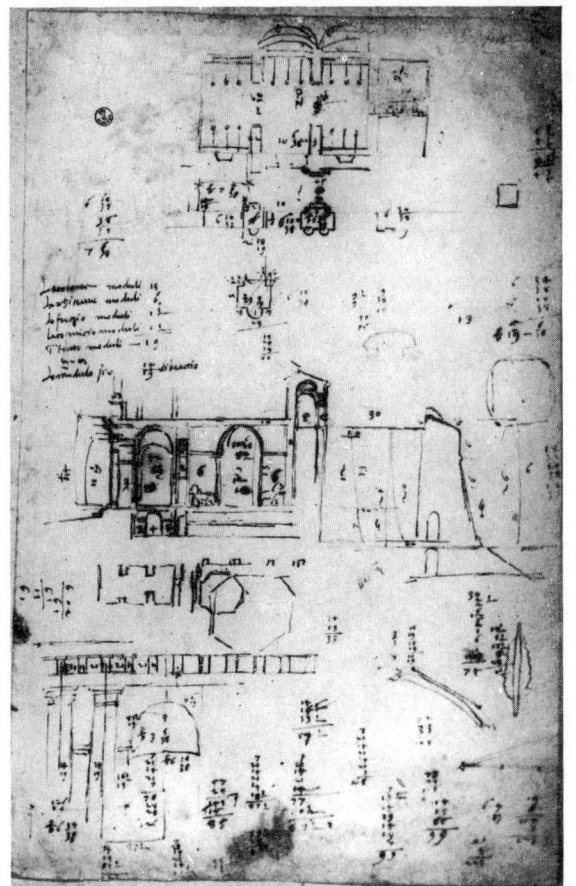

21. Antonio da Sangallo, Fortezza, plan of city front. Uffizi, 756 A.

22. Antonio da Sangallo, Fortezza, section through stables, rampart and wall. Uffizi, 1282 A.

23. Plan of sally port access

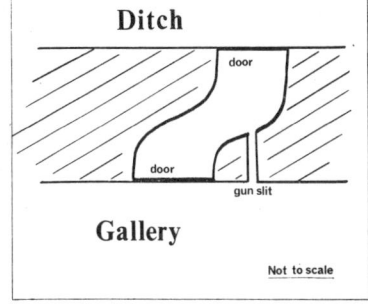

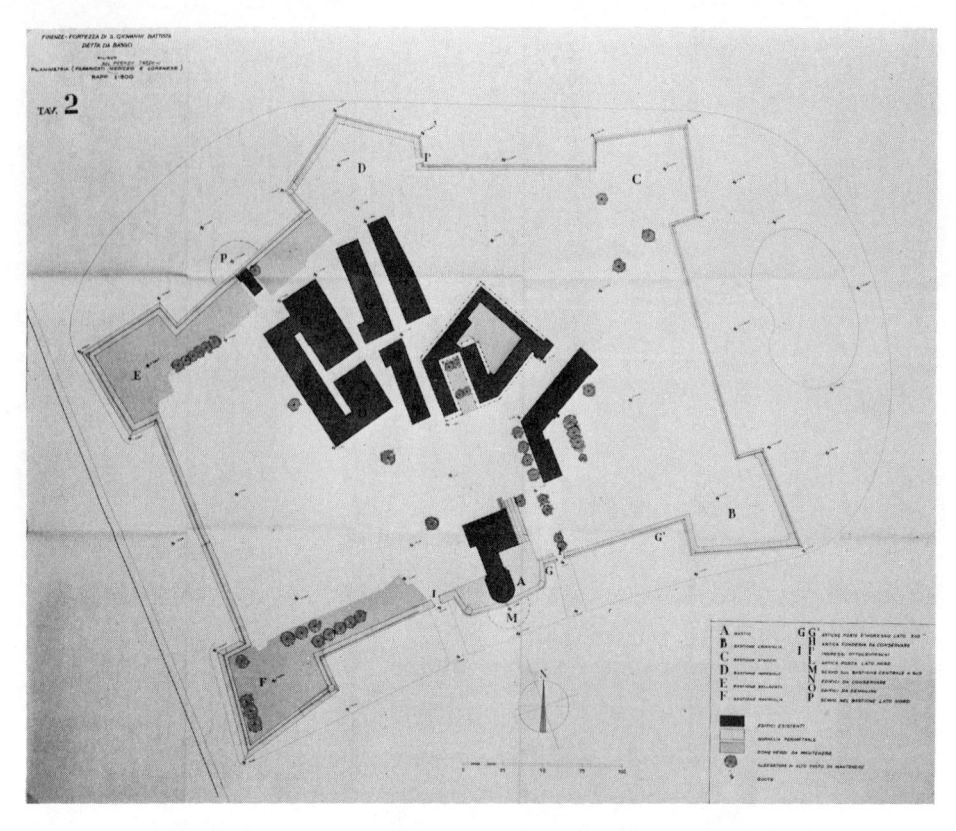

24. Fortezza, plan

25. Antonio da Sangallo, Fortezza, ink and wash plan of *mastio*.
'Torre de la porta a faenza' at bottom. Uffizi, 757 A.

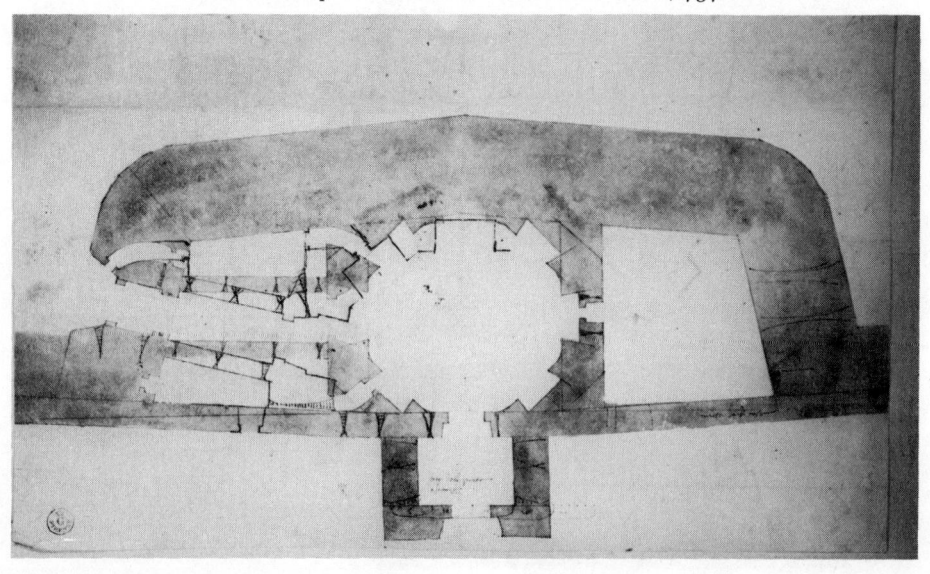

26. Pediment (at ground level) of original entrance to *mastio*

27. Top of early entrance, city front, right of *mastio*

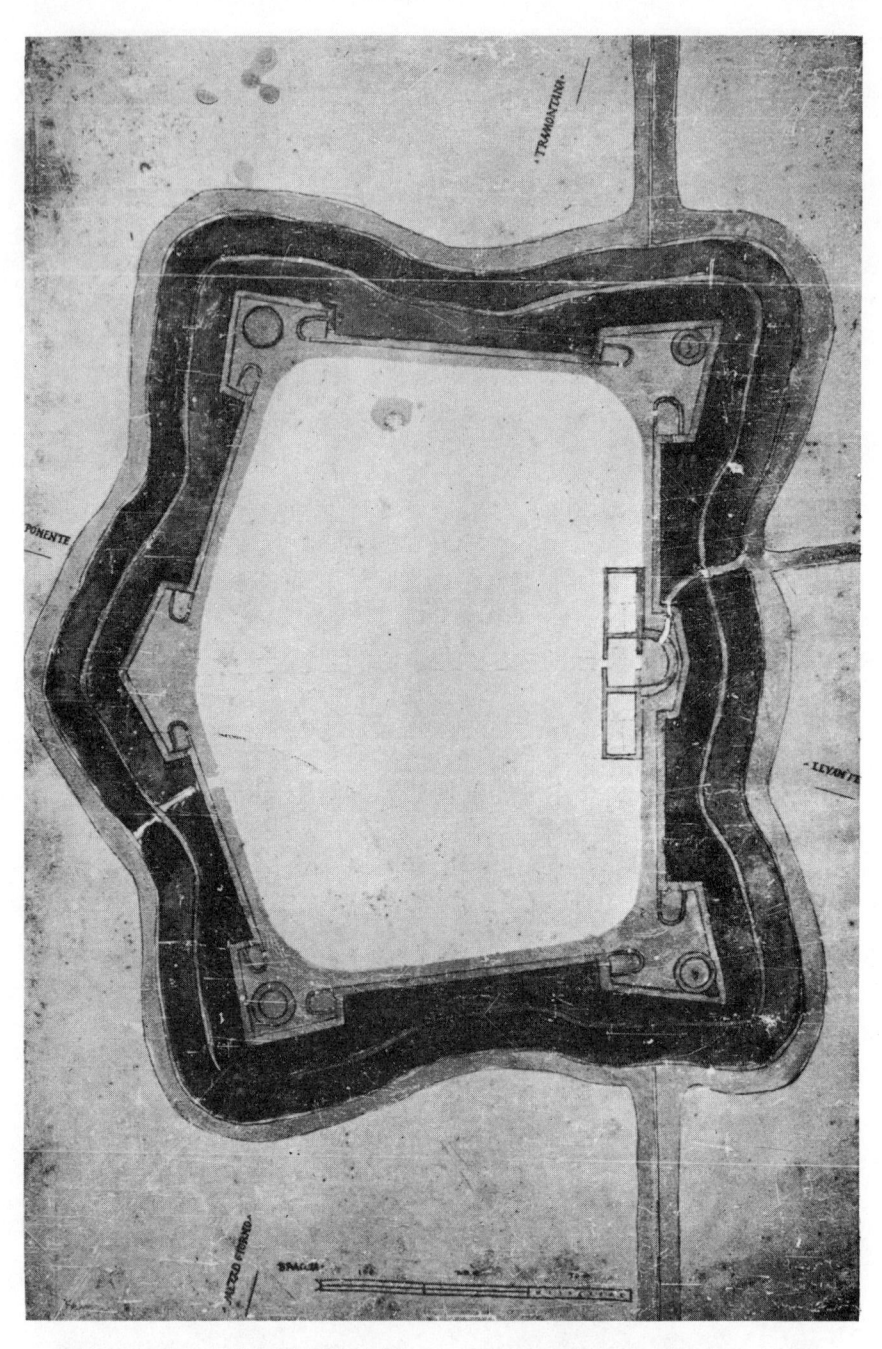

28. De Marchi, Fortezza da Basso. MS. cit., fol. 3r

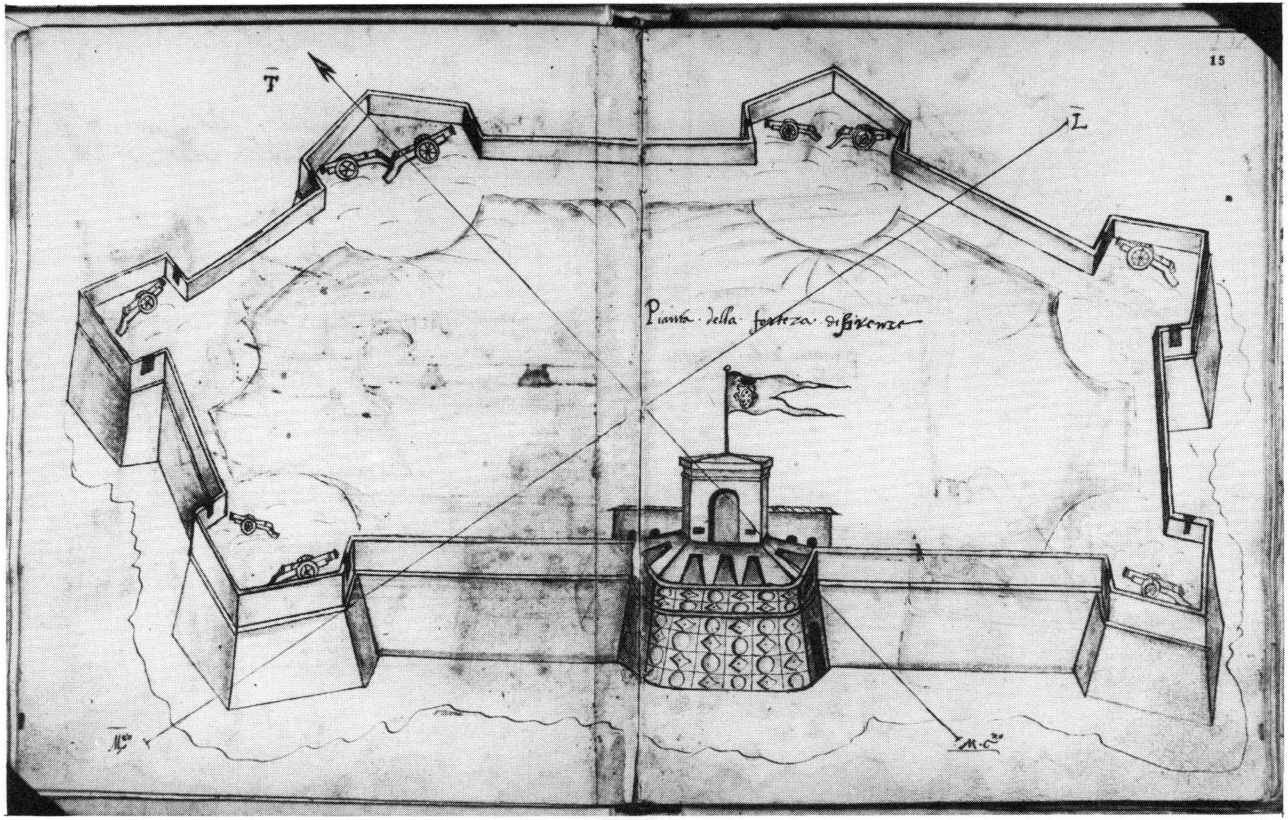

29. Fortezza da Basso. B.N.F., MS. XIX, 62, fols. 14v-15r

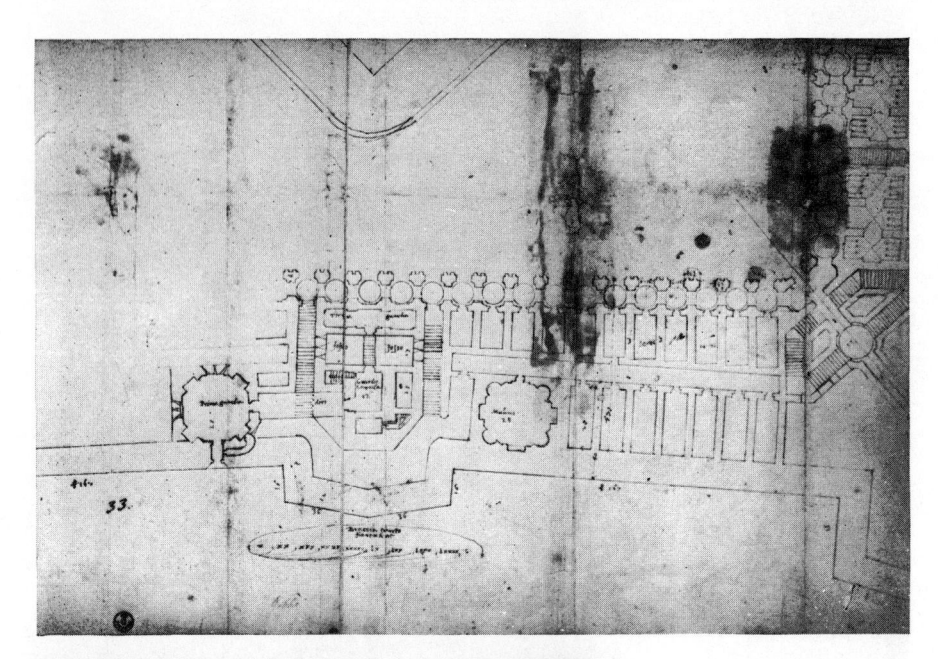

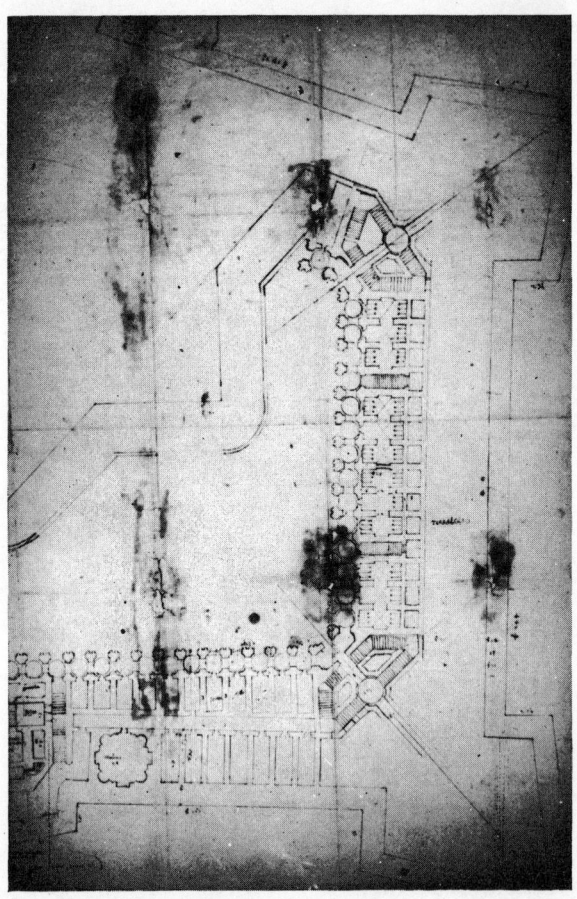

30 and 31. Bastiano da Sangallo, details from no. 20

32. Antonio da Sangallo, Fortezza, section. Uffizi, 931 A.

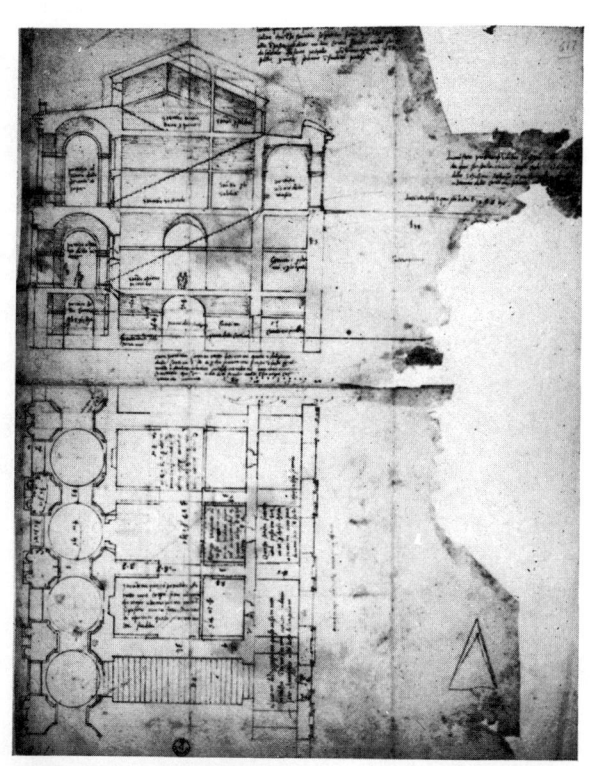

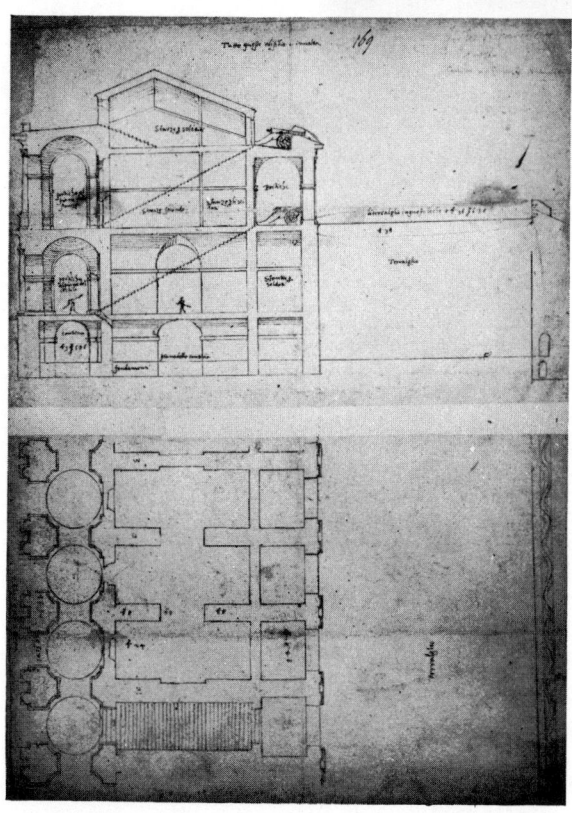

33. Bastiano da Sangallo, copy of no. 32. Uffizi, 1659 A.

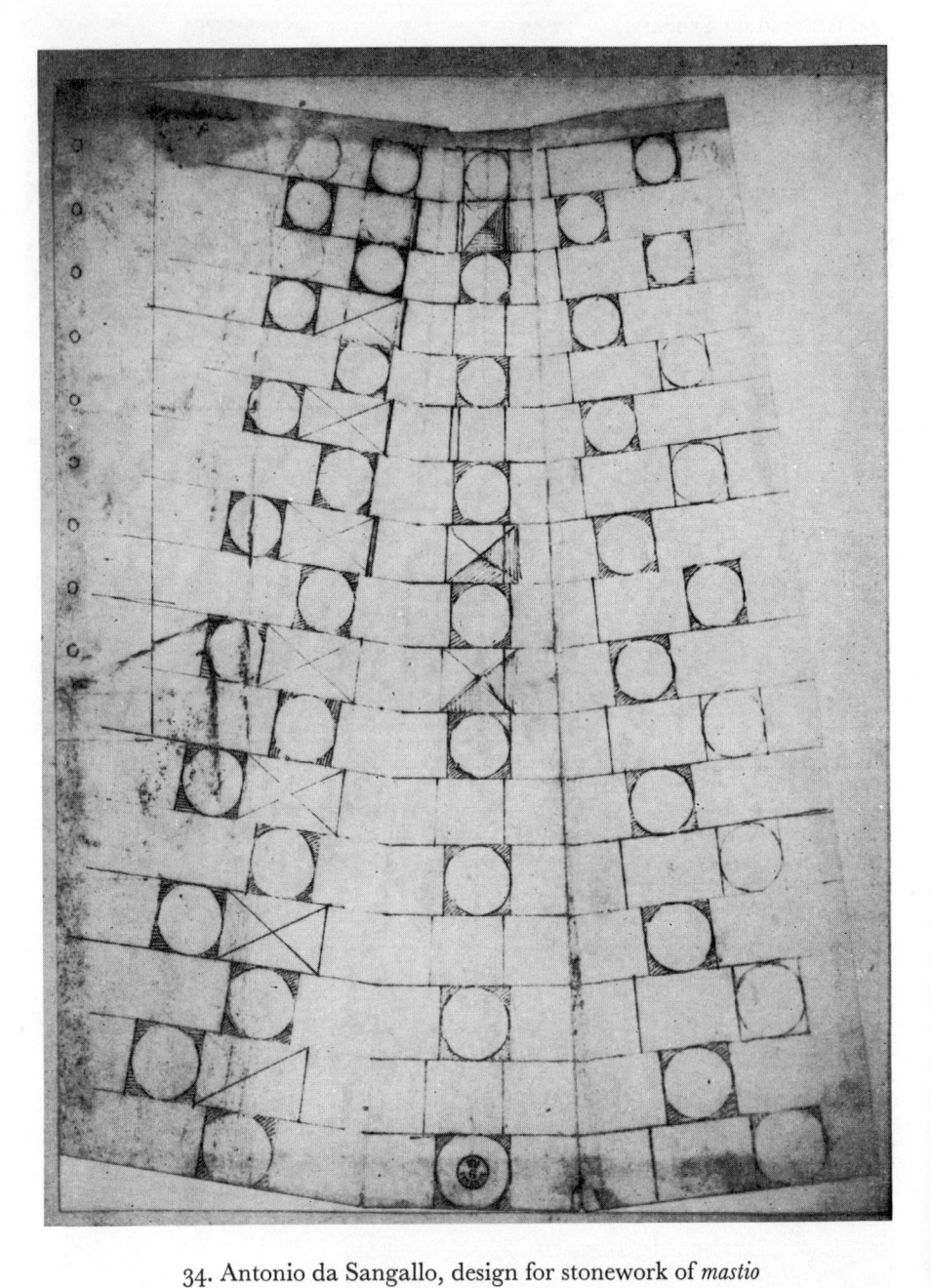

34. Antonio da Sangallo, design for stonework of *mastio*

35. (*opposite, above*) Fortezza, *mastio*. Uffizi, 762

36. (*opposite, below*) *Mastio* excavated to show stonework below modern earth level

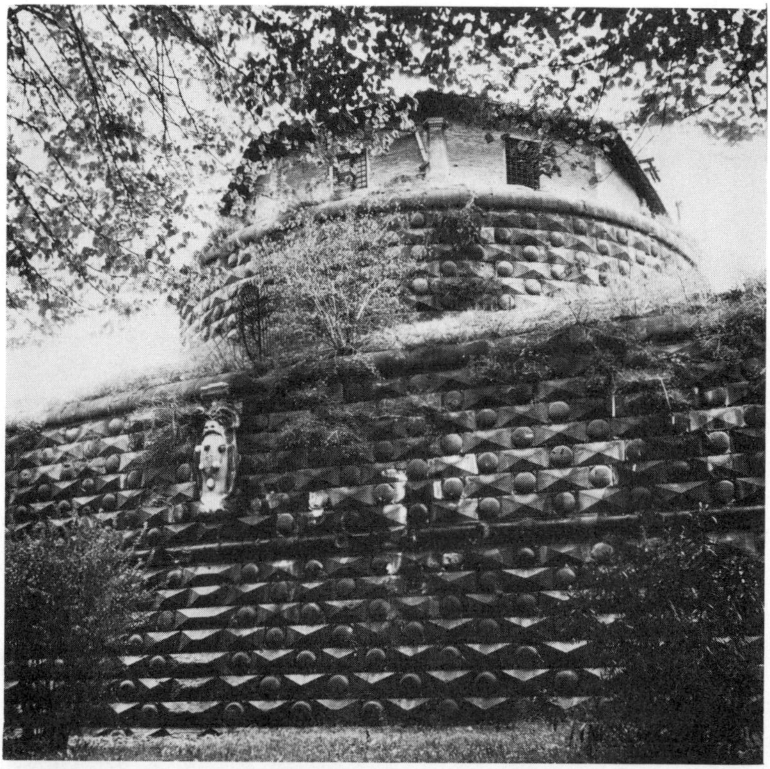

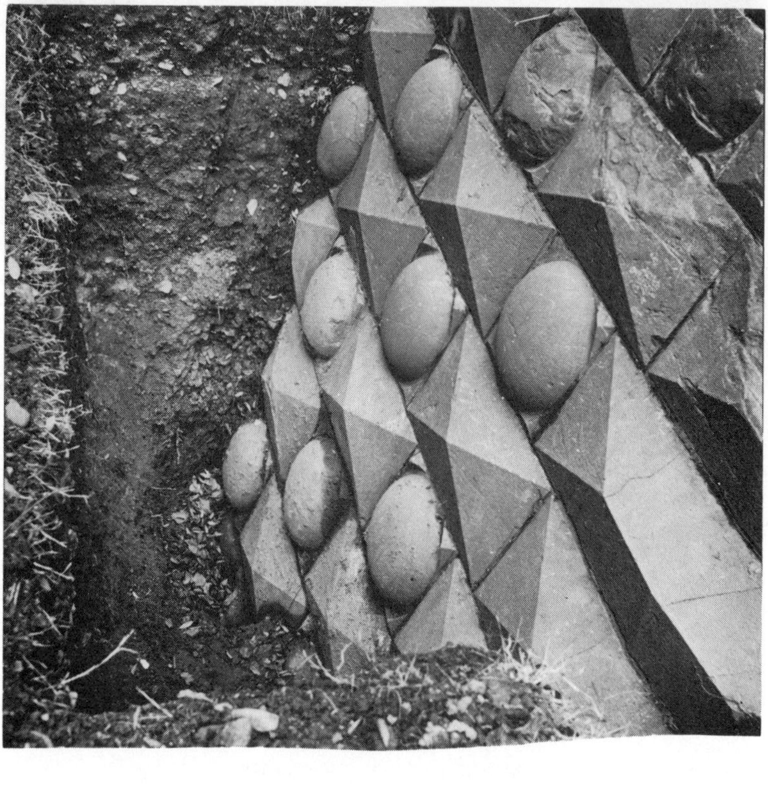

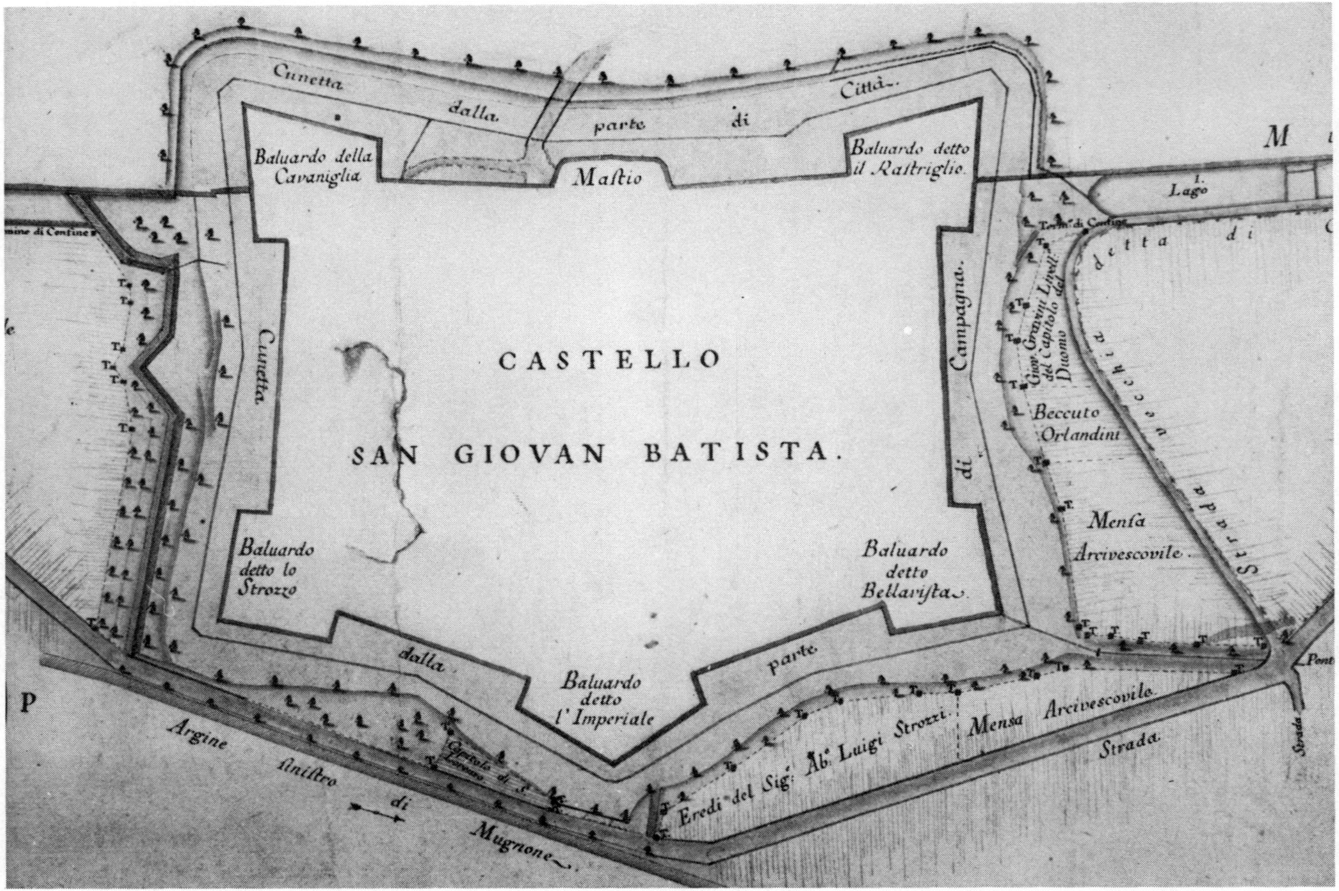

37. Fortezza da Basso, A.S.F., R. R. Possessioni, Piante, 536

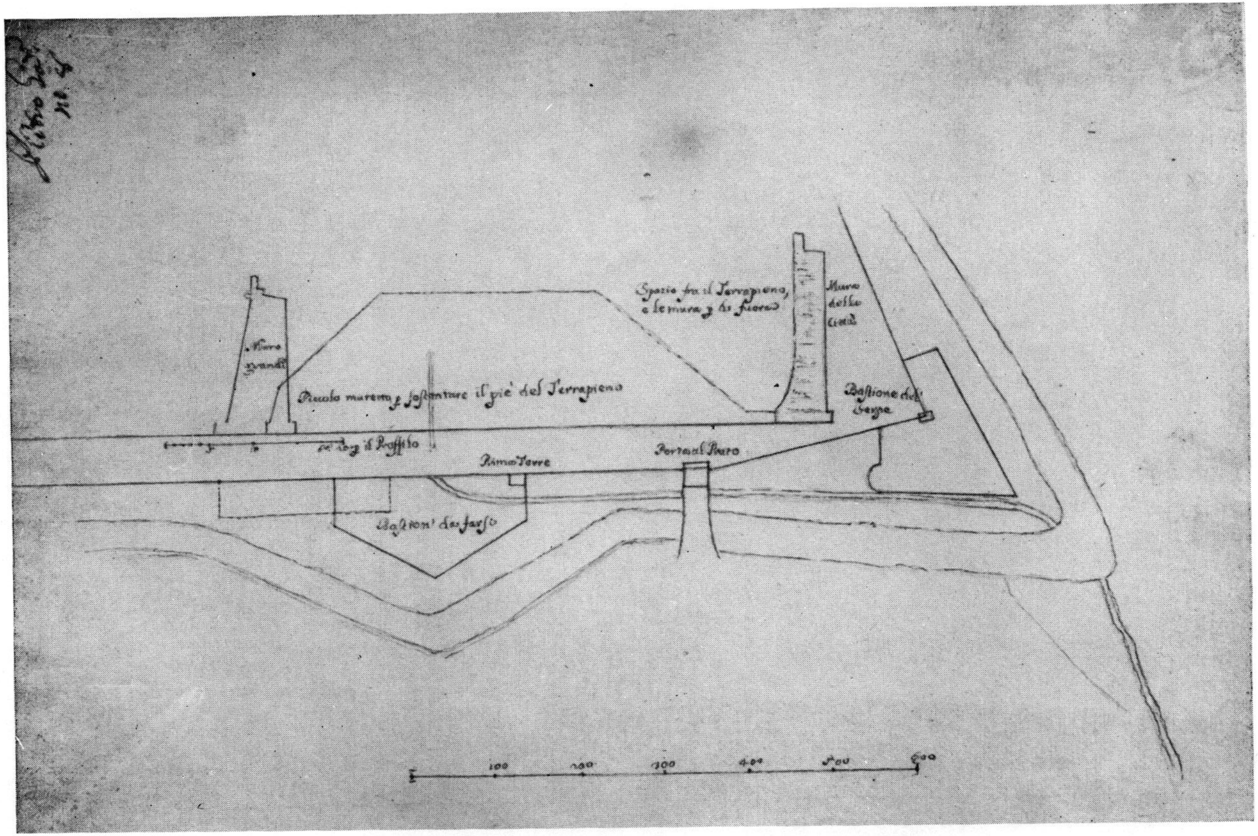

38. Project for new bastion between the Fortezza and Porta al
Prato. A.S.F., Capitani di Parte, cart. XIX, scaffale L,
palchetto 10, No. 58

39. Baldo de Paludi's inscription in the Fortezza

a sufficient state of readiness to receive a garrison. He went on to say that Porta a Pinti, on the north-east side of the city, had been decided on as its site, on the grounds that less destruction of private and ecclesiastical buildings would be involved than if the Porta San Gallo were chosen.[1] And on 30 March he repeated: the fortress is to be built, and at Porta a Pinti.[2]

Almost certainly it was at this time that Sangallo undertook the series of compass surveys[3] (plate 9) which led to the Fortezza's being sited neither at Porta a Pinti nor at Porta San Gallo but at Porta a Faenza. By 16 May the matter had been settled. On that day Vitelli wrote to Luigi Guicciardini, who was by now at Arezzo and concerned about his own citadel: 'I thought I would let you know that the fortress here will soon be begun. Its form and site is now decided.'[4] Why Porta a Faenza was decided on is not revealed, but this north-west front was clearly vulnerable to any enemy advancing across the plain either along the Arno or down the valley from Pistoia and Prato; a large bastion with earthern outworks had been built between Porta a Faenza and Porta San Gallo in preparation for the siege,[5] and, as we have seen, the gates on that side had been strengthened after it. Equally important, perhaps, was the fact that Porta a Faenza is nearest of all the city's gates to Palazzo Medici where Alessandro and his nervous court resided. Vitelli wrote to Luigi again on 1 June to say that he was sending 'the plan of the Fortezza of Florence' by the bearer and apologizing for the delay. In a few days he hoped to bring Antonio da Sangallo with him, so that they could all discuss the fortress at Arezzo.[6]

As soon as the site had been chosen, a formidable organization —

---

[1] *Op. ined.*, vol. IX, pp. 290–1.

[2] Ibid., pp. 293–4.

[3] Uffizi, Gabinetto dei Disegni, Arch. 771–4. Tribolo had used a compass during the siege (see below, p. 528), as did Vasari for the view of which plate 3 is a detail. See G. Boffito and A. Mori, *Piante e Vedute di Firenze* (Florence, 1926), p. 31.

[4] As this letter — or, rather, postscript to a letter — has not before been printed, I quote it in full: 'Post scripta, Mi e parso dar aviso che presto se dara principio alla fortezza di qui della quale e hormaj determinato la forma et sito suo. Et cosi ancora si deve far presto di cotesta di costi. Et iterum alla s.v. mi Racom do Idem S. ^{tor} Alex^o Vitello.' A.S.F., Carte Strozz., Ser. I, LXI, fol. 16r.

[5] Benedetto Varchi, *Storia fiorentina* (Florence, 1838–41), vol. II, p. 198.

[6] Again, I quote the relevant part in full: 'Per il Cap^o Biago presente exhibitore mando alla s.v. il disegno della fortezza de firenze quale non si e mandato piu tosto expectando questa occasione di venire al paese e non fo il debito mio in venir a farli Reverentia per non si dare molestia al presente. Per che alla tornata mia che sara fra pochi di faro il viaggio per costi, et menero m^o Ant. da San Gallo quale se ne va per la sua donna ch'e in Ancona et tornera per la volta di Castella [Vitelli's home]. Et alhora parlarimo a lungo della fortezza di costi, che la ex^{tia} del s. Duca nostro patrone vole che la si faccia ad ogni modo. Et me ne ha parlato di novo, in voler che la se disegni et dia principio et pero del tutto ne ci conferiremo con v.s. quando saremo li abocca ... Da Pōte Romito il 1° di Giug^o, nel xxxiiij.' A.S.F., Carte Strozz., Ser. I, LXI, fol. 25r.

of which, such are the archival lacunae for this period, we can know little — sprang into being. Progress went forward at a spectacular rate; Vasari's comment that the Fortezza 'was erected and completed with such expedition that no edifice of the kind, either in ancient or modern times, was ever brought to conclusion in so short a period',[1] was no hyperbole. The extensive ground clearing was done so swiftly that the foundation stone was laid on 15 July 1534, and on 5 December 1535 the first garrison was installed. And as the dome of the central hall (plate 10) shows, or an inspection of the galleries in the thickness of the walls, the work, though unfinished, was not skimped.

We know something about the architects involved. On 29 May 1534, the *Capitani* elected Antonio da Sangallo 'caput magistrorum fortilitii illustrissimi ducis' with a salary of twenty-five florins a month.[2] Antonio was the most expert and experienced of contemporary military engineers. In 1515 he had prepared a plan for Civitavecchia, in 1519 he worked on the fortifications of Montefiascone, in 1526 he had, at the Pope's bidding, inspected the fortified places of the Romagna, he began the citadel of Ancona in 1529, having in the meantime given advice on the defences of Parma, Piacenza and Florence itself.[3] In 1534 he was again working at Ancona (also for twenty-five florins a month) for the Pope.[4]

His chief assistant was Giovanni Alessio, better known as Nanni Unghero. Unghero had worked as a *capomaestro* for the *Capitani* since 1531.[5] He was apparently in charge of the works that transformed the Porta alla Giustizia into the Citadella Vecchia with a salary of £42 a month in 1532,[6] which was increased in October of the following year, 'viso quantum dictus Iohannes exercuit et exercet officium suum benediligenter et cum amore', to £54.[7] On 1 May 1534 he was appointed *capomaestro* with full responsibility for the new fortress at almost double his previous salary.[8] In 1535, when the foundations were completed,

---

[1] Tr. Mrs J. Foster (London, 1851), vol. IV, p. 13.
[2] A.S.F., Capitani di Parte, 14 rosso, fol. 209v.
[3] See Giovannoni, op. cit, 74 ff.
[4] James S. Ackerman, 'Architectural practice in the Italian Renaissance', *Journal of the Society of Architectural Historians* (Oct., 1954), p. 5.
[5] A.S.F., Capitani di Parte, 14 rosso, fol. 108v.
[6] Ibid., fol. 329r.
[7] Ibid., fol. 186v.
[8] 'Item deliberaverunt quod salarium Iohannis Alexii vocato Nanni Unghere, caput magistri dicte Partis et etiam habens administrationem fortilitii noviter incepti per illustrissimum dominum Ducham, sit et esse debeat pro uno anno incepto die primo mensis Maii proxime preteriti et finiendo per totum mensem Aprilis proxime futurum 1535, ad rationem florenorum centum sexaginta de libris 7 pro quolibet floreno, non obstante quod alias fuerit sibi factum salarium, quia voluerunt quod

and the actual construction work was going forward, Antonio's nephew Bastiano (Aristotile) da Sangallo was in Florence,[1] interpreting Antonio's drawings[2] and keeping him in touch with the way in which they were being executed. The *condottiere*-architect Pierfrancesco da Viterbo, who had previously worked with Antonio on the fortifications at Parma and Piacenza for Clement, was consulted at an early stage, but he died in 1534 and there is no clear evidence that he influenced the design of the Fortezza.[3]

The administration of the building operations was handled by the *Capitani di Parte Guelfa* through their *provveditore*, Bertoldo de Gherardo Corsini. Corsini had been the most active of the officials responsible for strengthening the walls before the siege and had worked with Sangallo when he was then called in to advise the Florentine government.[4] Afterwards he changed sides with alacrity, and from a *popolano* became for a while an assiduous courtier of the Medici.[5] In 1533 he was 'provveditore sopra le muraglie et fortificatione'.[6] From May 1534, as *provveditore* of the new fortress, he received a salary of £35 per month.[7] Under him was appointed a treasurer and officials responsible for building materials and for food (*pro distribuendo panem et vinum*) and lodging for the labourers.[8] The Medici family was, understandably, closely involved. Alessandro took a continuous interest in the works, Giulio was treasurer, and Ottaviano was mentioned in connection with the construction work in 1535.[9] While not formally part of the team responsible for the design and building of the Fortezza, Alessandro Vitelli, as confidant of Alessandro and captain of the guard, was

---

salarium alias sibi factum computetur in isto pro dicto anno. Nec pro dicto anno vel aliud petere vel habere possit nisi dictos florenos centum sexaginta ut supra.' Ibid., fol. 220r.

[1] He is mentioned in connection with a lawsuit on 26 April 1535, A.S.F., Capitani di Parte, 140 rosso, fol. 8r [unnumbered].

[2] Some of the Fortezza drawings in the Uffizi show traces of both hands. Plates 20, 30, 31, 33 are catalogued by the Uffizi as by Sangallo *detto il Gobbo*, i.e. Giovanni Battista, Antonio's brother. But his name is nowhere associated with the Fortezza in the documents, whereas Bastiano is mentioned twice in connection with its construction (Bottari, op. cit., pp. 330, 337). The first of these references calls him by his nickname Aristotile, which obviates a copyist's confusion with Giovanni Battista. And see the previous note for evidence of Bastiano's presence in Florence.

[3] Ed. Milanesi, vol. V, p. 458. The Florentines had asked for his services while they were preparing for the siege; Gaye, op. cit., vol. II, p. 177; Settimanni, MS. cit., fol. 83r. Varchi (op. cit., vol. III, p. 76) says that 'fece il disegno di questa muraglia' in connection with the foundation ceremony.

[4] Varchi, op. cit., vol. I, p. 108.
[5] Op. cit., 97–8.
[6] A.S.F., Capitani di Parte, 14 rosso, fol. 340r.
[7] Ibid., fol. 234r (for title) and fol. 292v (for salary).
[8] Listed ibid., fols. 207v–208r.
[9] Bottari, vol. III, p. 331.

concerned with the initial planning and continued to keep an eye on the eventual quarters for his troops. He had fought against the Florentines during the siege and had on one occasion been rumoured to have been killed;[1] he had a personal interest in having a safe refuge if the events of 1527 should recur.

The labour force was recruited from the *dominio*, each commune — even those for whom it meant a three days journey — sending three or four hundred men who were allocated an area of land to level or excavate before they were allowed to return home. There were no wages, each man receiving three loaves and a flask of wine a day. The numbers involved were as many as three thousand at a time, and the *Capitani* reinforced them by commuting fines to forced labour on the foundations. It was noticed with horror that work was not allowed to slacken on Sundays or on religious holidays. The citizens were rigorously excluded from the site: the penalty for peeping was ten florins, or, more appropriately, forced labour.[2] The speed with which work on the Fortezza went forward becomes more credible if we eke out our information with the description given by Bellucci of his completion of the fortification started by Nanni Unghero at Prato. He started work there in February 1545 and in spite of heavy rains completed the earthen bastions and ramparts in three months. He employed up to two thousand men at a time, and is full of praise for the abundance of transport and the strength of the oxen even at that 'weak' time of year, and for the supply of timber for use in strengthening foundations, reinforcing banks and for scaffolding.[3] About the organization of stone-cutting and masonry for the Fortezza we know almost nothing.

Unfortunately, information about its cost and the financing is equally obscure. On 7 July 1533, a forced loan (*accatto*) was raised to pay for grain purchases, for public works on the Arno and because 'it is still necessary to repair many of our fortifications'.[4] The sum raised was 35,000 ducats, to be repaid, with interest of 12 per cent p.a., using the income from the salt tax as guarantee. Settimanni recorded the opinion that this loan, though ostensibly for fortifications, was really to provide an adequately magnificent trousseau for Catherine de' Medici, about

---

[1] A.S.F., Carte Strozz., Ser. I, LXV, no. 124.
[2] The best accounts are in Settimanni, MS. cit., fol. 83r, Ughi, op. cit., pp. 172-3, and Segni, ed. cit., p. 176. These accounts (apart from the numbers involved) are borne out by A.S.F., Capitani di Parte, 14 rosso, fols. 210r–214r.
[3] MS. cit., fols. 32v–33v. On fols. 34r–38v he breaks down the costs, but as most of these are wages for earth-shifting and none were paid for the pre-masonry work at the Fortezza, they cannot be used to provide an analogy.
[4] A.S.F., Capitani di Parte, 10 rosso, fols. 89v–90r.

to be married to Francis I's son Henry.¹ Certainly Alessandro was short of money next year; on 27 June Luigi Guicciardini observed to his brother Niccolò that the Duke would have to disband some of his troops in order to find money for the Fortezza.² On 29 July came the news of a further *accatto*, specifically for the defence of the city, news that was greeted with gloom, not so much because the interest rate had dropped to eight per cent as because the chances of being repaid for either appeared nil, and 'the money was not going to protect, or be of any advantage to the city, but to confirm it in the servitude to which it had been recently condemned'.³

Somehow, from Florence — and possibly from Rome? — the money was forthcoming and the enormous task was taken in hand. The earth-shifting began in mid-May⁴ and, as we have seen, was sufficiently far advanced for the foundation stone to be laid on 15 July. Work started on the outer curtains and bastions, in order to leave the city wall intact as long as possible.

First it was necessary to clear buildings from the site outside the walls. The convent of S. Giovanni Evangelista, called the Monastero di Faenza from the city from which the founding nuns came (hence Porta a Faenza) was destroyed, and the nuns transferred to the Badia of S. Salvi.⁵ A comparison between plate 11 and plate 12 shows how much property had to come down when work began in June on clearing the inner side, and a special *provvisione* was passed exempting any householder who was affected from paying taxes to the city; it said nothing about compensation.⁶

Then began the digging of the broad ditch that was to surround the Fortezza, which was to be 50 *braccia* wide, together with the trench on its inner side, 6 *braccia* wide, which was to contain the foundations of the walls; these were to contain in their thickness not only a gallery giving on to a series of musketry batteries and sally-ports opening into the ditch but, at a subterranean level, a lower passage to serve as a listening gallery (countermine) and also, possibly, as a drainage sump. Drainage, throughout work on the foundations, was a major problem. The water table varied from $5\frac{1}{2}$ *braccia* below the surface towards Porta

---

[1] MS. cit., fol. 90r.
[2] A.S.F., Carte Strozz., Ser. I, CXXXV, fol. 144v.
[3] Settimanni, MS. cit., fol. 137v, and Varchi, op. cit., vol. III, p. 98, in almost identical words.
[4] 17 May, according to the anonymous diarist, B.N.F. Conv. Soppr., c.7. 2614, fol. 60v.
[5] G. Lami, *Lezioni di antichità toscane* . . . (Florence, 1766), vol. I, p. xxxiii.
[6] Exemptions were for those properties 'decimate et nella gravezza della Città'. A.S.F., Capitani di Parte, 10 rossi, fol. 93v.

a Prato (by the river) to 7 *braccia* towards Porta San Gallo, and it was only by the use of pumps and a diversionary ditch leading to still lower ground that the footings of the walls could be kept dry. Only excavation can reveal the drainage system that was inserted, but, whatever it was, it was cited as a model later in the century.[1] Another problem was the extremely varied nature of the ground, here stiff clay or gravel, there sand and soft silt which needed binding with timber. Just outside the walls the excavators uncovered a Roman cemetery: coins, glass, copper mirrors, lamps and marble inscriptions, one of which was to be later displayed in the Fortezza.[2]

By 6 July, most of the ditch outside the walls was completed, and the spoil thrown outwards to form a *glacis* and inwards to provide the earth core of the bastions. Meanwhile, lime (for mortar), bricks and shaped stones had been prepared so that Vitelli, in his progress report of this date on the 'Castello Alexandrino' was able to say that 'all is shaping splendidly (*gagliardamente*), so that when the foundations are finished we expect to be able to build the outer bastions up to the first gunports [when, by the standards of the time, they would be defensible] very shortly'. A beginning, too, had been made on the trace of the inner bastions, the south-western one encroaching on 'the garden of the Bartolini', and that of S. Antonio, the south-eastern, reaching into 'a field belonging to the Hospital of S. Bonifatio'. On that date 1200 men were working outside and 300 inside the city wall.[3] The work was not without danger; six men were killed and fourteen crippled when the embankment for one of the bastions collapsed.[4]

Absit omen, and the greatest pains were taken to ensure that the foundation ceremony should be as powerfully beneficial as possible. On 12 July Angelo Marzi, Bishop of Assisi and one of Duke Alessandro's most trusted advisers,[5] wrote in tones of great urgency to Francesco Guicciardini in Bologna. It had been decided that the foundation stone was to be laid in that month, but should it be on the 15th or the 19th? The astrologers of Florence were at a deadlock — was the Carmelite Giuliano da Prato right in choosing the 15th, or were his rivals? Would

---

[1] By Francesco de Marchi, *Trattato d'Architettura Militare*, B.N.F., II, I, 277, fol. 151v.
[2] A.S.F., Carte Strozz., Ser. I, CCCLXI, fol. 38v.
[3] All the details, unless otherwise noted, in this and the previous paragraph are taken from Vitelli's report, A.S.F., Carte Strozz., Ser. I, XCV, fol. 22 ff., printed (with a few errors, notably 'conducere' for 'canonier') by L. Dami in his pioneer work, 'La costruzione della Fortezza da Basso,' *Arte e Storia*, vol. VI (1915), pp. 165-6.
[4] Anon., *Diario* . . . , B.N.F., Conv. Soppr., 2614, fol. 60v.
[5] According to Ammirato (*Opuscoli*, Florence (1542), p. 154) 'suo Luogotenente nell' udienza di piati et differenze de sudditi'.

THE FORTEZZA DA BASSO 49

Guicciardini show Giuliano's diagram (plate 13) to the astrologers of Bologna and express back their opinion?[1]

Foundation stones were not laid lightly in the Renaissance. The last great building in Florence, Palazzo Strozzi, had begun to rise on 6 August 1489, at an hour determined by astrologers,[2] and only a fortnight before receiving Marzi's letter Guicciardini had been advising Luigi to observe this tradition before commencing the citadel of Arezzo.[3] Presumably the Bolognese astrologers supported the Provincial of the Carmelites, for the stone was laid on Wednesday morning, 15 July.

The ceremony was well attended, the citizens being for the first time allowed to see the site of their new citadel at close quarters. A moveable altar had been constructed and was placed beside the ditch where the point of one of the outside bastions was to rise.[4] To this moved a procession headed by Alessandro with Vitelli and 'the whole nobility of Florence', together with Marzi and his train and the city magistrates, followed by a large contingent of the guard. Mass was said by the bishop and then the altar was lowered into the ditch. It was thirteen hours after the previous sunset, and while hymns were sung and prayers chanted, the Carmelite astrologer and the famous astrological clockmaker Lorenzo dalla Golpaia watched 'the various instruments for telling the time' they held in their hands for the fortunate moment to arrive. Their instruments cannot have been properly synchronized, for there was apparently some disagreement between them; the moment when the signal was given was variously reported as twenty-five, thirty, forty-four and forty-eight minutes past the hour, and Giuliano is said afterwards to have prophesied that the citadel would fall in ruins at the end of ninety-three years, at which the clockmaker 'deservedly laughed'. However, the sign was given and Marzi at once laid the first stone at the point of the bastion. It was a marble slab one and a quarter *braccia* by one half and bore this inscription: ANGELUS MARTIUS EPS ASSISINATENSIS HUNC PRIMUM LAPIDEM PER EUM BENEDICTUM AD ARCIS FLORENTIE MEDICEE ALEXANDER IN FUNDAMENTO PONIT ANNO A SALUTE CHRISTIANA MDXXXIIII IULII DIE XV HORA XIII.$\frac{1}{2}$. At the same time Ales-

---

[1] Op. cit., vol. X, pp. 258–9. On 21 July he sent Giuliano's diagram to Luigi, remarking that the Bolognese astrologers thought it to be altogether the wrong month. *Op. ined.*, vol. X, p. 300.

[2] Guido Pampaloni, *Palazzo Strozzi* (Rome, 1963), p. 87.

[3] Op. cit., vol. X, pp. 295–6.

[4] 'Dove e l'arme di S. M. Cesarea', Settimanni, MS. cit., fol. 132v, but as the escutcheons have perished, we can only say that this was probably the central bastion on the north-west front, as its name 'Imperiale' (plate 37) implies.

sandro laid another of the same size, inscribed as follows: ALEXANDER MEDICES PRIMUS DUX FLORENTINAM ARCEM A FUNDAMENTIS ERIGENS PRIMUM APONIT LAPIDEM. QUEM ANGELUS MARTIUS EPS ASSISINATENSIS INVOCATO DIVINO NUMINE BENEDIXIT DEDICAVITQUE ANNO A SALUTE CHRISTIANA MDXXXIIII. CLEMENTE VII. PONT. MAXIMO ET CAROLO QUINTO IMPERATORE AUGUSTO.[1] After the slabs had been ceremonially tapped with a new mallet, guns and arquebuses were shot off and Alessandro threw three gold medals into the foundation, one with Clement's head, one with Marzi's and one bearing his own — again, in conformity with custom: medals had been placed in the foundations of Palazzo Strozzi, as they were to be at the Belvedere fortress.[2]

In spite of the speed with which the Fortezza was founded, its ground plan was the result of much preliminary thought. The first sketch that survives in Sangallo's hand represents the stage when the Fortezza was to be sited at Porta S. Gallo (plate 14). The bottom half of the sheet contains the preliminary doodling with ideal geometrical shapes that was common among military engineers at the time, but the regular pentagons at the top seem to take their cue from the angle at which the city walls met the gate, which is shown in the right-hand upper corner. The symmetrical pentagonal form was less suited to a fortress built in the middle of a long straight stretch of wall, and when the Porta a Faenza site was decided on, Sangallo settled for a rectangle with one side extended to form an irregular pentagon. From the first drawings associated with the new site (plates 15 and 16) we can see that while this basic shape remained, two drastic changes intervened before the work of clearing the ground began. He saw the fortress as straddling the wall in such a way as to be half in, half out of the city, and — taking the inscription 'parte della Città' to put the top half of the drawing inside the wall — as pointing menacingly inwards, though there was also a massive ravelin protecting the straight outer front from assault from the open country, and with (in plage 16) a second ravelin astride the wall to provide additional cover from an attack coming up from the river, either inside the wall or outside it.

It was probably at this stage that Alessandro's sense of urgency grew

---

[1] See Settimanni's corrected version, MS. cit., fol. 134r. M. Rastrelli, *Storia di Alessandro dei Medici* (Florence, 1781), vol. II, pp. 50–1, conflates his uncorrected with his corrected version.

[2] This description of the foundation ceremony is taken from: Letter from Giovanfrancesco Camaiani to Luigi Guicciardini, 15 July 1534, A.S.F., Carte Strozz., Ser. I, LXI, no. 51 (printed in the *Inventario*, p. 317); A.S.F., Carte Strozz., Ser. I, XCV, fol. 20r (printed, with omission of slab dimensions, in Dami, op. cit., pp. 164–5); Settimanni, MS. cit., fol. 132r–133r; B.N.F., II, IV, 339 (notes of A. F. Marmi), fol. 24r; B.N.F., II, I, 313, fol. 152v.

so great that it was decided to incorporate the recently strengthened Porta a Faenza, which Sangallo apparently thought of leaving to one side (plate 15), into the fortress itself and make it the nucleus of a *mastio* (plates 17 and 18, where Porta a Faenza is the high square-topped tower). This involved turning the entire fortress round, so that its straight front would be aligned with the city wall. A secondary advantage of this scheme is that less destruction of property within the city was entailed, but Sangallo appears to have thought that it weakened the fortress, for in the next surviving drawing (plate 19) he introduces a bastioned fort-within-a-fort which anticipates the possibility of having to retreat there after an attack from the city which might storm the southern front. Traces of such a defence are to be found on a subsequent, more finished drawing (plate 20), and the 'completed' Fortezza was indeed criticized for not having an inner retreat.[1] The city south front was, however, strengthened by building the *mastio* massively forward (compare plates 19 and 21) instead of using Porta a Faenza itself and presenting a withdrawn curtain to the city.

The decision to align on the city wall and build the Fortezza outwards gave time to refine the *mastio* front and the buildings within it while the three outer bastions were built, but one important feature of the design was fixed as soon as the foundation works began. This was the double tier of corridors in the thickness of the walls (plates 17, 22 and 33) which have already been referred to.

The lower, the top of whose vault coincides with the original level of the ditch, occupies what was to be the conventional position for a countermine gallery, though if the wall foundations really slope out as steeply as one of Sangallo's elevations suggests (plate 22) its value as a listening gallery would have been reduced. It seems more likely that its function was to act as a drain and to help ventilate the far more important gallery above it; as this contained musketry galleries and sally points a good circulation of fresh air was needed to clear smoke away and to prevent the soldiers mustering in that confined space from becoming stifled. The galleries communicate through a series of square traps in the floor of the upper one, and this, combined with chimneys rising at intervals from the upper gallery, keeps the air moving. The countermine is at present filled nearly to the top with mud, so its precise function cannot be established.

The upper gallery, however, though blocked in part by falls, can be examined. Large enough to let two men walk abreast without stooping,

---

[1] See below, pp. 60–1.

it contains, at intervals of some seven metres, musketry galleries scooped towards the outside of the wall in which firing slits are cut. There is also a series of sally ports, closed on the inside by a door and consisting of an S-shaped corridor in the thickness of the wall leading to a second door opening into the ditch and covered by musket slits cut through from the main gallery (plate 23). The filling-in of the ditch makes these invisible from the outside.

This nineteenth-century filling-in also conceals the way in which the Fortezza was entered. The present gates (plate 24, I and I[1]) were built when the original ones were buried. There are three early gates of which only one is shown in a contemporary working drawing, that of the *mastio* (plate 25), whose pediment can be seen at ground level immediately to the left of the present main entrance (plate 26). Recent excavation revealed the top of a second gate on the city front (plate 27, G[1] on plate 24). Until this is fully excavated, however, or associated with an inscription, it would be hazardous to attribute it to Sangallo. Two gates so near together would weaken the curtain between them and an entrance in that position is not shown on any sixteenth-century plan. De Marchi and the anonymous draughtsman of the Biblioteca Nazionale[1] (plates 28 and 29) show only the *mastio* entrance on the city front at mid-century, and so does Buonsignori in 1581 (plate 12). Finally, it would have been illogical for Sangallo to have lavished the precautions against effecting an easy entrance into the *mastio* (which has inner flanking fire positions and a succession of massive gates) while offering a head-on entrance in the adjacent curtain.

The obvious place for a second entrance was on the other side, for the admission of reinforcements and the launching of massive sallies. De Marchi indicates an entrance there, and the top part of a bricked-up gateway can be clearly seen. Set in a stone facing, which sets it off from the surrounding brick, topped with a massive straight pediment, and with a space for an inscription above the cordon, this is better suited for a ceremonial entrance than the more business-like entrance in the flanks of the *mastio*. And as the real 'master' of the Fortezza was not so much Alessandro as Charles V, it would have been natural to have the triumphal entrance on 'his' side, next to his imperial bastion, rather than in the direction of the city. This entrance is not shown by Buonsignori, possibly because after Cosimo's secure reign such a gate, necessarily vulnerable, was no longer necessary either as a symbol of

---

[1] Admittedly he is very inaccurate — showing four outer bastions instead of three, but he does have a good general notion of the city front.

Imperial power or to admit reinforcements to help the Medici overawe the populace. But until the gate is excavated, its date must remain conjectural.

Sangallo's plans for the interior (plates 30 and 31, and 32 and 33[1] which show a section across the righthand side of 31, modifying 22) envisaged elaborate and harmonious accommodation for men and horses, but they were never carried out, and *ad hoc* buildings in the interior (imaginatively rationalized according to the town-planning conventions of his day by Buonsignori) were put up instead. Nothing but the *mastio*, to contain quarters for the Duke himself, was completed in something like the form for which he had hoped. Apart from the stone façade in which the 'Imperial' gate is set, this provides the only decorative relief from the sombre brickwork of the rest of the Fortezza. Great care was taken over its design (plate 34) and even today its appearance is magnificent (plate 35), though lacking the impressiveness it must have had when the ditch was still void (plate 36). 'Vasari cited it as the finest example of rusticated masonry in Florence, and explained how the façade, "out of respect for the Medici emblems, is made with ornaments of diamond points and flattened pellets".'[2]

This failure to complete the fortress is explained by the events that followed the foundation ceremony. By July 1534 Clement VII's failing health was the subject of much concern in Florence, and the building of the Fortezza was pushed forward still faster — and faster yet on his death on 25 September: with the loss of a Medici pope, a Medici citadel became even more crucial to Alessandro. According to Segni, he clapped another heavy *accatto* on the Florentines, and called once more on the entire labour force of the *dominio*.[3] The work was driven on through the rain that winter, complicated somewhat by Antonio's absence in Rome, as we can sense from the letters to him from Giovanni delle Decime, who appears to have been clerk of the works under Nanni Unghero. Bastiano da Sangallo was invaluable as go-between and explicator of Antonio's drawings to Alessandro whose interest grew still greater as the *mastio* progressed, as it did this winter, for as the terms

---

[1] Among the mass of detailed information in Giovannoni (op. cit.) some small errors relating to the Fortezza have crept in. His fig. 377 is not Uffizi 931A but 1659A; on p. 81, for 791 read 761; on p. 421, 791 is confused with 761; on p. 415, for fig. 373 read 374 and change description to 'pianta di tutta quanta la fortezza' and draughtsman from Antonio to (assuming the argument of note 73) Bastiano.

[2] *Vasari on Technique*, tr. L. S. MacLehose, ed. G. Baldwin Smith (New York, 1940), 66–7. A detailed estimate of the Fortezza as a fighting machine must wait until the army leaves it, when further excavations can take place, gun embrasures be cleared out and parapets examined.

[3] *Op. cit.*, vol. II, pp. 415–16, 176.

used in connection with it show —*castello, palazzo del principe* — this part of the Fortezza was to double the function of a strong point with that of an armoured home for the Duke.

In January and February, the only months for which we have reasonably detailed information, the outer bastions with their ramparts neared completion, and work was concentrated instead on the inner ones. When the old city wall was torn down to leave the width of the ditch between it and the south-east bastions, the Fortezza, now to be seen as a growing whole for the first time was as Unghero exclaimed 'a superb thing'. It was, however, the *mastio* that especially preoccupied Alessandro. Unghero wrote to Antonio, with some of an expert's impatience of the layman, that he had had to have a model made as the Duke could not visualize it from the drawings; 'he says, "It is all very well to talk, but I don't follow it".' In particular Alessandro feared that the *mastio*, being so high, would be vulnerable, and Unghero explained how the lines of fire from the bastions would protect it, and that it would hardly be a conspicuous mark from the bottom of the *glacis* towards the town.[1]

At the same time, a fresh course was being dug for the Mugnone, the details of which are by no means clear. Early in the sixteenth century that stream came in from the north to Porta San Gallo and then flowed outside the wall past Porta a Faenza and so into the Arno. In preparation for the siege, however, its course was diverted so that it ran the other way, along the north-eastern and eastern walls, and thence to the Arno.[2] If Ughi is to be trusted this must have been a temporary measure, for he says that the building of the Fortezza made it necessary to turn it from its old bed along which it was now flowing again, and out past the Fortezza.[3] In this case it is difficult to understand why we first hear of this diversion in February 1535[4] and as an operation that was not yet completed. Perhaps it was deliberately turned back to its old route in February past the Fortezza and away on something like its present course to provide an obstacle to an army coming from Prato, and, a remote possibility, so that the Fortezza ditches could be filled from it if it were thought desirable: there was much debate at the time about the merits of a wet versus a dry ditch. Yet to flood the ditch would have been a desperate measure, for it would have rendered the ditch-

---

[1] Information in these two paragraphs from letters to Antonio da San Gallo from Giovanni delle Decime and Nanni Unghero printed in Bottari, op. cit., vol. III, pp. 329–37.
[2] Varchi, op. cit., vol. I, p. 109.
[3] Op. cit., pp. 172–3.
[4] Bottari, op. cit., vol. III, p. 337.

level musketry gallery and its sally-ports useless. However, the work was done, even if we cannot be clear about its purpose.[1]

All this activity continued through the spring and summer. By 5 November Vitelli is writing encouragingly to San Gallo, 'All goes well with the fortress (*roccha*) and procedes as ever with vigour and diligence.' But he added that they needed Antonio on the spot as quickly as possible.[2] This was for the last spurt before a garrison was able to take over on 5 December.

Once more the stars were consulted. 'On Sunday 5 December 1535 at eighteen hours Bishop Marzi said a solemn Mass at the new fortress of Florence by the gate [Faenza] at the moment fixed by the astrologers, and it was handed over by Duke Alessandro to the captain of the guard.'[3] Vasari was present at this ceremony, and he described the pageantry — the bishop's throne, the vestments, the musical instruments and the singing — with a mildly extravagant air of mockery to Pietro Aretino. The moment came for the elevation of the Host, and the officers began to appear, armed so divinely that they looked like the triumph of Scipio in the second Punic War, and they passed four by four to the left and drew up in line with their backs to the east. Last of all came forty pieces of artillery, all new, of beautiful shape, embellished with the ducal arms and wreathed with olive, drawn each by four yoke of oxen; then came carriages piled with cannon balls interspersed with mules laden with powder barrels and other warlike instruments, the appearance of all which might have struck Mars himself with fear. Then guns were fired, officers embraced, and the procession moved inside the Fortezza, where they shortly afterwards appeared on the ramparts, eight hundred of them, and the standards of Charles V and the Medici were for the first time seen displayed there.[4]

While Vitelli remained Alessandro's military right-hand man, the Duke appointed Paolantonio da Parma, 'a young man better known for loyalty than for reliability or judgment,'[5] as castellan, and at this installation ceremony Paolantonio had to take an oath, administered

---

[1] The earliest plan which gives the ditch system (plate 37) dates from the eighteenth century. It shows the ditch to be dry, save for a cunette — a narrow channel which combined the function of draining a dry ditch with making mining operations more difficult — running along the middle of it. The left bank of the Mugnone is shown outside the north side of the ditch. According to Fourquevaux (op. cit., p. 530, n.1), the cunette's function here was to drain the countermine. He says it was two paces wide.
[2] A.S.F., Carte Strozz., Ser. I, XCV, fol. 24r (printed in Dami, op. cit., p. 166).
[3] B.N.F., II, I, 313, fol. 153v.
[4] Frey, op. cit., pp. 40–2.
[5] Adriani, op. cit., p. 21.

by the Bishop in the presence of the Duke, the clergy of the Cathedral, and the large crowd of notables, in which he swore to guard the Fortezza with all its artillery, munitions, etc. for the Duke, to keep the password secret, and, if Alessandro should die, to hand it over only to the Emperor or his representative.[1] From this oath the status of the Fortezza becomes clear: it is a guarantee that the policy of Charles V, and not the will of the Florentine people, will prevail at any moment of constitutional crisis.

With the garrison installed, Alessandro felt safe in leaving Florence for an absence of two and a half months, during which he conferred with the Emperor in Naples and confirmed that in the event of his death his castellans in Florence, Pisa and Leghorn would take orders only from Charles.[2] It must have been at about this time that Baldo de Paludi's fervent tribute to the family he had served so long was set up in the Fortezza (plate 39): 'BALDO DE PALUDI SERVO FIDELE DELLA ILLUSTRE CASA DE MEDICI AL TEMPO DEL MAGNIFICO LORENZO DI PIERO DI COSIMO ET DEL MAGNIFICO PIERO DI LORENZO ET DI PP LEONE DI LORENZO ET DEL DUCA GIULIANO DI LORENZO ET DELLO ILLUSTRISSIMO DUCA LORENZO DEL MAGNIFICO PIERO ET DI PP CLEMENTE DEL MAGNIFICO GIULIANO ET DEL REVERERENDISSIMO HIPOLITO DELLO ILLUSTRISSIMO DUCA GIULIANO ET OGGI MDXXXV DELLO ILLUSTRISSIMO ET ECCELLENTISSIMO DUCA ALEXANDRO DELLA BUONA MEMORIA DELLO ILLUSTRISSIMO DUCA LORENZO ET GENERO DELLA CESAREA MAESTA DI CAROLO IMPERATOR INVICTISSIMO DELLA CASA AUSTRIA QUAL DETTO ILLUSTRISSIMO DUCA ALEXANDRO HA FATTO FONDAR ET FORNIRE QUESTO MIRABILE ET DIGNISSIMO CASTELLO ALEXANDRIA DI FIORENZA ET PER SE ET SEMENZA DI SUA ILLUSTRISSIMA ET EGREGIA SIGNORIA ET SUA FIDELISSIMI SERVITORI ET AMICI.'

Charles was sufficiently reassured to allow the marriage between Alessandro and Margaret to be celebrated in Naples, but when on his visit to Florence in May, which was celebrated with much pageantry, he was shown round the Fortezza by the Duke, he expressed unease that a contingent of the guard who were quartered there was commanded, under the authority of the castellan, by a Pisan, and suggested that one of his own officers might be more reliable. To which Alessandro is reputed to have replied that who could the Emperor trust if not his own son-in-law?[3]

Charles V and his successor took the tag *Quis custodiet ipsos custodes*

---

[1] Frey, op. cit., p. 45.
[2] G. Spini, *Cosimo I de' Medici e la indipendenza del Principato Mediceo* (Florence, 1945), p. 44.
[3] B.N.F., II, I, 313, fol. 155r, and Settimanni, MS. cit., fol. 317v.

with great seriousness: hence their nerve-wracked inability to delegate. The Fortezza was now Charles's guardian of the Florentine constitution, its political alignment and his daughter's safety. But — and this was the point of Machiavelli's reference to the Castello Sforzesco and its treacherous castellan — who was to guard the guardian? In this case, Paolantonio da Parma.

The test came in January 1537, when, for the last time, the Fortezza played a prominent rôle in the history of Florence. On the night of the 5th-6th, Alessandro's cousin Lorenzino assassinated him in the bed where he lay waiting for extra-marital entertainment. Cardinal Cybo, Charles V's political lieutenant, after consulting with Marzi and others, decided to keep the news as secret as possible until Vitelli, who was away from the city, could return. He feared a popular uprising. But this was not the only problem. Alessandro left no legitimate children. It was essential — if the exiles were not to gain the initiative and possibly win the armed support of France — to declare the nature of the new government as soon as possible. At the end of two days of constant debate, in which Francesco Guicciardini and Francesco Vettori played a large part, it became clear that rather than declare an interreguum under Cybo's temporary presidency it would be safer to declare at once for Cosimo, the eighteen-year-old son of Giovanni delle Bande Nere, the gallant *condottiere* whose career in arms and tragically early death had already made him something of a folk hero, and who, alone of the Medici, was not associated with any grasping political views. On the 9th, then, Cosimo was declared 'capo e primario della città di Firenze', a hedging title intended to contain two divergent political attitudes: that of the older generation of *ottimati* like Guicciardini, who wished to restore a muted republicanism and increase the independence of Florence from Charles V, and that of the Imperialists, who wanted a straightforward ducal government under Charles's protection and control.

The 'capo' title which was announced on the morning of the 9th was a victory for the more republican-minded party: that evening the advantage was annulled when Vitelli, by a trick, gained possession of the Fortezza declaring that he held it, not against Cosimo, but in pursuance of his oaths of allegiance — taken during the Naples conference — to Charles V. This redressing of the political balance within Florence, and its consequence, Cosimo's lifework of regaining Florentine independence, is not our concern,[1] but from the various

---

[1] See especially A. Rossi, 'L'elezione di Cosimo I de' Medici', *Atti del R. Istituto Veneto di Lettere, Scienze ed Arti*, 1889-90, pp. 369 ff., and Spini, op. cit. In his edition

accounts of Vitelli's occupation we can learn something of the state of the Fortezza in 1535.

These accounts differ, though they all argue that the Fortezza was far from finished according to San Gallo's designs. Ughi even makes the point that Lorenzino acted when he did because it would be easy to get possession in its uncompleted, and therefore undergarrisoned, state.[1] Whether Vitelli tempted Paolantonio out, or talked his way in and then, relying on a confederate, was able to subvert the garrison, is unclear. But these facts emerge: though the quarters in the *mastio* were adequate to house Cybo and Margaret, who fled there on the 8th with Alessandro's bastards, Giulio and Giulia, its external fabric was still uncompleted. A drawbridge was, however, in place.[2]

Later that year, Guicciardini, reviewing the city's finances in a memorandum for Cosimo, emphasized the need for economy and recommended that there should, while the present emergency lasted, be no further spending on the Fortezza,[3] though designs continued to pass between Unghero and Antonio da Sangallo.[4] However, if major work on the fabric was stopped, the embellishment of the exterior continued. Unghero said that the sculptor Raffaello da Montlelupo had received 130 soldi for carving the arms of Charles V — supported by two nude and life-sized Victories[5] — on one of the outer bastions, and those of the Medici, also 'with two figures', on the more southerly of those that faced the city. The sculptor Tribolo was also mentioned by Unghero as in receipt of 130 florins, presumably for the four arms he was commissioned to carve by the *provveditore* Corsini.[6] One of these was supported by nude Victories, the rest were '*mascheroni* supporting arms', of which the Medici coat on the *mastio* (plate 35) may be a survivor. Tribolo's connection with the Medici citadel is appropriate: in 1529 he constructed an elaborate model of Florence and its defences which was smuggled out to Clement who used it as a campaign map.[7]

(Florence, 1940) of Cosimo's *Lettere*, p. 22 n., Spini emphasizes Vitelli's rôle. 'In tal modo era divenuto quasi l'arbitro delle sorti di Firenze, potendo a suo piacere ceder la fortezza all' imperatore perchè vi mettesse dentro una guarnigione spagnuola, restituirla a Cosimo oppure consegnarla a tradimento ai fuorusciti.' Nardi describes how Charles's support of Cosimo was influenced by Vitelli's action, op. cit. (Florence, 1858), vol. II, pp. 296–7.

[1] *Cronica di Firenze*, in *A.S.I.*, Appendice, vol. VII (1849), p. 189. And Adriani, op. cit., p. 21.
[2] The fullest account is in Marucelli's *Diario di Firenze*, B.N.F., Magl., XXV, 274 (another version II, IV, 21), fols. 62r–63v.
[3] A.S.F., Carte Strozz., Ser. I, XIV, fol. 231v.
[4] Bottari, op. cit., p. 334; letter of 29 December 1537.
[5] Vasari, ed. Milanesi, vol. IV, p. 544. Neither has survived.
[6] Ibid., vol. VI, p. 66.
[7] Ibid., pp. 61–2.

In 1539 large-scale work was resumed, the *Capitani* being charged to organize labour from the *dominio* on the basis of three periods of work a year for the next three years for all men between the ages of fifteen and fifty, from which exemption could be bought at the price of seven soldi and six denari a time for *contadini*, and fifteen soldi for artisans. Those in the neighbourhood of Arezzo were exempt, for they were expected to work on the citadel which was at last going forward there.[1] Unfortunately no mention of the consequent works has, to my knowledge, survived. The next accounts which we have are for 1545–46[2] but though these contain tantalizing references to Pontormo and to the woodcarver Tasso, they include payments for work in the Boboli Gardens and the Palazzo della Signoria in a way that makes it difficult to isolate the payments for work done on the Fortezza. From the citadel's present state it seems unlikely that the internal fabric advanced beyond the condition in which it was left on Alessandro's death, that is, with the stables not begun, but with the guard rooms and state apartments in the *mastio* habitable; Cosimo, when eventually he was allowed to buy the Fortezza back from the Emperor in 1543, celebrated by taking up residence there for a short while.[3]

This was the last meaningful gesture in the context of the Fortezza's purpose; by the time Cosimo obtained possession he no longer needed a citadel, and the Fortezza started its long decline to the mock-military shambles it now is.[4] In 1554, Raymond de Fourquevaux, author of *Instructions sur le faict de la Guerre* and a keen commentator on military affairs, was taken prisoner at the battle of Marciano, during the French attempt to relieve Siena. He was brought back to Florence to await his ransom. He had to wait over a year, and while nominally imprisoned in Monte S. Miniato, he was given considerable freedom to move about the city, and on at least one occasion he made a careful inspection of the Fortezza. He considered it 'one of the finest and strongest strongholds in Italy', but was quick to point out its weak points. *The terreplain* which was to provide gun platforms within the walls was unfinished; the original city wall still connected the *mastio* with the south-western bastion; buildings on the town side had not been cleared back far enough to deprive an invader who penetrated the city of useful cover for his batteries. It was undergarrisoned — one hundred and twenty men (including fifty Spaniards) many of whom were hardly fit to bear

---

[1] A.S.F., Capitani di Parte, 10 rosso, fols. 109r–110r, *provvisione* of the 48, 11 October 1539.
[2] A.S.F., Capitani di Parte, 138 rosso.
[3] Segni, op. cit., vol. III, 639–40. [4] Now restored.

arms. But the Fortezza's weakest point, he told the French King, was the proximity of the new course of the Mugnone. 'On the side open to the country, there is a fair-sized stream called the Mognon, less than fifty paces from the ditch and which used to flow over the site of the citadel; so in an hour it could be turned back into the ditch to fill it and flood the countermines [in fact, the musketry gallery].' This would provide an alternative obstacle for a besieging force, but Fourquevaux's argument is of a different kind; the effect of the stagnant water would be, especially in the hottest months of summer, to spread disease by infecting the air, and this 'would, in a short time, kill the soldiers in the fortress'. Meanwhile the new, and now empty bed of the Mugnone, would provide cover for 'three or four thousand infantry', of the attacking army.[1] As we know from Strozzi's end and from the interrogations of other suspects it had already been used as a prison and place of torture.[2] Gunpowder was manufactured there,[3] and it was also used as the ducal treasury: on this point the annotation on Sangallo's drawing (plate 30) is confirmed by Menicuccio Rossi's reference to 'the new citadel where the treasure is'.[4] In 1608 an attempt was made to put an end to a period of growing neglect during which the Fortezza had been 'for long without a castellan', by reorganizing its administration,[5] but in the following century it seems to have become little more than a yard for the supply and repair of the machines, costumes and other equipment needed for entertainments in the Boboli Gardens, funeral processions and the like.[6] In the eighteenth century it was a house of correction, in the nineteenth a barracks, and in a few years it is planned to become a shop window for the work of those artisans whose sixteenth-century ancestors had helped to build it.

The Fortezza da Basso played a larger part in the political than in the military life of Florence; it was never put to the test of war. As a fortress it was criticized, by implication, by Vitelli himself who in 1542 asked a group of military engineers in Rome for a better solution than had yet been found to the problem of masking curtains from enemy guns while preserving their usefulness as firing platforms. De Marchi, who records this meeting, himself challenges the idea of having a citadel

[1] Raymond de Fourquevaux, *Information au Roy et à Monseigneur le Connestable touchant les affaires de Florence, avec ung discours pour entreprendre contre ledit Florence, Pize et Gennes s'il plaira à Sa Majesté. 1555*, ed. Raoul Brunon (Aix, 1965), pp. 55, 58–9.
[2] E.g. A.S.F., Carte Strozz., Ser I, XCV, fols. 191–4.
[3] Fourquevaux, op. cit., p. 56.
[4] *Lode di Firenze*, ed. M. F. Raffaelli (Ferino, 1887), p. 8. The editor's annotations are untrustworthy.
[5] A.S.F., Miscellanea Medicea, 805, fasc. 6.
[6] A.I., cat. CXLIV, codd. 126–33 and 150–3.

almost wholly outside the city wall, rather than having it half in, half out with the wall retained to provide a refuge in case the curtain were breached from either direction.[1] Sangallo later refined the placing of batteries and internal communicating ways in his Bastione Ardeatino (1536 ff.) in Rome,[2] and the problem of how best to relate a citadel to a town was first solved at Turin in 1564 and at Antwerp in 1567. But the Fortezza was the most advanced citadel of its time, and in an age where both princes and their architects looked on a citadel rather than a palace as the most striking symbol of their authority[3]—and a glance at the town plans of the second half of the sixteenth century will show how quickly this fashion spread throughout Europe — it was a formative influence. From a Tuscan and a Medicean, we may wish to take Vasari's comment, that 'it is celebrated today throughout the world and held to be untakable' with a grain of salt, but this was also the opinion of the Portuguese Francesco de Hollanda, who proclaimed the Fortezza to be 'the finest fortress in Europe'. The Florentines' yoke provided a model which was to bow many non-Italian shoulders, and it could be plausibly argued that the genius of Antonio da Sangallo was more baleful to the common man of sixteenth century Europe than that of Machiavelli.

Appendix: The Name of the Fortezza da Basso

What are we to call it? There are three alternatives. One, to associate it with Alessandro de' Medici, for whom it was built; two, to give it its official name of S. Giovanni Battista; three, to retain its popular apellation, da Basso. In 1534, when building began, it was known as 'Fortilitium illustrissimi ducis' (ASF, Capitani di Parte, 14 rosso, fol. 209v), 'novum fortilitium' (ibid., fol. 210r), 'Fortezza de Firenze' (A.S.F., Carte Strozz., Ser. I, LXI, fol. 25r), and 'castello Alexandrino' (A.S.F., Carte Strozz., Ser. I, XCV, fol. 22r); for both Lapini (*Diario Fiorentino di Agostino Lapini*, ed. G.O. Corazzini, Florence, 1900, p. 98) and Luca Landucci (*Diario Fiorentino*, ed. Iodoco del Badia, Florence, 1883, p. 371) it was the 'nuova citadella'. The *capitani* were calling it 'novus arx' in 1535 (loc cit., fol. 234r), and it was called 'nuovo castello di Firenze' in the oath administered to Paolantonio da Parma on

---

[1] MS. cit., fols. 93v–94r and 29r–32r, where he describes the Fortezza beyond doubt without actually naming it.
[2] M. Borgatti, 'Il bastione ardeatino a Roma', *Rivista d'Artiglieria e Genio* (1890), vol. II, pp. 325–403.
[3] Girolamo Maggi is eloquent on this theme. *Degli Ingegni Militari*, B.N.F., Palat. 464, esp. p. 309.

5 December 1535 (K. Frey, op. cit., p. 45), though on the newly discovered inscription of Baldo de Paludi of the same time (plate 39) it is 'Castello Alexandria di Fiorenza'. Usage remained uncertain during the rest of the sixteenth century. When Filippo Strozzi was imprisoned there in 1538 he wrote as from 'Castello di Firenze' (A.S.F., Carte Strozz., Ser. II, L, *Inventario*), and either this form or 'citadella di Firenze' (e.g. Ughi, op. cit., p. 189) was commonly used. In 1549 it was still 'la nuova citadella' to Menicuccio Rossi (op. cit., p. 8). But it was also commonly called after the Porta a Faenza, which it incorporated. Thus the anonymous author of the *Diario di tutti i casi eseguiti in Firenze* . . . called it 'Citadella della Porta a Faenza' (B.N.F., Conv. Soppr., C. 7. 2614 (s.a. 1537, fol. 67r), after having previously called it 'fortezza nuova' or 'citadella nuova', and for Adriani (Venice, 1587, p. 21) it was 'nuova fortezza di Faenza'. Both the modern formal and informal names appear late in the century. Mariano Borgatti ('Le mura e le torri di Firenze', *Rivista d'Artiglieria e Genio*, vol. IV (1900), p. 50, n.) cites a record of the *Otto di Guardia e Balìa* of 28 September 1573 to the effect that a criminal is to be 'rinserrato in una carcere fortissima della fortezza da Basso della città di Firenze', and this might seem to knock on the head any suggestion that 'da Basso' was used to distinguish this fortress from that of the Belvedere, built on the heights above the Boboli gardens in 1590. Another anonymous chronicler (B.N.F., II, I, 313, fol. 152v) referred retrospectively to the foundation ceremony of 1534 as at the 'citadella e fortezza di Firenze fatta dove era la Porta a Faenza detta di poi la fortezza S. Giovanni', and by the seventeenth century 'Castello di S. Giovanni Battista di Firenze' had become the official title (v., for example, the account books of clerks of the works in A.I., cat. CXLIV, codd. 126–9 and 150–3). There can be little doubt that from the beginning of this usage it was St John the Baptist, the patron saint of Florence, and not the Evangelist, who was referred to (cf. P. Moschella, 'Cenno storico-topografico di un'antica fortezza Florentina', *L'Universo*, 1943, p. 9, n. 9. 'Era così [S. Giovanni] chiamata dal convento di San Giovanni Evangelista' which was destroyed to make way for it.' This article is nevertheless the only serious study of the Fortezza since the article by Dami cited on p. 518. The current formula 'Fortezza di S. Giovanni Battista detta da Basso' is cumbersome; some case may be made for using the formula of the only inscription extant in the fortress, 'Castello Alexandria'; but 'Fortezza da Basso', with its respectable ancestry and universal popular acceptance would seem to have the strongest claim of all.

3

TUDOR FORTIFICATIONS:
THE DEFENCE OF THE REALM, 1485-1558

THE only successful invasion of England in Tudor times was the one that established the Tudors themselves as a dynasty: the landing in Pembrokeshire in August 1485 of Henry, Earl of Richmond, en route from France to Bosworth Field. As Henry VII his enormous island coastline was breached by the pin-prick incursions of his rivals: the Earl of Lincoln's Irishmen at Furness in Lancashire in 1487, Perkin Warbeck's men at Deal in Kent in 1495 and the pretender himself at Land's End in 1497; but no massive challenge to the change of dynasty appeared from abroad. When war fleets crossed the Channel it was the English who were the invaders: Henry backing his anti-French diplomacy with the siege of Boulogne in 1492, his successor, Henry VIII, embarking on mettlesome if unimpressive campaigns in Picardy in 1513 and 1522−3. It is true that Henry VIII, in a transient mood of good-housekeeping, had resolved in 1519 to check the security of his frontiers[1] and that similar expressions of intent were made by Thomas Cromwell after Charles V's indignant reaction to the annulment of the marriage to Catherine of Aragon in 1533.[2] But nothing was done on a national scale, very little on local initiative. Charles's long continuing conflict with Francis I and the grudging need of each to woo rather than subdue England seemed to promise immunity from all but the sparks of their conflict. England swept Romishness from its inmost rooms while confidently leaving its doors ajar. As Froude, speaking of 1536, put it: 'the French and Flemish ships of war captured prizes or fought battles in the mouths of English rivers, or under the windows of English towns.'[3] But actual invasion—and on the scale to be threatened in the Armada year of 1588—only emerged as a probability in 1538, with the signature of a peace treaty in June between England's ancient enemy, France, and the personally offended and militantly Catholic Charles V, and with the threatened publication of Pope Paul III's Bull excommunicating Henry and releasing his people from their allegiance to him.

Paul's hope was that the Catholic powers would first break off diplomatic and commercial relations with England and then, with the Bull as its banner, send a crusading army across the Channel; this, at least, was the form in which his intentions were expressed by his most fervid emissary, the exiled English cardinal, Reginal Pole.

Pole was only sent off from Rome to Spain on 27 December 1538, but a dispatch three days later from the French ambassador in London shows that the idea of

[1] *L. & P.* iii, 576.
[2] F. C. Dietz, *English Government Finance 1485−1558* (1920), pp. 105−6.
[3] J. A. Froude, *History of England from the Fall of Wolsey to the defeat of the Spanish Armada* (1870) iii, p. 63.

Additional Note: Cross-references in the foot-notes to the chapter refer to vols iii and iv of *The History of the King's Works* ed. Howard Colvin.

invasion was already taken seriously. To hurt the English through a blockade was something, he wrote to Anne de Montmorency, Constable of France, but why not aim for an outright conquest which would gain Francis I more glory than any of his precedecessors had won as well as gratifying the pope? 'True, there would be a fight, but it would be less dangerous than ever it was before, for the people are inconceivably discontented...Make spoil of this country between you [and Charles]. From the Thames the coast adjoins Picardy, Normandy, and Brittany as far as Brest, and is furnished with good ports, a great necessity to France... The other side of the Thames likewise lies convenient for the Emperor, adjoining Holland and Zealand. Hand over to the King of Scots the North, which is his ancient right and heritage.'[1] On 8 January 1539, Cardinal Farnese wrote from Rome that the pope already 'hopes that God will work some good effect for the reduction of that realm',[2] and news that Francis and Charles had bound one another through proxies at Toledo on 10 January not to make any separate agreement with Henry led to confident predictions of the impending division of England circulating on the continent.[3] On 3 March Sir Thomas Wriothesley, Henry's ambassador to Charles's regent in the Netherlands, Queen Mary of Hungary, urged Cromwell from Brussels to advise the king to prepare against an attack from enemies whose appetite would make a 'morsel' of England[4], and at the same time a spy, reporting on French preparations, urged that 'you must fortify your places and harbours.'[5] On the 8th a group of English Protestants wrote from London to friends in Germany, 'it is said we are to have war with the French, the Italians, the Spaniards and the Scots at once'. Henry himself, two days later, asked his ambassador in Spain to complain to Charles of the prevalence of the 'bruit' that French and Spanish forces were about to invade England with papal backing. Before a reply could be received came news from the English agents attending the Protestant Diet of Frankfurt that Charles had concluded a truce with the Turk to leave him free for the enterprise of England. Cromwell wrote back at once with the line they should take: 'although by the Grace of God he [Henry] will be able to defend his realm and offend the invaders', unity among the Protestant princes is essential.[6]

During April it became clear that Pole had been rebuffed by Charles V on the grounds that the Turks without and the Protestants within his own Empire gave him quite enough to think about. James V of Scotland let it be known that he, at least, if not his clergy, had no wish for war. After a long hiatus, Francis I that month sent another ambassador to reside in London who reported that 'his arrival rejoiced the English, who...thought war was already at their door.' And Paul III protested that all *he* had had in mind was a blockade which would irritate the English into settling their own destiny by civil war.[7] The troops and ships which had been reported as massing in the Channel ports of France and the Netherlands either seemed to have evaporated or had moved away to other destinations. But the scare had invaded the psyche if not the shores of England. 'These bruits be well laid', the Duke of Suffolk assured Cromwell, 'but the King does well to provide for the worst.' And Edmund

---

[1] *L. & P.* xiii (2), 1162.　　[2] *L. & P.* xiv (1), 36.
[3] *Ibid.*, 115, 158, 258, 288, 308, 372.　　[4] *Ibid.*, 433
[5] *Ibid.*, 418, 404.　　[6] *Ibid.*, 466, 487 (p. 190), 552, 580 (p. 228).　　[7] *Ibid.*, 603, 625, 669, 761.

Harvel, resident agent in that news-centre, Venice, also wrapped relief in caution; 'the babblings against England are everywhere ceased', but nevertheless Cromwell, he urged, should 'make strong and perpetual provision for the safety of the realm.'[1]

What the king had provided for the safety of the realm was admirably summarized by his contemporary, the chronicler Edward Hall.[2] Henry, he wrote, had been 'enfourmed by his trustie & faithfull frendes y^t the cankered and cruel serpent the bishop of rome, by [means of] that Archetraitor Reignold Poole...had moved and stirred diverse great princes and potentates of Christendome to invade the Realme of England, and utterlie to destroy the whole nacion of the same.' Accordingly, he reviewed the preparedness of the navy (in January) and ordered musters of men fit to serve in the army to be held throughout the county (in March).[3] 'Also', Hall went on, 'he sent dyvers of his nobles and counsaylours to view and searche all the Portes and daungiers on the coastes where any meete or convenient landing place might be supposed...And in all suche doubtfull places his hyghnes caused dyvers & many Bulwarks & fortificacions to be made.'

Here lay the innovation we shall be concerned with. Reviews of shipping and men were a commonplace of Tudor government, but not since the Roman fortification of the Saxon Shore or Edward I's castle-building in Wales had a general survey of coastal defence needs been called for. This time it was of almost the entire coastline subject to royal jurisdiction, and it led to a system of defense works being built larger in extent, if not in cost or the number of sites fortified, than those which would be devised against the threats of invasion by the first and third Napoleons in the nineteenth century (Fig.26). It has been justly described by the pioneer historian of post-medieval fortifications, B.H. St. J. O'Neil, as 'the one scheme of comprehensive coastal defence ever attempted in England before modern times.'[4]

Its plan emerged with remarkable speed. The founding document, the 'Device by the King',[5] was drawn up in February 1539, and probably early in that month because it does not include recommendations based on the advice of the Master of the Ordnance, Sir Christopher Morris, who was inspecting fortifications in the North between 8 January and 8 February.[6] It is largely a blue-print for survey and report, naming commissioners to advise on improvements at the outposts in France, Calais and Guines, and 'to search and defend' portions of the coast of England shire by shire, namely, Northumberland, Durham, Yorkshire, Lincolnshire, Norfolk, Suffolk, Essex, Kent, Sussex, Hampshire, Dorset, Devon and Cornwall, Somerset, South Wales, Lancashire, Cheshire, Westmorland and Cumberland. In addition the heads of actual construction teams were named for forts to protect the Thames as it narrowed towards the dockyards of Deptford and Woolwich — at Gravesend and Milton on the south bank and at Tilbury on the north; at Sandown, Deal and Walmer to defend the long, sheltered anchorage on the east coast of Kent known as The Downs; at Camber, facing Rye across a hospitable inlet now lost to silt; and at

---

[1] *Ibid.*, 749, 884.   [2] Ed. Sir H. Ellis (1809), pp. 828–9.
[3] *L. & P.*. xiv (1), 143, 643.   [4] *Castles and Cannon* (1960), p. 43.
[5] *L. & P.* xiv (1), 398 (SP 1/143, ff. 188–195).
[6] *L. & P.* xiv (1), 33, 58, 156, 187, 255. And cf. 37 (p. 18)

Calshot Point, guarding the access to Southampton Water. Work at these places was begun in March or early April, as it was at Sandgate, on the coast between Folkestone and Hythe, a royal project that, like the three blockhouses designed to defend Dover harbour, can only have been omitted from the 'Device' by oversight. The speed with which work could be started may well be connected with a report made by the French ambassador in London on 18 July 1538, when the first quavers of the invasion 'bruit' began to be heard, to the effect that 'the King is gone to visit his ports and havens.'[1] That September saw Henry at Dover, as did March 1539, when the blockhouses were begun. Indeed in these and previous visits to a harbour he was so determined to improve, his personal concern with plans, models, costs and construction teams may help to explain the speed with which the Device was drawn up and the forwardness of the projects it listed in Kent.[2]

March and April 1539 were months of intense military activity. The beacon early-warning systems round the coast were fuelled and manned, musters were held, arms, armour, gunners and mercenaries negotiated for through English agents in Antwerp and Hamburg, naval vessels were fitted out and suitable foreign merchantmen impressed for service with them. Reports and advice flowed in from the commissioners of border and coastal defences from Calais to Caernarvon and Carlisle. Pending the authorization of permanent works, defences of earth, turf and stones were rushed up at Portsmouth, Hurst Beach, East and West Cowes and at Harwich where, the Lord Chancellor Thomas Audley wrote to Cromwell, 'ye should have seen women and children work with shovels in the trenches and bulwarks'.[3] The mood of urgency is caught in a letter Henry, on a visit to Dover as his own chief commissioner of defence works, got his aide and future secretary of state, Sir Ralph Sadler, to write to Cromwell: there is not a moment to lose, 'for his Grace sayeth "diligence passe sence," willing me to write that French proverb unto your Lordship, the rather to quicken you in that behalf.'[4] The response lies among Cromwell's 'Remembrances' for that month, in a list of 28 sites 'where fortification is to be made.'[5]

In March 1539 Cromwell's protégé Richard Morison published *An exhortation to styre all Englishe men to the defence of theyr countreye*. This appeal for national support for Henry's war effort contains a list of fortification projects fuller than that given in any official document, and was designed to act as a reassurance as well as a challenge to Morison's readers.

> Is it possyble, that any his gracis subiecte, can refuse peyne, whan his hyghnes rydeth about from haven to haven, from castell to castell, dayes and nightes devisynge all the ways that wytte canne invent, for our assurance? What charges is his grace at, for the fortifyenge of Caleys, Hammes, Guysnes, for the repairyng of Dover haven, Dover castell, for buyldyng bulwarkes in the downes, bulwarkes at Folkestone? What a realme woll Englande be, whan his grace hath set walles accordyng to the dyches, that

---

[1] *L. & P.* xiii (1), 1405. He did not necessarily leave on that day. He was back on 25 July (*ibid.* 1451).
[2] Below, pp. 740–50.   [3] *L. & P.* xiv (1), 682.   [4] *L. & P.* xiv (1), 529.
[5] *L. & P.* xiv (1), 655. They are: Berwick, Carlisle, Holy Island, Tynemouth, Hull, Lynn, Yarmouth, Lowestoft, Aldeburgh, Orwell, Langar Point, Tilbury, Gravesend, The Downs, Camber, Calshot, Portsmouth, Southampton Water, Lyme, Tor Bay, Dartmouth, Plymouth, Falmouth, Fowey, Milford Haven, Calais, Guines and Hammes.

runne rounde aboute us. England wol than be moch liker a castel, than a realme. His grace hath devised a bulwark in the Camber, a bulwark at Calshottespoynte, a bulwarke at the East cowe, a bulwarke at the West cow. His highnes fortifieth Portismouth, Southampton, Weymouth, Portland rode, Torre baye, Plymmouthe haven, Dermouth haven, Falmouth haven. This ones done, what enemy, be he never so strong, wol thinke, he can invade England on those parties of it? Now, that ye may know, his highnesse careth for all, and not for some, he fortifyeth Barwycke, bothe towne and castelle, Carliel, towne and castel, setting men a worke for the repayring of Warke castelle, Bambrough castell, Alnwicke castel, Scarborowe castell, Powmfret castell, fortifying also Kyngston upon Hul, Grimsbye uppon Humber. Lynne also shall be made strong, Yermouth rode fortified, two bulwarkes set up at Lestoffe. Alborne Hoppe in Norfolke, Langeres poynte, Orwell haven, are to be fortifyed. ii blocke houses to be made at Tilbery. iii blockehouses at Graves ende, whiche with many other fortresses and munitions, for this our countrey, his grace woll shortely with all spede, to be set forwarde [sic]. If his highnes thus diligentely watche, that we maye safely slepe, spend his treasure thus largely, that we maye surely kepe our goodes, were it not our great shame, to suffer his highnes to travaile alone?[1]

The invasion scare both came to a head and was partially dissipated in the great parade of the Londoners under arms on 3 May. 'They were numbred by my Lord Chancellour', wrote the chronicler Charles Wriothesley, who watched them, 'to the number of 16 thousand and a halfe and more, howbeit a man would have thought they had bene above 30 thousand, they were so longe passinge by... There was never a goodlyer sight in London... which was a great rejoycinge to the Kinges Majestie.'[2] Thereafter, though the conduct of Francis and Charles was scrutinized with an at times intense anxiety, the sense of impending crisis faded until in May of the following year Henry sponsored the issuing of challenges for 'jousting, tourney, and fighting at barriers' to be held at the Palace of Westminster, 'it having pleased God to establish between Christian princes more concord than ever there was, so that in the idleness of peace there is danger that noble men may themselves fall into idleness.'[3]

By then the navy had been cut back, the shire levies disbanded. But there was no idleness shown in the sphere of coastal defence, and the king's 'Device' continued to be driven forward by the momentum acquired in the first feverish months of 1539. The Thames estuary forts were completed in March 1540, those at East and West Cowes in the summer, those in the Downs, at Sandgate and Calshot in the autumn, as was the impressive first stage of Camber. Work on forts at Portland and Sandsfoot (protecting the entrance to Weymouth Bay) had been started in the summer of 1539 and continued throughout the following year. What is more, the powerful forts controlling the entrance to Falmouth Haven at Pendennis and St. Mawes were begun in April and October 1540. Altogether the fortification scheme had advanced on a scale and at an expense which was thought in 1540 to merit an appeal to Parliament

---

[1] Sigs Diii^r–iiii^r. March is the date convincingly suggested by W. Gordon Zeeveld, *Foundations of Tudor Policy* (1948).
[2] *A Chronicle of England* ... ed. W. D. Hamilton (Camden Soc. 1875), i, p. 96.
[3] *L. & P.* xv, 616, 617.

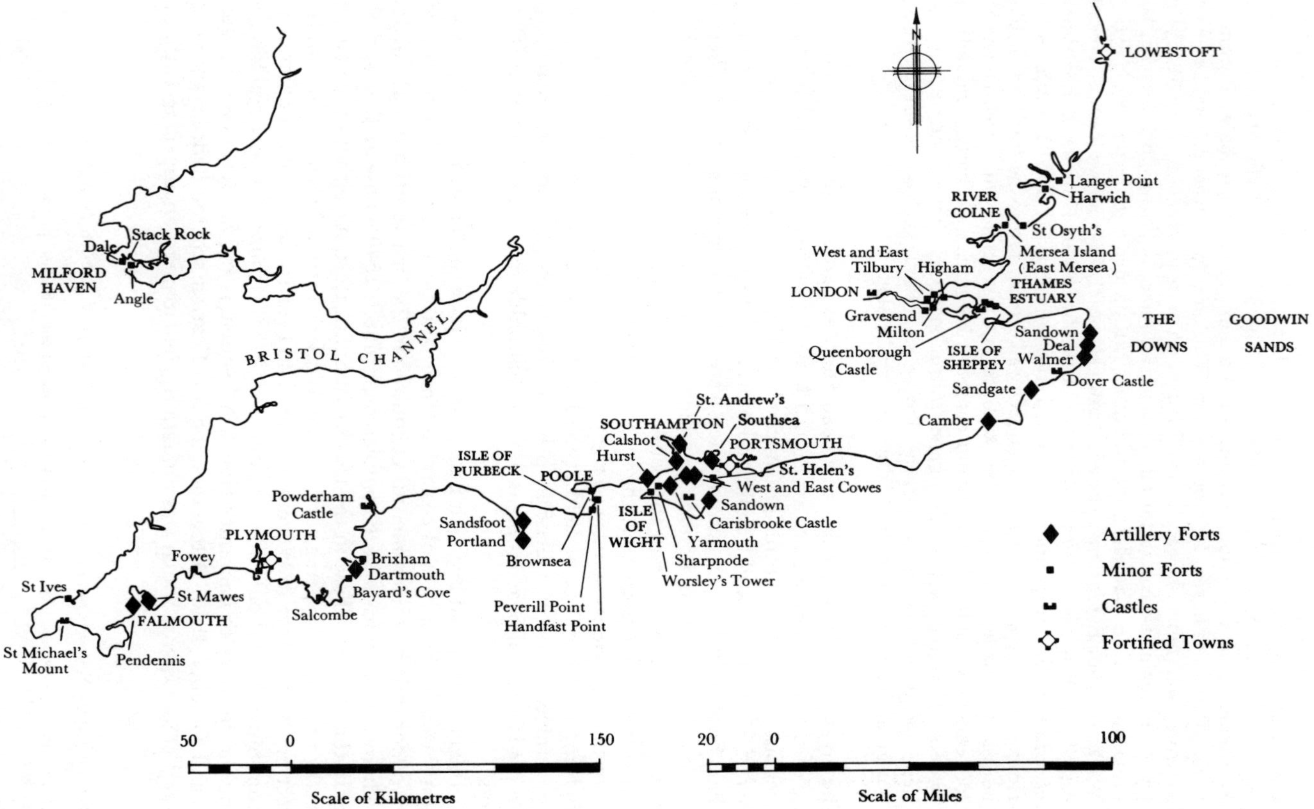

Fig. 26. The defences of the south coast in the reign of Henry VIII.

for a subsidy. The preamble to the statute granting the king four fifteenths and tenths mentioned the costs of naval and military preparations but concentrated on 'the great and most extreme charges, costes and expenses his Majestie hath susteyned, and contynueth dailye, in edifieng, new making, buylding, fortyfieng and preparing' the existing towns and castles in the Pale of Calais and on the Scottish border as well as 'the Castells, Blockhouses and Fortresses newlye made, edyfied and buylded'. These were all named. In addition, the preamble pointed out, there are 'the great charges that his Highnes must contynuallye susteyn in and aboute the munyting and fortifieng of the same... with all maner of habiliments of warre, with the great yerelye and contynuall charges for thengarnyshing of the same with Capetaynes, Lieutenantes, Porters, Souldiours, Gonners and Men of Warre for the sure defence thereof.'[1]

This addition was of great significance. It forced attention to the fact that the coastal defence scheme had been conceived as a permanent one. Hence the use from the start of brick and stone. Hence, when an appeal for parliamentary aid was first discussed — and dropped — in April 1539, Cromwell's alteration of the draft appeal 'let us lay up our sweet lips for three or four months, giving the overplus of our accustomed monthly charges to the present necessity of the common wealth' to 'three or four *years*'.[2]

A list of 31 December 1540 names 24 new fortifications, large and small, which were already garrisoned.[3] At this point, though other works were still under construction and yet others — in a way, as we shall see, the most interesting of all — were still to be planned, let us step back from chronology to review the development of the king's 'Device' from other points of view. But not without noticing the comfort it had by then brought to at least one admirer of a monarch who 'dothe dailie ymagine, devise and goe aboute on th'one side envyronynge and fortefyinge the bordurs and frountiers of this your realme with most strong castelles and fortresses able to withstande and expell all foreyn power, for th'other settinge furthe goddes most holy worde & your graces lawes.'[4]

To environ and fortify on such an unprecedented scale required a unique cluster of pre-conditions. One was a royal policy that consistently — through war, a goading diplomacy, or provocative religious change — invited reprisal. Another was an administrative stance that overrode (without absolutely ignoring) the older tradition that coastal defence was achieved piecemeal by strengthening castles belonging specifically to the Crown and subsidising local self-help elsewhere, and that now saw the coastline as presenting a strategic problem to be solved in an objective and unitary fashion.[5] This aspect of state planning could not have been conceived and carried through without the results of another Tudor revolution — that in car-

---

[1] *Statutes of the Realm* (1817) iii, 32 Henry VIII c. 50, pp. 812-3. For a list of works and garrisons possibly prepared for the subsidy bill: *L. & P., Addenda* i (2), 1446.
[2] *L. & P.* xiv (1), 869 (p. 407).
[3] *L. & P.* xvi, 372. In addition to works already referred to, the list includes earth bulwarks in the Downs and the gun emplacements covering Dover harbour.
[4] B. M., Harleian MS. 4990: John Hales's 'Oration to Henry VIII'.
[5] For coastal royal castles see vol. iii above, map on p. 227. For an example (Brownsea) of royal subvention of local initiative, see below, p. 468.

tography and surveying.¹ Thanks to this Henry and Cromwell had maps like those of the Dorset coast sent to Cromwell in April 1539 and of the Devon and Cornish coasts showing the progress on defence works in 1540.² When, at the height of the Turkish naval war of 1538, the French ambassador entered Henry's chamber, it was to find that 'the King had before him a map of the very place where the Armada of the Levant was.'³ And from some time before 1542, when it was inventoried, Henry possessed a 'large mappe of Dover and Calice of parchement sett in a frame of wodde.'⁴ The large scale maps at the king's and Cromwell's disposal were backed up by specially commissioned 'plats' of small areas and by verbal accounts such as the one submitted in March 1539, by the defence commissioners the Earl of Southampton and Lord St. John. Their recommendations for the Isle of Wight and the approaches to Southampton showed a highly developed strategic awareness of wind patterns, the navigability of channels and the ranges over which forts could cover one another.⁵

A fourth pre-condition was good-will. This Henry had, in spite of the northern rising only three years previously. Unlike many of his continental contemporaries, Henry had never seen fortifications in terms of a police function. He neither strengthened his inland castles nor strengthened and garrisoned inland towns. Only in the special cases of Berwick and Carlisle was a citadel within a town — always on the continent a symbol of governmental distrust — suggested: and at Carlisle it was emphasised that this was intended purely as a rallying point in case the Scots forced the town.⁶ Nowhere did corporations protest against damage to property, landowners against the loss of cultivable land. Nowhere was there any great difficulty about the enrolment or impressment of the often very large construction teams that were simultaneously required. Although, as from armies, there were desertions, there were only two 'mutinies' or strikes for higher pay, one at Deal in 1539, one at Guines in 1541. Both were speedily, if violently, settled without delaying the works.⁷ The 1539 'Device' was, of course, represented as being for the benefit of every subject who wished to be spared pillage, rape and the imposition of foreign control. And the construction workers were paid; even unskilled labourers received travel expenses and the five pence or sixpence a day of the ordinary foot soldier.

The wages of the 'crews', as the construction teams were called, were the major expense in each fortification. This brings us to another pre-condition: cash in hand and the expectation of more. The cost of implementing the 'Device' from 1539 to Henry's death in January 1547 was really formidable: some £376,500⁸ — a figure far exceeding the total expenditure on all non-military works in the entire lifetime of this giant among embellishers and palace-builders.⁹ Henry was well aware of how expensive military works were: after acquiring Tournai nearly £40,000 had been

---

[1] E. G. R. Taylor, *Tudor geography 1485–1588* (1930); A. H. W. Robinson, *Marine Cartography in Britain* (Leicester 1962).
[2] B. M., Cotton MSS. Augustus I. i. 31, 33 and 35–6, 38–9.   [3] *L. & P.* xiii (2), 748.
[4] Vol. iii above, p. 347, n.1.   [5] *L. & P.* xiv (1), 573.
[6] *Ibid.* 731. For Berwick, see below, p. 642.   [7] *L. & P.* xiv (1), 1103; vol. iii above, pp. 367–8.
[8] £181,179 in England apart from the Scottish border, £27,457 on the Border (vol. iii above, p.1 n.1), £120,675 on Calais and the March (*ibid.* 361), £47,166 in the Boulonnais (*ibid.* 392–3). Some garrison wages may be enwrapped in the total.
[9] Above, p. 5.

spent on remodelling its defences between 1515 and 1518.¹ Without engrossing church revenues formerly paid to Rome and dissolving and confiscating the properties of the monasteries the 'Device' could not ever have been imagined: it was funded and sustained largely by payments made through the new courts of First Fruits and Tenths and of Augmentations.² Peter with the keys was robbed to pay Paul with the sword. And there was a secondary advantage, the 'Device' devoured material as well as money: lead from Beaulieu Abbey clad the gun platforms of Calshot, stone from St. Augustine's, Canterbury, was shipped for the new bulwarks at Calais, rubble from Meaux Abbey was requisitioned for the fortifications of Hull.³

The last pre-condition was the personal interest of a monarch celebrated in the year before his death as 'a perfect builder as well of fortresses as of pleasant palaces,'⁴ and hailed in 1539 as constantly working for his country's good, devising 'in tyme of warre, plattes, blocke howses, bulwarkes, walles, castelles... and fortresses... Lorde, how may al englyshemen reioyce that your grace neyther spareth to vysite with your owne eyes the ruinous places of the see quostes, by which our enemies myght sodeynly invade us, neyther yet letteth to worke with your own handes, continually manegynge tooles, continually inventyng newe sortes of weapons, newe kindes of shyppes, of gunnes, of armure.'⁵

This was flattery. It was also very close to the truth. Whether or not Henry had been influenced by the propaganda that surrounded his first, and intensely glamorous military ally of 1512, the Emperor Maximilian, lauded not only for his prowess at prayer or in the jousting saddle but for being abreast of every branch of military science from gunfounding to the building of fortifications,⁶ there is no doubt about his interest in the design of warships, armour, ingenious firearms, or in the manufacture and performance of cannon. His interest even in fringe military technology was indicated by the French ambassador in London. Writing in 1541, and surely describing a pre-Galilean attempt at a telescope, he told Montmorency that 'there is an Italian here, aged about 70 years, who has shown this king that he would make a mirror and place it on the top of Dover castle, in which mirror could be seen all ships that leave Dieppe. Although that seems incredible, he has persuaded this king to provide money to make it, and left yesterday to fulfil his promise.'⁷ This interest was taken for granted by his commanders. The siege of the French town of Landrecy by an Anglo-Imperial force in the autumn of 1543 was to

¹ Vol. iii above, p. 381.
² See, e.g. below, pp.419 and 509. There were payments from the Chamber towards Sandgate and Camber. From 1544 payments were also made from the Exchequer, the Mint and the Court of Wards.
³ *L. & P.* xiv (2), 152; *ibid*, xvi, 733 (p. 345); vol. iii above, p. 353; below, p. 475. Typical was the application for lead for Berwick from the 'Receiver and Auditor of Augmentations in Northumberland' on 6 October 1539 (*L. & P.* xiv (2), 293).
⁴ William Thomas, *The Pilgrim* ...(1546), ed. J. A. Froude (1861), p. 78.
⁵ Richard Morison's translation of Frontinus, *The Strategemes, Sleyghtes and Policies of Warre* (1539), sigs a ii–iii.
⁶ The *Weißkunig*, the work which described his education and accomplishments, was composed between 1505 and 1516. The MS. was not published until 1775, but the splendid woodcuts which illustrated Maximilian's activities were widely circulated.
⁷ *L. & P.* xvi, 712.

be peppered by long-range advice on its conduct from Henry, who had been 'studying the plat of the town.'[1] Some of this advice was actually followed. In return, the English general, Sir John Wallop, persuaded Charles V to second to London a master gunner who, as he wrote, had invented 'a "fantasy" which would please the King', namely, a particularly dramatic form of explosive mortar shell.[2]

We should not, then, be too quick to dismiss references to Henry's personal role in the design of fortifications as mere flattery. A visit he made to Calais in 1532 led to the drawing up of 'A devyse made by the kinges highenes at his graces being at the towne of Calis...for the fortificacion of the said towne.'[3] This contains three references to gun embrasures which were 'to be made as the kinges grace hath devised' and another to a barrier across the haven 'to be made from the bulwerke in the bray wher the king did appoint.' From 1539 such references become frequent. In April 1539 170 men were building at East Cowes 'according to the platte devised by the King'.[4] In April 1540 Richard Lee, the engineer in charge at Newneham Bridge, to the west of Calais, described work in progress on an earthen bulwark 'where your Majesty hath devised the foresaid new tower.'[5] In February 1541 a survey party reported from Guines on 'the place where the King has devised to make the Cat and the travers wall by Whettelles Bulwark',[6] and the master mason in charge there, John Rogers, was recalled to London three times during the summer to confer with the king.[7] It was with some embarrassment that the Earl of Southampton and John Lord Russell wrote from Guines that they had been shown plans made by Lee and Rogers, 'and to be plain with your grace, by the faith, duty and allegiance which we bear unto your Majesty, . . . [if] you and six of the wisest men within the realm had been here a fortnight together, you could have devised your plats no better than they.'[8] In September 1541, the commissioners (including Lee) who were investigating Henry's scheme for a new settlement in the March of Calais reported that as for the church, which by the instructions was to be a 'refuge' [i.e. fortified], they had, considering the king's 'most excellent knowledge in devising of all kinds of fortifications . . . thought not meet t'attempt th'estimation of the charges thereof tofore his Highness shall have devised the plact of the same.'[9] It comes, then, as no surprise that when Hull—mentioned in the 'Device' of 1539 but passed over in the interest of concentrating on the south coast—was refortified in 1542 it was after a visit by the king and in accord with his 'device', as were the articles defining the organization of the garrison and the work force.[10] Indeed, ever

---

[1] *L. & P.* xviii (2), 293. 'The plat' is possibly B.M., Cotton MS. Augustus I, i. 49.
[2] *L. & P.* xviii, 310, 352. In the former the action of the shells is most vividly described.
[3] See vol. iii above, pp. 346–7. It is printed in full in *The Chronicle of Calais*, ed. J. G. Nichols (Camden Soc. 1846), pp. 125–9. It was endorsed 'For Mr. Amner, touching the fortification of Calais'. In 1530 a 'John Amynar' had been paid 30 angels 'for his costs coming from Norembarge to the King', 10 'for a bumbard for the King', and 5 'for the conveyance of certain ores from this realm to Norembarge, to be there tried to the perfection of their metals'.
[4] *L. & P.* xiv (1), 899.   [5] *L. & P.* xv, 527.
[6] *L. & P.* xvi, 547. See the plan in vol. iii above, p. 364.
[7] L. R. Shelby, *John Rogers, Tudor Military Engineer* (1967), p. 22.
[8] *Ibid.* pp. 12–13.
[9] *L. & P.* xvi, 1162 (p. 545) and vol. iii above, p. 374.
[10] *L. & P.* xvi, 1232; xvii, 140 (3); below, pp. 472–4.

since Cromwell's fall in June 1540 Henry had been recognized with increasing clarity as the chief director of his own programme of fortification.

This role, one in which we must see the king not, certainly, as a draftsman but as a copiously and deferentially referred-to expert, is crucial to an understanding of the architectural form of the structures planned between 1539 and 1542.

All the new free-standing fortresses, from the Sandown-Deal-Walmer-Sandgate-Camber group, through Calshot and Hurst and Portland to St. Mawes and Pendennis, display variations on the same theme: burly, rounded, hollow, roofed bastions expanding outwards from a tall cylindrical keep and either concentrically or at least symmetrically clustered about it (Figs. 28–36). The geometrical logic of the plan is reflected in the profile: rising tier by tier towards the keep to provide from three to five levels from which artillery could be fired. Parapets are curved, embrasures widely splayed on the outside to allow guns to traverse a broad field of fire. Moats, where the site permitted them, were dry, defended by loops for arquebus fire. The 'Device' fortresses were massively beautiful machines designed for the maximum emission of balls and bullets: at Sandgate there were over 60 embrasures for artillery and 65 loops for portable firearms. They were fire-power edifices representing, in a manner unique to England, a defensive style transitional between the medieval castle and the flatter profiled, angle-bastioned fortifications already established as an Italian speciality and soon to sweep across Europe and wherever Europeans dug themselves in overseas.

This is the nub of what has been seen as a problem. The Henrician designers were thoroughly alert to the power of cannon, the need for adequately splayed embrasures and for vents to clear gun-chambers of smoke. But to other, defensive, aspects of multi-storey gun houses they seemed indifferent: the structural weakness of bastions, however thick their walls, that were fenestrated with artillery apertures; the progressive masking of fire from platforms, tier by tier, as an assault edged forwards; the unflanked dead ground presented by any rounded surface that allowed miners to nestle against its snout and burrow down and explode their barrels of gunpowder. The 'Device' fortresses were urged forward at great expense and with complete initial confidence in the efficacy of their design. But why were they *transitional* when all the defects they presented had already been corrected in Italy? There, the 'transitional' phase of gunpowder fortifications had been over for a generation, and mutually supporting angle bastions, which solved the problem of dead ground, had become almost the norm for fortresses and town walls alike.[1] The importance of flanking fire was amply recognized, in Henry's 'Device' for Calais in 1532, for instance, or the orders for improvements at Guines in 1536,[2] yet all the bastions of 1539–42 were rounded, both in the coastal forts and in the new works at Calais and its March, and at Hull and Berwick, where Lord's Mount, begun in 1540 and 'devised by the kinges maiestie', echoed the segment-of-a-circle design of the new fort at Portland started in the previous year (Figs. 37, 58). Why were these buildings so *retardataire*?

---

[1] J. R. Hale, 'The early development of the bastion: an Italian chronology *c.* 1450-*c.* 1534', in *Europe in the Late Middle Ages*, ed. J. R. Hale, R. Highfield and B. Smalley (1965), pp. 466–94. Above. pp. 1–29.
[2] Vol. iii above, p. 366.

While much is known about the organization and functioning of the work-forces on these projects, sometimes with a month-by-month richness of detail,[1] very little can be glimpsed of their designers. Of the two men, both originally masons, who became deeply involved in the planning of fortifications in the mid-1540s, Richard Lee and John Rogers, the former was acting as surveyor in Calais from 1536 to 1542, but from 1537 to 1541, according to his biographer, 'Rogers disappears from the royal building accounts.'[2] Only in Stephen von Haschenperg, 'a gentleman of Moravia',[3] do we have a name directly connected with two projects, Sandgate and Camber,[4] as 'deviser' and closely associated with the creation of the earth and clay bulwarks that linked the great fortresses of the Downs.[5] A mysterious figure, nothing is known of his origins save that he was competent as a surveyor. In July 1541 he was entrusted 'alone [to] have the survey of the works at Carlisle'[6] but was called before the Privy Council two years later for having 'lewedlye behaved himself' and 'spent a great treasour to no purpose.'[7] Rather than producing the sureties the Council asked for he retreated to the Continent to await better days. Sir Edward Carne, Henry's agent in Brussels, described him in 1544 as 'a man that will pretend more knowledge than he hath indeed'. In 1545 he wrote from Lubeck appealing for a return of Henry's favour. In this letter he offered to reveal various chemical and hydraulic inventions, including one to convey water economically to serve the Palace of Nonsuch, but said nothing of fortifications.[8] In the absence of contemporary plans, elevations or working drawings, little can be concluded about Haschenperg's role save that Camber and Sandgate do share certain features which are not found elsewhere.[9]

Of the other foreigners employed by Henry, none can be connected with the designs associated with the 'Device'. In March 1538, a payment from the king was made to 'Ant. Fagion, Sicilian' for 'making of certain devices of bulwarks and blockhouses and other devices'; and in April 1540 among Cromwell's 'Remembrances' occcurs an equally enigmatic entry, just possibly referring to the same man: 'For the translations of the Neapolitan's device for a castle to be new made.'[10] But that is all. The gunfounder Archangelo Arcano, employed by Henry from 1538,[11] was sent in April 1541 to spy and report on the defences of Ardres and other French strongpoints around Calais,[12] but, again, that is all. The painter Girolamo da

---

[1] Vol. iii above, e.g. pp. 2, 21. For Sandgate see below, pp. 571–8 and a synopsis of Harleian MS. 1647 in *L. & P.* xiv (2), 645. For Calais *ibid.* 244 and xvi, 98.
[2] Shelby, *op. cit.*, p. 6.
[3] So described in a letter from the Regent of the Netherlands to Henry in 1544 (*L. & P.* xix (2), 94).
[4] That is, with the 1539–-40 version of Camber. See below, p. 422.
[5] Below, pp. 457–9. For a drawing showing their appearance, see J. R. Kenyon in *Antiquaries Journal* lviii, pp. 162–3, pl. li.
[6] *L. & P.* xvi, 958.
[7] *A.P.C.*, i, pp. 155–6.
[8] *L. & P.* xix (2), 131, 132 and xx (2), 37.
[9] On his career, see B. H. St. J. O'Neill, 'Stefan von Haschenperg, an engineer to King Henry VIII, and his work' *Archaeologia* xci (1945), pp. 137–55.
[10] *L. & P.* xiii (2), 1280 (p. 527, f. 7) and xv, 598.
[11] *L. & P.* xiv (2), 781 (f. 68ᵛ).
[12] *L. & P.* xvi, 711, 762.

Treviso,[1] who was in Henry's service by 1542, was almost at once sent to Calais on a similar mission,[2] but he cannot be connected with any feature of the 1539-42 building programme. In any case, Henry was more interested in what foreigners had to offer by way of 'machines of war and implements to project fire'[3] than of new styles of fortification. He had no specialist military engineers of his own and he did not instruct his diplomats to seek any out abroad.[4] When a Portuguese engineer turned up in 1541 and criticised the new works at Guines, the king dismissed him, 'calling him an ass who did not understand his business.'[5]

This petulant confidence is understandable. Henry had his own works organization, teams who could turn out palaces, hunting stands, dockyards, tennis courts: why not fortresses? Even in Italy the designers of the most avant garde fortifications were men whose practice included palaces, indeed, churches.[6] And the same was true of France, the only foreign country Henry had set foot in. Had he not strengthened Tournai without calling in outsiders to advise members of his own works team and the local master craftsmen?[7] And had anyone had the nerve to criticize the works he had recommended for Calais and left to his own men to execute?

Thus when works started at Sandown, Deal and Walmer in April 1539, it was Robert Lorde, the paymaster at Nonsuch and Hampton Court, who was given the same office there, while the comptroller, master mason, master carpenter and the surveyor, Richard Benese, were all men seconded from Hampton Court. Other royal master masons from the king's works at Whitehall and Windsor were deputed to Cowes in 1539 and to Hull in 1542.[8] 'Under the Tudors,' as has been said earlier in this *History*, 'it was the master-craftsmen who designed the king's buildings.'[9] But of course they worked in consultation with the king. And the king must have consulted his most favoured and experienced subjects. The list of commissioners sent into the shires in connection with the Device of February 1539 reads like a roll-call of veterans of England's past campaigns. Among them Sir Anthony St. Leger, sent to Kent, had reported on measures to strengthen the defences of Calais and the Pale in 1535; Sir Anthony Wingfield, sent to Suffolk, had been knighted for bravery in the French war of 1512-13, had served again in 1523 and was captain of the guard; Sir John Russell, sent into the west country, had fought in 1522 and was, in 1540, to become Lord Admiral. He had been one of those appointed to survey the

---

[1] Philip Pouncey, 'Girolamo da Treviso in the service of Henry VIII' [as a painter], *Burlington Magazine* (1953), pp. 209-11, R. W. Carden, 'The Italian artists in England during the sixteenth century', *Proceedings of the Society of Antiquaries of London* 1911-12, pp. 200-202. Pietro Aretino wrote from Venice to him in May 1542 asking him to prepare Henry to receive generously the volume of letters Aretino was intending to dedicate to the king (as he did in August): *Lettere*, ed. F. Flore (n.p., 1960), p. 875. His reward, £75, only came four years later (*L. & P.* xxi (2), 775, f. 94).
[2] *L. & P.* xvii, 387.
[3] J. Kaulek, *Correspondance politique de MM. de Castillon et de Marillac ... 1537-42* (Paris 1885), p. 243, speaking of 'aucuns maistres alemans et italiens qui sont ici.'
[4] No reply was given to the alert but anonymous correspondent who wrote from Augsburg on 25 April 1539 that 'if his Majesty wants ... fortresses made I can find the means to bring over the governor of the munition of war at Awspourg for three or four months' (*L. & P.*, xiv (1), 1076).
[5] Vol. iii above. p. 367.
[6] J. R. Hale, *Renaissance Fortification: Art or Engineering?* (1977).
[7] Vol. iii above, pp. 376-7.
[8] *Ibid*, pp. 15, 27-8, and below, pp. 474, 537.   [9] Vol. iii, p. 42.

defences of Calais and its marches in 1532.¹ So had the Earl of Oxford, sent to Essex, and the Duke of Norfolk, sent into the northern counties. The shared military experience of a peerage and gentry still heavily relied on for their traditional warlike skills² was represented by such names and it is not unreasonable to assume that the basic design of the new fortresses was worked out with the active advice of at least some of them, that it was determined, as was the practice elsewhere, including Italy, by a committee: men of political and military weight commenting on the practicability of ideas drawn for them by experts and adjusted until all parties were satisfied. And as the experts, the men to be put in charge of building projects, were not yet thought of as specialists in military engineering, the laymen were unlikely to be blinded by science, but to draw on their own experience of fortifications seen, attacked or defended. There was a real blurring of roles. Henry could represent the Earl of Southampton and John, Lord Russell, to Francis I as 'expert' in fortification.³ In 1538 a pier protecting Dover harbour which was known as the king's bulwark was described as being 'of Mr. Candishe's device', that is, designed by Richard Cavendish, a resourceful master gunner who had supervised new defence works at Berwick and Wark in 1522–3.⁴ In the following year a strengthened version was described as being 'devised' by the king and merely 'set forth' by Master Cavendish.⁵ In 1543 Cavendish was to be called from Dover to Guines as 'a discreet person in fortification' and to emerge in 1546 as a man whose specialist knowledge was respected almost as much as that of Lee or Rogers.⁶ But in 1539 men like Cavendish and his colleagues of the King's Works, even Haschenperg, who was sent off in 1540 to the March of Calais to draw maps (the only context in which he was described as an 'expert'),⁷ were no more likely to have determined the nature of the coastal fortresses than were men like Russell and Wingfield, and all deferred to a bullying monarch who saw himself as apprentice to no-one in any of the crafts of war.

From Deal to Pendennis, then, we can speak confidently of a Henrician style. Where did it come from?

Overwhelmingly the experience of Henry and his advisers had been restricted to England and northen France. In both countries the response to bombardment by cannon had been the cylindrical artillery tower. At the Tower of London two rounded 'mounts' or bastions guarded the landward approach from the north. Their date is doubtful, but almost certainly they were there when Henry came to the throne.⁸ Henry himself had incorporated half-round and cylindrical towers into the new defences of Tournai, where one still ponderously stands.⁹ They gleam romantically in the view of Guines in the Hampton Court painting of the Field of

---

[1] Names in *L. & P.* v, 1705.
[2] Graham McLennan, *Noble warriors: the military elite and Henry VIII's expeditions of 1513 and 1544.* Unpub. M.A. Thesis, Australian National University, March 1979.
[3] *L. & P.* xvi, 761.   [4] Below, pp. 630, 689.
[5] *L. & P.* xiii (1), 179 and xiv (1), 864.
[6] *L. & P.* xviii (1), 786 and xxi (1), 1234.
[7] *L. & P.* xvi, 248. However, Marillac seems to be speaking of Haschenperg when he reports from London on November 1540 that 'L'on faict icy venir un alemant qui entend à la fortification de Calès et de Guisnes pour désigner et y faire en diligence quelques autres boullevertz' (Kaulek, *op. cit.*, p. 243).
[8] Vol. iii above, p. 263.   [9] Vol. iii above, plate 39.

Cloth of Gold, where the artist represents Henry's castle as a cluster of rounded artillery towers.[1] Outside English territory, but at a port well known to the English, Mont St. Michel, round artillery towers were being built into a system which would be, in the opinion of an Italian visitor in 1517, 'impregnable'.[2] Other such towers were conspicuous at Saint-Malo. In England, the harbour entrances of Dartmouth,[3] Portsmouth,[4] Dover[5] and Hartlepool[6] were defended by such towers. And so was the entrance to an anchorage much used by local as well as foreign shipping, the Camber, near Rye. Here stood a tower built in 1512. It was a strategic area that evidently intrigued the king; in 1530 he paid for a map of it.[7] The tower remains the dominating core of the complex of defences that were built round it from 1539 onwards. It may well have been Camber that suggested the basis of the Henrician style: a cylindrical artillery tower extended outwards into sectors to house more guns and provide quarters for a garrison with its officers.

Tall in profile, hollow and rounded in their forms: hence 'transitional'. But the function of the Henrician fortresses must be remembered. They were to guard the coast. Everywhere in Europe, even in Italy, fortresses on low coastlines reached high so that enemy vessels could be spotted from a distance; only towns, with their spires and belfries, could affort to keep their defences inconspicuously flat. The solid bastion, filled with earth or rubble, was adopted because it was the best shock absorber for the punch of heavy artillery. But ships did not carry guns of the highest impact force: only with the Spanish armada of 1588 did a fleet transport a proper siege train. The round forms left areas of uncovered ground at their heads. But coastal fortresses did not expect to be subjected to a formal siege and to the laborious sap-works of miners. Why should an invading army bother about taking places whose garrisons were too small to provide any serious harassment to their advance? The fortresses' job was to make anchorages untenable and beat off raiding parties. That rounded forms were suited to the special conditions of coastal defence is suggested, surely, by the one hundred and three Martello towers built against invasion by Napoleon.[8]

In any case, Henry and his advisers in 1539 could not have realized that the angle bastion was to become the approved module for fortifications for centuries to come. Even in Italy it was only in the 1530s that its use became almost automatic. There, interest in the theory of fortification coincided with the revival of interest in Vitruvius who had claimed that while blows levelled at angles could shatter them, 'in the case of round towers they can do no harm, being engaged, as it were, in driving wedges to their centre.'[9] The resistance of the round to the advance of the angle bastion has, indeed, been underestimated. From 1509 Padua and Treviso and

---

[1] Sydney Anglo, 'The Hampton Court Painting of the Field of Cloth of Gold', *Antiquaries Journal* xlvi (2) (1966), pp. 287–307.
[2] *The Travel Journals of Antonio de Beatis*, ed. J. R. Hale, (Hakluyt Society 1979), p. 123.
[3] The tower was the dominating component of the castle: B. H. St. J. O'Neil, *Dartmouth Castle* (H.M.S.O. pamphlet 1951).
[4] Below, pp. 495–6.   [5] Below, p. 764.
[6] R. A. Skelton & John Summerson, *Maps and Architectural drawings ... at Hatfield House* (Roxburghe Club 1971), pl. 3.
[7] *L. & P.* v, p. 752.
[8] Sheila Sutcliffe, *Martello Towers* (Newton Abbot, 1972).
[9] *The ten books on architecture*, tr. M. H. Morgan (New York, n.d.), p. 23.

Cremona were refortified with round bastions. The huge round bastions at Loreto date from 1517. The round bastion 'delle Boccare' at Verona was finished in 1522. The round bastion flanking the entrance to the citadel at Assisi was constructed between 1535 and 1538. Round corner towers were built at Cortona as late as 1543. Even when victory had been conceded the Vitruvian point nagged, and argument shifted from the nose of the bastion to its ears: should these protections to the flanking batteries be squared off or curved?

None of this registered in England. Diplomatic representation in Italy was restricted to Rome, ceasing in 1536 before the angled defences of the Borgo emerged to distract attention from the circular *massif* of Castel S. Angelo, and to Venice, whence the resident, Edmund Harvel, wrote dispatches of imperturbable commonplace up to his death in 1550, and showed no awareness of the republic's growing leadership in the techniques of fortifying its borders by land and sea.[1]

Nor were hints to be gained from diplomatic correspondents or from travellers in Spain, Germany, the Low Countries or France. None, by 1539, had swapped their defensive curves for angles. As recently as 1537 the town walls of Ingolstadt had been strengthened with round bastions. In France the cylindrical artillery tower and the round bastion remained the norm, as they did in the Low Countries. Moreover, only two books dealing with fortification had yet been printed, Machiavelli's *Arte della Guerra* of 1522 and Albrecht Dürer's *Ettliche Underricht zu Befestigung der Stett, Schloss und Flecken* of 1527. There is no evidence that either had been read in England. In any case, the former makes no mention of angle defences, the latter constitutes a hearty endorsement of the curved bastion and describes and illustrates an ideal coastal fortress which is entirely circular.[2]

This excursus has seemed necessary as a gloss on the term 'retardataire', the reproach levelled against Henry for not building his fortifications in the style of Antonio da Sangallo or Michele Sanmicheli. Historians of ecclesiastical and domestic architecture do not reproach him for failing to imitate Bramante or Giulio Romano, yet fortifications are similarly the product of a complex interplay between tradition, function and appearance, and building for war as well as for praise and peace displays the hesitations, psychological and practical, which accompany any transmission and reception of a major new style. Brutal and straightforward the purposes of fortifications may be: but they are still subject to the whims of taste. Indeed, just as there could be no proof that a circular church engendered more effective prayer than a cruciform one, it would not be proved that an Italianate was more effective than a Henrician fortress: one could not be arrayed with equal armament against the other, and in any siege factors of morale, numbers and supply are as significant as those of design and construction. Prestige, the weight of fashionable endorsement, the theoretical probability of advantage: these are all filters between

---

[1] *L. & P. passim.* His funeral is described in *Cal. S.P. Venetian* v, 615.

[2] Nuremberg. Later eds. 1528, 1529, 1530 and 1538. Latin trans., Paris, 1535. Most conveniently read in the reprint of the 1527 ed., introduced by Martin Biddle (1972). It would be neat to show that these works had made some impact within a household hospitable, as Henry's was, to German painters, gunners and armourers, but the evidence is lacking. In any case, Dürer's detailed recommendations, for smoke vents, curved parapets, embrasures widely splayed externally, had already been employed in England and France, and his coastal fort bears no close resemblance to any built by Henry.

the pronouncement and acceptance of a new style — and affect the trust a government puts in its native converts and its imported practitioners.

We have seen that by 1539 England had, in any case, cut itself off from close scrutiny of the years during which the angle-bastioned enceinte moved most quickly to becoming an orthodoxy in Italy, and that other European countries had shown a similar preference for their own traditions. This gives — to anticipate for a moment — added interest to what happened during the next wave of defensive building, the programme that followed a renewed invasion scare in 1545 and beyond when assault from Scotland and France seemed at least as threatening as a Franco-Imperial invasion had seemed in 1539. What happened then was the adoption of an Italianate defensive style so swiftly dramatic as to suggest that some dam of national reserve had burst.

Meanwhile, the 1539 'Device' programme had rolled forward. The coastal defences culminated in Hurst Castle. Begun in 1541, Hurst's remarkable coherence owed much to work teams by now experienced in solving the problems encountered while building upwards from the ground-plans of 'devisors' too often absent from the site.[1] In the Calais Pale an enhanced recognition of the threat from miners to round bastions produced the Gothic (in plan, at least) answer of the trefoil. The Beauchamp bastion was completed in this shape in 1541 and pronounced 'such a piece of work both for beauty and surety as hath not been seen in this town before'; the similar Purton's bulwark at Guines, 'devised', it was said, by the king himself, led to the declaration late that year by the new ambassador to France, Sir William Paget, that the king's fortifications there were 'works of the greatest magnificence and force that ever I have seen or read of.'[2] And after an espial of the nearby French frontier town of Ardres John Rogers pronounced its fortifications 'nothing in comparison' to Guines.[3] Later in 1541 Rogers was transferred to Hull, where Henry, as we have seen, had planned new defences during his visit to the north. Here Rogers introduced, on the far side of the Hull River, a defensive line comprising a central strong-point with two hollow, multi-storied bastions, one facing the river and the other the open country to the east — both rounded but ending in points, connected by a wall with two terminal bastions which reflected the trefoil solution adapted at Calais and Guines[4] (Fig. 38 and Pl. 45). And in 1542, when the Hull trefoils were being built, the French at Ardres showed a similar new sensitivity to the problem of dead ground: they planned 'casemates of brick called *moyneaux*' to command the dry moats at Ardres:[5] a palliative that had been prescribed, and illustrated, by Dürer. Both nations were showing advanced symptoms of a readiness to be infected by the Italian solution.

It was in 1542 that Henry determined to move to the attack and for the first time since 1523 to involve himself and his nobility and gentry in the mood and methods of warfare on the continent. It was not to be done without taking precautions against

---

[1] Below, pp. 541–4.
[2] Vol. iii above, pp. 354, 367; *L. & P.* xvi, 1276. L. R. Shelby suggests that the three-lobed outer wall plans of Sandgate and Hurst Castle 'may have inspired the more precise trefoils of the new bastions at Guines' ('Guines castle and the development of English bastioned fortification'. *Chateau Gaillard: European castle studies*, iii 1969, p. 142).
[3] *L. & P.* xvi, 1036.   [4] Below, pp. 475–7.   [5] *L. & P.* xvii, 706 (2).

counter-attack, and with the Reformation booty almost devoured, raising money both for invasion and defence took time. The Chancellor's opening speech to Parliament at the end of January alluded to the expense of 'keeping up an army of 14,000 men for the new and old fortresses.'[1] The instructions given in March to the commissioners sent into the shires to raise a loan pointed out that 'the fortifications remain so imperfect that £100,000 would scantily suffice to expend upon them this year.'[2] It was not until the summer of 1543 that the king was able to send a token force of some 12,000 men[3] to support Charles V's campaign against Francis I in Picardy. They joined him at the siege of Landrecy, on the Sambre near the Hainault border, until both sides went into winter quarters in November. The invasion force came in the following March; an army with a book number of 38,865 and an estimated cost of £44,843 a month.[4]

While Charles fought towards Paris from the north-east, Henry's army divided to besiege Boulogne, which yielded on 14 September, and Montreuil, which held out successfully, secure in the knowledge that Charles, only a few days later, had signed a unilateral peace with Francis.[5] By then other English armies had twice invaded Scotland, in November 1542 and May 1544, and Francis, now free to turn against England, had an ally only too ready to back him. As a result, 1539 was come again: an English invasion of Scotland was checked by the Scottish victory at Ancrum Moor in February 1545, which drastically reversed the balance of power and confidence in the North, and independently, French naval raids along the south coast in July reawakened fears of invasion from the Continent. The scare continued until June 1546, when hostilities with France and Scotland were temporarily smothered by the peace treaty of Camp, or Ardres. And it was during this scare that fortifications were started (Portsmouth, Sandown, Sharpenode), modified (Southsea) or planned (Tynemouth) in a style totally breaking with the 'Henrician' model which had been so authoritatively re-affirmed in the 1543 modification of Camber,[6] a style recognizably and, after the fresh wave of building from 1547 (Eyemouth, Yarmouth, Isle of Wight) to 1550 (Berwick), unquestionably 'Italian'.

Only one causative factor can be traced in explanation of a change so abrupt and so complete: the experience gained in the 1543 and 1544 campaigns in France.

While a new venture for England, these campaigns represented for France phases in a series that had begun in 1536. In February of that year Francis I mobilized an army that invaded Savoy, halting only at the very border of Charles V's province of Milan. The emperor's reply was a holding operation on that front and a massive flanking assault in July on Provence. Forewarned, Francis had ordered Marseilles to be strengthened and his commander-in-chief, Anne de Montmorency, did the same to Arles, had the land stripped of crops and dug the main force of his army, some 30,000 men, into a fortified camp, built of earth, in the flat country between the Rhône and the Durance near Avignon. Deprived of food and foes, the

---

[1] *L. & P.* xvii, 63. [2] *Ibid*, 194.
[3] *L. & P.* xviii (i), 707, 763. [4] *L. & P.* xix (i), 271-6.
[5] Henry ordered the withdrawal of his troops on 26 September (*L. & P.* xix (2), 303).
[6] Below, pp. 445-7.

Imperial army was forced by sickness and misery to withdraw, leaving no sign of victory save the smoke from villages left deliberately undefended. Hardly had this pressure been relieved, however, than Imperialist troops under Antonio de Leyva crossed from Milan into Savoy, countered by Montmorency, who had been transferred from Provence, with a similarly defensive strategy. Exhausted, both sides agreed on a truce during the winter, a truce renewed in uneasy stages until hostilities recommenced in 1543.

Working fast in the latter half of 1536 and in 1537, and more slowly as money and labour became harder to come by thereafter, the French contrived a fortified southern frontier of strongly defended towns. In Piedmont, Vercelli, Moncalieri, Carignano and Savigliano defended the approaches to Turin from the Milanese. Westwards from Turin the line ran through Pinerolo and Susa to the French Alps, picking up beyond them at Gap and Sisteron and concluding beyond Marseilles with the barrier: Avignon, Tarascon and Arles.

Though unprecedented in scale, the work on this strategic frontier has never been studied.[1] Montmorency, its chief deviser, must have worked from maps like 'the map of the Alps and the lower regions of Provence' which Charles V early in 1536 studied with such avidity that 'he convinced himself that he already possessed the land in the same way that he owned the map.'[2] It also seems clear that it was this programme that first lodged the advantages of the Italian system firmly in the minds of the many noble French officers who served in the armies of 1536 and remained as military governors of the towns concerned. When the French took Turin they found it already surrounded by an Italianate enceinte, a rectangle with angle bastions at each corner and gun platforms in the middle of each stretch of rampart. This had been built in 1535 by the Duke of Savoy, Francesco I, in earth. The French merely faced the bastions in stone and completed the ditches; the original plan is shown in Niccolò Tartaglia's *Quesiti e inventioni diverse*, a work dedicated—though not until 1546—to Henry VIII at the instance of the author's mathematically minded English pupil Richard Wentworth.[3] These bastions quickly became famous enough for Rabelais to describe how Friar John 'brought in four tremendous pork pies, so large that they reminded me of the four bastions of Turin.'[4]

It is significant that this enceinte, apparently a novelty in Piedmont, was built in a medium that allowed new ideas to be tried out with a minimum of expense: earth reinforced with stakes and consolidated on the surface with turf. It was in earth that the fortified camp of late July to early August near Avignon was built. Laid out by Montmorency with the advice of two senior Italian members of the Provençal campaign's senior command, Caraccioli, Prince of Melfi, and Stefano Colonna,

---

[1] The main published source is Martin du Bellay, *Memoires*, Livres 6–8, which I quote from the ed. by J. A. C. Buchon, Paris 1836. Du Bellay served in Provence and Savoy-Piedmont. The fullest secondary work is Francis Decrue, *Anne de Montmorency, grandmaître et connétable de France* (Paris 1885). For the political background: Jacques Freymond, *La politique de Francois 1er à l'égarde de la Savoie* (Lausanne 1939).

[2] Du Bellay, *op. cit.*, p. 582.

[3] Published in Venice. In lib. 6, *quesito* 6, Tartaglia criticises the plan as already out of date, particularly because the curtain walls are too long in relation to the bastions. The book was sent to England with Captain Filippo Pini, who had been contracted in Venice by Harvel to serve Henry (*L. & P.* xxi (1), 666, 1482).

[4] *Gargantua and Pantagruel*, bk. 4, chap. 64.

Martin du Bellay's description makes it sound very much like Turin: ditch, rampart with flanking bastions and platforms—to which, he adds with provoking vagueness, 'time and experience added, practically daily, some new [element of] fortification.'[1] It was, too, in earth, that new bastions were built by the French at Fossano, Moncalieri, Savigliano and Carignano ('cinque beaux bastions de terre') in Piedmont, and ad hoc road-blocks like the ramparted ditch flanked by two bastions near Susa which were erected by the Imperialists as counter-measures.[2]

Shortage of time and money led to improvisation; that this led to Italianate solutions was due to the presence of Italian mercenary officers who held the respect of their French colleagues. The role of Stefano Colonna at Avignon was, for example, paralleled at Pinerolo by that of the garrison commander, Guido Rangone, a Modenese soldier whose expertise as a military engineer had been demonstrated in the remodelling of the defences of Piacenza. At Pinerolo his advocacy was the stronger for the presence of two Italian surveyors who had specialized in fortifications, the shadowy figure of Baldassare Azzale of Ferrara and the better defined one of the Bolognese Girolamo Marini,[3] who also worked at Moncalieri. And during the brief campaign of sieges in Picardy (March—July) which prefaced Francis I's leading reinforcements to Piedmont in the autumn of 1537, the king and Montmorency relied on the advice of another Italian, Antonio da Castello, in strengthening his northern zone of frontier towns: St. Pol, Thérouanne, Hesdin, Montreuil and Boulogne.[4]

Antonio had previously worked for Venice as captain of artillery and a fortifications consultant, advising the Republic in 1535, and in competition with men of no less stature than Michele Sanmicheli and Venice's commander-in-chief the Duke of Urbino, on the defence of the lagoon against Turkish attack. And it was with the paying-off of the large mercenary army that Venice maintained during the Turkish war of 1537—40 that unprecedented numbers of Italians crossed the Alps to take part in the next series of Franco-Imperial campaigns in 1542 and 1543—4.[5]

In all these years there was only one pitched battle, the French victory at Ceresole in Piedmont on 11 April 1544. These were wars of marches, sieges and reliefs, hurried preparations, usually in earth, for a renewed siege: wars of the spade rather than the sword and, as such, neglected by historians of war.[6] After 1536—7 they were, however, a crucial second stage in the conditioning of the higher commands of France and the Empire (a new bastioned enceinte for Antwerp was designed in 1542—3 by Donato Boni Pellezuoli of Bergamo)[7] to thinking of defence

---

[1] *Op. cit.*, p. 614. And see Decrue, *op. cit.*, pp. 271—3.
[2] Du Bellay, *op.cit.*, pp. 546—7, 566—8, 685, 691.
[3] Carlo Promis, 'Gli ingegneri militari che operarono o scrissero in Piemonte, 1300—1650', *Miscellanea di Storia Italiana*, xii (Turin 1871), pp 411—646, under names, and *ibid*. iv (1863), p. 614 et seq. Also Du Bellay, *op. cit.* p. 684.
[4] Du Bellay, *op.cit.*, p. 663; Ducrue, *op.cit.*, pp. 310—11.
[5] See E. Picot, *Les italiens en France au XVIe siècle* (Paris, 1901), revised and expanded in *Bulletin Italien* (1904), *passim*.
[6] The campaigns of 1544 are treated in some detail in Ferdinand Lot, *Recherches sur les effectifs des armées Francaises ... 1494—1562* (Paris 1962) but from a severely logistic point of view.
[7] L. Torfs & M. A. Casterman, 'Les agrandissements et les fortifications d'Anvers', *Annales de l'académie d'archéologie de Belgique*, 2e ser. vii (1871), pp. 69 et seq, with plans.

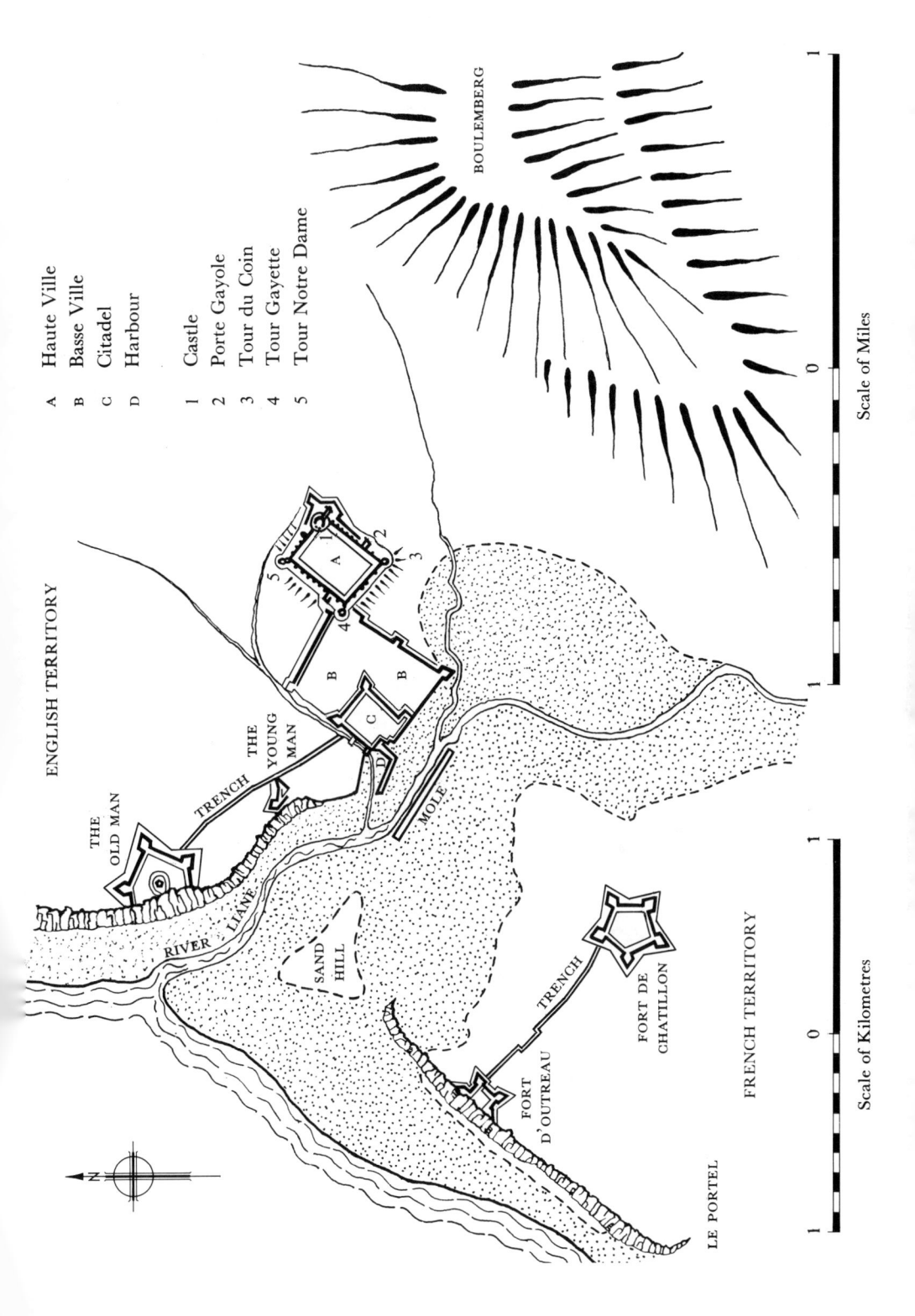

VOL. III, FIG. 19: BOULOGNE

A Haute Ville
B Basse Ville
C Citadel
D Harbour

1 Castle
2 Porte Gayole
3 Tour du Coin
4 Tour Gayette
5 Tour Notre Dame

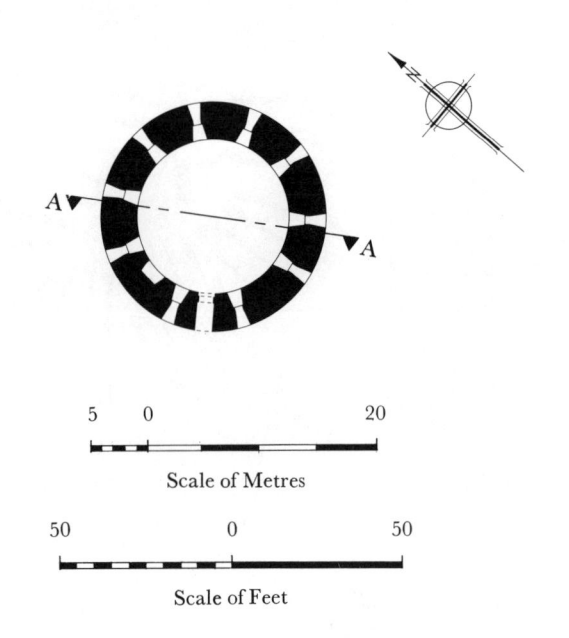

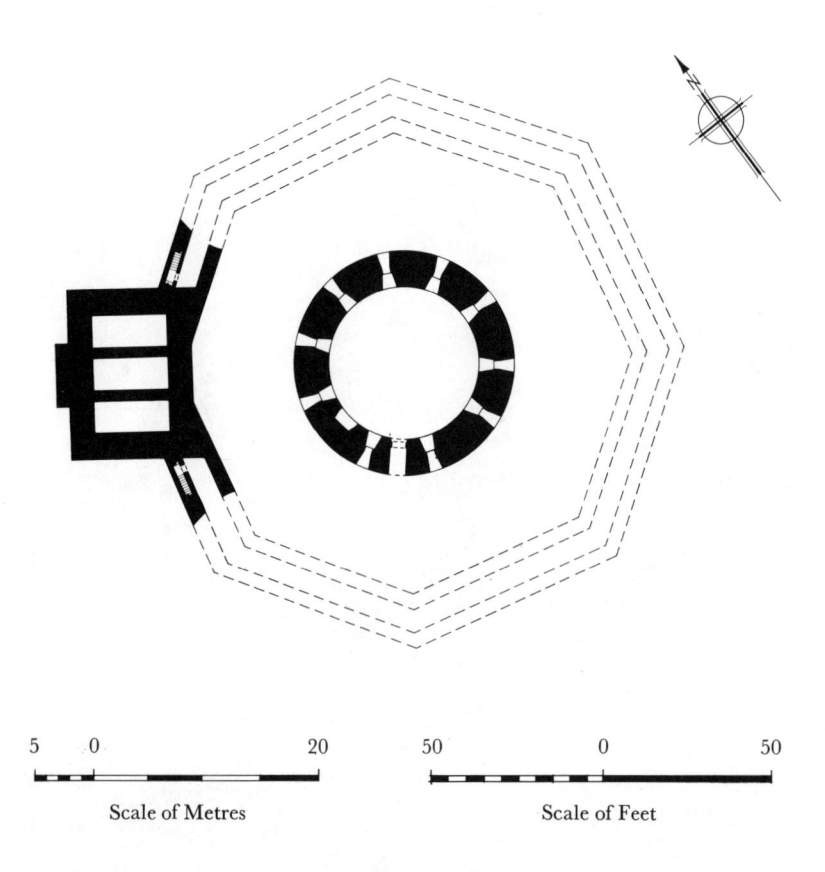

FIGS. 28 & 29: CAMBER CASTLE

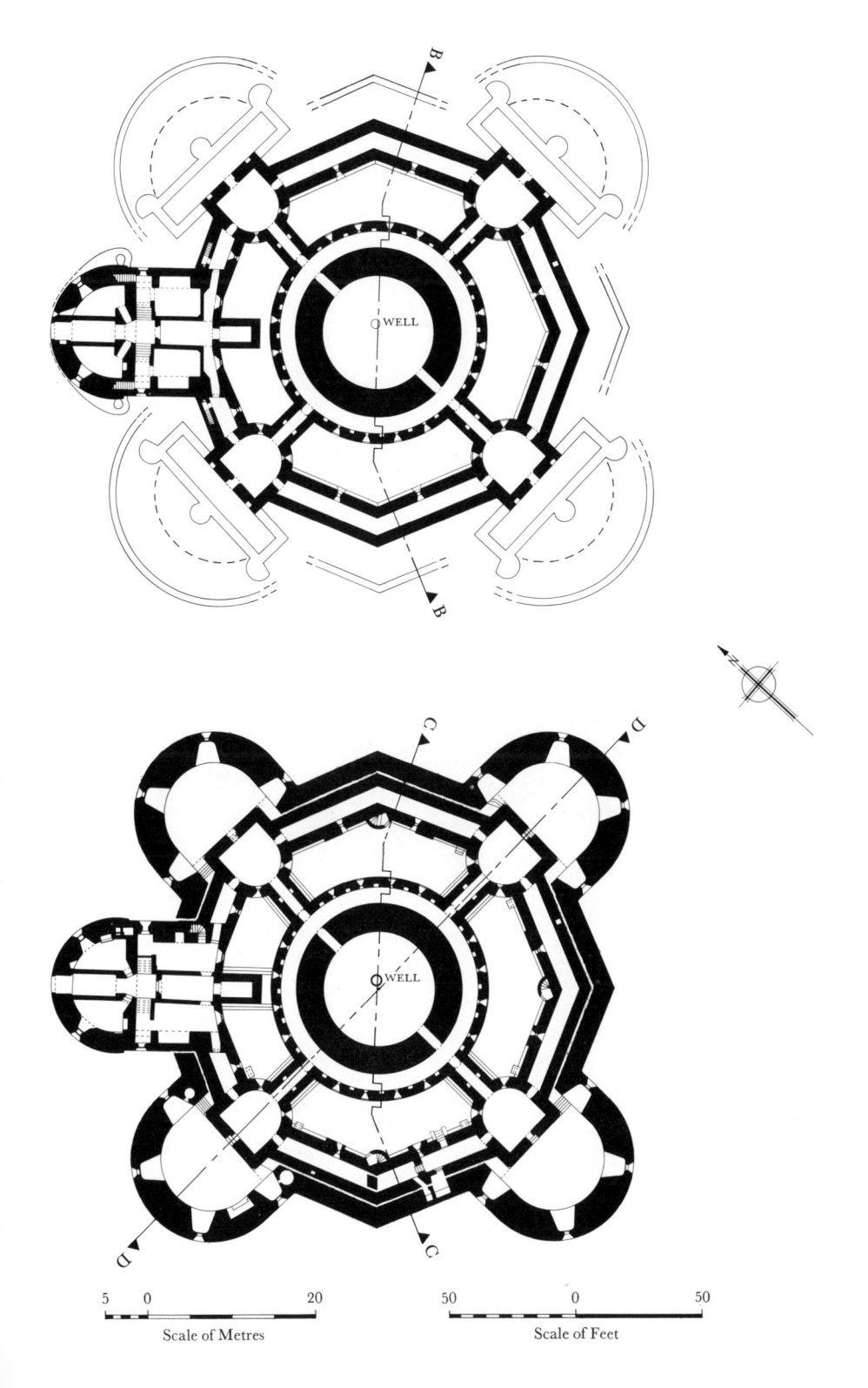

FIG. 30: CAMBER CASTLE

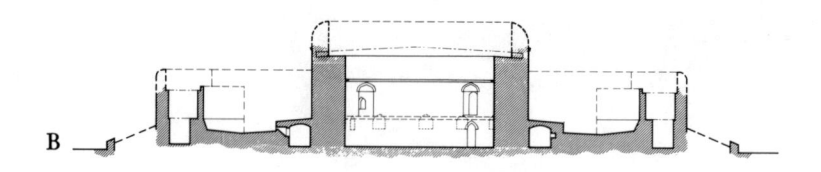

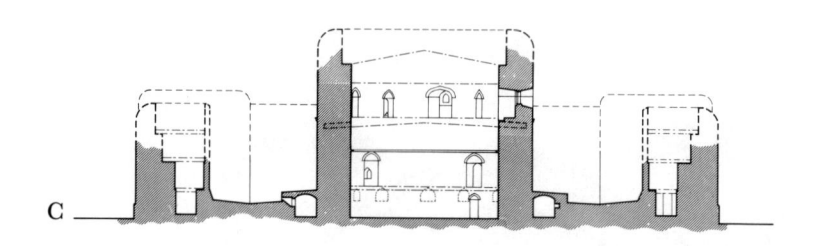

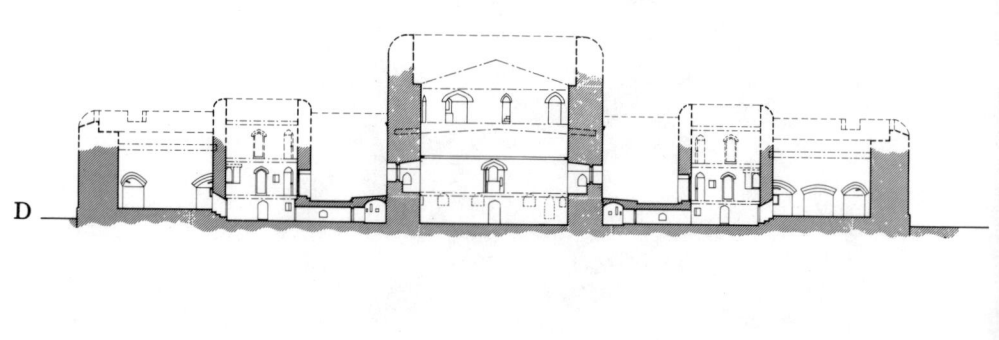

FIG. 31: CAMBER CASTLE (SECTIONS)

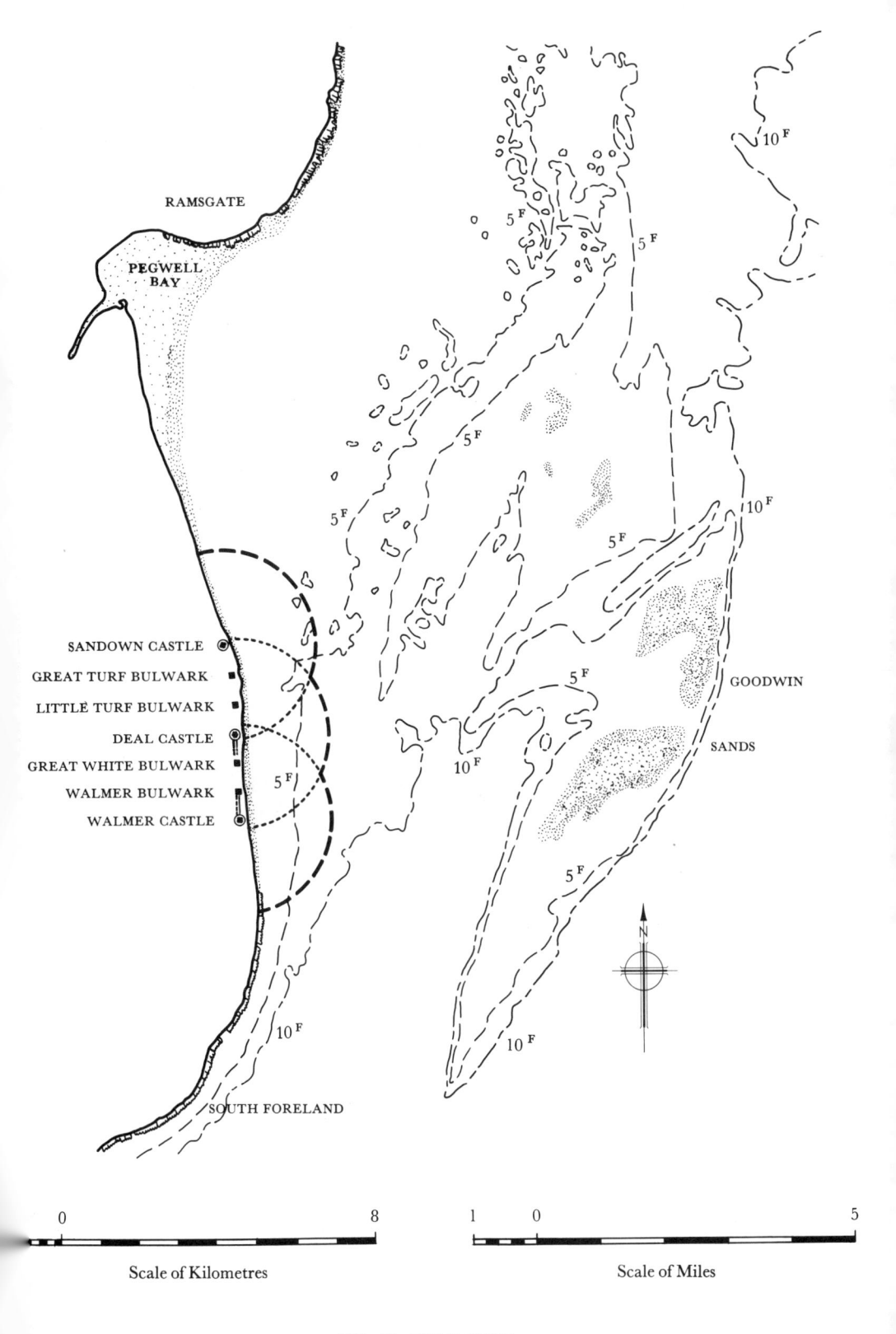

FIG. 32: THE DOWNS

FIG. 33: DEAL CASTLE (GROUND FLOOR AND BASEMENT)

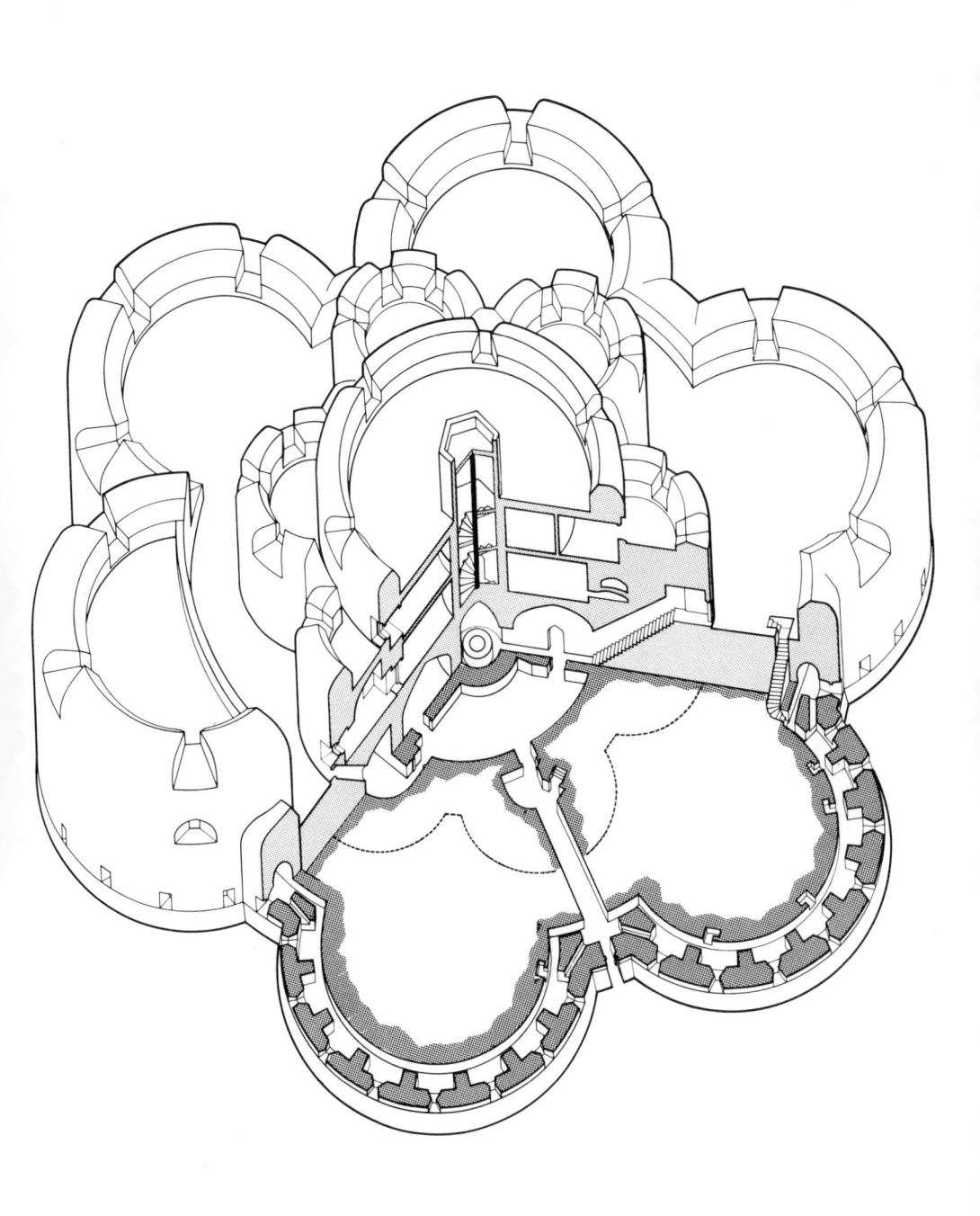

FIG. 34: DEAL CASTLE (PERSPECTIVE)

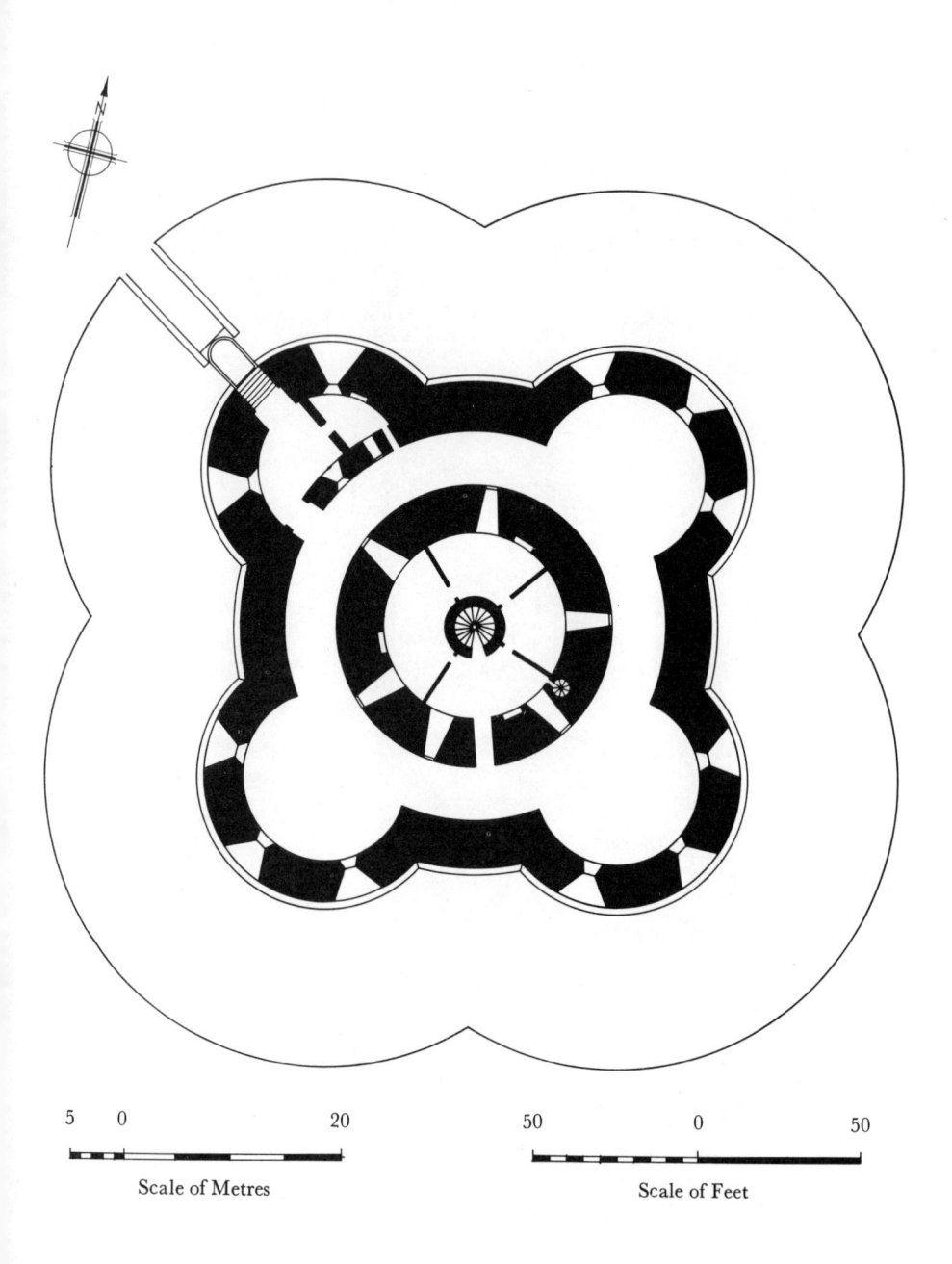

FIG. 35: SANDOWN CASTLE

Scale of Metres

Scale of Feet

FIG. 36: WALMER CASTLE

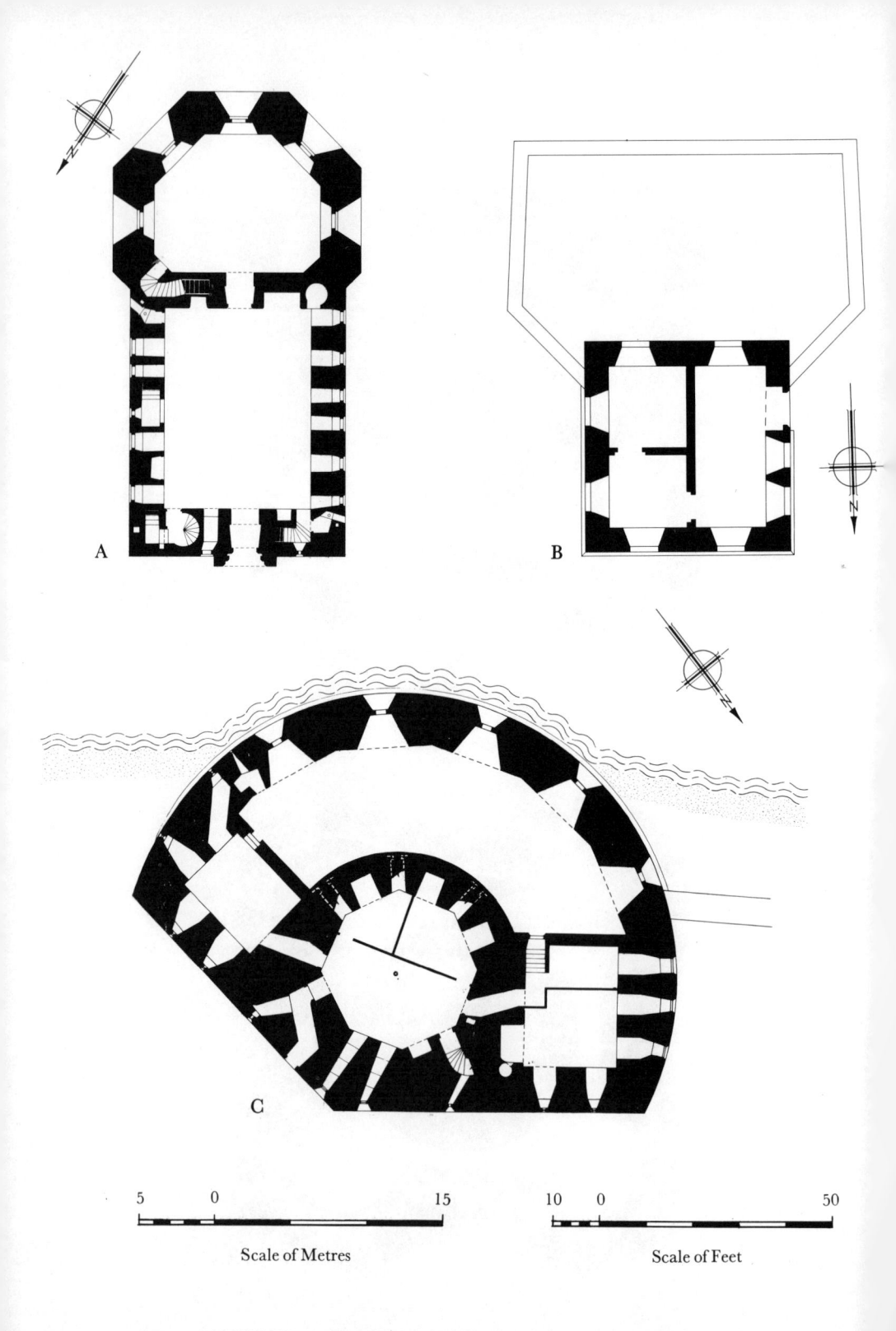

FIG. 37: A. BROWNSEA; B SANDSFOOT; C PORTLAND

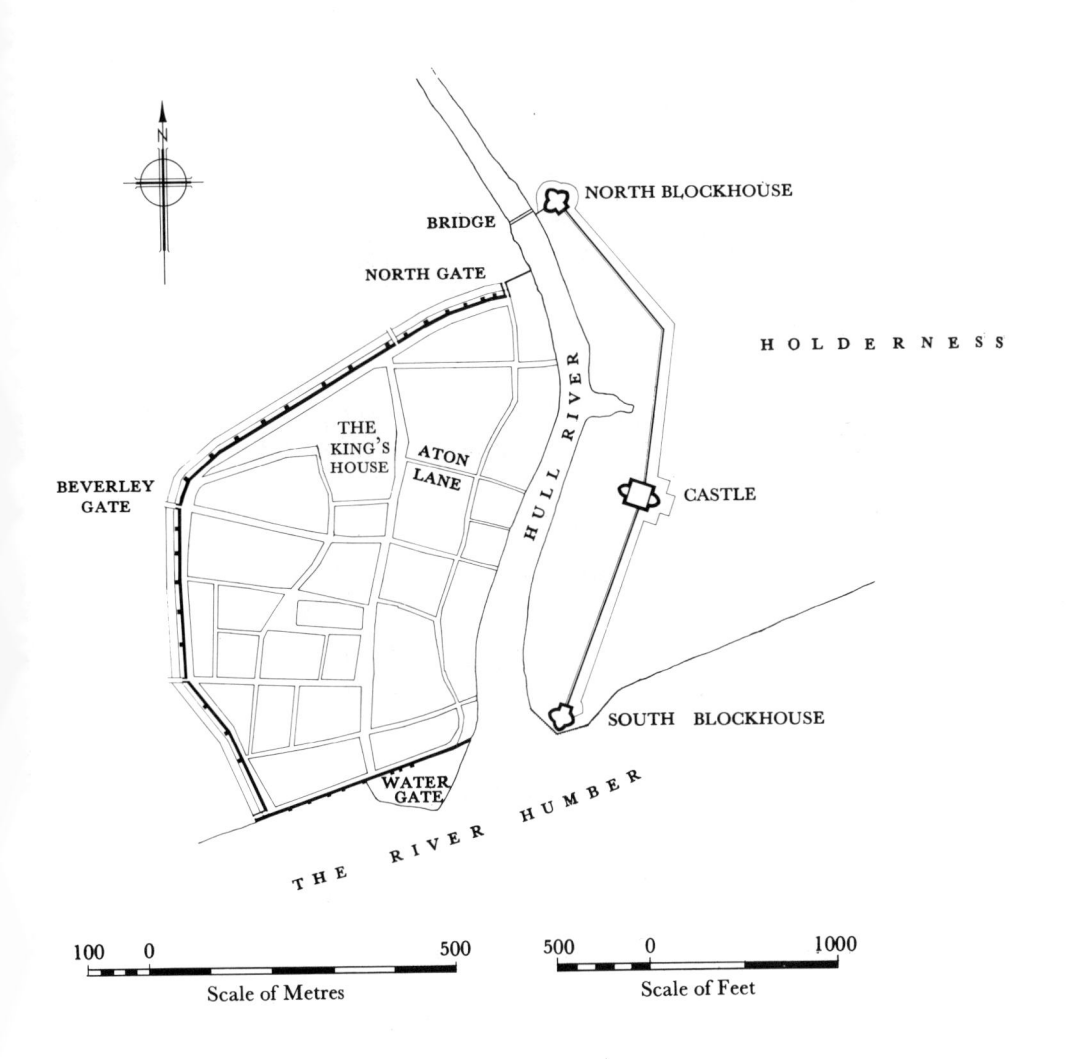

FIG. 38: HULL (TOWN PLAN)

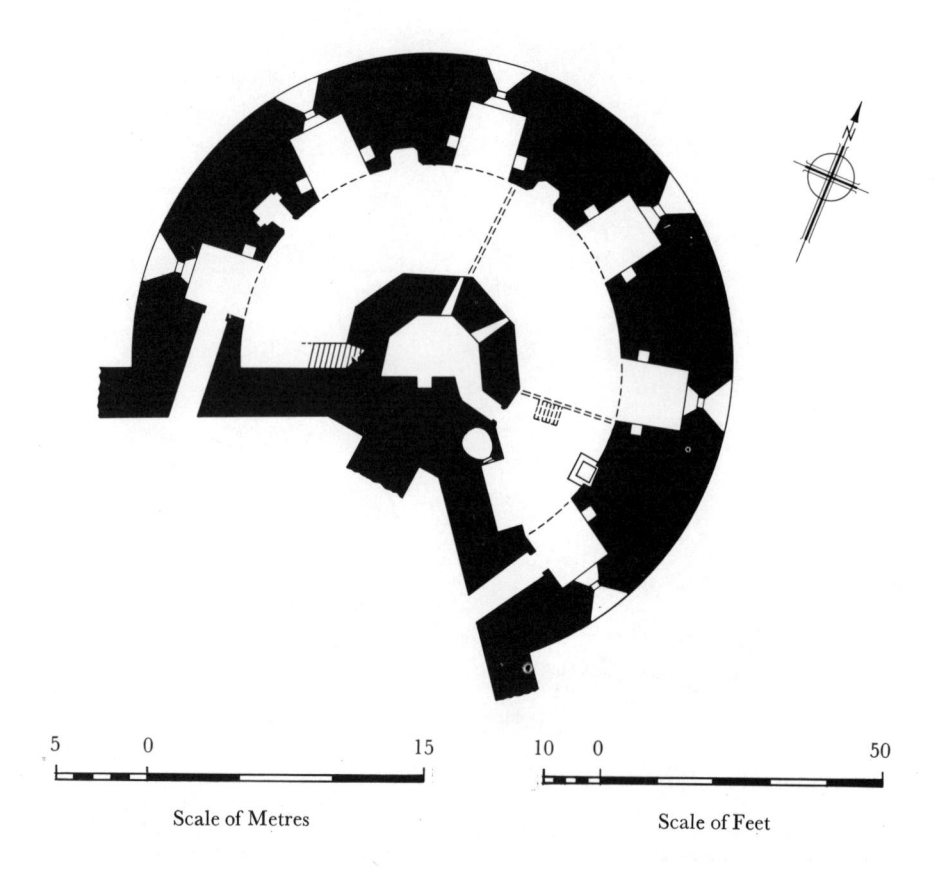

FIG. 58: BERWICK, LORD'S MOUNT

50   0   50

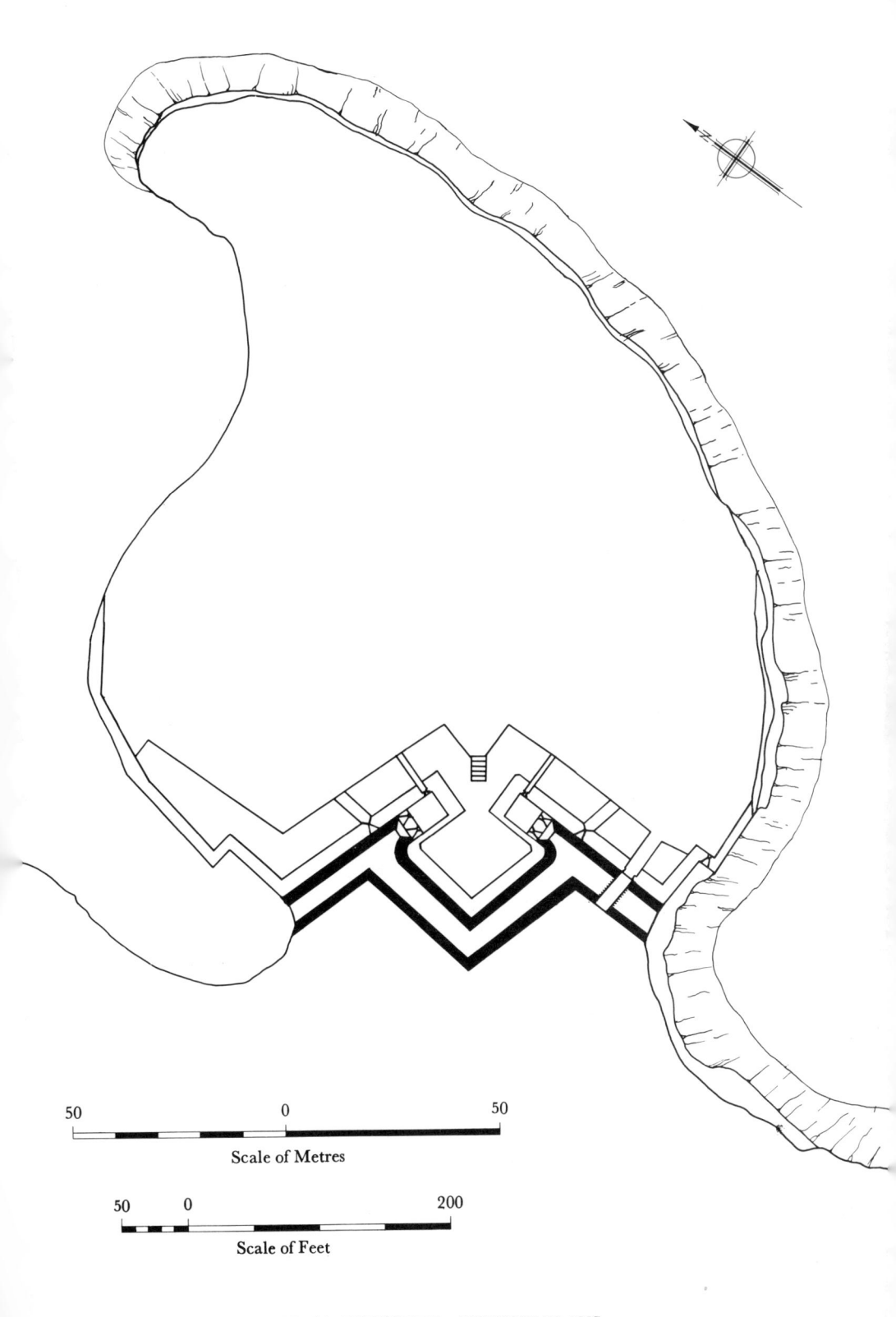

Scale of Metres

50   0   200

Scale of Feet

FIG. 64: EYEMOUTH – BELVOIR PLANS

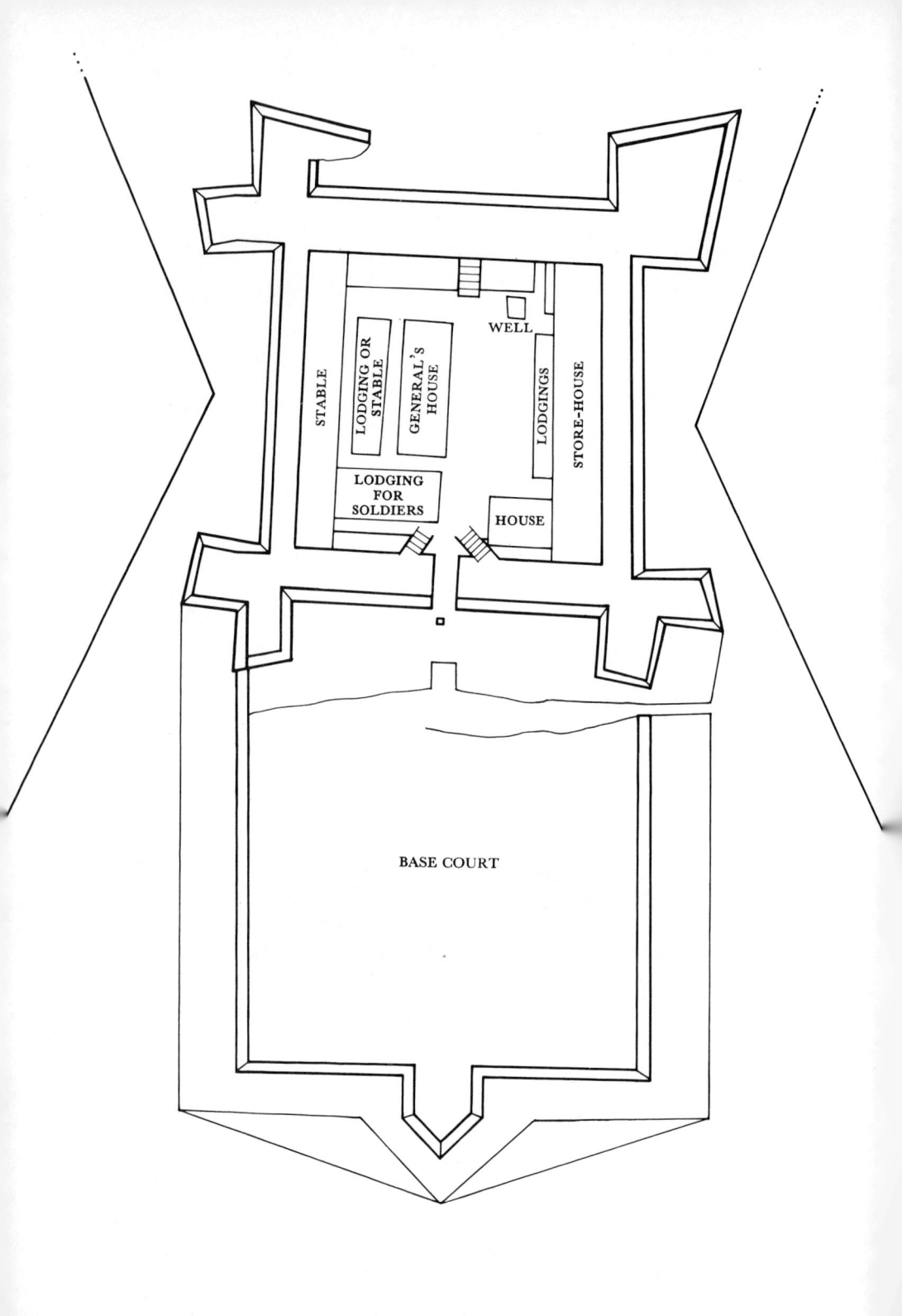

FIG. 65: BROUGHTY CRAG – BELVOIR PLANS

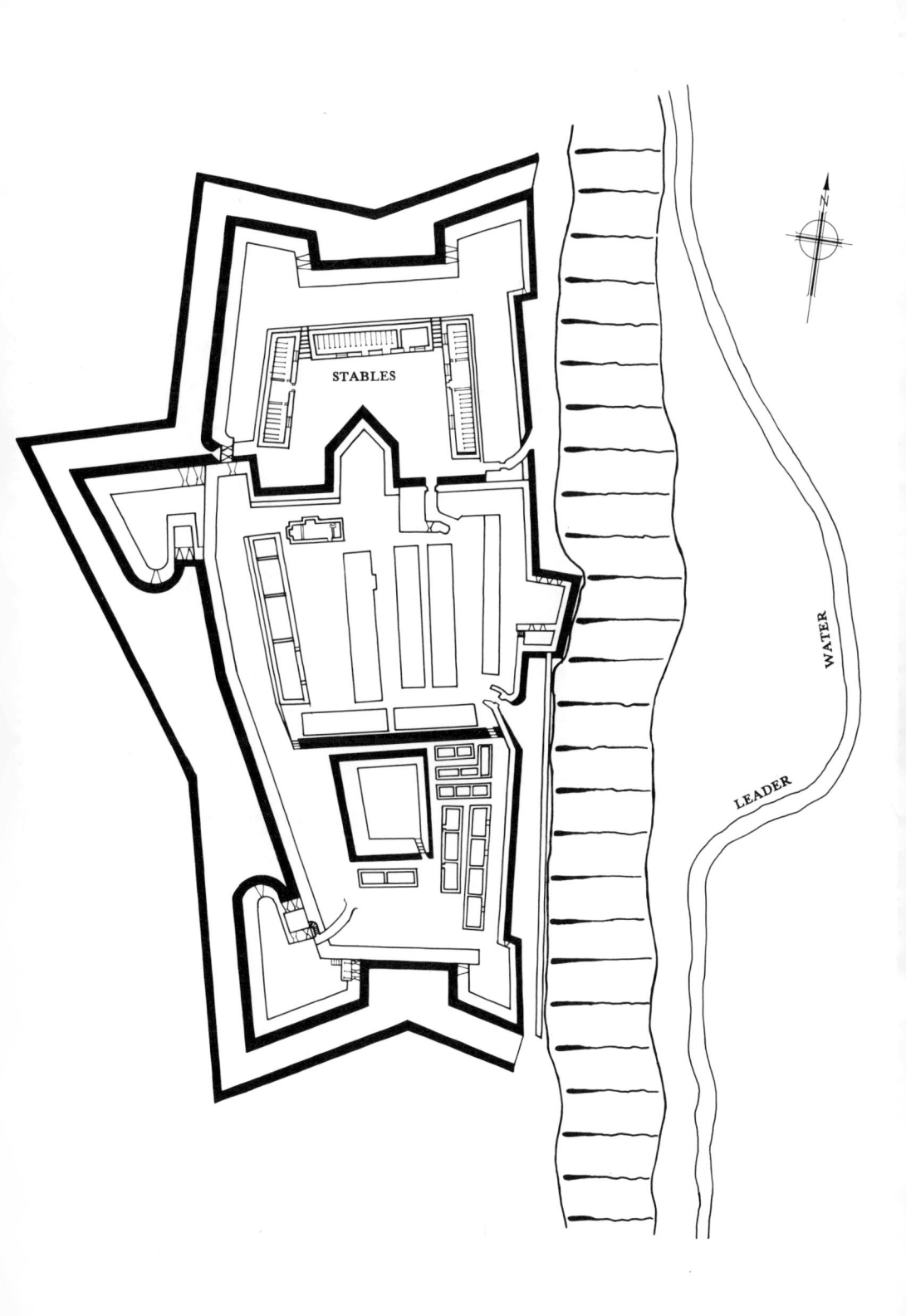

FIG. 66: LAUDER – BELVOIR PLANS

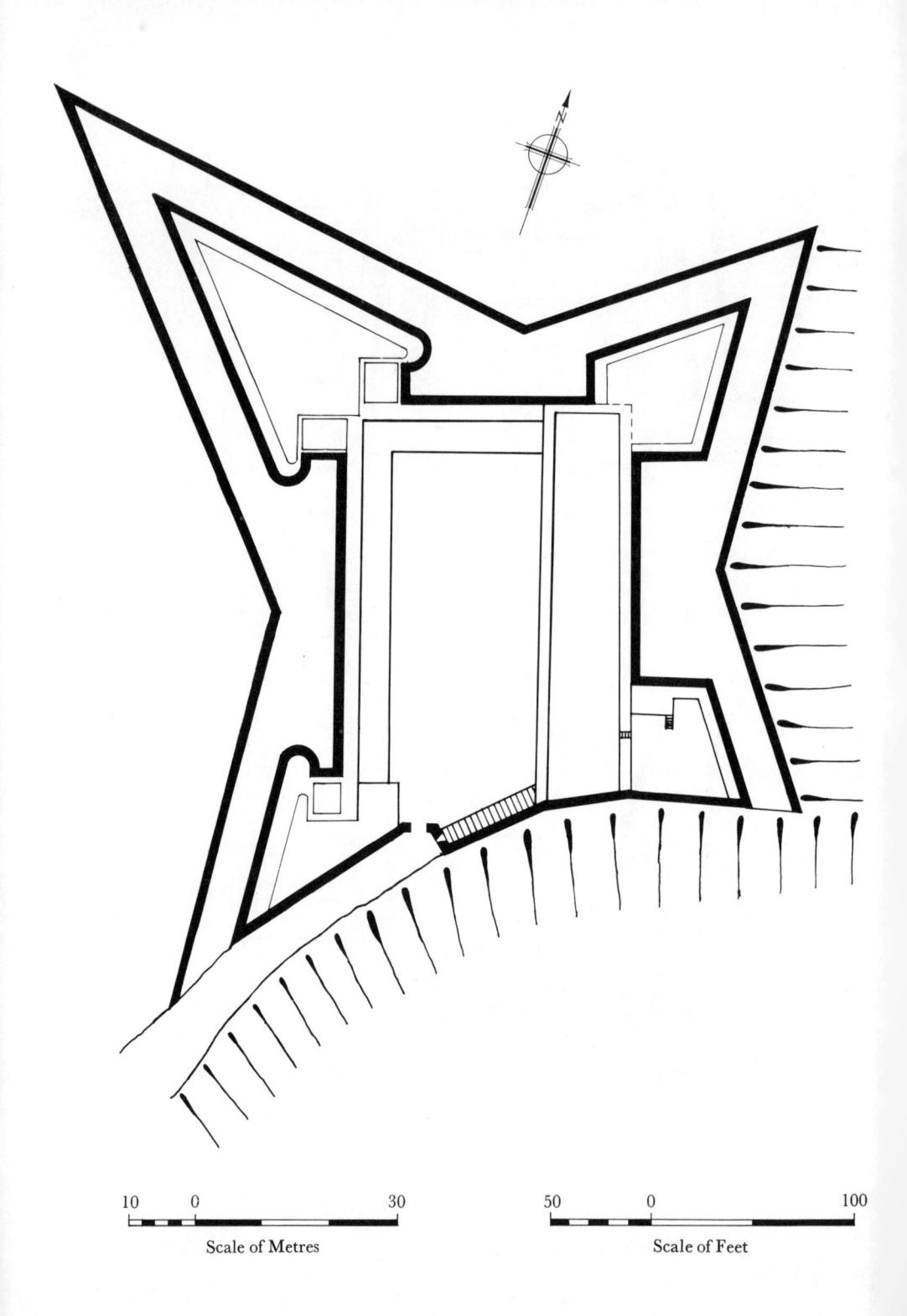

FIG. 67: DUNGLASS – BELVOIR PLANS

VOL. III, PLATE 42: PLAN OF AMBLETEUSE

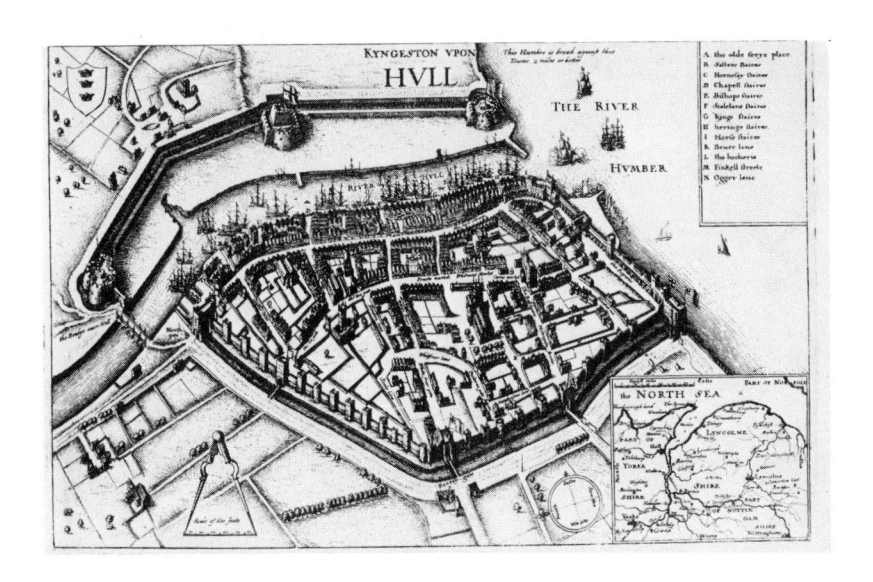

PLATE 45: HULL (SHOWING FORTIFICATIONS)

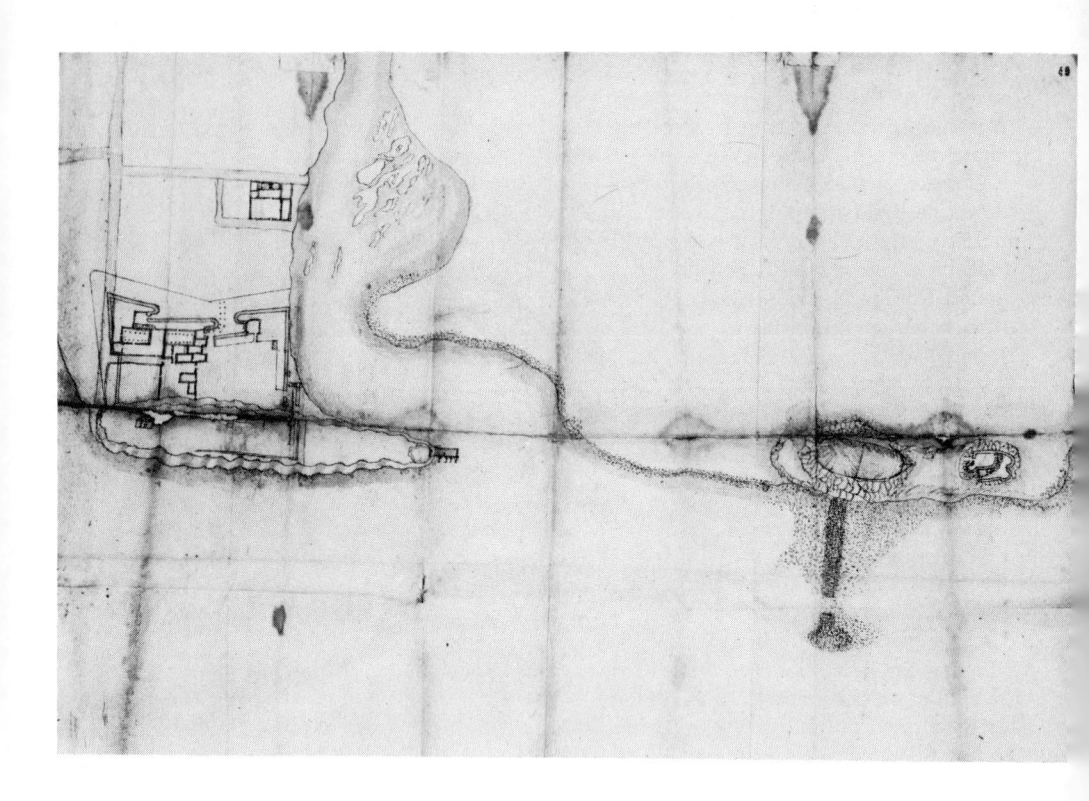

PLATE 51: PLAN FOR HOLY ISLAND (LINDISFARNE)
PLATE 52: PLAN FOR TYNEMOUTH (1545)

in Italian terms, and thus in affecting the ideas of English commanders re-entering what was, in this respect, a military atmosphere that was novel to them.

Francis I had followed his employment of Antonio da Castello by engaging Girolamo Bellarmato of Siena to enlarge Le Havre with an angle-bastioned enceinte in 1540.[1] He still continued to use French engineers. At the siege of Perpignan in 1542 he employed a Gascon 'called', as the English ambassador, Paget, reported, 'Sainct Romey, a great doer in his fortifications',[2] as well as Marini. Not all French officers were converted to the use of Italians. Blaise de Montluc checked the trenches designed by Marini, 'who is judged to be the best man in Italy in siegecraft', and decided that 'he was doing nothing that would be of any use.'[3] But Marini's influence grew, possibly because there was hardly a French council of war that did not contain at least one Italian senior officer. In the Luxembourg-Picardy theatre in 1543 Francis I employed him at Landrecy and at Luxembourg itself after its capture.[4] In 1544, while the English were besieging Montreuil and Boulogne, the English ambassador with the imperial army attacking St. Dizier wrote to Henry VIII of 'an Italian named Maryn who devised the fortifications', who had come out with the French commanders to discuss a truce.[5] In 1545, as a result of a tour of inspection with Martin du Bellay, Francis's lieutenant in Champagne, Marini was charged with the design of two new fortified towns, Vitry-le-Francois and Villefranche-sur-Meuse, to strengthen an area where the king's territory marched with that of the emperor.[6] And it is tempting to connect these essays in ideal fortified town planning with the ideas of the scholarly Italian architect Sebastiano Serlio, whom Francis had invited to France in 1541 and who was, at that time, working on illustrations of the *Castrametazione* of Polybius, with its descriptions of the ideally laid-out fortified camps of the ancients.[7]

It is not clear when Francis engaged yet another Italian engineer, Antonio Melloni, first mentioned as the designer of a five-angled bastioned fort (of earth) set over against the English occupying Boulogne in 1545 (see Vol. III, Fig. 19). Though it was criticised by Du Bellay both for its siting and workmanship,[8] Melloni was described in the following year by an English prisoner of the French as 'chief engineer to the French king'. The same informant told the Earl of Hertford, English commander-in-chief in the Boulonnais, that Melloni 'was half weary of serving France.' But Hertford did not follow up this hint.[9] Nor was an approach made by Henry or on his behalf for the services of any other of Francis's Italians, though the English agent in Antwerp, Stephen Vaughan, obtained leave to visit and question Giovanni di Salerno, a prisoner there whom he had gathered (erroneously, as it turned out) had 'devised the fortifications of Mutterell, Bulloigne and many other strongholds in France.'[10]

[1] Pierre Lavedan, *Histoire de l'urbanisme: renaissance et temps modernes* (Paris 1959), pp. 93 et seq. Bellarmato's (and later work) is recorded in B. M., Cott. MS. Augustus I. ii. no. 78, a plan of 1563.
[2] *L. & P.* xvii, 838, p. 459.
[3] *Commentaires*, ed. Paul Courtault, (2 vols. Paris, 1911) i, pp. 120–30.
[4] Du Bellay, *op. cit.*, pp. 737–8, 747. [5] *L. & P.* xix(2), 68.
[6] *Ibid.* pp. 797–8, 800. Lavedan, *op. cit.*, pp. 77–9, 83–4.
[7] W. B. Dinsmoor, 'The literary remains of Sebastiano Serlio', *Art Bulletin* (1942), pp. 84–5.
[8] *Op. cit.*, pp. 791–2. [9] *L. & P.* xxi (1), 981.
[10] *Ibid.*, xix (1), 1017, (2), 67, 96, 97. Vaughan obtained his release from the regent of the Netherlands and in December he was serving Henry in Boulogne, but as a captain in the garrison (ibid., 177, 799).

We are not, in any case, to suppose that the adoption of an Italian style depended on the employment of Italians. Henry was not unaware of developments on the Continent. In September 1536 Sir John Wallop, then ambassador to the French court, was instructed to examine such fortresses as he could visit without danger, carefully to examine the strength of them... 'to the intent ye may at your return hither... declare the same truly unto us.'[1] He went to the south of France,[2] but nothing he might have reported of the new defence works there was taken account of in the English fortifications of 1539. In May 1540 the French ambassador in London reported that the Lord Chamberlain, Lord Sandys, 'having informed himself about various fortresses in Italy, has left to reside in and fortify Guignes.'[3] But the work there reflected no such information. Henry may have received plans of Italian fortifications just as he did plans of Algiers in 1541 and of the siege of Perpignan in 1542,[4] but lacking Francis's instinctive sympathy with the cultural modes of Italy he needed to be converted first by the peers and knights on whom he relied to raise his men and lead them in war.[5]

For them, as the English commanding officer, Sir John Wallop, put it to Henry in November 1543, this had never been equalled as 'a war where there was so much for youth to learn, both at the being before Landrecy and then at the Emperor's coming [to support the English] with horse and foot of all nations.'[6] Even if Antonio da Castello's advice for strengthening Landrecy had been carried out in a scarcely Italian manner, as a contemporary plan suggests,[7] there was much to learn from England's new colleagues: in one assault, Wallop noted, there were 1200 English, 2000 Germans, 2000 Spaniards and 2000 Italians.[8] In the course of the siege, when Wallop returned to England to report progress, he brought Charles V's captain general, Fernando Gonzaga, with him.[9] Again, in 1544, the towns against which Henry was operating, Montreuil and Boulogne, probably had little that was Italianate about their fortifications, though the latter had been strengthened with an earthwork, the 'great bulwark', at the Abbeville gate and at Montreuil work had possibly been begun on the bastioned inner trace shown on an anonymous English plan in the Cottonian collection.[10] Certainly Henry had seen plans of both towns before he left to join his army in July.[11] But though Henry's and Charles's forces were now operating separately, the campaign continued to be a school of war. The English by now had numerous Italians in their own pay, thanks to Charles having dropped his embargo on their travelling through his domains. Indeed, their numbers increased to such a point that in the following year Paget was forced to complain of 'the coming of so many with which all here are wearied' and wrote to Lord Cobham at Calais: 'I beseech you send over no more strangers... for the King is not content.'[12] Moreover, in parleys over truces or the exchange of prisoners,

---

[1] *Ibid.*, xi, 445.
[2] According to *D.N.B.* he was in Valence-sur-Rhône on 2 October.
[3] J. Kaulek, *op. cit.*, p. 186. My translation depends on altering the editor's reading (adopted by *L. & P.*, xv, 697, p. 326) of 'des amys (*sic*) de diverses forteresses d'Italye' to 'des avys'.
[4] Both obtained by William Paget, ambassador to Francis I (*L. & P.* xvi, 1427, p. 667; xvii, 818).
[5] McClennan, *op. cit., supra*, p. 380, n.2, p. 46, reckons that 55% of the peers served in France in 1544.
[6] *L. & P.* xviii (2), 384.   [7] B. M., Cott. MS. Augustus I. i. 49.
[8] *L. & P.* xviii (2), 321.   [9] *Ibid.*, 218, 291.
[10] *L. & P.* xix (1), 907; ii, 4. B. M., Cott. MS. Augustus I. Supp. 11.
[11] *L. & P.* xix (1), 806, 882; ii, 497.   [12] *L. & P.* xx (1), 877.

English officers met their French opposite numbers and the Italian captains who fought with them. In 1543 Paget had been expansively shown 'all the castle and bulwarks' at Boulogne during a general muster by the French commander. In 1544, as diplomatic liaison agent with Charles V, Nicholas Wotton observed Marini's defence of St. Dizier.[1] Finally, the English were able to judge the effect on fortifications of heavier siege trains than they had used or seen before.

To this political diversion, which has taken us from Provence and Piedmont in 1536 to Picardy in 1543–4, one further element must be added before hazarding an explanation of the Italianate features that distinguished the fortifications planned or built from 1545–7 from those constructed between 1539 and 1543.

From the Peace of Crépy, by which Charles V freed Francis I from the threat of Imperialist aggression and jilted Henry on the very day (14 September) he entered Boulogne in triumph, England was on the defensive. In France there began at once a period of intense technological rivalry as the English built fortifications to protect the Boulonnais and the French built others to make the English positions untenable. In January 1545 Lord Lisle, High Admiral, was recalled from his lieutenancy at Boulogne because the French were preparing 'to invade our dominions.'[2] While the navy was readied, the Council obtained reports on the state of the coastal defences in the south and east and in the north, for Francis I's riposte would almost certainly combine landing an army to support the Scots with landings in England. These were not at all reassuring. In the north—at Berwick, Wark, Carlisle and elsewhere—the captains who had remained on duty there during the wars in France were pronounced sadly inexperienced in matters relating to siege and defence, and attention was drawn to 'the disfurniture of their fortresses, which have been kept more like gentlemen's houses.'[3] The Duke of Norfolk, who had served in France, was scathing about Yarmouth (in Norfolk): 'it is walled on all sides save towards the haven, but so weakly that a few shots of demi-cannon would make sufficient breach to enter. There are many small towers and evil walls, with neither bulwark outside nor rampart within, and the tower walls not above six feet thick; so that it is the weakest walled town he ever saw.' He also criticised the siting of the earthen bulwarks built on the coast in 1539 and had their guns moved nearer to the town.[4]

Once the reports were in and the Council had nominated gentlemen for local defence commands early in May,[5] there was time for little but repair works to be put in hand. Archangelo Arcano, who had been kept in England in the previous year, continued to advise on improvements at Wark and Holy Island and submitted (in February) a project for Kelso whose plan had at the corners 'four bulwarks to flank it',[6] Richard Lee was brought back from France to strengthen Queenborough and the blockhouses guarding the mouth of the Medway before being sent to Tynemouth and Berwick.[7] With many of the key members of the Works organization guarding the English possessions in France, recourse was once more had to the urging of local authorities to look after themselves, and blockhouses were built or town walls strengthened at Lowestoft, Rye, Plymouth and Falmouth. 'Gentlemen and

---

[1] *L. & P.* xviii (1), 295; xix (2), 68, 77.   [2] *L. & P.* xx (1), 121.
[3] *Ibid.*, 582.   [4] *Ibid.*, 717.   [5] *Ibid.*, 671–3.
[6] *L. & P.* xix (2), 653; xx (1), xx (1), 129, 141–2 (Kelso), 166, 698–9.   [7] Below, pp. 477–9.

commoners here,' Lord Russell wrote from Cornwall, 'are all diligent for the defence of the country. It is marvellous what a number of bulwarks, ditches and trenches they have made.'[1] Central administrative energy and money were concentrated on mobilizing local forces in the north (under the Earl of Hertford), the east (Norfolk), the west (the Earl of Arundel) and the south (the Duke of Suffolk) and readying them to move to any threatened area of the coast, and on manning and equipping the warships, converted merchantmen and galleys (for the French had brought up their own galley squadron from the Mediterranean) of the navy.

Henry happened to be at Portsmouth and on board its flagship, *Great Harry*, when the French entered the Solent on 19 July 1545. After a brief and huggermugger engagement they withdrew and, at their ease, landed on the Isle of Wight. There they decided not to attempt to capture Portsmouth because of the presence of the English navy and the uncertain nature of the currents (nothing suggests that the Solent forts were considered a serious obstacle). The pros and cons of occupying the Isle were then considered. This should lead in time to the capture of Portsmouth, would tie down a large English force and provide an ideal base for operations in the Channel. The Isle would, on the other hand, be difficult, expensive and time-consuming to fortify, would tie down a large number of their own troops and present, at least in the short term, a serious victualling problem.[2] Deciding to leave the decision to Francis I, the fleet sailed on 25 July to raid its way eastwards.[3]

By August the scare was over, but the crisis remained: the Scots, having already turned back an English punitive force at Ancrum Moor in February, had been heavily reinforced from France; the French navy remained intact; the pressure on Boulogne was so great that 5000 men had to be sent there; and large garrisons had to be maintained on the English coast because of the inadequate state of the fortifications.[4] The preamble to the subsidy bill that autumn referred to the king's expenses in protecting his subjects 'against the maine force and violence of our.... enemies, who against all honour and faith have attempted to make divers and sundry invasions and spoiles burnings and depopulations in this his Majesties Realme'. As a result of the measures he had taken, it continued, 'wee the people of this his Realme have for the most part of us so lived under his Majesties sure protection, and do yet so live out of all feare and danger as if there were no warre at all, even as the small fishes of the Sea in the most tempestuous and stormie weather doe lie quietly under the rocke or banke side, and are not moved with the sourges of the water, nor stirred out of their quiet place, howsoever the wind bloweth...'[5]

That the new 'rocks and banks' that had to be built turned out to be of a different shape, one that tentatively reached towards a fully Italianate solution, was due to the experience of the 1543–4 wars in France that had affected all of those connected with the planning of fortifications.

As in 1539, Henry's own conversion was essential, for his interest remained as strong as ever. In February 1543, Wallop wrote gratefully from Guines that thanks to 'the king's device' the formerly vulnerable Three Corner and Purton's bulwarks

---

[1] *L. & P.* xx (1), 717, 1159, 1254.
[2] Du Bellay, *op. cit.*, pp. 788–9.
[3] *A.P.C.*, i, p. 217.
[4] *Ibid.*, p. 218; *L. & P.* xx (2), 24.
[5] *Statutes of the Realm*, iii, p. 1019.

'now...cannot be mined.'¹ In April 1544 Hertford promised that he would 'accomplish the devices written in the King's own hand in the platte of Temptallen [Tantallon Castle, East Lothian],' and in May he sent Lee (whom he had recently knighted) and the Surveyor of Calais, William Burgate, to London from the army near Edinburgh so that the king could see 'vively what has been done here.'² Henry arrived in Calais on 14 July and was with the army besieging Boulogne on the 26th. He entered the town four days after its capitulation, on 18 September, and straightway set about 'fortifying it, and gathering his artillery, and viewing what works he would have done, until his departure into England.'³ On 4 October the Privy Council forwarded⁴ to the Council at Boulogne the first in a long series of royal criticisms, suggestions and demands to see plans and have the surveyors working in France sent over to explain and justify their designs to the king.⁵ The plans he backed were the increasingly Italianate ones of John Rogers and Sir Richard Lee, though in a letter of 8 October 1544 referring to both he was adamant that 'that knowledge that they have, they have learned only at oure hand'.⁶ It seems clear that his opinion was that the bastioned polygonal forts built by the French against Boulogne to the south should be answered by similar ones on the north bank of the estuary leading to the town, an opinion the easier to hold because all these forts were built in open country and of earth. And after the English occupation of Ambleteuse in March 1546, the polygonal earth enceinte built to defend the haven there was on an Italianate plan endorsed by Rogers and Lee but which reflected Henry's own insistence that it should have five rather than four bastions.⁷ It has been suggested on the basis of a plan for Ambleteuse that shows a radial street plan inside the enceinte (Vol. III, Pl. 42), that Henry was concerned to rival Francis I's fortress town of Villefranche-sur-Meuse, recently designed on similar lines by Marini.⁸ This cannot be substantiated. But it is not unlikely that Henry's renewed contact with the Continent made him anxious not to lag behind his rival's endorsement of a style which was also being introduced by the third and most powerful of western Europe's monarchs, his infuriating ally the Emperor Charles V.

As in 1539, decisions on each fortification project were made after considering plans submitted by the peers and knights with local military or para-military responsibilities who, in turn, had consulted experts with building knowledge. Though there is no suggestion that successive noble governors and commissioners—most of whom had been concerned with the operations at Landrecy, Montreuil and Boulogne—were averse to adopting the new style (William Lord Grey's complaints, when he was lieutenant of Boulogne in 1546, against Rogers were on personal grounds),⁹ it is noticeable that Henry dealt increasingly directly with those of them whose knowledge and sympathy with his own ideas he could rely on. Among them were Sir Thomas Wyatt, who had been at Landrecy

---

¹ *L. & P.* xviii (1), 216.
² *Ibid.*, xix (1), 432, 468, 535. Burgate went on to France and was killed at the siege of Boulogne (vol. iii above, p. 357).
³ *L. & P.* xix (2), 424, p. 242.   ⁴ *Ibid.*, 347.
⁵ Vol. iii above, p. 384 et seq.; Shelby, *op. cit.*, p. 53 et seq.
⁶ SP 1/193, f. 69 (*L. & P.* xix (2), 383).
⁷ Vol. iii above, p. 388 and Shelby, *op. cit.*, p. 75 et seq. and plates 15–18.
⁸ Shelby, *op. cit.*, p. 79 and plate 18.   ⁹ *Ibid.*, pp. 89–90.

in 1543, was made captain of Lower Boulogne in January 1545 and was praised by Paget, who of all Henry's political agents had had the best opportunities to keep abreast of continental military practice, as 'a great foreseer in fortification and [a man who] can make his plattes artificially';[1] Cavendish (now Sir Richard), made captain of Blackness (near Ambleteuse) in July 1546 with the assurance that Rogers was not to 'intromedle therin';[2] and Sir Thomas Palmer, treasurer of Guines from 1543. In 1545 Palmer was entrusted with the work going forward on the polygonal fort called the Old Man at the mouth of the Liane with the assurance that 'no officer of High Bullen should medle wyth any thing towching the sayde fortresse, my Lord Lieutenant [the Earl of Surrey] excepted.'[3] But by 1546 Henry was prepared to bypass both men in favour of his chosen expert, Rogers. 'Considering the uncertainty of the opinions of your lordship [Surrey] and Sir Thomas, his Majesty debated with Rogers and conceived certain plattes, the execution of which', Paget wrote to the Lord Lieutenant, 'he committed to Rogers... Your lordship knoweth that the man is plain and blunt, which must be borne withal as long as he is well meaning and mindeth the service of the King's Majesty.'[4]

Given the increasing burden of Henry's physical disabilities, this imaginative grasp of a new aspect of military technology, even if aided by the desire not to be left behind by his ageing fellow members of the college of militant monarchs, is remarkable, though it was combined with a conservatism which led him to entrust the domesticisation of the Italian style largely to native Englishmen.

Archangelo Arcano continued to be employed as a surveyor. After his plan of February 1545 for new fortifications for Kelso another was submitted to the king in September.[5] Nothing was done, however.[6] Girolamo da Treviso was sent to Calais with artillery and timbers for siegework in June 1544 and thence to advise on the attack on Montreuil. In reply to Henry's inquiry as to his competence, Lord Russell put him down as 'inexperienced in sieges' and one whose advice was given 'not as a man very skilful in such things.' Henry then suggested that he should be given a command of 100 arquebusiers, but he was transferred to Boulogne and was apparently engaged in mining operations before being killed in an assault there in September.[7] Gian Tommaso Scala had served Venice, and then, possibly, France before being employed by Henry in the north from the beginning of 1545. But it was not long before he returned to Venice.[8] Both he and Antonio da Bergamo had been described as 'Italians expert in fortifying' when Lee was sent with them to make recommendations for Tynemouth in January. A plan by Antonio showing some very shakily Italianate features for Wark may date from a later phase of this tour but his pay in July 1546 listed him among other foreigners who were obviously soldiers, and it was his last.[9] The 'John of Padua' employed from 1544, was referred to as '*architectus*' and on one occasion as 'engineer', but in a career in England that

---

[1] *L. & P.* xx (2), 919. [2] *A.P.C.* i, p. 476. [3] *Ibid.* p. 185.
[4] *L. & P.* xxi (1), 356. [5] *L. & P.* xx (2), 308, 328, 347.
[6] Carden, *art. cit.* (*supra*, p. 75), p. 199, says erroneously that he left English service in the following year.
[7] *L. & P.* xix (1), 746, 876, 1005; ii, 37, 216. Philip Pouncey, *art. cit.* (*supra*, p. 75).
[8] *L. & P.* xx (1), 99; Promis, *op. cit.* (*supra*, p. 386), pp. xii, 439.
[9] *L. & P.* xx (1), 99; *A.P.C.* i, pp. 256, 487. His pay was identical to theirs. The plan is Hatfield House, CPM I. 42. The name 'Antonio da Bergamo' is in the same hand as the Italian notations on it.

lasted until 1557 he is nowhere mentioned in connection with fortifications.¹ The last Italian to be named in this context is 'Giovan Rossetti Italiano', as he signed himself on an undated plan of that French threat to Calais, Ardres. Clearly showing the Italianate angle bastions that the French had added along one wall and at one corner of the castle enclosure of this much spied-upon frontier town, it is a reminder that the French stimulus towards adapting the new style was active in the Pas de Calais as well as in the Boulonnais.² Employed from 1543 he, too, was sent to work in the north.³

There is, of course, no necessary correlation between the employment of Italians and the adoption of Italian methods. Men paid by the Crown did as they were told. Henry's Italian engineers were often obliged to cooperate in works in the Henrician manner. Even when he became converted to the Italian style, his agent Nicholas Wotton turned down a Genoese soldier's suggestion that Henry should employ a companion who was 'an "ingiegnier" cunning in fortification', and 'showed him that the king was already provided with such men.'⁴ From 1545 the king's few Italians may have been listened to more attentively. From that year two plans, Antonio da Bergamo's for Wark and an unsigned one for Tynemouth⁵ (Pl. 52) have survived, both bearing additional notations in the hands of English colleagues. Contact with Antonio led one such colleague, John Man, to use an Italian term; in August the Earl of Hertford told Paget, not without a touch of insular superiority, that Man had made 'a dissegno (as he calleth it) of the new wall...at Warke.'⁶ But they hardly stand out among the native members of the works teams or the others who were employed about fortifications, like the John Brende, 'who is a wise and expert fellow', sent by Hertford to make a plan of Carlisle's bulwarks, or 'Giles, the King's servant' who made plans in Boulogne, or the renegade Scotsman William Wawan who 'understands fortifications and has drawn platts of...Hardeloo [Ardelot] and Estaples very perfectly.'⁷ And they are dim figures indeed in comparison to the *hommes à toutes affaires*, Rogers and Lee. At a time when in France, the Netherlands, Spain and Portugal (and in their overseas empires) and in Austria-Hungary Italians were more conspicuous than native engineers, England was a conscious exception.⁸

Indeed, in contrast to the well-grasped Italianate ideas that were being put into effect by English surveyors in the works in and near Boulogne and at Ambleteuse, very little was actually built in England according to the designs of Henry's Italians,⁹ and little, during the king's last years, that even echoed what had become standard practice in English France. And these echoes all sounded from the south coast, where Italians were scarcely in evidence.

The new fort at Sandown, built April—September 1545 to defend the most open landing on the east coast of the Isle of Wight, timidly flirted with current notions of

---

¹ Vol. iii above, pp. 43–4.
² B. M., Cott. MS. Augustus I. ii. 74. I have expanded the contractions in his signature.
³ In 1547. See below pp. 700–1.   ⁴ *L. & P.* xx (1), 1057.
⁵ B. M., Cott. MS. Augustus I. ii. 7.   ⁶ *L. & P.* xx (2), 87.
⁷ *L. & P.* xx (1), 1286; xxi (1), 18, 1095.
⁸ On southern and eastern Europe and overseas: Leone A. Maggiorotti, *Architetti e architettura militare. L'opera del genio italiano all'estero* (3 v., Rome, 1933–9).
⁹ The difficult cases of Holy Island and Tynemouth are discussed below, pp. 677, 683–4.

flanking cover.¹ With one square, one round and one angle bastion, its confusion reinforces the reflection that the presence of an Italian—in this case the soldier Giovanni Portinari (who had conducted mining operations at Boulogne)² in charge of the labour crew—does not guarantee the enforcement of Italian ideas. It is suggested below that Southsea Castle, on the Solent west of Portsmouth, the only work of fortification commenced in 1544, had from the start reflected 'a growing awareness of the new Italian ideas on fortification', though its two triangular bastions still lacked flanking batteries³. In the following July, after the king's visit to Portsmouth, changes were made which considerably improved the castle's flanking capacity, changes attributed to Henry's own intervention. Certainly the man in charge, Sir Anthony Knyvet, had from the beginning of the work in 1544 assumed that he was directly responsible to Henry himself for a work whose royal initiative he took for granted.⁴ Even if each of the two stages of Southsea's construction reflected the development of Henry's ideas more clearly than did any other defence work built in England during the renewed bout of siege warfare in France, the castle remained basically 'Henrician' and could not serve as a stimulus to more truly Italianate designs.

It should be remembered that Southsea was built of stone and roofed with lead. And in periods of transition the more expensive the building the more conservative the plan is likely to be. The period of experiment which made of Provence-Savoy-Piedmont the transmission chamber whence Italian ideas were pumped northwards was characterised by works in earth, as were the polygonal defences constructed at Boulogne and Ambleteuse. Yet even the little fort at Sharpenode, built from August 1545 cheaply in earth facing Hurst Castle across the Solent, was only feebly Italianate with its two little triangular bastions, without flank batteries and ending in vulnerably acute points.⁵

But if nothing really forward-looking was actually built in the south, plans were produced there that easily outdistanced those for Wark and Tynemouth in their grasp of the full Italian manner: the plans of new defences for Portsmouth.⁶ Dating from Henry's visit in July 1545 and the summoning of Lee to discuss the king's suggestions before he left for London, these sketched a new enceinte, to be built initially in earth, which incorporated angle bastions with batteries in their recessed flanks. Before his death in late August, the work was urged on by the Duke of Suffolk, the commander-in-chief of the army besieging Boulogne in the previous year. Other veterans of the French campaign, Lisle and Lord St. John, showed their interest. But the project was not carried out. Lee was called away after less than six weeks. There was a chronic shortage of cash. Disease cut the labour force. Before the danger of a new invasion receded with the treaty of 7 June 1546 little was done apart from the building of earthen ramparts and the reinforcing of the existing round corner bastions. But by Henry's death on 2 January 1547 the full Italian system of fortification had made at least the conceptual leap from the shores of his French territories to those of his native realm.

¹ Described below, pp. 552–5.   ² *Cal. S.P. For. 1553–8*, 196.
³ Below, pp. 562–3.   ⁴ E.g. *L. & P.* xix (1), 659, 660; (2), 476.
⁵ Below, p. 556.   ⁶ Below, pp. 504–6.

On 18 April 1547, Lord Grey and Sir Thomas Palmer wrote from Boulogne to Hertford, now Duke of Somerset and Protector, on behalf of the nine-year-old Edward VI, to report a conversation they had held with one of the officers in the French camp there. The Frenchman said that he had been present at the attack on the Isle of Wight; had this not been mismanaged, he declared, the Isle was so weakly fortified that it could easily have been overrun. Moreover, he added, 'all the other forts of the country were of small strength.' Grey and Palmer sought to disabuse him. 'We assure you that England is one of the most difficult realms to set foot on land for a foreign prince ... for he cannot come to the shore without likelihood of great loss in the landing, and when he is landed, he must come as to the sault the first day; and after that, if he pass it, he must yet look to fight every day, and to have battles offered to him without end. And as our fortifications are not so easy to be beaten as you think, so though they were never so strong, it is not England's profession to trust in lime and stone. And if there were want of anything when you were there, be you assured, it hath been seen and redressed since; for your sudden attempt in England, to be plain with you, warned us in some things; and therefore we say to you as to our friend, England needeth at this day as little to care as any other realm'.[1]

This answer recalls the role of the English coastal defences: to cause an invader 'the likelihood of great loss in the landing.' He will then break through, but thereafter he will have to deal with troops alerted by the early-warning system of beacons and moved into his path by the peers appointed to regional commands, as in 1545. The same point about lime and stone being only partially trusted was to be made in the Venetian ambassador Daniele Barbaro's *relazione* of 1551. After referring to the English fortifications, he emphasized that 'the chief strength of that realm consists in its inhabitants'. And he described the beacon and muster systems.[2] The same point was made again in George Rainsford's *Ritratto d'Inghilterra*, written for Phillip II's edification in 1556. 'They fear no foreign power because the places where ships can land are well fortified and guarded, and those that are not guarded are protected by high and strong cliffs. In addition the kingdom is strong because of the provisions it makes against unexpected attacks' — beacons and musters — 'so in time of danger the whole country can quickly take up arms.'[3]

We are not, then, to expect any major remodelling on Italianate lines in Henry's last years of works designed to check rather than to stop an invasion force. Under his successor one more fort was built in the south while the uneasy truce with France lasted: Yarmouth Castle, constructed May — November 1547 in the Isle of Wight to supplement Hurst Castle and the fort at Sharpenode in defending the western approaches to Portsmouth and to cover 'the movement of relief forces from the mainland.'[4] Another hybrid design, its single angle bastion was nonetheless the first actually built in England to contain batteries flanking the adjacent walls. But again, it is not to the design of coastal defences, with their need for unbroken, unflanked,

---

[1] *Cal. S.P. For. 1547–53*, pp. 333–5.
[2] *Cal. S.P. Venetian* v, pp. 353–4.
[3] Ed. P. S. Donaldson, *Camden Miscellany* xxvii (1979), pp. 104–5.
[4] Below, pp. 565–9.

firing platforms on the water-side and the scant necessity to provide against investment and assault from the land, that we should look for more than intimations of the Italian approach. The Old Man fort, on the English side of the Liane estuary in the Boulonnais, *was* polygonal, with three bastions on the land side (Vol. III, Fig. 19). But here, in occupied but not administratively reorganized territory, there was no beacon-and-muster to divert the pressure of an attack. And it was constructed of earth.

The Italian system had evolved not only from the structural challenge of bombardment but from the need to shelter heavy guns while they pounded a besieger's batteries, and, as we have seen, to provide flanking fire that could break up any attempt to mine (save through long, time-consuming tunnels) and enable assaults to be raked with fire from unexposed positions. This was true of town walls and of citadels designed to strengthen an enceinte as well as to repel attacks from a rebellious citizenry (or one responsive to, or overawed by an occupying force).[1] The mechanism of the bastion was comparatively easy to grasp—though the one built at Yarmouth had such short shoulders that the gun positions in the flankers were dangerously exposed. But for those to whom the system had not become habitual its geometrical logic was more easily grasped when designing fronts comprising more than two mutually supporting bastions. And the method spread northwards from Italy, as we have seen, not only because of its logic but because it lent itself, with its thick low walls and solid bastions, to construction cheaply and speedily in earth. Stone was only needed when gun batteries were incorporated low in the flanks of bastions.[2] Otherwise, once the trace had been staked out, local unskilled labour, including that of troops, could create a defensible position without the aid of carpenters, masons, lime-burners, smiths, plumbers or others of that host of craftsmen whose wage-bills had so inflated the costs of the fortifications of the 1539 Device. It is not surprising, therefore, that the system was not applied to the coastal fortresses but first notably emerged in England in the plans for Portsmouth, a town liable to siege as an important port and naval base; in the earthen fortifications associated with the Scottish campaign of 1547–50, which were designed to turn castles or villages into the equivalents of temporary but strongly defended armed camps; and, finally, in the plans of 1550 and thereafter for the enceinte and citadel of the often threatened frontier post and troop assembly centre of Berwick.[3] For after Henry's death it was in the north that new defence works were concentrated, first during Somerset's attempts to subdue Scotland, and then to protect the North of England, menaced by a French presence in Scotland during the decade 1550–60. In the south nothing new was built after Yarmouth until Elizabeth's reign,[4] though there were invasion scares, and some hasty repairs carried out, in 1548 and again in 1557–8.[5] In France work continued on the masonry inserts—flank battery chambers and gates—and on the cladding in turf of

---

[1] For an early (1534) example, see J. R. Hale, 'The end of Florentine liberty: the Fortezza da Basso', *Florentine studies*, ed. Nicolai Rubinstein (1968).

[2] As at Berwick in 1522 and at Roxburgh in 1548 (below, pp. 630, 706–7).

[3] For details of northern defences see below, pp. 607 et seq.

[4] For Upnor Castle on the Medway, begun in 1559, see below, pp. 478–9.

[5] *Cal. S.P. Dom. 1547–80*, pp. 7–8, *A.P.C.* vi, *passim*, January–April 1557; *Cal. S.P. Dom. 1547–80*, pp. 100–101.

Ambleteuse and its subsidiary fort at Blackness; the use of troops as labourers and the need to use them for repair work after rains showing the convenience as well as the major disadvantage of earth as a medium of construction.[1] In Calais and the March minor changes pointed to modernizations. The trefoil bulwark at Guines was ordered to be taken down in 1550 and the material used to make the semi-trefoil Purton's Bulwark 'pointed' and to improve its ability to provide flanking fire towards the keep; in the same year Thomas Petit, Surveyor of Calais, was charged to change 'the round boulwerk' of the Rysbank fort 'to a pointed one.'[2] But it was a still un-Italianised Calais that was taken by the French with such ease eight years later.

The new fortifications in Scotland followed Somerset's invasion and victory at Pinkie on 10 September 1547 and his determination to apply a new solution to the Scottish problem by leaving behind a permanent English presence in the form of garrisoned strategic points. From Broughty near the mouth of the Tay, through Haddington and Dunglass in East Lothian to Lauder and Eyemouth in Berwickshire, works were designed between September 1547 and August 1548 that as a group reflected a hitherto unprecedented dependence (in Britain) on Italian ideas[3]. At Roxburgh Castle, a narrow, precipitous site did not lend itself readily to Italian principles of fortification; but at Haddington the eastern defences (of which no plan remains) with their four corner bastions, were compared to those of Turin; Lauder, complete enough to receive a garrison in June 1548, was coherently flanked by a combination of full and demi-bastions, one of each having a curved orillon amply covering its flank battery (Fig. 66). The square fort on the rising ground to the north-west of Dunglass also contained a combination of full and demi-bastions and of square and orillon-shaped flanks (Fig. 67). The purest overall plan was that for the fort designed for the waterfront at Broughty: a perfect square with symmetrical bastions (albeit with rounded salients) which was dropped, however, for a site uphill of Broughty which could not be commanded by enemy guns (Fig. 65); The purest single bastion, and the earliest, was the one designed to defend the little port of Eyemouth (Fig. 64); with its pointed salient and two-abreast flanking batteries protected by rounded orillons and fronted, over a ditch, by what looks on the Belvoir plan like a counterscarp, this suggests a mastery of the chief component of the Italian system that was never quite expanded into the more comprehensive plans of this Scottish series of town enceintes and forts. It is likely that one project outside Scotland was associated with this series: the plan for a broken front of two demi-bastions defending the abbey church of Holy Island (Lindisfarne) from attack from the landsward (Pl. 51).

These works were urged forward by the threat of French intervention. In March 1548 Wotton warned from Paris that 'a French painter named Nicholas has given the French King pictures of all the havens in England, by means of which they may land their men that go into Scotland easily',[4] and in June 1548 6000 men and artillery for siegework were landed from France at Leith. The emphasis was on defence against artillery from the start, and this meant building afresh: before

---

[1] Vol. iii above, pp. 388–9. [2] *Ibid.* pp. 369, 357.
[3] For details of this group see below, pp. 694–725. [4] *Cal. S.P. For. 1547–53*, 70.

Somerset's campaign began the walls of a typical Scottish strongpoint, Langholm in Dumfriesshire, had been reckoned tenable for four or five days against small guns but only one against canon or culverins.[1] The absorbency of earth was pointed to from the first—with the option (as in the plan for the sea fort at Broughty) of subsequent cladding in stone—and earth was also indicated by the need to provide large and speedily built areas to accommodate both troops and friendly Lowlanders.

That the designs (for not all the plans referred to above are known to have been executed) were Italianate is once again only in part due to the continued employment of Italians. Though Archangelo Arcano, Giovanni di Rossetti and Gian Tommaso Scala were all active in the North (notably at Broughty, Holy Island, Tynemouth and Wark), they were only one element in a loose organisation headed by Sir Richard Lee as 'generall surveyour' of works and fortifications, which included such experienced English engineers as Petit and Ridgeway[2]. They were, moreover, working for an English command which was by now familiar with Italian conceptions in fortification, for several of its officers had served at Boulogne in 1544–6, notably William Lord Grey and Sir Thomas Palmer. The decisions were theirs, and they were in constant touch with Somerset, whose own prominence had been aided by his recent military commands: Lieutenant-general in the North early in 1544 and then service with Henry at the siege and taking of Boulogne; commissioner of fortifications in the Pale of Calais and subsequently Governor of Boulogne and, once more, Lieutenant-general in the North in 1545; back as Captain-general of Boulogne in 1546. Though his role in the actual design of fortifications was less direct than Henry's had been, it is not inappropriate to describe the works carried out in Scotland in 1547–8 as 'the Protector's device'.

Though the king in whose name the works of Somerset's device were carried out was only nine years old on his succession, his chronicle-journal reflects, as early as 1550, an interest in fortification inherited from Henry and probably fostered by the Protector. His report of Petit's commission for Calais and the Pale in 1550 is fully abreast of the current jargon about flankers and their function 'to beat' (i.e. cover) adjacent walls and projecting works. In 1552, when he was fifteen, an entry neatly sets out the procedure adopted before making decisions about defence works, in his father's reign as well as in his own: 'There were sent to Guines Sir Richard Cotton and Mr. Braye [Sir Edward Bray, Captain of Calais Castle] to take a view of Calais, Guines and the marches, and with advice of the captains and engineers to devise some amendment, and thereupon to make me certificate, and upon mine answer to go further into the matter.'[3] Later in the year he complained that the bulwarks at Portsmouth were 'il facioned, il flanked, and set in unmete places.'[4]

By then his interest had become academic in both senses of the word. In 1550 Somerset's political leadership was replaced by that of the Earl of Warwick, who was supported by his colleagues in the Council in settling the hostilities which had flared up in France in the previous year. By the treaty of Boulogne the French were left in possession of Ambleteuse, which they had captured, and the English surrendered

---

[1] *A.P.C.* ii, pp. 485–6.   [2] Below, pp. 698–702.
[3] *The Chronicle and Political Papers of King Edward VI*, ed. W. K. Jordan (1966), pp. 35, 104.
[4] Below, p. 513.

Boulogne itself. In a further reversal of Somerset's policy, garrisons were withdrawn from Scotland.

While both moves were designed to placate France they reflected the Crown's now desperate need to economize.[1] In February 1551, before the decision to withdraw from Scotland had been reached, the Council ruled that 'wheare there were a numbre of Bulwerkes and other fortresses upon the sea costes and other wheares within this realme whiche stoode the Kinges Majestie in very great chardges and in no service at all, nor coulde serve at any tyme to any purpose ... those whiche were superfluouse shulde be dischardged' and inquiries were to be made to this effect throughout southern England from Cornwall to Essex.[2] The reason given was that 'the Kinges ordonance was so dispersed for the furnyture of them that presently he hathe no ordonance for the felde.' This shortage of artillery was borne out by the meagre list of guns ordered in July 1549 to be prepared 'for the field'[3] and repeated a theme sounded in 1545 both with respect to the fleet, whose needs were in competition with the forts, for both guns and gunners, and to the army in the North where 'when the fortresses are furnished with the powder which was sent hither, little remains for the field.'[4] But if it was not only the expense of Somerset's legacy of 'sumptuous endles vayne Fortificacions'[5] that led to the desire to decommission some of them, this was certainly the main motive.

How many were actually decommissioned is uncertain. Another inquiry was ordered for Kent in May 1552[6] and it was not until the following year that the ordnance was withdrawn from seven bulwarks in Essex and shipped to the Tower.[7] In 1552 there were small cuts in garrisons in the west at Portland, Sandsfoot, St. Mawes, and Pendennis[8] but no work is mentioned as being disestablished. Indeed, in November 1553, soon after Mary's accession, the Council recorded that 'the Lord Treasourour hath taken uppon hym, with thadvise of other experte personages, to make an accompt of all the Queenes Blockehouses within the realme ... with a consideration and full reaporte whiche and howe many of the said Blockhouses be necessarie still to be reteyned, and whiche of them to be rased and utterly defaced.'[9] Again, no decisions suggest that this survey was actually carried out.

Financial retrenchment meant that nothing came of plans for fortifications in Ireland to forestall French intervention there in 1551[10], and little of the connected plans to improve the defences of the Scilly and Channel Islands. On St. Mary's Isle in Scilly the new fort begun in 1551, and almost identical with Lee's Berwick citadel, was abandoned half finished[11]. In Jersey, the churches were despoiled of their bells to pay for defence works[12], and in 1554 the Council resolved to urge Mary to consent that to save 'a mere gulfe of charges no purpose' the defences of Alderney

---

[1] See Dietz, *op. cit.*, p. 188 et seq.   [2] *A.P.C.* iii, p. 225.
[3] *Ibid.*, ii, pp. 301–2.   [4] *L. & P.* xx (1), 950, 1221.
[5] *Statutes of the Realm* iv (1819), p. 176. The preamble to this subsidy bill (7 Ed. VI c. 12) continues the indictment of Somerset's warlike policy by pointing out that 'no smalle sommes of treasure were ... waasted in Armies and Fortyfycations.'
[6] *A.P.C.* iv, p. 34.
[7] *Ibid.*, pp. 139–40, naming them, and 286. But it was not until October 1552 that Edward noted that the soldiers guarding them were discharged (*Chronicle, cit.* p.147).
[8] *A.P.C.* iv, pp. 33–4.   [9] *A.P.C.* iv, p. 369.   [10] Shelby, *op. cit.*, pp. 116–7.
[11] Below, pp. 588–9.   [12] *A.P.C.* iii, pp. 248–9.

'be utterly rased and defaced.'[1] It was in this year that Wotton met in Paris one of Henry's and Edward's Italians, the ex-captain of Sandown, Portinari; deprived of his post he had been forced by poverty to serve France 'one the fortifications in Piedmont' and begged to be re-employed lest he be made to serve in Scotland against his previous masters. Two years later he was still pressing his cause, telling Wotton that he had 'at length discovered how to make a fortification such as no battery shall be able to prevail against it, though there were 150 cannons continually beating upon it.'[2]

By then England had no need even of the little assistance Italians may have provided in the Italianising of new fortifications. In July 1550 Lee and Palmer were sent north to report on the Border defences. Specifically they were to select in Berwick a site that 'may both master the towne and kepe the haven', and have it staked out under the direction of the two most experienced of the Border surveyors, Thomas Gower and William Ridgeway.[3] The plans that evolved were for a square citadel in a thoroughgoing Italian style, with acute angled bastions at the corners and two-abreast flank batteries protected by substantial orillons. In the event, however, a compromise was worked out whereby only the western half of the citadel was retained to master the tówn while a new enceinte, comprising five full bastions, was designed to keep the haven and protect the eastern and northern land fronts, with a grasp of the geometrical logic of flank support surpassing that of the projects for Portsmouth initiated by Henry in 1545.[4]

These plans, too, suffered from the financial exigencies first of Edward's and then of Mary's reign, though the sum spent on getting the citadel ready for a garrison — between £16,000 and £17,000 — in 1551-2 and the amount allocated for the citadel and the new enceinte during the renewed fears of French intervention in 1556-8 — £12,000[5] — show the outstanding priority given to Berwick over all other fortified places. With plans unsigned and undated it is difficult to allocate the responsibility for projects whose lineaments only developed recognizably in Elizabeth's reign. But they suggest that Rogers (who was sent in November 1556 to urge on 'the newe fortificacions'[6]) and Lee (sent again to Berwick in January 1558[7]) worked harmoniously within a system that was now accepted as a norm for fortifications not built directly on a shore-line where, as we have seen (and as Lee's Upnor Castle of 1559 was to affirm), there were special reasons for not adopting the ideal Italian plan.

It is impossible to judge how far the ideas of English engineers and surveyors continued to be stimulated by their opposite numbers who worked with the French in Scotland both before and after Warwick's withdrawal, or by new fortifications at Dieppe[8] and in the area Pas-de-Calais — Hainault — Namur — Luxemburg that was still contested between Valois and Habsburg: Renty[9] and the frontier towns

---

[1] *A.P.C.* v, pp. 5-6.   [2] *Cal. S.P. For. 1553-8*, 196 (1), 470.
[3] *A.P.C.* iii, pp. 90-1.   [4] For Berwick, below, pp. 642 et seq.
[5] *S.P. Dom. Add. 1547-65*, p. 465.   [6] *A.P.C.* vi, p. 22.
[7] *Ibid.* pp. 245, 326, 393; *Cal. S.P. Dom. Add. 1547-65*, p. 467.
[8] Whence Sir John Masone reported in October 1550 that 'a fort is being erected ... which it is thought will cost 100,000 crowns before it is completed.' (*Cal. S.P. For. 1547-53*, 248).
[9] Projected by Charles in 1547 and still under construction in 1554 (*ibid.*, p. 34 and *1553-8*, 26 September 1554).

Marienbourg and Philippeville.[1] Certainly, Sir John Mason, writing in 1554 from the area's listening-post, Brussels (itself being re-fortified at the time) wrote scornfully of how the French have bragged of taking Dinant and Bouvines 'as if they had been two castles of Milan, and Got wot they were two very weak pieces builded altogether *à l'antiqua*, without any kind of such defences as are requisite for the wars now-a-days.'[2] All that can be said is that among the drawings at Belvoir Castle connected with the Scottish war of 1547–50 there is a design for an unidentified coastal fort that is based on the ideal fortified town plan of Italian inspiration and French and Imperial practice. It represents a symmetrical angle-bastioned citadel encompassed by a square bastioned enceinte containing regularly arranged blocks of barracks or other service buildings intersected by diagonal pathways leading from the citadel to the external bastions (Fig. 27).[3] Nothing of the sort was ever built in the British Isles. Nor did anything come of Rowland Johnson's plan of about 1560 to stamp a rigorously symmetrical enceinte over the wandering lines of Norham's medieval walls with a ruthlessness that went further than the projects for Portsmouth and Berwick.[4] All the same, by the accession of Queen Elizabeth the Italian system of fortification had at last been assimilated into English practice.

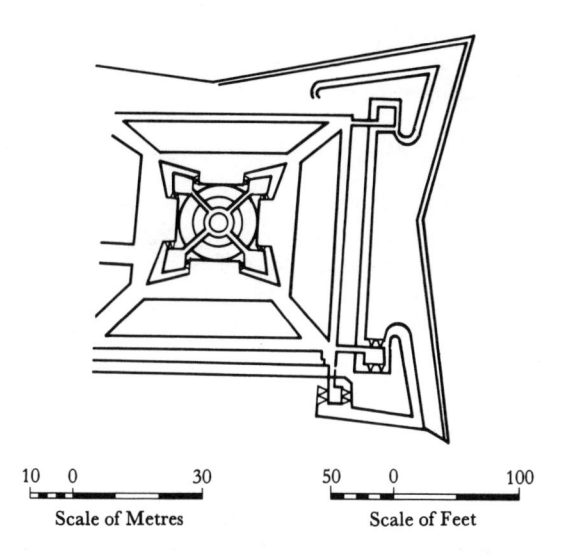

Fig. 27. Design for an unidentified Tudor fort in Scotland (redrawn from part of a damaged plan at Belvoir Castle).

---

[1] Lavedan, *op. cit.*, pp. 84–86.
[2] *Cal. S.P. For. 1553–8*, 253.
[3] Rutland MSS., Misc. MS. 36, map. no. 121. The scale is inscribed in English.
[4] Hatfield House plans, ii, no. 59 (O'Neil, *op. cit.*, plate 19c).

1

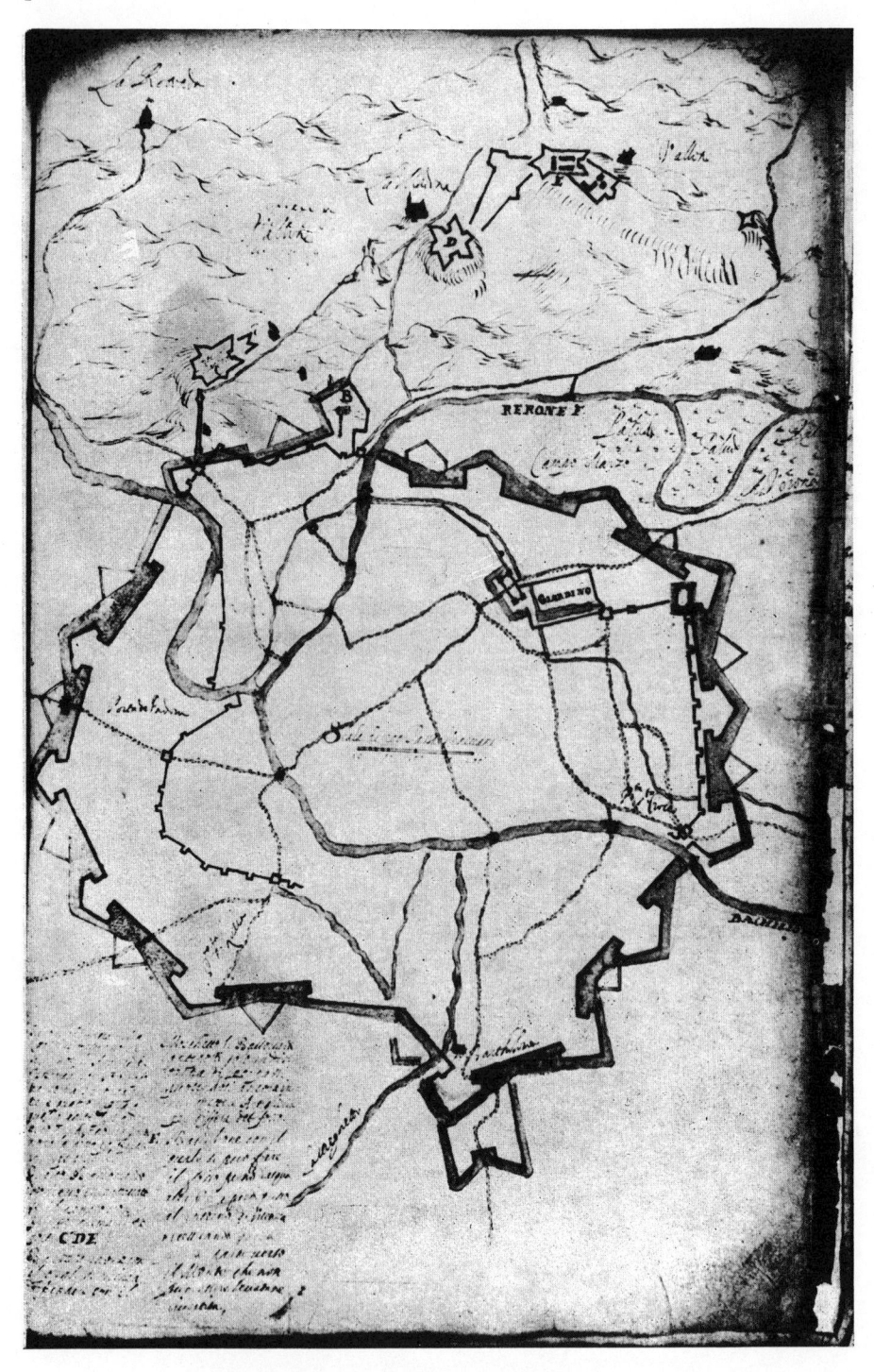

FRANCESCO TENSINI, *Plan of Vicenza, 1631.*
(Crema, Biblioteca Comunale, F. Tensini, *Trattato...*, c. 135 r).

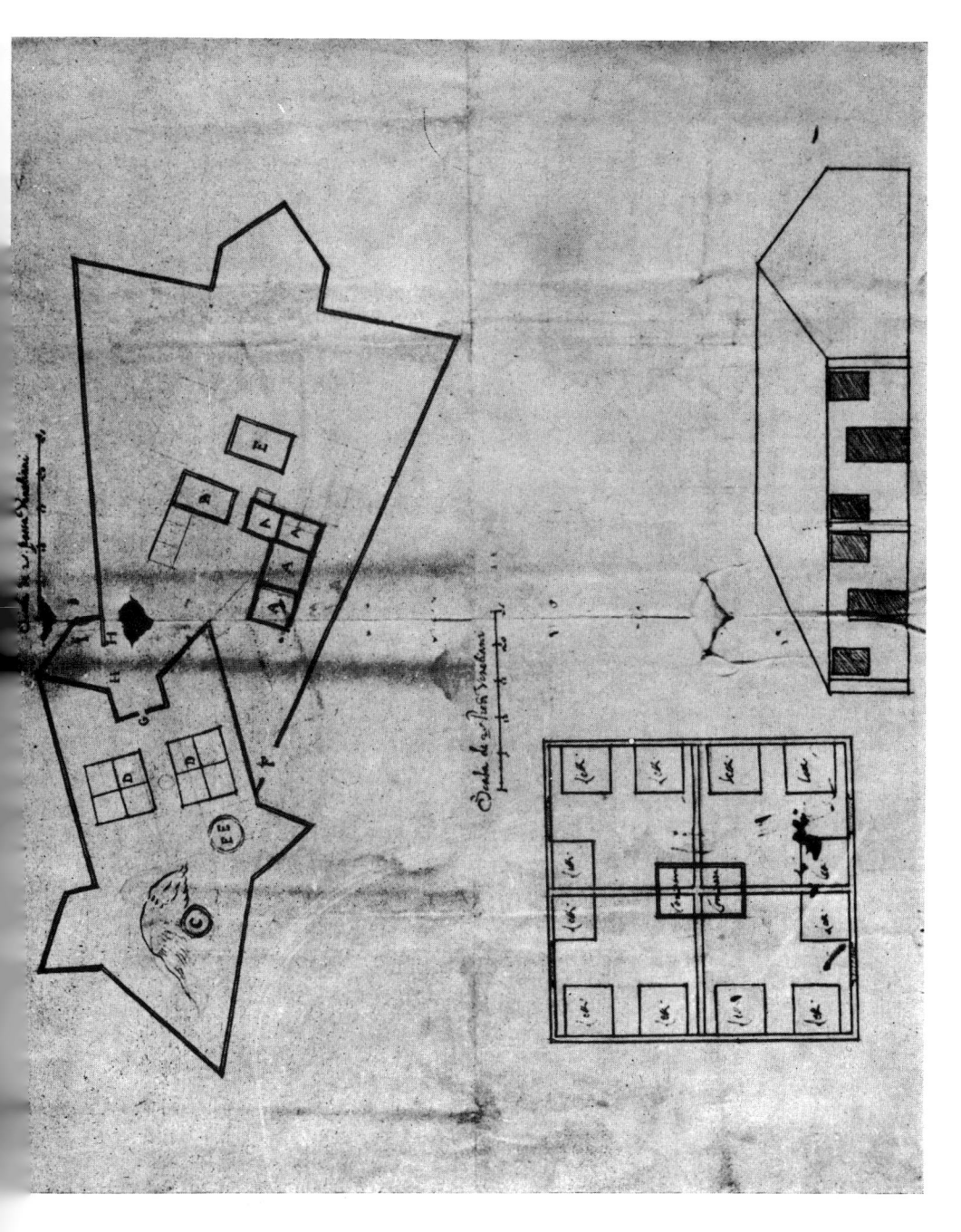

FRANCESCO TENSINI, *Plan of Fort Cornaro*
(A.S.V., *Senato Rettori. Dispacci Vicenza e Visentino*, f. 18, lett. october 8, 1630)
Key: AA Lodging for garrison of fifty; B Officers; C Munitions;
D Lodgings for additional one hundred horses; E Chief well;
EF Subsidiary well; F Main gate; G Connecting gate:
H,H Double flank

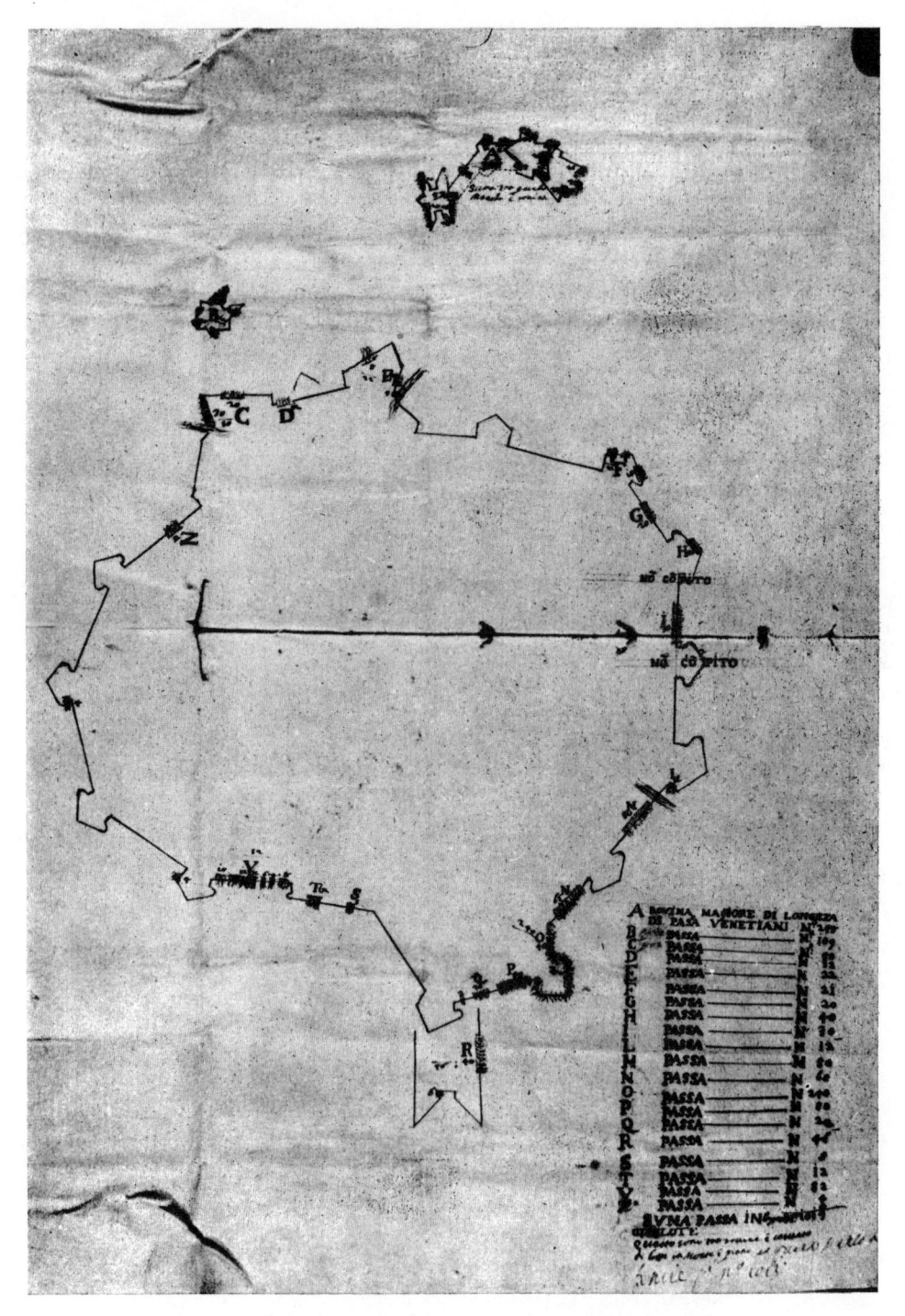

FRANCESCO TENSINI, *Plan of rain damage.*
(A.S.V., *Senato Rettori. Dispacci Vicenza e Visentino*, f. 18, lett. Jan. 14, 1631).

FRANCESCO TENSINI, BARBACANNONE
(*La fortificazione*, Venice 1624, plate 10).

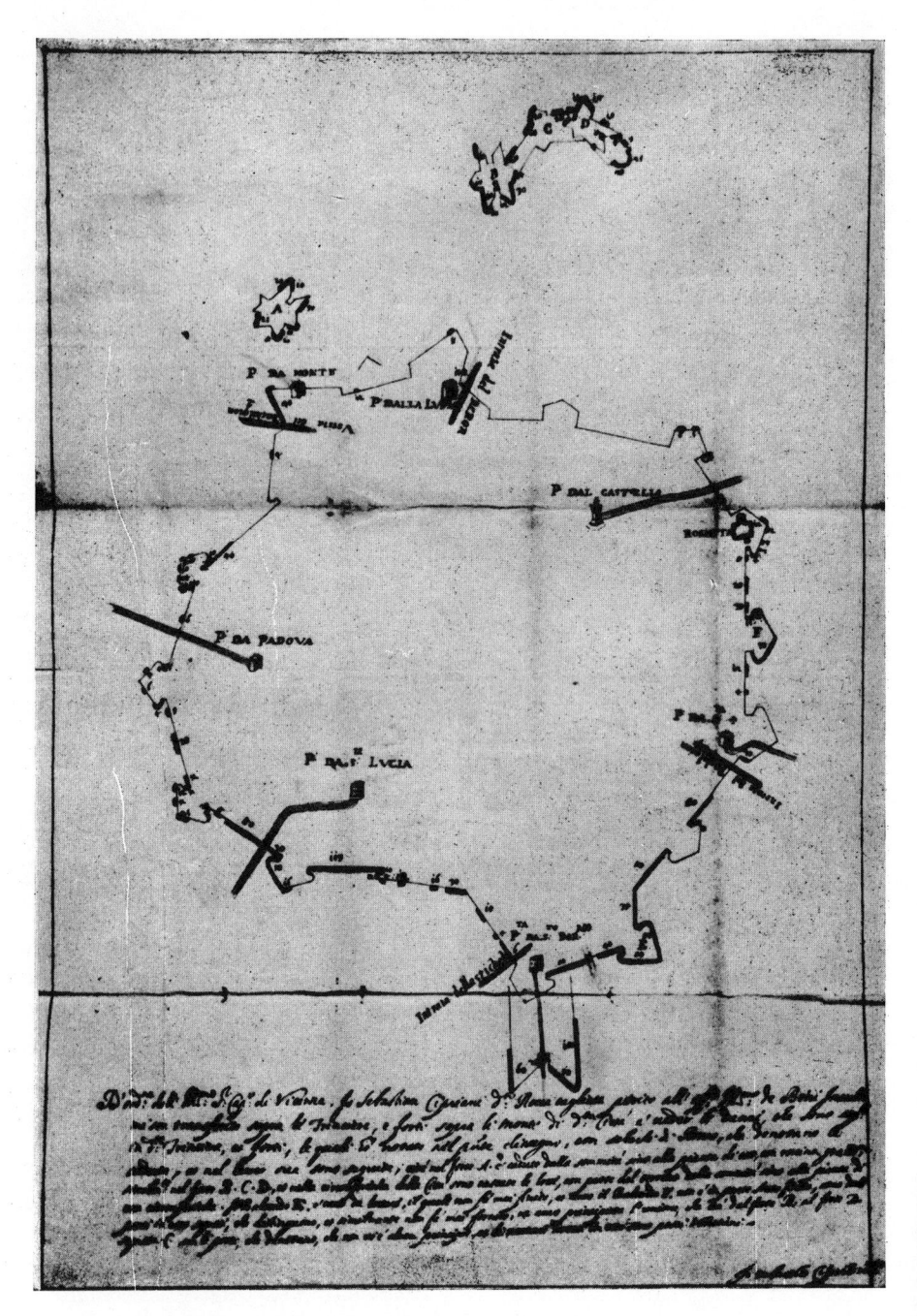

SEBASTIANO CIPRIANI, detto Roccatagliata, *Plan of rain damage.*
(A.S.V., *Senato Rettori. Dispacci Vicenza e Visentino*, f. 20, lett. Feb. 4, 1633).

4

FRANCESCO TENSINI
AND THE FORTIFICATION OF VICENZA*

At the extension of the War of the Mantuan Succession to the Veneto (September, 1629), Vicenza was alone among the important cities of the *terraferma* to be virtually defenceless. The work of modernising the fortifications of the mainland which had begun during the recovery from the wars of the League of Cambrai and had continued sporadically, but at immense cost, for a century, had left Vicenza protected only by two much-breached stretches of medieval wall, to east and west [plate 1], and by ditches clogged with refuse. Early in 1630 the Venetian government resolved to correct this omission by setting in motion one of the most grandiose public building operations in its history. Planned by Francesco Tensini, the most trusted and experienced of the Republic's engineers, the new fortifications, comprising a bastioned *enceinte* of five miles around the city and a complex of forts on Monte Berico, were almost completed within the year and awaited little more than their revetment. Yet within a generation these works had decayed, leaving so little trace on the ground or on maps that to remind the Vicentines of today that their city was once surrounded by one of the more impressive pre-Vaubanesque fortifications in Europe is to be met with unbelief.

The records are, however, copious, and because we lack detailed descriptions of the building of fortifications in this period I have treated this essay as a narrative, following closely, at times from day to day, the initial planning, the construction and the welter of conferences that attended the works' demise. This demise was due to a complex of causes, among them: the com-

---

* I should like to acknowledge the advice so unstintingly given to me while working in the Venetian Archivio di Stato by Dott. Paolo Selmi and the generous watchfulness of Professor Gaetano Cozzi. Neither, of course, is responsible for what errors may remain.

peting demands for manpower during the war; the devastating effect of the plague, which struck the Vicentino in July 1630; controversies among experts about the technical merits of Tensini's designs and between the Italian and French *capi di guerra* employed by the Venetians over expenditure on fortifications as against keeping armies in the field; and the opposition of powerful Vicentino families to a scheme imposed on them by the government in Venice. The narrative takes us, then, well beyond straightforward architectural history; it throws some illumination on the working of the command structure of the Venetian military machine and on the relations between Venice and one of the most important (and, from 1509, the most consistently cantankerous) of its mainland cities. Tensini, with his career in jeopardy, added to the physical causes which prevented the completion of the scheme – labour shortage, exceptional rains, his own absence on other duties for long periods – an accusation of treachery among certain members of the senate itself. With this attack on ' l'interessi di moltissimi gentiluomini Venetiani e senatori che hanno le lor possessioni nel Vicentino '[1] this study broadens to one of the crucial themes of Venetian history: the relations between the city and its *terraferma*.

The 1630 scheme was not the first attempt to strengthen the defences of Vicenza. In 1509 Bartolommeo Alviano, as Venetian governor general, seeing the city ' richissima, pomposissima, abbondantissima e piena di valorosa gente ' called up pioneers and ordered work to begin on an enlarged *enceinte* and on defensive works on Monte Berico. Little was done, and Luigi da Porto's letter makes it clear why; to fortify the city it was necessary ' rovi-

---

1. Crema, Biblioteca Comunale, FRANCESCO TENSINI, *Trattato sopra delle città e fortezze che possiede la Serenissima Signoria di Venetia in terraferma...*, f. 34r. I have to thank Dr. Gino Benzoni for sending me photographs of this ms. and inviting me to write about it. It is undated, but on internal evidence the Vicentine section (the longest) can be placed in mid-August to early September, 1631. It refers (see below, p. 147) to the *consulta* at Vicenza of August, 1631 and to Giustiniani as *capitano* of Vicenza; he was replaced by Zaccaria Mocenigo on Sept. 8. In quotations from documents capitalization, punctuation and dates have been modernized.

nare molte belle case, distruggere molti bei giardini e guastare molti bei campi vicini alle mura, e ... tagliare innumerabili gelsi ',[2] and the Vicentines did not want protection at such a price. The same complaints were to recur whenever the 'valorosa gente' were called on to adapt their city to the overall defensive strategy of the *terraferma*. Venice required a check to German armies which slipped past Verona. The Vicentines wanted neither the expenditure nor the destruction of property this would involve, nor, it would seem, did they welcome the loss of independence that would follow their being walled-in, as it were, to the strategic interests of the lagoons. Their equivocal stance with regard to Venice and the Empire, shown so clearly in 1509,[3] persisted until 1630 if Tensini is to be believed in his statement that his plans were sabotaged by certain Vicentines 'e de più principali, mossi dell'affettione che portano a casa d'Austria e del desiderio che hanno di retornare sotto al Imperio '.[4]

A second attempt, in 1528, this time based on plans drawn up by Francesco Maria della Rovere, duke of Urbino,[5] was similarly abortive. The city loudly protested against the expense and destruction of property that would be involved[6] and remained with its ditches choked and mostly dry, its walls part fallen, part incomplete and part holed 'a comodità de' privati'.[7] In 1544 Michele Sanmicheli was sent to inspect Vicenza and four years later submitted a report recommending ' che la se doveria fortificar, perchè essendo lei apperta da ogni banda, et vicina... al territorio di Trento, un esercito nemigo che s'annidasse dentro

---

2. *Lettere Storiche*, ed. B. BRESSAN (Florence 1857), p. 33. For the 'Alviano' fortifications, see also S. CASTELLINI, *Storia della Città di Vicenza* (13 vols., Vicenza 1783-1822), Lib. XVI, p. 13.
3. DA PORTO *op. cit. passim*.
4. Ms. cit., c. 31v.
5. Letter from Alvise [Luigi] da Porto to Agustin Abondio, 11 April, 1528, in SANUTO, *Diarii* (Venice 1879-1903), XLVII, col. 222-3, reprinted in G. BROGNOLIGO, *Studi di Storia Letteraria*, (Rome 1904), pp. 128-9.
6. Vicenza, Bertoliana, Archivio del Comune [V.B.C.], 160, 1, *passim*.
7. *Relatione del N. H. Ser Agostino Contarini podestà di Vicenza, 11 Aprile 1541*, (Nozze Rossi-Bozzotti, Venice 1877), p. 9.

metteria in confusione tutte le cose di Vostra Sublimità'. If Vicenza remained open, he continued, Venice would have to keep a large army hovering outside the city instead of a small garrison within it' and Venetian policy should be to deploy its troops along the *confini* – ' la qual cose è laudata da tutti i gran capitani '. Following the general lines of Alviano's and the duke of Urbino's projects, he suggested a new and extended *enceinte* of three miles (3000 *passi*), to consist of thirteen bastions with an extension to command Monte Berico. Such a system, he claimed, could be built by two thousand pioneers in four months and would be in the first instance of turfed earth, a method of construction (adopted by Tensini) which he defended vigorously as not only quick and cheap but, if properly supervised, durable.[8]

Thereafter, though the city spent an exiguous sum on ditch clearing in 1570 and ordered property owners to restore the ditch to ten feet wide and at least five feet deep in 1611,[9] on the eve of the Mantuan war Vicenza remained ' come aperta '.[10] In September 1629, when work was going forward on the fortifications of Crovara, Asola, Verona, Bergamo, Mantua, Sermione, Peschiera, Crema, Goito, Lonato, Legnago and Castel Gioffrè,[11] the defenceless state of Vicenza, so obviously a key point in any defense against the Imperialist thrust towards Mantua, was an anomaly too striking to ignore.

Nevertheless, it was not until November 18th that Francesco

---

8. *Del Fortificare Vicenza*, (Nozze Marzotto-Caotorta, Vicenza 1879), p. 12. Tensini deals briefly with earth construction in his *La fortificatione guardia difesa et espugnatore delle fortezze...*, (Venice 1624), cap. XXX, and concludes that though there are some advantages in using brick or stone, ' havendo buona terra, lotte, & acqua sortiva nel Fosso, per schifare la spesa, la farei di sola terra '. He will not give fuller directions, however, ' per non havere occasione di mostrarne una mia inventione, in questo particolare, con la quale si spendeva sempre [changed in ink in the Marciana copy from the erroneous ' prendera senza '] la mita meno di quello, che si fa lavorando all'ordinario; riservandola per servirmene alla prima occasione, che comporterà il palesarla. '

9. V.B.C., 160, 11.

10. Antonio Lando, *Sommario di tutte le città et fortezze di la da Menzo...*, Correr, Cicogna 2854, XXXVI, c. 188 v.

11. Venice, Archivio di Stato, [A.S.V.], *Senato, Dispacci, Provveditori da terra e da Mar* [P.T.M.], 74, *passim*.

Erizzo, *provveditore generale*, wrote to the doge announcing that in accordance with his orders, he was sending Tensini within a few days ' a rivedere tutto quello si potesse operare per la difesa di quella città '.[12] At the beginning of September a conference (*consulta*) had been held in Verona, presided over by Erizzo and attended by Zaccaria Sagredo, the *provveditori del lago* and *di Salò*, the *commissarii in terra ferma*, the commander of the artillery, Giorgio Martinengo, and by ten of the non-Venetian *capi di guerra* on whom the Venetians relied to do the actual fighting, headed by Prince Alvise d'Este and Count Ferdinando Scotto. Tensini, who that August had been working on the fortifications of Mantua at the request of the duke of Mantua himself,[13] was at this conference, which discussed the raising of troops and the state of fortifications throughout the *terraferma*. Erizzo's despatch of September 3rd does not reveal whether Vicenza were discussed or no, but clearly the sealing of the *confini* was the first preoccupation, and during the next two months the work on the frontier was held up by an unhappy series of illnesses among Venice's skeleton staff of engineers. On September 9th Erizzo reported that Tensini was ill and unable to join the duke of Mantua for a conference on the defences in the Mantovano. Bernardino Mariani was reported sick on September 13th and Giorgio Martinengo on the 17th. Bewailing this series of misfortunes Erizzo explained that ' these are the men who, with incessant labour and hardship, constantly hurrying from one spot to another to work on so many fortifications, have born the full weight of this emergency '. It was the same on September 28th; with three ' such important officers ' out of action, ' matters cannot but go slowly '. By October 10th the sick list included Niccolò Candido, and Erizzo was having to fortify the new headquarters camp at Valeggio without expert advice. On October 23rd Erizzo heard from

---

12. A.S.V., P.T.M., 74. Reference to dispatches will be by date: where the dating of a reference is indicated in the text it is not repeated in footnotes.
13. R. QUAZZA, *La guerra per la successione di Mantova e del Monferrato*, (2 vols., Mantua 1926) I, p. 130, fn. 1, and pp. 419-420.

Sagredo that yet another engineer, Antonio Sarti,[14] had gone on sick leave. Candido was getting up that day, but the only other engineers available for duty were Pompeo Targone, Giovanni Giacomo Marchese, Beato, Murmori and ' un Tedesco ',[15] and all were fully occupied on the *confini* except Beato, who had been sent to Valeggio, where the Venetian forces were already beginning to assemble.

Engineers were needed not only to strengthen frontier posts and improve the fortifications of the large towns from Bergamo to Palmanova but to travel with the armies in order to supervise their field fortifications. The planning of the new works at Vicenza must be seen against the background of a harrassed and over-stretched technical corps – and of demands constantly outrunning the supply of pioneers and cash. Erizzo wrote in panic on November 26th of the lack of men, money and time to prepare adequate defences ' in ogni sito, in ogni posto, ad ogni città et in ogni fortezza dello stato '.

When Tensini did return from recuperating in Crema, his home, he was sent not to Vicenza but to Castel Gioffrè; Goito had fallen on November 22nd and the relief road to Mantua (already under siege) lay open to imperialist reinforcements. He reported to Erizzo in Valeggio on the situation at Castel Gioffrè on November 29th; meanwhile Marcantonio Canal, *provveditore in Vicentino*, to whom, in the shortage of experts, the task of reporting on Vicenza had been referred, rode round the city on horseback and confirmed its vulnerability in a letter to the doge of November 28th, apologizing for his dilatoriness (he too had been ill) and proposing a modest and by no means specific programme of building and ditching works whose cost he estimated at no more than four thousand ducats.[16]

---

14. Author of *La reale et regolare fortificatione descritta in quesiti et risposte* (Venice 1630).

15. The first three were experienced men; Murmori had worked recently at Crovara. On Feb. 28th Sagredo referred to ' un tal Tedesco, il quale, non havendo la lingua nostrana, si crederia nel resto ben atto e sofficiente.' A.S.V., P.T.M., 76.

16. A.S.V., *Secreta, Materie Miste Notabili* [M.M.N.], 144 olim: Misc. Cod. 355. This volume, important to this article, was drawn to my attention by Contessina Maria

Tensini was to be sent to follow up this report, but not immediately. Senior engineers at this time were not mere construction experts; Tensini himself, in an unpublished work of 1618, had (understandably enough, as he had only entered the Venetian service two years previously[17]) stressed the importance to a ruler of engineers who not only know fortifications by the book but whose experience enabled them to give advice on the broader strategic issues of siege or defence.[18] Erizzo held a conference at Valeggio on December Ist which decided that the risks involved in raising the siege of Mantua were too great and that attempts should be made instead to introduce reinforcements. Among the ' capi... soliti a chiamarsi in affari simili ' were Tensini and Candido. On December 4th the senate wrote in reply to a report on Legnago from its *provveditore* Basadonna that they would send an expert to help him and on the same day told Erizzo to send ' Tensini o Candido ' to Vicenza, ' restandoci pur a cuore il veder assicurata Vicenza, del tutto aperta '.

Erizzo had already sent Tensini to help the *provveditore di Verona e Veronese*, Michiel Priuli, in preparing the defenses of Verona and dispatched Candido to Legnago, and though he notified the doge that he would get Tensini to visit Vicenza, the needs of Verona were paramount. Verona was still Erizzo's chief preoccupation towards the end of the month, when Tensini drew up the plans decided on after an inspection by him, Priuli, the *capitano* of Verona, Cosimo del Monte, Benedetto Spinola and Martinengo,[19] but on January 1st, 1630, Tensini

Francesca Tiepolo. It contains correspondence and reports (but no plans) relating to the fortifications of Vicenza, and is referred to in A.S.V. *Senato, Rettori, Deliberazioni*, Registri, [S.R.D.R.], 2, c. 42r, under the date May lst, 1631, as ' un libro legato in materia di queste fortificationi '. References in this article to Senato, Registri, are to the *old* folio numbers in ink, and not the new ones in pencil.

17. A.S.V. *Senato, Deliberazioni, Secreta*, Registri [S.D.S.R.], 108, c. 225r.
18. *Relatione...*, Marciana, mss. It., 9557, 29. f. 3v. This ms. is dedicated to Francesco Errizo.
19. A.S.V., *Senato, Dispacci Rettori, Verona*, 27, Dec. 26. Martinengo, as responsible for the supply and placing of artillery was a key member of such conferences. About del Monte's previous career I know nothing. Spinola entered the Venetian

wrote to Erizzo that he, Martinengo, and Spinola, joined by Antoine de Ville,[20] Canal and the *podestà* of Vicenza, Giovanni Grimani, had at last examined the possibilities of fortifying Vicenza.[21] His report referred to a coloured map (now lost) and quoted a figure of 6,000 ducats to patch up the walls, clear and extend the ditch and thus give some protection from raids. This covers the brief Erizzo had received from the senate, which had asked for an opinion of how best ' assicurar quella città dal pericolo almeno delle incursioni '.[22] But Tensini went much further. Pointing out the strategic importance of Vicenza, which could be used by an enemy to split the *terraferma* into two halves, he suggested diverting the river to create a wet ditch, building three small forts on the Monte and constructing a new *enceinte* of *tenailles* and demilunes[23] backed by a stoutly terrepleined rampart. He rejected the idea of strengthening the northern side of the city (from which an attack in force might be expected to come) with a citadel because though this would serve ' per tener in freno il popolo ' it would not add to the role better played by the forts on Monte Berico; he proposed a large detatched *tenaille* beyond Porta S. Bartolomeo instead. The whole operation would require 2,000 pioneers for four months and would cost, he reckoned, 60,000 ducats. Erizzo, passing on this opinion to the doge on the 4th, also stressed the strategic importance of the city, its vulnerability to an attack from Germany – as had been shown ' in altro tempo ', i.e., in 1509 – and its cash value to Venice: 300,000 ducats a year. Much of this came from taxes levied on goods entering the gates, and Erizzo poin-

---

service in February 1629 (A.S.V., *Senato, Deliberazioni, Terra,* Registri [S.D.T.R.], 102). Like Tensini, he had seen service in Flanders and central Europe.

20. Author of *Les Fortifications* (Lyons 1628) and *De la charge des gouverneurs des places...* (Paris 1639). His major work in Italy was the refashioning of the *castello* of Pola, 1630-2.

21. A.S.V., M.M.N., 144.

22. A.S.V., S.D.S.R., 133, 41v, Dec. 14th.

23. A *tenaille* was an M-shaped outwork, a demilune a triangular one, Tensini describes and illustrates them in caps. XXVII and XXVI of the first book of his *Fortificatione...* (1624).

ted out that to close the fortifications would stop the lively smuggling that took place through gaps in the walls.[24] It can be seen from this first investigation that there would be opposition from the citizens: loopholes in *dazii* payments would be closed, there would be (Tensini drew attention to this) destruction of property, and the city would be subject to the control if not of a citadel, at least of the forts on Monte Berico. The thorny question of financial contributions had not yet been raised.

The senate acted with untoward promptness. On January 8th dispatches were sent to Erizzo telling him to set in motion ' con ogni prontezza et sollecitudine ' plans for defending Vicenza not only against mere raids, but whole armies; to Priuli bidding him transfer himself to Vicenza to explain the decision and see it implemented; and to the *rettori* of Vicenza preparing them for Priuli's coming. It is difficult to explain this sense of urgency, and the extension of the Senate's earlier design, without turning to Castellini, the contemporary historian of Vicenza. He says that certain captured German soldiers had given information, ' finta o vera ' that the Imperial commanders were determined to broaden their aims from the seizing of Mantua to a general attack ' contra lo stato Veneziano, e spezialmente contro Vicenza ', and this explains why ' i Veneziani prendessero subito la deliberatione di fortificare la città '.[25]

Priuli had the unenviable task of pointing out to the Vicentines that they would have to raise the greater part of the money. He was to explain to the *deputati* and then to the council of 150 that the senate had taken this decision not only to defend them, but to ensure that their sons would be able to live in security; surely they could be expected to pay for so precious a boon. In presenting the senate's case Priuli was to use all his dexterity.[26] He would need it.

He reached Vicenza on the 14th (Tensini should have been

24. A.S.V., M.M.N., 144.
25. *Op. cit.*, lib. xix, p. 210.
26. A.S.V., S.D.S.R., 133, cc. 128r-v.

there to help him but was laid up by a fall from his horse[27]) and found that rumour had come before him. At a hasty *consulta* between the *deputati*, the council and some of the leading citizens it had been decided to send a deputation to the doge before his representative had had a hearing and in defiance of the prohibition of the *podestà*. The council met again on the 14th and answered Priuli's appeals to their well known generosity and nobility of spirit with pleas of poverty and the argument that they had already helped the war effort to the tune of 60,000 ducats: 24,000 as a donative on September 6th, and 36,000 towards the cost of transport for the army. They also pointed to the destruction of property that would ensue. Priuli reported this meeting with the convinction that his arguments ('dolci e lusinghiere parole', as Castellini put it) had done no good at all.[28] He was also hampered by the fact that he had no engineer to advise him and no plan, indeed no 'lume della volontà publica'.[29] This appeal crossed with a senate dispatch saying that Erizzo had been told to send an engineer who was to proceed at once with staking out the trace of the new fortifications; when work had started, Priuli was to hand over its supervision to Canal and return to Verona.[30] Erizzo, too, was acting as though the goodwill of the Vicentines had already been obtained. On January 16th he held a conference at Valeggio attended by Martinengo, Spinola, Tensini (brought in a litter because of his injury) and others which decided to proceed at once with diverting the rivers into the ditches, fortifying Monte Berico and constructing a strong point at Porta S. Bartolomeo; a new *enceinte* could then be completed at leisure. Tensini was to get the work started and Spinola to keep a professional eye on its progress. But Erizzo pointed out that everything depended on money being forthcoming.[31] Priuli

27. A.S.V., P.T.M., 74, Jan. 13th.
28. A.S.V., M.M.N., 144, Jan. 15th.
29. Ib., Jan. 16.
30. A.S.V., S.D.S.R., 133, c. 141v.
31. A.S.V., P.T.M., 74.

can hardly have been comforted by the senate's belief, expressed in a letter of the 17th, that the objections to voting money were merely the voices of certain 'interessati' who would certainly be won over by a sense of public duty, nor by the fact that the senate had decided that the costs were to be born by the Venetian government, the city of Vicenza and its *territorio* in equal thirds, and that he was to explain that the initial instalments of 6,000 ducats each would be due on February 1st.

Tensini arrived on January 23rd. Three days previously the council had confirmed, by one hundred votes to one, the proposal of the *deputati* to elect four *oratori* to put their case to the doge, and this in spite of Priuli's efforts to dissuade them. The *territorio*, too, expressed alarm in a petition to the doge drawn up on the 23rd. It was a vivid piece of writing. The 'poveri, estenuatissimi sudditi' of the *territorio* pleaded that in these difficult times, when they had already had to contribute so much money and so many men as soldiers and pioneers, it was 'assolutamente impossibile' that they could find the payment 'senza l'ultima rovina et total desolatione'. Besides, as they pointed out in terms that would hardly have commended themselves to their colleagues in the city council, the *territorio* had been, as far back as 1518, 'in stato molto florido', retaining two thirds of its own produce. In 1564, however, this had been reduced to one quarter, and now it had declined to one tenth, 'essendo tolto il restante de beni passato nella Magnifica città, che sopra la miseria de' contadini ha stabilita la sua grandezza et opulenza'. They concluded by claiming – erroneously[32] – that in all other cases when similar

32. The fortifications proposed for Vicenza itself in 1528-9 were to have been paid for on the thirds basis - the *capitano* of the city showed Priuli the senate's order of Dec. 26, 1529. (A.S.V., M.M.N., 144, Jan. 16). On Dec. 17th 1629 the same apportionment was enforced for improvements in the fortifications of Udine. (A.S.V., S.D.S.R., 133, c. 68r). On the other hand, the Vicentine *territorio* had been charged 290 ducats a month towards the works at Legnago in 1527 and were still paying in 1577! (A.S.V., *Provveditori alle Fortezze*, 36, 1, May 24), and money was raised, eg., from Asola, for the building of Palmanova in 1594. (ib., 36, 4, Nov. 23.) Legnago, a poor town, and Palmanova, a new one, were special cases. A good parallel is the case of Bergamo in 1575, when the *territorio* did contribute. (Prov. Fort. 36, 1, Nov. 8.)

fortifications had to be built, the cost had been spread over the whole *terraferma* in recognition that the works were for the common good; could the same not be done for the fortifications of Vicenza?[33]

Two days later, however, the council of 150 agreed[34] (by 66 votes to 21) to produce the 6,000 ducats,[35] and the council of the *territorio* decided that evening to follow suit. Priuli implied that this was due to his own wearing down of the opposition, and that he had not been untouched by the citizens' arguments is implied by the terms in which, on the eve of his departure for Verona, he forwarded the council's own petition – ' degno d'ogni pieno riflesso ' – to the doge.

The *territorio*'s petition had stressed the sorry economic state of the countryside; the *consiglio*'s dwelled on the damage to civic property that would be caused by Tensini's ' imperfetto disegno '. Building ramparts behind the city walls to make them canon-proof would involve the destruction of ' undici monasterii ripieni di virgini nobili ' and three great religious houses for men. Creating a glacis and building outworks – the *tenailles* and demilunes – would wreck havoc in the suburbs (for Tensini's *enceinte* was based on that of the medieval walls) and would leave part of the large *borghi* that had grown up, especially to the east, unprotected. It would be sad, the petition pointed out, if protection had to be bought at the price of desolation, if great sums were called for at a time when large numbers of tax-payers would be driven away by the ruin of their homes, and if, in the cause of the safety of the city and its *territorio*, an *enceinte* were proposed too small to contain the refugees from an emergency. If not without self interest, it was a shrewd document, worthy, indeed, of mature consideration.[36] And this it received; the final plans were not to be approved until early in April.

33. A.S.V., M.M.N., 144.
34. V.B.C., 869 (Parti, 1630-1644), and A.S.V., M.M.N., 144, Jan. 25.
35. To be borrowed on the security of the *estimo*.
36. A.S.V., M.M.N., 144, Jan. 26.

On January 29th Canal was ordered to report, with an explanatory drawing, on the destruction to property that would be involved were Tensini's plan to be implemented. Tensini himself was in Mantua, following repeated requests for his presence from the duke, and Candido, the only suitable engineer within reach, was discounted because he had not been present at the *consulta* and might produce contradictory plans. Matters were further confused by Erizzo's begging to be relieved ' doppo 22 mesi di incessanti et intollerabile fatiche ' and his replacement by Sagredo on February 1st,[37] but the senate's pressure was maintained. The *provveditori alle fortezze* were ordered to send five hundred wheelbarrows, and Spinola, with the command of two companies of cavalry, was deputed to prepare the report with the aid of a local surveyor. Work was meanwhile to begin on the Monte, on stopping up breaches in the walls and on temporary defences in the wide gap between the gates of S. Lucia and S. Croce.[38] On February 11th, to the sound of trumpets, Canal posted a proclamation in the *loggia del Capitanio* ordering the owners concerned to restore the walls to their original state on pain of a 500 ducat fine (to go towards the fortifications), or prison, the galleys or death.[39]

On the same day Tensini returned to Verona from Mantua and wrote on the 12th to Girolemo Roccatagliata, *agrimensore* – the surveyor used by Canal – in Vicenza to say that he had been thinking over the fortifications and had formed a rough plan which would not only include the suburbs but make the whole scheme ' four times stronger than the original one '. To push this through, however, it was necessary that the city should back it and send him to explain it to the doge.[40] In fact on April 5th Tensini's new scheme was approved, and on the 8th he was granted a contract for the whole operation, but his success was

37. A.S.V., P.T.M., 75.
38. A.S.V., S.D.S.R., 133, cc. 179r, 180r, 198r-199r.
39. V.B.C., 160, 6.
40. Ib. Autograph.

gained in the teeth of prolonged opposition from the city, and a long debate between him and rival planners. Castellini casts him as the villain of this interim period (together with Spinola and the Vicentine noble Francesco Caldogno), as intriguing, with a fat contract in mind, to prevent the Venetian government from paying sympathetic attention to the objections raised in Vicenza.[41]

Spinola was named because on February 20th his report[42] to the doge effectively undermined the Vicentine argument, drawn up by Scipione Ferramosca, based on destruction to property. Together with the *rettori* he had visited the eleven nunneries and three monasteries named by Ferramosca and showed that the damage to be incurred in the city – mostly to gardens, outbuildings, dovecotes and the like – would be unimportant. He was scathing about Ferramosca's second category: property and churches in the suburbs, pointing out that many of the threatened houses were small and old, 'more suited to horses than to men' and that according to the neighbours one of the churches was not even used for divine service. He had started full of compassion, he said, but having now checked Ferramosca's claims he was convinced that the 'destruction' argument was purely factious; the people as a whole wanted the fortifications, so did some of the nobles, the rest opposed them because of 'the expense, the presence of soldiers who would bring them to their senses and make them obedient instead of walking about bristling with guns', and because they would no longer be able to slip in and out of the town by night, thus defrauding the customs posts.

If the Vicentines saw Tensini as an enemy because he was a professional putting his own trade before the interests of the city, they saw Spinola as a representative of the traditional contempt of the military for free institutions. In his eyes, Vicenza needed fortifying because it was 'non solita alle guarnigione ne a capi

---

41. *Op. cit.*, lib. xix, p. 213.
42. A.S.V., M.M.N., 144.

di guerra per disciplinar i popoli'. It is not surprising that the party represented by Ferramosca and Castellini saw the issue as a crisis in the relationship between Venice and her subjects on the *terraferma*.

In an appendix to his report Spinola reaffirmed his faith in the policy determined at the Valeggio *consulta*: a minimum of work on the walls and a dependence on a fortified Monte, plus the turning of the old *rochetta* which abutted on to the city wall to the south west into an effective citadel. Tensini, on the other hand, in a report dated February 21st,[43] developed his idea for an *enceinte* of thirteen bastions ' al mio modo ', each connected to the next by a *barbacannone*,[44] as an improvement on his earlier idea of a smaller circuit of *tenailles* and demilunes. He enclosed a plan and profile (lost) and estimated that, together with three forts on the Monte, the cost would be 100,000 *scudi* for ' the finest fortress that your serenity would possess '. With two thousand pioneers he claimed that he could bring the fortifications to a state of defence effective against cannon in three months and finish them within a year. He made a direct bid for the contract and suggested that it should be based on the costings used for Mariani's contract for Verona.

Both men argued their case before the *collegio* on the 26th, and, according to Tensini,[45] Spinola allowed himself to be won over. Another plan, for forts on the Monte *plus* strengthened walls *plus* citadel had been submitted by de Ville.[46] Tensini repeated his point that while a citadel would serve ' per tener in freno il popolo ' this purpose would be served equally by forts on the Monte, and that a citadel, without a bastioned *enceinte*,

---

43. Ib.
44. A long, thin defence work, lower than the counterscarp, built between the curtain and the ditch, and designed to give fire support to the flanks and faces of adjacent bastions. V. note 163 and plate 4.
45. Crema, ms. cit., c. 27v.
46. Known only from Tensini's autograph attack on it in A.S.V., M.M.N., 144, Feb. 26. De Ville's ' citadella ' was to have been ' tra la chiesa di S. Francesco e le convertite '.

would not prevent an enemy from ravaging the suburbs or even part of the city itself, ' che saria al contrario del intention publica, che e di conservar li suoi subditi '. The citadel element in Spinola's and de Ville's plans clearly made them politically unacceptable at this point to a senate which contained spokesmen for the Vicentine point of view, and this must explain Spinola's own support for Tensini, whose revised project, though elaborate, combined a maximum of protection with a minimum of damage and retained an element of control from the Monte which could be represented to the Vicentines as being designed to command not the city but its potential assailants. No plan to fortify Vicenza could avoid the stigma of tighter control from Venice, however, and on March 2nd the senate ordered Canal to draft troops into the city ' in modo che non possino nascer disordini ', to take over the command of horse and foot himself and to entrust the keys of the city to the *capitano*[47] – keys that would be useless until some form of circuit were locked in place.

Encouraged by the discussion in the *collegio*, Tensini drew up a formal proposal on March 3rd for the three forts and the *enceinte* of thirteen bastions.[48] He repeated his undertaking to get the fortifications into a state of defence in three months and to complete them within a year were he given the necessary materials, tools, transport, pioneers and adequate administrative and judicial control over the whole operation. His offer now stood at 107,000 *scudi* and he declared himself ready to sign an agreement on these lines as soon as he had refined his drawings on the site.

This was to go too fast. With characteristic caution the senate on March 4th determined to order only the construction of the three forts on the Monte, ' restando da consigliarsi sopra il corpo maggiore della fortificatione per la totale sicurezza della città '. To assist them in coming to an opinion on the *enceinte* they ordered the election of ' tre signorevoli nobili nostri con titolo di

47. A.S.V., *Senato, Deliberazioni, Terra,* Filze [S.D.T.F.].
48. A.S.V., M.M.N., 144.

Provveditori Generali' who were within eight days to go to Vicenza to discuss the whole matter with Tensini, Spinola and any other experts whose opinions they might wish to invite. After mature discussions with the *rettori* and Canal they were to return either with a joint report or a series of personal recommendations. They were to receive twelve ducats a day for their expenses and were to take with them a secretary from the ducal chancery.[49] Tensini and Spinola were ordered on the same day to leave Venice and begin work on the forts.[50]

On receipt of this news Canal, who had set four hundred pioneers digging ditches in the large gap between the walls on the north side of the city, suspended operations until the two men should arrive,[51] and the council of 150 hastily elected six *oratori* to greet the *provveditori*. One of them was Scipione Ferramosca.[52]

The *provveditori* were named on March 9th: Geronimo Corner, Simeon Contarini and Antonio Barbaro, and Sagredo was asked to send Martinengo to meet them in Vicenza.[53] Meanwhile, in the wake of Tensini's arrival on the 10th,[54] two proclamations were issued by Canal. One forbad the breaking of ground – 'nissun imaginabilmente eccettuato' – within two miles of the city's boundaries in order to conserve the supply of turf for facing whatever fortifications were made, and the other provided for the striking of lead tokens to serve as a special temporary coinage for the 'poveri che lavorano nelli forti sopra il monte Berico.'[55] And because Canal was still responsible for the Vicentino as a whole and therefore had to be mobile, Spinola was made 'generale dell'armi in Vicenza', ranking immediately below the *ret-*

---

49. A.S.V., M.M.N., 144.
50. A.S.V., S.D.T.F.
51. A.S.V., *Senato, Dispacci di Rettori, Vicenza* [D.R.V.], 18, 1630, Mar. 4 and 7. There is no volume for 1629, possibly because so much of the material was diverted into A.S.V., M.M.N., 144.
52. V.B.C., 869, March 7.
53. A.S.V., S.D.S.R., 134, 20v.
54. A.S.V., D.R.V., 18.
55. V.B.C., 160, 6, Mar. 12 and 14. See Appendix I.

tori, according – as the senate patent tactfully pointed out – to precedents accepted in other principal cities of the *terraferma*, Crema, Brescia, Bergamo and Verona among them.[56] Order was also given that all Vicentine citizens who were living elsewhere should return to their homes at once.[57]

A flood of opinions, verbal and written, began soon after the arrival of the *provveditori* on the 14th.[58] The first, on March 18th, came from a Vicentine, Ottavio Bruto Revese. He declared himself a ' large circuit ' man for three reasons: Vicenza should be secured against full-scale attacks as well as raids; the principles of modern fortification demanded a bastioned *enceinte*; and the larger it was the less damage to property it would cause. He submitted a design for an *enceinte* of seventeen bastions which would include the suburbs of Casale, Padua and S. Lucia and part of the buildings beyond the Castello gate. In the light of later criticisms levelled against the excessive length of Tensini's curtain walls, Revese's explanation of his choice of seventeen bastions is of some interest. He says he originally decided on twelve, but found that this would make the space between them 200 *passi*, ' which contradicts the good rules of the best modern writers, according to which the distance should be about 130 from the flank of one bastion to the outer angle (' angolo della contrascarpa ') of the next '; the defence of one bastion from another, he explained, depends on frequency of fire rather than the weight of single projectiles, and 200 *passi* is too far for accurate quick fire either from muskets or small pieces of artillery charged with

56. A.S.V., S.D.T.F., Mar. 14.
57. According to Castellini, *op. cit.*, lib. xix, p. 214. It is the same author who gives March 14 as the date of arrival of the *provveditori*.
58. A.S.V., M.M.N., 144. Revese's has been printed in A. Mogrini, *Scritture inedite in materia d'architettura di Onorio Belli, Ottavio Bruto Orifeci, Ottone Calderari* (Padua, 1847, Nozze Zanella-Turra), pp. 29-42. ' Ottavio-Bruto Revese, nell'anno 1606 leggeva filosofia nell'Olimpica Accademia; nel 1620 publicava un disegno della scena del Teatro Olimpico. ' Barichella, Vittorio, ' Vicenza difesa dalla Republica di Venezia ', *Corriere del Brento*, I, 1865 - [1866. But I have been unable to find this volume. 1865 is in the Bertoliana]. Barichella is, to my knowlegde, the only writer to have paid serious attention to Tensini's fortifications at Vicenza. All the proposals refer to plans, none of which has, so far as I know, survived.

grapeshot. The *deputati* replied to this enemy from within by submitting to the *provveditori* a long-winded and pathos-laden plea to be released from the financial burden *any* large-scale plan would involve.

The next opinions came from Canal, Camillo Valle, Roccatagliata, Martinengo and Spinola, all argued before the *provveditori* on March 22nd and 23rd. Martinengo began by setting out the three alternatives which had been put forward. One, to complete the existing *enceinte* and supplement it with sixteen or seventeen *tenailles* or demilunes. Two, to build a large *enceinte* that would include the suburbs; this, with sixteen *baloardi reali* would be of about the same total circumferences as the former, because bastions do not extend outwards so far as do *tenailles* and demilunes. Three, to build a rampart to fill the gap between S. Lucia and S. Bartolomeo, mend the walls, clear out the ditches and flood them by diverting water from the Bacchiglione, Rerone and Seriola rivers. He then ruled out one and two on grounds of time, pointing out how long it was taking to get the camp at Valeggio fortified, and not even then to proof against cannon, and to the èxample of Nicosia, ' which, being begun as an *enceinte* of eleven bastions and not completed, was of more service to the Turks than to us. ' He ruled them out too on grounds of expense, instancing the ' immense cost ' of Palmanova and concluding that it would cost less to keep six infantry regiments in the field each year ' con assai meno incomodo del stato. ' So the third alternative should be preferred, coupling with it, of course, the forts on Monte Berico which were essential to all these projects, and adding – on lines discussed at Valeggio – a strong point at Porta S. Bartolomeo capable of being developed at some later time into a proper citadel. Canal also recommended sticking to the original plan of the Valeggio *consulta* on grounds of time and expense, though he added in a postscript that were time no object, then he would support Tensini's designs. Spinola's submission was curiously indefinite. Starting with the premise that the doge had to decide between giving his daughter a ' marito vecchio ' (the old circuit) or ' giovane ' (enlarged circuit), he praised Tensini's plan as being 'pui secondo la grandezza dell'animo di Vostra Serenità', doubted whether it could be achieved with the money or in the time proposed but, assuming Tensini to have calculated accurately and 'non esser pazzo', he would give it his support. His conclusion, however, was that it would in fact be better to start with the Monte forts and with a citadel of five bastions at S. Bartolomeo.

Praise for Tensini came less equivocally from Camillo Valle, Venetian *fiscal di camera* in Vicenza. This is probably because of his reading, for Valle's proposal has the effect of light relief, so clearly does the picture emerge of the armchair expert delighting in the harmonious geometrical forms of the text books and thrilled with the opportunity to put his learning into practice. The *enceinte*, he said, should form a perfect circle with fifteen equally spaced bastions, thus obeying the canons of the profession and 'appearing beautiful to the eye.' If the bastions proved to be too far apart, then in time of war (what was it, if not that?) demilunes could be inserted between them; what is more, money could be saved by digging the ditches to only half their proper depth in the first instance. Finally, calling to mind, no doubt, his true avocation, he claimed sternly that the cost must be spread over the whole *terraferma* and not borne by Vicenza alone with its *territorio*, already 'essaustissimi et debolissimi.' Roccatagliata supported Tensini's plans as an ideal, but suggested that the Valeggio plan should be proceded with so long as the S. Bartolomeo strong-point were such that it could be incorporated readily into Tensini's *enceinte* were that to be built later. Canal and Martinengo were recalled for further discussions. Canal stuck to his original opinion. Martinengo was asked which – time and money permitting – he would prefer of his first and second alternatives. He chose the second because the larger circuit would produce a more regular shape with more obtuse (and therefore stronger) bastions and, above all, because it would lead to least damage to property both immediately behind the city wall and in the suburbs.

All these spokesmen had discussed the forts on the mountain: how many, and where, and how large they should be. Valle made the only non-technical point, arguing for one large fort rather than several small ones on the ground that the morale of small garrisons easily cracked under pressure and that this would lead them to surrender.

It would be disingenuous to suggest that the *provveditori* were influenced towards the number three because the forts were to be called after them, but Tensini, in his own evidence submitted on March 24th, was already calling them forts Cornaro, Contarini and Barbaro. He exuded confidence, picking holes in his original scheme for an *enceinte* based on the old circuit with disarming brio. It would have cost 70,000 ducats and still have been ' campale et di non molta resistenza ' because the old wall, even with an earth embankment behind it, would not be as strong as a properly constructed curtain. Much property would have been destroyed and the outworks (the *tenailles* and demilunes) would have presented too sharp an angle to stand up to enemy fire. No, the best circuit would be one of fifteen bastions (including two more than in his proposal of March 3rd, to reach into the foothills of the Monte) which, together with the three forts and a defense work linking Cornaro with Contarini, would cost 115,000 ducats; in addition six new gates, with their drawbridges, would have to be made at 6,000 ducats each. The new *enceinte* would be 5,400 *passi* in circumference. Cornaro would have a circumference of 375 *passi*, Contarini of 320 and Barbaro of 240, the linking defence of 475. In time of peace Cornaro would have a garrison of 150, the others fewer, and in war their total complement would be 600 men. He poohpoohed the notion of a citadel at Porta S. Bartolomeo. It would cost 50,000 ducats even in *terreno*[59] plus another 35,000 in compensation to the adjacent church and monastery which would have to be destroyed. In addition, it would require a garrison of 500 men even in peace-

---

59. Earth consolidated with stakes and covered with turf.

time, costing 35,000 a year, whereas a bastioned *enceinte* would need no garrison at all in peacetime (because it could not be seized by a political faction). To repair the walls and ditches was not an unsound idea: he would do it himself in fifteen days for 15,000 ducats – as a second line of defence within his main *enceinte*.[60]

On March 30th the *provveditori generali sopra la fortificatione della città di Vicenza* presented their opinion on the city which they termed ' propugnacolo della Lombardia, del Polesene, del Padoano et si può dire della stessa città di Venetia. '[61] They had arrived at a decision about the Monte without difficulty: there should be three forts, the higher two to be connected, and they should all be equipped with lodging for garrisons, munition stores and wells, ' et in questo particolare ci rimettiamo alla scrittura et alli calcoli più distinti del Tensini. ' Turning to the *enceinte* they pointed both to the different opinions of the *capi di guerra* and to the split between the city and the *territorio*, the former wanting to make as few alterations to the existing circuit as possible, the latter, since they had to help pay for whatever as done, wanting a circuit large enough to receive as many refugees from the countryside as possible. We, the *provveditori* said, were not swayed by private interests but considered only the public good, ' imitando il medico, il qual risolve far tagliar il brazzo per dar la vita all'un infermo. ' Their recommendations were, in brief: get on with the forts; begin two bastions and a *tenaille* at S. Bartolomeo; repair existing walls and ditches; be ready to implement Tensini's fifteen bastion circuit (which they explained consisted of thirteen full, and four half bastions: fifteen for costing purposes) as soon as circumstances permitted; put all the work out to contract, the example of Palmanova having shown this to be the cheapest method. They ended by saying that they had brought Tensini back with them – who had ' pienamente confirmata

60. Ib.
61. Ib.

quella buona opinione che habbiamo sempre havuto della sufficienza, virtù et integrità di lui' – to explain technical details, and by suggesting that Revese's help should be compensated in cash.[62]

Seizing this opportunity, Tensini drafted a new contract on April 2nd[63] with the aid of the *secretario* Giovanbattista Patavino.[64] Retaining his estimate of 115,000 *scudi*, he now broke the operation into two stages. For 65,000 ducats he undertook to complete the three forts and to bring an *enceinte* of thirteen full and four half bastions and a *tenaille* outside Porta S. Bartolomeo to a state of defense against canon, all to be of earth covered with turf, the work to be done within three months were the men and equipment he stipulated forthcoming. Then, if it were wished 'ridurla in perfectione' he would complete the *enceinte* and add its covered way[65] for a further 50,000 *scudi*. He would need an advance of 2,000 ducats, then 5,000 each week, also paid in advance; 2,000 pioneers; the necessary stakes and fascines for consolidating the earth; 1000 wheelbarrows, 1000 *zerletti*, 500 shovels and 200 picks. He also stipulated that whenever he was called away from Vicenza the work should be supervised by Giovanni Giacomo Marchese, 'mio alievo'.

When this contract was under discussion, the comment – the irony seems to have been lost on Tensini – was made that if he could keep to these terms he would deserve a statue in bronze 'come quella di Bartolameo Coleone,'[66] but on April 5th Tensini's proposal was accepted in its entirety, the senate resolution[67] stressing that 'sopra tutto ci debba principalmente attendere all'amplificatione della città... et ridurla in Fortezza Reale con tredici balloardi intieri et quattro mezi balloardi, oltre li forti

---

62. He was granted 200 ducats on April 8th. A.S.V., S.D.S.R., 134, c. 85r.
63. A.S.V., M.M.N., 144. Appendix II.
64. Crema, ms. cit. c. 27v.
65. The covered way is a path cut into the counterscarp, with the top of the glacis as its parapet.
66. Crema, ms. cit., c. 27v.
67. A.S.V., S.D.S.R., 134, 70r ff.

sopra il monte.' The short-term need was to consolidate the existing walls and build the strong-point at S. Bartolomeo, but this would leave the suburbs unprotected and deprive the people of the *territorio* of a refuge. Moreover, Venice should not consider only one emergency but look to the future, so the forts and walls should be proceeded with ' senza pretermettere di fortificar anco immediate il recinto al piano con li quindeci balloardi ', the whole operation be ' in appalto dato... all'istesso Cavaliere Tensini, ' with the undertaking that when the decision came to be made to bring the *enceinte* to completion, this would also be entrusted to Tensini. And, conscious of the ill-will this decision would arouse in Vicenza, the resolution concluded, ' sia oltre di ciò tolto nella Signoria Nostra il castello della detta città, insieme col luoco della Rochetta, per potersi valer dell'uno et dell'altro secondo che ricercherà il bisogno.' This was twice voted on inconclusively (62 for, 7 against, 69 *voti dubii*; then 42, 2, 89), but on April 8th, after Tensini had again been questioned by the *collegio* on the 7th, and with the addition of a clause giving priority to work on the two bastions and the *tenaille* at S. Bartolomeo, the resolution was passed, though by a somewhat grudging margin: 108, 7, 41. Tensini had won, but against an opposition that would watchfully bide its time.

At this point, then, the decision was taken to fortify Vicenza in two phases. Phase one provided for bringing the *enceinte*, the Monte forts and the S. Bartolomeo bastions and *tenaille* to a minimum state of defence. The decision mentioned the repair of walls and ditches but did not budget anything towards them in addition to the 65,000 ducats stipulated by Tensini. Work on the forts was to be suspended and he was to be charged with one half of the sum already disbursed on them. Moreover a new clause was introduced on the 8th; as a guarantee that the work was actually done in the time promised, Tensini was to pledge ' tutti li suoi beni, presenti et futuri, di qualunque sorte, et specialmente una casa et possession da lui acquistata in Crema ', and he was also liable to a fine of 5,000 ducats for breach of contract. The government undertook on its part to supply him with labour and, were it not possible to raise the 2,000 pioneers from the Vicentino, ' come è credibile ', to secure them from the Padovano, Trivisano or elsewhere. Phase 2 would be to bring the *enceinte* as a whole to a state of perfection.[68]

A copy of the contract was sent to Vicenza the following day and Canal and the *rettori* were told to order the dismantling of houses along the line of the new *enceinte* within fifteen days.[69] They were also told to urge the city and the *territorio* to pay the first instalment on their contributions of one third each.[70] The auspices were not encouraging. On presenting the March accounts for the city the *capitano*, Giovanni Giustiniani, had complained that payments towards the forts were already leading to a reduction in the sum he could send to Sagredo for the army,[71] and on April 9th two tearstained appeals were sent to the doge from the *territorio*. One catalogued the burdens under which the countryside was already tottering: customs duty, the subsidy, taxes for troops, payments for their commuted pioneer service at Legnago, the quartering of soldiers – demands which had already in this new year[72] totalled 15,000 ducats. To find another 6,000 would be ' veramente insopportabile '. Vicenza was ' oppulentissima ': why shouldn't it pay it all? Or couldn't the cost be spread over the whole *terraferma*, as were contributions to the subsidy? Or, at least, if the cost had to fall on city and *territorio*, could not the city's contribution be much the greater part? At the very least, the petition urged, nothing should be demanded until the harvest was in.[73] The second petition was a furious denunciation of Canal's failure to control the extortions made by his soldiery and on his drafting poor peasants from the borders of the *terri-*

---

68. Ib., 84r ff. Orders were also sent for *zerletti* and wheelbarrows to Verona, Padua and Rovigo. A.S.V., M.M.N., 144, April 9.
69. V.B.C., 160, 7.
70. A.S.V., M.M.N., 144, Apr. 9.
71. A.S.V., D.R.V., Apr. 4.
72. Vicenza and its *territorio* dated the new year from Jan. lst.
73. V.B.C., 160, 16.

torio, instead of men who worked in or near the city whose lives would scarcely be interrupted by work on the fortifications. Every part of the countryside resounded, they protested, with the sobs and groans of Venice's afflicted subjects.[74]

Canal himself wrote to say that he was heartily sick of his connection with the fortifications. He was attacked on all sides by interested parties, those whose property or pockets were threatened or did not want to work, and he begged to be relieved of ' questo grandissimo peso. '[75] The doge sent Bernardo Marcello, *avogador di commun*,[76] to investigate, and the charges turned out to be justified, though Canal blamed it all on the evil atmosphere in and around Vicenza and on the peculations – without his knowledge – of his chancellor.[77] His inefficiency was proved when Giustiniani held a snap muster of one of the cavalry companies in Vicenza and found seventeen dead pays in a muster list of fifty four.[78] Canal was not censured, however, merely released back to his duties in the Vicentino where, near Schio, he died, probably of plague, that September.[79] The Canal affair was a storm in a teacup, significant only in that it reveals how much ill-will attached to those involved in the government's scheme. The *territorio*, meanwhile, was temporarily calmed by the issuing of a proclamation stating the legitimate charges that could be levied for the provisioning and lodging of troops in the villages and farms of the countryside.[80] Nor was the *territorio* the only vocal partner in this unpopular enterprise; on April 14th the city elected two more *oratori*, Scipione Ferramosca and Giulio Volpe, to plead its ' povere et exhauste fortune ' before the doge.[81]

A further obstacle was the competition of other interests in

74. A.S.V., S.D.T.F., Apr. 9.
75. A.S.V., D.R.V., Apr. 10.
76. A.S.V., S.D.T.F., Apr. 11.
77. A.S.V., D.R.V., Apr. 18 and May 26.
78. Ib., Apr. 15.
79. Ib., Sept. 26. He did not actually leave until June lst.
80. Ib., Apr. 15.
81. V.B.C., 869.

the war theatre as a whole. Tensini had hardly arrived in Vicenza[82] and had time to complain of the way in which the money for the preliminary work on the original forts had been mispent[83] than he was asked for by Sagredo to help Martinengo with the artillery at Valeggio. Sagredo also complained that the fortifications there were held up for lack of engineers, with Marchese reserved for Vicenza, Sarti away he knew not where, and only Candido to hand. He asked urgently that de Ville be sent to him and reported the need for more pioneers at Asola, Castel Gioffrè, Verona and elsewhere.[84] Hardly had he written this when news came that the Venetians had re-taken Ponte Molino, and Candido was sent to confer with Beato about improving its defences.[85] Marchese's transfer to Vicenza was countermanded[86] but Tensini, haunted no doubt by the short time allowed by his contract, turned a deaf ear to repeated summons to Valeggio[86a] until May 3rd, when the transfer of Martinengo to Brescia (replacing Cosimo del Monte, who was ill) left the artillery in desperate need of its lieutenant.[86b] Tensini's position, as he later complained, was an extremely difficult one. On the one hand he was responsible to Venice for the progress of the works at Vicenza, on the other he was responsible to Venice's general for the protection of the army. Sagredo left him in no doubt where, in his opinion, the priority lay ' Naturalmente nemico delle fortificationi, ' as Tensini reported, he resented losing money that Vicenza could otherwise have spent on troops, as well as the services of Tensini, who found it awkward to slip away from time to time to look after his contract; ' if you wish to be my friend, ' he reported Sagredo as saying, ' never mention your fortifications. '[87]

82. On April 10th. Crema, ms. cit., c. 27v.
83. A.S.V., D.R.V., Apr. 14.
84. A.S.V., P.T.M., 76, Apr. 15.
85. Ib. Apr. 16.
86. Ib. Apr. 21.
86a. He had the excuse of fever on April 21. A.S.V., D.R.V.,
86b. A.S.V., S.D.S.R., 134, May 4 and A.S.V., D.R.V., May 6.
87. Crema, ms. cit., c. 27v.

The *deputati* of Vicenza were meanwhile writing round to their opposite numbers in other fortified cities, Bergamo, Orzinovi, Asola and Brescia among them, collecting information about how their works had been paid for, and obtaining, in the main, reassuring news. At Orzinovo and Asola, some of the fortifications had been paid for by the state, at Bergamo neither city nor *territorio* had paid for the defense works of 1561, except through ' the destruction of an infinite number of houses and shops and the ruin of many gardens. '[88] Though reassuring, this surreptitiously gained information was not conclusive, and as if sensitive to the unconvincing nature of a case founded on partial evidence, on May 3rd the council of 150 passed, by seventy seven votes to eighteen, a special tax on all citizens, resident or non resident, except ' i miserabili '.[89] Approved by the Venetian senate on condition that really poor artisans, shopless and without property, who lived merely by ' i proprii sudori ' should also be exempt,[90] the tax was confirmed in Vicenza on May 13th, the income to be anticipated by a loan of 12,000 ducats from the Monte di Pietà, ' essendo molto urgente il bisogno di far il pagamento della portione che potesse toccare a questa città per cause delle sue fortificationi. '[91] No notice was taken of a petition – unsigned, but prepared in multiple copies – to substitute a property tax to be paid only by those who would directly profit from the protection offered by the new works.[92] A small pamphlet was printed describing how the ' tansa estraordinaria ' was to work.[93] It was to be paid within two years; ten per cent would be deducted if payment were made within four, six per cent if within eight months. Defalcation would involve an extra

88. V.B.C., 160, 6.
89. V.B.C., 869.
90. A.S.V., S.D.T.R., 103, May 11, c. 123r-v.
91. V.B.C., 869. Voting: 82 for, 8 against. They were borrowing from the Monte by May 13th (2, 500 ducats to make up their first instalment of 6, 000).
92. V.B.C., 160, 6.
93. *Parte presa nel consiglio della città di Vicenza et confermata nell'Eccellentissimo Senato per distributione della spesa del nuovo recinto della medesima città*, (Vicenza, Francesco Grossi, n.d.).

ten per cent plus the penalties of the law. The preliminary assessment would be made by two citizens in each *sindicaria*, accompanied by a notary, and the final amount to be paid by each family would be determined by a committee comprising the *deputati*, one of the *rettori*, the *signori conservatori degli leggi*, together with eight leading citizens and four merchants from each *quartiere*, to be elected by the *consiglio*.

The *rettori* themselves, who behaved as model public servants throughout their term of office, after some girding at the favourable terms Tensini had obstained for himself,[94] had spoken in terms of muted optimism in their progress report of May 1st. They praised unreservedly the energy with which Tensini was forcing the work ahead on the Monte but pointed out that it would be necessary to draft pioneers from the Padovano, the Trevisano and even the Feltrino in order to keep to his timetable; so many men in the Vicentino had been drafted into the army or enrolled in the militia that they had only been able to engage one thousand, and most of these 'vecchi poverazzi' who were of little use.[95] It was a warning note they were to sound in dispatch after dispatch, and Tensini, looking back on his failure to earn a Colleone monument, was to lay much of the blame on the Venetian government's inability to supply him with sufficient labour.[96]

Within three days of Tensini's departure from Vicenza the *rettori* were expressing alarm that there was no one capable of directing what labour there was, and, shortly afterwards, that unless more labour were forthcoming he might invoke the clause in his contract stipulating that he would not be financially responsible unless 2,000 pioneers were provided.[97] Work was nevertheless proceeding on the forts, where Revese was giving a helping hand, and on the *enceinte*, though the pioneers had run into trouble on the S. Rocco section where the soil proved to be soft and

---

94. A.S.V., D.R.V., 18 Apr. 25.
95. Ib.
96. Crema, ms., c. 27v.
97. A.S.V., D.R.V., May 6 and 12.

sandy, and On May 20th they reported with relief that Marchese had at last arrived.[98] Tensini meanwhile had been sent to report on the recently retaken, and considerably damaged ostiglia. He reported back to Sagredo on May 23rd,[99] was sent to Marmirolo[100], and returned from there just in time to witness the notorious retreat. From this action, which led to the disgrace of Sagredo and was the biggest blow to Venetian armed prestige since Agnadello, Tensini firmly disassociated himself: it was made ' senza mio consenso e saputo '.[101] On May 31st the *podestà* of Verona and Priuli reported that ' vi si è ritirato il cavaliere Tensini '.[102] Tensini's own account was that this was his own decision; he went because he knew it to be weakly guarded and in sad need of someone to help its fortifications and artillery, so at hazard to his life he made his way there accompanied only by one servant.[103] Priuli, who had in fact asked for Tensini on the 21st,[104] put him in charge of the fortifications gratefully,[105] the city being threatened by raiding parties that came right up to its walls.[106]

Not surprisingly, the news of Valeggio, which reached Vicenza by courier during the night of 30th-31st May, threw the city into alarm. The pioneers were reorganized to work on the main danger points, on the Monte, at S. Bartolomeo, the Castello Gate and the Rochetta, and a further 600 hundred men were summoned from the ' esaustissimo territorio '; together with two hundred who had arrived from the Feltrino this made a total of some 1,800. Marchese, however, declared that he could not guarantee the safety of the city with less than 3,000.[107] The senate, besieged by

---

98. Ib. May 18; May 20.
99. Plans in A.S.V., P.T.M., 76, with Sagredo's dispatch of May 23. One shows the whole area between Ponte Molino and Ostiglia, the other Ostiglia itself. Both are signed, the latter is dated May 21.
100. Ib. May 25.
101. Crema, ms., c. 28r.
102. A.S.V., D.R. Verona, 29.
103. Crema, ms., c. 28r.
104. A.S.V., D.R. Verona, 29.
105. Ib. June 2.
106. Ib., May 31.
107. A.S.V., D.R.V., June 1.

similar requests, ordered Bassano and Belluno each to send two hundred pioneers to Vicenza[108] while the *rettori* lost no time in writing to Erizzo, Sagredo's successor, begging him to urge the government to make up the toll of pioneers they had promised.[109] Erizzo replied in a letter full of goodwill, and though one of his first actions on taking command had been to ask for the services of Tensini,[110] he released him so that he could pay a visit to his fortifications for one day, June 10th, before sending him to report on Legnago. Tensini had only time to write out, in a hurried hand, a list of the guns needed for the forts on the Monte and to add that the need was now for 4,000 pioneers: with these, ' in meno di uno mese rendirò tutta la città in difesa. '[111] Tensini had just left for Legnago when an order came from Venice for him to go back to Verona where his services were urgently needed;[112] the senate was being bombarded with requests for engieers and pioneers and Vicenza was competing with other places of equal strategic importance, particularly Verona and Peschiera. Harvest time, moreover, was just beginning, and it was impossible to draft the few able-bodied men left on the land away from their only means of livelihood.[113] Giustiniani had managed to scrape together 3,000 pioneers, but as he was also responsible for raising more troops in the *territorio* he admitted that he conscripted for the fortifications only those who were not fit to carry arms[114] and who were thus not likely to be ideal pioneers. Towards the end of June the fortifications were struck by the advance guard of yet another enemy: plague. Tensini returned from Verona on June 27th and had to go straight into quarantine.[115] On July 6th Vicenza was sealed off, with guards on all roads leading to

---

108. A.S.V., S.D.T.R., 103, June 6.
109. A.S.V., D.R.V., June 6.
110. A.S.V., P.T.M., 77, June 5.
111. A.S.V., D.R.V., June 10, enclosing Tensini autograph.
112. A.S.V., S.D.T.F., June 10.
113. The point is made in A.S.V., D.R.V., June 13.
114. Ib., June 17.
115. Ib., June 27.

the city to turn back possible carriers of the infection.[116] On July 16th the first case was suspected within the city itself.[117]

After giving quarantine orders, the *rettori* rode round the city and reported on the progress of the fortifications. Marshy land on the north was proving an obstacle, but work on the *enceinte* as a whole was reasonably well forward. The stretch Porta del Monte – Porta della Lupia – Rochetta – Porta S. Croce – Porta S. Bartolomeo was three-quarters finished; the next stretch, from Porta S. Bartolomeo to Porta S. Lucia rather less so; and the section enclosing the eastern suburbs was about half finished; the Rochetta bastion was almost complete, as was the *tenaille* outside Porta S. Bartolomeo. On the Monte, Cornaro was three-quarters, Contarini and Barbaro were two-thirds finished. On the other hand work was slowing down: the harvest had led the men from Bassano and Feltre to desert and the long-promised help from Padua had not yet turned up. Tensini pointed out (rather late in the day) that the forts would need gates and drawbridges. These had not been allowed for in his contract; the senate was asked for its advice on this point, and also to ask the *provveditori alle fortezze* to send a specialist mason to build the well in Fort Cornaro.[118]

This reiterated request for more pioneers was bound to fall on deaf ears. So great was the shortage that troops were working on the defenses of Verona under Tensini's supervision and the more immediate concern, both of Erizzo and the government, was not Vicenza but Mantua, which seemed on the point of falling to the Imperialist siege. Tensini had attended a gloomy conference at Monteforte on July 14th where any large-scale relief of the city was discounted because the army had been weakened so much by plague.[119] On July 20th Mantua fell, and Tensini, the duke of Candales and Baron Louis de Sciaban were

---

116. Ib., July 6.
117. Ib., July 16.
118. Ib. I conflate the report of July 6 with that of June 30.
119. A.S.V., P.T.M., 77, July 14.

sent to find a suitable rallying place for the army between Verona and Peschiera.[120] The news caused such alarm in Vicenza that the *rettori*, consulting with Marchese, impressed the services of ' gente di conditione ordinaria... come gl'artiggiani et altre minute, benche poco frutto se ne posia attendere per inabitudine della meglior parte nell'essercito della terra ', and summoned another thousand from the *territorio* in spite of the protest to which this would give rise.[121]

Nor had the financial position improved. The impressment of men for military service had caused not only personal hardship but a falling off in productivity (for instance of silk) which had badly hit the revenues of the city. There was widespread ill will towards the tax of May 13th. On June 3rd the council passed a law to compel those who had been elected as ' liquidatori et estimatori ' to serve on pain of a fine of one hundred ducats to be paid towards the fortifications[122] and there were bitter wranglings between the city and the religious bodies, who were claiming exemption. By June 12th the *rettori* reported that the only monies raised amounted to 5,500 ducats from the city and 2,000 from the *territorio*. On June 20th the council decided, by a margin of seventy four to thirty two votes, to offer a further donative of 12,000 to the doge to show their ' incomparabile divotione et inviolabile sua fede verso il Serenissimo nostro Prencipe ', but the *rettori*, enclosing a copy of this decision, sourly drew attention to the condition that the money would only be forthcoming ' finita che sia però di pagarsi la fortificatione ' and when a new *estimo* had been drawn up, ' essendo il presente estimo pieno di errori et confusioni. '[123] By July 4th the balance sheet stood as follows: expenditure on the fortifications 35,220 ducats (including pre-contract work, six

---

120. Ib. July 20 and 21. Candales was *Governatore generale delle fanterie*. Sciaban published in Venice, in 1631, *Il Bombardiero veneto essaminato dal suo Generale, dialogo fatto Francese, & in Italiano*.
121. A.S.V., D.R.V. July 22.
122. V.B.C., 869.
123. A.S.V., D.R.V., June 30 and V.B.C., 869, same date, where the voting is given as 79:32.

payments of 5,000 ducats to Tensini and his initial payment of 2,000); income, from the city, 10,000, and from the *territorio*, 3,180 ducats.[124] While the city could just cover its debt, the *territorio* could not and in response to a request from the *rettori* to be allowed to secure it with public money the senate agreed, subject to this being done secretly and to repayment before the end of the *rettori's* term of office.[125] The efforts of the *capitano* to raise the income from the *dazii* proved vain; production was still falling off, interregional commerce was severely cut down by quarantine regulations and it was impossible to persuade business men to take on the taxes at farm. The *deputati* of the city, urged to use the old *estimo* instead of their dodging device of waiting for a new one, expressed their willingness–but any decision, they pointed out, would have to be ratified by the council, most of whose members had left the city to avoid the plague![126]

The plague was not actually confirmed in Vicenza until August 4th. By the end of the month it had put the affairs of the city into the greatest confusion; ' rende ', as the *capitano* put it, ' le facile dificilissime, et le difficile riduce all'impossibile '.[127] The greatest difficulty was still the financial one. The senate had authorized the council to make decisions with a restricted quorum but such decisions as it did make merely used the plague as an excuse for cutting down expenditure or for continuing its legal battle with the clergy, who by August 22nd owed 2,657 ducats towards the fortifications and were still refusing to pay.[128] At the end of the month disbursements for the fortifications had reached a figure of 53,114 ducats (including 49,800 to Tensini), while the city's contribution stood at 16,000 and that of the *territorio* at 3,180. The balance of 33,934 was charged against the public revenues owing to the *camera*.[129]

124. A.S.V., D.R.V., July 6, enclosing accounts of July 4.
125. A.S.V., S.D.S.R., 135, July 11, c. 34v.
126. A.S.V., D.R.V., July 12 and 19
127. Ib., Aug. 29.
128. Ib., Aug. 22, enclosing petition to doge from *deputati*.
129. Ib., Aug. 26.

Work went forward, however, punctuated by appeals to the *provveditori alle fortezze* for masons and to the *provveditori all'Arsenale* for artillery[130] and spurred by rumours eminating from Germany that a full-scale assault on Vicenza was being planned.[131] Tensini was absent throughout the month of August, ill for part of the time in plague-ridden Verona, though not of the plague itself.[132] Ambitious as ever, while he turned down an appointment as *ajutante dell'artiglieria* because of Vicenza (and to the relief of Erizzo, who wanted to offer it to Sciaban ' per non dare luoco all'instabilità natturale de' francesi ')[133] he applied for, and was granted, the title of *sopraintendente delle fortificationi*.[134] He was sorely missed in Vicenza, and at the end of the month the *rettori* begged for his presence ' per quatro o sei giorni '. Subject to the agreement of Francesco Zen, who had been sent as *provveditore per la sanità* in Vicenza and the Vicentino, they were sure that it would be possible for him to inspect the fortifications as long as he remained on horseback, escorted by the *guardie della sanità*, while actually inside the city.[135] By this time the forts and *enceinte* were well advanced. The half bastion and bastion between Porta del Monte and Porta della Lupia were complete except for the demilune between them and the face of the half bastion. The two bastions and the half bastion between Porta della Lupia and the road to Verona, together with their curtain walls, were finished. The two bastions at the Rochetta and Porta S. Croce with the one between them only required work on their flanks, which the *rettori* reckoned could be completed in ten days. Also nearly com-

---

130. Ib., Aug. 20. Request for ' 24 cannoni, 12 mezzi cannoni, 4 colubrine, 6 mezzi-colubrine, 10 quarti di cannoni ' and 4 smaller pieces, together with the appropriate powder, shot and implements.
131. Ib., Aug. 17. *Capitano* reporting information derived ' dal solito mio confidente '.
132. A.S.V., P.T.M., 77, Aug. 6.
133. Ib., July 31.
134. Ib., Aug. 19, and A.S.V., S.D.S.R., 135, Aug. 21, c. 170r. This was an honorific title only, and it is not clear how large was the area involved: probably only the immediate theatre of war, in which Tensini had become the chief strategic adviser for permanent and temporary fortifications.
135. A.S.V., D.R.V., Aug. 30.

plete were the next three bastions, including the *tenaille* at S. Bartolomeo. From S. Bartolomeo to S. Lucia only part of the turf covering was lacking and the completion of the next stretch, to Porta di Padova, was envisaged within ten days. The last section, from Porta di Padova to the Bacchiglione, again required only the completion of its turfing. Fort Cornaro would be completed – *its enceinte*, at least – in a week or so, apart from a cavalier which Tensini had decided to insert to strengthen its defence; Barbaro, Contarini and the linking defences between Cornaro and Contarini were within a fortnight of completion according to Marchese, and work was about to begin on quarters for a garrison in Cornaro. Work on gates and drawbridges was ready to go ahead, but would have to wait for the instructions of Tensini himself. The *rettori* permit themselves for the first time to refer to Vicenza as a *piazza*, a term reserved for towns surrounded by up-to-date defences, but end with a request that is highly significant in the light of the criticism that was later to be brought to bear on Tensini's designs: they ask for a large number of spingards, ' mentre particolarmente le cortine fra un balloardo et l'altro sono molto lunghe... onde le spingarde saranno molto a proposito per valersene ai fianchi de' balloardi. '[136]

On August 30th Zen reported ninety one deaths from plague in the city on that day alone, and on September 2nd the *capitano* asked for permission to use criminals to bury the dead as it was becoming increasingly hard to find free men prepared to face the risk of infection. On that day the toll was ninety six; thereafter it declined and towards the end of the month steadied to between forty and fifty.[137] On the 11th the *capitano* himself begged permission to leave the city – the infection was raging in his own house – as long as he merely went beyond the *enceinte* to a spot whence he could continue to keep an eye on the fortifications.[138] The answer was a suave negative: we do understand,

136. Ib., Aug. 26.
137. Ib., Sept. 2, 5, 6, 10 and Oct. 2.
138. Ib., Sept. 11.

but you are too valuable a public servant for us to consider being deprived of your services amid ' l'urgenza di tanti publici bisogni '.[139] Indeed, Giustiniani's situation was not so tragic as that of his colleague Grimani. On September 19th the *podestà* reported that he had lost a child as well as four servants and had moved into one of his judge's houses in order to continue to serve the state.[140] Not surprisingly, the council of 150 was more concerned, at its skeleton meetings, with finding money for building isolation sheds and burying the dead than with the fortifications, the only contribution in that direction coming from the clergy, who at length agreed to give three thousand ducats – but payable at five hundred a year. Assailed again, this time by the *rettori*, the synod raised its offer to five thousand, but would not budge from the principle of producing only five hundred per annum.[141] Worst of all, the early Autumn rains began to produce falls of earth where the turfing was not complete. Deaths among the pioneers slowed progress and brought work on Fort Barbaro to a standstill. Marchese himself fell ill. In almost every despatch the *rettori* called for Tensini until the senate ordered Zen to make the necessary quarantine arrangements, to which the *provveditore* reluctantly (he was proud of the strict measures which had reduced the daily mortality) agreed.[142] But Tensini was ill again in Verona, ' a letto con febbre '[143] and meanwhile ' le continue et incessante piogge che tutti questi giorni sono cadute dal cielo ' led to the partial collapse of the bastion at Porta S. Lucia, part of the curtain at S. Bartolomeo and damaged the northern front of Fort Cornaro, where the well site still awaited the specialist promised by the *provveditori alle fortezze*.[144]

Tensini arrived at the beginning of October and, together

---

139. A.S.V., S.D.R.R., 1, Sept. 21, c. 22v.
140. A.S.V., D.R.V., Sept. 19.
141. Ib., Sept. 18. But the *territorio*, with the harvest coming in, produced 5, 000 ducats. Ib., Sept. 25.
142. A.S.V., S.D.R.R., 1, Sept. 20, c. 15r; A.S.V., D.R.V., Sept. 23.
143. A.S.V., P.T.M., 77, Sept. 25.
144. A.S.V., D.R.V., Sept. 25.

with Giustiniani, made frequent visits to the fortifications, concentrating on plans for getting Fort Cornaro ready for its armament and garrison [plate 2] and for clearing a glacis round the *enceinte*. Proclamation had already been made that property owners should cut trees and tear down buildings obscuring the line of sight between one bastion and the next, but Tensini declared that this was not enough; the flanks of the bastions being low, the field of vision was poor; for this reason, and to deprive an enemy of cover, it would be necessary to clear a glacis of at least one hundred *passi* beyond the ditch. This issue, though inherent in any scheme for artillery fortifications, had been consistently burked. Now it could be put off no longer the *capitano* pointed out nervously to the doge that it would not cause too much damage to property, ' andando a basso pochissime case et di poco rilievo '.[145] The administrative life of the city was almost at a standstill, however, and the council was hardly in a position to voice the complaints of property owners. The *deputati* had fled, so had consuls, notaries, even the officials of the *palazzo* itself.[146] The financial situation was worse than ever: by October 24th, when the end of the infection was in sight (the deaths had dropped to 21, 16, 13 and 8 in the previous days) the city estimated that it had spent 29,000 ducats on hospitals, doctors, medicines and food for the poor.[147]

Rain continued to fall throughout October and the turf facings of the bastions and curtains, heavily waterlogged, began to slip down into the ditch, leaving the banked earth vulnerable to the weather. The largest falls of turf and earth occured in the sections between Porta di Padova and Porta S. Lucia and between S. Bartolomeo and S. Croce, the areas where the earth was most sandy, but almost every section suffered some damage. Faced

---

145. Ib., Oct. 3, 8. The folding plan of Fort Cornaro, with a written key is enclosed with the dispatch of Oct. 8.

146. Ib., Nov. 4.

147. Ib., Oct. 24. On Nov. 24 (Ib.) the *capitano* reported that, from deaths and the general exodus, the population in the city had fallen to something over 6,000.

by this spectacle on his next visit to Vicenza, Tensini addressed an urgent petition to the doge on November 4th.[148] ' This city, ' he began, ' is completely surrounded by fortifications, seven feet high and eighteen thick, with a thirty foot ditch, and its forts are almost completed, according to my undertaking.' But, he continued, because of ' queste straordinarie e quasi continue pioggie ' the *incamisiatura* has suffered damage in various places for the following reasons: the turfing was not completed on time because I was not given enough workmen; there was a shortage of stakes for pegging the turves into place; proper attention was not paid to drainage, ' which would not have happened had I been present.' And he went on to say bitterly that the doge ' should never have given me such a task only to force me to be away so long, for in five months I have only been here eleven days, eight of them shut up in quarantine.' He has paid out money for work that, thanks to the effect of plague on his labour force, has not been carried out, and is left with barely enough men to work on Fort Cornaro. To try to repair the damage, even were skilled pioneers forthcoming, would be a waste of time. With the banks of earth so waterlogged, new turf would not stay in place; with the next fall of rain the work would be to do all over again, ' per il che li guastadori buttano via il tempo et io consumo li danari senza alcun profitto.' Soon frost will come and, without time to bind, the turf will be sprung loose again and slip off when the ground thaws. He begs, then – throwing in ' si dice che la pace sia fatta, che dio voglia ' as an added persuasion – to be allowed to suspend work for the three winter months. He still has 5,700 ducats owing to him; with this sum he promises to repair and complete the works when spring comes. Also, he is still under orders to Erizzo, who has summoned him back to Verona.

The government answered him with silence. It was not until the *capitano* forwarded a plan showing the great extent of the

148. Ib., Autograph, forwarded with *capitano*'s dispatch of Nov. 4.

damage [plate 3][149] that the senate, on January 21st 1631, drawing attention to defects in the defences, ' in particolare della poca loro scarpa ' (which had not been mentioned by the *rettori*), ordered Erizzo to carry out an investigation on the spot; as soon as his duties permitted, he was to take Sciaban and Tensini and other experts to Vicenza and submit a full report, ' acciò opera così principale non riesca imperfetta '.[150]

Though Tensini returned to Verona from fifteen days leave in Crema on January 24th and Sciaban was also there on his return from a tour of inspection in his capacity as adjutant of artillery,[151] Erizzo was not free to begin the investigation until April. The *rettori* used this delay to try to pay off some of the huge debt standing against the fortifications in the *monte*. Not unnaturally both city and *territorio* both pleaded the effects of the plague, and the *dazii* proved especially difficult to get in ' per la mortalità de datari et de ministri ' and the difficulty of finding replacements for them.[152] The *capitano*, indeed, forwarded a table of incomes from the chief *dazii* which showed a slight overall decline from 1628 to 1629, a steeper one from 1629 to 1630 and anticipated a calamatous one from 1630 to 1631; *vino a spini*, for example, showing an estimated drop from 16,480 ducats to 10,700, *porte* from 19,200 to 13,500 and *panni* from 2,950 to 1,850.[153]

Erizzo did however send Sciaban on his own to make a preliminary examination in the middle of February. As Tensini must have feared, the Frenchman extended his brief to include a criticism of the fortifications as a whole. He declared the *enceinte* to be altogether too big – a fault he attributed to most of the *piazze* of the *terraferma* – and in design too irregular and ' lontana dai termini della scuola megliore '; he particularly criticised the southern front for approaching too near to the commanding

149. Ib. Enclosed with *capitano*'s dispatch of Jan. 14, 1631.
150. A.S.V., S.D.R.R., 1, c. 106v.
151. A.S.V., P.T.M., 77, Jan. 24.
152. A.S.V., D.R.V., Feb. 2.
153. Ib. Feb. 14.

slopes of the Monte Berico, and concluded that it would have been much better to have had merely ' una citadella di quatro balloardi '. He also criticised the forts as being too small, their interiors cramped by too complex an outline and their bastions vulnerable to mining because their angles towards the field were too acute.[154] Erizzo had warned the doge that Sciaban was on his way to Venice ' per mero fine di cavar sodisfattione d'alcuni interessi ' and that he was a troublemaker, threatening to return to France unless he were made general of artillery.[155] He did not take Sciaban's criticisms of Tensini very seriously, then, when they were reported to him by Giustiniani, pointing out that the Frenchman always criticised the Venetian preference for a town wall over a citadel, a point of view which might suit the political temper of the French, but did not square with that of Venice, ' il qual consiste nella difesa de' sudditi e dello stato '. The *collegio*, however, gave a sympathetic hearing to Sciaban, noting particularly two criticisms: that Tensini's curtains were too long for effective musket cover from flank to flank (hence, indeed, the earlier request for *spingardi*) and that his embarkments were sliding because he had omitted to foot them with a step (*banchetta*). Erizzo was ordered to begin his investigation without more delay,[156] but because of the difficulty in assembling his experts, and then because he himself was ill, the inquiry did not get under way until April 7th.

Sciaban then developed his case at considerable length and with considerable energy,[157] making his points about the forts being too small and the *enceinte* unstepped, but concentrating on the distance between bastions; this was a mistake ' fuor di tutte le regole dell'arte '. To remedy it, he said, Tensini had suddenly come up with the idea of inserting *barbacannoni* in the ditch in

---

154. His views reported (ib.) by *capitano* on Feb. 18.
155. A.S.V., P.T.M., 77, Feb. 20.
156. A.S.V., S.D.R.R., 2, Mar. 1, cc. 1v-2r.
157. A.S.V., M.M.N., 144, n.d., at end of volume.

front of each curtain, a notion 'partorito in un giorno[158] dall'imagination, non mai visto in pratica, non che nominato fra tutti li antichi o moderni capi di guerra'. Referring to a (lost) model Tensini had made to demonstrate his *barbacannone*, Sciaban declared that in any case this 'non è altro che una falsabraga stroppiata, et priva della sua parte essentiale, cioè di quella che circonda li balouardi'. As a *faussebraie*[159] he criticised it on two grounds; that it would be composed not of solid earth, left uncut, but of loose earth piled up, and that it was below the level of the outer edge of the ditch and thus incapable of giving fire over the counterscarp and fulfilling its role of supporting the fire from the ramparts; it would also be easily dominated by an enemy who reached the counterscarp. 'Queste regole', he continued, 'sono talmente chiare che le più bellicose nationi del mondo, et le più perite nell'arte della guerra, cioè la Francese, Spagnola et Olandese le tengono inviolabile'. This was not only tactless but untrue, as the treatise of Sciaban's fellow-country man de Ville shows;[160] there was much controversy among engineers about the best form a *faussebraie* should take. He then turned to the question of what could be done to repair Tensini's monstrous errors. Instead of *barbacannoni* it would be necessary to construct a large demilune and crownwork in front of every curtain. To keep the walls from collapsing still further they could either be sheathed in stone (the best solution, but costing 300,000 *scudi*) or cut back to provide a *banchetta* at least six feet wide. As for the forts, they would have to be clad in stone and enlarged as much as possible. Best of all would be to improve the forts and let the *enceinte* crumble away; 'per assicurarsi in ogni avvenimenti del popolo et per difenderlo, anch'esso et i suoi beni' it would be a thousand times better to make a four-bastioned citadel, utilizing two of the best of the new ones. 'Alle oppositioni che si

---

158. Tensini had, in fact, suggested them in his project of February 21st, not as a spur-of-the-moment answer to Sciaban's criticisms.
159. A defensible platform stepped out from the curtain.
160. *Op. cit.*, pp. 123-6.

potranno far contra la cittadella,' he concluded, 'si risponderà con ragion di guerra, et di stato, et con l'essempio di tutti li Principi della Christianità.'

It is easy to see how Sciaban got on Erizzo's nerves, and it was probably Erizzo who showed Tensini a copy of the report.[161] He wrote a rebuttal at once.[162] It was not an impressive one. The size of the forts was determined by the nature of the terrain, as was the angle of their bastions; all were at least 60º, 'accutezza tolerabile'. A *banchetta* was not necessary. As for the size of the *enceinte*, it was made so extensive to avoid damage to property and provide a refuge for families from the countryside together with their possessions and livestock; 'ne era di raggioni che li cittadini e paesani pagassero li dui terzi della spesa e rovinare agl'uni le case et privare gl'altri del comodo del potersi retirare in sicuro'. In any case, the extent of the *enceinte* was not unreasonable – the fortifications of Genoa spread over ten miles – and his *barbacannoni*, with fifty musketeers in each, would give ample defence to the ditch and flanks, If Sciaban had only read the chapters on the length of curtains and on the *barbacannone* in his book,[163] these objections would not have been made. Commenting on the suggestion that the *enceinte* might have to be clad in stone, he pointed out that if the works had been finished by the end of the previous July, as he had planned, the embankments would have had time to settle and the turf to become rooted.

161. Crema, ms., c. 28r.
162. A.S.V., M.M.N., 144, Apr. 9. Copy, but corrections and postscript autograph.
163. *Fortificatione...* (1624), lib. I, caps. XI and XXII. He admits that the curtain length he recommends (217 *passi*) is open to two objections: bastions tended to be too acute and musket fire (taking point-blank range to be 150 *passi*) not effective from flank to flank, but defends the long curtain on three grounds; musket fire from the flank of a bastion is usually impracticable: there is no room for musketeers in the canon embrasures and they have to fire over the parapet, thus exposing themselves hazardously; long curtains mean fewer bastions, and thus less expenditure on men and of money for construction. Besides, he claims, his *barbacanone* [plate 4] provides adequate musketry support for the flank and face of each bastion. The ends his account of it as follows: 'Credo di haver fatto veder à bastanza, quanta utilità, e difesa apporti alla Fortezza questo mio Barbacannone; però io lo farò sempre nelle mie Fortezze, & essorto gl'altri a farlo nelle loro'. (p. 51).

The damage could be repaired, and the works made permanent, without difficulty. As for Sciaban's preoccupation with citadels, ' la mente di Sua Serenità non e statta di fare una citadella per tener in freno li cittadini ma bene di fortificar Vicenza e conservar la città '. Sciaban had also made another familiar ' French ' point that it would have been better to have put the money into an army and thus into strengthening the whole *terraferma* rather than one single town. Tensini replied with the standard ' Italian ' answer: what would happen if that army were defeated? Then not only would Vicenza fall, but all other cities of the *terraferma* be in jeopardy.

Armed with models and drawings, Tensini, Sciaban, the Duke of Rohan and Larochetta[164] discussed the fortifications during several sessions of the *collegio* at the end of the month, finally producing a joint report drawn up by the three Frenchmen, countered by a minority report from Tensini. All were in agreement about the need to cut back the west flank of the bastion at Porta del Monte and substitute a bastion for Tensini's demilune between that bastion and the one at Porta della Lupia; about compensating for the length of curtains elsewhere by reinforcing them with demilunes, and not *barbacannoni*; and about cladding forts Cornaro and Contarini with stone. Tensini dissented from the others' recommendation that a *banchetta* should be made and wanted the flanks of the demilunes to come back to the covered way[165]; the others preferred them set forward on the glacis. He had not suggested demilunes as part of his *enceinte*, he said (not altogether ingenuously), because they would have added 27,000 ducats to the cost and could always have been added subsequently. He reserved his scorn for the *banchetta* notion: for works of low profile, like those at Vicenza, he had never seen such a thing ' in trenta

---

164. ' della Roccetta ' in the joint report. ' Monsu Larochetta ' in Tensini's minority report; both are in A.S.V., M.M.N., 144, Tensini's dated Apr. 29 (autograph) the other undated. Henri, duc de Rohan, was the author of *Le parfait Capitaine. Autrement, l'abregé des... Commentaires de Cesar...*, Paris 1636. It was translated into English (1640) and Spanish (1652).

165. There is no evidence that a covered way had been started.

doi anni che io ho fatto fortificare, in undeci guerre dove son statto'

On May Ist the Senate findings[166] were reported to Alvise Zorzi, successor to Erizzo who had been elected doge on April 10th. The dispatch is openly hostile to Tensini, listing the criticisms made of his designs and adding ' a tutto ciò risponde il Tensini e porta i rimedii; ma non son certamente la maggior parte tali che possino acquietare il senso nè anco di una mediocre intelligenza '. The decisions reached were these: to build the new bastion between Porta del Monte and Porta della Lupia; to add eight demilunes;[167] to clad the two forts; and to add a *banchetta* by reinforcing the lower part of the scarp of the *enceinte*. Zorzi was asked to estimate the cost of these changes, to bring the accounts for the fortifications up to date, and to find out whether Tensini had fulfilled the terms of his contract or not. The issue was so important that as ' nostro supremo e savio rappresentante ' he was to hold yet another conference in Vicenza, taking care to invite, among others, Cosimo del Monte and Brancaccio, and to consult the duke of Candales. The French experts would join him from Venice, and his report should reach the senate if possible by May Ist.

All this represented a major blow to Tensini, a possible turning point in a career which had hitherto been remarkably successful. His own explanation of what happened in those last days of April is thus of special interest.[168] He claimed that Sciaban had been ' instigato dall'Ill.mo et Ecc.mo S.r ...... Senatore di auttorità e di eloquenza all'hora di Collegio '. The senator's name is left blank in the manuscript, and Tensini leaves unsigned two letters from the senator, dated May 6 and October 17th, which he quotes. Their language is veiled, but clearly Tensini was being asked to adjust the fortifications to save an unnamed Vicentine ' cavagliere ' from the destruction of his property

---

166. A.S.V., S.D.R.R., 2, cc. 41r ff.
167. The term used here is *rivellini*, but ravelin and demilune were treated as loosely equivalent terms.
168. Crema ms., cc. 31r-34r.

threatened by the levelling of the glacis. Tensini represents Erizzo as standing up for him in the *collegio* while Sciaban and Rohan continued to attack him in order ' gratificar al sudetto senatore che ardentemente portava l'interessi de Vicentini essendo stato suo Podestà,[169] e facendo professione di essere suo particolare protettore. ' During their meetings together at Rohan's house, however, a considerable area of agreement began to emerge; Sciaban dropped his citadel idea and all were agreed on improving the fortifications by extending them. This introduced a new atmosphere into the *collegio* discussions, for the ' senatore protettore de' Vicentini ' and ' altri interessati ' wanted the works to halt, not to be strengthened with demilunes which would greatly enlarge the amount of ground that would have to be cleared outside the city.

The interests the protector of the Vicentines had in mind, Tensini claimed, did not only concern land and houses and the smuggling of silk past the customs houses, but the political sympathies of those who were ' mossi dell'affettione che portano a casa d'Austria e del desiderio che hanno di retornare sotto al Imperio '. When to this was added the pressure of ' molti nobili Venetiani e senatori che hanno delle possessioni in sul Vicentino ' and who did not want their property taxed or their *contadini* impressed for the fortifications, it is not surprising, Tensini suggests, that the *collegio* decided to play for time by calling yet another commission of inquiry. He himself was the immediate victim of this treacherous faction largely because he had offended the unnamed senator (and, by implication others) by condemning his cowardice at Valeggio, but the ultimate victim was designed to be the whole notion of an effectively walled Vicenza. The real issue was not being fought over *banchette*, or the length of curtains, or whether demilunes were preferable to *barbacannoni*, but whether private interests or public ones were to prevail.

169. Dr. Selmi has established that this was almost certainly Vincenzo Gussoni who had been podestà 1606-7.

Intentionally or not, the senate's decision certainly led to delay. The experts named were widely scattered, Brancaccio in Brescia, del Monte in Bergamo; Zorzi himself was busily occupied with organizing the shadowing of the German army's withdrawal and dealing with the skirmishes which attended it.[170] Tensini, no longer in demand, showed his model to Candales in Verona ' che... lo lodo grandemente, particolarmente il *barbacannone* ' and took it to Zorzi, who (Tensini adds: there is no confirmation in Zorzi's dispatches) went with Candales to inspect Vicenza and congratulated Tensini for having ' fatto miracoli ' in so short a time and with so little expense.[171] But May went by without any official move and so did June, until on the 30th the *rettori* were asked for a report on the fortifications by the senate.[172] Their reply, if there was one, is not preserved, but the situation in the Vicentino was not very different from that of Verona, whose *rettori*, on July 1st, sent an eloquent essay on the effects of the plague. City and *territorio* together had lost ' sopra i due terzi delle persone, diminutione che poi ha tirato seco altre dannose consequenze, e particolarmente la distruttione de' trafichi per la morte de' mercanti e d'operai, la incoltivatione de' terreni per la desolatione de bestiami e delle gente del contado, la declinatione dell'estimo... et un insopportabile acrescimento di gravezze a sudditi mentre rimanendo ferme le spese '.[173] Tensini had reckoned the cost of the extensions and alterations at Vicenza at 61,500 ducats.[174] The times were favouring the ' interessi privati '.

On July 12th, however, the *rettori* of Vicenza were told to make quarantine arrangements for Sciaban and Rohan (they were in Venice, where the plague still lingered) and Zorzi was told to summon Tensini, del Monte and Brancaccio.[175] ' Capacissimo et honorevole ' lodgings were reserved for the Frenchmen and their

---

170. A.S.V., P.T.M., 78, May 6, 11, 16.
171. Crema ms., c. 30v.
172. A.S.V., S.D.T.R., 105, c. 119v.
173. A.S.V., D.R. Verona, 30.
174. His minority report, A.S.V., M.M.N., 144.
175. A.S.V., S.D.R.R., 2, c. 90v.

suites; Rohan, in particular, was accustomed to receive considerable deference, so much so, in fact, that on the eve of leaving for Vicenza, Candales called on Zorzi to express concern lest the Frenchman expect to take precedence over him. Zorzi referred the matter to Venice and was told to give Candales precedence if matters became deadlocked. They did. The Frenchmen arrived on July 27th. Zorzi, Candales, Tensini, Brancaccio, del Monte, Candido, the *commissario in campo* Antonini and Count Giovanbattista Polcenigo assembled there on August 11th, only to find that Rohan refused to meet them unless he were guaranteed the status of *capo della consulta*. At length a compromise was reached whereby Candales should draw up the report as *capo*, but Rohan should submit an independent report of his own.[176]

Tensini, though under a cloud, did not come as a prisoner to the bar of his colleagues' judgement. At the end of July Zorzi had taken him, with Candido, Candales and Antonini to consider the state of Forte Santa Maria degli Angeli, near Crovara, and the fort was later visited by Polcenigo, del Monte and Brancaccio. The last two, with Candido and Tensini, submitted written reports.[177] Tensini's opinion showed that he was not afraid of challenging comparisons with his own fortifications at Vicenza. S. Maria had been designed by Candido, and of earth. Because the quality of the embankments was so poor and because the fort was too large, he suggested that a strong point should be made of one bastion and the rest allowed to decay. The others wrote in similar vein (with the exception of Cosimo del Monte, who was for finishing the fort as a whole).

To arm himself for the fray, Tensini asked for the model he had shown the *collegio* to be sent to Vicenza.[178] He found that opinion had hardened against him. Dining with Zorzi, Sciaban and Rohan not only brought up their old objections but introduced new ones. Tensini defended himself as best he could. That

176. A.S.V., P.T.M., 78, July 26, Aug. 5, 11.
177. Ib., Aug. 1, 9.
178. A.S.V., D.R.V., Aug. 7. It arrived on the 20th. P.T.M., 78.

was on August 15th.[179] Five days later it was clear that Zorzi, represented by Tensini as previously friendly to him, had been won over to the other side. There had been several inspections on the spot, in the course of which Tensini 'vedendosi irreparabilmente scoperto, declinando dal rigore con che professava sostenere l'opera sua, è passato a nuove proposte d'aggiunta d'altri balloardi per ridur la fortificatione a giusta misura'. His nerve cannot have been strengthened by the careful survey of the fortifications that was being carried out at the same time by a local surveyor, Giovanbattista Dante, under the supervision of Polcenigo, in order to check his contract work.[180]

The Dante-Polcenigo report cleared Tensini of any suspicion of peculation. Some work mentioned in the contract remained undone, particularly on the inner side of the rampart and its parapet, but this, plus some building work still remaining at the forts, could be met by the 6,900 ducats still owing to him. Summing up, Zorzi, in his covering report, said the contract had been fulfilled 'canonicamente', and 'se alla perfettione di questo corrispondesse la qualità del dissegno, ne rimarrebbe la Serenità Vostra ottimamente servita'. But the measurements and cost calculations that cleared Tensini's character as a contractor luridly condemned, it seemed, his opinions as a military engineer. If his designs were to be corrected in the way the *consulta* recommended, the total cost would be 1,436, 470 ducats; that is: adding a *banchetta* and extending the ditch so that the demilunes could cover the adjacent bastions properly without being too far in advance of the counterscarp; building them; cladding the walls to a height of four *passi*, with one of foundation (necessary because of the soggy nature of much of the ground). This did not include the forts; to bring them to the pitch of perfection envisaged by the *consulta* would cost another 135,000 ducats. A round one and a half million: that would be the consequence of making Tensini's

---

179. A.S.V., P.T.M. 78.
180. Ib., Aug. 20. Dante and Polcenigo are named on Aug. 26.

115,000 *scudi* design into a thoroughly respectable defence system.[181] Allowing for considerable inaccuracies in both mensuration and cost estimation the moral was inescapable: it would be better to write off Tensini's scheme and begin again from scratch. Or almost: the figures played into Sciaban's hands; the obvious solution was to salve two bastions and incorporate them into a citadel. This was the opinion of Giustiniani, who swung against Tensini as Zorzi had done. Writing to the doge on August 30th he said he much regretted that the opinion of the ' prima consulta ' had not been adhered to, that is, to build one large fort on Monte Berico, restore the old wall and ditches and construct ' una citadella di cinque balloardi alla porta di S. Bartolomeo che haveria valso ad una più valida difesa di questi cittadini '.[182] The over-simplification in this view does not need underlining. It was echoed in an instruction from the government to Zorzi three days later, asking him to send a plan ' della nuova citadella che viene proposta, et il conte della spesa ' as soon as possible.[183] Zorzi obeyed on September 7th.[184] Giustiniani also pointed out, in a letter very similar to the one from the *rettori* of Verona, that the plague had wiped out more than half the population; the city's income had dropped from 72,000 ducats to an estimated 38,000, possibly less. And the fortifications were partly to blame; Tensini's large circuit had eaten up a large area of the Campo Marzo which the city had formerly let out for grazing at a good price.[185] The climate, moreover, continued to be anti-Tensini. That July-August saw one of the worst harvests in recent emory.[186] The city was 8,000 ducats behind in the payments of its original donative (September 6th, 1629); there was no talk of paying the

181. Ib., Aug. 26.
182. A.S.V., D.R.V.
183. A.S.V., S.D.R.R., 2, Sept. 2, c. 123v.
184. A.S.V., P.T.M., 79. The plan is lost, as are the records of the *consulta*.
185. A.S.V., Aug. 30. In 1629 the population figures for city and *territorio* were 31, 897; 164, 286. In 1635 they were 19, 000; 97, 000. A.S.V., *Senato, Relationi*, 51, Basadona and Bragadin.
186. Ib. passim for these months.

second one. Vicenza was also in the grip of a crime wave which occupied the energies of the *rettori* to the full. In late November they were forced to ask the Council of Ten for permission to grant immunity to informers and to take evidence in secret from them. The streets were full of swaggering groups of armed men; murders, rapes, robbery with violence were an everyday occurence: and all this just when 'speravimo che, cessato il flagello dell'ira di Dio in questa città e territorio, gli huomini si dimostrassero grati riconoscitori del beneficio ricevuto, astenendosi da delitti e da sceleratezze '.[187]

The question now was not how to improve Tensini's *enceinte* but whether to demolish it or not. Fort Cornaro, though not entirely finished, was at least occupied by a garrison of forty infantry,[188] but the rest of the works, with labour suspended, continued to decay. It was not until January 26th, 1633 that the senate ordered another report.[189] The *capitano*, Zaccaria Mocenigo had Sebastian Cipriani produce a plan [plate 5] showing the existing state of the fortifications and pointed out that the damage was entirely due to the weather; in spite of many requests from citizens to demolish the embankments on their property he had steadfastly refused.[190] It was not until May that the senate ordered Zorzi to organize another conference on the spot, to which he was to invite de Ville and others but was to exclude those who had played any part in the construction of the fortifications,[191] and it was not until late September that de Ville and Candido produced opinions[192] and until October that Zorzi commented on them.[193] He said that the wisest measure would be to

187. A.S.V., Capi del Consiglio di Dieci, Lettere Rettori, Vicenza, Nov. 29.
188. A.S.V., D.R.V., Sept. 19, 1631.
189. A.S.V., S.D.T.R., 108, c. 533r.
190. A.S.V., D.R.V., 20, Feb. 4, enclosing coloured plan, signed Sebastian Cipriani detto Roccatagliata. Bastions E and F had remained unfinished, the *unione* between Cornaro and Contarini hardly begun. Dotted lines show projected, but uncompleted work. He is presumably a relative of Tensini's correspondent of February 12, 1630.
191. A.S.V., S.D.R.R., 4, May 21, c. 33v.
192. Ib., c. 80r. Their opinion is not preserved.
193. A.S.V., P.T.M., 85, Oct. 6.

reform the forts into a large defence embracing the whole summit of the Monte and to build a citadel at S. Bartolomeo: the two works being essential complements to one another. As for Tensini's *enceinte*, because of its low profile, too narrow ditch, long curtains, ' et per altri mancamenti che non hanno alcun rimedio ', it should be left to decay. It would be too expensive to level it, so it would be best ' che si lascino distrugger dal tempo, o che la Serenità Vostra, benignamente consolando i patroni del fondo, permettesse ad essi di spianarle et valersene come prima, a lor gran sollievo '. Zorzi also pointed out, however, that the Monte and the citadel between them would cost something like 300,000 ducats, plus the maintenance of their garrisons, so he could not unreservedly commend their construction. After all, he pointed out, a threat like the recent war might never recur, and would be all the more unlikely if the government kept an adequate army ready for the field.

The senate replied that ' ne' tempi presenti l'entrare in considerabili dispendii non è di nostra volontà ', and that they were only prepared to make a decision on the existing works, which should meanwhile be preserved. With the assistance of de Ville, Zorzi was to make a clear decision: improve them, leave them as they were, or demolish them?[194] Once more there was delay, and when Zorzi finally received de Ville's opinion (and those of Candido and Brancaccio, whom he had sent to give force to the Ville's findings) it was May 1634, and the tone of Zorzi's report is that of a man sick and tired of the whole issue of the Vicenza fortifications.[195] Wearily he sums up yet again the objections to that miserable *enceinte* ' falso, contro ogni regola, generalmente diffettoso et inutile in tutto '. Better no fortifications at all than this *enceinte* as it stood, good only to provide lodgement for an enemy. If the doge insists on refortifying Vicenza it is not for him to object, but it is his duty to point out that the sums involved

---

194. A.S.V., S.D.R.R., 4, Jan. 12, 1633, cc. 121r-v.
195. A.S.V., P.T.M., 86, May 6, 1634.

will be large and that Venice already has more fortifications than it can afford to maintain. Was it really necessary, in fact, to fortify Vicenza at all? (Not having been involved during 1629-30, Zorzi could afford to put the question). It is already 'i diffesa per levante da Padova, Treviso et Palma, per mezzo dì dal fiume Po et fortezza di Legnago, et per ponente da Peschiera et Verona di quà da Menzo, senza parlar di Crema, Bergamo, Brescia, Asola et Orzi piazze fortissime oltre il medesimo fiume per consumar gl'eserciti intieri; et per tramontana da sterilissime montagne et passi stretti'. Besides, not only would it cost 'milioni' to put Vicenza into a state of perfect defence, but money would still have to be spent on an army to relieve it in case it came under siege. He has been asked for a firm opinion on the fortifications of Vicenza, and here it is: 'lasciarle cader da se stesse, senza spendervi un soldo'.

This could almost be the fortifications' epitaph were it not for a prohibition against levelling them at once. Not an effective prohibition: by August 1634 animals were wandering in and out of forts Contarini and Barbaro and part of the *enceinte* had come under the plough.[196] A year later the works were judged to be no longer of any defensive use,[197] though the possibility of further work was still used as an excuse by the *consiglio* for non-payment of its 12,000 ducat donative.[198] Early in 1636 the *capitano*, Francesco Corner, inspected the *enceinte* and the forts and was alarmed by the speed at which they were deteriorating. Four soldiers were living in the only two habitable rooms in Fort Cornaro amid fallen earthworks and looted quarters.[199] His successor, Francesco Loredano, explained at the end of his term of office, in September, 1640, that he had done his best to prevent the citizens from reclaiming the parts of the fortifications which had originally belonged to them, but somehow it had become taken

---

196. A.S.V., D.R.V., 21, Aug. 13. Report of *capitano*, Agostini Nani.
197. A.S.V., *Senato, Relazioni*, 51. Nani's *relazione*, Dec. 1635.
198. A.S.V., D.R.V., 22, Sept. 1635.
199. Ib., Jan. 22.

for granted that Venice would do nothing more and the *rettori* were helpless in the face of public opinion, their proclamations ignored.[200] In the mid-1640's yet another proclamation was published because the Vicentines had continued 'senza alcun riguardo di propria auttorità occupare con passaglie, & in altre maniere qualque parti delli Terrapieni, Baloardi, Cortine, & Fosse delle fortification di questa Città, nel circuito da basso, & delli forti del Monte,' ploughing, sowing, reaping and grazing 'non ostante precedenti prohibitioni.'[201] But the habit of treating Tensini's fortifications as though they had never existed was already too strong to be broken. When Napolion Francesco Eraut visited them briefly before July 1682 in order to fill out his account of the fortifications of the *terraferma* they had vanished save for 'qualche semplice vestigie'.[202]

And what of Tensini himself, who had been preremptorily excluded from the *consulta* of September 1633? Vicenza had not, in fact, been his ruin. He was employed at Mantua in June, 1632, when the duke was seeking advice on making the city stronger than it had proved to be in 1630.[203] More significant was the renewal of his *condotta* on November 18th of the same year.[204] The resolution was warmly worded, referring to his fifteen years of faithful service 'particolarmente nel riconoscer et fortificar la maggior parte delle nostre piazze, riveder artiglierie, munitioni, passi et confini di Terra Ferma, havendo in tutt'occasioni datto saggio dell'isperienza sua militare, acquistata in lunghi anni et assedii nelle guerre esterne, et essercitata in quelle del Friuli, Valtellina e Mantova, dove nel maneggio dell'Artiglieria et nelle fortificationi ha adempito i numeri di buon soldato'. His salary

---

200. A.S.V., *Senato, Relazioni*, 51, Sept. 25.
201. V.B.C., 160, 11. No date, but published in the name of Lorenzo Barbaro, *capitano* 1644-6.
202. Marciana, Mss. It., 5093, *Racolta delle piante d'alquanto delle più considerabili et forti piazze dello stato...*, Brescia, 29 July, 1682.
203. A.S.V., S.D.R.R., 3, June 3, 70v.
204. A.S.V., S.D.T.R., 108, c. 430v.

was increased from 1,000 to 1,200 ducats a year[205] and the renewal was for the usual ' anni cinque di fermo et due di rispetto '. Vicenza was not mentioned, but it must have been in the minds of the *collegio* who had passed it on November 9th by thirteen votes to two *voti dubii* but referred it to the Senate, where the voting was unusually close for a renewal of *condotta*: eighty nine for and twenty one against, with eleven *dubii*. This is not the place to follow the rest of Tensini's career;[206] suffice it to say that, as far as I know, he did not revisit the place which he had hoped to make ' una delle più belle e forte città - non dire che habbia Sua Serenità, ma che sia al mondo '.

---

205. Sciaban was getting 3, 000 ducats a year. A.S.V., S.D.T.R., 104, c. 560v.
206. I hope to do this in a biography for which I am working, and for which I should be grateful for any advice readers of this essay could give me.

APPENDIX 1

Vicenza, Bertoliana, Archivio del Comune 160, 6.

Havendo l'Illustrissimo Signor Marc' Antonio da Canal... per maggior commodita delli poveri, che lavorano nelli forti sopra il monte Berico, fatto fabricar delli ferlini, o monete picciole de' piombo, & quelle valutate a soldi 20. l'uno, fa percio publicamente intendere & sapere, come ogn'uno può liberamente, & sicuramente pigliar detti ferlini in pagamento per soldi 20. l'uno tanto quanto se fosse moneta corrente, e che ogni Sabbato di sera saranno dalli deputati da Sua Signoria Illustrissima permutati li detti ferlini in tanti buoni danari correnti in ragion come di sopra.

14 Marzo 1630

APPENDIX 2

A.S.V., M.M.N., 144.
Endorsed: « Capitoli con li quali si è acordato Sua Ser^{ta} col Cavalier Tensini in matteria del fortifficare la Città di Vicenza.

Serenissimo Prencipe

Io Francesco Tensini, umilissimo servatore della Serenita Vostra, dico che toro a fare in apalto la fortificacion di Vicenza, cio e li tre forti sopra la somita del monte vecino coll'unione delli doi piu alto, et da basso al intorno della cità li tredici baloardi intieri con li quatro mezi, conforme ho disignato sopra il sito et al disegno datto alli Illustrissimi et Eccellentissimi Signori Cavalieri Procuratori et Generali Girolamo Cornaro, Simon Contarini et Antonio Barbaro, a cio deputati della Serenita Vostra, cio è di dare del tutto fenito di terreno li tre forti sopra il monte, con la sudetta unione delli doi piu ad alto, in termine di tre mesi, obbligandomi anco nel istesso termine di dare in diffesa et a prova di canone, li sudetti tredici baloardi et quatro mezi, con il tenaglione davanti alli doi di porta di Santo Bartolameo, cio è alti sopra la superficie del tereno sette piedi, et grossi alla superficie deciotto, con il suo fosso largo 30, et il tutto incamisiato della superficie del terreno ad alto di lotte di prato vecchio [cancelled; in margin: con lotte buone et consistenti] con l'erba, potendone anche tore sopra le rive e ne' fossi della cità ben batute, impironate piedi per piedi, et li pironi distanti l'uno dal altro uno piedi e mezo, dovendo anco battere il tereno piedi per piedi per il spacio di deciotto piedi. Facendo li forti del monte alti nella parte più bassa quindeci piedi sopra la superficie del sasso o fosso dove saranno fondati, et li soi parapetti verso la valle et verso dove possano ragionevolmente esse batuti, grosso alla superficie quindeci piedi, bastando che delli altri parti siino grossi alla superficie sei piedi, che chi li volesse far grossi ugualmente quindeci piedi si veniria a ristringere troppo le piazze d'alto, non havendosi potuto fare li forti più grandi per la stretezza del sito, dovendo io prima con accurata diligenza fenire la fortificacion del monte et fare li doi baloardi col suo tenaglione davanti la porta di Santo Bartolameo et, in caso che io non complisse cio che io prometto, possa Sua Serenita farla fare lui, ad'ogni mio danno et interesse. Et fenita questa opera risolvendosi Sua Serenita del fenirla e ridurla in perfecione con che mi sia datto il piu delli 65 miglia ducati sino alli 115 miglia scudi, con li quali ho detto che si puo fenire di tereno la sudetta fortificacione; li quali 115 miglia scudi fanno 129,838 ducati di 4 lire e otto soldi, delli quali ribatendone li 65,000 che mi danno di presente restaranno 64,838 ducati et 8 soldi, con tutto cio che mi sia scordado a fare questo conto la scavacione e spesa del fare la strada coperta, che costera piu di 15 mille ducati, ma io torei piu volontieri a perfecionare la fortificacione a solo 5 lire e meza al passo cubo venetiano, dandone hora à Verona al Apaltador Mariani 6 et meza.

Toro a fare cio con le seguenti condicioni: che la Sua Serenita mi dia in soma sesantacinque miglia ducati di moneta corente in Vicenza, cio è cinque miglia alla setimana anticipatamente; mi dara medesimamente Sua Serenita anticipatamente doi miglia ducati per poter fare le provisioni di ta[v]ole, travi, chiodi et altre cose necessarie per la sudetta fortificacione di essermi questi discontati [?] nel fine del opera.

Mi fara comandare Sua Serenita 2.000 guastadori, a li quali pagaro giornalmente per il primo mese e mezo una lira al giorno, et l'altro mese e mezo un mozanigo a 24 soldi, bene spero che incominciata l'opera con il bon ordine che teniro nel pagarli veniranno voluontariamente come io feci al forte di Tirano in Valtelina. Delli quali guastadori comandati mi sia datto la poliza, che non venendo ne daro la notta al Illustrissimo Signore Provveditore affine che siino castigati li inobediente, facendo alcun guastadore o altro sotto al mio comando alcuna cosa ingiusta debba l'Illustrissimo Signore Capitano farli mettere pregioni et castigarli conforme al delitto.

Mi dara Sua Serenita la fasina, et il legname per fare li pironi per impironar le lotte et mettere nella fortificacione delli forti si per andare le ponte di questi molte alte come per non esservi sopra il monte cosi buon tereno come al piano, condotto sopra il luogo per niente, come si fa di presente a Verona et in ogni altro luogo che io ho fatto fortificare.

Sua Serenita m'imprestara 1,000 cariole, 1,000 zerletti della forma che io li ho fatti cominciare, 500 badili et 200 piconi, li quali mi obbligo di ritornare fenito che sia l'opera, et essendovene dispersi comperarne delli altri, et essendovene dirotti farli accomodare, cose necessarie di tenersi di monicione in una fortezza.

Non cominciando l'obbligo di dare la fortificacione in diffesa et a prova di canone se prima non mi saranno consignati la meta delli sudetti istrumenti, et l'altra meta in 20 giorni appresso.

Mi fara dar Sua Serenita ne borghi allogiamenti per li guastadori, capi mastri et altri officiali solo con paglia.

Che niuno senza mia licenza ne venda ne facia vendere pane ne vino fori della cità a' guastadori, e quello che con mia licenza li sara venduto sia del istesso peso, qualita e bonta di quello che si vende nella cita et venduto al istesso precio, e cio a giudicio di uno eletto diputato a cio de Signori Vicentini.

Mi concedara Sua Serenita l'ingegnero Giovanni Giacomo Marchese mio alievo per assistere alla sudetta fortificacione, dovendo io alcuna volta andare a ordinare e rivedere quella di Verona, dovendosi subito mandare a dimandare e far venire a Vicenza il sudetto ingegnero. Intendendomi di non haver altro sopraintendente alla detta fortificacione che l'Illustrissimo Signore Provveditore, Capitani o Podesta, che devano vedere s'io facio l'opera bene e conforme alli capitoli.

Che sia subito sospesa la fabricha del forte Contarini, ordinando che subito l'Illustrisimo Signore Capitano si faccia dare il conto del danaro speso al intorno del sudetto forte, della qual spesa io ne pagaro la meta nel fin del opera.

Che subito gionto il Cavalier Tensini a Vicenza sia fatto proclama che li patroni delle case che necessariamente vanno a basso per fare la fortificacione, le faciano disfare subito, altramente pasati 15 giorni le fara disfare sua Serenita o vero il sudetto Cavalier Tensini, ma con perdita delli patroni di tutti li materiali, si per la inobedienza come per la spesa che vi andera a farle disfare, le qual case le saranno mostrade del medesimo Cavalier Tensini o suoi officiali. Che subito si faccia proclama che per doi miglia lontano della cità niuno facia rompere alcun prato o rive et fossi dove si possano far lotte.

Potendo il nemico levare l'acqua del Astighello, per magior sicurezza del potere havere e dare 5 piedi d'acqua al intorno della fortificacione tra porta Santo Bartolameo al Bachilione, si deve un ponte Canale di legno sopra l'Astigello, affine che con l'acqua del Bachilione la qual il nemico mai la puo levare, si possa dare nella sudetta fortificacione l'acqua necessaria: il qual ponte farò à mie spese.

Del qual accordio s'ne deve fare tre copie, havendone di restare una in mano di Sua Serenita, l'altra all'Illustrissimi Signori Representanti a Vicenza et l'altra a me, sottoscritta coi nome di Sua Serenita et da me. Dovendosi medesimamente fare tre copie simile della sudetta fortificacione, dovendone restare una in mano di Sua Serenita, l'altro al Illustrissimo Signore Proveditore di Vicenza et una a me, sottoscritto in nome di Sua Serenita et da me, assicurando Vostra Serenita che io faro quanto ho promesso, et risolvendosi con il tempo di ridure il tutto in perfecione, lo prenderò a fare con la soma datta in notta nelle mie scriture alli sudetti Illustrissimi et Eccellentissimi Signori Cavalieri Procuratori et Generali, diffalcando la soma delli presenti sesanta cinque miglia duchati intendendomi di non esser obbligato il fare la sudetta fortificacione in tre mesi se non mi vengano osservati pontualmente li sudetti capitoli, particolarmente quelli del danaro e guastadori; con che facio umilissima reverenza alla Serenita Vostra et a tutti questi Illustrissimi et Eccelentissimi Signori Senatori.

In Venetia li 2 Aprile 1630.
[Signed] Il Cavalier FRANCESCO TENSINI

5

THE FIRST FIFTY YEARS
OF A VENETIAN MAGISTRACY
THE *PROVVEDITORI ALLE FORTEZZE*

> Per certo se con giusto giudicio si vorrà andar considerando con quanta grandezza, con quale illustre apparato, e regale spesa siano state molte fortezze dalla Republica in questi tempi fabricate, e che per quanto comporta la diversa usanza di tempi faranno queste a quelli più famosi edificij presso all'antichità paragonate, troverassi, che per respetto così della spesa, come della grandezza dell'opera, non minor laude di magnificenza devono haversi i Vinetiani acquistata di quella, che si dia a gli antichi Romani ....
>
> (Paolo Paruta, *Historia Vinetiana*)

After its recovery from the sickening defeat at Agnadello, the Venetian government adopted a generally defensive and neutral posture in international affairs. Commercially, this meant the guarding of its sea lanes with no attempt to extend them by force. Territorially it meant that the medieval concept of a border, something flexible, responsive to the losses and gains of inheritance and war, changed towards that of a frontier enclosing a changeless homeland. Encircled by two active enemies, the Turks in the east, the Austrian archdukes in the north, and two potential ones, Spanish Milan in the west and the papacy in the south, Venetian neutrality had perforce to be armed. Venetian diplomacy, moreover, dedicated to an active policy of sowing discord among these enemies and distracting them by bringing pressure to bear on their potential adversaries from England and France to Persia, required a strong base to give it credibility. The sixteenth century, therefore, saw a marked increase in the attention Venice paid to its fortifications.

The chief new works undertaken were: in the east, Candia (Herakleon), Canea (Khania) Corfu and Zara (Zadar); against the north, Peschiera and Verona; in the west, Bergamo and Brescia; in the south, Legnago. But because of the effects of weather and ground subsidence, and because of pressure to revamp old fortifications ' alla moderna ', less costly work was carried out intermittently at — to box the compass once more — Cephalonia, Famagosta, Suda, Spinalonga, Dulcigno, Budua, Novigrad, Trau (Trogis), Cattaro (Kotor), Sebenico (Sibenik); Capo d' Istria, Treviso, Cadore, Marano, Anfo, Chiusa; Crema and Orzinovi. Venice itself acquired the Lido forts of S. Andrea and S. Niccolò and a defensive system at Chioggia. The list could be considerably extended if it were to include fortifications like Naxos and Padua, where improvements were discussed and prepared, but not carried out.

These are the sites that were the major preoccupation of the period with which this essay is concerned, the fifty years between 1542 and 1592. But already in the years since Agnadello the burden of static defense had been growing too heavy for the crowded agenda of the *collegio*. The absence, too, of a connecting link between site works and the *collegio* led to delays and misunderstandings. An attempt to counter this difficulty was made tentatively in 1527, when a senator was elected to act as a contact between the *collegio* and the work going forward at Legnago. Foreshadowing the work of the *fortezze* magistracy, the duty of this individual, who was given no title, was to remain in Venice and see to the execution of all orders relating to the fortifications [1]. Administrative problems were thrown into especially high relief by the widespread reconstruction work needed after the Turkish war of 1537-1540, especially up the length of the Adriatic from Corfu to Zara. The problem was all the greater for the administrative disarray in which the coastal towns had been left and an economic plight which led them to plead for relief from taxation. In 1542 the senate acted as it traditionally did when one of its spheres of competence was swelling to unmanageable proportions: it released the pressure by creating a new magistracy.

After drawing attention to the fact that fortresses are « as everyone knows very well » the foundation of the state, and citing the unprepared condition in which Corfu had had to face the Turk, the decision of September 25th laid the blame for past inefficiency on the lack of a body specifically concerned with fortification and the pressure of other business on the *savii*

---

[1] Senato, Deliberazioni, Terra: Registri [S. D. T. R.], 24, f. 161 v. All documents cited are in the Archivio di Stato, Venice.

of the *collegio*. Two senators were therefore to be elected annually with the title of *provveditori delle fortezze* [2]. Their responsibility, which extended to both *Terra* and *Mar*, was to ensure that fortresses (the term included town walls and citadels as well as isolated strong points) were adequately maintained. The *provveditori* were limited in their freedom of action. They had to refer the orders they gave to the *savii* of the *collegio* who could countermand them, though only after explaining their reasons to the senate.

To keep themselves informed they were to be present when *rettori* reported on their terms of duty and they were to receive reports on matters concerning fortifications and stores from other returning officials — castellans, for instance, or *provveditori in terra ferma* — whose duties had kept them in touch with fortified places. On the sixth of October the first two *provveditori* were elected by the senate and *zonta*: Alessandro Contarini and Filippo Cappello.

The lack of continuity caused by having both *provveditori* quit office at the same time was corrected in 1551 [3]. At the election in October of that year the *provveditore* chosen with the fewer votes was to remain in office only for six months; thereafter the terms of office were to overlap. The same decision spelled out the period of disqualification before a man could be re-elected — equal to the number of months he had held office — and laid down penalties for a *provveditore* who accepted another commission before his term was completed [4]. Two later pieces of legislation stressed the importance of the magistracy. In 1566 it was coupled with the magistracies *all'Arsenale* and *all'armar* as being one of the key organs elected by the senate, and, with them, its officers were to be chosen before the balloting took place for other posts. It was further decided that a man could be appointed no matter what other post he already

---

[2] See Appendix. 'Alle fortezze' only became standard form in the seventeenth century; before that they were referred to as *provveditori alle*, or *delle*, or *sopra le fortezze*. The Latin form was *super fortilitiis*.

[3] S. D. T. R., 37, ff. 154 r-155 r, 6 July.

[4] Re-elections were common, helping sustain the continuity of administration. Thus Alessandro Contarini was reappointed in 1544, 1547, 1549 and 1554. Antonio Cappello, first elected in 1550, served again in 1552, 1556 and 1558.

held, unless it were that of *conservatore delle leggi* and as long as he was not a member of the *collegio* [5]. In March 1579 the council of ten had introduced new accounting procedures as part of a general re-allotment of funds among the magistracies [6]. A counter-signature was now required before *fortezze* money could be disbursed. The indisposition of one of the *provveditori* could (and repeatedly did) hold up the business of the office, and in 1580 it was decided that henceforward there were to be three *provveditori*, two holding office for a full year and one for six months [7]. Finally, the importance of the magistracy was once more stressed in 1585, when it was laid down that a *provveditore* could only leave his post for that of ambassador or *provveditore generale*, or were he appointed to the *collegio* [8]. Like other legislation of the period, this reflects the strain on the restricted membership of the senate caused by the multiplication of offices and the principle of rotation.

While the Venetian constitution could throw out new limbs at need, it was less good at putting them to effective use. The policy of appointing amateurs to specialist duties, and for only a short period, meant that while their responsibilities were heavy, there were continual checks on their freedom of action. These checks were particularly hampering in the case of the *provveditori alle fortezze*. Partly this was due to the large sums involved. Control over expenditure was kept in the hands of the senate and the ten not only so that the spending of the state's annual income could be kept under review, but because the imposition of special taxes and labour services in the territories affected by works of fortification involved political decisions; they touched on the perennially nervous relationship between Venice and the *terra ferma* and its overseas possessions. Politics, as well as purely military decisions were involved in two further respects. Military engineers might decide that the best way of defending a town was by building a citadel within it; the inhabitants might interpret this as a threat to their own liberty. (This

---

[5] S. D. T. R., 43, f. 74 v, 3 October.
[6] See below, p. 184.
[7] Provveditori alle Fortezze [P. F.], 2, f. 29 r, 31 January. (All dates in this essay are modernized).
[8] S. D. T. R., 56, ff. 70 v-71 r, Oct. 2.

issue led to no action being taken on the proposal to build a citadel in Padua in the 1540's.) And the responsibility of the *provveditori* for military security had to be balanced against the ten's responsibility for political security, which led them to send out inspectors of their own and to correspond directly with *capitani* about the ability of a town's defenses to keep out spies and malcontents [9].

The *provveditori* were, in effect, a committee of the senate, and they suffered to some extent from the rivalry between senate and ten that was to lead to the constitutional friction of 1582-83 and the redefinition of that council's powers. In a decision supplementary to that setting up the *fortezze* magistracy, the senate had noted that « the chief fortresses of the state are under the control of our council of ten, as are the most important and necessary artillery and munitions; the provision of money, moreover, is for the most part determined by that council ». To establish a line of communication for the *provveditori* between discussions concerning 'senate' fortifications and those of the ten, it was decided that one of the *savii del consiglio* and one of the *savii di terra ferma*, who had access to the meetings of the ten, should be responsible for liaison in matters of fortification between the ten and the *collegio* and thus keep the *provveditori*, who sat with the *collegio* when their duties were discussed, and the senate informed. Similarly one of the *savii agli ordini* was entrusted with reporting any discussion in the ten dealing with fortification in the *Mar* zone. It was possibly on the insistence of the ten, and certainly to the detriment of the clarity with which the duties of the *provveditori* had just been defined, that the three *savii* were entrusted with the « specific charge of ensuring that all our fortresses are provided with the things appropriate and necessary to them » [10]. While the implication is that the *savii* were to check the allocation of guns, powder, foodstuffs and other supplies, the planning of fortifications was at all stages involved with quarters for garrisons and with food and arms stores; the *savii* thus amounted to a body shadowing the *provveditori* at every point of their duties.

---

[9] E. g., Consiglio di Dieci, Deliberazioni [C. D. D.], Secreta: R., 1539-46, ff. 107 v, 165 v, 72 r, and C. D. D., Comune, R., 62, f. 103 r.
[10] S. D., Secreta, R., 62, f. 59 v-60 r.

The ten continued to order cannon directly from the *patroni* of the arsenal and have them transported to fortresses with only a rare stipulation that a copy of the inventory should be sent to the *provveditori*. They continued to receive reports on the state of artillery and of powder stores direct, and give instructions without reference to the *provveditori* even when repairs and alterations supervised by their magistracy were going forward. As a result, there was no one office that could give a clear overall account of a fortress's state of readiness.

On the other hand, the ten appear only to have maintained control over the full range of operations involved in planning and arranging for the execution of fortifications in the case of those within the *dominante*, those of immediate concern to the protection of the city itself. In 1543 the council asked for advice on the fortification of Chioggia from the duke of Urbino, Michele Sanmicheli, and Antonio da Castello, interviewed them, and gave orders for the work to be carried out — only then entrusting the organization of the labour force to the *provveditori*. The single note of dissent to this procedure was sounded by Antonio Priuli, who proposed that the matter should be postponed and raised at a later time « in the *consiglio de' pregadi* [senate], where other matters concerning fortifications are discussed »[11]. The decision to fortify the Lido had already been taken in 1534 and subsequently dropped. It was therefore appropriate that the council of ten should take the initiative again in 1543, and had it not been divided on the issue of which fort should be begun first, S. Andrea or S. Niccolò, it would doubtless have acted as it did at Chioggia. As it was, the controversy was referred to the *collegio* with the intervention there of the three *capi dei dieci* and the *provveditori*. The decision to build S. Andrea first (on the designs of Sanmichele and Castello) and then S. Niccolò (according to the duke of Urbino's model) was then taken by the ten [12], and at least until 1579 they continued to make the decisions affecting these fortresses « important above all others »[13]. After 1542, apart from their interest

---

[11] C. D. D., Secreta, R., 1539-46, f. 91 r. The money was sent to the *podestà* of Chioggia by the ten; the *provveditori*, however, were to be accounted to for its disbursement.
[12] *Ibid.*, f. 101 v and 104 r-v.
[13] C. D. D., Comune, R., 34, f. 164 v.

in the *dominante* forts, and a few additional works [14] for which the council had allocated money before the creation of the *fortezze* magistracy, the ten appears to have surrendered its initiative in proposing fortifications, though it continued to answer letters about defense works sent directly to the *capi* without consulting the *provveditori*, particularly when too much sharing of responsibility might lead to the leaking of secrets « to the ears of the Turk » [15].

Thenceforward the *collegio* remained the principal locus where information was gathered and projects planned before being passed to the senate for decision and to the *provveditori* for execution. Information about the state of fortifications came from *rettori* and castellans, local *provveditori*, *sindici*, and *provveditori generali*: any of those officials, that is, whose commissions, roving or stationary, called for reports on military preparedness. Occasionally a community would raise a question, like the repair of its walls, directly. Those reports and suggestions were addressed — when in written form — most frequently directly to the doge, whose secretariat diverted them to the *collegio*, rarely to the doge and the *signoria*, and fairly commonly to the *savii* ' dell'una e dell'altra mano'. As the *signoria* and the *savii* normally made up part of the *collegio*, these addresses all led to the same place. On receipt of information the *collegio* discussed it. Commonly more information was called for at that point, in writing were the informants *en poste*, personally in the case of recently returned officials or when, say, engineers could be reached who had experience of the site in question. This was the point, too, at which models and drawings were discussed, the doge himself sometimes intervening. The *collegio* might ask for oral opinions to be put in writing; experts could ask permission to speak again at a later meeting: these few days represented, in fact, a crucial point in the process of decision-making, for they culminated, after a vote had been taken, in the making of a specific recommendation to the senate [16].

The *collegio's* ' bill ', as it were, was sponsored in the senate by the three *savii* — one from each *mano* — responsible for in-

---

[14] E. g., Cerigo, *ibid.* 62, ff. 115 v-116 r.
[15] Secreta, Materie Miste Notabili, 1, (Asso = Naxos, 1577).
[16] For the role of the *collegio* v. *ibid.*, 1 and 2, *passim*, but with special reference to Crete and Cyprus.

forming themselves about fortification matters [17]; and the 'bill' was supported by the reading of passages from reports and, if necessary, by the production of models. As far as it is recoverable, discussion in the *collegio* appears to have been primarily technical. In the senate the recommendation was discussed against the general background of the current financial and political position. Either it was approved, and orders given for its implementation, or — and this is true of most proposals involving large expenditure, especially on the *terra ferma* [18] — doubts were expressed which led to control of the investigation being taken over by the senate. From this moment it was that body which determined the supplementary fact-finding procedure, electing, it may be, a special investigatory commission from its own members, writing to officials on the spot and summoning new engineers. While the *collegio* might be asked to digest the fresh information and report back its findings, the senate was henceforward the directing agency until a firm decision had been reached.

Before seeing what part the *provveditori* played in this decision-making structure, there is a further body to be considered which had a short life, but was highly characteristic of the politico-administrative mentality of the Venetian patriciate. Little more than a month had elapsed since the setting up of the *fortezze* magistracy when another body was created to deal with fortifications: the *collegio sopra le fortezze* [19]. The senate decision drew attention to the complexity of the issues involved in the planning of new fortifications for Zara, and the number of persons from whom expert advice had to be sought. A body of twenty-five senatorial 'nobili nostri' who were familiar with

---

[17] They are sometimes named; e. g., P. F., 2, ff. 92 r, 102 r, 108 r.

[18] 'Mar' decisions were straightforward in that they were directed against a traditional and openly acknowledged enemy, the Turk, and involved labour, the provision of which was, in the main, welcomed rather than resented. 'Terra' decisions led to speculation and resentment on the part of Venice's neighbours, and frequently involved local protest based on legal precedents, 'hard times' or resentment at being keyed in more firmly to Venetian political-military domination. See, though for a later period (the 1630's), my « Francesco Tensini and the Fortification of Vicenza », above, 99, ff.

[19] So-called in S. D. T. R., 33, f. 127 v, Oct. 6, 1544. Up till then they were referred to simply as the 'XXV nobili'.

the subject was to be elected. A majority vote of this body, together with the 'normal' *collegio* was to be « as firm and binding as if it had been taken in this council » — i. e. the senate [20]. The new *collegio* was reconvened to discuss reports on Padua in the following year. In 1544, because of the difficulty of getting together the necessary quorum of twenty, the membership was enlarged to thirty [21]. In 1547, because a series of reports on Padua, Verona and Legnago had revealed that due to faulty organization certain works had been begun without careful planning while others had been left incomplete, the senate ordered that in future no work was to be undertaken until a model or drawing had been passed as satisfactory « either by this council or by the *collegio nostro sopra le fortezze* » and that works so licensed were to be completed before others were commenced [22].

This, to my knowledge, is the last reference to this new *collegio*. Trouble with the quorum suggests one explanation, the fact that it did not in practice prevent an overlap with the senate suggests another [23]. Designed to cut down a very time-consuming aspect of senatorial work without deputing a zealously guarded legislative function to a chiefly advisory body, the *collegio*, the new body's failure demonstrates the disinclination of senators to delegate power over issues involving large sums of money or to accept decisions (as opposed to recommendations) which incorporated the votes of non-senators. From 1547 the senate relied on the election of *ad hoc* bodies of *provveditori generali* [24] to report back to the *collegio* when works on a large scale

---

[20] Senato, Deliberazioni, Mar: Registri [S. D. M. R.], 26, f. 145 r, Nov. 2. The record of the first meeting is headed « In Collegio cum additione xxv nobilium habente autoritatem consilii rogatorum ». And in addition to the two colleges the following are noted as attending: *consiliarii, capi della quarantia*, and one of the *provveditori*. Twenty-three members of the *collegio sopra le fortezze* are listed. Thirty-nine votes were cast in all and one minority opinion recorded. *Ibid.*, f. 149 r-v, Nov. 31.

[21] S. D. T. R., 33, f. 127 v, Oct. 6.

[22] *Ibid.*, 34, ff. 182 v-183 r, Feb. 3.

[23] S. D. M. R., 28, f. 164 v, May 29, 1546, where the senate amends a *collegio* decision in light of fresh information from Zara.

[24] The number varied. Two were appointed to visit Bergamo in 1585, four to inspect Brescia (together with Savorgnan) in 1588, three to advise on the proposed new fortified town of Palmanova in 1592. P. F., 2, f. 41 r; *ibid.*, 60; S. D. Secreta: Registri, 89, f. 82 v.

were under consideration. In 1587, still in pursuit of that elusive goal, a total expert oversight of fortifications, it appointed Giulio Savorgnan ' sopraintendente general di tutte le fortezze del stato nostro così da terra come da mar ' [25].

The creation of the *collegio sopra le fortezze* throws into relief, however, the restricted nature of the role the *provveditori alle fortezze* were expected to play in the making of decisions. They were present at meetings of the *collegio* when fortifications were discussed, as they were when the senate discussed them. Very rarely they were sent to discuss plans on the spot [26]. The records of *collegio* and senate meetings are such that only dissident opinions are noted, and then only infrequently. No *provveditore* is cited as advancing a minority view. Their role was not to argue, but to assemble records, provide information and to administer and put into effect decisions proposed and ratified by others. Inevitably, as their files thickened and as the precedents they established became part of the routine administration of building projects, their magistracy increased in stature, but still as a provider of services. Indeed, as its efficiency grew in this respect, the *provveditori* were called upon less and less frequently for their advice [27].

Essentially the *provveditori* were building contractors, responsible for the most costly aspect of the state's public works programme. As such they were involved in a policy of retrenchment in government spending which spanned the second half of the sixteenth century. Already in 1540 the *savii sopra la mercantia* had been instructed to conduct a purge of public officials throughout the *terra ferma* [28]. In 1558 garrisons on the *terra ferma* were cut down, in 1560 it was the turn of those on the Dalmatian coast [29]. In 1564 the *provveditori* were made responsible for a

---

[25] P. F., 2, 49 r.

[26] Both were ordered by the senate to go to Padua, Legnago and Verona with experts of their own choosing in 1546; one was sent to Peschiera in 1549. S. D. T. R., 34, f. 166 v; *ibid.*, 36, f. 132 v.

[27] At least, in the marginal notes which record attendance in senate registers and *filze*, they appeared less frequently from the late 1560's and very seldom from the late 1570's.

[28] The principles behind this purge long continued to be invoked. E. g., S. D. T. R., 53, f. 4 r, March 7, 1580.

[29] *Ibid.*, 41, ff. 113 r-114 r; S. D. M. R., 35, f. 10 r and 51 r ff.

second purge of officials — accountants, building subcontractors, carpenters, masons, storekeepers — who were no longer essential to the fortification work then going forward. Within two months all such officials were to turn up in Venice to be interviewed by the *provveditori* (six months in the case of those in the *Mar* jurisdiction) and with their help the *collegio* was to determine who would be retained and who would be fired [30].

This order was sent to *rettori*, but it was above all on these individuals that the *provveditori* were expected to check. Within months of the establishment of their magistracy they were being called upon to make sure that *rettori* did not spend the money sent to them for fortifications on anything other than walls, ditches and gun emplacements — « as has been done until now by many of our representatives » — and to be especially vigilant that public money was not spent on personal display, such as the putting up by *rettori* or *provveditori sopra le fabriche* [31] of their own coats of arms or names on gates or bastions. The *provveditori* were to check the accounts of all *rettori* or *provveditori sopra le fabriche* returning from duty, and were there any discrepancy between the record in the *fortezze* office of the sums which they had been licensed to spend and their actual expenditure, the *provveditori* were to refuse to issue the receipt (*bolletino*) without which they were left without voting rights [32]. Consequent legislation in which the *provveditori* were involved supports the view that the patricians who served as *rettori* and in other positions of responsibility outside the city were not always ideal public servants. It was deplored that they were prone to leave their posts without permission [33], that they handed out more jobs than were strictly necessary [34], that they made contracts with individuals for lime and stone without inviting bids and accepting the lowest [35], that they ordered more material than they could afford so that the *fortezze* office was plagued with unpaid bills [36]. In the inspection of public accounts throughout the

---

[30] S. D. T. R., 45, f. 45 v-46 r; 63 r ff.; 76 r ff.; 83 v.
[31] Officials responsible on the spot for a particular building programme.
[32] S. D. T. R., 32, 113 v ff.; 197 r.
[33] *Ibid.*, f. 113 v.
[34] *Ibid.*, 36, f. 6 v.
[35] *Ibid.*, f. 110 r.
[36] *Ibid.*, f. 170 r.

terra ferma made in 1547 by the *sindici inquisitori*, a number of other fraudulent practices were turned up [37], and where a flood of regulations had failed, the government tried the opposite approach by nearly doubling the *rettori's* allowances. This was in 1549 [38]. Complaints continued to flow in. The *rettori* were paying for lime without checking to see whether it had been watered (it was bought by weight) en route from the furnace [39]. They were even taking personal advantage of the difference in the rate of exchange between Venice and the Levant [40]. In many cases the *rettori* were merely guilty, of course, of a lack of vigilance, as when forged requests for money were made in their name [41], but complaints about their mis- or overspending were constant, and the *provveditori* were used as one of the chief means of controlling it.

From 1543 all payments to *rettori* for fortifications had to be authorized by the *camerlengo de commun* responsible for the *fortezze* account with his signature countersigned by one of the *provveditori*. *Rettori* were to send monthly statements to the *fortezze* office and if a *rettore*, on returning from duty and being denied a *bolletino*, wished to justify himself to the senate he could only do this when the senate had obtained the opinion of the *provveditori* [42]. From 1555 *rettori* were subject to similar checks by the *provveditori* on the grain store it was their responsibility to preserve against an emergency, and on building materials, even though these had been acknowledged on receipt in a note describing quality, quantity and condition on arrival. Thus any discrepancy between the money and materials sent to a *rettore* and the accounts he brought back at the end of his term of duty, could lead to deprivation of voting rights until the discrepancy was made good. And the penalty for not sending monthly accounts — the form of which was carefully spelled out — to the *provveditori* was dismissal and a five hundred ducat

---

[37] *Ibid.*, f. 53 r.
[38] *Ibid.*, f. 160 v-163 r.
[39] S. D. M. R., 31, ff. 122 v-123 r.
[40] *Ibid.*, f. 52 v.
[41] *Ibid.*, f. 97 v. On May 16, 1551, the *camerlenghi di comun* were instructed to keep specimens of *rettori*'s hand-writing so that forgeries could be detected.
[42] S. D. T. R., 32, ff. 174 v-175 r.

fine, half of which was to go to the arsenal and half to the *fortezze* office [43].

A handful of examples will show how difficult it was to enforce the letter of this efficiency-economy drive. In 1551 Niccolò Rimondo, on his return from a period as *conte* of Traù was refused his *bolletino* because he was unable to account for twenty-five ducats that had been sent in the early days of his office. He claimed that he had not received it; the *collegio* accepted his case (represented to them by the *provveditori*) and the sum was charged to his predecessor. In 1561, Gian Domenico Manoleso, ex-castellan of the Castel Vecchio of Verona, was short forty-four *stara* of grain, claiming that the loss was due to damp. As three keys were needed to get into the store (the others held by the *capitano* and the storekeeper) the claim was allowed. In 1565, Piero Emo, returned from being *provveditore sopra le fabriche* at Legnago, could not account for 320 ducats worth of timber. So much timber, however, had been rushed to shore up a collapsed *cavaliere* that the storekeeper may well have been confused. The senate ordered the *provveditori* to give him the benefit of the doubt and make up the loss from *fortezze* funds. Paolo Zorzi returned in 1566 from his post as *capitano* of Candia without any certified accounts. He was given his *bolletino* on payment of an 800-ducat security and eight months in which to have them sent to Venice. In 1573 returning — and accountless — *rettori* from Corfu, Tine and Micone, were excused because they pleaded the dislocating effects of the recent Turkish wars [44]. These cases (which are, I think, reasonably representative) reveal the nervous financial mood which prompted the economy regulations rather than the existence of peculation on a large scale.

The *provveditori's* office [45] was itself run with a minimal and poorly paid staff. It started with an accountant to record monies paid from the *fortezze* account at the *cecca* into the working account at the office, and the sums forwarded and the goods and salaries paid for from that. He was also responsible for checking the monthly statements sent in by *rettori*. Elected by

---

[43] S. D. M. R., 33, ff. 27 v, 35 r, 56 v-57 r. Accounts had to be sent in monthly by *Rettori di Terra*, every four months by *Rettori di Mar*.
[44] P. F., 20 (1), f. 37 v; *ibid.*, f. 47 r; S. D. T. R., 45, ff. 134 r-v; P. F., 20 (1), ff. 51 v-52 r; *ibid.*, f. 96 r.
[45] The records do not show where in Venice it was located.

the *collegio* and paid fifty ducats a year from the *fortezza* account [46], he was assisted by a clerk whose salary of twelve ducats a year came from the same source [47]. For the part-time services of a notary in the chancery the account was charged twenty-four ducats a year [48], a sum which was slightly raised in 1547 by which time the need for his services had risen to a point at which « he needed almost always to have his pen in hand » [49]. In 1562 the accountant, Stefano Spiera, was given an assistant bookkeeper (at one ducat and sixteen grossi a month), because of the increasing load of his work. Traditionally in Venice jobs like clerkships and overseerships in the building trades were handed down from father to son. When Alvise Stella resigned from being clerk in 1553 at the age of eighty, the *provveditori* replaced him with his son. But for the younger man the salary, which had risen to twenty-four ducats a year, was no longer enough. He soon handed it to *his* son, but he, too, found it insufficient. Ten years later, in 1565, Zamaria Dalla Piazza was making the same complaint that the salary was too low for such a « heavy and insupportable » job. Initiating a new dynasty of resignations, he was succeeded by his son [50].

In 1589 the establishments of all magistracies were challenged by an inquiry into government spending conducted by *revisori sopra la scansation delle spese superflue*. By this time, besides an accountant and his assistant and a clerk, the *provveditori* had acquired an overseer whose duty was to inspect the materials — timber, nails, clamps and so forth — purchased by the office and sometimes to inspect construction work on the spot. His salary was fifty ducats a year. Since the council of ten had handed over to the *provveditori* responsibility for the maintenance of S. Andrea and S. Niccolò, they had appointed a custodian to the former, and a foreman to the latter, whose chief job was to see that the mud excavated from the canals of Venice was used to consolidate the land surrounding the fort. The *provveditori* managed to persuade the *revisori* that all these posts were ne-

---

[46] S. D. T. R., 32, Jan. 30, 1543.
[47] P. F., 20 (1), f. 3 r.
[48] *Ibid.*, f. 3 v.
[49] *Ibid.*, f. 21 r.
[50] *Ibid.*, ff. 40 v, 44 r, 49 r.

cessary [51]. The total wages bill of the office was under 350 ducats per annum.

While suggestions for the repair or modification of fortifications most commonly came from the reports of *rettori* or *provveditori generali* and thus came before the *collegio* in the first instance, *rettori* (or representatives fulfilling similar functions under another name) increasingly wrote to the *provveditori* directly [52], as did various public-spirited individuals [53]. Such suggestions were referred at the discretion of the *provveditori* to the *collegio*. Until a decision had been reached by that body and the senate, the *fortezze* office functioned as an archive for the relevant drawings and models [54] and the *provveditori* kept in touch with the engineers and captains who were investigating the situation on the spot, sometimes summoning them to a conference in Venice the results of which would be duly reported in the *collegio*.

Once a decision had been made to proceed, the relevant documentation which had remained in the hands of the *collegio* or senate for the purpose of debate was transferred to the *fortezze* office [55]. A local construction hierarchy was then set up on the spot. Commonly this was supervised by the *capitano* [56] or his

---

[51] P. F., 2, ff. 91 r-92 v and P. F., 36 (1), April 16, 1590. The custodian of S. Andrea got 10 ducats (reduced by the *revisori* from 12) a month; the foreman at S. Niccolò, 6.

[52] E. g., P. F., 36 (4), Dec. 7, 1590.

[53] « I am making so bold [to give an opinion on Verona, in September 1583] both for the zeal I bear towards the illustrious signory of Venice, my patron, and because I have found in the books of the Romans that they listened to anyone, however humble, who spoke to them of matters of concern to the republic ». Anon., P. F., 37 (4), f. 149 r. In 1556 a crank, Joan. Battista de Lion, wrote to say that he had discovered a fatal flaw in the defenses of Padua. Michele Sanmicheli, who was sent to investigate, wrote a report of contemptuous rebuttal. P. F., 65 (1).

[54] The archivio of the *fortezze* survives, unfortunately, in a maimed form. There are very few drawings from this period and no models. I cannot trace the ' cattastico modelli e dissegni ' cited in an inventory of 1798, P. F., 69 (5). The *fortezze* office obtained a part-time curator of models and drawings in 1566, S. D. T. R., 46, f. 17 r. It is not clear how long he served there.

[55] E. g., when, after long discussion, the senate decided to go ahead with plans for improvements at Brescia in 1591, the copy of the minute was endorsed « Le scritture sono state mandate all'offitio delle fortezze ». P. F., 2, f. 110 r.

[56] Occasionally, as at Sebenico, the *capitano's* salary was charged to the

equivalent. Alternatively a *provveditore* was appointed by the *maggior consiglio* to take charge. In peace time the engineer responsible for the plans stayed on the site long enough at least to see the trace drawn (possibly with the aid of a local surveyor) and returned to check progress from time to time, in war time — or indeed when many projects were going forward simultaneously — the engineer could be out of touch with his work for long periods. The actual work programme was organized by a site overseer (*proto*), with deputy foremen in charge of the masons, carpenters and blacksmiths. He directed the labourers (raised by local authorities on the orders of the senate) and was assisted in keeping a labour roll, an inventory of materials received, and a record of work performed, by one or two bookkeepers [57].

The *provveditori* sent drawings and models (in *gesso* or wood) to the site to act as guides during the absences of the engineer, and they also supplied overseers and specialist craftsmen if these could not be recruited locally. The demand came particularly from overseas, where local craftsmen were not familiar with Venetian construction techniques and where there was a shortage of trained overseers and bookkeepers [58], but the *provveditori* also provided trained personnel for works on the *terra ferma* and in all cases their ratification of locally-made appointments was necessary [59]. Most frequently, these jobs were filled by transfer, or by a relation of a man known to the *provveditori*, but occasionally they were advertised by a written announcement displayed « on the Rialto steps » [60]. The *provveditori* were also responsible for sending small change (*sesini*) for the labourers'

---

fortifications while work was proceeding on them. S. D. M. R., 33, f. 157 v, 29 Sept. 1557.

[57] P. F., 2, f. 26 v and 20 (1), f. 3 r for examples from Zara and the Lido. Salaries for these posts varied from 3-11 ducats per month, depending on the amount of work involved and responsibility.

[58] E. g., S. D. M. R., 30, f. 29 r; P. F., 2, f. 8 r and 10 v; S. D. M. R., 35, f. 164 r, and P. F., 20 (1), ff. 31 r-v for examples from Corfu, Cattaro and Candia.

[59] P. F., 20 (1), ff. 40 r and 49 r (Peschiera); *ibid.*, f. 45 v (Legnago). The files kept on such men — P. F., 36 (1), 14 Feb. 1596 — have disappeared. Where really large sums were involved, the *collegio* itself would appoint a bookkeeper: S. D. T. R., 37, f. 17 r (Peschiera).

[60] P. F., 20 (1), f. 139 v. Copy of advertisement for a *proto* in 1585.

weekly pay and could use their judicial powers to settle labour disputes [61]. Meanwhile the bookkeepers on the site reported on the arrival of all supplies to the *provveditori's* accountant, who was required by law to mark these receipts against his record of goods dispatched, and they furnished the *capitano* — or, rather, an accountant from the local *camera* — with the details he was expected to send month by month to the *fortezze* office.

On the *terra ferma* building supplies were usually obtained by the *capitano* or *provveditore* in charge; the *provveditori* were normally only concerned when operations were under their direct supervision; thus they bought Istrian stone for S. Andrea. Within the *stato de Mar*, however, their activities in connection with the purchase and dispatch of supplies were considerable. From Capo d'Istria to the Aegean they were responsible for keeping fortified places equipped with timber (mainly planks of various sizes), bricks, nails, angle-irons and clamps (and pigs and bars of iron for forging on the spot) and with tools, especially picks and shovels. These materials were sent not merely for fortifications, but for constructing and repairing quarters for troops and food and munition stores. Orders for the purchases were given by the senate or, more rarely, the council of ten, in the light of requests made by *rettori*, the costs — in which freight charges figured largely [62] — being worked out with the advice of the *fortezze* office. The *provveditori* then bought and sent the goods, obtained receipts for them [63], dealt with complaints [64] and with the consequences of vessels being sunk,

---

[61] I know of only two examples, however. In one they threaten a recalcitrant subcontractor with a 25-ducat fine, three months in prison and three « squassi della corda »; in the other they insist that a galley loaded with *fortezze* supplies sail in spite of the vessel's being the subject of private litigation: P. F., 20 (1), ff. 57 r, 60 r.

[62] The space occupied by timber made these charges high. Some examples (chiefly from P. F.): freight charge 421 out of a total of 4,506 lire, 114 out of 658 ducats (Zara); 620 out of 3,212 lire (Sebenico); 651 out of 8,145, 1,271 out of 9,663, 700 out of 4,177 lire (Corfu); 780 out of 2,387, 500 out of 1,330 ducats (Candia); 680 out of 2,228 lire (Zante).

[63] One of the difficulties of keeping track of these supplies is suggested by an order of 1575 which specifies that the receipt should be enclosed in a wind- and water-proof cover. P. F., 2, f. 21 r.

[64] E. g., a cargo of bricks which en route from Treviso to Zara were largely « reduced to powder », *ibid.*, f. 41 v.

diverted by storms or having their cargoes forcibly unloaded at ports of call where the local authorities were themselves desperate for supplies.

The *provveditori* were occasionally called upon to dispatch materials other than building supplies, from guncarriages, powder and shot to medicines and boots, caps, and cloth for soldiers' uniforms. But what added more heavily to the administrative burdens of the *provveditori* was their responsibility for victualing. « Fortified places cannot truly be said to be fortified », as a senate preamble put it in 1547, « unless they are provided with an adequate food supply »[65]. Before this date victualing had been organized on an *ad hoc* basis, *rettori* reporting to the *collegio* or the council of ten and receiving from them money for purchases and licenses for the sale of stocks threatened by damp. From 1547 this procedure was rationalized, a lump sum being allocated to the *fortezze* account (though with a separate accounting procedure) and the *provveditori* were empowered to negotiate directly with *rettori* and introduce an accounting procedure parallel to that used for construction work. *Rettori*, at the end of their term of duty, had to satisfy the office on this score, too, before the *provveditori* could supply them with a *bolletino*; the procedure applied both to *Terra* and *Mar*[66]. This meant that the *provveditori* inherited part of one of the more complex areas of governmental administration, for the state granaries, in Venetian territory as elsewhere, were involved not only in the socially nervous business of price-fixing, but were subject to pressure in times of dearth and could not, therefore, be managed merely in terms of military preparedness[67].

The original brief to the *provveditori*, to ensure that fortified places were defensible for at least a year ahead, now involved making sure that a starving population would not force a garrison to surrender. For the people as a whole this was almost exclusively a matter of grain for bread, and grain, from wheat to millet, was thus the *provveditori*'s chief concern. But they were

---

[65] S. D. T. R., 35, f. 41 v.
[66] See esp. S. D. T. R., 35, f. 33 r., 36, f. 108 r. The account was called the « a comprar vettuarie per le fortezze » and from the point of view of overall budgeting remained a sub-account of the *cassa delle monitioni*.
[67] See P. F., 36 (1) for some of the problems involved.

also responsible, within this overall concern, for the detailed diet of the garrisons themselves [68]. As itemized by one of the government's most trusted advisers in military matters in the 1540's and 1550's, the duke of Urbino, this included, besides grain of various sorts for bread: beans, rice, oil, salt, cheese, salt meat, fish, vinegar, wine, and wood for fuel [69]. From 1552, moreover, the *provveditori* were entrusted with obtaining enough hand-and horse-driven mills to grind flour for garrisons [70]. This soon involved them in the installation and maintenance of water mills as well [71].

Assistance in the planning of fortifications, the supply of building materials and grain: while these were the major concerns of the *provveditori*, they were far from exhausting the list of their duties. They were responsible for — or at least their aid could be invoked for — the water supply of fortified places, and thus with the construction of wells [72] and indeed with fountains if to bring water meant a temporary breaching of a city wall [73]. If a town wished, for the convenience of trade, to open new gates in its walls and thus weaken the defenses, it had to obtain permission from the *provveditori* [74]. They were concerned with the design, supply and installation of defensive chains across rivers for riparian fortresses [75]. Where town ditches were filled with running, as opposed to stagnant water, there was a demand to use it for irrigation purposes by individuals farming outside the counterscarp and *glacis*; it was for the *provveditori* to supervise this and determine the charges [76]. They might be called on to provide equipment and trained men for dredging work at fortified sea ports [77]. The council of ten was reluctant to allow

---

[68] S. D. T. R., 36, ff. 189 v-190 r.
[69] P. F., 37 (4), f. 72 r, Dec. 16, 1551.
[70] S. D. T. R., 38, f. 159 v and S. D. M. R., 32, f. 53 r. They had formerly been instructed to provide mills only from time to time, e. g., for Legnago in 1547, S. D. T. R., 35, f. 40 r.
[71] *Ibid.*, 41, f. 119 r (Padua); P. F., 2, f. 33 r (Traù).
[72] E. g., P. F., 36 (1), 9 Mar. 1588 (Corfu).
[73] *Ibid.*, July 9, 1594 (Asola).
[74] E. g., *ibid.*, June 12, 1551 (Capodistria).
[75] S. D. T. R., 41, f. 68 v (Chiusa), f. 120 r-v (Verona), P. F., 37 (4), Apr. 13, 1593 (Legnago).
[76] P. F., 2, f. 60 v (Legnago).
[77] *Ibid.*, ff. 34 r, 37 r, 87 v (Canea, Zara, Candia).

markets to be held inside certain fortifications because of the security risk of an influx of strangers; even markets held outside the walls were not looked on with favour, so local communities petitioned for them via the *provveditori* [78]. As well as being responsible for the building of garrison quarters within fortifications the *provveditori* could be asked to construct them outside, as when in 1572 they were charged with providing transit accommodation on the Lido, near the S. Niccolò monastery, for troops en route for, or returning from, overseas [79].

The earth-shifting, labouring work on a fortification was deputed through a quota system to neighbouring territories charged by the senate with supplying so many men for so many months, the details having been worked out by the *collegio* with the *provveditori* [80]. This system led to loud complaints, especially from the territories farthest away and least likely to benefit personally from the work, and especially in harvest time when men were reluctant to leave the land. These complaints were referred, in the first instance, to the *provveditori*. Again, part of the costs of major fortifications were charged against other towns on the theory that the strengthening of any one part of the Venetian dominions was for the benefit of the whole. This also led to protests, and it was the duty of the *provveditori* to investigate them and, indeed, to call the senate's attention to towns that were defaulting on these unpopular payments [81].

Unpopular, too, was the *provveditori*'s responsibility to advise against granting building licenses where the internal functioning of a fortification might be impeded (especially near gates

---

[78] *Ibid.*, f. 65 r; P. F., 36 (1), Mar. 22, 1590 (Legnago and Peschiera).

[79] Troops in transit had formerly been billeted in monasteries within the city — and this order was the result of the monks' protests. P. F., 2, f. 2 v and 104 v-105 r.

[80] E. g., S. D. T. R., 51, f. 47 v (Bergamo).

[81] E. g., *ibid.*, 32, ff. 162 v-163 r (Vicenza behind with payments for Corfu). There are numerous examples in P. F., 36 (1), *passim*. Earth-shifting was allocated on the basis illustrated by these two cases: Bergamo — figures refer to *perteghe* — work divided between the Bergamasco (5,000), Bresciano, including Asola (5,000), Veronese (2,000), Vicentino (2,000), Cremasco (1,000); Verona — Veronese (7,000), Colognese (500), Vicentino (3,500), Bergamasco (3,500), Bresciano (5,500). P. F., 2, f. 24 r and S. D. T. R., 33, ff. 23 v-24 r.

and munition stores) [82] and to prevent any building or planting from interfering with its external functioning. In spite of heavy penalties [83], buildings had been erected outside town walls which impeded the field of fire from battlements or ramparts. One of the earliest duties of the *provveditori* was to ensure that *rettori* carried out the order to clear away all buildings within half a mile of the walls, and any building or any planting of trees or crops that could block the operation of platforms for cannon or gun emplacements in the flanks of bastions [84]. In 1551 this legislation was repeated and strengthened. If returning *rettori* could not prove to the *provveditori* that ramparts, curtains, bastions and ditches were free from any impediments, they could be denied voting rights [85]. This legislation proved extremely difficult to enforce. In peace time the *glacis* of a fortification was a standing temptation to plant and cultivate, especially to those citizens who had owned the land before it was taken over by the state. The ramparts and the earthen tops of bastions tempted soldiers from the garrison to grow fruit and vegetables there. A more thunderous version of the law of 1543 and 1551 was issued in 1588, repeating the need for sworn and witnessed testimony from *rettori*, and empowering the *provveditori* to impose a fine of fifty ducats on anyone contravening the order [86].

Another issue in which the *provveditori* were involved and which brought public and private interests into conflict was corcerned with riparian property rights. In 1565, for instance, the Adige flooded and damaged the fortifications of Legnago. The *provveditori* were sent by the senate to inspect the course of the river and the streams that ran into it and report any construction that had altered the water flow — mills, weirs, fish-traps, and the like [87]. So many were discovered that the senate decided to elect a panel of twelve from among its members to formulate specific proposals, restricting eligibility to those who

---

[82] E. g., P. F., 36 (1), July 16, 1584 (Verona).
[83] In 1512, a year in prison and 200 ducats fine. S. D. T. R., 18, f. 24 r.
[84] *Ibid.*, 32, f. 118 v, Feb. 15, 1543. The order repeats one of Nov. 1513.
[85] Minute of decision of *maggior consiglio* (26 June) in P. F., 1. The returning *rettore* had to bring a declaration to this effect countersigned by his successor and by an official of the *camera*.
[86] P. F., 2, ff. 72 v-73 r.
[87] S. D. T. R., 45, f. 167 r.

did not possess property, nor were related to anyone who had property in the area « between the Po and the Bacchiglione or in the Veronese, Vicentino or Colognese » [88]. That was on February 19, 1566. Four days later, however, it was noted that « because the number of interested parties turned out to be so great, the election could not be made », and it was decided to try again, excluding only those who owned land themselves, or were the fathers, sons or nephews of those who did [89].

This, of course, is but one aspect of a problem which increased in magnitude during the course of the sixteenth century. As more and more of the senatorial class acquired land in the *terra ferma* it became more difficult to pass legislation in the interest of the state itself. The *fortezze* records have already suggested that the *rettori*, who came from this same class, showed some inclination to protect the *terra ferma* from the full rigour of regulations emanating from Venice. A final example of the *provveditori's* ' occasional ' functions throws an interesting pencil of light on the interrelationship between the legislative and executive functions of the *ceto dirigente*.

The authority of the *provveditori* had not proved sufficient to enforce the senate's order to *rettori* of January 1543, that they should not divert *fortezze* money to the repair and decoration of their own *palazzi*. They had, moreover, been plagued by requests for money for this purpose, and in 1585 the senate moved to put teeth into their original order. *Rettori* were to be deprived of voting rights if they could not satisfy the *provveditori* on this score and all proposals to spend public money on *rettori*'s own residences had to be approved by the *collegio* and senate. The sums involved were, in fact, never large, but the fact that the issue had a considerable symbolic importance is evidenced by the provision that assent to such requests had to be passed — unusually — by a five-sixths majority in both bodies [90].

---

[88] *Ibid.*, f. 217 v.
[89] *Ibid.*, f. 218 v.
[90] *Ibid.*, 56, f. 86 r. The distribution list for the promulgation of this law gives a useful view of what were considered to be the key *fortezze* on the *terra ferma*: Padua, Treviso, Peschiera, Verona, Orzinovi, Bergamo, Brescia, and Crema, and overseas: Zara, Sebenico, Cattaro, Corfu, Candia, Canea, Spinalonga, Suda, Grabusa. By 1589 the necessary majority had been chan-

The duties of the *fortezze* magistracy frequently involved cooperation with other magistracies. Before timber could be felled permission had to be obtained from and trees selected by either the *patroni all'arsenal* or the *savii alle acque*; the *savii* had to be consulted when water courses were changed for the cleansing or filling of wet ditches. The *savii alla mercanzia* had a general oversight of salaries during work on fortifications. Victualing led to cooperation with the *provveditori alle biave*. Artillery was supplied by the *provveditori all'artiglieria*; they employed munition storesmen and in some places, but not all, were responsible for the fabric of powder magazines. The closest relations were with the *patroni all'arsenale*, from whom the *provveditori* on occasion borrowed craftsmen and overseers and obtained a large part of the material and supplies they dispatched to their fortresses [91]. The two magistracies were sometimes charged to work together on some aspect of defense works, such as the installation of a chain « in all secrecy » between the Lido forts [92].

Inventors who approached the government in the hope of selling some new way of defending or constructing fortifications were referred to the *provveditori*, who interviewed them, examined models and drawings and, if the ideas seemed practicable, arranged trials before making recommendations. The inventions submitted during the period covered by this essay were not impressive [93]; a new method of making lime, an unspecified weapon proposed by an ex-slave of the Turks, a way of fixing the chain in the Peschiera channel, devices for strengthe-

---

ged to four-fifths, but it is interesting that the names of the *savio* of the *consiglio* and the *terra ferma* with special responsibility for *fortezze* issues were — against the common practice — entered in the records of these decisions. P. F., 2, ff. 95 r (Asola), 96 v (Oderzo), 97 r (Cittanova), f. 108 v (Lendinara).

[91] The procedure varied. Normally the *provveditori* approached the *patroni* for materials stored in the arsenal. Sometimes the *patroni* were ordered to dispatch supplies without reference — on occasion even without sending an inventory — to the *provveditori*. Sometimes an order was broken down between them, as in 1578 when the *provveditori* were given money to buy nails and timber for Budua while the *patroni* were made responsible for tools, wheelbarrows, barrels and a « great bell ». S. D. M.: Filze, 72, Oct. 5.

[92] C. D. D. Secreta, R., 1539-46, ff. 96 r-v.

[93] P. F., 36 (1), *passim*.

ning walls. Only one, so far as I know, was adopted [94], though not all were written off as peremptorily as were certain « secrets » as « problematical, impossible and incapable of success ». But this was another aspect of the *provveditori's* function which could invoke cooperation with, or at least reference to, other magistracies. Battista Scarpa, for instance, claimed to have an infallible method of securing the Lidi which he refused to reveal to the *provveditori*. If the doge (i. e. the *collegio*) nevertheless resolved to give him a trial, the *provveditori* suggested that it should be entrusted to them together with the *savii alle acque* [95].

Far more important was the role of the *provveditori* in the selection of military engineers. As in other levels of the building trade, preference was given to dynasties; thus in addition to the great military architect, Michele Sanmicheli, whose services they inherited, the *provveditori* also employed his son, Zuan Hieronimo, and his nephews, Alvise and Bernardino Brugnoli. Other men either approached the government directly or were recommended by *provveditori alle fabriche* or *in terra ferma* who had employed them on a temporary basis. In either case the *collegio* asked the *provveditori* to take up references and interview them. Thus, petitioning for permanent employment, Giovan Battista Bonhomo of Brescia had enclosed testimonials which praised his work at Zara and Corfu and the *provveditori* contacted three ex-*capitani* of Zara to confirm them. They also requested candidates to bring models and drawings; in one case an applicant was told to draw the Lido forts. They then reported back to the *collegio*. Because, after Sanmicheli, he was the most outstanding of the sixteenth-century Venetian military engineers, their report on the Florentine Bonaiuto Lorini is worth quoting. « We summoned him before us and he showed us drawings and other designs in his own hand from which, and from his accompanying remarks, we could see clearly that he is professionally competent, quick to apprehend, of solid and mature judgement in his replies and suggestions, and, lastly, full of excellent and useful new ideas » [96]. They supported his request

---

[94] Bonaiuto Lorini was granted a patent in 1580 for « edificii per lui ritrovati da cavar canali et fossi et terrapienar le piazze delle fortezze, et per portar polvere et ogn'altra cosa ». S. D. T. R., 53, f. 5 r.
[95] *Ibid.*, Aug. 4, 1578.
[96] On these interviews, P. F., 31 (1), *passim*. For Lorini's, Jan. 18, 1581.

for a *condotta* also because there were then only three engineers who were employed on a permanent basis: Bonhomo, Francesco Malacreda, and Zenese Bresciano.

The government, indeed, was extremely grudging in its employment of permanent military engineers. Three of four was the usual number, at a salary which began between 120 and 200 ducats a year and normally leveled off at between 280 and 340. Requests for increases were usually supported by the *provveditori* who were reluctant to lose the few men on whose services they could always rely, but they frequently led to close or adverse votes in the senate or council of ten. An attempt to raise Malacreda's salary from 340 to 400 ducats was turned down four times by the latter body [97]. The motive for keeping the engineer corps so small was doubtless primarily one of economy, but the design and supervision of fortifications was not entirely dependent on them. Many designs were submitted by high ranking *capi di guerra* in the Venetian service, like the duke of Urbino or Marcantonio Martinengo, for whom the planning of fortifications was one of the talents expected of the well educated, all-round soldier. Much of the bread-and-butter work of supervision and the provision of working drawings was carried out by engineers employed often for long periods, but always on the basis of one job at a time, men whose earnings varied between sixty and 144 ducats a year. It was not a satisfactory system. The high ranking amateurs had many other duties. The part-time engineers lacked authority and prestige. The few professionals had constantly to be switched from one site to another and, moving between the *terra ferma* and the fortresses overseas, were sometimes out of reach for months at a time. The cost of correcting mistakes and rebuilding walls and bastions that collapsed from the lack of consistent expert supervision far outweighed the money saved by keeping the corps small and added considerably to the administrative burden of the *provveditori* [98].

---

[97] C. D. D. Comune, R., 33, f. 48 v; 34, f. 164 v. Even Sanmicheli had had trouble in getting his traveling expenses reimbursed: P. F., 20 (1), ff. 10 v and 14 v.

[98] E. g., S. D. T. R., 39, ff. 192 r-v (Orzinovi); *ibid.*, 44, f. 44 r and 45, f. 156 r (Peschiera).

This is not the place in which to treat the financing of Venetian fortifications in any detail. The raising of money from taxation and from cameral dues remained complex even after the « nova regolatione » of 1579 [99]. This reform purported to ensure a steady annual income of some thirty thousand ducats for the *fortezze* account. The actual income was more like twenty-two thousand. Fortifications were expensive. Between 1543 and 1546, 7, 332 ducats were spent on one bastion alone at Verona; the bastion at the Campo Marte there had cost 20,416 ducats by 1574 [100]. *Provveditori* returning from Asola complained regularly about the old-fashioned state of its fortifications; simply to improve them, it was estimated, would cost sixty thousand ducats. Figures between one hundred and one hundred and fifty thousand ducats were quoted for Cerines in Cyprus [101]. Neither of these schemes, nor many of the others that were proposed, were undertaken. Yet by the end of our period, mainly thanks to extensive works from the mid-1580's at Bergamo and Brescia, the *fortezze* office had run up a debt of one hundred and fifteen thousand ducats at the *cecca* [102]. The *provveditori* had no say in the apportionment of public monies to the *fortezze* account; any disbursement from it of more than one hundred ducats had to be approved by a three-quarters majority in the *collegio*. Their responsibility was for seeing that the sums granted for fortifications were spent carefully and accounted for exactly. In an atmosphere of almost continual cheese-paring they spent far more time checking their accounts, dealing with protests about labour allocations, and harassing local *camere* to pay their dues than in discussing those ideal geometrical forms which in the eyes of all Europe had coupled the name of Italy with the art of fortification.

It is, of course, arbitrary to close this sketch of the *fortezze* magistracy in 1592. At the beginning of the next year the senate proposed « in the name of the Holy Ghost and for the benefit

---

[99] Printed in *Bilanci Generali della Republica di Venezia*, vol. 1, part 1 (Venice, 1912), pp. 605-606, from C. D. D., Zecca, R., IV, ff. 22 v-23 r.
[100] P. F., 37 (4), ff. 26 r and 132 r.
[101] P. F., 36 (4), Dec. 20, 1589; Secreta, Materie Miste Notabili, 1 (unfoliated, undated, but apparently 1558).
[102] P. F., 2, f. 104 v. This was in July 1591. Further borrowings were necessary in the next months, *ibid.*, ff. 113 r-v and 118 r-v.

not only of ourselves but the Christian Republic as a whole to construct a *fortezza reale* in the *patria* of Friuli » [103]. This proposal set in motion the most grandiose public works operation ever undertaken by Venice, the construction of the fortress town of Palmanova. But the implementing team decided on by the *savii* of the *collegio* and three *ad hoc provveditori generali* who had inspected and chosen the site did not include our magistrates. At its head was Marcantonio Barbaro (who had not been a *provveditore alle fortezze*); subordinate to him, with responsibility for construction work, was Marcantonio Martinengo; Giulio Savorgnan was to act as general adviser; there was to be a site engineer, a secretary and an accountant [104]. The role of the *fortezze* office remained, as it was to continue, that of a subordinate factotum, arranging supplies, querying traveling expenses and, eventually, helping in the government's prolonged attempt to persuade families to settle within the giant harmonies of this most rationally designed of fortresses, least rationally located of towns.

---

[103] S. D., Secreta, R., 89, f. 82 v, Jan. 29. The actual decision was not confirmed until Oct. 19. *Fortezza reale* = a fortification entirely in the 'modern' style.

[104] *Ibid.*, ff. 137 v-138 v.

APPENDIX: THE FOUNDING DOCUMENT
S. D. Secreta, R., 62, ff. 59 r-v

[Sept. 24, 1542]

Sono di tal qualità li tempi presenti che sì come alla giornata si vede non solamente per ragion di guerra, over per forza di arme, ma etiamdio con fraude si cerca di occupare le città et loci che non sono ben guardati et moniti, al che dovendo quelli che sono al governo di questa republica, con ogni suo spirito et diligentia attender et proveder che tali disordini non seguino nel stato nostro, il fondamento del quale, come a tutti è notissimo, sono le fortezze sì da mar come da terra, le qual in molti loci, perchè non hanno quelle provisione et cose che necessariamente per la summa importantia di esse doveriano haver, potriano in diversi modi pericolare con grandissimo danno et interesse della signoria nostra, sì come in manifesto pericolo stete la importantissima fortezza nostra di Corfù al tempo che l'armada del signor Turcho se li presentò sotto, il che tutto procede perchè questo cargo, che è di savii del collegio, per le molte et continue occupatione non può esser essequito secondo che ricerca il publico bisogno, et etiam per non esser ditto cargo particolarmente applicato ad alcun magistrato di questa nostra città; et però:

L'anderà parte che non derogando all' auttorità di savii del collegio nostro, siano eletti per scrutinio di questo conseglio doi honorevoli zentilhomini nostri che siano del corpo di esso conseglio de pregadi et zonta et de là in suso, eccettuando quei del collegio per le ragion ditte, con titolo de proveditori delle fortezze, sì da mar come da terra, i quali siano per un anno, et in suo loco se debbi elezer altri successive di tempo in tempo, et possino esser tolti de ogni loco et officio etiam continuo, et con pena nè possino refutar sotto pena di ducati 500 oltra le altre pene comprese nell'ultima parte contra li refudanti; habbiano auttorità di aricordar, procurar et proveder che tutte le fortezze nostre et terre che a loro paresse esser de importantia siano fornite delle cose opportune et necessarie alla conservation di esse al meno per uno anno, et in questa materia possino in nome della signoria nostra scriver di fuora a chi serà bisogno et ricever lettere et metter le parte che li parerano in questo conseglio, cosi uniti come separati, a beneficio di esse fortezze, ben però che le lettere et parte siano prima vedute et ben considerate per li savii del collegio nostro, li quali se ben fussero de altra opinione non li possino impedire salvo con deliberation di questo conseglio, il qual non possi esser negato alli preditti proveditori sempre che in tal materia lo rechiederano; et siano etiam obligati ditti proveditori essequir quanto più presto li serà possibile tutte le deliberation di qualunque conseglio nella detta materia; et acciochè li ditti dui proveditori habbiano bona informatione de ogni cosa, sia etiam preso che alle relation delli rettori nostri si debbano ritrovar presenti in collegio, et da tutti essi rettori, capitanei, proveditori, castellani et altri ministri che venirano de cadaun loco nostro li sia dato una nota particolare delle cose che bisognerano, a fine che possino far le debite provisione, et il presente capitolo sia aggionto in tutte le commissione a ziò habbino a essequir quello; dechiarando che la elettion delli detti dui nobili sia fatta il mese di ottobre da poi fatte le zonte, et così successive de anno in anno.

105
[no adverse or doubtful votes]

6
To fortify or not to fortify? Machiavelli's contribution to a Renaissance debate

Machiavelli's straightforwardly technical writings on fortification provided no stimulus to thought or action in later generations. Book seven of the *Arte della Guerra* contained the longest discussion of the subject that had yet appeared in print, but this was based on his knowledge of the sieges of Pisa and Padua,[1] which had ended in 1509, eleven years before he wrote. Both had seemed to show the greater effectiveness of internal defences, while—as was recognized in the much briefer contemporary treatment of the subject by Battista della Valle[2]—future practice was to stress the walls themselves and the building of outworks; and he gave no hint of the importance of geometrically computed proportions which came to play so prominent a role in the literature and practice of fortification. Neither of the two men who later independently claimed to be the pioneer authors dealing with fortifications adjusted to the challenge (fully accepted by Machiavelli) of gunpowder mentioned him, nor did they incorporate any of his suggestions.[3] The terminology and the proposals made in his *Relazione di una visita fatta per fortificare Firenze* of 1526 were more up to date than those of the *Arte della Guerra*, doubtless because he was chiefly recording the comments of the professional soldier and engineer Pietro Navarra. But this was a governmental report and remained unpublished.[4]

In neither work did Machiavelli attempt to put his subject into any sort of political framework, though in the *Arte della Guerra* he made one psychological point: that the existence of successive rallying points within a circuit of walls weakened the resolve of the defenders. It was when he treated fortifications in terms not of ramparts and ditches, but of statecraft and morale, that posterity listened.

In *Il Principe*, before completing his survey of different kinds of principality with the ecclesiastical variety—a topic which, in the circumstances, could hardly be left out but seems to have caused him the same sort of embarrassment that he felt about the most up-to-date section of his Medici-commissioned *Storie Fiorentine*—he pauses to consider in chapter ten 'how the power of every principality should be measured.'⁵ He is mostly concerned with princes who do not have armies capable of defending the whole of their territories from invasion, and his advice is that they should 'strengthen and fortify their own towns and not worry about the country around.' Emphasizing the reluctance with which an enemy faces the prospect of besieging a well-defended capital he points to the cities of Germany: they fear neither the emperor nor their neighbours because they have citizen armies, ample stocks for eating and working and 'excellent moats and walls'. This defensive posture has, it is true, its risky side. Ignoring any tactical or technical hazards that can arise from a siege, however, Machiavelli concentrates on the effect on the morale of the defenders of watching their possessions outside the walls being pillaged and burned. Because of the psychological trait that makes men loyal to a leader they have made sacrifices for, and because he is assuming the qualities of bravery and energetic authority in that leader, Machiavelli concludes that 'it should not be difficult for a prudent prince to inspire his subjects with determination during a siege, so long as he has adequate provisions and means of defence'. But this conclusion has been prepared by another assumption, twice repeated: that we are dealing with a prince 'who is not hated by the people', who 'does not make himself hated.'

When Machiavelli returns to the question of fortifications in *Il Principe* it is not in connection with the three chapters he devotes to military affairs, but after five dealing with the qualities and attitudes that are desirable in his ruler. And here, in chapter twenty, after looking back to Rome and across to contemporary cases when walls and citadels have or have not protected princes, he re-formulates that last assumption as a general rule: 'the best fortress that exists is to avoid being hated by the people.' That stone walls have on occasion provided protection, he concedes, nonetheless 'I censure anyone who, putting his trust in fortresses, does not mind if he is hated by the people.'

This treatment of fortification in psychological and political terms, with no hint of the technological interest he was to show in the *Arte della Guerra*, recurs in the extended discussion of the subject in chapter twenty-four of the second book of the *Discorsi*.⁶ Fortresses 'cause you to be more violent and audacious towards your subjects', so 'a good and wise prince, desirous of maintaining that character, and to avoid giving the opportunity to his sons to become oppressive, will never build fortresses, so that they may place their reliance upon the good will of their subjects, and not upon the strength of citadels.' Though for the Roman and contemporary instances he cites the chapter is basically an amplification of what he had said in *Il Principe*, the tone has markedly changed. In the earlier work he had not been dogmatic about the disadvantages of fortifications; their usefulness depended on circumstance. His discussion of them in chapter 20 is, indeed, one of the most carefully balanced arguments to be found in the work as a whole. Now there is an unyielding prejudice against fortifications. There is no more mention of the walls and provisions of the German towns; fortifications are lost 'by the violence of the assailants or by famine.' In the *Ritratto di cose di Francia* he had said that France feared no invasion from Italy because of her fortified towns, to pass which, without conquering them, 'would be madness'.[7] In the *Discorsi* border fortresses may serve to gain the invaded ruler a little time, but 'even if they are so strong that the enemy cannot take them, he will march by with his army and leave them in the rear'. Now, as he had not in *Il Principe*, Machiavelli links armies with fortifications. Again, the effectiveness of the latter is disparaged; 'they are not needed by those peoples or kingdoms that have good armies; for good armies suffice for their defence without fortresses, but fortresses without good armies are incompetent for defence...A prince, then, who can raise a good army, need not build any fortresses; and one who cannot should not build any.' Now, once more in contrast with what he had said in *Il Principe*, while it is wise for a prince to fortify his capital, this is only 'so as to be able to resist the first shock of an enemy, and to afford himself the time to negotiate, or to obtain aid from without for his relief.' No: the really wise prince will rely on the love of his people and on his armies in the field. 'Experience proves this to be the case with those who manage their government and other affairs well, as was the case with the Romans and Spartans; for whilst the Romans built no fortresses, the Spartans not only refrained from doing so, but even did not permit their city to be protected by walls, for they wanted to rely solely upon the valour of their men for their defence, and upon no other means.'

There it is. The future chancellor of the *Cinque provveditori delle mura della città di Firenze* decides that fortifications are 'unnecessary' against a foreign enemy and 'injurious' against one's own subjects. The latter point he returned to a few years later somewhat by way of self-quotation. In the *Istorie Fiorentine* he puts a speech into the mouths of a group of citizens who warn the Duke of Athens to moderate his invasions of their traditional liberties; however much he trusts in allies, guards and *cittadelle*, these are no sure defences for a tyrant who has alienated his people.[8] And in a letter to Guicciardini of 1526, referring to plans to strengthen the spur of San Miniato, he warns of the danger to a republic of establishing a potential fortress within its defences; 'if ever in any disorder a powerful man should come to Florence, as did the king of France in 1494, you would become slaves without any way of escape.'⁹ If only Machiavelli had lived to see out the siege of 1529–30, the stoutness of the modified walls, the initial successes of the supporting army, the reactions of the wealthy to the destruction of their property in the *contado*, the effect on morale of famine, plague and fear, the loyalty and treachery that make the story of the Last Republic so suggestive and so haunting a study! We might then have had an account of fortification that balanced the pros and cons of a rapidly changing technology against the aims to be pursued by a ruler and the conditions making for loyalty and self-sacrifice among subjects. Such a work, combining the subject matter of *Il Principe* and the *Discorsi* with that of the *Arte della Guerra* might have added to his repute in our days, but it would have reduced his reputation and influence in the century that followed his death. Balanced views have a tepid *fortuna*, if they have one at all.

Machiavelli's writings prior to 1513 anticipate his later concern with fortifications in a political context hardly at all, though his missions for the Ten took him to many walled towns and citadels. An exception is the reference to Duke Guidobaldo of Urbino in his account of Cesare Borgia's drastic dealings with his untrustworthy captains.[10] When Guidobaldo retreated to Venice, Machiavelli records, he destroyed the fortifications in his duchy which he knew he could not defend, lest the invaders should use them to bridle the loyalty of his subjects. This point, made at some time after 1503, was so pertinent to his views as they developed that variants of it were employed again in *Il Principe* and in the *Discorsi*.

As far as his reading is concerned, influences can, in the main, only be guessed at. But there was, I think, little in the writings of the recent past to act as a growth-point for his observations, especially for the sweep of arguments he mustered in the *Discorsi*. In their treatises on architecture Francesco di Giorgio mentioned the need to protect the seat of government against conspiracy while Filarete's ideal city was unquestioningly surrounded by strong walls; the military writers Valturio and Cornazzano described siegecraft. None, however, can be seen as a precursor of Machiavelli's point of view. Leon Battista Alberti comes nearer. In his *De re aedificatoria* (1449, printed 1485 in Florence) he contrasts the good ruler, who will build a palace in the centre of a city, with the tyrant who, because of the inconstancy of the people, will build a fortress athwart its walls. He also cites the Spartans, who 'gloried in having no walls at all about their city; for confiding in the valour and fortitude of their citizens, they thought there was no occasion for any fortification besides good laws.' Alberti took issue with this openness: 'what is there to be said against adding security to security?'[11] Here, at least, were hints which, if known, could have been more suggestive than anything to be found in pre-Machiavellian writers on politics: the occasions and justification of war; the use of armies and the character of the soldier; the need for and the nature of defences, the qualities of the tyrant and discussion as to whether it is better to be loved or feared: these topics, already rather fully dealt with by Egidio Romano in the thirteenth century, were not linked as Machiavelli was to link them. To turn back to the ancients is to come closer to Machiavelli. Aristotle had raised in the *Politics* the doubts expressed (notably by Plato in the *Laws*) as to the military and psychological effectiveness of fortifications, and had disposed of them. 'It is sometimes argued that states which lay claim to military excellence ought to dispense with any such aids. This is a singularly antiquated notion—all the more as it is plain to the eye that states which prided themselves on this point (an allusion to Sparta) are being refuted by the logic of fact.' Again: 'To demand that a city should be left undefended by walls...is like refusing to have walls for the exterior of a private house, for fear they will make its inhabitants cowards.' And these gruff dismissals might have carried even more weight to an early sixteenth century reader because he could see a parallel between the race mentioned in the *Politics* between new siege 'engines' and wall design, and the situation in his own day. 'It is always the concern of the offensive to discover new methods by which it may seize an advantage,' Aristotle wrote 'but it is equally the concern of the defensive, which has already made some inventions, to search and think out others. An assailant will not even attempt to make an attack on men who are well prepared.'[12] This point of view could well have acted as a goad. Machiavelli would also have responded to the passage in the *Laws* where the Athenian stranger praises weapons rather than walls, and lauds the Spartan practice. 'It is a fine saying of the poet, and often repeated, that walls should be made of bronze and iron rather than of earth'; to build a wall 'usually causes a soft habit of soul in the inhabitants, by inviting them to seek refuge within it instead of repelling the enemy.'[13]

In connection with Machiavelli's key phrase 'la miglior fortezza che sia, è non essere odiato dal popolo', the pioneer English editor of *Il Principe*, L. A. Burd, cites three Roman parallels: Seneca's 'unum est inexpugnabile munimentum, amor civium'[14]; Cicero's 'caritate et benevolentia civium saeptum oportet esse, non armis';[15] and Cornelius Nepos' 'nullum est imperium tutum nisi benevolentia munitum.'[16] While the last two occur in a police or military context, only the first is associated with the needlessness, for the merciful king, of fortifications. Professor Gilbert adds a passage from Pliny the younger: 'The unassailable fortress, the impregnable castle is to have no need for protection. In vain he encircles himself with terror who is not surrounded with love, for arms are roused up by arms.'[17] Again, in chapter 24 of the *Discorsi*, Machiavelli writes: 'when a Spartan was asked by an Athenian whether he did not think the walls of Athens admirable, he replied, 'Yes, if the city were inhabited by women.' Father Walker suggests that this could be modified from three similar remarks quoted in Plutarch's *Moralia*.

Even granted the stimulus of Aristotle's summary discussion and a building block or two from elsewhere, Machiavelli's approach to the role of fortifications was so naturally related to the contemporary situations he described, to his enrichment of the theme of effective political and military control and to his constant preoccupation with morale (evinced in his attitude to religion, for instance, or to the use of native troops, or to the de-personalizing influence of firearms), that readers of *Il Principe* and the *Discorsi* were faced with opinions apparently new and all the more provocative because closely integrated into an overall vision of the nature of political life. And his approach seemed all the more provocative to succeeding generations because it not only contradicted a re-installed Aristotle but collided with an enthusiasm for the theory of military engineering that was amounting to a cult, and with a wholesale building and re-designing of city walls and citadels. The topic acted, moreover, as a hinge between his fascinatingly frank exposition of princely self-interest and his emphasis on enlisting the willing support of subjects and entrusting them, and not hired mercenaries, with arms. On the one side Machiavelli gave encouragement to the spokesmen for an increasingly 'absolutist' age, on the other he challenged them with his doctrine of the open city.

The new style of bastioned fortification, designed to answer and make use of provenly effective artillery, was largely an Italian development[18] and became an acclaimed orthodoxy in the 1530's. Geometrically based, it depended on the architect-engineer's intelligence because 'forma' was now more important than 'materia'.[19] No longer simply utilitarian, it was looked on as an art in its own right. With printing and overseas exploration it was seen as one of those few areas in which the moderns had outdistanced the ancients,[20] and it made works of the fourteenth and fifteenth centuries seem crassly out of date. And from the mid-sixteenth century interest in refurbishing fortifications or founding them 'alla moderna' was increased by a growing promotional literature. At its end, the debate preceding the construction by Venice of the frontier fortress town of Palma took account of cost, and the usefulness of armies as against fortifications, and the danger of provoking an enemy by a stone show of force, but, on the other side, as well as the favourable strategic argument were others drawing attention to the glory it would bring its sponsors and designers—and to the fact that all princes nowadays protected themselves with fortifications.[21]

For while architects and engineers and *capi di guerra*, supplemented by a growing number of armchair enthusiasts,[22] formed a highly vocal pro-fortification lobby for reasons of up-to-dateness and prestige, governments were in any case building at a hitherto unprecedented rate for severely practical reasons, to stabilize frontiers and to control their populations: the Spaniards in Lombardy, the Venetians in their *terra ferma*, the popes in the Church States—and the Medici in Tuscany. An anecdote told by Bishop Gian Girolamo Rossi points up the contrast between Machiavelli's views and the political inclinations of the time. He describes how he went to see Pope Clement VII (probably towards the end of 1531) and found him reading chapter 24 of *Discorsi*, book two, and, Rossi reports, 'he gave a great laugh, and said "Look at this scoundrel and the fine way in which he would like to dissuade me from building the fortress in Florence. But he will not succeed."'[23] Three years later, after delays caused, in part at least, by the doubts expressed by Machiavelli in his 'fine way', Duke Alessandro's Fortezza da Basso began to be built athwart the city wall. To enemies of the Medici it was 'a thing totally inappropriate to a free city', 'a prison and slaughter-house for the distressed citizens'. To their friends it was a necessary 'yoke for their critics'; the Emperor Charles V made its completion a condition of his continuing support of Alessandro.[24] On the opposite side of Florence, S. Miniato, strengthened as a quasi-independent fortress by Michelangelo and others for the siege of 1529–30, was maintained and garrisoned under Cosimo I, so that in 1576 a Venetian ambassador could report that while both fortresses could be used against an invading army 'they were principally built to keep the people in check' ('per freno dei popoli').[25] In the same year Jean Bodin made the same point; the grand duke needed the fortresses, 'having found out that it was impossible to live securely in the midst of his subjects once he had converted the popular state into a monarchy.'[26] And by the end of the century one arm of the pincers had been reinforced by building the superb Belvedere fortress to strengthen the role hitherto played by S. Miniato. In the *Discorsi* Machiavelli had attacked the view of 'our wiseacres in Florence that Pisa and other similar cities should be held by citadels'. With citadels now gripping Florence itself, and the countryside and frontiers weighted down by the most radical defence programme Tuscany had ever known,[27] Machiavelli's case for the open city and sparsely defended *dominio* might have seemed buried by the evidence.

From a miscellaneous, and by no means systematic, scattering of sources, I shall suggest that it was not. But first the routine cautions of any *fortuna*-hunter must be emphasized. When an author deals with fortifications in what seems to be a Machiavellian way but without mentioning Machiavelli, three points must be borne in mind. Plagiarism was still rife. The citation of classical sources became more usual in the sixteenth century, but contemporaries or near contemporaries were commonly pillaged without acknowledgement, especially if, as was the case with Machiavelli after his works were placed on the index published in 1559, they had provoked scandal or censure. Secondly, the classical sources open to Machiavelli were open to all; others may have arrived independently, with their aid, at Machiavellian conclusions. Borrowing from medieval sources does not, I have suggested, present a similar problem. Thirdly, events, actual situations, produced opinions that could sound like Machiavelli's. Given the financial burden of supporting armies and of building fortifications, there was much debate as to which should be favoured at the expense of the other; it was an argument that delayed the building of Palma for half a century. Or again, if the Fortezza da Basso was seen as a prince's vote of no-confidence in his subjects, the same opposition prevented Venice from proceeding with plans for a citadel in Padua in 1517 and again in the 1540s. The citadel in Antwerp became a notorious symbol of Spanish oppression, as did that of Milan and its guns 'whereof part', Thomas Coryat noted, 'are planted Eastward against the towne, to batter it if it should make an insurrection; and part on the country side Westward against the country if that should rebell.'[28]

It is useful to start by looking at that notorious piece of plagiarism, the *De regnandi peritia* (Naples, 1523) of Agostino Nifo. The clumsy style, the plodding accumulation of gobbets from 'authorities', above all the impertinence of rushing a version of a manuscript of *Il Principe*, all unacknowledged, into print, has secured its author a uniformly bad press. But as an example of how suggestive Machiavelli's treatment of a subject could appear to lesser, if conventionally better-trained minds, Nifo's work is instructive. He sees the importance of the treatment of fortifications in a political context and gathers what Machiavelli had spread between two chapters into one dealing solely with that topic.[29] This was an example Machiavelli himself had by then anticipated in the *Discorsi* and was to be followed, as we shall see, by others. Nifo recognizes the disputative attraction of the subject—'de arcibus semper dubitatum est an construendae ne an destruendae sint a regibus'—and its impetus not only leads him to add to Machiavelli's list of illustrative examples but to filch others from elsewhere in *Il Principe* and adjust them to their new context.[30] He senses the resonance of a central proposition—his version is 'regis enim arx munitissima est ut a suis subditis ametur'; his reading enables him to develop the subsidiary themes hinted at by his author (the relationship between armies and fortifications, the question of martial spirit: 'muri timidos tutantur et arces'); he chops up his chosen text, adds chippings from elsewhere, and there is a *discorso* (indeed, his chapter gives the impression of drawing more on the *Discorsi* than on *Il Principe*) worth offering to a king. To placate his contemnors, it can be pointed out that in spite of his dedicating his book to a monarch, Charles V, Nifo is if anything more outspoken than Machiavelli in connecting fortresses with tyranny. More to the point, however, is Nifo's demonstration of how an old topic, re-handled in a way that made it relevant to contemporary circumstances, could be absorbed into an argumentative mode which, though its roots lay in the techniques of medieval scholasticism, was to remain characteristic of much sixteenth century scholarly discourse.

With Guicciardini we move from the atmosphere of the schools to that of the court-house, and to another work. In his *Considerazioni sui discorsi del Machiavelli* (c. 1530) he cites chapter 24 of Book II and one-sidedly rends its arguments. Just because the Romans did not build fortifications in their subject cities, it cannot follow that those who do so now are at fault. However well treated, men are not basically rational, they pine for change; they can yearn after the memory of their last prince, or the sort of liberty they used to enjoy. No ruler, besides, can afford always to adopt measures that are popular. So some element of force is essential. Having hemmed in the open city argument, he turns elsewhere. Fortifications tempt rulers to swagger, to be overbearing? What a frivolous idea! If you follow it, why not insist that they give up guards, weapons, armies as well? Should medicines be jettisoned because their existence can give a sense of false confidence? And after dismissing Machiavelli's contemporary examples for his not taking account of the military and political situation as a whole, he reasserts the usefulness of fortresses to protect against insurrection, to serve as a bridle ('freno') to revolt and to help recover territories that have been lost.[31]

Proceeding chronologically, and taking a group of military writers whose reluctance to name names, other than those of military commanders, was to remain typical of the *genre*, we find Zanchi in 1554 referring to the argument as to whether it is better to trust walls or hearts ('gli animi de' cittadini') as though it is perfectly familiar. The preference for trusting to hearts he credits to 'many wise men and judicious philosophers' but as he proposes to write for those who need help in putting the opposite contention into effect he brushes their view aside.[32] Writing at about the same date, Francesco de' Marchi gives the opposition more of its due, gives, indeed, the impression of having *Il Principe* beside him as he writes. It is hazardous, he says, to build fortresses in cities or places that have been used to determine their own political fortunes ('città o luoghi che sono usi di vivere liberi') because the resentment they cause can lead to revolt. Moreover, some have suggested that if a prince has a large army he has no need of fortifications. However, an additional form of control is needed where cities have been taken by force or guile or where populations are particularly seditious. In these cases fortresses act as the bit ('freno') in a wild horse's mouth. And as an example he cites the Fortezza da Basso.[33] Both Zanchi and de' Marchi were professional military engineers. Ascanio de Hortensii Centorio was not; perhaps that is why his *Il quinto discorso sopra l'ufficio d'un capitano generale di essercito*, published in Venice in 1562, appears more sympathetically Machiavellian. He cites Lycurgus to the effect that stone walls are useless unless the men within them have adequate martial qualities, but then he points out that the Romans relied mainly on their armies, and that fortifications were chiefly useful in frontier zones or in mountain passes, so that rulers had time to mobilize. Apart from these, given loyalty, men and cash, it would be best not to build them.[34]

After Guicciardini, the first fairly detailed (five pages) treatment of the utility of fortifications known to me occurs in Gianfrancesco Lottini's *Avvedimenti civili* (Venice, 1575). Those who challenge their usefulness, he writes, have to reckon with the authority of Aristotle in the *Politics* as well as 'the universal opinion that security is something you can never have enough of.' However, many join Socrates in praising the Spartan point of view that reliance on walls emasculates the fighting spirit of a people. By referring to the 'ancient verses' about walls of bronze and iron being better than those of earth, he makes it clear that, directly or indirectly, he is citing the *Laws*. And, he goes on, if anyone wishes to save the contradiction by allowing fortifications in frontier regions while forbidding them to capital cities, then his argument is risible ('cosa degna di riso'); in that case, why not give up lances, heavy armour, fortified camps? No, fortifications must be built, though the prince must garrison them wisely to prevent their falling into the wrong hands.[35]

In the next year support for Machiavelli's view in chapter 20 of *Il Principe* that only princes who feared their people should build fortresses came from a curious quarter. It was characteristic of Innocent Gentillet's attack on Machiavelli that when he agreed with any of the opinions expressed in *Il Principe* he misrepresented its intention so sharply that he could, while in fact glossing it, appear to warn his readers against it. Thus he misrepresents Machiavelli as recommending the use of fortresses as the culmination of advice to would-be tyrants. However, as his opinion reflects one view of the experience of his generation, it is worth quoting at some length.

> The invention of citadels (which in our time princes have builded against their subjects) hath bin cause of infinit evils: For all commerce and traffique hath been & is greatly diminished in towns where they have been builded, and there have been and are committed infinit insolences by souldiers against citizens; and there neither hath come nor will come to princes which have builded them other good than great expences and evill will of their subiects. For this construction of citadels is an apparent shew that the prince trusteth not his subject, but especially where they are builded any other where than in the limits and borders of kingdoms and countries against strangers. When the subiects know that their prince distrusteth them they also esteem that he loveth them not. And when the subject is not beloved of his prince, he cannot also love him, and not loving him, he obeys not, but is constrained, and in the end will get his head out of the yoke as soone as there wil fal out a fit occasion. Here is the profit of citadels.[36]

Also in 1576 appeared Bodin's more comprehensive treatment of the subject. In republics only the capital city need be strongly walled, otherwise 'one may be sure that ambition will move someone or other to seize a fortified place and then convert the popular state into a monarchy.' It is at this point that he refers to Duke Cosimo. In a princely state, especially in a large and long-established one, 'it is never expedient for a prince to erect citadels and strongholds except on the frontiers, lest his subjects suspect that he intends to become their tyrant. But if he encircles his kingdom with strong frontier posts, his subjects will believe that they are directed against the enemy, and the prince, at need, can use them either to repel the enemy, or master his subjects should they rebel.'

These crisp, and highly politicised, conclusions are only reached after a general discussion of the pros and cons of building fortifications. Like Machiavelli (whom he nowhere mentions), he sees the subject as one calling for a presentation of alternative views before he gives his own opinions, for 'this is one of the most important problems of policy, and one of the most difficult to solve, because of the disadvantages of either course of action.' Against fortification there is the Machiavellian point that 'citadels and defence works encourage bad rulers to oppress their subjects' and the Machiavellian marginal rubric 'La plus belle forteresse est l'amour des subiects'. Then it is claimed both that 'they turn the inhabitants into cowards' and that they enable subjects to rebel against their rulers; 'for this reason the kings of England do not allow any of their subjects to fortify their houses, even with a moat.' If these arguments are valid, then fortifications 'are harmful and destructive of the commonwealth.' On the other hand, open towns tempt aggression and 'to say that men are the best defence against the enemy is only applicable on the field of battle'; because of age, sex or infirmity, only a quarter of the inhabitants of a city are available to fight, the rest need the protection of the walls. 'It is, moreover, ridiculous to say that men are more valiant if they have no fortifications to rely on... Logically we should then prohibit men from fighting otherwise than quite naked.'[37] So fortifications will have their use, and this will differ according to the nature of a country's political institutions, monarchical, tyrannical or republican.

In 1577 Raphael Holinshed's *Cronicles* accept that 'it hath beene of long time a question in controversie, and not yet determined, whether holds and castles neere cities or anie where in the hart of common-wealths are more profitable or hurtful for the benefit of the countrie.' But he has no use for balanced arguments. He points to that blatant symbol of oppression, the citadel at Antwerp. He cites Aristotle and 'Timotheus of Corinthum'[38] as being uncompromisingly opposed to the building of fortresses in a commonwealth. And he clearly would not have agreed with Bodin's interpretation of the comparative paucity of fortifications in England. 'I need not to make anie long discourse of castels, sith it is not the nature of a good Englishman to regard to be caged up as in a coope and hedged in with stone walls, but rather to meet with his enimie in the plaine field at hand strokes.'[39]

Two works of 1589 show, in varying degrees, how the subject of fortification was now taken for granted as a suitable topic within the treatment of political themes. For the authoritarian Brabanter, Justus Lipsius, the question was straightforward. In his *Politicorum Libri sex* he assumes that rulers will need to take precautions against revolt. The wars in France and the Netherlands, however, have shown that siegecraft has overtaken military architecture. While fortresses are useful in frontier zones, within his realm the wise ruler should therefore plant colonies rather than trust to walls.[40] Discussing fortification in *Il Principe* and the *Discorsi*, Machiavelli had not mentioned the rival advantages of establishing colonies in conquered territories. In both works this topic was dealt with in other chapters, without cross-reference. As the arguments for and against building fortifications developed, however, his readers began to exploit the potential relevance of the two themes and set them together.

Thus, in his *Della ragion di stato libri dieci*, Giovanni Botero, an avowed, if rarely overt, anti-Machiavellian, also expressed a preference for using colonies rather than fortresses to hold down a militant people. He cites the ancient example of the Romans and a modern one: 'Calais, a colony of English men...was the last place which that nation lost there on the continent.' But he adds that it is not just a question of a simple antithesis. Colonies imply fortresses as well. And because colonies plus fortresses take a long time to become established, advice to a present ruler must concentrate on fortresses alone. There is, certainly, the case of Sparta. 'When Agesilaus was asked why the city of Sparta had no walls, he pointed to the armed citizens and said "here they are!", adding that cities should be built, not with wood and stone, but with the strength and valour of their inhabitants.' Yet valour by itself will be worn down in the end, so 'I do not know why anyone should doubt the utility of fortresses to a prince...There is no empire, however great and powerful, which has neither fear nor suspicion of the inclination of its subjects or the intentions of neighbouring powers. In both cases fortresses are a safeguard.'[41]

For Scipione Ammirato, snug in the possession of a grand-ducal pension guaranteed by those bridles against change, the Fortezza da Basso and the Belvedere, Machiavelli's wrong-headedness is an article of faith. He does not name him in the *Discorsi...sopra Cornelio Tacito* (Florence, 1594), but he quotes from *Discorsi*, II, 24, and point by point he refutes its author. He begins by accepting the embarrassing discrepancy between Plato's views and those of Artistotle. Aristotle is in the right, but Plato was more in the right than those who distrust fortifications have been willing to concede, for when he commends the Spartans he is talking about the desirability of a valorous civic spirit in a people rather than criticizing walls as such. The following advantages of fortified places he assumes to be unchallengeable: an enemy will hesitate to attack them; they can be defended against many by a few; they are essential places of refuge in adversity; they weary an invader; they serve, in defeat, as a means of extorting better terms; the argument that they can all be eventually taken is less important than the fact that they help you 'to benefit from the advantage of time' and the unguessed-at changes in fortune it can bring.

Now come his direct challenges to Machiavelli. First, the notion that fortresses so encourage rulers to oppress their subjects that they should not be built, lest their sons come to rely upon them rather than on the good-will of their subjects. Not so, counters Ammirato; possession of a standing army is more likely to make a ruler oppressive than are fortresses. Then he [Machiavelli] says that fortresses are useless because they can be betrayed by their castellans. But far more examples can be found of princes who have been betrayed by the commanders of their armies. Next he [still the unnamed Machiavelli] cites examples of famous men whose actions appear to support his distrust of fortifications: Guidobaldo, duke of Urbino, Niccolo da Castello, Ottaviano Fregoso. Again, wrong: what actually happened shows that our author is misinterpreting the events in which they were concerned. And Ammirato brings in Guicciardini as witness for the prosecution, quoting at length from the *Storia d'Italia*. And yet again, 'voglio mi basti l'autorità de' Romani', says our author. But he cannot make the authority of the Romans support him because even if they employed colonies they did not, in fact, distrust fortifications; they employed them, they refined them. Ammirato then concludes by observing that, thanks to all the new fortifications that have been built in Italy, the peninsula has never been so safe from foreign invasion.[42]

Three years later, another commentary on Tacitus was published in Florence. As Filippo Cavriana dedicated his work to Grand Duke Ferdinando, his point of view can be anticipated. A new prince, he writes, cannot expect to be completely safe, because he comes to power either at the expense of an aristocratic or a popular form of government. Even an Augustus (who, thanks to assiduous propaganda had become almost the tutelary deity of the Medici dukes), 'amabilissimo principe' as he was, had to reckon with potential discontent. Certain precautions, then, are necessary, not only the employment of foreign bodyguards, the use of spies, the exiling of seditious persons and the forbidding of subjects to carry arms, but the building of fortresses. And these measures (and he has described those adopted by Ferdinando's predecessors) cannot be dubbed tyrannous, for if well and peacably intended they offend neither the people nor the laws of nature.[43]

With the *Discorsi politici* of Paolo Paruta, published in 1599, shortly after his death, we find the century's most concentrated discussion of the advantages and disadvantages of fortifications. He was at home among the literature of the ancients. He had pondered the *Discorsi*, at least, of Machiavelli, though he affected to ignore rather than to appear to draw back in revulsion from him. He had been an active government servant, had, indeed, been a member of the three-man magistracy that supervised fortifications throughout the Venetian empire. A scholarly man of affairs, he could draw at will on antiquity, Machiavelli and experience.

'Forts and strong holds,' he begins, are of late grown into so great esteem as princes seem now adaies to mind nothing more than these for the security of their states.' But to say whether they are right is a matter of some complexity. He then sets out the arguments against fortifying. Though fortifications are more skilfully designed than they ever have been, the race between attack and defence goes on, and they could, after a crippling expenditure of money, become anachronistic, or, at least, involve continuous extra expense for modifications. By themselves, they are inert and useless, their effectiveness depending on the quality of those defending them, and men of the requisite quality might well be better employed in the field; besides, unsupported by armies to relieve them, the strongest fortress must fall at last. An army is, after all, a sort of fortress itself, but one that can move, can seek out, head off or avoid the enemy as it chooses, rather than waiting to be assaulted or by-passed. Even if, technically, a fortress is invulnerable to attack from without, there is always the possibility of its falling to treachery or heedlessness on the part of those commanding it, or through the insurrection of the inhabitants who may hand it over to a rival prince. 'But if the state be open and not pestered with fortifications, though it may the more easily be lost by sudden assaults, or by ill affected subjects, it will be the more easily regained.' This is why the Duke of Urbino slighted his strong points when he recovered the territories taken from him by Cesare Borgia. It was because Venice had not yet invested heavily in elaborate fortifications for her subject cities that she had been able to recover so quickly the mainland empire she had lost to the allies of Cambrai in 1509. Paruta returns to the question of cost, 'for who can deny but that the excessive charge which princes are at, not onely in building fortresses, but more in muniting and guarding them doth sufficiently exhaust the publick exchequer and necessitate the disbursing of such moneys in times of peace as ought to be kept for the more urgent occasions of war.' And, winding up the case for the prosecution, he says that dependence on walls can lead a ruler to neglect his army and citizens to lose their martial spirit. The walls of iron rather than stone motif is introduced, and Plutarch's anecdote: 'A Spartan being demanded by an Athenian what he thought of the walls of Athens? answered that he thought they were very handsome for a city which was to be inhabited by women.' Finally, a prince 'who thinks he shall be able to curb his subjects, to govern them and rule them as he pleaseth by means of bulwarks and castles, and that therefore he needs not the love of his subjects, is much less mindful of those things which become a good prince, and which purchase affection...And it may be generally observed, that such governments as have lasted longest, have been preserved not by the advantage of strong holds, whereof some have not had any, but by vertue of a good militia, and of the subjects love.'

In favour of fortifications Paruta brings forward five arguments. Both nature and reason prompt us to adopt defences, and men have constructed them from the earliest times. Their design, if not yet perfect, is at least more effective than hitherto. Without them, a country is constantly vulnerable to enemies 'who, whilst they may safely at unawares enter thereinto, not meeting with any obstacle, have it alwaies in their power, if not to prejudice the main affairs of that state, at least to vex the people by fire and rapine, of whose safety and preservation the prince ought alwais to be careful.' Armies cannot be so large as to be in every threatened zone; fortresses act as refuges and rallying points all the more effectively because enemy forces are unwilling to have them in their rear. Lastly, the very existence of fortifications can give a potential enemy pause, for 'in the condition of the present affairs and times, it is seen that as much time is spent in the taking of one onely fort as in former ages... was spent in taking whole provinces.'

'What then is to be resolved upon in this diversitie of allegations?' First, one must distinguish between the policy to be adopted by large states and small ones. The former, especially if they have large armies, should concentrate their fortifications along the frontiers, to give time for mobilization. The latter need fortifications at the centre; their forces will be too small to defeat an enemy in the field, so they must rely on the deterrent effect of well garrisoned defences. All princes must guard against spending so much money on fortifications in peacetime that they cannot find the large sums necessary in an emergency. No prince should trust entirely to armies. Suppose his army should be defeated? He will be utterly lost, 'wheras by the help of fortresses a few are able to resist many and to gain time, the only true remedy of him who is the weaker.' No weight need be attached to the example of the Spartans. Their neighbours were weaker than they, and the whole nation was uniquely dedicated to the art of war. Neither need any heed be paid to the argument that fortifications tempt princes to be harsh to their subjects. Quite the contrary, 'the prince is so much the more bound to preserve the love and loyalty of his subjects in that he stands in the more need of them for the safety of the city thus fortified, for if it should fall into the enemies hands by the peoples rebellion, the loss would be the greater.'[44]

Lest the influence of Machiavelli in shaping discussion of the subject should seem to be either habitual or to be assumed, two more works of 1599 may be mentioned, Cino Spontone's *Dodici libri del governo di stato*, published in Verona, and Girolamo Frachetta's *Il prencipe*...which appeared in Venice. Spontone's book takes issue with Machiavelli, but while he praises the defensive value of fortifications he betrays no response to Machiavelli's having placed their utility in a political context, nor does he compare their value with that of armies. Frachetta lists his sources, including Plato and Aristotle among the ancients, Guicciardini and Bodin among the moderns, without mentioning Machiavelli. He discusses the various zones, one or all of which may be fortified according to the prince's power vis-à-vis his neighbours: cities, *dominio*, frontiers. He compares their value with that of armies—using the image of their likeness to mobile fortresses ('come fortezze vive et mobili'). He points out that while the prince's best protection comes from 'la benevolenza' of his subjects, men are fickle and untrustworthy, so an armed guard is always necessary as a precaution against revolt. But he does not mention walls or citadels in this connection, nor is it easy to see Machiavelli himself as a point of departure for his discussion of the other themes. It is probable that Frachetta omitted Machiavelli from his sources not out of deference to the censorship but because he had not read him.

With the more widely diffused *Tesoro politico*, a collection of tracts and *relazioni* originally compiled by Comin Ventura, we slip back into the mainstream of overtly anti-Machiavellian polemic—at least as far as the anonymous section on fortifications, which first appeared in the edition of 1600–1601, is concerned. Once more, colonies on the Roman model are considered before the author moves to fortresses, those essential 'bridles' for the discontent of both long-established and newly acquired lands. Machiavelli has rejected them as useless, 'but for reasons so feeble and frivolous that one brushes them aside as one would a spider's web.' The lessons of recent history are such, the author goes on, that he merely invites our ridicule. Machiavelli's opinion is as follows: if you have sufficient men under arms you have no need of fortifications; if you do not, they cannot protect you. He posits extremes. Wisdom is to be found in a middle ground. If a prince can raise enough troops to meet a danger at once from his own resources or with the aid of allies, then fortresses are at least no disadvantage to him. If he cannot, then fortresses are essential to delay the enemy: 'as the Venetians say, "who has time, has life."' And if we have to answer the question: which is better for a prince, to build fortifications or maintain a large standing army to control and defend his territories? experience directs us to the former course. Fortifications cost less, and thus the ruler does not have to tax his subjects so heavily. And whereas large numbers of troops quartered around the countryside behave like criminals, rioting and laying waste, as well as forgetting all military discipline, a small force garrisoned in fortified places behaves better and retains its soldier-like qualities.[45]

With a foot over into the next century, let us turn back to review the significance of these references. Of his most famous phrase, 'la miglior fortezza che sia, è non essere odiato dal popolo' we can say little more than that Machiavelli found an already current idea, gave it a little twist (that negative 'not to be hated') and imparted some momentum and accretive power to its passage through other men's thoughts. Burd quotes, without giving the source, a fifteenth century rhyme that had jingled to the effect that princes are busy constructing fortresses and city walls, 'Mais si n'est-il muraille que de gens.' Pre-Machiavellian, again, was Diomede Carafa's advice of c. 1485 to a ruler that 'no castles, no walls will be more nearly impregnable than the defence which consists in having the spirits of your people friendly to you, and to have all your subjects wish you well.'[46] After Machiavelli the instances multiply. In his commentaries on Aristotle, Louis Le Roy mocks the naivety of this Spartan ideal[47], but trust in men rather than walls is expressed again in D'Aubigné's scornful reproach to his mortar-mad fellow countrymen 'Vos ayeux desdaignoyent forts et villes frontieres...Nos cœurs froids ont besoin de se voir emmurez.'[48] On the other side of the channel Thomas Digges stoutly claimed that 'we have no such multitudes of strong townes as other countries: our armes and weapons are our wals and rampires',[49] and it was a fervent royalist, the poet Francis Quarles, who was to declare that 'the surest fort is the hand of thy souldiers, and the safest citadell is the hearts of thy subjects.'[50] Quarles knew both *Il Principe* and the *Discorsi* well,[51] but there are some ideas whose neatness conceals so complex a suggestiveness that the study of their transmission is the province of the folklorist rather than of the historian.

Taking his arguments as a whole, we can say, I think, that Machiavelli moved the issue of the significance of fortifications nearer the centre of current political as well as military debate, and enriched its scope. What he had to say was relevant, in the directest way, to a reawakened interest in the way in which fortifications were constructed, a lavish building programme of citadels, town walls and frontier fortresses, and to a comparatively new feature of contemporary warfare, long sieges which received more publicity than did the pitched battles of the period. He sharply increased the topic's theoretical relevance to those revitalized stand-bys of the medieval schools, whether it is better for a ruler to be loved or feared, and what distinguishes a monarchy from a tyranny. He brought it firmly into connection with another debate, anticipated in the fifteenth but rampant in the sixteenth, about the rival trustworthiness of national as opposed to mercenary armies; and here, as in connection with the reflections we have noted on the rival merits of colonies or fortresses in the retention of new conquests, we must bear in mind the magnetic power of ideas he isolated in separate chapters but which sprang together in the minds of his readers. Finally, the topic was respectable, because it had provoked conflicting views in antiquity, and attractive to those who took it up because it lent itself (if the tone of *Principe* chapter 20 was followed) to judicious parades of pros and cons or (if *Discorsi*, II, 24 were the point of departure) to strenuous concurrence or rebuttal: and in both cases because it enabled scholars to display examples of their knowledge of events both ancient and modern.

'Politike affairs', Montaigne remarked, constitute 'a large field open to all motions and to contestation.... As, for example, Machiavel's *Discourses* were very solid for the subject, yet it hath been very easy to impugne them, and those that have done have left no lesse facilitie to impugne theirs.'[52] The *Discorsi* did not stop Clement VII from sponsoring the Fortezza da Basso (nor the French from relying on the Maginot Line) and Machiavelli's views on fortification were impugned by arguments as well as, apparently, by events. But our impression of the past, the issues that concerned it, the modes of thought in which they were expressed, relies in some part on our reading of its contestations. And when they concern fortifications it is legitimate to suspect that they concern Machiavelli, too.

NOTES

1. Giancarlo Severini, *Architetture militari di Giuliano da Sangallo* (Pisa, 1970) 51–2; V. Bertolini, 'Niccolò Machiavelli a Verona durante la lega di Cambrai', *Atti e Memorie della Accademia di Agricoltura, Scienze e Lettere di Verona* (1959) 273–301.
2. *Libro continente appertinentie ad capitanii, retenere & fortificare una citta con bastioni* ... (Naples, 1521).
3. Giovanni Battista Zanchi, *Del modo di fortificar le citta* (Venice, 1554)4, and Giacomo Lanteri, *Duo libri . . . del modo di fare le fortificationi . . .* (Venice, 1559). In the dedication he is writing about 'la ... materia delle fortificazioni moderne. . . . per non essersi fino a questo tempo trovato chi ne habbia scritto.' Two years earlier, in his *Due dialoghi . . . del modo di disegnare le piante delle fortezze secondo Euclide . . .* (Venice, 1557) he had been more modest: 'vedendo io quanto pochi siano fin ad hora stati coloro di ciò habbino scritto ...'.
4. Now most easily consulted in *Arte della guerra e scritti politici minori*, ed. Sergio Bertelli (Milan, 1961).
5. Quotations from *The Prince* are from George Bull's translation in the Penguin Classics series.
6. Quotations from tr. by Christian E. Detmold (New York, Modern Library, 1940).
7. In Bertelli, ed. cit., 172.
8. Book 2, section xxxiv.

9. In Allan H. Gilbert, *Machiavelli's* Prince *and its forerunners* (Durham, N. C., 1938) 159.
10. *Descrizione del modo tenuto dal duca Valentino nello ammazzare Vitellozzo Vitelli* . . ., in Bertelli, ed. cit., 44.
11. I quote from the translation by James Leoni, (repr. London, 1955) 82, 86–7.
12. Book 6, ch. xi.
13. Loeb ed. (London, 1967) i, 481. The 'poet' has not been identified. Plato did recommend the ditching and fortifying of frontiers.
14. *De clementia*, i, 19, 6.
15. *Philippics*, ii, 44, 112.
16. *Dion*, 5, 3. He also cites Isocrates, who certainly stresses the need to win the hearts of the masses: 'consider your surest body-guard to be the virtue of your friends, the goodwill of the citizens, and your own wisdom.' 'To Nicocles', *Orations*, tr. J. M. Freese, i. 22–3. But again, there is no connection with fortresses.
17. Op. cit., 160–1; *Panegyricus* (Leipzig, 1933) 49.
18. So, at least, I have argued; 'The development of the bastion, 1440–1534', in *Europe in the late middle ages*, ed. J. R. Hale, Roger Highfield and Beryl Smalley (London, 1965). See *supra*, 1–29.
19. Niccolo Tartaglia, *Quesiti e inventioni* (Venice, 1546) 69^{r-v}.
20. G. Zanchi, op. cit., 59.
21. Maria Grazia Sandri, 'La progettazione di Palmanova', *Castellum* (1973) ccclxxxix–ccxc.
22. Eg. the complaint from the Venetian *proveditore* in Candia (1591) that his task is complicated by the fact that 'hoggidi pare che ogniuno voglia esser professore della scientia del fortificare'. In Giuseppe Gerola, *Monumenti veneti nell'isola di Creta*, i (Venice, 1905) 352.
23. In Luigi Firpo, 'Le origini dell'Anti-Machiavellismo', *Il Pensiero Politico* (special fascicle, 1969) 37.
24. J. R. Hale. 'The end of Florentine liberty: the Fortezza da Basso', in *Florentine Studies*, ed. Nicolai Rubinstein, (London, 1968) 502–3 and passim. See *supra*, 31–62.
25. Eugenio Alberi, *Relazioni degli ambasciatori veneti al senato* (Florence, 1839–63) Ser. 11, vol. ii, 363.
26. *Les six livres de la republique* (Paris, 1576). I quote here (p. 170) as later from the translation by J. M. Tooley (Oxford, 1955) and give page references (in this case 764) to the ed. of Paris, 1583.
27. See Raymond de Fourquevaux, *Information au roy* . . . *touchant les affaires de Florence* [1555], ed. Raoul Brunon (Aix-en-Provence, 1965) esp. 76–7, and G. Spini, 'Architettura e politica nel principato mediceo del cinquecento', *Rivista Storica Italiana* (1971) 797–8 and 827.
28. *Coryat's crudities* [1611], (London, 2v., 1905) i, 249.
29. Lib. II, cap. xvii. No pagination.
30. He names Aristotle, adds Pedianus, Timoleon of Corinth and Pyrrhus, and cites Fabius Maximus in connection with armies versus fortifications, not, as in *Il Principe* chap. 17, with military discipline. He uses Machiavelli's examples of Milan and Forlì, and re-writes the argument of chap. 4, where Machiavelli deals with the conquests of Alexander the Great and the Turkish sultan, in terms of the connection between conquests and fortresses.
31. *Opere inedite*, i (Florence, 1857) 70–74.

32. See note 4. I paraphrase from the Venice, 1560, ed., 3–4.
33. *Della architettura militare* . . . (Brescia, 1599, written 1546–60) book one, ch.s 13 and 18, 3^v and 5^{r-v}.
34. 62–69.
35. Ed. B. Widmar in *Scrittori politici del '500 e '600* (Milan, 1964) 593–597.
36. *Discours . . . contre Nicolas Machiavel, Florentin* (written 1575, first printed, s.l., 1576). I quote from the translation of Simon Patericke (London, 1602), 348. The translation was made in 1577.
37. Op. cit., French ed., 756, tr. 167–8.
38. Presumably Timoleon, who destroyed the tyrant Dionysius' citadel in Syracuse in 343 B.C.
39. I use the London, 1807–8, ed.; i, 326–7.
40. *Opera omnia* (Wesel, 1675) iv, 73–4.
41. *The reason of state*, tr. P. J. and D. P. Waley (London, 1956) 117–120.
42. Lib. XIX, discorso 4 (Padua, 1642) 393–403. Francesco Patrizi the younger's *Paralleli militari* was published in the same year, in Rome. Patrizi also notes the number of new fortifications: 'Delle fortezze, tante n'hanno fatto a prencipi fabricare, in si picciolo paese quanta è Italia, che il resto del mondo tutto non n'ha altretante.' But he points out that many ('passato il numero di xc') have changed hands. What is the use of them if men ignore the example of the ancients, if good military discipline is lacking?
43. *Discorsi . . . sopra i cinque libri di Cornelio Tacito*, 40–41.
44. Venice, 1599, 577–597. Quotations from the tr. by the Earl of Monmouth (London, 1657) 168–178.
45. *Tesoro politico cioè relationi, instruttioni . . . discorsi varii*. There is no mention of fortifications in the first (Cologna, 1589) or second edition (Cologna, 1598); the discussion summarized here occurs in the Milan edition in two volumes, 1600–1601, ii, 49–57 and is repeated in subsequent editions and translations, e.g. *Le tresor politique* (Paris, 1611) 410–415.
46. Burd, op. cit.; Carafa quoted from *De principis officiis* (ed. of Florence, 1558) 652 by Allan Gilbert, op. cit.
47. *Les politiques d'Aristote* (Paris, 1568) 890. He dedicated the book to the Duke of Anjou, the King's brother.
48. *Les tragiques* (1st ed., 1616), *Oeuvres*, ed. Henri Weber (Paris, 1869) lines 663–9. The passage continues: 'Et comme les veillards, revestus et fourrez / De rempars, bastions, fossez et contre-mines . . .'
49. *Four paradoxes or politique discourses concerning militarie discipline* (London, 1604, but written before 1595) 69.
50. *Observations concerning princes and states* . . . (London, 1642) no. 66.
51. Felix Raab, *The English face of Machiavelli* (London, 1964) 110.
52. '*Of presumption*', Florio's translation in the Everyman edition (London, 1910)ii, 381–2.

7

THE ARGUMENT OF SOME MILITARY TITLE PAGES OF THE RENAISSANCE

ON THE TITLE PAGE of the French translation of Matthias Dögen's seventeenth-century treatise on fortification, *L'Architectvre militaire moderne* . . . . ,[1] [plate I] two groups appear to be discussing the plan of a curtain and two demi-bastions which the architect holds in his hand. He is in the group on the right, between a common soldier and a somewhat foppish officer with long curling hair. The other group includes an elderly, soberly-dressed man who listens intently to the woman standing on his left. Her left hand holds over her shoulder a spear with a flag attached to it, her right rests on a table, on whose top are some mathematical instruments. Listening to her also, with his back to us, is a workman. He is standing bent forward in a litter of surveying instruments, his right hand holding a spade touching a large rectangular block of stone, behind one corner of which appears the right foot of the architect. Out the window, we see a siege in progress, with trenches zigzagging up to the walls of a town, whence the defenders' cannon are replying. Beneath the surface of this relaxed and apparently naturalistic conversation piece lies an allegorical argument of some complexity.

* Mr. Hale is a Fellow of Jesus College, Oxford. He wishes to acknowledge the assistance of Professor Edgar Wind, from whose criticism and discussion of the present article he gained much.

[1] *L'Architectvre militaire moderne. . . . Mise en François par Helie Poirier*, Amsterdam, 1648. (The illustrations, except for Plate VI, are from copies in The Newberry Library. Plate VI is from the author's copy.)

By the middle of the sixteenth century the Italianate ideal of the cultivated warrior was in general currency. Sir William Patten, writing in 1548 of the prowess shown by Sir John Luttrell in the battle of Pinkie, said "for his wit, manhood, good qualities and aptness to all gentle feats beside, I have good cause to count [him] both a good Captain at warfare in field, and a worthy courtier in peace at home," and added in the margin, "I mean such a one as Count Balthazar the Italian in his book of Courtier doth frame."[2]

Of the intellectual attainments of the courtier-soldier, those most commonly taken for granted were skill in music and poetry and a knowledge of history and classical literature. But during the sixteenth century mathematics was taking its place beside them, as can be seen from the account by John Dee, English mathematician and astrologer, of one of Luttrell's contemporaries, John, Earl of Warwick who died in 1554.

> This John by one of his acts . . . did disclose his hearty love to virtuous sciences and his noble intent to excel in martial prowess, when he with humble request and instant soliciting got the best rules (either in time past by Greek or Roman or in our time used, and new stratagems therein devised) for ordering of all companies, sums and numbers of men (many or few) with one kind of weapon or more appointed; with artillery or without; on horseback or on foot; to give or take onset; to seem many, being few, to seem few, being many; to march in battle or journey—with many such feats to fought field, skirmish or ambush appertaining. And of all these, lively designments most curiously to be in vellum parchment described, with notes and peculiar marks as the art requireth. And all these rules and descriptions arithmetical inclosed in a rich case of gold he used to wear about his neck, as his jewel most precious and counsellor most trusty. Thus arithmetic of him was shrined in gold.[3]

This picture of the mathematical warrior reflects the emphasis, which gathered momentum from the end of the fifteenth century, on the usefulness of mathematics in war. The

---

[2] *The Expedition into Scotland,* . . . . London, f.Hvii^r. (I have modernized the spelling and punctuation of all English titles and quotations).

[3] The "Mathematical preface" to H. Billingsley's translation of Euclid, *The Elements of Geometry,* London, 1570, f.ai^r.

excellence of mathematics was deduced from three great founts of authority: Nature, the classics, and the early Fathers. A knowledge of numbers, declared an early English textbook, "is the only thing (almost) that separateth man from beasts."[4] For the ancient world, Plato spoke through the inscription over his Academy, "Let no one enter here who is ignorant of geometry"; and, endorsing the numerological researches of both philosopher and divines, St. Augustine had declared *nemo ad divinarum humanarumque rerum cognitionem accedat, nisi prius annumerandi artem addiscat.*[5] All this was familiar from the middle ages. The extension of this cult of mathematics to war, and particularly to fortification, was the contribution of the Renaissance. Of all the liberal arts, an Italian teacher declared, arithmetic and geometry are the most excellent.[6]

The earliest printed military treatises contain eulogies of mathematics, and the earliest mathematical books stress their relevance to the subject of war. In his *De re militari* (1472) Roberto Valturio wrote so eloquently on arithmetic and geometry that Roger Ascham quoted him as an authority on mathematics, and Luca Pacioli, in the preface to his *De divina proportione* (1509) reminded Lodovico Sforza, Duke of Milan, that the military art was impossible without a knowledge of geometry, arithmetic, and proportion: in particular, how without geometry could fortifications of all sorts be properly constructed?[7]

As military architecture became increasingly symmetrical, and as the relationships between curtain and bastion, bastion and revelin, on the one hand and between the fields of fire from the various levels of cavalier, curtain, and outwork, on the other came to be more carefully measured, the relation-

---

[4] Robert Record, *The Ground of Arts, teaching the Work and Practice of Arithmetic*, London [1542], f.aiiii^v.

[5] Repeated, for instance, in the preface (f.A6^r) to William Bedwell's translation of Ramus' *The Way to Geometry*, London, 1636.

[6] Francesco Feliciano da Lazesio, *Libro di'Arithmetica e Geometria . . . Intitolato Scala Grimaldelli*, 1560, f.Ai^v.

[7] Ed. 1956, p. 10.

ship between geometry and fortification drew ever closer. Most textbooks on military architecture contained sections on geometry, and a number of geometers found their studies leading them to fortification.[8] In the same way, as tactics came to involve refinements in the combinations of specialized arms and the marshaling of men in a number of small, or eccentrically shaped, units, the arithmetician came to the aid of the camp marshal, and the soldier turned increasingly to the arithmetician.[9] In his preface to the first English translation of Euclid, John Dee coined the term "Stratarithmetrie" to describe the technique of ordering an army on mathematical principles.

In 1571, Thomas Digges, writing the introduction to a mathematical book designed to be of use to gunners and military engineers, could refer to men who did not appreciate the importance of mathematics as "two footed moles and toads, whom destiny and nature hath ordained to crawl within the earth and suck upon the muck."[10] The extent to which this represented current doctrine is made clear by the thoroughly conservative and sober *Book of Honor and Arms* (1590) in which Sir William Segar asks "who without learning can conceive the ordering and disposing of men in marching, encamping, or fighting without arithmetic? Or who can comprehend the ingenious fortifications of instruments apt for offence or defence of towns, or passing of waters, unless he hath knowledge of geometry?"[11] The demands of war stimulated the arrival in London of a number of self-appointed "professors" of mathematics.[12] Sir Humphrey Gilbert's plan for an academy for the children of noblemen and gentlemen provided for a professor of geometry to teach the theory and prac-

---

[8] For an example of this process, v. Giacomo Lanteri, *Due Dialoghi . . . del Modo di disegnare le piante delle Fortezze secondo Euclide*, Venice, 1557, f.iv^{r-v}.

[9] A typical instance is Alexandre Vandenbyssche, *L'Arithmetique militaire*, Paris [1571].

[10] Leonard Digges' *A geometrical practise, named Pantometria . . .* , London, f.Aiv^r.

[11] Pp. 66–7.

[12] V. E. G. R. Taylor, *The Mathematical Practitioners of Tudor and Stuart England*, London, 1954, p. 9.

tice of gunnery.[13] The war scare of 1588 led to the appointment of a mathematical lecturer to give instruction to the trained bands,[14] and the Frenchman Jean Chesnel, planning a military academy, had learned enough from the chaotic handling of men in the wars of religion to provide for adequate mathematical teaching. The mathematical teachers and lecturers catered to all grades, and the standard was not particularly advanced. Leonard Digges' problem for would-be masters of the victuals was typical of the genre. "If 1200 quarters of corn suffice 400 soldiers for 9 weeks, how much ought to be provided to serve 25,000 soldiers for 40 weeks?"[15] In a period when the profession of arms was under strong attack because of the disorders of contemporary armies, soldiering gained some added prestige from its association with the liberal arts, while mathematicians flourished as the instructors of warriors. Their influence even extended to the most individual of weapons, the sword, and a gratulary set of verses addressed to the author of a fencing manual in 1639, began:

> Thanks mathematic fencer, that dost tie
> The sword of th' book and fight in geometry.[16]

The strongest mathematical link with war, however, was with fortification. It was symbolized by the *Nieuwe Maniere van Sterctebou* (1617) of the great Dutch mathematician, Simon Stevin, and by the lectures on fortification given by Galileo at Padua.

Just as the status of mathematics had been rising, so the art of the military engineer had come to be held in growing repute. There was no split between the military and the civil architect; men like Francesco Laparelli or Philibert de l'Orme were expected to provide for palaces and public fountains as well as bastioned *enceintes*. The new gunpowder fortification, harmonious, symmetrical, mathematical, not only suited

---

[13] *Ibid.* p. 321-2.
[14] F. R. Johnson, "Thomas Hood's inaugural address as mathematical lecturer of the city of London, 1588," *Journal of the History of Ideas*, 1942, pp. 94–106.
[15] *An arithmetical military Treatise, named Stratioticos*, London, 1579, p. 67.
[16] Verses by D. Vivian in G.A., *Pallas Armata*, London, 1639, f.A8ʳ.

the aesthetic code of the Renaissance but its taste for rational town planning, from the imaginary Sforzinda of Filarete (c. 1460) to the real Sabbioneta (c. 1577) and Palmanova (c. 1593). The respect accorded to architecture rubbed off onto military engineering, especially as an interest in fortification became increasingly fashionable in the sixteenth century. The popularity of engraved views of fortified towns enables us to imagine the decorations in the galleries of Rabelais' Thélème, "all painted with ancient feats of arms, histories, and views of the world," and the same interest prompted the decorative scheme of Eleanora de Medici's *Stanze delle città* in the Gonzaga palace in Mantua, with its views of bastioned cities. Tourists began to look around fortifications as naturally as around churches or galleries. Villamont, for instance, visiting Milan in 1588, mentioned the cathedral and then went on, "There are several other churches and objects of interest which I will pass over in silence in order to speak of the almost impregnable castle of Milan, which is situated at one corner of the city, and surrounded by deep ditches *à fond de cuue*, and with ravelins armed with heavy pieces of artillery."[17] Country villas, like Caprarola or Verdala (in Malta), came to copy features of the new fortification for no purpose other than to be in the mode. Yet for all the princely patronage extended to military engineers, and the respect granted by government to the inventors of new, increasingly horrific weapons, there remained a faint but definite stigma attaching to the exploiters of gunpowder. It was recognized that the new weapons had come to stay and that defenses had to be designed to meet them, but the values of the gentry and nobility of Europe still accorded pride of place to personal combat with sword and lance in the open field, and those who wrote of firearms and defenses, while technically avant-garde, found themselves morally on the defensive.

It became common for works on firearms to begin with a justificatory preface explaining that God had permitted man to invent new weapons with which to preserve peace and jus-

[17] Jacques de Villamont, *Voyages*, Arras, 1605, p. 19.

tice or that, though invented by the devil, guns were now in everyone's hands, and it would be foolish not to know how to use them to the best advantage. Books on cavalry or infantry tactics contained no such apologies. Niccolò Tartaglia claimed to have already torn up one treatise on gunnery on moral and humanitarian grounds and only to have published his *Nuova scientia* in 1537 because of the need to teach Christians how best to arm themselves against the Turk; and as late as 1629 Francis Malthus defended himself in a "Preface Apologetique" to his *Traité des feux artificiels pour la guerre* against "those ignorant persons who condemn me for revealing the means to ruin and destroy what art and nature have laboured to create. . . ." And though books on fortification might be thought to be less objectionable, they were concerned with defensive systems which could mount a maximum of destructive firepower; most of them described siege techniques, and a considerable number had a section on artillery. Thus Dögen's translator could refer to

> Ses cruels appareils de l'horrible Sciance,
> Qui n'a rien de commun avec l'humanité [18]

though justifying its study as helping to protect the weak and punish the wicked.

To protect themselves from this impotent but galling criticism, the authors of books on gunnery and fortification invoked Olympus and the Liberal Arts. On Malthus' title page [19] Vulcan, the arms-smith, is shown next to Minerva, protectress of arts and crafts. In front of Minerva is the plan of a fortification; before Vulcan smolders a bombshell. Each points to the other's symbol, and the arms, as they cross, teach that the study of artillery involves a combination of strength and skill. The title page of Hanzelet Lorrain's *La Pyrotechnie* (Pontamoussin, 1630) [plate II] makes the same point by combining Mars with Ars, ferocity with intelligence, and strengthens the

---

[18] Prefatory sonnet, f.4ʳ.
[19] Reproduced in my Folger Booklet *The Art of War and Renaissance England,* 1961, p. 17.

argument by placing the inscription in an architectural setting in which cannons support the canons of classical taste and also by including the device of a large explosion issuing from a tiny space, a symbol of man's intelligence and its effects, already familiar from emblem books.[20]

The range of justificatory imagery used for works on fortification was wider than that for artillery manuals, partly because they were more commonly dedicated to the princely exemplars of the morality of the *arme blanche*. The classic portico on the title page [plate III] of Galasso Alghisi's *Delle fortificationi* (Venice, 1570) advises the student, as did the Platonic Academy, that the subject to be studied within should not be approached except with adequate intellectual preparation, in this case the full Quadrivium, with Architecture (familiar as a personification since the early middle ages) deputizing for Music. The Virtues on the pediment are a reminder that fortification is above all an art for the good prince, attentive to the well-being and protection of his people.

The title page [plate IV] of Daniel Speckle's *Architectura von Vestungen* (Strassburg, 1589) shows Geometry as an active force, for her set square and dividers have produced the plan of a fortress, while the figure of Architecture, who confronts her, also holds the dividers, symbol of pure mathematics. Architecture is further burdened by the half-intellectual, half-practical tools of the surveyor, the rule and level, and beneath her foot is a pickaxe, the purely practical tool of the builder. It was, of course, self-evident that military architecture involved more labor and brute mass than other branches of the art, and the fortification title pages capitalized what might have been a reproach by dwelling on the contrast between intelligent conception and massive execution rather as the artillery writers stressed the massive destruction that resulted from an idea. In title pages like that to Nicolas Goldman's *La Nouvelle fortification* (Leiden, 1645) [plate V] Hercules, pausing heavily in the course of his labors, is a more dignified and resonant version of the pickaxe, while the aerial

[20] V. Edgar Wind, *Pagan Mysteries in the Renaissance*, London, 1958, p. 96.

Mercury represents intelligence and skill. The god had appeared in the Roccabianca frescoes (c. 1460)[21] holding dividers and set-square, and as patron of the Quadrivium on the title page of W. Cunningham's *The Cosmographical Glasse* (London) in 1559 and Billingsley's *Euclid* of 1570. His ambassadorial caduceus was of sufficient independent force as a symbol of peace for it to be transferred on occasion to Pax herself.[22] Here it serves as a reminder that all this grim activity is in the cause of security, and the page as a whole, dominated by the figure of a matronly Bellona, holding a wreath and a statuette of Victory, asserts the military engineer's triumph through a union of strength and skill.

The same point is made, more elaborately, by the title page [plate VI] of Antoine de Ville's *Les Fortifications* (Lyon, 1629). The imagery on this densely didactic gateway is an extended comment on its dedicatory inscription to Mars and Ars but extends, nevertheless, the implication of the Ram and Scorpion in the pediment, for if war has a bad, Saturnian, side because it involves death and destruction, it has too a good Jovial aspect, for it brings glory both to the victor and to the deity who has thus demonstrated which cause was in the right. The comment begins on the panel immediately above the inscription, where the rule and dividers (over a bomb, itself a symbol of a statesmanlike combination of power and restraint[23]) bridge the gap between the implements of labor and strength (gabion, pick, spade) and those of intelligence and action (petard, firearrow, incendiary tube). On the right side, that of Labor, the lounging figure of Time declares with *Oppidum tandem sensum* that buildings rise by degrees; below him the tortoise and the pick and spade echo the sentiment on his scroll. The figure of Labor holds both his own shovel and Time's scythe, while the windlass perfectly exemplifies the tag *Ubi tempus, ubi vis*. The other side

---

[21] Now in the Castello Sforzesco, Milan.

[22] On the title page of A. Carnero, *Historia de las Guerras civiles que ha avido en los Estados de Flandes des del año 1559 hasta el de 1609*, Brussels, 1625. Peace has a down-turned torch in one hand and a caduceus in the other.

[23] Wind, *op. cit.*, p. 97.

is dominated by Jupiter, whose statement *Aliis leth [um] mihi gloria* is a less important part of the argument than his thunderbolt-bearing eagle and his sceptre, symbols (like the bomb) of vigorous execution and wise restraint. The gun and feathered casque are opposed to pick and tortoise, while in contrast to Labor stands Ingenio, dressed with modish nonchalance and holding rule and dividers. Below him is a windmill which, unlike the windlass that works whenever brute force is applied to it, obeys a power as insubstantial as thought. This composition, designed by de Ville himself, proclaims that fortification is the product of both strength and intellect; to preside over it, with plumed helm and with baton in hand, he has chosen not Mars or Bellona but Minerva, most rational of war deities.

Whereas Mars, during the Renaissance, had lost some of his medieval ferocity, he remained a somewhat colorless personification of the rough-and-ready side of war.[24] Bellona had come to take his place as representing war's cruel aspect, but as this was a side of war seldom stressed by artists working for a militant aristocracy, she seldom appears at her most bloodthirsty on the title pages of expensive books. The most popular female representative of war on military title pages was Minerva, whose spear, according to Ripa "signifea l'acutezza dell'ingegno."[25] The "great mistress of both Arms and Arts," as an English author called her,[26] was a natural complement to Mars, and it was both appropriate and highly conventional for a laudatory sonnet to de Ville to declare him "Avoir un coeur de Mars, un esprit de Minerve." The title page [plate VII] of Pietro Sardi's *Corona imperiale dell'architettura militare* (Venice, 1618), then, makes the by now familiar point that the victor's crown in war goes to one who

---

[24] Except of course, when some eminent person was portrayed in the guise of Mars, the associations then being nobility and courage.

[25] Cesare Ripa, *Iconologia*, Padua, 1611.

[26] [Sir Francis Kynaston], *Corona Minervae*, London, 1635, f.A3ʳ. Vincenzo Cartari's *Le Imagini . . . degli dei degli Antichi*, Venice, 1556, f.LXXIʳ, had made the point "che Minerva mostrasse l'accorto provedimento, il bon governo e il saggio che usano i prudenti e valorosi capitani nel guerreggiare, e Bellona le uccisioni, il furore, la strage, a la roina, che ne i fatti d'arme si veggono."

combines force with intelligence, and by adding set square and dividers to the goddess's equipment, Minerva is identified with the intellectual basis of military engineering, geometry.

Mars and Minerva were but the most popular of a set of variations of the Force-Intelligence theme. Others were Hercules and Minerva, Jupiter and Juno, and Guerra and Ingegno. The last variation is splendidly expressed in the title page [plate VIII] of Francesco Tensini's *La Fortificatione* (Venice, 1624), where Guerra, with smoking torch and dart, confronts the winged rider, Ingegno. Both these figures are taken directly from Ripa with a literalness that is extraordinary, considering the harmony and life of the design as a whole, and so is the female figure who sits at the top of the composition, her hand on a lion, her foot on a half-hidden book inscribed IUS. She is Ragione di Stato, and Ripa explains that the book is half hidden because statecraft demands that the ordinary processes of the law should be from time to time withdrawn. And just as the book is contrasted with the lion, and the violence of war with the power of thought, so Arithmetic's hook[27] suggests that she can grapple with more than a problem in simple addition and Geometry holds a surveyor's level as well as her dividers. The art of the military engineer, like that of the statesman, and of war itself, depends on a combination of the intellectual and the practical.

If we now turn back to the conversation piece on Dögen's title page we can see that this too may well be a commentary on the qualities required in the military engineer. The general on the left (possibly William II of Orange (d. 1650), to whom the book was dedicated), is himself placed beside a somewhat schoolmistress-like Bellona and is reminded by the goddess that neither the attack nor the defense seen in the background would be possible without the union of the dividers of geometry and the spade of industry. The same point

---

[27] 'L'uncino di ferro, e la tavola imbiancata dimostrano, che con quelli istrumenti si fa la cagione in diversi generi d'essere, e le cose composte per lo numero, peso, e misura de gli Elementi.' Ripa, *ed. cit.*, p. 30. For his descriptions of Ragione di Stato and Guerra, see pp. 452ff. and 213ff.

is made by linking the spade through the block of stone with the architect (? the author), the effectiveness of whose plan is dependent on its geometrical basis. And it may not be entirely fanciful if we see in his being placed between an elegant youth (? the translator) and a tough soldier a reminder that, just as the good general combines force with wisdom, so the good military engineer unites strength with Ingegno.

The main purpose of this essay has been to draw attention to the beauty and interest of the title pages of Renaissance works on fortification, a branch of military literature of which The Newberry Library possesses an unusually rich collection. But I should like to feel that it has, in addition, added a footnote to that still unwritten survey of the Renaissance controversy Art versus Letters, and perhaps another to an account of how the conscience of Europe adjusted itself to use of gunpowder; and I hope it may show that, to the historian of ideas, the title page of a technical work can sometimes have as much to say as the text.

L'ARCHITECTVRE MILITAIRE MODERNE, Ou FORTIFICATION:

Confirmée par diverses histoires tant anciennes que nouvelles, & enrichie des Figures des principales Forteresses qui sont en l'Europe, par MATTHIAS DÖGEN, Natif de Drambourg en la Marche. Mise en François par HELIE POIRIER, Parisien.

à Amsterdam,
Chez Louys Elzevier. 1748.

MARTE — **ETARTE**

LA
PYROTECHNIE
DE
HANZELET LORRAIN
ou sont representez les plus
rares & plus appreuuez
secrets des machines &
des feux artificiels.
Propres pour assieger battre
surprendre & deffendre
toutes places.

AV
PONT A
MOUSSON PAR
I. & Gaspard
Bernard.
1630

avec. — permission.

DELLE FORTIFICATIONI

DI M. GALASSO
ALGHISI DA CARPI
ARCHITETTO
DELL' ECCELLENTISS.
SIGNOR DVCA
DI FERRARA.
LIBRI TRE,
ALL' INVITTISSIMO
IMPERATORE
MASSIMILIANO
SECONDO,
CESARE AVGVSTO.

M.D.LXX.

D   O   M
CHE DIFENDERA SIGNORI ET CH'AVMENTARA GLI VOSTRI
IMPERI, VOI SOLE VERTV, ET ARTI INSIEME.

ARCHITECTVRA
Von Vestungen.

Wie die zu vnsern zei-
ten mögen erbawen werden / an
Stätten Schlössern / vñ Clussen / zu Wasser /
Land / Berg vñ Thal / mit jren Bollwercken / Caualiren /
Streichen / Gräben vnd Leuffen / sampt deren gantzen anhang /
vnd nutzbarkeit / auch wie die Gegenwehr zu gebrauchen /
was für Geschütz dahin gehörig / vnnd wie es ge-
ordnet / vnd gebraucht werden soll /
alles auß grund vnd deren
Fundamenten.

Sampt den Grund Rissen / Visierungen / vnd
Auffzügen für Augen gestellt.

Durch Daniel Speckle / der Statt Straßburg
bestellten Bawmeister.

Mit Röm: Key: May: Freyheit / auff
zehen Jar.

Gedruckt zu Straßburg / bei Bern-
hart Jobin.
Im Jar M. D. LXXXIX.

LA
Nouvelle
FORTIFICATION
DE
NICOLAS GOLDMAN
A LEIDE.
Chez les ELSEVIERS.
1645.

Adri. Matham fecit

LES
FORTIFICATIONS
DV CHEVALIER
ANTOINE DE VILLE
THOLOSAIN,
AVEC
L'Ataque & la Defence
des Places.

A LYON,
Chez Irenée Barlet.
M.DC.XXVIIII.

CORONA
IMPERIALE
dell'Architettura
militare
DI PIETRO SARDI
ROMANO
Diuisa in due Trattati
Il Primo contiene la Teorica
Il secondo contiene la Pratica
Il Primo Trattato si diuide in sette libri
Il Primo libro tratta de Fini
Il Secondo dei siti
Il Terzo delle offese
Il Quarto delle Forme
Il Quinto delle Materie
Il Sesto del modo di presidiare, monitionare, e
Vettouagliare il sito fortificato
Il Settimo del modo di difendere la Fortezza
Il Secondo Trattato della Pratica dimostra in
figura il modo di formare con somma facilità ogni
genere di Fortieze, loro Perfettioni, et imperfettioni
DEDICATA
Agli Ill.mi SS.ri Pni suoi Oss.mi
Bartolomeo Lomellino del S.r Agostino
Giouan Domenico Pallauicino del S.r Tommaso
Giacomo Cattaneo del quondam S.r Filippo
Giorgio Doria del quondam S.r Ambrogio
Stampata in Venetia à spese dell'Autore MDCXVIII
Con licentia de Superiori, e Priuilegi

LA FORTIFICATIONE
GVARDIA DIFESA
ET ESPVGNATIONE
DELLE FORTEZZE
ESPERIMENTATA IN DIVERSE GVERRE
DEL CAVALIERO FRAN.co TENSINI
DA CREMA
GIA INGEGNERO CAPITANO, ET LOGOTENENTE
GENERALE DELL' ARTIGLIERIA DEL
DVCA DI BAVIERA DEL RE DI SPAGNA,
E DELL' IMPERATORE RODOLFO
SECONDO.
ET HORA PERSONAGGIO CONDOTTO DELLA
SER. SIGNORIA DI VENETIA
AL SER.mo PREN.pe ET ECCLE.mo
SENATO VENETO
IN VENETIA.
1624.

II

TRAINING AND RECRUITMENT

8

THE MILITARY EDUCATION OF THE OFFICER CLASS IN EARLY MODERN EUROPE

INTRODUCTION

THE CREATION OF institutions for the formal military education of potential and serving army officers is rightly associated with the period 1650–1750, with large native standing armies and with the widening influence of scientific and technological ideas.[1] The nature of these institutions (and of the conservatism they had to overcome) was, however, prepared for by earlier suggestions, detailed projects and actual experiments which, taken together, form both an introduction to the later period and an extension of the research carried out by historians of Renaissance humanism and of its implications for educational theory and practice.[2] The process whereby the notion of institutionalised military education began to erode that of the well born individual's right to command on the basis of birth and a familiarity with horse and sword has not yet been charted. This essay provides a preliminary survey of the subject, followed by a narrative check list of proposals and institutions which may act as a guide to a fuller and more satisfactory account.

TRADITION AND REFORM

In 1497 Giovanni Sabadino reminded his patron, Ercole I d'Este, how he had been prepared as a warrior: 'venuto in la adolescente estate cominciasti scrimire e cavalcare armato sopra legiadri e potenti cavalli, correndo con la lanza con altri nobilissimi toi equalli in la augusta corte de Alphonso de Aragonia.'[3] At the age of eighty-five Giulio Savorgnan, reviewing in 1595 a lifetime devoted to the military service of Venice, described himself as a pupil of the *condottiere* Duke of Urbino, and his nephew Germanico as 'degno scolare della militar disciplina del Signor Duca di Parma'.[4]

Swordplay and riding, skills learned at home if adequate masters were available, otherwise in a household or court distinguished for its martial tone; then experience in the field under a commander of fame: the late medieval syllabus for a military career survived radical changes in the qualities and skills required in army officers with remarkable consistency. Lacking adequate masters, proposals to train young Venetian patricians for military commands in 1515 envisaged sending them at once into the field under the supervision of the republic's captain general, Bartolomeo d'Alviano.[5] Having them available in Florence, the Grand Duke Francesco turned them on to his young bastard brother, Giovanni, and then, when he was nineteen, sent him off to put his skills into practice in Flanders—skills and practice which were to make Giovanni in his turn captain general of the Venetian forces during the 1615–17 war of Gradisca. In a century that inherited and widely developed a belief in the value of education, Pietro Aretino, friend of the great soldier Giovanni delle Bande Nere and himself a professional man of letters, wrote to a young nobleman in 1549 with advice of unflinching conservatism. 'I consider it of little importance or none that Your Excellency has set yourself to studying treatises and compendiums upon the art of war. A man of your talent and your valour should rather have some great captain for his instructor. . . . You should study and consider things military in actual warfare and not in the classroom.'[6]

At about this time, however, increasing concern was coming to be expressed for the adequate preparation of army officers for their combat duties. For the reformers with whom this essay will be concerned it was no longer enough simply to be brave and a gentleman, to know how to ride and to use a lance and a sword. Weapons were changing and so, in their wake, tactics. 'The art of war is now such that men be fain to learn it anew at every two years' end,' as Granvelle pointed out to Sir Thomas Chaloner in 1559.[7] And the pace of change increased after the mid-century. There are 'evrie day newe inventions, strategems of warres, change of weapons, munition, and all sorts of engins newlie invented and corrected dailie', Sir Roger Williams warned in 1590.[8] Well before the radical tactical innovations associated with Maurice of Orange and widely discussed early in the seventeenth century, the untrained captain, however courageous, was seen as a source of confusion and of potential risk to the lives of others; do not make men captains, Blaise de Monluc pleaded with Henry IV, simply on account of their birth or 'à l'appetit d'un monsieur ou d'une madame'.[9] And the need for officers who could use their heads as well as their hands was still further emphasised by changes in the nature of fortifications and the consequential shift from open battle to campaigns of siege and skirmish. The potential officer needed to know more about a more complex and a more disciplined craft of war than had his late medieval predecessor.

The recognition of this need was supported by the wider concern with the condition of the traditional officer class, a concern expressed in three ways: a desire to moderate its lawlessness; an urge to protect its status as the natural leader of society; and—allied to this—worry about its decreasing militancy. The worry here was not that men who a century before would have been warriors were turning to the law or civilian court service but that those who did not bring themselves forward in these ways were becoming drones, guzzling and hawking themselves to the very margins of social usefulness.[10]

Not all military commands went to nobles, aristocrats and gentlemen. Men from other backgrounds became ensigns, lieutenants and captains, if the senior ranks were largely closed to them. But a concern for the methodical education of potential officers was linked to a concern for sobering and instructing the whole class which formed the traditional reservoir of military leaders, and the proposals for reform discussed here related only to them, either as an adjunct to a general education or as a specialised way of finishing it. These proposals were strengthened by the growing conviction that a country's army should be nationally officered, independent of the expertise of foreign mercenaries. And although they anticipated the lines along which the formal military education of the future was to develop, and to a significant effect conditioned that development, they had little practical impact; they remained on paper or affected small numbers. But before turning to the traditional ways of becoming prepared for a military career let us look at three attempts to canalise them into a formal curriculum, one English, one Italian and one German.

The first is well known, though its military scope has never, I think, been sufficiently emphasised: Sir Humphrey Gilbert's proposal of 1570 for 'the erection of an academy in London for education of her maiestes wardes and others the youth of nobility and gentlemen'.[11] It was to cater for boys from twelve years old, but its facilities were also to be open to 'gentlemen of the Inns of Cowrte which shall not apply themselves to the study of the lawes' and to 'cowrtiers and other gentlemen . . . all which now for the moste parte loose their times'. Its purpose was fourfold: to deliver boys from *ad hoc* and often careless private tuition; to break down clannish antipathies by bringing up young aristocrats together—putting age group before family loyalties; thirdly, in contrast to the universities, to provide youth with an education suited 'for the service of their countrie'; finally, its non-academic subjects were to constitute a finishing school 'in qualities meet for a gentleman'.

The syllabus was to include Greek, Latin and Hebrew; divinity; civil and common law; natural philosophy and medicine; cosmography and astronomy. There were to be teachers of French, Italian, Spanish and High Dutch. The military relevance was to be provided by a mathematician or engineer who

shall one day reade arithmetick, and the other day geometry, which shall be only employed to imbattelinges, fortifications, and matters of warre, with the practiz of artillery, and use of all manner of instrumentes belonging to the same. And [he] shall once every month practize canonrie (shewing the manner of underminings), and train his awditorie to draw in paper, make in modell, and stake owt all kindes of fortificac[i]ons, as well to prevent the mine and sappe as the canon, with all sorts of encampinges.

A teacher of logic and rhetoric was chiefly to teach through 'orations made in English, both politique and militare, taking occasions out of discourses of histories . . . with the examples and stratagemmes both antick and moderne'. A reader in moral philosophy was to devide his readinges by the day into two sortes, the one concerning civill pollicie, the other concerning martiall pollicy ... Touching warres he shall also particulerly declare what manner of forces they [all monarchies and best known common wealths] had and have, and what were and are the distinct discipline and kindes of arminge, training and maintaining of their soldiers in every particuler kind of service.

On the less academic side there was to be instruction in music, dancing and gymnastics ('vawlting'). Also 'there shalbe one who shall teache to draw mappes, sea chartes, &c., and to take by view of eye the platte of any thinge, and shall reade the growndes and rules of proportion and necessarie perpective and mensuration belonging to the same'. There was to be a master of defence to teach the handling of weapons: rapier and dagger; sword and target; the use of dagger, battle-axe and pike. In addition there was to be a

perfect trained sowldiour who shall teach them to handle the harqubuz, and to practize in the same achademie all kindes of skirmishinges, imbattelinges, and sondry kindes of marchinges, appointinge amonge them some one tyme, and some another, to suply the rooms of captaines and other officers, which they may very well exercize without armes and with light staves in steade of pikes and holbeardes.

And finally

there shalbe entertained into the said achademy one good horsman to teache noble men and gentlemen to ride, make and handle a ready horse, exercising them to runne at the ringe, tilte, towrney, and course of the field, if they shalbe armed. And also to skirmish on horsbacke with pistolles.[12]

The combination of the trilingualism of northern humanism with the Castiglionesque range of polite accomplishments plus mathematics and applied science is remarkable in itself. Even more remarkable is the width of the programme's relevance to the military needs of the day. It keeps the three gentlemanly career options—law, war, politics—open, while offering both a general understanding of warfare and an up-to-date practical knowledge that would stand any officer in excellent stead when he saw action for the first time. But its implementation would have been expensive, it poached on jealously guarded educational monopolies all the way from the universities and the Inns of Court to the private riding and fencing masters of London, and the queen at no time showed any interest in professionalising the leaders of her army. Her academy remained a paper one.

Between 1608 and 1610, on the other hand, four academies were actually set up in Padua, Verona, Udine and Treviso. Subsidised through judicial fines, their purpose was to provide an outlet for the violence of the young nobles of the Venetian *terraferma* and a pool of trained recruits for the republic's permanent force of heavy cavalry. Each had a riding and a fencing master. In addition each had a mathematics lecturer, whose duties, as set out by Piero Duodo, the moving spirit behind the Paduan Academia Delia, were as follows: to teach the theory and design of fortifications and armed camps, the elements of ballistics and rangefinding, and the use of square roots for planning troop formations.[13] This addition of mathematics was not surprising in Padua, where Galileo was already lecturing on fortification in the university and giving private tuition in his home on the military applications of arithmetic and geometry. That similar instruction should be offered to the still largely feudalised young bloods of Udine is more revealing evidence of the extent to which mathematics were taken for granted as a desirable element in a potential officer's education.

The third example is a full-fledged professional military college, the first of its kind in Europe: John of Nassau's *schola militaris* at Siegen in Westphalia. Opened in 1617, it drew students between the ages of seventeen and twenty-five from as far afield as Holland and Bohemia. It was socially exclusive. Its descriptive brochure invited applications only from 'Fürsten, Grafen, Adeliche and Patriziersöhn'. But while it provided opportunities for riding and fencing, its chief emphasis was on turning out technically competent infantry officers. More time was spent on the parade ground than in the classroom; the only frills promised were Latin, Italian and French, and probably only the last was actually taught.

Tirelessly propagandist for the reforms of Maurice of Orange, John either wrote or directed the writing of a play about the college's activities. His spokesman lists six, all severely practical: the handling of weapons, including the pike; drill 'auf niederländsch manier'; marching and battle formations; their variation under combat conditions, including the use of reserves; the defence and siege of fortifications, including the use of artillery. The play then introduces an old soldier, Octeranus, who has learned his craft the hard way by fighting in Poland, Sweden and Hungary. He regards this school in Germany with heavy scorn:

> Daß ich dennoch in so viel Jahrn
> Von Kriegssachen fast wenig erfahn,
> Solt man denn in so kurzer Zeit
> Erlangen solch geschicklichkeit
> In dieser Schule?—Das Glaub ich nicht.

Nor is he convinced when the training programme is explained to him.

> Ha, ha, ha! Das wüßt ich gern,
> Wie man ohn Krieg kriegführen lern!

But after watching their weapon training and drill on the parade ground, followed indoors by war games with cards, each representing a tactical unit, which they combine into various formations, he is converted. He is forced to admit that

> auch ein junger Knab
> Von Kriegssachen mehr Wissen hab
> Als mancher der viel Jahr und Tag
> Die Krieg gebraucht selbst haben mag.

And John has made this defeat of a representative of the conservative majority all the more significant because Octerarus, when quizzed by the students, is unable to justify his own military practice. He defends, for instance, the old massive formations of pike. But most of the men are just passengers within them, the students point out. The aim should be to enable every man to bring effective pressure to bear on the enemy. This means using many small formations, thoroughly drilled to work effectively in mutual support. Hence the need for many well trained officers and for training establishments to prepare them.[14]

The Siegen *schola militaris* apparently ran into administrative difficulties and closed even before John of Nassau's death in 1623. It was a logical adjunct to the advanced military practice of the time, but Octeranus had been routed only on paper. For most soldiers combat experience was the only worthwhile tutor. 'A campe continuallie maintained in action,' as Sir Roger Williams put it, 'is like an universitie continuallie in exercises.'[15] Writing of Maurice's reforms a year before Siegen opened, John Bingham paid tribute both to him—'a prince born and bred up in arms'—and to the United Provinces, 'which countries at this day are the scoole of war, whither the martiall spirits of Europe resort to lay down the apprentiship of their service in armes'.[16]

The vast majority of well born recruits first saw action—some as gentlemen rankers but many already with the rank of captain and with responsibility for a hundred or more men—with little or no formal preparation for war. Apart from those who had first joined the permanent establishment of princely guards and garrison forces which all countries maintained, the nearest approach to handling a body of men they could have gained was at musters of the local militia, and here more time was commonly spent checking names and equipment than performing drill and evolutions. Only the Spaniards, from the middle of the sixteenth century, systematically sent recruits to train in garrison before sending them into action,[17] at the same time encouraging the enlistment of gentlemen rankers in the infantry by allowing them special baggage and transport privileges. Nor did the page system, the apprenticeship served by young aristocrats in a military household, guarantee more than a prior acquaintance with horses, weapons and stories of past campaigns.

In order to estimate the degree of preparedness a young officer brought with him to siege or battlefield, therefore, we must concentrate on his *in*formal military education, a matter of family tradition and class expectation, private tuition and reading, and of such paramilitary activities as riding and swordsmanship.

To the extent that the tuition given a youth had a humanistic flavour, it would almost certainly have stressed military matters.

Arms and methods of warfare change from age to age . . . But whatever the method or the weapon of the time, let there be ample practice for our youth, with as great variety of exercises as can be devised, so that they may be ready for combat hand to hand or in troop, in the headlong charge or in the skirmish. We cannot forestall the reality of war, its sudden emergencies, or its vivid terrors, but by training and practice we can at least provide such preparation as the case admits.[18]

Thus Vergerio, in his pioneering treatise on education of about 1392. And whether written by a Palmieri for a republic or by an Aeneas Sylvius Piccolomini for a prince, the sword was prominently displayed alongside the pen by Vergerio's Quattrocento successors.[19] The extent to which a young noble should learn every aspect of warfare, from swimming and riding to the casting of artillery, was set out in prose and woodcut in Maximilian I's *Weißkunig* and elaborated in Rabelais's account of Gargantua's education.[20] And to the humanistic strain and the technologically conscious chivalric strain in educational thought was added the balanced range of accomplishments attributed by Castiglione to his *Courtier*. When in 1615 Sir George Buc was justifying his calling London the third university in England, he pointed out that it was possible to study not only the traditional liberal arts there but also the more up-to-date ones. And

in the choice of the arts of this kind I will not be mine owne carver but will receive them of the recommendation and warrant of that most learned and iudicious noble gentleman the Count Baldesser Castilio, who, recounting the qualities and arts necessary and properly appertaining to a gentleman (and so consequently to be esteemed liberall and ingenuous) giveth to the arts gladiatorie, or of defence, and of ryding, and of paynting and of pourtraying, and of dauncing, place amongst them.[21]

Blending the Castiglionesque canon with the Maximilian one, Sir George also described where instruction in swimming and the firing of artillery was to be found. It was not only in Spain, where the aristocratic ideal remained ostentatiously militaristic, and where the Jesuit Juan de Mariana advocated mock battles to prepare young nobles for cavalry and infantry combat,[22] that educational theory took the military potential of the aristocracy for granted. Renaissance theory required more learning, and allowed for a greater variety of careers, without eroding the medieval connection between high birth and arms. If anything, it played up the theme of military responsibility in order to increase the socially distancing image of the Second Estate, to help to distinguish its members from the thriving urban bourgeoisie and the wealthy farmers who had risen from peasant stock. And this educational theory, with its emphasis on an 'all round' self-development—increasingly within a group—became more and more widely accepted during an age which saw the progressive breakdown of the page system of early entry to a military career.

The age at which boys went to serve as pages in the late fifteenth and during the first half of the sixteenth centuries varied. Bayard, the future 'chevalier sans peur et sans reproche', was sent as page to the Duke of Savoy at thirteen; Dürer's friend Willibald Pirckheimer was sixteen when he became a page at the chivalrous court of the Bishop of Eichstätt; Peter Ernest of Mansfeld was only eleven when he became a page. In return for serving at his lord's table a boy could expect to learn horsemanship and the management of weapons from the *escuyer* into whose charge he was placed, to compete in wrestling, jumping and running with the other pages, and to learn to dance. In theory the *escuyer* should encourage his charges to read 'une ou deux heures du jour . . . en quelque beau livre'; when this did happen the book was commonly a chivalrous romance or chronicle of wars.

After two or three years the page would be promoted 'hors de page' and given a junior command or sent to a garrison for further training. If fighting were going on during his pageship a boy would accompany his lord. At the age of fifteen I set off, recalled Jean de Mergey, 'sur un petit cheval barbe, mais fort viste, ayant en ma teste mon morion à banniere avec un beau panache, et un javelot de Brezil, le fer doré bien tranchant, avec belle houppe d'or et de soye, ma casaque de page, belle et bien estoffé de broderie, de sorte que je pensois estre quelque petit dieu Mars'. Normally the young page was not expected actually to fight. On one occasion, however, de Mergey's company was surprised and was forced to charge as a whole. He himself ran one of the enemy through and then found that he could not pull the lance out of the man's stomach before he was forced to retreat. The reaction of this little Mars was not pride but fear: fear that he would be whipped for losing his weapon.[23]

The gallantry and personal initiative fostered by the page system was taken for granted. But as the century wore on, doubts were increasingly expressed about its effect on character and its suitability as a preparation for wars where there was less and less need for the individual daring of a cavalryman. The system was also collapsing from within. The military training in great households was becoming more perfunctory; pages were being exploited as servants; their morals were ignored, their education skimped; their irresponsibility when given a command was deplored. From 1530 the emphasis was on later entry to a military career after a broader education.[24]

The part that reading could play within that broader education is revealingly described by that tough and conservative old soldier Sir John Smythe, who was born in 1531.

I even from my very tender years have delighted to hear histories read that did treat of actions and deeds of arms, and since I came to years of some discretion and that by my father's rank I was brought up to school and brought with time to understand the Latin tongue somewhat indifferently, I did always delight and procure my tutors as much as I could to read unto me the commentaries of Julius Caesar and Sallust and other such books. And after that I came from school and went to the university ... I gave myself to the reading of many other histories and books treating of matters of war and sciences tending to the same.[24]

The relevance of classical to contemporary warfare was sometimes queried but never denied. Paradoxically gunpowder, by reducing the role of heavy cavalry and encouraging the introduction of less bulky, less vulnerable infantry formations, had led sixteenth-century tactics actually to resemble those of ancient Greece and Rome more closely than those of the Middle Ages; the Ancients' stress on morale and training was also directly relevant to the contemporary situation. Towards the end of our period John of Nassau, founder of Siegen and contemporary of Galileo, listed among the books which, if read *ex fundamento* 'einen rechtschaffenen Capitein machet', works by the following authors: Livy, Polybius, Appian, Dio, Josephus, the emperor Leo, Xenophon, Thucydides, Vegetius, Tacitus and Aelian.[26] And because, as the Italian translator of Frontinus put it in 1574, 'Latin is not widely understood today, especially by the majority of those who make a career of arms',[27] there was a steady flow of translations of classical military texts, most of them dedicated to princes and prominent soldiers.

The demand for Smythe's 'other histories' was catered to by printed accounts of contemporary campaigns. An author in 1546, commenting on his fellow countrymen's thirst for news, wrote that 'we will not sticke to spend a quarte of wyne or two of a caryer or serving man that commyth out of the northe partyes to heare tel what skyrmishes hath been betwixt us and the Scottes',[28] and two years later, by spending a few pence, they could read a full and lively account of the Pinkie campaign by Sir William Patten, illustrated with battle plans.[29] The demand for newsletters describing battles had become so great that the author of an account of the actions round Noyen in 1591 was forced to protest that it 'is not forged or fained ... neither is it fetched from flying and fabulous letters, ordinarie reports on the Exchange, or published uppon rash warrant as some, I know, will not stick to utter'.[30] In more considered vein, a translation of a Spanish narrative of the Flanders wars from 1567 to 1577 advertised itself as 'convenable à ceux qui suyvent le train de la guerre, font profession des armes & manient les affaires d'Estat'.[31]

As for the third category of books mentioned by Smythe—'books treating of matters of war and sciences tending to the same'—there is need to do little more than note in passing the flood of books dealing with the conduct and technology of war that steadily mounted in volume through the sixteenth and early seventeenth centuries.[32] The problem is to know who read them, at what age, and with what effect. It is from the last quarter of the sixteenth century that authors stress and cater for the need to keep informed and up to date through books during the lulls between wars,[33] and that there is an increase in the number of books not only aimed at the inexperienced would-be officer but likely to be actually comprehensible to him;[34] and by now the use of that valuable explanatory aid, the diagram, had become habitual. All the same, writing in 1607, John Cleland takes a somewhat moderate view of the young nobleman's appetite for book learning: 'for military affaires yee maie read the Lord of Noue, who is somewhat difficil for some men, & also the commentaries of the L. Monluc which are good both for the younge soldier and an old captaine'.[35] Autobiographical evidence is scanty. All, perhaps, that can be concluded is that the enduring controversy between these who stressed the need for preliminary study before reaching the battlefield and those who relied wholly on combat experience suggests—as do the economics of the book trade and the number of reissues of military works—a body of readers some of whom, at least, must have been young men who had not yet gone to the wars.[36]

With increasing regularity sixteenth-century travellers had paid attention to fortifications, armouries and musters of troops, as well as to antiquities, religious relics, feather beds and pretty women. And as a hortatory literature of travel developed towards the end of the century one of the reasons suggested as compensating for the moral and physical dangers of foreign travel was that it enlarged the military education of the potential as well as of the serving officer. 'What captain of warre is to be appointed over an army,' asked Hermann Kirchner, 'if not he that hath searched the manners of other people, & hath scene their skirmishes and exercises in military affairs?'[37] Cleland's advice is specific almost to the point of positive hazard.

When you are in Hungarie, mark the forts; and if the Christian army be in the field, observe their order and fashion of martial exploits.... Come to Flanders ... you shall not spare to salute the Arch-Duke and to see his forces, aquainting yourselfe with his Spanish captaines, ever to learne some good observation in martial affaires. ... This [he goes on] is the place where you maie learne to be perfect in militarie discipline; there you shal be moved by example & encouragement to be valiant: yet I wish you not too rash in endangering your life and reputation, where neither your death nor wounds can be either honourable or profitable.[38]

The commonest form of preparation for war arose, however, from the nature of the physical pastimes of the class from which officers were drawn. The relevance of hunting was taken for granted throughout the period. 'Hunting is a military exercise,' as Lodowick Lloyd put it; 'the like strategems are often invented and executed in warres against soldiers as the hunter doeth against divers kindes of beasts.'[39] There were complaints that men were so besotted with the music of hounds that they stopped their ears to the trumpets of war,[40] and that hunting took up time which could have been spent reading about war or studying mathematics,[41] but no one queried its relevance to the physical fitness, the eye for terrain or the bloodthirsty *brio* needed in war.

The tournament, which at times—as at the court of Henry II of France— became *the* obsessive aristocratic pastime,[42] was increasingly looked on less as a preparation for the shock of encounter in battle than as an occasion for the display of physical strength and skill. This paralleled the decline of the heavy lancer in war, and as the tilt came to be overtaken by running at the ring, and still more when the pistol quintain took the place of the ring, the relevance of this form of entertainment to the actual practice of light cavalry remained close. However, it was not quite true to say, with an Italian enthusiast in 1600, that 'every form of mounted game of skill [*giostra*] and combat has real combat as its end and purpose',[43] because a number of these 'combats' were horse ballets pure and simple, designed to show off the riders' exquisite management of specially schooled horses.

The breeding of horses for looks, strength and intelligence, while not new, took on a special significance from the mid-century. Horses became a cult— that is, the Great Horse of the *manège*. Instead of talk about the merits of different strains, the names of individual outstanding beasts were breathed with reverence. And with the cult of the horse came the cult of the riding master and the riding school. 'The professors of this art,' wrote one of them, 'truly deserve higher praise than those who teach any other art in the world.'[44] Sir Philip Sydney was hardly exaggerating when he said of his Italian riding master in Vienna that 'to so unbeleeved a point hee proceeded as that no earthly thing bred such wonder to a prince as to be a good horseman. Skill of government was but a pedanteria in comparison.'[45] Throughout the later sixteenth century Italians were considered the supreme masters, and though they set up establishments as far afield as Vienna and London, Italy itself remained the Mecca of the aspirant horseman. Within the peninsula state competed with state both to attract free-spending foreigners and to prevent their own young bloods from seeking instruction elsewhere.[46] The Neapolitan master Pignatelli, who died in 1596, was cited as a familiar symbol of the teacher of a physical skill as late as 1668.[47] But even his fame was eclipsed when his pupil, Antoine de Pluvinel, established his school in Paris early in the seventeenth century, and while status-conscious painters could point to the emperor Charles V picking up Titian's brush for him, future generations of riding masters could henceforward fondle the pages of de Pluvinel's books, where in one sumptuous engraving after another Louis XIII is shown in close conversation with the author, or touching his arm with eager and deferential attention.[48]

Even before 1600 the riding masters were having to counter complaints that their caracoles and standing jumps were irrelevant to war.[49] 'The principall use of horsses,' wrote Thomas Bedingfield in the most moderate of the answers to this charge, 'is to travell by the waie, & serve in the war: whatsoever your horse learneth more is rather for pompe or pleasure, than honor or use.' He merely maintained that riding the great horse should be continued for motives of delight, prestige and horse-breeding.[50] Few men, however noble, could in fact afford to master the art, let alone buy its instrument, but at least it raised the reputation of horsemanship in general and probably encouraged the recruitment of men and mounts to the cavalry, that branch of military science which was still essential even if it did not in fact 'surpasse de beaucoup toutes les sciences du monde (excepté la Theologie).'[51]

It was again from the mid-sixteenth century, and once more under Italian influence, that fencing joined riding as an accomplishment to be expected of a young man of good birth. Fencing guilds, with their degrees of membership corresponding to the student, Bachelor and Master of the universities, were flourishing earlier in the sixteenth century: the *arte palestrinae* of Spanish Perpignon, the *Marxbrüder* of Frankfort, the *Federfechter* of Prague, the Masters of Defence of London.[52] And instruction was not available only in large cities. 'For of fence in everie towne,' wrote Roger Ascham in 1545, 'there is . . . maisters to teach it.'[53] Nor was this surprising at a time when much of the execution in war, by horse and foot, was accomplished by the sword, when roads and forests were haunted by footpads and outlaws, and when one of the privileges of gentility (and of gentlemen's servants) was licence to carry a sword.

It was the mid-century honour code that promoted swordsmanship from a necessity to an art, from habit to fashion, the honour code with its dubiously glamourous companion, the duel. The result was that the fencing master acquired the title 'professor', which he has retained ever since, and a spate of books in which one new method trod with a nice sense of malice and superiority on the heels of the last. These books may have warned their readers against the duel, but they knew the social tide was with them. Arms, cautioned one Italian author, may be used only 'in defence of the faith, one's country, one's person, and in the last resort one's honour', but he also invited the reader to consider that 'this science is chiefly practised in royal courts, in those of every prince, and is studied in the most famous cities by barons, counts, *cavalieri* and persons of outstanding distinction'.[54] And this was not unjustified. James I, in spite of his dislike of the duel, recommended fencing in his *Basilikon Doron*, and Louis XIII allowed himself to head the illustrious list of sponsors of Girard Thibault's *Academie de l'espée*, a work dedicated to 'Empereur, Roys, Princes, Ducs, Comtes et toutes autres seigneurs et nobles fauteurs & amateurs de la tresnoble science de manier les armes'.[55]

For the gentleman, fencing as a social accomplishment became increasingly identified with the rapier, or at least with rapier and dagger; in any case, with the use of the point rather than of the edge. And it was for this reason that a science which, according to the fencing master George Silver, was 'noble, and in mine opinion to be preferred next to divinitie'[56] came under attack for no longer being relevant to war, even though the authority of Vegetius favoured the point.[57] By this time, however, deaths in combat were increasingly caused by guns, pistols, pikes, halberds and lances rather than by swords. In any case, edged weapons were not neglected by the schools of fence, though they were given less prominence than the foil-like employment of the rapier. Moreover under the influence of the fencing schools wrestling, which was declining in repute as an exercise for gentlemen, was modified into a respectable and useful form of judo, with special emphasis on the unarmed man's defence against an armed assailant.[58] And any sort of fencing helped promote the sort of physical strength and dexterity—with, in the case of one author,[59] the help of setting-up exercises—that the military life called for.

In 1596, at the age of seventeen, François de Bassompierre and his brother travelled to Italy to round out the bookish education they had had at school and from tutors. At Naples they attended Pignatelli's riding school. Then they moved to Florence, 'ou nous demeurasmes à apprendre nos exercises, moy sous Rustier Picardini à monter à cheval, mon frère sous Terenant. Pour les autres exercises, nous eusmes mesmes maistres, comme Maistre Agostino pour dancer, Mr Marquino pour tirer des armes, Julio Panigy pour les fortifications.'[60]

Ten years later he might well have stayed in Paris. De Pluvinel's accomplishment was to bring together at the Louvre the sort of teaching talent that de Bassompiere described as scattered through Florence or Sir George Buc through London. De Pluvinel's academy became the best-known martial finishing school in Europe.[61] There a man could learn to ride with the controlled nonchalence that had become the hallmark of gentlemanly accomplishments,[62] as well as fence, do gymnastics, dance and learn mathematics and military drawing.[63] For however far the great horse and rapier were removed from remount and pistol, the pursuit of these activities was associated with the possibility of a future military career, and it was accepted that for such a career mathematics was needed as a background to fortification, gunnery and the marshalling of troops (and, it might be added, for fighting according to certain schools of fence[64]), and also enough

THE MILITARY EDUCATION OF THE OFFICER CLASS

drawing to design a fort and map a plan of campaign.[65] The idea of the many-sided officer recruit arose within the conservative fostering of 'politeness' as well as among the more progressive spokesmen for a professionalised army. And both schools of thought moved in the direction of institutionalisation.

A NARRATIVE CHECK LIST, c. 1530–c. 1630

This, then, is the background against which we can pass in brief review a mixed bag of suggestions, projects and experiments bearing on the military education of the potential officer class. They are numbered (in square brackets) in chronological order.

Sir Humphrey Gilbert's proposals of 1570 were not without precedent in England. [1] In the mid-1530s Thomas Starkey had deplored the irresponsibility of an aristocracy amongst whom 'every man privately in his own house hath his master to instruct his children in letters'. These children should be brought up together in 'the discipline of the common weal'. Where? Well, there are 'over-many' monasteries and abbeys, so 'to this use turn both Westminster and St Albans, and many other. . . . Here they should be instruct not only in virtue and learning but also in all feats of war pertaining to such as should be hereafter, in time of war, captains and governors of the common sort.'[66]

[2] A few years later Sir Nicholas Bacon, Thomas Denton and Robert Cary submitted a memorandum relating to Henry VIII's proposal to erect a college in London 'whereby your grace hereafter might be the better served of your grace's own students of the law, as well as in forein countries as within this your grace's realm'. While agreeing that the main emphasis should be on law, Latin and French, they urged that the students should also acquire 'some knowledge and practice in martial feats, whereby they may be able to doo the king's grace and the realm service both in time of peace and war'. They also suggested the erection of an archive of military science. Whenever war broke out between princes on the continent a number of suitable students were to 'repair into those parts not only to view themselves the order and fashion of their camps, and assaulting and defending, but also to set forth in writing all the whole order of the battel, and this to be registered in their house, and to remain there for ever'.[67]

[3] In 1561 Bacon wrote on his own account to Sir William Cecil a proposal for 'the bringing up in vertue and lerning of the queenes maiesties wardes'. There were to be five schoolmasters, one for Latin and Greek, one for 'frenche and other languages', one for music, one to teach the boys 'to ryde, to vawlte, to handle weapons and such other things as thereto belongeth'. And 'every Tewsdaie and sattersdaye all the wardes that be XVI years of age and upwards shall spende the daie as he that teacheth to ryde and to handle weapons shall appoint'. The fifth was 'to reade a lecture of the temporall or cyvill lawe' each other working day between eight and nine in the morning and 'a lecture *de disciplina militari*' every afternoon between four and five—again, for boys of sixteen and over.[68]

[4] In 1563 Giovanni Maria Memmo pleaded that his fellow countrymen should not confine their military role only to naval warfare but that Venetian citizens should be trained to take the place of the mercenaries used on land. His proposals do not include the setting up of a formal academy, but the regular use of an open space where physical training and weapon handling can be carried on in the manner described by Vegetius—even to the use of dummies on which to practice swordplay, and vaulting horses to prepare for the agile mounting of real horses—with the addition of training in the handling of the arquebus. To this classical curriculum *à la* Campus Martis he adds drills and manoeuvres as practised by the contemporary militia of the Venetian Terraferma, and a knowledge of arithmetic and geometry to aid in the brigading of troops and the construction and siege of fortifications. Though as a project for military education his ideas are blurred by an aspiration to create religious and virtuous citizens as well as trained soldiers, and though no notice was taken of them in Venice itself, Memmo's ideas form part of the body of opinion that was to lead to the setting up of formal academies on the Terraferma.[69]

[5] In Paris in 1570 (for Gilbert's proposal of the same date [6] see above, pp. 442–3) Jean Antoine deBaïf's academy was founded as 'an institution in which all subjects were studied, natural philosophy no less than poetry, mathematics as well as music, painting in addition to languages, even military discipline and gymnastics'.[70] [7] In his *Discours politiques et militaires*, written between 1580 and 1585, Francois de la Noue proposed the setting up of academies first in four cities—Paris, Lyons, Bordeaux and Angers—and in four little-used royal *châteaux*—Fontainebleau, Moulins, Plessis le Tour and Cognac, and then in the chief town of each province. Here, from the age of fifteen, young members of the *noblesse* would follow a syllabus comprising the following subjects: riding and running at the ring, both with and without armour; the handling of weapons; gymnastics, swimming and wrestling; music and painting; possibly dancing. There would be lectures, all in French, on the writers of Antiquity 'qui traitent des vertus morales, de la police & de la guerre', and on ancient and modern history. Each academy would have from eight to ten teachers, paid well and in proportion to the importance of their subject, 'car chacun sçait qu'un qui monstreroit à manier chevaux meriteroit plus qu'un peintre'. He reckoned the cost at 3,000 écus per academy.[71] [8] In the late 1580s Scipio Ammirato, fired by Pope Sixtus V's grandiose crusading plans, suggested that a number of Italian orphanages should be turned into military academies.[72]

These schemes all remained on paper. [9] However, from 1589 the Collegium Illustre of Tübingen was combining riding and fencing with a syllabus heavily biased towards law, history and modern languages, while [10] with Maurice of Hesse's foundation of the Collegium Mauritianum in Kassel in 1599 Gilbert's plan appeared to come to life in Germany. It offered a secondary education to young aristocrats 'in allen Ritterlichen Thugenden und Übungen'. Four masters taught theology, moral philosophy, medicine (*Physices*) and dialectic and rhetoric. Four others taught languages:

two for Latin, one for Greek, one for French, Italian and Spanish. One of the eight had also to teach the military applications of mathematics with special reference to fortification and siegecraft and to the planning of troop formations. Another of the eight also taught history. There were instructors in dancing, music and drawing, riding, the handling of weapons for horse and foot, and the principles of military evolutions.[73]

[11] At about the same time Henry IV of France attempted to rationalise the education of the young nobles at his court by establishing what his panegyrist, Jean-Baptiste Legrain, calls an 'Academie pour la noblesse & autre ieunesse. . . . Ayant ordonné une compagnie de maistres, les uns pour les lettres, les autres pour les armes, autres pour monter à cheval, autres pour l'escriture, autres pour la musique, les instrumens, & la dance, bref, pour tout honeste exercice.' First mooted in 1594, the academy was designed to provide a training in skills that had hitherto been sought abroad, especially in Italy, and was seen by mathematical practitioners as a natural market for their wares, 'qui ne proffitent pas seullement durant la paix, mais produisent leurs plus beaux effects en temps de guerre.' By 1598 the king's chief riding master gave lessons every day, and from the fees paid him by the academicians he engaged masters of fence, dancing, music and mathematics; moreover the example of Paris had been followed in Rouen and Toulouse.[74]

[12] Far more hazy is the evidence suggesting that at this court at Nonsuch Palace the king's namesake, Henry, Prince of Wales, was being brought up in a similar atmosphere. In 1607 Sir Thomas Chaloner, the prince's tutor, an ex-soldier and something of a scientist, described Henry's household as 'a courtly college, or a collegiate court',[75] and in the same year Cleland wrote 'without offence to either of the famous universities here, or our colleges in Scotland, for all sorts of learning, I recommend in particular the academie of our noble prince, where young nobles may learne the first elements to be a privie counseller, a generall of an armie, to rule in peace, & to commande in warre'.[76] (The Venetian academies [13] of 1608-10 are described above, pp. 443-4.) Finally, at some time before his death in 1612, when still only eighteen, Prince Henry was associated with proposing yet another scheme for the education of royal wards: [14] an 'academy for the learning of the mathematiques and language, and for all kinds of noble exercises, as well of arms as other'. Its expenses were to be defrayed from an increase in the fines imposed in Star Chamber[77]—a suggestion paralleling the method of subvention used to support the contemporary riding academies in the Veneto.

Cleland's picture of a milieu that can produce instant privy councillors and instant generals is at least evidence of a growing faith in institutionalised education for young gentlemen. It was echoed across the Channel by Jean de Tavannes. [15] The educational whims of fathers and tutors could no longer be trusted, he wrote. The page system had degenerated into producing mere 'valets et macqueraux'. Travel to seek the riding and fencing masters of Italy led to youths returning 'plus chargez de vices que de vertus'. What was needed was 'colleges de noblesse' where 2,000 young gentlemen could be educated at the expense of the king or the Church: 'seroit-ce une grande gloire de voir sortir à vingt ans des generaux d'armées de ces escolles'.[78] And if courts like those of the two Henries were reflecting—or were being interpreted as reflecting—academic theories about the relevance of education to responsible public life, learned academies themselves were affected by the pastimes and interests of courtiers. [16] In 1612 David de Flurance Rivault, tutor to the young Louis XIII, set up a short-lived academy which not only allowed 'the methods of warfare of different peoples' to be discussed on an equal footing with questions of theology and literature, but was to provide for the teaching of 'military exercises and the art of war'.[79]

[17] It was quite in keeping with this atmosphere that Jean Chesnel, Seigneur of Chappronnoye, should, with the young Louis's encouragement, found in 1614 a new military order. Named after the Magdalen, it had three purposes: to maintain the Catholic faith, to suppress irresponsible duelling and to train a military *corps d'élite*. Its members were to fall into two categories: knights (those with three generations of noble blood) and 'brethren servants' ('from the most honorable families in townes and cities, next to the nobility'). The headquarters was to be in Paris, where 500 knights could be accommodated during the two-year period of probation before they were admitted to vows of charity, obedience and conjugal chastity; and those who so chose could stay on longer. They swore loyalty to the king and to avoid duels unless they were forced on them. Between eighty and 100 were to wait upon the king daily as a sort of special guard, and the motherhouse was to employ 'esquires, maisters in actions of arms, learned mathematicians, and some numbers of well experimented souldiours to enstruct military agilities and exercises fit for horse and foot'. Moreover there was to be a fund to help 'poore gentlemen'—not members of the order—'to the exercises that have no means for their learning'.[80] The project was never realised, though as proof his sincerity Chesnel spent the rest of his life as a rather prestigious hermit.

[18] In that same year, 1614, the English Privy Council allowed an increase in the membership of the London Artillery Garden to 500. With its armoury and practice fields, this institution was to be referred to as a 'nursery of military discipline' and a 'shoole' which taught 'martiall policy or discipline'. Its members were proud to reflect that, like the Greeks and Romans 'we [have] our academies and military schooles; witnesse our Artillery Garden ... wherein the choice and best-affected citizens (and gentry) are practised and taught the rudiments of our militia'.[81] Its members had weapon training in the use of halberds, pikes and muskets, drilled and practised evolutions and possibly carried out mock sieges. They also tried out new weapons, like William Neade's combination pike and gun. There were training periods each fortnight (sometimes once a week), and at least once a year these future officers could expand their evolutions with the whole of the local trained bands. They kept abreast of Continental tactical changes and followed the postures and written directions of the drill books seriously enough to stir the

mockery of Jonson and his fellow dramatists. Translations of ancient writers on the art of war were dedicated to them. Clearly there were far more citizens than gentry among their members, and though Prince Charles and various sheriffs and deputy lieutenants attended some of their meetings neither the Artillery Garden nor the other training establishments modelled on it had either the aristocratic enrolment or the polished and learned emphasis required to justify the term 'academy' save in partisan eyes.[82]

The Siegen academy ([19], see above, pp. 444-5) closed with the death of its founder, John of Nassau, in 1623. [20] In 1624 came another French proposal, this time from the man who had for many years run the nearest approach to a school for officers which France had produced, de Pluvinel. He was, he represents himself as saying in a dialogue with Louis XIII, dismayed at the extent to which the aristocracy had slid into idleness and vice. Let the king, therefore, found academies in Paris, Bordeaux, Lyons and in Tours or Poitiers. Those who could afford to pay, would; but the sons of impoverished aristocrats should be subsidised. The syllabus reads like a more serious version of the courses available at his own establishment. In the mornings, tuition in riding and practice in running at the ring. On Monday, Wednesday, Friday and Saturday afternoons, lessons in weapon management, dancing, gymnastics and mathematics. On Monday and Thursday afternoons, lessons in moral philosophy, drawn from ancient and modern history, and in politics tailored to the needs of future army officers, governors of towns and provinces and ambassadors. Once a month, moreover, there should be something more like modern field exercises,

> pour leur apprendre la maniere d'aller au combat, le moyen d'attaquer une escarmouche, la forme de se retirer. Bref, tout l'ordre de la guerre, & faire ces combats tantost à cheval tantost à pied, en faisant faire des forts de terre, & les faire attaquer et deffendre à ceste ieunesse (selon leur force) pour leur enseigner à bien attaquer une place & à la bien deffendre; donner les commandemens alternativement aux uns & aux autres, afin de les rendre tous dignes de bien commander & bien obeyr.

Such academies, he guaranteed, would create a loyal and law-abiding aristocracy 'capables de servir leur prince soit en paix, soit en guerre'. At this point the king breaks silence to ask how much it would cost. Thirty thousand livres a year, Pluvinel replies, and the dialogue closes with the king making non-committal noises of approval.[83]

[21] From 1628 the Friedländische Akademie provided the sort of education for aristocratic boys between nine and seventeen that was to be continued by the numerous German *Pagenakademien* or *Ritterakademien* of the second half of the seventeenth century: religion, mathematics and other 'nützlichen Studien', riding, the handling of weapons, dancing. But it died with its founder, Waldstein, in 1634.[84]

[22] Similarly short-lived was my last example, Louis XIII's establishment in 1629—at Richelieu's instance—of an Académie des exercises militaires. How large its enrolment was is not clear, but Richelieu added scholarships for twenty sons of poor gentlemen aged fourteen or fifteen. These awards were for two years, and as well as following the standard courses given at the

academy in riding, gymnastics, mathematics and fortification, and so forth (for the syllabus seems close to that of Pluvinel's private school), they were to learn the elements of logic, physics and metaphysics and moral philosophy—all taught in French. They were also to learn some geography and the outlines of universal history 'comme aussi de l'histoire des principautés modernes, singulièrement de l'Europe, dont les intérêts nous touchent de plus prés pour leur voisinage'. At the end of their two years the scholarship youths were to spend two years in the king's service, 'dans le régiment de ses gardes, en ses vaisseaux, ou autrement'.[85] This school also died with its founder, but, as with the other proposals listed here, the momentum of its intention helped to support the institutions that were later to endure.

NOTES

[1] See Frederick B. Artz, *The Development of Technical Education in France, 1500–1850*, London, 1966, and the papers by David Bien, John Shy, Thomas Hughes and Gunther Rothenberg in *Science, Technology and Warfare: Proceedings of the third Military History Symposium*, U.S.A.F. Academy, Washington, D.C. [1970], pp. 51–84.

[2] This essay owes its origin to the encouragement I received at one of Professor Kristeller's seminars at Columbia University.

[3] *Art and Life at the Court of Ercole I d'Este: the 'De triumphis religionis' of Giovanni Sabadino degli Arienti*, ed. Werner L. Gundersheimer, Geneva, 1972, pp. 39–40.

[4] Archivio di Stato, Venice, Materie miste notabili, 18, f. 66*v*.

[5] Marin Sanuto, *Diarii*, Venice, 1879–1903, xx, cols. 116, 149, 151, 185–8; xi, 147–9.

[6] T. C. Chubb, 'The Letters of Pietro Aretino', n.p., 1967, 280.

[7] J. A. Froude, *History of England . . .*, London, twelve vols., 1870, vi, p. 286.

[8] *A Briefe Discourse of Warre*, ed. John X. Evans, in *The Works of Sir Roger Williams*, Oxford, 1972, p. 27.

[9] *Commentaires*, ed. P. Courteault, Paris, three vols., 1925, iii, p. 389. He accepts that higher commands—generals of cavalry and colonels of infantry—will still go to men of noble blood, experienced or not; but the risks are reduced if they rely on well trained marshals and junior officers.

[10] One complaint can stand for many. 'A great sort of our gentlemen . . . doo take more comfort to be called good faulkners or expert woodmen than either skilful souldiers or learned scollers.' (Sir William Segar, *The Booke of Honor and Armes*, London, 1590, p. 72). His point is that gentlemen should exert themselves in either arms or learning or both.

[11] *Queen Elizabeth's Academy*, ed. F. J. Furnivall, E.E.T.S., extra series, viii.

[12] The academy was also to have the first copyright library in Europe, for 'all printers in England shall for ever be charged to deliver into the library of the achademy, at their own charges, one copy well bownde, of every booke, proclamacion, or pamflette, that they shall printe'. And it was to inaugurate the policy of 'publish or perish'; every six years each teacher was to produce one work of his own and two translations of foreign works.

[13] A. Favaro, *Galileo e lo studio di Padova*, Florence, two vols., 1883, ii, p. 331. Galileo was one of three candidates voted on for the position of mathematics lecturer to the Delia; he received the fewest votes. (Archivio di Stato, Padua, P.V., 2610, libro secondo ff. 12r f.) And see J. R. Hale, 'Military academies on the Venetian Terra ferma in the early seventeenth century', *Studi Veneziani*, 1973.

[14] Extract from the 'Festspiel' are quoted in Max Jähns, *Geschichte der Kriegswissenschaften*, Munich, three vols., 1889, ii, pp. 1026–9, and in W. Hahlweg, *Die Heeresreform der Oranier und die Antike*, Berlin, 1941, p. 148.

[15] *Op. cit.*, n. 8, p. 27.

[16] *The Tacticks of Aelian*, London, 1616, sig. A 2v. Sarpi, too, wrote of the Netherlands as 'the learnedest schoole for that kind of discipline, that at this time is in all Europe, yea in the whole world'. (Tr. Bishop William Bedell as *The Free Schoole of Warre*, London, 1625, sig. B iiiv. When Thomas Hood was appointed in the Armada year to give lectures in London on 'mathematicall science, a knowledge most convenient for militarie men', he anticipated the reaction of the conservatives. 'But heer some men per happes will say, what needeth this cost? what? those famous captaines of ours now in the Low Countries, or those of ancient time before ... were they trained up in this kind of learning?' (Sig. A iiir–v.) Only his first lecture, in fact, had a military bias; as the war scare eased, he devoted himself increasingly to the mathematics of navigation. The lecture is reprinted in F. R. Johnson, 'Thomas Hood's inaugural address ...', *Journal of the History of Ideas*, III, 1942, pp. 94–106.

[17] Geoffrey Parker, *The Army of Flanders and the Spanish Road*, Cambridge, 1972, pp. 32–3, and see also 40–1, 118–19.

[18] Translated in W. H. Woodward, *Vittorino da Feltre and other Humanist Educators*, Cambridge, 1897, p. 115.

[19] W. H. Woodward, *Studies in Education during the Age of the Renaissance*, Cambridge 1924, p. 71; *De liberorum educatione*, ed. J. S. Nelson, Washington, D.C., 1940, pp. 105–7.

[20] The *Weißkunig*, though composed between 1505 and 1516, was not published until 1775. Gargantua's education is described in book 1, chapters 23 and 24. There are, however, some remarkable similarities between their descriptions of their heroes' military education.

[21] Appendix to John Stowe, *Annales ...*, London, 1631, p. 1087. First printed in the edition of 1615. 'Paynting and ... pourtraying' was, as in Castiglione, for military purposes; see *Il Cortegiano*, trans. G. Bull, London, 1967, p. 97. By 1615 dancing had become accepted as giving a bodily grace that helped in the handling of weapons. The Academy at Treviso employed a 'ballarino'. (Archivio di Stato, Venice, Senato, Dispacci Rettori, Treviso, 28 March 1610.) Aristocratic foreigners presented their coats of arms to record their visits to the chief dancing school in Padua. (L. Pearsall Smith, *Sir Henry Wotton*, London, two vols., 1907, I, p. 458.)

[22] *De Rege*, trans. G. A. Moore, Washington, D.C., 1948, p. 113.

[23] *Mémoires*, in M. Petitot, *Collection complete des mémoires relatifs a l'histoire de France*, Paris, 1832, p. 18.

[24] For a retrospective glance at the system see Salomon de la Broue, *Le Cavalerice françois*, Paris, 1602, pp. 2 and 18–22. For the unreliability and thoughtlessness of young officers see Agrippa d'Aubigné, *La Vie*, in *Oeuvres*, ed. H. Weber *at al.*, Paris, 1969, p. 393, and Jean de Tavannes, *Mémoires* (of Gaspard by Jean, but containing much comment by Jean) in Petitot, *Coll., cit.*, Paris, three vols., 1822, I, p. 319. The latter sets out a preferable programme, under the charge of private tutors, on pp. 157–8 and 168–73.

[25] Quoted in *Certain Discourses Military*, ed. J. R. Hale, Ithaca, N.Y., 1964, p. xv.

[26] Hahlweg, *op. cit.*, p. 128.

[27] *Stratagemi militari*, trans. M. A. Gandino, Venice, 1574, sig. a 2v.

[28] Paolo Giovio, *A Shorte Treatise upon the Turkes Chronicles*, trans. P. Ashton, London, 1546, f. ivr, preface.

[29] *The Expedition into Scotlande* [no place, no date].

[30] Anon., *A True Declaration of ... the Winning of Noyan, August 1591*, London, n.d., epilogue.

[31] Title page of Bernadin de Mendoce, *Commentaires memorables ...*, Paris, 1591.

[32] See generally M. J. Cockle, *A Bibliography of English and Foreign Military Books up to 1642*, London, 1900; repr. 1957. For England, Henry J. Webb, *Elizabethan Military Science: the Books and the Practice*, London, 1965.

[33] E.g. Sancho de Londoño, *Discurso sobre la forma de reduci la disciplina militar ...*, Brussels, 1589, epistle dedicatory.

[34] A generation later, titles begin to stress the 'do it yourself' approach, e.g.

J. Jacobi von Wallhausen, *Alphabetum . . . der Soldaten zu Fuess ihr A.B.C.*, Frankfurt, 1613, and J. T., *The A.B.C. of Armes . . .*, London, 1616; C. Köber, *Tyrocinium militare . . .*, Danzig, 1616; Anon., *Scola militaris exercitationis. Das ist ein schul darinnen die angehende Soldaten zu Fuß . . . auff die newe und jetzundt ubliche Weiß gemunstert . . . gelehret und underricht werden . . .*, Cöllen, 1619.

³⁵ *The Institution of a Young Noble Man*, Oxford, 1607, p. 153. The works he refers to are *The Politicke and Militarie Discourses of the Lord de la Nove* (François de la Noue), trans. E. A., London, 1587. Cf. Roger Williams on la Noue: 'the little experience I got was from him, and from such others as himself' (*op. cit.*, p. 33). And Blaise de Monluc, *Commentaires . . .*, Bordeaux, two vols., 1592; no English translation until 1674.

³⁶ The debate, as far as England was concerned, was opened in 1562 by John Shute: 'I desyre of god that this [military] disciplyne maye be better knowen in oure countrie than it is, so shall we not have so many as we have that shall saye, give me the untrayned souldiour and take the trayned that lyste'. *Two very Notable Commentaries*, London, 1562, sig. ii*v*. See also Anthony Esler, *The Aspiring Mind of the Elizabethan Younger Generation*, Durham, N.C., 1966, *passim* but especially p. 109; F. de la Noue, ed. F. E. Sutcliffe, Geneva, 1967, pp. 161-2, 175.

³⁷ Trans. in Thomas Coryat, *Coryat's Crudities . . .* [1611], Glasgow, two vols., 1905, I, p. 191.

³⁸ *Op. cit.*, pp. 267-8.

³⁹ *The Practice of Policy*, London, 1604, pp. 10-11.

⁴⁰ Thomas and Dudley Digges, *Foure Paradoxes, or Politique Discourses*, London, 1604 (written before 1595), p. 79.

⁴¹ Tavannes, *op. cit.*, p. 291.

⁴² See E. Bourciez, *Les Moeurs polies et la littérature de cour sous Henri II*, Paris, 1886, pp. 18 ff.

⁴³ A. Massari Malatesta, *Compendio dell'heroica arte di cavalleria . . .*, Venice, 1600, f. 51*v*.

⁴⁴ Claudio Corte, *Il cavallerizzo*, Venice, 1573, sig. b 2*v*.

⁴⁵ Quoted in Clare Howard, *English Travellers of the Renaissance*, London, 1914, p. 127.

⁴⁶ Thus the Grand Duke Francesco set up a riding school under Rustico Piccardini in 1585, 'quod nobilissimorum adolescentium qui equestri splendore se ornari cupiunt in primisque Joannis fratris'. G. Sommi Picenardi, 'Don Giovanni de' Medici', *Nuovo Archivio Veneto*, new series, XIII, p. 115.

⁴⁷ Chevalier de Méré, *Les Conversations* [1668], ed. C. H. Boudhors, Paris, 1930, p. 69.

⁴⁸ *Le Maneige royal*, Paris, 1624, extended in *L'Instruction du roy . . .*, Paris, 1625.

⁴⁹ Malatesta, *op. cit.*, attempts an answer, f. 20*r*.

⁵⁰ *The Art of Riding* (trans. Giulio Corte, cited in n. 37 above), London, 1584, sig. A ii*v*.

⁵¹ J. Jacobi von Wallhausen, *L'Art militaire pour l'infanterie*, Paris, 1615, sig. 3*r*. From the letter to the reader in which he describes his other books.

⁵² Egerton Castle, *Schools and Masters of Fence*, London, 1892, pp. 41-5; J. D. Aylward, *The English Masters of Fence*, London, 1956, ch. 2.

⁵³ *Toxophilus*, quoted in Alyward, *op. cit.*, p. 18.

⁵⁴ Almoro Lombardo's preface to Nicoletto Giganti, *Scola . . . e modi di parare et di ferire di spada . . .*, Venice, 1606, sig. b 3*r*.

⁵⁵ Paris, 1628.

⁵⁶ *Paradoxes of Defence*, London, 1599, quoted in Ruth Kelso, *The Doctrine of the English Gentleman in the Sixteenth Century*, Urbana, Ill., 1929, pp. 151-2.

⁵⁷ Achille Marozzo, *Onera nova . . .*, Venice [?1517], could claim ('Proemio') that of G. A. de Lucha's *scuola* 'si puo ben dire che sieno piu guerrieri usciti che dal Troiano cavallo', but later writers are forced to plead the military relevance of fencing, e.g. G. dall'Agocchie, *Dell'arte di scrimia . . .*, Venice, 1572, sig. A iii*r* and f. 5*r*.

Some books have illustrations (in the Thurber 'Touché!' vein) to show what bloody damage can be done with the point: e.g. N. Giganti, *Scola overo teatro* . . ., Venice, 1606. Montaigne thought that the 'turnings, windings, and nimble-quicke motions, wherein youth is instructed and trained in this new schoole, are not onely unprofitable, but rather contrary and damageable for the use of militarie combate.' (trans. Florio, lib. II, ch. 27.)

[58] See illustrations in A. Marozzo, *Arte dell'Armi*, Venice, 1568, and J. Jacobi von Wallhausen, *Art de Chevalrie*, Frankfurt, 1616.

[59] Giacomo di Grassi, *Ragione di adoprar sicuramente l'arme* . . ., Venice, 1570, trans. I.G., ed. T. Churchyard, as *Giacomo di Grassi his true Arte of Defence*, London, 1594, sig. Ee, 1r f.

[60] *Mémoires*, Cologne, two vols., 1665, I, pp. 38–9.

[61] Howard, *op. cit.*, 121–2; John Walter Stoye, *English Travellers Abroad, 1604–1667*, London, 1952, pp. 56 f.

[62] The influence of Castiglione's notion of *sprezzatura* is very strong in the riding literature, e.g. riding 'deve adoprare arte & industria, ma in termine che dimostri esser fatta senza fatica e sforzo, quasi dotato natural gratia, coprendo l'arte con l'istessa arte'. (A. Massario Malatesta, *Compendio* . . ., Venice, 1600, f. 6v.) In his *Il cavallerizzo* (Venice, 1573) he says he is going to describe the perfect riding master 'per essere il modello, l'esemplare, & il bersaglio' on the lines of Plato, Xenophon and Castiglione. See especially ff. 128v f.

[63] Pluvinel employed Crispin de Pas the younger, who later produced the magnificent folio *La prima parte della luce del dipingere et desegnare*, Amsterdam, 1643, a teaching manual in Italian, Dutch, French and German, concerned with the correct drawing—by relating real to geometrical forms—of human figures, animals, birds and insects. In the preface he explains how he taught de Pluvinel's students how 'ils peussent facilement ordonner les bataillons & fortifier des places regulierement.' (Sig. A 4r.)

[64] It was works by authors like C. Agrippa, *Trattato di scientia d'arme* . . ., Rome, 1553, and Thibault, *op. cit.*, that prompted these lines in a prefatory poem to 'A.G.' in *Pallas Armata*, London, 1639: 'Thankes, mathematic fencer, that dost tye/The sword to th' booke and fight in geometry.'

[65] An idea urged previously, e.g. D. Mora, *Il soldato*, Venice, 1569, pp. 219–26.

[66] Thomas Starkey, *A Dialogue between Reginald Pole and Thomas Lupset*, 1553–56, ed. K. M. Burton, London, 1948, pp. 169–70.

[67] Edward Waterhous, *Fortescutus illustratus*, London, 1663, pp. 539 and 542. The memorandum is here acribed to 1539–42.

[68] J. Conway Davis, 'Elizabethan plans for education', *Durham Research Review*, 1954, p. 2. The proposal is described by J. P. Collier in *Archaeologia*, 1855–56, pp. 343–344.

[69] *Dialogo nel quale . . . si forma un perfetto principe ed un perfetto republica, e parimente un senatore, un cittadino, un soldato e un mercatante*, Venice, 1563, pp. 132–7, 182. For the academies, see above, pp. 473–4.

[70] F. A. Yates, *French Academies of the Sixteenth Century*, London, 1947, p. 25.

[71] *Ed. cit.*, pp. 152–5.

[72] Eric Cochrane, *Florence in the Forgotten Centuries*, Chicago, 1972, p. 127.

[73] F. Paulsen, *Geschichte des gelehrten Unterrichts auf den deutschen Schulen und Universitäten*, Leipzig, second edition, two vols., 1896, I, pp. 503–6.

[74] *Decade contenant la vie et gestes de Henri le Grand* . . ., Paris, 1614, p. 428; J. Errard, *La Géometrie* . . ., Paris, second edition, 1602, dedication; E. Albèri, *Relazioni degli ambasciatori veneti al Senato*, Florence, 1839–63, xv, appendix, p. 103.

[75] T. Birch, *Life of Henry, Prince of Wales*, London, 1760, p. 97. The household accounts (*ibid.*, pp. 449 f.) only mention, as relevant to this description, a music teacher, a librarian (the mathematician Edward Wright), a master of the horse and the 'keeper of the riding-house at St James's', George Blastone.

[76] *Op. cit.*, p. 35.

[77] *Collecteanea Curiosa*, ed. J. Gutch, two vols., Oxford, 1718, I, pp. 213–14.
[78] *Op. cit.*, p. 175.
[79] Yates, *op. cit.*, pp. 277–8.
[80] Andrew Favyn (= André Favine), *The Theatre of Honor and Knight-hood*, London, two vols., 1623, trans. from Paris edition of 1620, I, pp. 55–65.
[81] Henry Petow (1622), quoted in G. Goold Walker, *The Honourable Artillery Company, 1537–1926*, London, 1926, p. 30; Edward Cooke, *The Character of Warre*, London, 1626, sig. A 3v; William Bariffe, *Mars his Triumph*, London, 1638, sig. aa 2v.
[82] In 1636 Sir Francis Kynaston announced the setting up (with royal assent) of his Musaeum Minervae. It offered instruction from teachers of philosophy and medicine, astronomy, geometry (including fortification), music, languages, weapons, instruction, dancing, painting and riding. He justified it by saying that 'hitherto no such places for the education and trayning up of our own young nobilitie and gentrie in the practise of arms and arts have been instituted here in England'. (*Constitutions of the Musaeum Minervae*, London, 1636, sig. C 2r–4r.) The work was published to reply to criticism of his scheme. He stresses the fact that he intends no competition with the universities or the Inns of Court.
[83] Antoine de Pluvinel, *L'Instruction* . . ., Paris, 1625, pp. 191–204. The work is posthumous. Apart from this dialogue, it reproduces *Le Maneige* . . .
[84] Max Jähns, *op. cit.*, II, p. 1030.
[85] F. Funck-Brentano, 'L'Éducation des officiers dans l'ancienne France', *Réforme Sociale*, 1918, pp. 21–2. The Assembly of Notables had proposed a military school for young nobles in 1626. (Frederick B. Artz, *op. cit.*, p. 43.)

9

ON A TUDOR PARADE GROUND
THE CAPTAIN'S HANDBOOK OF HENRY BARRETT 1562

For the student of Tudor military affairs, the middle decades of the sixteenth century are dark. The records are fragmentary. Moreover, between Henry VIII's Boulogne campaign of 1544—6 and the beginning of English intervention in the Netherlands in 1572, military activity in Scotland, Ireland and France was not on a scale, nor had lasting enough results to have encouraged its investigation in depth. Nor has the student of military organisation found much to relish between the Henrician statutes regarding military service and the setting up in 1573 of an effective neuclus within the national militia reserve, the trained bands. What is clear, however, is that when Elizabeth came to the throne in 1558 the country was felt to be dangerously vulnerable both to sedition at home and invasion from abroad.

Apart from the royal guard, the Yeomen, and a scattering of garrisons in the north, based on Berwick, England had no standing force of professional troops. Mercenaries had been employed, but their cost, and still more, their unpopularity, had led this solution to be rejected; and English forces had been found to operate uneasily with troops supplied by allies — with auxiliaries, to use Machiavelli's term. Indeed, it was while translating Machiavelli's *Art of War* during his service with Charles V's armies in North Africa that Peter Whithorne was converted to his belief that the only satisfactory troops were to be found among one's own countrymen. And it was with this in mind, and knowing that the young queen was urgently concerned about military preparedness, that he dedicated his translation to her in 1560. The idea of a national force was, however, already in being. By statute, all able-bodied men between the ages of 16 and 60 were liable for military service except the clergy, lords of parliament and their servants, privy councillors and justices of the peace. As it happened, this militia force was called on for the fumbled Scottish campaign of that same year, 1560, and both the system and the troops it produced were found wanting.

The investigation Sir William Cecil called on magistrates to make into the working of the militia statutes only confirmed the doubts expressed by individuals who had the cause of military reform at heart.

Too doggedly insular, in spite of recent campaigns in France, the English had not kept abreast of European developments. Only two years before, in 1558, one of the continent's foremost military reformers, Lazarus von Schwendi, had told an Englishman 'that we stoode to moch on our owne conceitte.'[1] This fault arose chiefly from the absence of a programme that would not just muster and count the militia units but train them to use their weapons and drill them to perform evolutions both on their own and in conjunction with others. Such a programme would need a set of uniform and up-to-date instructions. The 'articles devised for the manner of musteringe' produced in Mary's reign noted that 'yt shall not be a mysse that the muster mayster have ready in rightinge aforhande certeyne preceptes and rules meete for everie capteyne and his officers.'[2] But nothing had been done.

It was the need to instruct the captains that was the basic and most frequent explanation of what was wrong with the militia system. Thinly scattered among the rustic manors of England were men who had fought the Scots at Solway Moss and Pinkie, had vainly defended Calais and won and lost Boulogne. Others, like Whithorne, were seeking cash and glory in the domestic broils of the French and in the Emperor's wars against the Turks and the Moors. But there were not enough of them to pass on their experience to the militia. The decline in numbers and possessions of the militant territorial landlords of a previous generation meant that comparatively few of those responsible for local musters and training had any military knowledge.[3] 'The moost part of gentlemen', wrote Richard Barkhede, 'ar and have ben of laite dayes brought up so deyintely and in such vanities that they can little skill of the service of their countree . . . I cannot passe over with silence (for the worlde doth se) what tenderlinges the greatest part of our younge gentlemen be.'[4] There were many ex-servicemen enrolled in the militia, but neither were they of much use. The ex-soldier could teach nothing because he had learned nothing. Why was this? asked Thomas Audley,

---

1 Richard Barkhede, *A brief discourse for the mayintenaunce, exercise and trayning of a convenient nombre of Englishemen wherby they may be the soner made souldiours for the redier deffence of this realm of England.* British Library [B. L.], Harleian Ms. 68, 4r. N. d. but c. 1560.
2 B. L. Egerton Ms. 2790, 94r.
3 Jeremy Goring, 'Social change and military decline in mid-Tudor England', *History* (1975), 185-97.
4 *Ms. Cit.*, 3r.

who had served in Henry VIII's later wars in France. 'Because his captain is as ignorant as he ... I wyshe ... that captaines would be as readie to take paynes to traine their men as thei be readie at the paie daie to take paynes to tell mony, for it is a grevouse payne to sett a bataill with untrayned men.'[5] And Sir Thomas Gresham, closely aware of military developments in Germany and the Low Countries wrote to Cecil to urge a training programme for the militia. 'If this were put presently in use, and good captains appointed to train them up, the news of that once spread throughout all Christendom would be terrible.'[6]

It is against this background, and that of the assembling of a new army to assist the Huguenots in France in 1562, that we should imagine the motives of one Henry Barrett who in that year wrote a handbook which took account of the fact that 'the practises of the warres dothe daylie alter and chaunge', which emphasized the importance of training recruits to handle weapons and get themselves in and out of tactical formations, and which was not addressed to professional soldiers but was 'A briefe booke unto private captaynes.'[7]

We can see why such a book was written at this particular time. We shall look at the light it throws on military thought and practice in the dark decades. But first, who was Henry Barrett and what were his qualifications to write it?

It is perhaps surprising, but it is not untypical of the period, that he appears to emerge from total obscurity as the author of a very different sort of work. In 1549 Thomas Berthelet printed in London a tract entitled *The armyng of a Christen warrier readie to fyghte with the enemies of our captain and savioure Jesus Christe, to the whiche soldiers, Henry Barret, the writer of this rude boke, wisheth health and muche increase of faith*. The tract was written to tell the good protestant soldier how to equip himself for the battle against the Devil and the doctrines of Rome, and it is remarkable not for what the author says, but how he says it.

At a later date, the use of a technical military vocabulary to describe the struggle of the soul towards perfection was to become

---

5 'A treatise on the art of war', *Journal of the Society for Army Research* (1927), 69.
6 Quoted by Lindsay Boynton, *The Elizabethan Militia* (London, 1967), 57.
7 Folger Library, Washington D. C., Ms. V. a. 455. Full title: *A briefe booke unto private captaynes leadinge ffootemen, their officers necessary. In[s] tructinge to marche, trayne and imbattell their noumbers as to service ys convenient*. Set furthe by thands of Henry Barrett one of the yomen of the Queenes Maiesties moste honnorable chaumber. Anno Domino 1562. 'Private' = individual. *Cf.* Audley (v. note 39, Tanner Ms. 103, f. 34r): 'Everie private captein shall swear his souldiours one by one ...'

commonplace.[8] Such a use of martial imagery was less usual at the mid-century and it was rare indeed to use it as lavishly. 'First put on your greaves and queshes [cuisse: thighpiece] ... and ye shall arme your self with a coller [gorget: protection for throat and upper chest] ... and beware of excessious drynkynge whiche oftentymes maketh an unable souldier, and causeth his captain to put hym out of his boke [remove his name from the muster list], and then he becometh a venturer [unattached volunteer] which when he is taken is not sure of his raunsome ... Then put on your corsolat with a reste [support for a lance projecting from the breastplate of the corslet, or suit of body armour], basses and tasses [protections for the upper leg] ... Then put on your vanbrasses [vambrace: armour for lower arm] and gantlets ... then locke down your bavier and moffle [eye cover and lower face piece of the visor] ... then set one youre graunde garde and polgremes [shoulder pieces] ... ' Those that fail in their service shall 'enter into the continual payne emonge the forlorn hope [advanced party] of lost soldiers.'

The Christian soldier might have been thus armed by a writer who had not served as one himself. But near the end of the work the author turns to veritable soldiers and addresses them as though from one professional to others. This closing section is headed — similarly to some of the headings in the *Breife booke* — 'The souldiers charge'. 'Now verely', he writes, 'there is a faut emonge many soldiers, as well emong some English soldiars as other nacions, which when they be once chosen to goo agaynste the Kynges ennemies whether it be in Scotland or Fraunce or else where, they do use such ungodlye usages within the Kynges realme both out warde and home wardes as ys great shame to reherse, for some wyll take their neyghboures cattayle and vittayle and will paye nothinge, and some wylle procure mens wyves and servantes to ungodlye livinge and some useth excessious drynkynge and other some abhominable sweryng ... wherfore good Christian soldiers let us praye to our graund captayne ... so that from this tyme forward no Englishe soldier shalbe worthy of reproch in the offence aforesayd and that we may live only by the Kynges wages and by hys conduct money [travel allowance] which we have according to his graces godly custome ...'

The extreme rarity of this little volume can plead some excuse for these extracts. They show that the author had a grasp of military terminology and a knowledge of how soldiers behave, and they at least

---

8 See J. R. Hale, 'Incitement to violence? English divines on the theme of war', below pp. 487-517, esp. pp. 491 seq.

imply that he took the King's wages as a soldier himself. And they make more readily understandable the assumption in the handbook of 1562 that the good soldier should be equated, at least potentially, with the good Christian.[9]

Nor, indeed, should we be surprised at a soldier writing a religious tract. John Shute, who, also in 1562, produced what we now know to have been misleadingly called 'the earliest English composition on military discipline',[10] published in 1565 a translation from Pierre Viret, *The firste parte of the Christian instruction* ... In the dedication to Leicester, Shute refers to himself as 'a simple souldior better practised abrode in martiall matters then furnished at home with cunnyng of the scoole ... yet do I not thincke it a matter unmeete for my profession and callyng to knowe the truthe of Gods holy worde ... A souldior is not excluded from this band [of Christians], he must needes in this battell keepe his order and do (by grace) his uttermost endevoure, leaste the muster maister, Christe, do casse [discharge] him.'

The armyng of a Christen warrier, was dedicated to Sir John Markham, lieutenant of the Tower of London, and it was in 1549 that the guard there became incorporated into the larger body of Yeomen of the Guard to which, as we shall see, Barrett was mentioned as belonging in 1553.

The next witness to his activity is a large diagram [Plate 1] endorsed as 'Set fforthe by the han[de] of Henry Barrett Anno 1550.'[11] The identity of the author of the tract cannot be proved, but spelling and phraseology make it clear that this diagram is by our Henry Barrett, as do the table of square roots and products and the numbered grid: both are features that recur in the handbook of 1562. Apart from the table, the page contains a squared grid, numbered from 5 to 101 at the top and left-hand side, with a diagonal line of corresponding odd numbers. On this grid is superimposed a diagram showing the order of an army on the march, moving to the left of the page. In the van is the artillery ('ffawconnets, ffawcons, sakers, bastard colveringes, colveringes, deme canons, canons' — the full range of Henrician field and siege artillery from small to large, excepting mortars), followed by pioneers and officers of the ordnance. The main body is an infantry square surrounded by a hollow square whose corners are protected by bands of shot. Behind come the cattle, provision carriages, more pioneers and a guard for the supplies, also a square of 'all kynde of men

9 See Appendix, 'Captaines ... charge'. 'Priest ...'. 'Trueth'.
10 The Epistle prefacing his translation, *Two very notable commentaries* ...
11 B. L. Harleian Ms. 309. 84-5.

extraordenarye as well shott as other men.' In the rearguard follow units of heavy and light cavalry and of archers and hackbutters. It is a remarkable work for its time and place, possibly the earliest, certainly the first so elaborate English diagram of a troop formation to have survived.

We are left with a few fragments of information. On September 14th, 1553, in Star Chamber, 'Henry Barrett, one of the garde, [was] committed this daye to the custodie of John Piers, to be fourthcomyng the next daye by ix of the clock.'[12] John Peers was Clerk of the Check of the Yeomen, a civilian responsible for handling the chamber account whence the guard was paid and equipped. It is more likely, therefore, that Barrett's attendance as a witness was being ensured than that he was accused of a crime. The early months of Mary's reign were charged with uncertainty – it was decided in Star Chamber on that same day to send Cranmer to the Tower – and members of the guard were well placed to overhear gossip in corridors and anterooms. Indeed, if only Barratt had committed a crime we should know more about him. In 1562 the title page of *A breife booke* tells us that he was 'one of the yomen of the Queenes Maiesties moste honnorable chaumber' and its preface that he had gained experience and knowledge 'by my few years travaile amongest dyvers nacions.' On October 21st of that year a Henry Barrett was licensed to marry Margaret Webster at St. Sepulchre's in London. This is probably our author. Finally, a soldier called Barrett[13] was lieutenant to the captain of the troops guarding Mary Queen of Scots at Carlisle castle in 1568.[14] As we shall see, it was not unusual for yeomen to be detatched for specially responsible duties of this kind. The information comes, moreover, from Sir Francis Knollys who was not only Mary's custodian but Captain of the Yeomen of the Guard.

With biographical evidence so scanty it is important to see what significance attaches to Barrett's being a member of the yeomen from at least 1553 to 1562 (and possibly from 1549 to 1568). This royal bodyguard had been instituted by Henry VII in the late summer of 1485. In 1550 it numbered only 105.[15] In the following year Edward VI noted in his *Chronicle* that he had been so delighted by a display of their archery that 'it was appointed there should be ordinary 100

12 *Acts of the Privy Council* [A. P. C.] 1553, 347.
13 *London marriage licences*, ed. Joseph Foster (London, 1887), 86.
14 *Queen Elizabeth and her times*, ed. Thomas Wright (2 vols., London, 1838), i, 290. References in muster and chancery records mention Henry Barrett of Hereford and Shouldham (in Norfolk) respectively; both
15 *A. P. C.*, n. s., iii, 54.

archers and 100 halberdiers, either good wrestlers or casters of the bar, or leapers, runners, or tall men of personage.'[16] Accordingly, by 1553 there were 200.[17] By the early 1560s the number had declined to 146.[18]

In time of war or of domestic crisis when the sovereign's person was in danger, or when an army was being disbanded and it was thought politically wise to offer interim employment to at least a small proportion of the troops, extraordinary yeomen of the guard were enrolled. Thus the guard attending Henry VIII on the campaign that led in 1513 to the occupation of Tournai numbered 600.[19] In the anxious year 1550 Edward VI was given 300 'yeomen extraordinarie to attende on his highnes person';[20] these were chosen from men returned from the Boulogne campaign 'to thentent they shulde not have cause to murmour, and that the kinges majestie may be the better furnished of men.'[21] Most famous of the yeomen 'extraordinary' were the guards at the Tower of London, who became yeomen of the guard in 1549 and have come to represent the corps as a whole.

The ordinary were much better paid than the extraordinary yeomen; in c. 1562 they got 16d. a day as opposed to 4d. or 6d. – the pay of the common soldier as well as of the extraordinary yeomen.[22] The yeomen of the chamber appear as distinct from the yeomen of the guard only occasionally; normally, payments are recorded to the yeomen of the guard as a whole, but it seems reasonably clear that the former were chosen as being especially responsible for the sovereign's privacy and safety. They could, however, be seconded for special duties. In 1562, for instance, the captain of Rye castle was a yeoman of the chamber, Philip Chute.[23] All the yeomen were foot soldiers. After 1550 the new weapons ordered for them were halberds and 'javelinges' rather than bows. They wore full body armour underneath ceremonial coats of velvet decorated with silver gilt. But in spite of the fairly

---

16 *The chronicle and political papers of King Edward VI*, ed. W. K. Jordan (Cornell U. P. for Folger Library, 1966), 63. That the archers were members of his 'ordinary guard' we know from Sir John Hayward, *Literary remains of King Edward VI*, ed. J. G. Nichols (2 vols., London 1957), i, ccxii.

17 Sir R. Hennell, *History of the King's bodyguard* (London, 1904), 103.

18 *Calendar of State Papers Domestic*, ix, p. 507. No names are given in the document cited (Public Record Office, S. P. 15, 9, 203r).

19 C. G. Cruickshank, *The English occupation of Tournai, 1513-1519* (Oxford, 1971).

20 *A. P. C.*, n. s., iii, 45.

21 *Op. cit.*, 29.

22 P. R. O., *doc. cit.*

23 A reference I owe to Martin Biddle's account of Camber, forthcoming in vol. IV of *The History of the King's Works*

frequent orders for 'silver spangelles' and 'spangelles gilte' for their uniforms, they were very much a working guard. Their captain was invariably a man of aristocratic birth – Knollys was succeeded by Sir Christopher Hatton – and the names and possessions of the yeomen (leases of land, houses, occasionally advowsons) amply justify the title of their office.

Apart from their duties of watch and ward wherever the sovereign happened to be residing, yeomen were employed to arrest suspects and escort prisoners, attend executions or protect unpopular preachers from the mob. Not all yeomen escaped suspicion of treason, one was even convicted of 'conjuration for treasure in the ground'[24] but there is no doubt that they were looked on as a *corps d'élite* who formed the small but prestigious nucleus of the armies that crossed to France or Ireland and whose parade exercises were expected to impress visiting dignitaries. And as a crack corps their training and drill could be seen as a model for the militia and their captains. In 1585 the Commissioners for the Musters were apprised that Elizabeth had seen fit to send round as muster-master a yeoman to assist local captains to train men 'in a uniforme sort', a man likely to 'answeare her expectation, being appoynted for the guard of her own person.'[25] This is a late date, but it is quite possible that yeomen had been sent out in this capacity before.

The need for a practical handbook for amateur captains in 1562 was apparent. It was still apparent in the 1570s, when Thomas Proctor complained of 'the necessitie and scarcitie of writing in this matter'[26], and in the 1580s, when Nicholas Lichefield translated a military manual 'lately found in the forte in Ireland where the Italians and Spaniards had fortified themselves ... chiefly because in our English tongue I finde not the lyke extant for the necessary instruction and generall commoditie of our common souldiers.'[27] It was not, however, apparent to the government. The first practical manual to be licensed for the press came as late as 1600.[28] and the first official drill-book was not issued until 1623.[29] So to extend the context within which Barrett produced his handbook we may picture a government reluctant to put any information about its armed forces into print. And we can add this: the very general psychological and linguistic inability on the part of his

24 *A. P. C.*, n. s., vi, 306.
25 B. L. King's Ms. 265, 264v-265r.
26 *On the knowledge and conducte of warres* (London, 1578), sig. vr.
27 Luis Gutierrez de la Vega, *De re militari* (London, 1582), sig. A iir. Original published Medina del Campo 1569.
28 Sir Clement Edmonds, *The maner of our moderne training, or tacticke practise.*
29 *The military discipline ... to be exercised in musters.* Thus the engraved title page, dated 1623; the printed title page reads: *The military art of trayning*, and is dated 1622.

contemporaries to produce a thoroughly practical and elementary account of any technical subject whatsoever, from commercial mathematics to metallurgy or building, and the inability of military writers in particular to stick to the local parade ground without veering away to discuss ideal battle formations for whole armies, the morality of war and its practitioners, or the lessons to be learned from studying the campaigns and the military leaders of antiquity. It is Barrett's attempt to cater for the needs of local units of the militia, his comparative lack of fascination with the evolutions of whole armies and his absolute lack of interest in antiquity - combined with (for England) an unprecedented use of explanatory diagrams - that make his book a uniquely practical answer to the needs of the time.

Were a non-professional captain to have received a copy of Barrett's book he would have read first an account of his own responsibilities and how to deal with his men in general terms, next an account of the command structure of a company, with enough about the duties and qualities of each officer to aid him in choosing them from the men at his disposal. A surgeon and a priest were added for the sake of completeness though they would only have been made available on active service, and in general it would be a lucky captain who could cast the roles to perfection — how many drummers and fife-players were also 'ingenious of sondery languages'? (In this section Barrett does show signs of being infected by the age's craze to depict ideal types and its virtual inability to stick strictly to the matter in hand.) After sorting his men, the captain is helped to 'see them furnished', the weapons, defenses, and roles of hackbutters, archers, pikemen, and halberd-iers being described, and he is then ready to lead them 'to some convenient grownede', where the sergeant puts them in ranks as their names are called from the roll, and marches them into a ring-like formation where they wait ready for the captain to harangue them [Plate 2].

At this point Barrett gives the captain some background information from which he can explain some of the purposes of the drill that is to follow. He points out the importance — a theme to which he recurs more than once — of being on higher ground than the enemy and having the wind at your back. To gain, or having lost, recover one or both of these advantages is a prime reason for learning to manoeuvre together. It is essential to learn the dense defensive posture, edged with pikes crossed and levelled, that is used when attacked by horse or heavy infantry, and to learn how to form squares and rectangles from the column of march. Finally, the practical use of formations such as the one the men are already in is explained. While the men are still around him, the captain reminds them of the qualities that make the good soldier:

soldier: he must be silent, so that he can hear orders while the enemy cannot hear him, he must obey orders, keep all military secrets, be courageous and always be trustworthy; those who are false will go after death to everlasting darkness, 'from the which God save all true Christian soldiers.' The material provided for his harangue concludes with a recital of some of the clauses relating to discipline and good order that were commonly read out to troops at the commencement of a campaign.

At this point the training proper can begin, first shot (archers and hackbutters) alone, then shot, pikemen and halberdiers together in increasingly large numbers, the formations being described in words and illustrated by diagrams. Their relevance to actual combat conditions is pointed out and the general point made that 'all thoughe the same seeme paynfull at the firste, it wilbe profitable in tyme of service.' In theory, company drill was the sergeant's responsibility, but it was as likely as not that the captain would first have to train his sergeant, so these sections are an essential part of the manual. Again, although the largest group a captain would be responsible for was the company (which at the mid-century could be anything from 100 to 200 men) or the ensign (which Barrett puts at 300 men), he needed to know how to cooperate in the brigading of larger formations. The largest formation Barrett describes are those of five ensigns, 1500 men. Where Barrett does ride a hobbyhorse beyond the bounds of what could have taken place at a training of the militia is in the mathematical tables with which his book concludes, three of which run to numbers that could only be the concern of the sergeant major of a whole army.[30]

The drill described in the long illustrated section devoted to evolutions commenced with marching in column of three files. The men were then taught to 'augment', first by bringing up two files from the rear, creating a rank of five, then by bringing up two more, making a body of seven files which, faced left and right, formed the rectangular

---

30 Table 1 (36r-v), 10,000; table 4 (40r-v), 8, 181; table 5 (41r *seq.*) 2,700. That these tables in their higher reaches are more suited to a sergeant major than to a captain can be appreciated from Sir Robert Constable's description (1576) of his function. When the high marshall of an army has decided where the battle is to take place, 'the serjant major muste then repare also unto the said fielde, there to set the order of the batailes [*i. e.* vanguard, main body, rearguard] to the most advantage according to the grownde. And first of all he must divide his weapons and appoint every rancke withe weapon most convenient accordinge to order. That being done and the battailes being set and everie weapon placed in everie rancke most convenient, then must the said serjaunt major se that the kinges standard be placed in the middest of the mayne battaile ... '. Eventually he allocates places to individual captains in the 'battailes' in the wings and in the advance party or 'forlorne hope'. *The order of a campe and armye royall*, B. L. Harleian ms. 847, 54r-55r.

body known as a 'hearse' (Plate 3). Further augmentation produced the other basic formation of the period, the 'square' or 'quadrant'. Column, hearse and square then had to practise moving from side to side or, face about, to the rear. The only order quoted is 'instruct to augment' which, given by the captain, must have involved much rushing about and gesticulating by the sergeant, for 'augmenting' progressively fractured the organization of the company by platoons or 'vintaines' and threw into disarray the ideal disposition of arms in any formation: short-arms (halberds and bills) protecting the ensign in the middle, pikes next, front and rear, and at head and tail, hackbuts and bows which could split off into advance and rearguards or fan out as skirmishers. Nor had the concept 'half-left' 'half-right' been born, so oblique movements must have involved further gesticulation or have been left to common-sense when the transition was made from parade ground to battlefield.

Of all arms, Barrett devotes most space to the training of the shot; not so much to archers, whose role is restricted to harrassing the enemy in small mobile groups or to covering hackbutters while they reload, but to the users of the hackbut or arquebus, the rough, sturdy matchlock gun that was the age's chief hand firearm. Whatever the formation in which they found themselves, hackbutters were conceived as either working in pairs, the 'loadsman' firing first, then falling back to recharge while his 'follower' fired, or in small groups, one firing, the other 'reskewing' or relieving it with their newly charged weapons. Hackbutters were also drilled in the process Barrett called 'wading', that is, passing quickly through the ranks and files of other weapons in order to bring their fire to bear wherever the attack was pressing home. Finally, when forced back by cavalry, hackbutters were to be trained to pass within a formation of pikemen who crouched with their weapons crossed to form a continuous hedge of steel, and to fire over their heads. As he reassuringly says, 'the shott, which some call the forlorne hope, needeth not that name amongest Englishmen, thear ys so many wayes provided for their savegarde'.

Typical diagrams show a column of two hundred men, five in a rank, being split into three groups, each taking up a position on the other's flank while the shot separates out into detatched wings to protect the formation as a whole [Plate 4]. There are a few others showing formations on the move: in open order while under canon fire from the flank, in closed order on a wider front when escorting 'poulder, treasure or suche lyke', a time when, Barrett warns, the enemy may well feign small infantry attacks in order to tempt part of the escort to pursue them, thus leaving gaps into which the cavalry, hiding in ambush, can charge. To keep formation at night or in wooded country, each pikeman is to hold the butt of the weapon of the man in front of him. But there is no hint, in text or diagrams, of what might happen if defence were tested more deeply than by an initial cavalry charge. And there is no mention of formations actually attacking an enemy force. Indeed, as was perhaps inevitable at a time when open manoeuvres or campaign simulations were not envisaged, the emphasis, formation by formation, was on defence, on falling back either to rally against a natural obstacle or to present a symmmetrical body capable of resisting assaults on all its fronts.

Such an emphasis, then as later, was also one of the normal limitations of parade ground practice, but though Barrett refers to the 'beutie' of one formation and of another writes that 'sometymes soldiers must remove by ranckes or bandes to strengthen or beutiffie as neede shall requier', he does not yield to the temptation either to treat his recruits as a corps du ballet or to spend time on purely academic formations like the wedge, saw and shears. He recommends bending a column of pikes and bills into an 'ess' to provide inlets of shelter for hard-pressed hackbutters. He does portray triangular formations for wings of shot. But this is as esoteric as he gets. A curl-shaped formation is in fact his notation for a column of shot wheeling rank by rank after firing, in order to reload, a perfectly practical manoeuvre though one as he notes 'not a common practise amongest Englishmen'. And though he describes field formations of up to 1500 men, his tone remains reassuringly local. Such formations would be arranged by 'the chieftaynes or sargent major', but within them 'captaynes accompany their owne men' so that — as he puts it on another occasion — 'captaynes maye see the service of their whole members, accordinge to the desire of Englishmen.'

To sum up: with due allowance for some turgidity of language, *A breife booke* would have enabled an English country gentleman to organize a couple of hundred farm labourers and tradesmen into an infantry company, give them a notion of a soldier's duties, and encourage them to fit with some degree of preparedness into an army should the occasion come for actual combat. And all this in the congenial tones of a modest professional, an ardent patriot who feared God and honoured the queen, a man who, aware that there were lessons to be learned from abroad did not put foreigners on a pedestal and who, though alive to the advantages of firearms, did not scorn the longbow, 'that arte which ys onely by God his provydence given to Englishemen.'

Given the timeliness of the book, the appropriateness of Barrett's profession and the work's potential practical value, what were its precedents and sources? Compared with the continent, the production of books on warfare in England was meagre. Certainly there was nothing approaching a practical manual in print. Vegetius had been translated and published by Caxton in 1489.[31] It is true that Vegetius had advised that a commander should know the proportion of ground required for armies of different sizes and had stressed that a captain should make sure that the sun was behind him and the wind at his back and that he should be on higher ground than the enemy; so had Frontinus, who was published in English in 1539. But these authors had been so widely read and points like this one had become so commonplace that there is no need to assume a knowledge of the sources themselves. Nor is there any indication that Barrett had read the work published in about 1550 as *An order whych a prince in battaylle muste observe* ... or *The preceptes of warre* by Jacopo di Porcia, translated in 1544[32], both of which drew heavily on Vegetius and Frontinus. There is, indeed, no trace in Barrett of the classical fad from which no printed book on warfare was immune. Even the first substantial book on a military theme by an Englishman, William Patten's 1548 account of the battle of Pinkie, had a long preface stuffed with classical allusions.[33]

Only two other works of a military nature were published before 1562. The first printed English military code was issued in 1544, as *Statutes and ordynances for the warre*, in connection with Henry VIII's projected invasion of France. In five instances Barrett's 'paynall ordenances' deal with similar points of discipline, order and hygiene, but even in these cases the correspondence is not close enough to suggest that he had a copy under his eye. Nor are there any parallels between his book and the completest foreign treatment of warfare that had yet appeared in English, Whithorne's translation (1560) of Machiavelli's *The arte of warre*. Finally, he shows no sign of having seen the four works published on the continent which were nearest to his own in tone and subject matter: Battista della Valle's *Vallo: libro contenente appertenentie ad capitanii* ... (Naples, 1521; French translation, 1529), the anonymous *Familiere institution pour les*

31 *The boke of the fayt of armes and of chyvalrye*, tr. from the French of Christine de Pisan.

32 From *De re militari liber* (Venice, 1530).

33 *The expedicion into Scotlande*. There is no reflection of this book in Barrett's work, nor of the far slighter anonymous account of Somerset's Scottish campaign, *The late expedicion in Scotlande* (London, 1544). I have not been able to trace a copy of ...*the order or trayne of warre* ... (London, ?1525-30). See Maurice J. D. Cockle, *A bibliography of English military books up to 1642* (London, 1900), no. 2.

legionaires (Lyons, 1536); Raimond de Fourquevaux's *Instructions sur le faict de la guerre* (Paris, 1548); and the anonymous *Institution de la discipline militaire au royaume de France* (Lyons, 1559).

Either through ignorance or choice, then, Barrett appears to have avoided any borrowing from printed sources. This is in strong contrast with two military books that were published in the same year as *A breife booke*. John Shute, whose work we have already glanced at, listed among his sources Livy, Plutarch, Caesar and Valerius Maximus as well as the works of della Valle and Fourquevaux.[34] His book was of no practical utility whatever, though at one point he wrote what amounts to a synopsis of Barrett's book and implies the usefulness of such a work. Talking of military discipline — by which he meant efficiency — he said 'the roote therof is the perfecte judgement of the captaine. The branches are these: the good choise of the newe souldiours, obedience of the souldiour, the contynuall exercise of the souldiour, order wherin the souldiour must be instructed, furniture wherwith the souldiour must both defend and offend, and then the severitie of the captaine in seinge this discipline truely observed and kept.' At first sight, utility does appear to be the hallmark of the other work, Peter Whithorne's *Certain waies for the orderyng of souldiers in battleray and settyng of battailes after divers fashions, with their maner of marchyng . . .* [35] The author tells the reader that he has written in order to teach men how to become skillful in arms even if they have never had any military experience, there being ample evidence in the past to show 'how daungerous and pernitius it is for a prince and his realme to be driven to truste to the servis of straungers for lacke of sufficiente skilfull men of their owne for their defence.'

Whithorne has sections on fortification, the making of saltpeter and gunpowder, on aspects of gunnery and the making of fireworks, and on coding secret messages. Only the first, on troop formations, resembles any part of Barrett's book, a resemblance strengthened by the use of diagrams, the first to appear in England in print. But in contrast to *A breife booke* any attempt on the parade ground to follow

34 He has 'Monsieur de Langie', *i.e.* Guillaume du Bellay, to whom Fourquevaux's work was then attributed. In old age, Shute wrote *A faithful frende and remembrancer to a generall of an armie in divers respects* [1598]. This remained unpublished. It is a rambling and impractical work, full of references to the ancients. B. L. Royal Ms. 17. E. xxi.

35 Though dated April, 1562, no edition is recorded which is not bound with the author's translation of Machiavelli, *The arte of warre*, which is dated (by the same publisher, John Kingston) July 1560. It is perhaps more likely that the appearance of *The arte of warre* was delayed (pending approval of the dedication to the queen?) than that *Certain waies ...* was foredated. Errors of dating were less likely with the use of Roman numerals which were employed in both these cases.

Whithorne's directions would have led a normally non-numerate captain into confusion, a confusion derived from the closeness with which Whithorne followed his (unacknowledged) source, the fourth book of *Quesiti et inventioni diverse* (Venice, 1546) by Niccolo Tartaglia. Tartaglia was an author with a lively interest in war, but first and foremost he was a mathematician. He was also a student of the tactics of the ancients, so Whithorne describes and illustrates formations like the wedge, the shears and the saw which had featured in one of Tartaglia's own sources, the first century A.D. treatise by Aelianus Tacticus, but were never used in contemporary warfare. In only one respect does this dependence on a doctrinaire source give a note of realism that Barrett's diagrams lack: the recognition that a 'square' of men cannot occupy a 'square' of ground because more room is needed between ranks than between files. Both Shute and Whithorne, then, pillaged printed books and thus lost contact with reality.

Barrett did not. But no-one wrote without some precedent to draw on, so we must look elsewhere for what did influence him. It would have been difficult for a yeoman at court, member of a unit constantly refreshed by other men returning from service overseas at a time when the need for military reform was very much in the air, to remain isolated from the verbal discussions, circulated instructions and unpublished treatises passed from hand whence emerged the corpus of military lore that was to feed the increasingly lavish military literature of the later decades of the century.[36]

The discussions have evaporated in talk. I have not found instructions for this period, though later ones suggest that they were issued.[37] But manuscript treatises do exist which show what military topics were being aired before Barrett wrote, and one of them is very close indeed to certain sections of his work.

Toward the end of Henry VIII's reign, Thomas Audley dedicated *A booke of orders for the warre both by sea and land*[38] to the King. This

---

36 *Cf.*, G. G. Cruickshank, 'when they [Tudor military manuscripts] are taken as a whole it is not easy to sort out who wrote what; and it may be that a detailed study of the manuscript treatises of the earlier part of the century and the military books of Elizabeth I's reign would reveal that some of them have so much in common that they could readily be conflated into a single 'Great Tudor Military Book'.' *A Guide to the Sources of British Military History*, ed. Robin Higham, (London, 1972), pp. 74-5. I am grateful for the kindness Mr. Cruickshank has shown in reading the ms. of this lecture.

37 *E. g.* those sent to commissioners for musters or to armies collected for active service. B. L. King's Ms. 265.

38 B. L. Harleian Ms. 309, 5r-14r. The author's identity is unclear. He was not Sir Thomas Audley who was Lord Chancellor and died in 1544, and 'confusingly enough, Audley's own brother and two of his nephews were also named Thomas' (Arthur J. Slavin, *Tudor men and institutions ...*, Baton Rouge, 1972, 10). A Thomas Audley was, intriguingly, a 'gentleman usher of the chamber' in 1545 (*L. and P., Foreign and Domestic*, xx, pt. 1, no. 1325 item 54).

is primarily a work of opinion and exhortation which does not prefigure Barrett, but shows in which way the wind was blowing. Audley, too, is uninsular: he favours the 'broade square' rather than the 'iuste square' because it is favoured in France and Germany, and he emphasizes how much England has to learn from 'the almaynes, who be accepted among all nations the flower of the world for good orders of footemen.' He is anxious that the companies formed from the militia should be systematically armed, and uniform in their combination of arms. He was also concerned that the proportion of shot to *armes blanches* should be fixed at a third of a small, a quarter of a medium and a fifth of a large army — and that there should be either equal numbers of archers and hackbutters or a proportion of three to two, depending on the number of men in a rank. Another version of this work was copied for Edward VI and yet another in Mary's reign.[39]

A similar reforming zeal marks *A brief discourse for the mayintenaunce, exercise and trayning of a convenient nombre of Englishmen wherby they may be the soner made souldiours for the redier deffence of this realm of England*. Written very early in Elizabeth's reign, the author, Richard Barkhede, dedicated it to the Queen. We have seen his dismay at the unwarlike spirit of the English gentleman. He also points gloomily to the recent lack of success of English armies in France and Scotland. The country may be at peace, but, as the Romans knew, this is the very time to prepare for war — and so he proposes a reserve of 15,000 men organised in bands of 500 and trained at least twice a year. The Queen (as he rightly foresaw) might shrink from the expense, but he assured her that this would be small and would, in any case, be happily shouldered by 'your willing subjects'. The second part of his little work is, indeed, about how the cash could be raised, and in the third and last he lauds the strength and security, and the abolition of the vagrancy problem, that would follow from the adoption of his scheme. Again, there are no diagrams or details of 'exercise and trayning', and the strongly hortatory tone is that of a petition rather than of a handbook.

We are in a completely different atmosphere when we turn to a treatise written this time in the reign of Mary, in 1557, by Robert

---

39 The second has been printed as 'A treatise on the art of war' in *Journal of the Society for Army Historical Research* (1927), 65-78 and 129-133; it concludes: 'This booke was made by Mr. Thomas Audley and geven to King Edwarde the sixte, he being one of his graces gentleman ushers of his privey chamber'. The third (Bodleian Library, Tanner Ms. 103) is endorsed in a contemporary hand on a separate slip of paper as follows: 'An introduction or A. B. C. to the warre dedicated to Kinge Edward the VI the first yeare of his reyn by Thomas Audley, newelie corrected in the first yeare of Queene Marie by the sayde Thomas Audeley'.

Hare.[40] The manuscript appears to be prepared for the press. It has no title, dedication or preface but has an index with page references at the front and it is written in a steady hand throughout, without corrections. The book consists of short sections with headings, as does Barrett's, but Hare's work is much larger in scope, containing sections on – to give only the chief additional topics – prisoners, the provost marshal, encamping, scouts and watch parties, the ordnance, harangues to be made on the battlefield, conduct after a battle, the management of cavalry. He has three sections on the German 'Trosshe' [*Trossmeister*], an officer responsible for the non-combatants who follow an army. Though very sparing in classical reference, Hare does refer to 'Alexander Magnus' and cites Vegetius. But where he and Barrett cover the same topics the parallels are very close indeed. These topics comprise the duties of officers (though Hare omits the lieutenant and the priest and includes the muster master and officers of the higher command; nor does he have any discussion of the captain himself that resembles Barrett's long section on this officer); weapons and their use (Hare has sections on hackbutters, archers, 'morespikes', and on halberdiers or billmen, in the same order that Barrett employs); the qualities required in the good soldier (Hare has silence, obedience and truth but omits secrecy, sobriety and courage). And there are parallels between the two texts with respect to some of the penal ordinances and the treatment of pike tactics as well as to certain phrases in sections which do not overlap closely in subject matter.[41]

I said that this treatise was written by Robert Hare. Of this there is no doubt. It ends, firmly enough, with the assertion 'scriptus et finitus per me Robertu Hare ultimo die Junij 1557.'[42] But Hare's manuscript is, in fact, an excellent example of the hazards confronting the student of Tudor military literature. In spite of its self-sufficient air, apart from its spelling, some altered phraseology, the reordering of a few sections, and its index, everything in it is taken from an earlier manuscript in the Bodleian Library. This has no title, dedication or author's name, but is endorsed on the verso of the first page: 'This booke was composed by Sir Thomas Audley, who was so wise, so valiaunte, and so sufficient a man of warre as that in Kinge Edward the sixthes time Sir James Wilford, Sir James Crofts and Sir Thomas Wiatt, Coronell Randall, and

40 B. L. Cotton Ms., Julius F, v.

41 *Cf.* especially: on hackbutters, Hare 7r, Barrett 7r; on archers, Hare 7v, Barrett 7v; on the 'Ensygne bearers charge', Hare 8v, Barrett 4v; on surgeons, Hare 10r, Barrett 6r; on 'trewth', Hare 11r, Barrett 13r; on military law, Hare 14v, 15r-v, 19r and 20r, Barrett 14r-v and 13v; on pike tactics, Hare 32v, Barrett 10r.

42 On f. 1r, in a different hand, is 'Roberti Hare, 1556'.

all of the rest of our best soldiers of that time termed him their father, and father of the English soldiorie. And he died in Queene Maries tyme in Sowthwarke.' Even this endorsement, because it is in a somewhat later hand, cannot be said to clinch the matter of authorship beyond all shadow of doubt, let alone the date of the treatise's composition or the originality to Audley of all its material.[43] Clearly, however, we should now speak of a second Audley treatise (substantially independent of *A Booke of Orders* and of Hare's copy of it.

I have quoted from the work at such length in order to justify speaking of parallels rather than plagiarism. Barrett, it seems to me, is not copying Audley. Both men, rather, drew, at least to some extent, on a common source (or, again, cluster of sources). Sometimes they select from it (with reference to the surgeon, Barrett has more about his equipment, Audley more about his pay), sometimes they modify it.[44] The nature of the convergencies and divergencies between the passages quoted from Hare's copy of Audley and the equivalent passages in *A breife booke* coupled with phrases through which Barrett seems to dive back into much older texts ignored by Audley ('the captayne ys bothe loved and feared. Suche be to their prince a treasure', or 'when perill ys pondered') and Audley's use of texts which Barrett does not appear to have used,[45] suggest that Barrett may not have known of the earlier treatise and that both men were picking and choosing from and adding to a body of manuscript material about war that contained many chronological strata and included practical memoranda and instructions, humanistic strains and homespun moralising culled from

---

43 Bodleian, Rawlinson Ms. 363. The endorsement would appear to date from Elizabeth's reign. Wilford († 1550) was knighted for his services as provost marshal at Pinkie in 1547. Croft was knighted in the same year after service in France and Scotland; Lord Deputy of Ireland from 1551 he died in 1590. Wyatt (the Younger) served in France 1543-50 and was beheaded in 1554 for his rebellion against Mary. 'The noble Captaine Randall' is mentioned as serving in Scotland and Ireland by Thomas Churchyard: *A generall rehearsall of warres* ... (London, 1579), sigs. Hivr, Pir.

44 *Cf.* Audley's 'trompettes and drommes which serveth to caule as the mowths of men', with Barrett's 'drommes and fyffes which warneth as the mouthes of men'. Speaking of the halbardiers guarding the ensign in the centre of an infantry formation, Audley comments that they are 'usually cauled the slaughter or execusyon of the battell', while Barrett has 'suche be the garde to the ansaigne or execution to the battell'. The interest here is that in the diagram of 1550 he had the annotation 'there shalbe plased the ansaynyes, dromes and fyffes garded withe halberds usually called the execucyon of the battaile', so that if there is a debt to Audley, a version of his treatise must be pushed back to 1550 or earlier.

45 Audley's passage (9v; Hare 20r) about the disposal of excrement in camp, for instance, is nearer to the 1544 printed code (or *its* source) than is any of Barrett's 'paynell ordenances'. Another example is Audley's passage on having feigned 'casualties' as part of an exercise to teach men to pass forward to keep the ranks full (9v; Hare 14r). Barrett does not have this, but Whithorne does (11v), though not precisely in Audley's words.

homilectic literature. Essentially the works are different in spite of the parallels I have cited. Audley pays little attention to the role of the captain and has only some thirty lines about training inexperienced men; his treatise is a survey of military practice as a whole, apparently unique in its scope and practical value. It is a field manual, while Barrett's work is a manual for training.

So much for Barrett's text and its precedents. Now let us consider in turn two of its special features, first the mathematical tables with which it concludes, then its wealth of diagrams illustrating troop formations.

The Audley manuscript contains four mathematical tables designed to help an officer set out his men in various formations and combinations of arms and to judge the numbers of the enemy. Hare copied only one of them, and in an incomplete form. Of Barrett's five tables, one duplicates most of Audley's, a second bears a fairly close resemblance to another, a third conflates two into one; two have no precedent in Audley. The space allocated to such tables by Audley, and, still more, by Barrett, is surprising. The earliest continental printed books to include such tables are Girolamo Cataneo's *Tavole brevissime per sapere con prestezza quante file vanno a formare una giustissima battaglia*, printed in Brescia in 1563 and Giovan Mattheo Cicogna's *Il primo libro del trattato militare, nel quale si contengono varie regole & diversi modi per fare con l'ordinanza battaglie nuove di fanteria ...*, printed in Venice, in 1567[46]. The earliest English works are a translation of Cataneo in 1574 and, four years later, William Bourne's *Inventions or devises* ... So again we are sent to an uncharted manuscript tradition, this time one whose implication that battle was a matter for precise calculation[47] was becoming almost as pervasive as the suggestion that it could not be waged successfully without a knowledge of antiquity.[48] The sort of manuscript that lies behind Audley and Barrett was described by John Dee, the mathematician and astrologer, in his account of John Dudley, Earl of Warwick, who had served in France in 1523 and 1544—46, from 1545 as Lord Admiral,

---

46 Not seen by Cockle, *op. cit.* I amend his citation from a copy in the Newberry Library.

47 Alexandre Van den Byssche's *L'arithmetique militaire* (Paris, 1571) and Thomas and Leonard Digges's *An arithmeticall militare treatise, named stratioticos ...* (London, 1579).

48 A pleasant example is Tristram Tirwhyt's *Rules apperteyning to a generall or lieutenant*, written 1577. B. L., Harleian Ms. 2326. This was written as a new year's gift to Leicester in the hope that he would achieve his desire to be put at the head of an army for the Low Countries. In this case, the author hoped 'that by thexample of Alexander the renowned and victorious prince, you would carie the same in your hands by the daie, and laie it under your pillowe in the night'. It is entirely devoted to the moral qualities required in a military leader, with many examples drawn from antiquity, and ends with 'general rules of warre, taken out of Vegetius'.

and in Scotland in 1547 and 1549. In 1551 he had become Earl Marshal. 'This John by one of his actes ... did disclose his harty love to vertuous sciences and his noble intent to exell in martiall prowesse, when he with humble request and instant solliciting got the best rules (either in time past by Greke or Romaine or in our time used, and new stratagemes therin devised) for ordring of all companies, summes and numbers of men (many or few) with one kinde of weapon or mo appointed; with artillery or without; on horsebacke or on fote; to give or take onset; to seem many, being few, to seem few, being many; to marche in battaile or jornay — with many such feates to foughten field, skarmoush or ambushe appartaining; and of all these, lively designementes most curiously to be in velame parchement described, with notes and peculier markes as the arte requireth. And all these rules and descriptions arithmeticall inclosed in a riche case of gold he used to weare about his necke, as his juell most precious and counssaylour most trusty. Thus arithmeticke of him was shrined in gold.'[49]

It is likely that some of these 'lively designements ... with notes and peculier markes' were diagrams. The Audley manuscript has six diagrams of troop formations,[50] occupying four pages. Together with Barrett's large diagram of 1550 they constitute (to my knowledge) the earliest English examples of the military diagram yet recorded. On the continent, from the mid-1450s manuscripts of Theodore of Gaza's Latin translation of Aelian had included the diagrams of troop formations found in the earlier Greek manuscripts,[51] and these were carried over to the printed editions of the end of the century. Della Valle's work of 1521 contained more complicated diagrams, as did Machiavelli's *Arte della Guerra*, printed in the same year. At least in Italy, then, the military diagram was well established before Warwick's participation in the Anglo-Imperial campaign around Boulogne in 1544—46. In charge of the battle formations of the Italian troops who fought on the English side was their sergeant major, Giovacchino da Coniano, some of whose manuscripts containing diagrams came after his death into the hands of the military theorist Girolamo Maggi, who printed them.[52] These are of considerable interest. They show not only the formations set by Giovacchino for his own troops but how the

---

49 The 'Mathematicall preface' to H. Billingsley's translation of Euclid, *The elements of geometrie* (London, 1570), sig. ai,r.

50 Ff. 64r, 66r, 66v and 67a,v.

51 *E. g.* (Latin) Bodleian Ms. lat. class. d. 38 and (Greek) Marciana Library, Venice, Ms. Venetus 904 of *c.* 1330.

52 *Della fortificatione delle citta ... Trattato dell' ordinanze, o vero battaglie del capitan Giovacchino da Coniano* (Venice, 1564), 118vseq.

English were formed up: archers and hackbutters combined in wings, a rectangle with pikes on the outside, halberds in the middle, and shot between — somewhat on the same principle as that shown in one of Barrett's diagrams.[53] Giovacchino says that he had asked his English opposite number why the shot were placed behind the pikes, and was given the explanation (given also by Barrett) that the pikemen stoop while the shot fired over their heads. Thsi is not the only example of how military ideas were exchanged. Giovacchino notes that one day he was told that 'l'amiraglio di sua maesta', that is the Earl of Warwick, was coming to inspect the troops and that he should set his own troops in battle array for review by the admiral, 'who was an experienced soldier'. This he did and 'it greatly pleased him ... and he saluted me on His Majesty's behalf and said that he would carry a favourable report back to the king.' And this gives added interest to the fact that William Patten, who was known to Warwick and was with him during the Pinkie campaign, included in his account the three crude woodcuts which are the first battle plans to be printed in England.[54] Somewhere behind Audley's and Barrett's diagrams, as behind their texts and mathematical tables, must lie the circles of experts known in England or encountered abroad, who were associated with men like Warwick, and the manuscripts that incorporated their ideas.

Barrett's diagrams are close in manner to Audley's. They use the same squared paper and the same symbols for the different arms; the use of captions is similar. There is an especially close resemblance between Barrett's diagram of 1550 and the double page in Audley reproduced here [Plate 5]. But in no case does Barrett portray any of the formations shown by Audley, and in contrast to Audley's six, Barrett illustrates no fewer than forty-four. His diagrams are not like Patten's, which deal with units scattered over a battlefield. They are not like Machiavelli's, known in England from the 1560 translation. Nor do they resemble those in Whithorne's *Certain waies* ... which are adapted and sometimes copied from Tartaglia's *Quesiti et inventioni diverse*. They are unlike those in other books published before 1562 on the continent, Fourquevaux, for instance, or the mid-century editions of Aelian, or the semi-official *Institution de la discipline militaire au royaume de France* of 1559. They are closely integrated with the text, each being explained either on the same or on an adjoining page, and

---

53 The graphic conventions used by the two men are too distinct for it to seem likely that Barrett had seen any of his diagrams.

54 Reproduced in Cockle, *op. cit.*, between pp. 8 and 9. Again they bear no resemblance to the conventions used by Barrett. The third is signed 'S. Cromes [or croomes] ins'.

there is a key to the symbols employed. Barrett explains that a man can be substituted for each letter, and while there are a few discrepancies, in the main this is true: the number of each type of soldier mentioned in the text fits the appropriate symbols. Uniquely, the diagrams are all in coloured inks. However, while colour is used sometimes to distinguish the different arms, in general it is employed as much for decorative effect as for helping the eye to see where the different weapons are placed.[55] Certainly Barrett intended the diagrams to have a thoroughly practical value, hence his use of 'voyde lynes', spaces inserted to show how a formation is created from different units marching into place and then joining up. The major drawbacks from a captain's point of view would have been the lack of consistent guidance as to which way a formation was meant to be facing, and, as we have seen, Barrett's failure to indicate that a 'square' of men could not function effectively within a 'square' of ground.

Apart from printed works already mentioned, the next that claims to deal in practical terms with the training of infantry and their employment on the battlefield[56] is Thomas Styward's *The pathwaie to martiall discipline* ... (London, 1581). The author says that he has been persuaded by friends to publish the work 'the which this three or four yeares I have kept in secret', and justifies publication by saying that the present peace cannot last; it is thus essential that the country prepare for war. The institutional framework of a militia is there, but at present it cannot produce good results. Captains are inexperienced, muster masters are appointed not from men who know drill and training but from those who have 'good skill in the lawe, the flieng of a hawke, or experience in choosing of a fat bullocke or sheepe.' So he has turned to what he revealingly calls 'these my collections, gathered from most excellent souldiers, as Italian, Germaine, Swizzers, French, and English ... the fruits fathered from most excellent souldiers, also from the best writers in Europe' and has produced a volume in two parts:

> 'Two bookes I have therefore set foorth,
>   to shew thee how to traine,
> To march, incampe, and battels make,
>   with tables verie plaine.'

---

55 Audley used only black ink save for the grids, which are in red.
56 The 1579 ed. of Digges's *Stratioticos* has a diagram, or 'battaile in portraiture', between pp. 184-85. It employs different conventions from those used by Barrett. T[homas] P[rocter], *Of the knowlege and conducte of warres* ... (London, 1578) sounds practical but is not.

At first sight it appears that Barrett's book has at last found its way into print, within a larger framework, and under another name. After a description of the higher command and the officials – provost marshal, purveyor of victuals and the like – we come to the infantry company, to 'The captaines charge', 'The lieutenants charge', 'The ensignebearers charge' – just as Barrett lists them save with the addition of a corporal and a clerk and the substitution of a 'disner' (in charge of 24 men) for a 'vintaine' in charge of 20. Styward next describes the four arms: calivers (an improvement on the hackbut), longbows, pikes and bills. He then has the men marched off 'to some ground necessarie to muster, march and traine.' The six military virtues are then expounded to them: silence, obedience, secrecy, sobriety, courage and truth, and certain 'lawes and constitutions of the field' are explained before they are set to their drill. The different formations they are taken through are illustrated by diagrams. Then come tables of mathematical calculations. This is all very close to Barrett, but it is Barrett with a difference.

Where Styward's sections correspond to Barrett's the subject matter is very close. So, sometimes, is the phraseology, though it is very seldom exactly the same; on occasion it echoes Audley rather that Barrett, as when Styward refers to the guard surrounding the ensign as 'usuallie called the slaughter of the field, or execution of the same'. But throughout one has the sensation that he is not directly copying either Barrett or Audley but turning to manuscripts in 'these my collections' that antedated both and were the common inheritance of all three of them. Similarly with the diagrams; some follow Barrett very closely in subject and convention [Plate 6], others do not. Similarly, lastly with the mathematical tables[57];; three resemble Barrett's, three do not. In addition Styward has a more complex version of Barrett's computation grid; he endorses it as useful 'also to tile and measure ground of like proportion'. Reflecting the 'by the same rewle you may tiell, pave or measure grounde of lyke proporcion' of Barrett's preface, which in turn echoes the 'allso to tyle, pave or measure ground of lyke proporcion' of one of Audley's tables, this surely sends us past all three men to one of those builders, architects and military maids-of-all-work employed by Henry VIII who worked now at a royal palace in England, now on a

---

57 Both begin with Ring, Snail, and Ess. Barrett then has units of shot only; Styward does not. Both then proceed from formations for 100 to others for 300, 400, 500, 900, 1,200 and 1,500. Here Barrett stops, but Styward continues, though using a different convention based not on letters but on numerals. Even when convention and subject are similar, however, there is no straightforward copying. One of Styward's diagrams is reproduced in my *The art of war and Renaissance England* (Folger booklets on Tudor and Stuart civilization, 1961), 49, which corresponds to Barrett's on 34v., shown in plate 6.

fortification in France and who mingled freely with native officers and their foreign allies. And the same sensation of dipping into an accreting body of 'fruits gathered from the most excellent soldiers, also from the best writers' occurs when reading — to mention only those works nearest to *A breife booke* in language and organisation — books like Sir George Carey's manuscript instructions for training in the Isle of Wight of 1585,[58] or two works printed in London in 1591, Gyles Clayton's *The approoved order of martiall discipline* . . . and William Garrard's *The arte of warre* . . .[59]

Because he deals with the largest single formations, Barrett does not deal with the vanguard, main body, rearguard formation into which English armies as a whole were then divided on the march or in combat. Nor does he deal with artillery or with cavalry save from the point of view of defending infantry against them. Within the limits of its subject matter, however, and despite its indebtedness to earlier sources, it gives a useful and reliable insight into contemporary English military practice.[60] I hope that by being released, at least in part, into print, it may help others bring to light more about its sources and the atmosphere in which they were gathered together and thus further illumine our understanding of military moods and methods near the mid-century. Certainly that understanding is helped by a professional soldier's idea of what should happen on the village greens and meadows that were the parade grounds of Tudor England.

[58] B. L., Lansdowne Ms. 40/48, ff. 13-22. *See* Boynton *op. cit.* 117-18. No tables, but five diagrams, four of which parallel diagrams in Barrett.. After those the text has 'Item. Sondrie other formes there be of reducing an hundred, ttwoe or three hundred men and upwardes into good strengthe, which I for brevities sake omytte, referringe you [but giving no references] to the workes of sondrie writers thereof'.

[59] With Garrard we at last have a specific acknowledgement: 'I have thought good to borrow out of Master Styward's booke of martial discipline his maner and forme of trayning'.

[60] His proportion of shot to pikes and halberds — 30 to 70 — is if anything rather advanced for the time (*cf.* Audley's 20 to 80).

APPENDIX

In this appendix, which contains all passages from Barrett's text which are not dependent on an accompanying diagram, the following conventions have been used in the transcription: contractions expanded except for '&c.'; 'ye' rendered as 'the', 'y^t' as 'that'; i/j, u/v and long 's' normalized: punctuation and capitalization modernised; spelling and word division as in the original; sub-titles in bold.

The Preface

Consideringe how throughe mutacion of tymes and invencions of menns wittes the practises of the warres dothe daylie alter and chaunge to the greate perill of the ignorante in suche behalfe, the zeale I beare unto my native contrie hathe moved me to write of suche experience or knowledge as I have by my few yeares travaile amongest dyvers nacions obteigned and gotten. And [I] have collected, gathered together and ruedly set fourthe a fewe shorte poyntes touchinge thoffices and dueties of private captaynes, their officers and soldiers, the furnitures of armures, weapons and municions and the usinge of the same to battell convenient. Ffirste instructinge archeres and hagbutters to the skirmishe, as to their place apperteyneth; the morrishe pikes and halbardes in whose force the battaile[a] consisteth, shewinge suche in broade[b] or square; with a kallender[c] discoveringe noumbers in suche arraye assembled from one hundred unto ten thowsand in one battail contayned. By which you may perceive every particuler weapon with their noumbers in their place. By the same rewle you may tiell[d], pave or measure grounde of like proporcion. And althoughe my laboure hearin be not of suche skyll ne perficte to service as others can set furthe yf it please them, yet I humbly requier all noble soldiers and readers hearof to beare with my ignorance, acceptinge my good will in this behalfe, who wissheth unto Englande and Englishmen honnor, victorye and noble successe. Amen.

a = Main combat formation.
b = Rectangular with long front. The formation then known as a 'herse' or 'hearse'.
c = Table.
d = Tile.

Captaines of bandes' charge[e] (2v–4r)

When captaynes of Englishemen receive that noble charge to leade souldiers in the fielde in their prince's affaires, they muste firste consider their owne deuties and experiences, ponderinge how many wayes they have to answer unto almightie God and their prince for the good goverment of the same, consideringe for the tyme of warres soldiers be committed unto them as their chiefe governours and teachers; whearfore they will not suffer any of their souldieres to lyve in idlenesse, untraynde and unexercised in suche good, stronge and warlyke poyntes as [to] their callinge appertaynethe, but will see the same often trayned, exercised and instructed by woordes and deedes tyll they be perfecte: chusinge and advaunsinge the experte and willinge accordinge to their demerittes[f] into the offices of leutennantes, ansiaigne berer and sergeantes of bandes, &c. Of whose dueties hearafter followeth some mencion, with certayne practices to trayne and instructe all soldiers to their leadinge committed, so that none be ignorant in tyme of service.

Also, good captaynes be ever myndfull to sarve their prince with honnor, not regardinge proffict or paynes in comparison of service. The good soldier he gratifieth courteouslye and rewardeth lardgely accordinge to his power. The evill man, slouthefull and unjuste, he punisheth extremely accordinge to his aucthoritie; by which meanes the captayne ys bothe loved and feared. Suche be to their prince a treasure. Yf soldiers throughe their good desertes merite prayes or rewarde, he dothe ever to the higher powers make relacion[g] of the same, so that they may be preferred. Any merritinge preferment of office within his bande, he distributeth the same, not after affection, but demerittes. Many poyntes of service unto captaines are committed, secret and chargeable,[h] which sometymes requireth counsaile of the experte soldiers, and the better to know suche, they will frequente and talk familierly with them, fayninge causes or matters of exploytes which they pretende not willinge[i] the same to be kepte close, which beinge reveled will trie the trueth and punishe the disclosers accordinge to suche greate offences as they shall thinke meete; and they fyndinge soldiers secrett, experte and ingenious will gratifie and advaunce them to the vallue of their counsaile.

e = Duty, responsibility.
f = Merits.
g = Relation, report.
h = Weighty.
i = Give the impression of not wanting (?).

Theye be myndefull to se provision made for victualles and victulers, and the order of the same. Also the furnitures of armure, weapons and municions to the bandes belonginge. And to procuer wages for soldiers when the same ys dewe and to see the same payde and distributed unto victulers and others trustinge[j] armure, weapons, apparrell or suche lyke, that soldiers may have creditt for the same at reasonable prises at their neede.

Thear be often times committed unto captaynes' charge and leadinge, soldiers of great honnestie, substance and creditt. So be thear others of small regarde, wilfull and ignorante, rather adictid to evill then good, whome by the sapiente goverment, diligent trayninge and instructinge of captaines be converted and broughte to the order and worthie name of soldiers. And douptinge[k] that some woulde geve them selves by liberties of the warres from the office of soldiers, hearafter[1] dothe follow a fewe preceptes or ordinances to be observed uppon payne. Considering the noumbers experte within this realme, heare needeth none other resitall of captaynes' charge, althoughe unto suche apperteynith more than can in this small volume be expressid, seinge how the practises of the warres doo daylie alter and chaunge accordinge to the devises of the practisers of the same; althoughe to the ignorante, thease aforesaid maye seeme convenient for remembraunce of officers and soldiers.

Leutenants of bandes' charge (4r)

Suche be chosen men of greate experience and knowledge of service in the fielde, able to trayne and instructe soldiers in poyntes to them belonginge, whose aucthoritie extendith in the abcence of their captayne to examyn, trie and reforme any falte within the bande committed, ofte call fourth their companyes, muster, marshe and trayne them till they be perfect; any resistinge hym in suche behalfe shall receave suche punishment as agaynste his chiefe captayne.

Thansaigne berer's charge (4v)

Hee ys chosen a man of greate experience and of able personaige, hardie of couraige tadvaunce and spleye[l] the same, which at the receivinge

j = Extending credit.
k = Anticipating.
l = Display.

1   See below, 'Paynalles'.

therof professeth rather to loase his lyfe thear in then to neclecte his duetie in service of the same. He must be secrett, scilent and zealous, ofte mayntayninge, anymatinge and comfortinge the company with his discreete woordes never to retier but when of noble pollacie the higher officers commaundeth the same.

Drommes and fyffes (4v–5r)

Suche be chosen men of able personaige, hardy of couraige, secrett, and ingenious of sondery languages, able to use and instructe the soundes of their instruments [that] the company dothe diligiently learne, know and observe the same. Suche be often tymes sent on messaiges, to sommon fortes and holdes,[m] to carry ransomes and redeeme prisoners, which of necessitie requireth languages. Many soundes and callinges[n] of their instrumentes ys needefull of knowledge: aswell to marshe, aproche, assaulte, allaro[m], a retreate and many otheres which for tediousness in this place I doo omitt. Yf they shoulde fall into thandes of enimies they may not for any cause discover secrettes to them known. Suche be prooved by enemies; as by promises, gyftes and greate rewardes, allso by bankettes[o] and plentie of wyne. Sometymes by paynes and cruell tormentes, to make them disclose as aforesaid, which in any wise they may not doo the same.

Sargant of bandes' charge in tyme of trayninge (5r)

Suche muste instructe soldiers aswell by signes[p] from them framed, as by woordes and deedes how to trayne, marshe and use them selves in all poyntes accordinge to the signes aforesaid; that ys, layenge the staffe on his shoulder marshinge forthe, the company doinge the lyke, sometymes he traileth the same on the grounde, sometymes coucheth[q] the same as it wear to incounter enimies, some tymes retireth so couched, still his face towardes the enimies, some tymes standeth still advancith his staffe on highe, the company standinge still geveth silence, and accordinge to every signe by hym framed they doo the lyke. Any soldier usinge hym selfe to the contrary, or not kepinge his arraye, he reproveth, accordinge to his aucthoritie. Many woordes by his mouthe unto soldiers be resited, to longe in this place to expresse[2], which soldiers muste dilligiently observe.

m = To summon forts and strongholds to parley.
n = Notes and phrases.
o = Banquets.
p = Signals conveyed by raising or pointing a weapon, etc.
q = Lower and prepare for assault.

2   For a list of spoken field orders *see* Clement Edmonds, *op. cit.* above, note 28.

Vintaines (5v)

It may seme good the captayne chewse of his owne company, unto every hundreth, fyve honest and circumspect soldiers, placinge them in the office of vintaynes, that every of them have the leadinge of xx men[3], of whose weaponns they have beste skill. They shall ofte assemble their noumbers to see their furniture of armure and weaponns or any other thinges to them necessarie, practisinge them in the necessitie of the same. And fyndinge any fallte needefull of reformacion they shall amende the same or else shewe it furthe to the sargent, so to the leutennante, and so to the higher power, that justice and dignitie of office may be mayntayned and faltes amended.

Surgions (6r)

Niedfull yt ys that every company have a surgion skilfull in that science, able to cuer and heale all kinde of sores, greifes and woundes, specially to take a pellet oute of the ffleshe and boane and to slaike the fyer of the same.[r] See them furnished furnished [sic] with all their tooelles[s], instrumentes and necessary stuffe to them belonginge, as salves, balmes, oyells, rowlers, stoppers[t] and all other thinges to them convenient. Spare them carriages aswell for their pacientes as for the stuffe aforesaid. Regarde suche surgions be payde truely for their cuers and of their wages to them dew. So muste they imploye their industrie uppon the sore and wounded, not intermellinge with others to their charge noysome.[u] Necessary it ys that they weare their baldrykes, which by the lawe of the fielde ys their charter in the daye of fighte.[4]

Preiste or minister (6v)

Necessarie yt is that every company have one honest and christen minister to communicate in times convenient, also to use daylie prayer with the same, ofte prechinge, teachinge and instructinge them the lawe and feare of God, with which soldiers, as holy scripture mencioneth in many places, God ys pleased. Yf soldiers be sicke or hurte, or otherwise in extremitie, they will them to fighte agaynste the fleshe, the worlde

r = Reduce the pain and/or inflammation.
s = Tools.
t = Bandages and (uncertain) stoppers for jars and vials.
u = 'not meddling with other cases outside the scope of their employment'.

3 Presumably including the 'vintaine', otherwise the company would number 105.
4 *I.e.* the baldrick, or distinctive belt (worn over one shoulder and across the chest) identifies them as noncombatants and they are thus protected by convention from attack or imprisonment.

and the devill. Sufferinge none to their knowledge to lyve contrary to the lawe but will reforme them accordinge to their knowledge and callinge. Thus I presume not to teache them their office, but praye God to sende good ministers to instructe and teache captaynes, officers and soldiers, that the more boldely in this worlde they may doo their dueties, and the lesse to feare to departe from the fleshe, hopinge to receive everlastinge lyfe, which God sende to all soldiers.

The furniture of the iv weapons, and usinge of the same to battaile convenient (7r)

Those leadinge hagbutters muste have regard that every of them have a good currier or hagbuse, flaske and poulder in the same, pellottes, moulde and rammer, prymynge iron, fyer iron;[v] teache them to charge and discharge, marshe and retyre in good distance asonder, their faces towardes the enimies. In rayne, mist or wynde, their peces charged and prymed, cary their toucholles under their harmholes, their mache lighte under or within the palme of their handes.[5] Regarde they keepe matche and poulder drye, so be they furnished at every suddayne, and alowable[w] at the musters. Suche muste know they be the firste that begynneth the skirmishe and the laste in campe or harbor.[6]

Suche muste not use to spoyell or ryffell, neither carrie anythinge to them noysome, nor yeat in place of service be uncharged nighte or daye. Regarde that every follower be reskewinge his loadesman[x] and charge when the sounde ys discharged[y] as appertayneth and ys hearafter more playnely shewed.

Archers (7v)

Those leadinge longbowes muste regarde that every man have a good and mete bowe accordinge to the drawghte[z] and strengthe of the man,

v = 'pellottes ... fyer iron'; pieces of lead to be shaped in the mould, bullet mould, rod for pushing bullet and sealing plug down the barrel, wire to keep touchhole free, iron for striking sparks from flint to light the match.
w = Recognized as adequately equipped.
x = Backing up ready to relieve (take place of) the man in front.
y = Load when the order is given (by fife or drum).
z = Drawing power.

5 When expecting action the match (a length of material impregnated with saltpetre and twisted into a thick cord) was kept glowing. In rainy weather Barrett recommends that it should be cupped in the hand, and the touchhole (the hole between the pan containing the priming charge which is ignited by the match, and the interior of the barrel where the main charge lies) kept dry underneath the armpit.

6 *I.e.* they open an attack and cover a retreat.

their stringes whipped or trenched in the nock and myddes, waxed on the glew,[a,] a braser[b] and shooting glove, a sheafe of arrowes in noumber xxiv whearof I wishe viii of them more flighter[c] then the reste to gall and annoy the enimyes farder of then the usuall custom of the sheafe arrowes, whose sharpe hallshot[d] may not be indured, neither may thenimyes putt up hande or face to incounter the same — so that the archers draw their arrowes to the hedd and delyver the same accordinge to that arte which ys onely by God his provydence geven to Englishe men, who geve us grace to mayntayne the same as our elders have donn before us. Such weareth lighte armures or else none, a burganet or huslyn,[e] a maule [f] of leade with a pyke of five inches longe, well stieled, sett in a staffe of fyve foote of lengthe with a hooke at his gyrdell to take of and mayntayne the fighte as oure elders have donn, by handye stroaks.

Morrispykes (8r)

Those leadinge morrispikes muste instructe the soldiers that every man keepe his pike faire and straighte, of usuall lengthe, for the strengthe consisteth in the lengthe of the same, with brighte headdes and well nayled. Traile, beare, pushe, warde, couche, crosse and defende[g] in skirmishe or battell agaynste horsemen and footemen. Such must be fayer armed with corselettes,[h] longe tasses,[i] vaumbrases,[j] burganettes, sworde and dagger. Theyr orders in arraye and goverment in the same ys hearafter more playnely set furthe by proporcions of battailes and other strengthes in the fielde. The strengthe of the battailes chiefeley consisteth in the lengthe of the pykes,[7] and the good goverment of the same. Suche be often tymes appoynted to the skirmishe wheare they meete with the lyke, hand to hande. At suche tymes they pushe and

a = I. e. the strings were to be soaked in glue and subsequently waxed. The loops at each end and the place where the arrow was fitted were then strengthened by being whipped with thread.
b = Bracer, guard (commonly of leather) for forearm and the wrist of the hand holding the bow.
c = With thinner feathers, to achieve longer range at some expense of accuracy.
d = Hail-shot: descending in steep trajectory, the flight of arrows resembles a squall of hail.
e = Synonyms for a helmet which protected the neck.
f = Combat hammer.
g = Lower from the shoulder and carry horizontally in one hand, arm extended downward; grasp firmly in both hands; thrust; knock aside; for 'couche, crosse and defende' see f. 10r.
h = Generic term for an armour protecting body and arms.
i = Defence for upper part of thigh.
j = Armour for forearm.

    7   Barrett has in mind the 'couche, cross and defende' defensive posture, in which the pike had to be long enough for the pikes of the men in the third rank to project beyond the men in the first two ranks. This meant a pike 18-22 feet long. Hence the emphasis on making sure the shafts were 'straighte'.

warde, with the one hand bearinge their pike, with thother hand travisinge of grounde.^{k} Quicknes of foote and hand ys muche adveilable.^{l} Sometymes, by ranckes, greater noumbers dothe meete, unto which the practise of the pyke is very helpfull. Whearfore pykemen muste use the practise of the same in tymes convenient.

Halbarders (8v)

Suche be the garde to the ansaigne or execusion to the battell,^{m} who be armed with corselettes as aforesaide or suche lyke, of which noumber the captayne chueseth a certayne to accompany hym selfe whose experience and counsaile he will sircumspectly examyne and trie, and sometymes use accordinge to their devises. Suche be oftentymes for their experience appoynted to assiste and geve orders in arraye with the sergentes. Many poyntes of service are to them committed which in this place I doo omitt. Suche, accompanynge thansaigne in tyme of extremitie, as to their place apperteigneth, will advertise thansaigne berer, drommes and ffyfes to use as ys ment,^{n} be it to advaunce and mayntayne the exploites or, perceavinge the company to travaile to their discomoditie, as followinge the enimyes oute of course, loosinge the wynde and hill, &c., they will cause to stopp and sounde the retret whearby the company kepeth together in order as ys moste convenient.

Musters and trayninge of bandes (9r)

Thus furnished with men, armure and weapons, resorte to some convenient grownede,^{o} thear muster, marshe, trayne and instructe them by woordes and deedes as followith. Firste the byll shalbe called; every man muste answer to his name, none absente excepte lycence by pasporte,^{8} which byll ys framed as thus: hagbutters be firste called, seconde archers, thyrde pyke men, then byll men, laste halbarders accompanynge the ansaigne and officers of the bandes. The sargent passeth furthe the company in order as they be called. Be yt in iii, v, vii &c., bringe them into a rounde rynge, then place thansaigne and garde

k = One hand supporting the weight of the pike, the other determining the direction in which it is to point.
l = Is of great advantage.
m = The sense is that of a corps d'élite within the formation.
n = To act as is resolved upon.
o = Ground.

8 A written exemption had to be obtained if a man were unable to present himself at the muster on account of illness, etc. Otherwise he was liable to a fine of twenty shillings or ten days' imprisonment.

to the same in the myddest of the pykes, then deviude the shott halfe in the vowarde halfe in the rerewarde. Beinge thus in rynge or lymason,^{p} meete it ys some tymes to resite suche charges, preceptes, paynall ordinances and poyntes of dissipline as hearafter ys sett furthe for their instruction.

Recoveringe^q wynde and hyll (9v)

At all tymes of assembly agaynste enimyes, in what sorte you marshe or imbattell, the officers and leaders muste have alwaies speciall regarde above other thinges that you may have the wynde and hill yf it be possible to recover bothe. In wynninge of the wynde, a small noumber may so annoye their incountre^r by smoke, douste and other thinges that they shall loase bothe sighte and breath. Other difficulties by such meanes may be wroughte, which nedeth not hear to be expressed. Yf officers shoulde approche loosinge the same, the experte soldiers leadinge in ffrountes will staye tyll all the officers hath consulted to travail till they may recover a syde wynde, but as neare as they may they will marshe full upon the wynde. The enemise practisinge the lyke, the[y] will skirmishe with shott whiles longe weapons recovereth as aforesayde aswell in Ess^s, lymason or any other strengthe hearafter followinge, which sheweth dyversly in order as to sondrie intentes ys necessarye.

[No heading in ms.] (10r-v)

In exercisinge or imbattelinge noumbres in order followinge, the sergent major^9 chuseth oute of the beste armed and moste skilful soldiers, placinge the same on the uttermoste partes of the battelles on all sydes, which perceavinge enemise approche, will sarr^t close close [sic] to gether agaynste horsemen. Fyve ranckes will couche, crosse and defende as followith. Two ranckes crosseth by the mydd pike, the thirde rancke coucheth fourth righte betwixte the two aforesaid, holdinge their pykes faste with bothe handes, stay the same agaynste their lyfte knee, kneele on the same with righte knee firmely. The other two ranckes beareth their pykes above hande, reddie to pushe with the

p = A formation resembling the whorls of a snail's shell; Fr. *limaçon*.
q = Gaining (the advantage of).
r = The enemy force they encounter.
s = An S-shaped formation.
t = Audley/Hare *(op. cit.* 32v) has 'farre' = fare or move in a similar passage, as does Styward *(op. cit.,* 83). Barrett has possibly misread his source.
9 The officer responsible for arranging the formation of several companies.

righte hande at the whole lengthe of the pyke. In this sorte defende on all sydes. Beinge incountered with ffootemen they sarr very close, ioyne shoulder to shoulder, the follower so close to the loadsman that the same cannot retyre or fall backwarde. Suche havinge thadvantaige of the hyll beareth their pikes towardes the enimyse, pusshinge with their mighte, weyinge forwardes with their weighte so that the [soldiers] approchinge towards the hyll hath greate disadvantaige. At suche tyme those armed with faier corslettes, bases and longe tases be agaynste other not so armed muche available, for that they be as profitable to footemen as barbde[u] horses in the frountes of horsmen. At suche tymes of imbattailinge drawinge towardes the incounter the politike and wise perswasions of auncient[v] soldiers be unto the ignorante much advailable, incoraginge the same to fighte which else mighte wishe to flee; which wordes in another place in this booke ys more playnely declared.[10] Thus soldiers be kepte in order reddie to advaunce or retier, still chasinge with their faces towardes thennymyes. Sometymes instructe them by marshinge to augmente their ranckes from three to fyve, seven, nyne, etc. to hersse or quadrantes convenient. Sometymes in order usually accustomed bringe them in proporcion of Ess and the shott within the same, for doupte of[w] horsemen, which, so placed, fyndeth place convenient to shoote to the enymies, not molestinge their owne company, &c.

Sometymes in lymason or snailes, usually called ringes, necessary to the intentes aforesayde. In travalinge to make this same and others the leaders muste travaile towardes the wynde and hill to obteyne the same, in which consisteth great advauntaige aswell in makinge quadrantes, herses and many other thinges to battell appertayninge.

Six principall poyntes to soldiers belonginge.[11] Any offendinge to the contrary ys not worthie that noble name. (12v-13r)

Silence.

In all places of sarvice suche silence muste be used that soldiers may observe any charge geven to their dueties appertayninge, in watche, ambushe or elsewheare. They muste heare enymyes but not be hearde. Ofte tymes the assuraunce or perdiscion of the whole campe and

u = Barded, armoured. A barded horse had mail or armour plate on chest and flanks.
v = I.e., experienced.
w = When anticipating attack by.
    10   Barrett probably had in mind model harangues of the sort included by Audley/Hare and frequently given in different versions in later military books. He does not go on to give such 'wordes' himself.

company consisteth in thobservac[i]on of silence.

Obedience.

Souldiers of all estates muste be obedient and observe any poynte of sarvice by the officers commaunded nighte and daye. Who resisteth to the contrary ronneth in daunger of the lawe. Lenger then obedience ys used thear ys no hope of good successe.

Secrett.

Souldiers muste be secrett and have greate regarde that they disclose not suche thinges as some tyme to them shalbe reveiled, for longer then secrettes be kepte thear ys no assuraunce from perdicion.

Sober.

Sobrietie in a soldier ys suche a vertue that those which use the same be ever in state of preferment, but the rashe and unadvised, busibodies, hunters of harlottes and dronkerdes be ever in reproofe and punishment. The sober soldier ys ever myndfull of his owne charge, reprovinge others to the contrary offendinge.

Hardie.

The hardie and valiant couraige of captaynes and soldiers ys unto their prince a greate treasure, specially suche as dothe sircumspectly ponder and waye what effect may growe of onhardie, as some in tymes paste have hardely geven thonsett and for lack of circumspection hath repented the same. But when perill ys po[n]dered, then the hardy onsett and pollitike mayntenance of the same ys to sarvice muche advailable and bringeth honnor to those usinge the same.

Trueth.

The verteous that consisteth in trueth cannot be expressed in a whole vollume. Soldieres using the same shall have their rewarde in everlasting lyfe, and the fallse shall loose the fruission of the same in continuall darknes. From the which God save all true Christian soldiers.

11   This extends to the ranks the much older recital of the virtues required of the knight. Thus, after the colophon in the Paris, 1488 edition of Christine de Pisan's *L'art de chevalerie* there is 'Icy sont declairees les douze vertus que ung noble homme et de noble couraige doibt avoir en son coeur et en sa memoire et en user.' There follow verses headed 'Foy', 'Leaulte', 'Prouesse', 'Soubresse', etc.

Hear folloeth certeine preceptes or paynall ordenances necessarie to be observed by soldieres of every estate, or else to suffer suche payn as by the hygher officers shalbe devised.

Paynalles (13v–15v)

Souldiers muste be faithefull and obedient unto their owne captaynes, ever supportinge, mayntayninge and defendinge their owne ansaignes nighte and daye, and at the firste warninge resorte unto the same, and not to departe till yt be broughte in savetie, uppon payne.

Souldiers muste be instructed and diligently learne the soundes of drommes and fyffes which warneth as the mouthes of men to dyvers and sondery intentes, be yt to venders of bootties, to watche, warde, or reliefe of the same,^{x} to marshe, musters, convey, or other exploytes, to assaulte, skirmishe, alarom, battaile, or retreate, with dyvers others whearof they may not be ignorante, uppon payne.

Privat captaynes, their officers and soldiers muste resorte to their watche or warde in order of arraye, ansaigne, drommes and ffyfes, none abcent withoute licence, uppon payne.

Beinge in watche they muste silently herken for treadinge of horses, looke oute for matche light &c. Regarde none make alarom upon their owne scowtes or sarchers of the same but espyenge enymies shall brute^y oute the usuall woorde of 'bowes, bowes' or 'arme, arme' to soldiers beste known, which may not be neclectid nor necligently bruted, uppon payne.

Souldiers muste keepe their armure and weapons fayer and cleane, placinge the same in suche a redines to service at every soddeyne that none be to seeke, or intermell but with his own^z, uppon payne.

None may make bruite or noyes uppon the sighte of hare, foxe or deare, or breake their arraye for sleyinge of the same, uppon payne.

Beinge in camp or garrisson none may fyell^a or annoye the same with garbaidge or filthe other^b washe, trouble, or file the waters thearto

x = To proceed to their place of guard duty or relieve others there.
y = Call.
z = or meddle with anyone else's.
a = Defile.
b = Or.

adjoyninge, but in the lowest partes appoynted for the same, uppon payne.

Soldiers travailinge within the queenes maiesties realme or dominions of the same may not slaye any cattell or pullen,[c] take any thinge to another appperteyninge to use the same as his owne, starte oute of the waye to fyghte, quarrell or defraude, uppon payne.

None may carry any mannes wyffe travailinge within the bande or armye excepte suche as be well known and allowed by the provoste marshall or others in aucthoritie to be victulers or launders, uppon payne.

Soldiers muste honestly intreate victulers and truely payenge the same for their victuales, thoughe they be enymyes beinge so appoynted by the provoste, &c. Lykwise they must receave and salfely [sic] conduct such as desire to speeke with those in chiefe aucthoritie. Regarde they bringe not them whear they may see any secrettes leaste they be dubble espies,[d] uppon payne.

Soldiers muste content them selves with their places to them appoynted by the harbyngers[e] without resistance or dispute to the contrary, uppon payne.

The officers of bandes muste ofte resorte unto the cabbaynes and lodginges of soldiers, regarde they place their armure and weapons in a redynes to sarve at every soddeyne, spendinge their tyme in preparinge all their necessaries as to the necessitie of the same belongeth, as hagbutters skouringe their peces cleane within and withoute, castinge their shott,[f] &c.; archers whippinge and trenchinge their stringes, tryminge their fethers, ofte rubbying their arrowes, &c.; halberders and byll men kepinge their weapons brighte and sharpe, their armoure in warlyke manner; the pykemen kepinge their pykes fayer and straighte with brighte headdes and wel nailde, their armures well buckled, lethered and nailed, uppon payne.

Thofficers muste ofte call furthe the company aswell to vew their

c = Fowl.
d = Deceitful spies.
e = The officers responsible for arranging lodgings for the troops.
f = Making lead bullets in their moulds.

aredines^g and helthefull estate, furnitures of necessaries to them needfull, as also to muster, marshe and trayne the same. Fyndinge any sycke, hurte or not servizable, advertice the higher powers which muste see reformacion in that behalfe that the prince be not deceived nor company lost throughe suche defalte, uppon payne.

Soldiers muste not goo a forraginge or for booties withoute lycence or garde of ordenance, horsemen or bandes of footemen attendinge in order whiles other be occupied aboute the same, uppon payne.

Mayny poyntes to service needfull mighte hear be resited exceeding the paynall preceptes aforesaid, but for that suche apperteyneth not to the knowledge of every private soldier the writer hearof spareth to set furthe the same, wisshinge and prayenge all soldiers circumspectly to regarde those aforesaid and diligently to observe the same, to the increase of good and honnorable service to our queene, and their owne savitie of lyfe. Which doinges may move hyr grace to provide lyvinges for those justeley servinge,[12] which, when warrs be ceased, may continually praye for hyr good successe, joye and felicitie in this earthe and afterwarde to be partaker of the kyngdome of heaven, which the lyvinge father graunte for his sonne Ihesus Christe sake. Amen.

Certayne practises to trayne, instructe and exercise hagbutters and archers as to the skyrmishe appertayneth (16r)

Suche shotte be oftetymes in warelyke poyntes ignorant, althoughe to other uses they can right well use the same. They be of the nomber to the battell appertayninge but not of the body of the same but to the skyrmishe, whearfore they muste be instructed in dyvers poyntes: to marshe, invaide towardes thennymyes, followinge the same some tymes retyer in pollitike manner, still their faces towardes their incounter. Regarde the follower be reskewing his loadesman, any stiringe from place to place notwithstandinge, as to such ys meete. And for that the noble assistance of longe bowes be so adveylable to those usinge the same when tharrowes be drawn to the headdes, sent from the man with strengthe and arte, that their sharpe and manyefolde hailshotte may not be indured, heare followith certayne ruelles in order of arraye to exercise the same: some tymes in winges or bandes by them selves and sometymes mixed togethere with hagbutters, as ofte ys necessary and advayleable.

g = State of preparedness.

12 There was no regular provision for discharged or wounded soldiers save transport and enough money for them to return to their homes as directly as possible. The lawless behaviour of the troops was – along with the high cost – employed as an argument against providing pensions for the disabled.

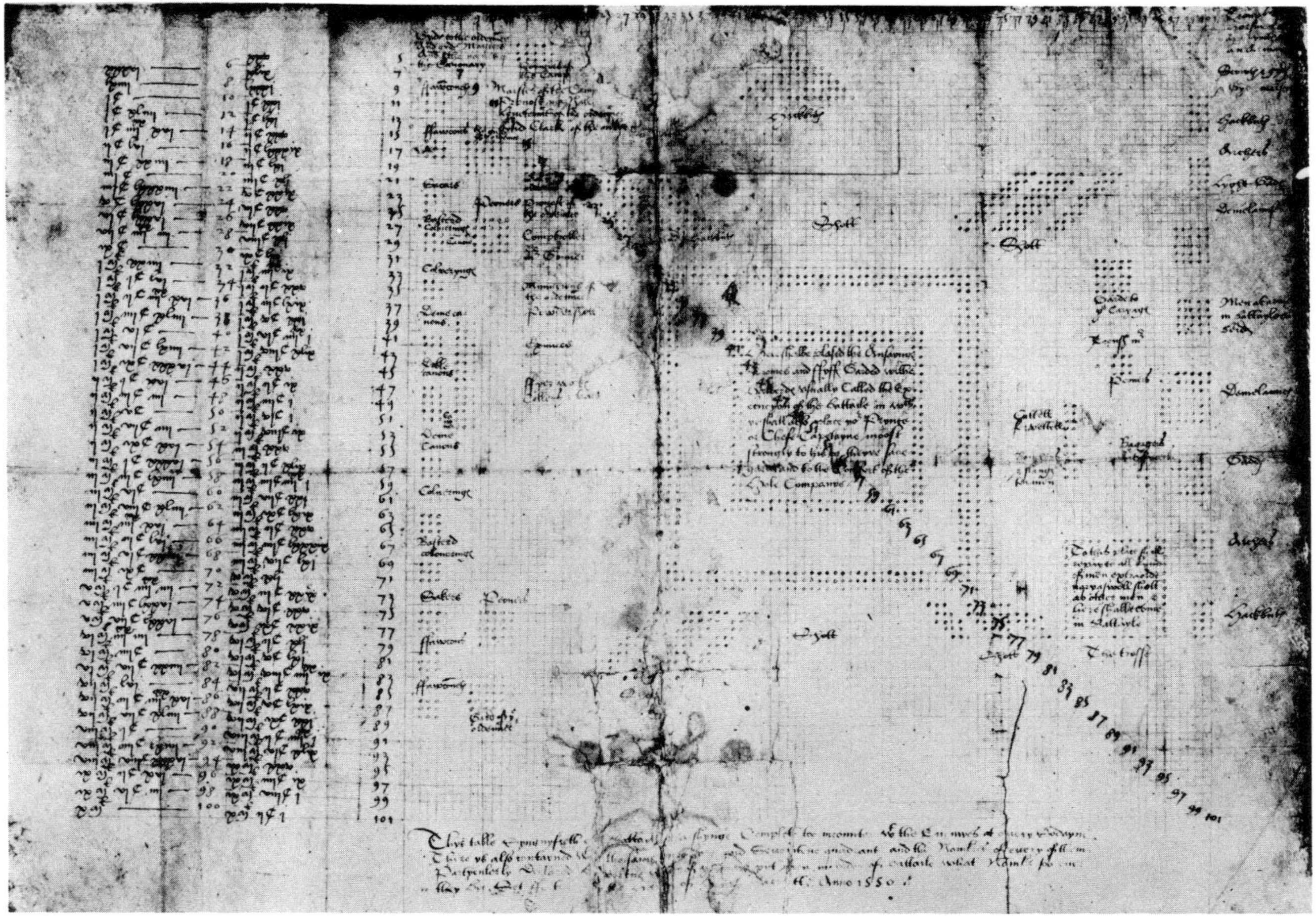

Plate 1

This Lymason or snaile ys not to be vsed for any
intente exepte it be to exersise the arrey. yt
bringeth halfe the sort from place of strenie
and leaueth the Ansaigne open to the enimyee.

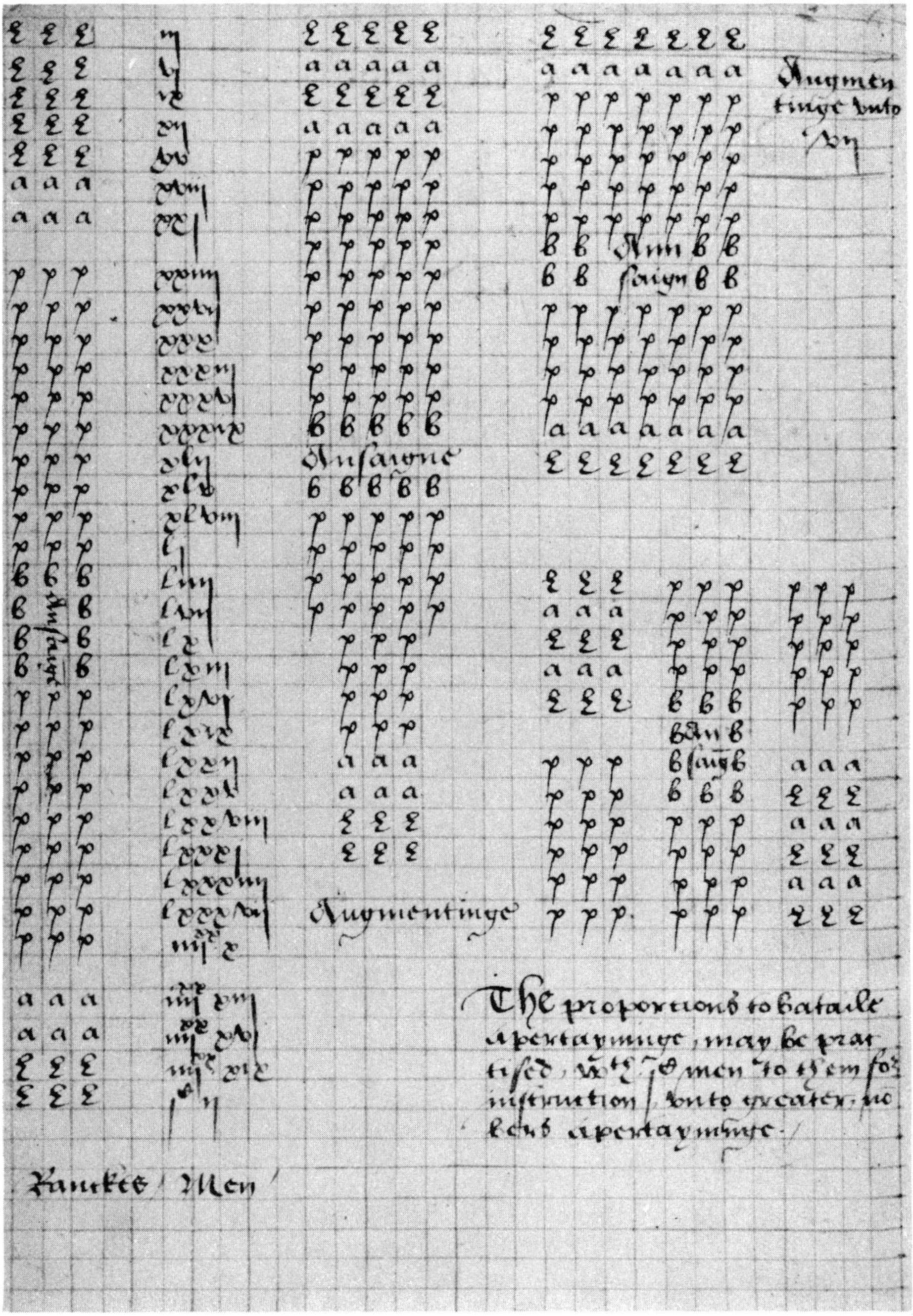

> The proportions to batalle apertayninge, may be practised, w'th 70 men to th'em for instruction, vnto greater no bers apertayninge.

Plate 3

25

This battaile shewith ij men quadrantly proportioned, in y͞e bodye & y͞e fett. & ꝑ placed in iiij wings, to sense convenient

This battaile shewith xiiij brode, ix thike batl of longe weapones, & ꝑ in the bodie, fett & ꝑ placed in iiij wynges.

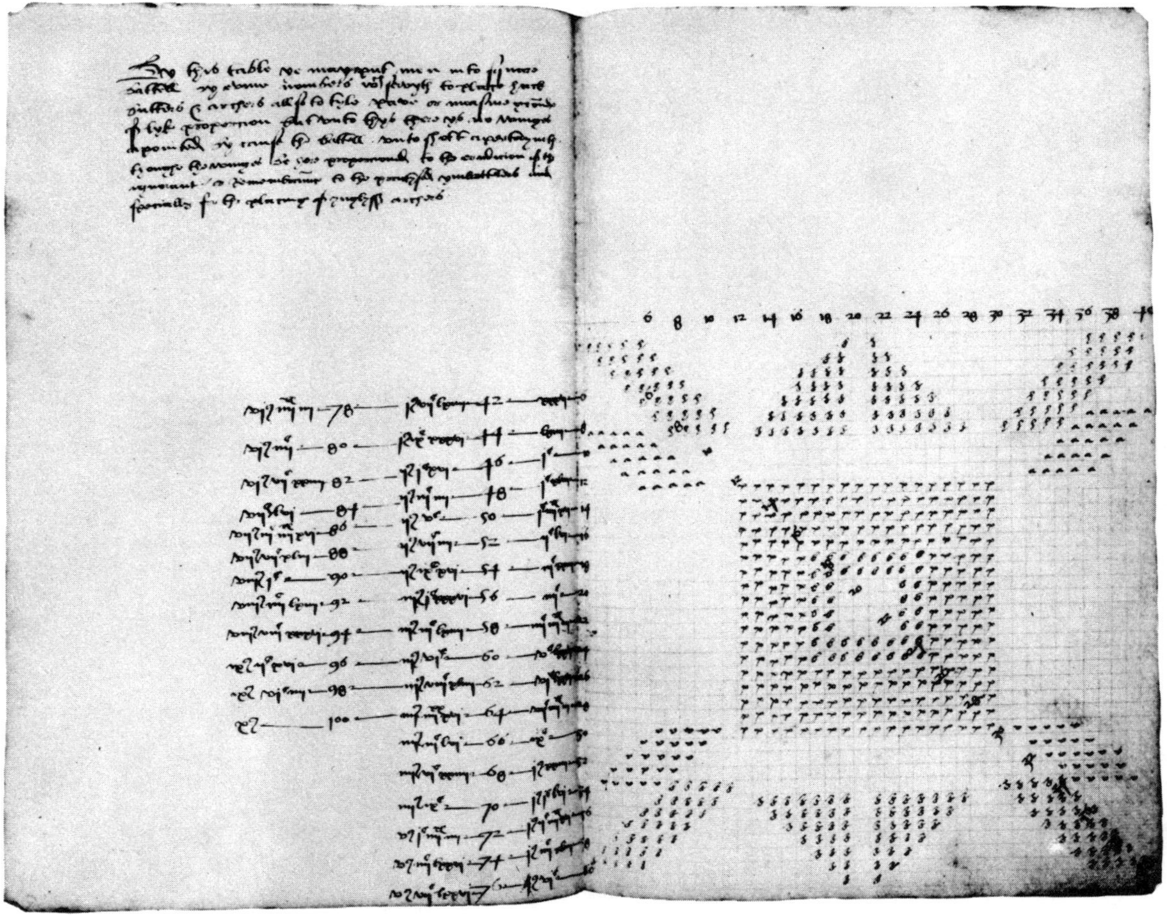

Plate 5

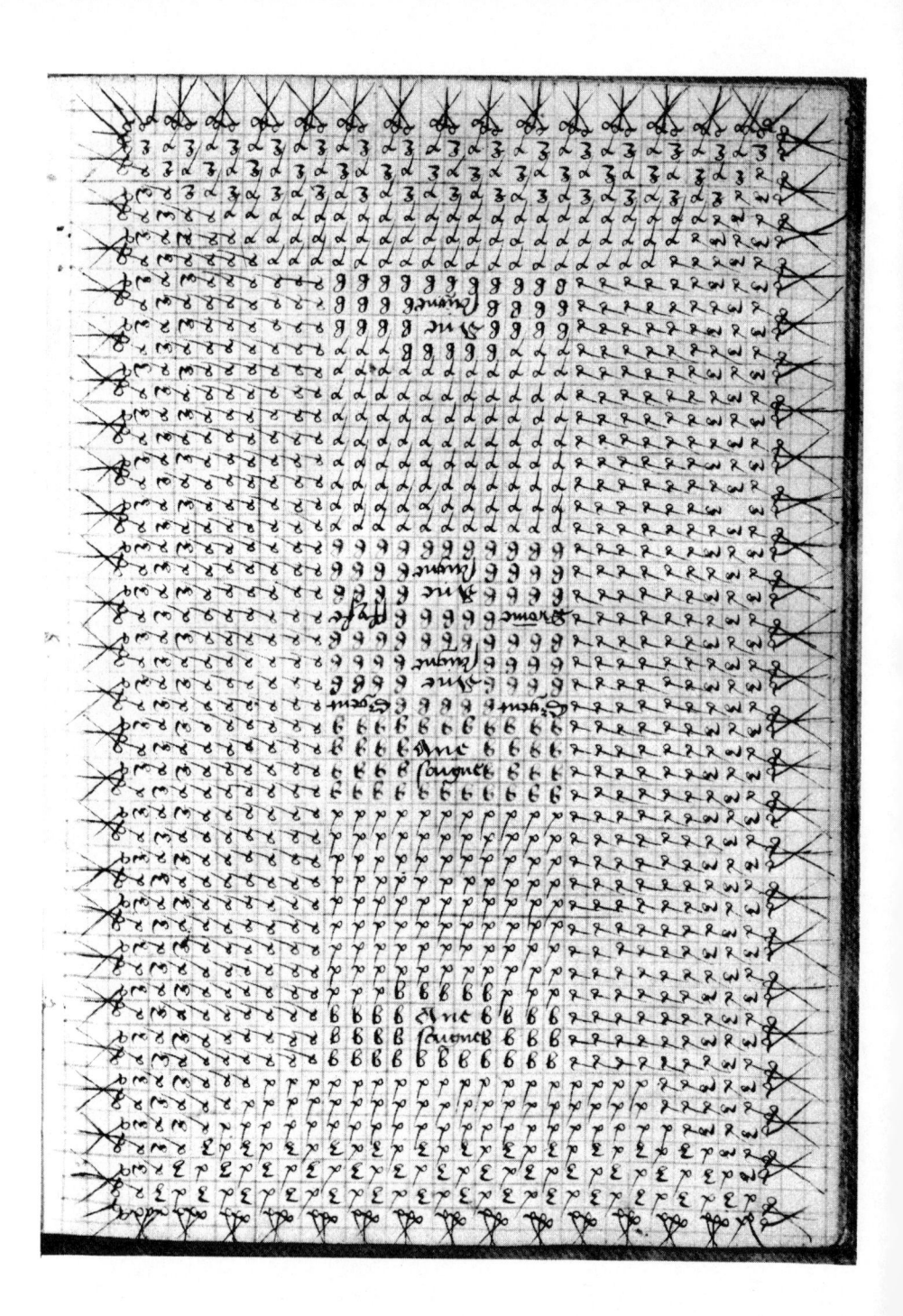

Plate 6

10

MILITARY ACADEMIES ON THE VENETIAN TERRAFERMA IN THE EARLY SEVENTEENTH CENTURY *

Among the problems facing the governors, the *rettori*, of the chief Venetian cities on the mainland in the early seventeenth century was the riotousness and restlessness of the younger members of noble families. Debarred from the political life of the capital, excluded for the most part from local government and disencouraged and sometimes debarred from studying abroad, their energies had few responsible outlets. They consumed the swelling literature on points of honour and the duel, abused their right to carry arms by adding the wheel-lock pistols proscribed by law as the age's most potent murder weapon,[1] and constituted a pool of violence all the more disturbing because of the local prestige of their ancestry and a still smouldering resentment that such families should be subordinated to the "foreign" control of the lagoon. A traditional outlet for their ambition had been service in the permanent force of heavy cavalry maintained by the republic. From the point of view of military efficiency, this force was an anachronism; contemporary warfare had little place for the heavily armoured man at arms and his two mounted supporters.[2] Chiefly employed in garrison service in time of peace, in

---

* My interest in the academies was roused by the references to them on pp. 411-412 of Professor BRIAN PULLAN's *Rich and Poor in Renaissance Venice: the social institutions of a Catholic state, 1500-1620*, Blackwells, Oxford, 1970, and on p. 109 of his *Service to the Venetian state: aspects of myth and reality in the early seventeenth century*, « Studi Secenteschi » 5 (1964), and this sketch has been aided by his generously providing me with further references.

[1] Eg., Venezia, Archivio di Stato (= A.S.V.), *Consiglio dei Dieci, Lettere di Rettori*, busta 86, Padova, 14 May, 1608.

[2] Writing from long professional experience, Lodovico Melzi was dogmatic on this point; " lascio del parlar de gli huomini d'arme, l'uso de' quali si può dire, ch'a

war they were frequently transferred to infantry units or kept at home to carry out a police, rather than a military function. There is little doubt that the heavy cavalry was kept in being largely because of its political and social usefulness. The ancient prestige of horse, armour, lance and squire encouraged nobles of the *terraferma* to bind themselves by contract to the state, and the government was always careful to preserve the illusion that the heavy cavalry was the most honoured part of its military machine.

From the 1520's, however, Venetian wars had for the most part been waged overseas, in the empire *da mar*, and while the local cavalry of Dalmatia, Cyprus and Crete had been used, the cavalry of the *terraferma* were too expensive to transport; rather than fighting the Turks they had been left to patrol resistance to war taxation. By the beginning of the seventeenth century, generations of under-use had led to an inevitable decline in discipline. There were complaints that training was desultory, that captains neglected their men, that recruitment was difficult because fewer noblemen kept horses and learned to ride, that instead of promoting order the men at arms disturbed it. Whereas formerly captains had been selected from volunteers, the government was now reduced to asking *rettori* to suggest names.

The subject of this essay is an attempt to solve this problem by establishing military academies that would provide an occupation for young nobles and a source of trained recruits for the cavalry arm of the republic. Between 1608 and 1610 such academies were set up in Padua, Udine, Treviso and Verona. The method of foundation was similar in all of them: local interest encouraged and formalized by the *rettori*, followed by governmental subvention. The programme drew on precedent; previous societies of nobles had been formed to do honour to the horse. It drew on an atmo-

---

tempo nostro sia quasi del tutto dismesso". *Regole ... cavalleria*, Antwers, 1611, *proemio*. The more conservative Bartolomeo Pelliciari regretfully agrees, not on tactical grounds but " per desiderarsi all'incontro nell'huomo d'arme molti nobili esserciti cavallereschi, et destrieri esquisiti, et piu d'uno, et di gran costo '. *Universale instruttione ... cavalleria*, Venezia 1617, p. 34.

sphere of romantic chivalry breathed even in Venice itself. Thomas Hoby had watched running at the ring in Campo S. Stefano in 1549,[3] and in 1606 Sir Henry Wotton quoted an unknown senator deploring the decadence of modern Venetian youth, "la veggiamo inamorata negl'essercitii cavallereschi, odiar la toga, mormorar de' brogli, darsi alle spese sontuose, invillarizzar tele, nutrir cavalli... Se havremo la guerra, si divertiranno virtuosamente tutti questi cattivi humori fuori di casa in servigio publico".[4] The solution offered in 1608-10 was less drastic, but though it followed precedent it was new not only in scale but in the thoroughness with which the new academies were organized, the scope of their curricula, the closeness of their links with the central government, and their comparative longevity.

There had been three local precedents, at Verona, Rovigo and Padua.[5] On September 16th., 1566, the *podestà* of Verona, Alvise Grimani, reviewing his term of office, said that in the previous year " una academia d'huomini d'arme " had been set up and, after a somewhat shaky and unenthusiastic beginning, had secured premises and horses, elected officers and was one hundred strong. He added that among their regulations was one that obliged them to serve the government for four months at their own costs in case of need.[6] More details were added at about the same time by the *capitano*, Marco Antonio Morosini. He says

---

[3] *Travaile and lief*, Camden Miscellany, London 1902, p. 14.
[4] London, Public Record Office, S.P. 99/3, c. 280.
[5] Among the Accademie Cavalleresche or de' Nobili in other parts of Italy (Faenza, Pavia) the closest analogy to those described in this essay was the Accademia de' Cavalieri del Sole of Palermo (1567-1636), on which see M. MAYLENDER, *Storia delle Accademie d'Italia*, 5 voll., Bologna 1926-1930, Vol. 1, pp. 523-5. For an example of a *giostra* organized by an otherwise purely literary academy in the Veneto, see A. RIOS, *Giostre a Conegliano nel carnevale 1604*, in « Nuovo Archivio Veneto », Ser. 1, 12 (1896), pp. 79-81.
[6] A.S.V., Collegio, Secreta, Relazioni (= C.S.R.), busta 33, under date. G. DALLA SANTA and G. NACCARI, in *Una accademia cavallaresca di Verona* (Venice 1901, *per nozze*), p. 7, give the date of the academy's foundation as 2 May, 1565. They add "ebbe il nome di Filotima perché si doveva ispirare al desiderio della gloria ed all'amor dell'onore". This short account is too brief and too vaguely referenced to be of much use for the period covered by this article.

that the academy was founded by Astorre Baglione (then military governor of the city) ' so that the youth of the city should be trained in the use of weapons and in horsemanship to the effect that this virtuous exercise would deliver them from idleness and other, less honourable, forms of activity as well as make them ready to render some service to the state when it was needed.' He was its ' protettore' and the academy had four other officers, including Captain Ludovico da Monte, chief of the republic's light infantry. The members numbered 60, all young nobles of the city, " from whose virtuous and loving association arises the fact that the city is united and that there are neither disorders nor quarrels ".[7]

The academy did not prosper, nor was there any attempt to obtain a financial grant. The records do not furnish an explanation, but one can be hazarded. With its founder and one of its officers being non-Veronese members of the republic's military higher command, and with the insertion of the clause about four months compulsory service, the academy may have seemed too closely geared to the ordinary recruitment procedures of the state to satisfy local pride. A last feeble echo sounded in August, 1607, when twenty " cavalieri della compagnia " contracted with the riding master Baldessare Mazidore for three years at 400 ducats a year " per ravivar per quanto sia loro possibile l'honorato essercitio della cavaleria in questa città ".[8]

The Academia dei Cavalieri in Rovigo, founded in 1595, lasted for only three years, but the nature of its statutes and its close links with its " protettore ", the *podestà* and *capitano* Benedetto Tagliapietra,[9] may have provided a model for the first for-

[7] C.S.R., busta 33, no date but probably some time in 1566.
[8] Verona, Archivio di Stato (= A.S. Ver.) Academia Filotima busta 237. In 1607 the returning *podestà*, Giulio Contarini, reported that ' i primari cittadini ... sentono grande amaritudine di non poter, né per nobiltà di sangue, né per eccellenza nelle lettere, né per esperienza e valore nelle armi conseguir di quelle dignità et di quegl'honori che a lor pare di meritar '. Quo A. VENTURA, *Nobiltà e Popolo nella società veneta del '400 e '500*, Bari, 1964, p. 344. Military academies were to form a sop to this discontent without prejudicing the Venetian reluctance to give actual power to the mainland nobility.
[9] MAYLENDER, *op. cit.*, vol. 1, pp. 525-7.

mally organized military academy in Padua, that of the Oblosofisti, founded in 1600.[10]

Padua was traditionally to the north what Naples was to the south of Italy, the centre of private tuition in the chivalric arts. "Non tutti che hanno nome di scolari e che vanno a Padova", wrote Pietro Bucci in 1576, " ci vanno per istudiar lettere, massimamente la maggior parte de Franzesi studiosi d'imparar a cavalcare, a ballare, ad esercitarsi nel maneggio di qualunque sorta d'arme ".[11] The variety and flavour of the numerous *giostre* performed in the 1590's is well conveyed by A. Massari Malatesta's book on horsemanship, completed in 1599. He prints a typically flowery challenge from " Don Gilidoro l'Ardito " to " Cavaliere Pistofilo il Costante ", mentions Sartorio Orsati as one of the leading spirits of Paduan chivalric pageantry and dedicates part of his book to the *capitano*, Antonio Priuli.[12] And in the following year, with Orsati as a prominent member and Priuli as its " protettor, principe et patron", the academy of the Oblosofisti devised its statutes and declared its intention of remaining in existence for at least five years.[13]

It was open by election, and on payment of a subscription of twelve *scudi* a *year*, to Paduan " gentil'homeni d'onore et natti gentil'homeni " and was to engage a riding master and a *mastro d'arme*. In addition to Priuli, now returned to Venice, whence he approved the thirty three clauses of the constitution on May 2, 1600, it was to have three " padri ", " duo cavallieri principalli per nobiltà et valor millitare... et similmente uno per lettere

---

[10] My authority for giving the 1600 academy this name is an anonymous but contemporary (because he studied under Giacomo Tron, the academy's riding master) author of a memorandum on the origins of the 1608 Accademia Delia. Padova, Archivio di Stato (= A.S. Pad.), P.V, 2604, filza h.

[11] *Le coronationi di Polonia, et di Francia, del Christianiss. Re Henrico III...*, Padova, 1576, p. 137.

[12] *Compendio... cavalleria*, printed 1600, c. 41r: "tutto ciò procedeno dal splendore et magnanamità de Vostra Signoria".

[13] A.S. Pad., P.V, 2601, a. In the statutes and minutes of meetings it is only called "questa accademia" and "accademia stabilita et formatta in questa citta per honoratto cavalaresco esercitio ".

famoso ", and was to be governed by a committee (" banca ") of five comprising a president, two councillors, a syndic and a " contradittore " whose duty was, by attacking each motion as it was proposed, to ensure a balanced and informed debate. Accounts were to be kept by a treasurer, minutes taken by a chancellor and errands run by a *bidello*. Each new member was to be welcomed with a mass held in the Santo to which the *rettori* were invited, and while Priuli remained the academy's protector, incoming *rettori* were to be asked to take it under their wing and meetings were held in the palace of the *capitano*. The chief business of the academicians was the planning of *giostre* in which they displayed their skill under such names as " Orso il crudele ", " Sfortunato " " Furioso " and " Dell'Ardente Spada ". Their riding master, Tron, resigned on account of his age in 1603 and the last surviving minute of a meeting is dated 18 April, 1605.

It was against this background that the first of the new, durable and more serious military academies was to be planned under the influence of another Venetian patrician, Pietro Duodo, himself *cavaliere* and a man whose unusual interest in both criminal and military natters had been made clear in the lengthy *relazione* he submitted in 1598 on returning from his embassy in France and by his speeches in the Senate before his appointment as *capitano* to Padua, as well as by the letters he wrote after his arrival. In the palace of the *capitano* and under Duodo's chairmanship, sixty three Paduan nobles, many of them (including Orsati) members of the defunct Oblosofisti, met on February 7th, 1608 to discuss the formation of " una nova accademia di cavalieri et di cavalaresca disciplina ". Three were elected to draw up its constitution and worked to such good effect that at a subsequent informal meeting on March 13th, it was resolved " that the academy should open on the 25th of March of the current year 1608 ".[14]

---

[14] A.S. Pad. P.V. 2610, liber primo cc. 1r-8r. In his *relazione* of 1598, Duodo had described Henry IV's establishment of an academy in Paris where young nobles not only learned to ride but had instruction from ' maestri di scrimia, di ballo, di musica e di matematica '. Similar academies had been started in Rouen and Toulouse, ' e

The statutes of the academy [15] are recognizably a development from those of the Oblosofisti. There were to be sixty members, " gentil'huomeni Padovani onorati et nati gentil'huomeni " paying a subscription of 60 *lire* a year, and they were to engage not only a riding master and master of arms but also, " perchè il fine principale di questa onorata academia deve esser non solo nell'ammaestramenti nelli essercitii semplici cavalereschi, ma ancora nelle buone discipline militari per potersi render in ogni tempo più fruttuosa al Serenissimo Nostro Principe, et più utile et honore alla patria nostra, sia condotto un soggietto di valor et principale nella professione delle matimatiche ". While Duodo was acknowledged as the chief inspirer of the academy, three protectors were appointed, two, as in the case of the Oblosofisti, renowned in war, the other in letters.[16] The governing " banca " was to comprise a *principe*, four councillors, a syndic and a *contradittore*, and there was to be a treasurer, a " notaro legale " as chancellor and two *trombetti* to summon members to meetings, distribute their challenges and act as doorkeepers and ushers. On the Venetian model, the members of the " banca " were elected " per scrutinio ", served only for four months at a time and were subject to penalties if they refused office. And on January 4th, 1609, after much debate, the society decided on its name: the Academia Delia, after Delos, the floating island which only acquired a permanent site in the Mediterranean after the birth there of Diana and Apollo.[17] As with the Oblosofisti, incoming *rettori* were

---

se lo stile continuerà, si può creder che verrà assai minor numero di francesi in Italia di quello sia venuto per il tempo passato; di che sentirà anco la città di Padova qualche maleficio '. ALBÈRI, *Relazioni...*, Appendice, p. 103.

[15] *Ib.*, 2601, d.

[16] The warriors were Giovan Battista da Monte and Antonio Collalto, the man of letters the humanist Giovan Francesco Mussato. As far as I can discover, Mussato's only connection with the academy was the composition of "un elogio" on Duodo's retirement from Padua. *Ib.*, 2610, liber primo, 40v.

[17] The rejected names the academicians suggested for themselves were Immobili (27 pro to 17 con), Concordi (24 to 21), Rincorati (18 to 20), Constanti (4 to 33), Arestatti (2 to 35). Delii scored 32 to 5. *Ib.*, liber secondo, cc. 42r and 44r. The name expresses the determination that the academy will be a permanent residence for the followers of arms and letters.

to be greeted with due obedience and begged to take a benign interest in the academy's activities.

Is was, indeed, the *rettori* who suggested a form of subvention which was chiefly responsibile for the Delia's long life and which would place no additional charge on public revenues: an addition of two *soldi* per *lira* to judicial fines. On average, this would bring in some 800 ducats a year, to the disadvantage only of malefactors.[18] This device, the *rettori* pointed out, had been recently applied to pay for the restoration of the Roman amphitheatre – the Arena – of Verona. And while it was a worthy purpose to restore so impressive a memorial of antiquity, could money spent on something "inanimate and ruinous" compare with money used "to preserve the coming together and exercising in military and mounted discipline of so many gentlemen" who would thus be prepared to serve the state in its times of need? The argument was accepted. On March 10th 1609, the Senate granted the 2 *soldi* per *lira* to the academy as long as it continued to perform "gli esercizi cavallareschi", on condition that the money was spent on the salaries of qualified instructors and that the *rettori* and their successors kept a careful eye on the running of the academy; the decision was by no means unanimous: there were 89 votes in favour, 32 against and 20 abstentions.[19] On July 1st 1610, Francesco Morosini, the new *capitano* of Padua, reported to the doge that the academy inspired by his predecessor Duodo was being run "con molto splendore", having a highly paid riding master, an instructor in the managing of arms and a lecturer in mathematics. Thus employed, the academicians "conservano mutuo amore, et in ogni evento potranno impiegarsi in servitio della Serenità Vostra".[20]

---

[18] "Et per il più facile che ci si representa è che ella si compiacia di conceder ad essa Academia fin che durera doi soldi per lira sopra le condennagioni che saranno fatte di tempo in tempo dalli rettori di questa città, da esser pagati alli condennati oltre quello che al presente sono obbligati di pagar", A.S.V., S.D.R., 17 Dec. 1608.
[19] A.S.V., *Senato Terra*, reg. 79, c. 5v.
[20] A.S.V., C.S.R. busta 43, under date.

It cannot have been long after the founding of the Paduan academy that under the leadership of Federico Savorgnano, a member of one of the leading military families of Friuli, a number of young nobles in Udine decided to follow its example. On August 2nd, 1609, the *luogotenente* of Udine, Antonio Grimani, reported to Venice that there were some thirty academicians under their " principe ", Savorgnano, that they had held several meeting in the lieutenant's palace and had raised and sent 200 ducats to cover the travelling expenses and six months advance salary of a riding master from the Kingdom of Naples. But, he pointed out, they would need a subvention from the state, and while the sum obtained from an additional two *soldi* per *lira* on fines would not compare with what this brought the Paduan academy, still, even at about 150 ducats a year this would be worth having. And the project was well worth supporting in this way. As well as bringing the young nobles together " in amore et mutua benevolenza " it did away with the need some of them felt to go to learn the art of riding at the courts of the archduke or other nearby foreign princes and would form " un seminario de fedeli et honorati vasalli di Vostra Serenità ".[21] This time the senators' agreement was more whole-hearted: 92 votes in favour, 3 against, 6 abstentions, though it was emphasized that this contribution toward " attioni virtuosi et nobili " would only last as long as riding practice actively continued.[22] In the letter of thanks he was asked by the academicians to write, Grimani replied that they were already purchasing horses for this purpose.[23]

The next city to establish a military academy was Treviso.[24] On March 28th, 1610, the *capitano* and *podestà*, Marc Antonio Michiel, wrote to say that in repeated conversations he had found

---

[21] A.S.V., S.D.R., *Udine e Friuli*, 1608-1609, under date.
[22] A.S.V., *Senato Terra*, filza 191, 8 Aug. 1609.
[23] A.S.V., S.D.R., *Udine e Friuli*, 1608-9, 13 Aug. 1609.
[24] The Modenese fencing master GIACOMO DI GRASSI dedicated his *Ragione di adoprar... l'Arme*, Venezia 1570, to thirteen "molto magnifici signori" there who had paid him to act as their master of arms.

a number of lively young nobles anxious " to find some way of avoiding idleness, the chief cause of many evil consequences, and devote themselves to some virtuous activity, especially to the art of riding, in emulation of other cities in the vicinity ". Now they have founded, at their own expense, an academy of seventy gentlemen, and not only elected officers and found a meeting place but hired a riding master, a master at arms, a mathematics lecturer and a *ballarino*.[25] They were also providing themselves with horses. Would the doge now authorize a contribution on the same terms as those of Padua and Udine had received? Two *soldi* in the *lira* of additional fines would only bring in about 300 ducats in Treviso, but it would be of the greatest encouragement to the academicians. Besides, their academy was worth supporting because it would not only provide trained men in times of emergency but " maintain harmony among keep them and keep them well away from any dissidence ".[26] The Senate's reply, which praised Michiel's initiative, was again favourable: 133 to 6, with 10 abstentions.[27]

The last military academy to receive public support was that of Verona, granted the two *soldi* per *lira* by the Senate on July 3rd., 1610.[28] On June 15th., 1610, the *capitano* of Verona, Zuan Mocenigo, wrote that with the aid of the Veronese nobleman Ferrante dei Rossi he had persuaded 37 young nobles and three survivors of the original foundation to restore the academy of 1566. A further encouragement was that building works on the new *palazzo publico* on the Brà had gone far enough for it to be used as the academy's headquarters and for its riding lessons in wet weather. Mocenigo concluded by saying that the purchasing of horses and weapons was under way, as was the appointment of teachers " per decoro et ornamento della Academia ", and by

---

[25] Dancing was by now well established as part of the training for the martial gentlemen of western Europe, the grace and suppleness it provided being seen as an adjunct to the physical *sprezzatura* advocated by riding masters.
[26] A.S.V., S.D.R., *Treviso*, 1610, under date.
[27] A.S.V., *Senato Terra*, reg. 80, F. 25r, Mar. 31, 1610.
[28] *Ib.*, filza 195. The voting was 127; 4; 2.

hoping that the doge would not be less generous to Verona than he had been to Padua and Treviso.[29] The letter of thanks which answered the Senate's grant on July 3rd, 1610, of two *soldi* per *lira* – which in the case of Verona came to something like 1,000 ducats a year – was written in the name of " Gl'Accademici Filotimi ", and praised the role played by Mocenigo in giving life to " questa rinnascente accademia ", and pledged support to him and his successors as well as – " per debito di vassalaggio " – to the doge.[30]

The statutes of the Academia Filotima [31] explain that the academy has been restored " a fine che li giovani di questa città possino essercitarsi in opere virtuose et spetialmente nella disciplina militare, accio fugino li vitii nei quali incorreno per non haver essercitii ne intertenimenti convenienti a gentil homeni ". At an annual subscription of fourteen *scudi*, membership was open to those " nato nobili, con dichiaratione che s'intenda tale se non haverà essercitio ne egli, nè il padre nè l'avo arte o mercanzia. " Each member was to maintain a good war horse and two armours, one for use at the barriers – that is, personal combat – one for riding at the ring or quintane. They were to engage a riding master and a master at arms, and a teacher " per legger publicamente nel nostro ginnasio istorie, aritmetica, geometria, matematica, astronomia o altra sorte di lettera. " Moreover, the academicians were to practice " ogni altro essercitio del corpo, come saltare, correre, trar il pallo di ferro, lottare, et altri simili essercitii. " Zuan Mocenigo was to remain their protector after his return to Venice,[32] and the governing " banca " was to comprise a " principe ", two councillors, a " governatore " or effective chairman, a " contradittore ", and a " censore ", whose function was to see that the statutes and regulations were observed, to inspect the academi-

---

[29] A.S.V., *Senato Terra*, filza 195, under date. Mocenigo encloses a list of the names of the academicians, which is also printed in dalla Santa and Naccari, *op. cit.*, 8-9.
[30] A.S.V., S.D.R., *Verona*, 1610, 16 July, 1610.
[31] A.S. Ver. *Academia Filotima* 1.
[32] *Ib.*, 3.

cians exercises " acciò non segua scandalo fra essi et acciò il tutto si faccia con modestia ", and in general to ensure that " gli cavalieri vivono secondo gli ordini et la creanza et costumi che appartengono alla profession loro. " There was also to be a treasurer, book-keeper and chancellor, a *tamburro*, and an *armarollo* to look after arms and armour and help members to prepare for *giostre*. Finally, there were to be four " padri " of over forty five years of age " che habbiano cura che tutti quelli della compagnia vivono costumatamente, et che le loro operationi siano tali quali à cavallier ben creato si convengano, ammonendo con paterno affetto ciascuno che ritrovassero viver altramente. "

There was to be an annual mass, and members were to attend the funerals of academicians. As in the case of the other academies the religious note in the statutes is a faint and conventional one. It is the moralistic and disciplinarian tone that distinguishes those of the Filotima. Members must not wear swords to meetings " perche dove sono l'armi et la forza, di rado suole havervi luoco la ragione. " Only when called upon by the *governatore* may they come up to the *catedra* to speak, and then no one may interrupt them, but remain seated in the place appointed him and maintain " modesto silentio. " There is even a seating plan for the " banca ", chancellor and treasurer. Duels were licensed if they could not be avoided, but there were stern injunctions against lobbying or building up parties to support particular measures, and it was emphasized that such crimes as rape and murder were as unbecoming to a *cavaliere* as was cowardice. The academicians were expected to live as saints as well as fight as heroes. The Filotima was also unique in the emphasis it still placed on service to the state. Statute 56 read: " Che essendo il desiderio di servire questo Ser.mo Dominio uno delle principali cause che mossi ci ha a porsi sotto questo ordine, si statuisce che in occasione di guerra aperta in terra ferma, quando via sia persone che porti nome di generale, siano mandati dodeci della compagnia sotto il governo di uno de gli altri, da esser elletto a bussoli et ballotte, ad assistar all'Ecc.mo S.r Generale per mesi sei senza stipendio. " And leave to serve

" potentato alcuno straniero " had to be granted by the *rettori* or the doge as well as by the academy itself. In the same spirit, the Filotima was the only academy to insist on annual public musters in the presence of the *rettori*.

With four academies in being, all promoted and supported by the Venetian government and its representatives for the double purpose of promoting law and order and providing trained cavalrymen in time of war, it is time to look more closely at what actually happened in these institutions.

Apart from the " ballarino " maintained at Treviso, all the academies retained instructors in the same subjects: riding, the handling of weapons, and mathematics. Of these, the riding master, without whom a military academy would be " come un corpo senz'anima ",[33] was far and away the most important. Local instructors were available, but the academies wanted the best, and such men were not easy to find. We have seen that the academicians of Udine had to send to Naples for one. The Veronese academy also sent to Naples, for Fulvio Cardone, but the negotiations were given up after two lingering years. The Delia offered the Neapolitan Horatio Pentrasci 700 ducats a year in vain. When they hired " il Picardini ", " huomo celebre nella professione " he was recalled to Tuscany by the grand duke after only a short stay. Two years later the *capitano* reported that because a successor had not been found at once the academy " era quasi per decadere ", but that after a round of letters to Venetian ambassadors he had located and engaged one at Turin.[34]

The riding master, who was expected to bring and maintain from two to six horses of his own, according to his salary, not only taught the academicians to ride but broke and trained their horses, the hours at which he could train non-members and their horses being carefully spelled out in his contract. The style of riding taught is never mentioned. A pupil of Giacomo Tron, the riding

[33] *Ib.*, c. 5v.
[34] A.S.V., C.S.R., busta 43, 21 may. 1616.

master of the Oblosofisti, said he trained a horse to be obedient and agile in all the manoeuvres needed in war, and a rider to be well-seated and graceful,[34a] but in general the emphasis was likely to have been not on ordinary military techniques, for which the local riding masters would have been sufficient, but on the more esoteric art of " riding the great horse " described in a number of contemporary textbooks.[35] This art, highly valued for its difficulty, its expense and the social exclusiveness it implied, was practised above all in princely courts which had for centuries associated aristocracy with a good seat. For Venice and its consciously defeudalized subject cities, it was an exotic export. And it was expensive not only because of the riding masters' salaries (800 ducats a year for Picardini, 1000 for his successor, Lelio dall'Agno) but because only carefully trained horses of special breeds could be used. In 1614 the *podestà* of Padua rejoiced because thanks to the academy, the public interest was being advanced with the importation of " molti nobilissimi polledri et cavalli del Regno et d'altre razze generose et famose ",[36] but more commonly the news was that the academies were in difficulty because of the expense of purchasing suitable mounts.

Riding the great horse was primarily a decorative art, though so high a degree of horsemanship was also held to be an excellent preparation for war. Similarly, though the Filotima statutes specified competence in " tutti le sorte d'arme ", it is likely that the master at arms was primarily responsible for teaching the various forms of fencing – on one occasions he was described as " maestro di scrimia " – as well as the use of the normal cavalryman's weapons, lance and sword: significantly, given the intention of the academies' sponsors, there is no mention of the by now much used pistol. Great care was taken in their selection, the

---

[34a] A.S. Pad., P.V., 2604, h.
[35] Eg., in his *Disciplina del cavallo*, published in Udine in 1636 but written in Padua, the Cavaliere Aquino explains how for many years he had taught " mediante il piliere ", the most difficult and artificial method of all.
[36] A.S.V., C.S.R., busta 43, 16 Sept., 1614.

choice at times being determined by setting two candidates to fight in front of the academicians.[37]

By the early seventeenth century it was established that the military man needed arithmetic (adding, subtraction, multiplication and square roots) to understand the brigading of troops, and that the art of fortification was based on geometry. Any well-informed military man was by now expected to be reasonably numerate.

It was not until May 12th, 1609, that the statute respecting " un soggietto di valor et principale nella professione delle matimatiche " was commented on in a meeting of the Academia Delia,[38] and not till December 27th. that two members, Girolamo Salvatico and Ciro Anselmo were elected to recommend names. On March 20th, 1610 they put forward that of Conte Giulio Zabarella. At the same time another member suggested that of Ingolfo de Conti. Salvatico and Anselmo at once protested; *they* had been deputed to suggest names and it made nonsense of their function if others could make suggestions on the spur of the moment – " sopra che fu detto et replicato molte cose ", as the chancellor dryly minuted. They appealed to the " banca " for a ruling; it went against them and was upheld by a majority vote of the members present. Salvatico at once put forward another name, " nominando anco il M.^{co} et Ecc.^{mo} S.^{re} Galileo con provisione di ducati 150 all'anno. "

This was the moment that justified such fragile attention as posterity has accorded the Academia Delia: the opportunity to engage the world's most famous scientist as a mathematics lecturer. It was not taken. The bench proposed electing de Conti, and in the absence of Salvatico and Anselmo, who left the room in a rage, the academicians voted as follows:

---

[37] Eg. A.S. Pad., P.V., 2604, k.
[38] *Ib.*, 2610, liber secondo, c. 12r. What follows is taken from subsequent entries in the same minute book.

	For	Against
Zabarella	17	21
Galileo	15	23
de Conti	28	12

Galileo, who obtained least votes, was then forgotten. Zabarella, who had offered to donate his services gratis if he were made an honorary member, was asked to "legger matematica nell'accademia tre giorni della settimana ... et in oltre insegnerà a quelli che si compiaceranno andar a casa sua". But, as the academicians were in honour bound by their vote, the official title was offered to de Conti, who recorded in his diary against that date, " io fui eletto lettor delle matematiche et altre scientie militari nell'Accademia Delia di Padova in concorrentia del Sig.^{re} Galileo Galilei et C. Giulio Zabbarella." [39]

He was granted the salary asked by Galileo, 150 ducats a year, and he was charged to lecture three times a week on the following subjects: " Quella parte di Euclide che le parerà piu necessaria; la sfera et la geografia; un trattato delle mechaniche; uno delle ordinanze; uno delli instromenti militari; uno delle fortificatione; uno delli stratagemi militari; l'uso delli instromenti mathematici; l'uso della bussula; il modo di disegnare; un trattato della virtù del cavaliero et del capit°." [40] This panorama, based doubtless on his suggestions and previous works, was narrowed to a more realistic compass in a letter of congratulation sent him by Duodo from Venice on March 29th, 1510. " Il carico è nob.^{mo} e dignissimo ", wrote the academy's protector, " e per me loderei che in questo principio si atendesse a dissegnar fortezze e paesi: prenderne in dissegno et alle cose della fortificatione. Trattar della castramentatione, essercitare li Ss.^{ri} Academici nella inventione della radice quadrata che è tanto necessario. Sara anco necessario inse-

---

[39] A. FAVARO, *Galileo e lo Studio di Padova*, II, Firenze 1883, p. 336.
[40] A.S. Pad., ib., c. 22v.

gnar la materia delle artiglierie et altre cose appartinenti alla opugnatione e difesa di fortezze, e queste sono in effetto le materie proprie per quei Ss.ri perche quanto a theorica, io l'ho tutto e per tutto superflua al presente. " [41]

Two years after *their* foundation, the academicians of the Filotima also engaged a mathematics teacher. Referred to simply as Alfiero, a pupil of the well-known engineer and fortifications expert Malacreda, his salary was, at 120 ducats a year, less than was the case at Padua, and his duties more elementary: he was merely required " di far li figuri secondo al bisogno nella matematica. " [42] I have found no details of the appointments made at Udine or Treviso. But that the records should be fullest for Padua is not surprising. The holder of the mathematics chair at the *studio* was expected to lecture on the theory of fortification. Since he had come to it in 1592 Galileo had given public lectures on fortification, writing two treatises on the subject, and had given regular private tuition in his house to young noblemen, many of them foreigners, on the military use of the compass in surveying, on perspective drawing and on fortification as well as on Euclid, arithmetic and cosmography.[43] He had submitted a plan of study for the academy,[44] but his own name was not the first suggested to the Delia perhaps because of his known restlessness in the little university city. He wanted to be employed by the Duke of Tuscany. " I have many and most admirable plans and devices, " he wrote to a Florentine friend in May, 1610, " but they could only be put to work by princes, because it is they who are able to carry on war, build and defend fortresses, and for their royal sport make most splendid expenditures, and not I or any private gentleman. " [45]

The military academies of the *terraferma*, then, were rather more

---

[41] FAVARO, *op. cit.*, p. 331.
[42] A.S. Ver., *Academia Filotima*, 3, c. 9r, Jan. 26, 1612.
[43] FAVARO, *op. cit.*, I, pp. 183 sgg.
[44] " Racolta di quelle cognizioni che a perfetto cavaliero e soldato si richieggono, le quali hanno dependanza dalle scienze matematiche". Printed in vol. 2 of the national section of his *Opere*, pp. 607-8.
[45] G. DIAZ DE SANTILLANA, *The crime of Galileo*, London 1958, p. 3.

in the nature of finishing schools for young nobles and clubs for their elders than training establishments for future cavalry officers. The potential military usefulness was there, but it was chiefly expressed in the *giostre* on which the academies spent so much of their time and money.[46] Long subjection to Venice, and the security and adequate prosperity this had brought with it, had not quenched the nostalgia the nobility of the mainland cities felt for the more swashbuckling way of life they now associated with the aristocracy of Austria and the Tyrol. The academies enabled them to play at being northern nobles with Venice's benign approval. It was not for their eyes that the *capitano* of Verona, Girolamo Correr, expressed the view that a military academy was primarily " un seminario d'ottimi soldati ", and that their members would serve the state more faithfully than foreign *conduttieri* (who then comprised the great majority of captains of cavalry companies), and that the government could henceforward rely on the service of " questi academici cavallereschi " because of their gratitude for the two *soldi* per *lira*.[47]

In the same year, 1612, a gloomier view was expressed by Vicenzo Pisani, *capitano* and *podestà* of Treviso. " For the last eight months there has been no riding master, nor have the academicians maintained horses for practice or any other noble use. Most of them show only the feeblest intention of keeping the academy in being and the strongest reluctance to pay the miserable twenty ducats a year which each is obliged to contribute... And I take it that this derives from the fact that the people of this city do not have the least taste for taking horsemanship seriously."[48]

Treviso was not a rich city. Nor was Udine, whose academy was, in 1629, only confirmed in its subsidy if it actually employed a riding master.[49] In neither did the two *soldi* produce anything

---

[46] See eg. A.S. Ver., *Academia Filotima*, 3, cc. 2r and 8r, and A.S. Pad., P.V., 2601 f, passim, for the organization of *giostre*; the points method of scoring, and the festivities which followed them.
[47] A.S.V., C.S.R. busta 50, 5 May 1612.
[48] *Ib.*, busta 48, 10 May 1612.
[49] A.S.V., *Compilazioni Leggi*, busta 1, c. 545.

like the sum required to hire specialist riding masters from outside the Veneto. As important in explaining the decline of their academies is the fact that neither city was so closely in touch with the aristocratic values of the politer elements of the northern aristocracy as were the far more cosmopolitan Verona and Padua, and neither was the centre – as those cities were – of the annual cavalry musters and training periods of the republic's professional cavalry.

Even in Verona the academy limped along uncertainly. In 1612, its numbers were growing and henceforward it was regularly coupled in the end-of-term reports of the *capitani* with the other Veronese academy, that of the Filarmonica, as one of the " chief ornaments that make the city so noble and so respected ". But by 1629 the state of the military was falling behind that of the musical academy because of the expense of obtaining suitable horses.[50] The Delia was reported on far more frequently by the *rettori* in the first generation of its existence than was the Filotima because of its relationship to the university and the profit it brought to the town. Reporting in 1614, the retiring *podestà* of Padua, Giovanni Battista Foscarini, barely mentioned the encouraging number of local nobles who used the academy, but devoted considerable space to describing the " many leading *signori* and *baroni* among the *oltramontani* who come here for the lessons in horsemanship, such as the " Principe di Hannalt " and some of the ruling family of Saxony. "[51] By 1616 the *capitano* had hit on a formula gratefully repeated by his successors: " there are two major ornaments of this city, one is the university, the other is the riding academy (*accademia della Cavallerizza*) ".[52]

The fullest account is given by Giovanni Dandolo on his return to Venice from his term of office in Padua in 1617. The Paduan academy had 60 members, many too old or infirm to use it themselves; they let their sons and nephews use their subscriptions of seven

[50] A.S.V., C.S.R. busta 50, 7 Dec., 1629.
[51] A.S.V., C.S.R. busta 43, 16 Sept. 1614.
[52] *Ib.*, 21 May 1616.

ducats a month. The riding master was a Neapolitan, Lelio dall'Agno, who had recently been in the service of the duke of Savoy. He was paid 1,000 ducats a year out of which he had to maintain six horses for the use the academicians. He gave riding lessons in the mornings. In the afternoon there were lessons from the *maestro d'arme* who taught " il gioco dell'arme " and was paid 160 ducats a year. There were also afternoon mathematics lectures by Zabarella, who gave his services free. These lessons took place in the academicians' own headquarters, which had already cost them over 5,000 ducats. There was a secretary (*cancellero*) who did the paper work and kept the accounts for 40 ducats a year, and three servants – two *trombetti* and an *araldo* – to look after the building and equipment. All these salaries were paid from subscriptions and from the two *soldi* per *lire*, the money being deposited in the monte di Pietà until it was needed. For some years afterwards the reports remain encouraging. Considerable numbers of German aristocrats attending the university wanted riding lessons, and though some of them patronised private riding schools, they helped to keep the academy, few of whose membership of sixty actually used its training facilities, in a flourishing state. In 1629, however, both the *podestà*, Antonio Canal, and the *capitano*, Marco Priuli, sounded notes of gloom. As far as the native members are concerned, wrote Canal, the numbers were falling off because men were too stingy to pay the fees, and unless they had a change of heart and learned to imitate " li loro maggiori " the academy would have to close. And as for the fee-paying honorary members from the German-speaking countries, their numbers, too, were falling off, partly because the expenses of attending the university were rising too steeply and partly because the growing crime rate was scaring potential students away. In the same moralistic vein Priuli added that men simply used the academy's horses as a convenience, rather than bringing their own mounts to the lessons, because they lacked " the necessary spirit of liveliness and responsibility ".[53]

---

[53] *Ib.*, 20 Mar. and 28 Aug. 1629. The point about the crime rate was repeated

The drift towards the academy's facilities being used chiefly by German students at the university was speeded by the catastrophic effects of the plague in 1630, which cut the city's native population from more than 30,000 to something over 12,000.[54]

When the plague and the War of the Mantuan Succession were over, however, in spite of the academies' past record of dwindling enthusiasm, narrower interests and chronic indebtedness, the government was still strongly in favour of their continuance. In October, 1632, the Senate dispatched a round of letters to all the *rettori* concerned, urging them to restore the academies to full activity again, " ravivare essercizio cosi degno et azione tanto virtuosa et onorata ".[55] By this time there were two more academies. In September, 1626 the Academia della Cavalarizza of Vicenza had been granted the conventional two *soldi* per *lira* " delle condanne pecuniarie " imposed in the city and its territory.[56] The Academia degli Erranti of Brescia, though still in search of a headquarters, had been granted its two *soldi* at least by October, 1632, when the Senate welcomed " la prontezza de molti cavallieri in voler applicarsi all'antico lodevoli istituto di essercitii cosi degni et virtuosi, per ornamento di se stessi et a decoro di quella nobilissima citta. " [57] While the *rettori* of all six cities, Padua, Udine, Treviso, Verona, Vicenza and Brescia, were called on to reanimate the academies, only Padua was offered more money: an additional 600 ducats a year from fines. Nor did senatorial urging stop here. In January 1633 another round of orders was despatched and once

---

by the *podestà* Giovanni Pisani, in 1638 (*Ib.*, 9 Nov.). He said that parents were sending their sons to Bologna and Perugia because of student riots in Padua.

[54] The *podestà's* estimate. He noted that " the academy has lost its riding master and many academicians and has quite given up its usual activities ". *Ib.*, 7 Jan. 1632.

[55] A.S.V., Senato Terra, reg. 108, cc. 375-378. Oct. 16th.

[56] A.S.V., Compilazioni Leggi, busta 1, f. 566. This then brought in 400 ducats. There had been many privately organized *giostre* in Vicenza, one of them, held in the Teatro Olimpico, had been attended by a challenger from the Filotima. A.S. Ver., *Academia Filotima*, 3, c. 9r, Feb. 13, 1612.

[57] A.S.V., Senato Terra, eg. 108, c. 376r. A site was found in the next year (*Ib.*, c. 542r.). In 1535 the *capitano* of Brescia wrote to the Delia asking for guidance as to the relationship between himself, the city authorities and the members of the academy, A.S.P., P.V., 2604, m.

more the Delia alone was singled out with a further 200 ducats a year, primarily so that the *capitano* could help them secure the services of an outstanding riding master with the help of the Venetian representatives in Naples and Florence.[58] The tone of the correspondence of 1632-3, however, had changed from that of the founding years 1608-10. The emphasis was no longer on public service or recruitment to the republic's army.[59] Mathematics was now seen as a dispensable frill. The aim was no more than to flatter and harness the fashionable energies of the local nobility.

Even much favoured Padua remained indifferent. There were only thirty subscribers in 1637, none of whom owned horses or went for riding lessons. " I have urged them to take it up again ", reported the *capitano*, Giacomo Soranzo, "stressing the honour and prestige the academy brings to the city as a whole and how dear its preservation is to your serenity, but where the spirit is lacking and there is no willingness to cooperate, exhortations can have no effect ".[60] His successor's exhortations were scarcely more successful. Though the number of subscribers had fallen still lower, to twenty, a few horses had been imported from outside the Veneto and exercises were being carried out " et in publico et in privato ". All the same, he added, there was no sign of gratitude for the governmental subsidy which alone kept the academy in being.[61] In general, the correspondence of *rettori* from the 1630's suggests that the establishment of military academies on the *terraferma* was an experiment that by now had failed. They lingered on as social institutions [62] but they could no longer be seen as contributing to public order by keeping young nobles usefully occupied or as

[58] A.S.V., *Senato Terra*, reg. 108, cc. 491v-492r.
[59] The Delia kept a list of members who serves the Republic between 1608 and 1621. It contains 13 names. A.S.P., P.V, 2604, i.
[60] A.S.V., C.S.R., Busta 43, 12 May, 1637.
[61] *Ib.*, 28 Sept. 1638.
[62] The Filotima lasted until 1797, the Delia until 1801. The academy at Treviso was still functioning in 1701, the one at Brescia in 1700, those of Vicenza and Udine were limping along in 1664. For the last four, I do not know the effective date of their demise.

providing a source of eager recruits to the republic's cavalry force. They turned out to have suited neither the temperaments nor the purses of the class they were aimed at.

The story of this brief and artificial experiment may end with an odd postscript. In 1654 a new academy was founded, which likened itself to those of Udine, Treviso, Padua and Vicenza. But this time it was set up in Venice itself. In 1658 it had some twenty members paying one hundred ducats a year subscription. A list of half " gl'illustrissimi academici della cavallerizza di questa città " includes some of the famous of Venetian patrician names: Nani, Donà, Giustinian, Morosini, Contarini, Barbarigo, Tiepolo, Molin, Loredan. They had a riding master, Nicolo Paulina, but apparently no other instructors, nor any revenue from public sources.[63] In 1663 there were said to be twenty four members who stabled their horses near the Ospedale de' Mendicanti on a site which " contiene luogo capace per settantacinque cavalli altre à spatiose terreno scoperto ". Their riding master was then the Florentine Vincenzo Simani.[64] The academy was still in being in 1664, but unfortunately the records do not reveal whether riding the great horse had a palmier future among the citizens of the lagoon than among those of the pastures and hills of the *terraferma*.

---

[63] Biblioteca Correr, *Cod. Cic.* 3160/16 and 23.
[64] F. Sansovino, *Venetia città nobilissima et singolare*, Venezia 1663, p. 396. I owe this reference to Dr. Gino Benzoni.

11

MEN AND WEAPONS: THE FIGHTING POTENTIAL OF SIXTEENTH-CENTURY VENETIAN GALLEYS*

The Venetian oared fighting vessel has attracted considerable, sometimes rapt, attention from historians.[1] There has not yet, however, been an attempt to estimate its overall effectiveness in attack or defence. Hesitation in making such an attempt is all too justified. Fire has devoured, and occupying forces (French and Austrian) have dispersed, the greater part of the archival sources dealing with the fitting out, manning and supplying of Venetian warships. The nonchalance of men who took for granted what we long to know has impaired the usefulness of many of the documents that survive. There are more records saying what should have been done than what was done or how it was done. The shortage of crew lists, punishment sheets and take-home pay slips, let alone of supporting biographical information, prejudices one of the very topics with which this publication is concerned — the links between a fighting unit and the society from which it is manned. It is difficult for the historian to believe that it is better to travel hopefully than to arrive, but it is necessarily in this spirit that the following observations, limited to crewing, armament and morale, and ignoring tactical practices and strategic intention, are made.

That a ship is a microcosm of society is so much a cliche that it needs to be demonstrated. Here, then, is a list (of 1601) of those who crewed the most populous of Venetian warships, a great galley flagship.[2]

	No. on board	Venetian term	Approx. trans.	Wage (*lire* per 'month' of 11 p.a.)
1	1	Capitano	Commanding officer	620
2	2	Capellan	Chaplain	20
3	4	Nobeli	Patrician volunteers	62
4	1	Fisico	Physician	60
5	1	Segretario	Correspondence clerk	36
6	1	Rasonato	Book-keeper	49½
7	1	Armiraglio	Chief navigating officer	72
8	1	Comito	For'ard deck officer	60
9	1	Huomo da Conseglio	Navigating officer	48

	No. on board	Venetian term	Approx. trans.	Wage (lire per 'month' of 11 p.a.)
9	1	Huomo da Conseglio	Navigating officer	48
10	1	Paron	Aft deck officer	40
11	2	Pedotti	Pilots	40
12	1	Ceroico	Surgeon	31
13	1	Capo di Bombardieri	Chief gunner	30*3
14	8	Sotto capi di Bombardieri	Gunners' mates	24*
15	12	Bombardieri	Gunners	18*
16	1	Marangon	Carpenter	24*
17	1	Calafao	Caulker	24*
18	1	Remer	Oar-wright	24*
19	4	Penesi	Storesmen	24*
20	2	Compagni di stendardo	Masters-at-arms	20*
21	36	Compagni d'alboro	A.B.s	20*
22	1	Botter	Cooper	18*
23	1	Corazzier	Armourer	18*
24	1	Scrivanello	Copy-clerk	15
25	2	Barberotti	Barber-medical aides	12
26	2	Capitanei di soldati	Captains of soldiers	90
27	130	Soldati	Soldiers	12*
28	1	Patron di gondolieri	Chief longboatman	36*
29	12	Gondolieri	Longboatmen	12*
30	10	Prouieri	Strokesmen	12*
31	4	Fanti del marangon et calafao	Carpenter's and caulker's mates	12*
32	12	Mocci	Cabinboys	6
33	290	Galeotti, 25 de respetto	Oarsmen, incl. 25 reserves	10
34	1	Mistro de casa	Chief steward	28
35	1	Scalco	Steward	21
36	1	Cuogo	Cook	21
37	1	Sotto cuogo	Asst. cook	18
38	1	Canever	Wine steward	21
39	1	Spenditor	Purser	21
40	1	Caneverolo	Asst. wine steward	18
41	4	Servatori del Capitano	Personal assistants/servants	21

	No. on board	Venetian term	Approx. trans.	Wage (*lire* per 'month' of 11 p.a.)
42	2	Servatori de nobeli	Personal assistants/servants	21
43	1	Servatore del fisico	Personal assistants/servants	21
44	1	Servatore del Segretario	Personal assistants/servants	21
45	1	Servatore del Rasanato	Personal assistants/servants	21
46	1	Aguzin	Crewminder	31*
47	4	Trombetti	Trumpeters	24*
48	2	Fanti dell' armiraglio	Chief navigating officer's assts.	10
	572			

With an annual wage and food bill of 31,929 ducats, it was essential that the great majority of the crew, not just the gunners and soldiers, should be able to fight the ship. Here Venice was able to call upon a long tradition of trusting subjects with arms and training them in their use. In 1506, when ordering the reconstruction of shooting yards, so that men from each *sestriere* could practise regularly with bow and crossbow for the periodical shooting competitions on the Lido, the Council of Ten stressed the need for all classes — patricians, citizens and workers — to be ready to defend the city.[4] The threat of invasion from the land was then very much in mind, from Maximilian's Austria, from the Turkish Balkans through Friuli, but the tradition originated in the custom of requiring evidence of military competence from those who wished to sail in merchant galleys (and obtain the perquisites of a niche of freight free cargo space and customs exemption) whether as oarsmen, craftsmen, mariners or deck officers; the positions reserved for young patrician traders were, indicatively, called *balestrerie*, crossbowman's places.[5] Merchant galleys were seldom convoyed. They had the benefit of naval galley squadrons patrolling the red sectors, as it were, of their routes, the 'Christian' corsair area south of Istria, the Turkish corsair zone in the southern Adriatic, the waters off Crete, but for the most part they were on their own, and cargo privileges had, literally, to be fought for. When, in 1509, the allies of Cambrai rolled Venice's armies towards the brink of the lagoon, this sea tradition came ashore. Patricians, mariners and craftsmen from the *arsenale* (the Venetian dockyard) were sent to defend positions the government felt to be too crucial to be entrusted to mercenaries: the town gates of Venice's nearest subject cities, Padua and Treviso.[6] The tradition continued throughout the sixteenth century, whether on great galleys, or on the far more numerous light galleys (150 or 160 oarsmen); clerical, ecclesiastical and medical staff apart, practically every man on board was expected to fight when occasion demanded. The patrician commander directed his vessel in armour,[7] crossbow in hand. Craftsmen and storekeepers were expected to be qualified marksmen.[8] Oarsmen rowed into action wearing sallets and reinforced canvas jacks, one third with swords at hand for the moment of boarding or repelling boarders.[9] A.B.s were ordered to have arquebus and morion 'as the *scapoli* do'.[10]

Scapolo was a chameleon-like term. There are traces of its earlier sense of 'volunteer'. It was occasionally used to describe all crew members in receipt of food allowances above the basic ration (the asterisked items on the crew list above) who were not clerks, chaplains or senior officers. But the technical significance of *scapoli* is best expressed as 'marines', the fighting men ('homini da spada' was a frequent synonym) enlisted as part of a galley's normal complement; and — except in the later crew lists of great galleys, where the distinction is seldom made — *scapoli* are to be clearly distinguished from *soldati*, the supplementary troops raised in time of war, with amphibious operations and full-scale combat at sea in mind.[11]

Up to 1542 the number of marines on a light galley was set at forty-two. From then until 1550 two marines were to be replaced by mariners, to mitigate the unemployment caused by the demobilisation that followed the Turkish war of 1537-40.[12] In 1565 there was another reduction of two, this time to increase the opportunities for young gunners to obtain sea experience,[13] but by the end of the century the standard number was forty-four.[14] These were peacetime numbers, calculated in terms of anti-corsair patrol, harbour guard and on-board discipline. They were increased when especially notorious corsair squadrons were known to be cruising,[15] in vessels serving in the Usock-ridden headwaters of the Adriatic, or when galleys were carrying cash from Venice for the payment of salaries *da mar*. On the other hand, Donato Gianotti, writing in 1525-6,[16] had suggested 80-100. A generation later Cristoforo da Canal, a serving naval commander, reckoned seventy to be necessary for patrol duty.[17] One hundred was the number recommended in a treatise of 1614 largely based on Venetian example.[18]

The discrepancy between the ideal and the actual is partly to be explained in terms of space and expense, but also in terms of the difficulty of recruiting sufficient men. The pay was low — 120-132 lire a year[19] — and remained constant throughout the century. Any proposals to alter it deliberately ignored the upward creep of prices and, by suggesting an increase in pay coupled with the abolition of the ration allowance, threatened a reduction in take-home pay.[20] The official free ration allowance (on top of biscuit) does not sound so bad on paper. Sunday, Monday, Tuesday and Thursday, six *onze* of meat and two glasses of 'honestly' watered wine; Wednesday and Friday, two sardines with oil and vinegar, plus soup; Saturday three *onze* of cheese and soup.[21] To purchase this, captains were advanced a sum roughly equivalent to a marine's cash pay.[22] But when in 1573 Venice was having a hard time recruiting marines and turned to the Mantovano, the Senate was forced to admit the justice of rumours that captains were not honouring their obligations, and not only to offer fifteen lire instead of twelve, but to suggest to the Duke of Mantua that galleys chiefly crewed by his oarsmen and marines should be commanded by Mantuan nobles who could ensure that rations were issued in accordance with regulations.[23] It was, doubtless, the persistent defaulting of Venetian captains in this respect that led marines to jump ship in the War of Gradisca (1615-17) in order to join the republic's land army.[24]

Information regarding the recruitment of marines is scanty. Though Venice maintained in readiness a militia on the *terra ferma* that from 1560 numbered 20,000 men, the government was reluctant to draw on it for service at sea.[25] There was more drafting of men from the militias of the ports and islands *da mar*, but here too the militia organisation was seen as an essential supplement to the republic's small core of professional troops in garrison. There is an occasional reference to recruiting drives by individual *entrepreneurs*,[26] but for the most part the government seems to have relied on volunteers, and the loan of arms and armour to newly joining marines suggests that many of these men were not among the roaming professional or semi-professional soldiers who made up the bulk of land armies. From a bare handful of references the chief recruitment areas can just about be guessed at: Venice itself, the *terra ferma*, Romagna, Apulia, Dalmatia and Albania, Crete; there was the odd northerner – 'Zuane Springal, fiamingo'.[27]

Before turning to the other straightforwardly military component of a normal galley crew (i.e. a crew not supplemented with additional professional soldiers), the gunners, it would be as well to consider the armament for which they were responsible by means of some typical equipment orders.

Light galleys

1540[28]	1571[31]	1600[32]
1 culverin of 50[29]	1 cannon of 50	1 cannon of 50
2 sackers of 12	2 asps of 12	1 falcon of 6
6 asps of 12	3 falcons of 6	1 falconet of 3

4 falconets of 3	3 falconets of 3	10 perriers of 6
1 musket 'da zuogo'[30]	3 perriers of 6	8 perriers of 3
36 muskets 'da braga'	12 perriers of 3	

Great Galleys

1570[33]	1587[34]	(weight in lb.)[35]
2 culverins of 50	2 culverins of 60	10,407
2 culverins of 30		10,282
2 culverins of 20	2 culverins of 30	5,832
4 culverins of 14		5,773
4 cannons of 30	4 cannons of 30	5,976
4 falcons of 6		4,876
2 falconets of 3		3,831
2 perriers of 30		3,920
12 perriers of 3	6 cannons of 20	3,420
		3,210
		3,072
		2,989
		2,939
		2,918
	4 culverins of 14	3,212
		3,211
		3,185
		3,181
	5 perriers of 3	About 150 each

From these and other inventories some generalisations may cautiously be made.

The types of artillery of a calibre equivalent to more than a single pound ball numbered twenty-one. Allowing that guns of similar calibre, though different types, could share projectiles, this leaves twelve varying weights of ball. Seventy balls was standardised as the issue for each piece of artillery in 1617.[36] In sieges, each side reckoned to recover by night a proportion of the balls fired during the day; armies could receive fresh supplies; navies, however, lost every shot fired and could place much less reliance on receiving more. The growing cost of metal and powder led to suggestions towards the end of the sixteenth century that both in fortresses and at sea Venice should concentrate on smaller guns from two to fourteen calibres;[37] no mention was made of the inconvenience involved in having so many sorts of incompatible missiles, but it must at times have been formidable. The liveliest debate concerning naval armament was about the substitution of breech- for muzzle-loading guns in the interest of giving gunners less occasion for exposing themselves to enemy short range fire.[38]

More important is the lack of contemporary discussion (to my knowledge) about the purpose of naval artillery: to what extent was it intended to sink the enemy at a distance, how far to maim his vessel and his crew during closing and grappling?

By applying a crude arithmetical test to a sample of equipment orders between 1540 and 1600, and taking point-blank ranges,[39] we get the following distribution of weapons:

Long range	(300 *passi*[40] and over)	42
Medium	(200-300 *passi*)	145
Medium-short	(100-200 *passi*)	112
Short	(0-100 *passi*)	62

Short range weapons must, of course, be supplemented by muskets, arquebuses, bows and projectile incendiary weapons, but ship artillery seems concentrated on the hope of sinking or disabling at 100 *passi* plus. There are supplementary pieces of evidence that point in the same direction. In 1537, at the beginning of the Turkish war, when the reserve of guns and metal was low, the Arsenal was nevertheless ordered to concentrate on cannons and culverins of fifty[41] and the Duke of Ferrara was asked to loan fifty pieces of forty and fifty.[42] In 1590 it was proposed that all cannons and culverins of fifty to one hundred should be transferred from the *terra ferma* to the fleet.[43] And in 1607, orders to replace perriers of six with a new type of falcon of six, replaced a short with a medium range weapon.[44]

The men in charge of the choice and production of naval guns, as *proveditori* of artillery or of the manning and armament of ships or as members of *ad hoc* committees to supervise the testing of new weapons,[45] were, on the whole, men with sea experience of their own. Changes in gun design were, perhaps, slow in being adopted, but experimentation was constant and the Republic's dynasties of gunfounders — Alberghetti, de Conti — were among the most progressive in Europe. At Lepanto, a booty of some 225 Turkish guns had been sent back to Venice. These the Arsenal had melted down and recast 'al moderno' until, in 1601, the Senate decreed that the thirty-four still left should be preserved 'to keep alive the memory of so worthy and famous an event'.[46] We may assume that naval armament, if conservative, was the result of practical and frequently reviewed experience.

We may also assume that, as in the matter of fortifications, the Venetian government was readier to invest in hardware than in manpower. The armament of galleys was not only as numerous and powerful as the vessels' manner of construction could well bear, but it demanded a variety of skills: calculating the charges for different calibres,[47] manipulating heavy guns recoiling on sleds (which could only be aimed by moving the ship as a whole) as well as the lighter swivel guns, loading some weapons by the muzzle, others at the breech, timing each shot with reference to the vessel's motion. Yet manning never approached even a one man per gun basis. In light galleys, with a minimum armament of eleven three-pounders and up, the number of gunners of all ranks was seldom more than eight. In great galleys, where such pieces varied between twenty-two and forty-two, gunners seldom exceeded the twenty-one given on our crew list. And these figures take no account of the non-portable versions of the *moschetto*. To load and fire these, and to get the heavy guns back into position after recoil, recourse must have been had to non-specialists, from cabin boys to officers' and master craftsmen's servants. In 1533, when there was still considerable competition from craftsmen in the Arsenal to go on trading voyages, carpenters, oarwrights, caulkers and sailmakers (*filacanevi*) had first to qualify as prentice gunners;[48] it is doubtful how long this regulation remained effective.

Graded by pay and responsibility into three ranks, *capi, sotto capi* and *scolari*, gunners were drawn from artillery companies which, since the establishment of the *Scuola* of St Barbara in Venice in 1500, had been set up in nearly all the cities of the *terra ferma* and in many of the islands and fortified ports of the empire *da mar*. Volunteers were attracted by exemption from personal taxation, the right to carry arms and exemption from sales taxes on certain quantities of grain, wine and wood. Attendance at training periods under full-time chief gunners was encouraged by prizes for marksmanship, patrician military governors (*capitani*) were required to keep an eye on the efficiency of their local company, general army officers to examine them during tours of inspection. As a precaution against slack training in the *terra ferma* all gunners coming to serve on galleys were in 1534 ordered to be re-examined in Venice. As a result of this system, gunners both full and part-time were looked on as the most reliable of the military components in warship crews, and from 1556 fines of 500 ducats were to be imposed on any official who tried to detach them from ship- to shore-based duties.[49] Gunners were responsible not only for a ship's artillery but for signal rockets and for incendiary devices. There was, however, some difficulty in recruiting men for naval, as opposed to trading voyages. In 1539 the Council of Ten (responsible as they were until 1588 — when control passed to the Senate — for gunners as well as for artillery) ordered that prior service of at least two years in the army or in a naval squadron was a prerequisite for obtaining a place on a trading vessel.[50] The order to ships' captains of 1565 to take two extra gunners in place of two marines arose from fears of a shortage of men with sea experience. The 'monthly' wage of a chief gunner remained constant at thirty lire plus food from at least 1531;[51] that of a gunner's mate is obscured by conflicting terminology; the ordinary gunner continued to get eighteen lire plus food throughout the century. All the same, the problem of recruiting only became really serious late in the century when Spain and Austria became consistently hostile to Venice. In order that the fortress towns of the *terra ferma* should not be left vulnerable by drafting gunners to the fleet, urgent but not entirely successful attempts were made to keep up the numbers and intensify the training of the artillery companies.[52]

Far graver than the problem of recruiting marines and gunners was that of obtaining enough oarsmen. The numbers involved were large. From 1537 Venice decided to have 100 light galleys at sea or in readiness: this would require some 16,000 oarsmen. The 106 light and 6 great galleys at Lepanto in 1571 were rowed by about 18,140 oarsmen; an even larger force was envisaged by the treaty of 1573 with Spain and the Papacy.[53] And these figures take no account of *fuste, briganti* and oared galleons.

In 1522 it was decided that even with the manpower of Dalmatia and the Mediterranean islands to draw on, swift mobilisation required a reserve of local oarsmen. On 18 March[54] the Senate decided to enroll 6,000 men in the cities and territories of the *terra ferma* who would be liable, when called upon, for paid galley service. Targets for volunteers from between 18 and 40 years of age were set for each administrative centre.[55] The inducements offered were these: freedom for life from personal taxation,[56] permission to wear arms (a much coveted privilege for reasons not only of status but personal safety),[57] freedom during service and for six months afterwards from prosecution for debt.[58] Once enrolled, the men were to be given and taught to use firearms (the *schioppo*, a simpler version of the arquebus) 'which will be of great benefit to us in time of need both by land and sea', though their chief contribution would be to the motive force of the galleys they were called up to. It was anticipated that this measure would enable the Republic to crew fifty galleys from the city of Venice and the *terra ferma*. The initial response, however, was so poor that the government accepted an offer by a *condottiere*, Giulio de Bruna, to raise 1,200 men himself; there were to be eight companies of 150 men each with an ensign in charge of it and six corporals. On being called up, the ensigns would serve as gunners (one per galley), the corporals as *schioppettieri* (six per galley), the rank and file as oarsmen. This blueprint for a private enterprise system of raising *scapoli* and oarsmen together seems to have come to nothing, and though sporadic attempts were made in subsequent years to enroll the 'Ordinanza da Mar', in September 1534 it was acknowledged to have been a failure.[59]

A number of men, noted the Senate, had been raised, but they had been put aboard in groups of forty or fifty 'together with Dalmatians who had treated them badly', and they had been made to winter abroad, as a consequence of which 'many had died and the rest had undergone much suffering'. These experiences had discouraged others from coming forward. The Senate then voted the reimposition of the scheme of 18 March 1522, with two changes: men from one area were to form the entire rowing crew (150) of one galley under a prominent local resident who would command the vessel, and they were to serve only for six months at a time. It was also decided that men already enrolled in the militia of arquebusiers (24,000 strong at that time) could change to the sea militia, but this provision was cancelled later in the year and, more important, the first note of true conscription was sounded. Provincial military governors were to spread enrolment equally among families in each community, to forbid enrolled men to change their place of residence without permission, and to transfer those whose ineptness with pike or firearm disqualified them from serving usefully in the militia of arquebusiers to the sea militia.[60]

In February 1537, half of the 6,000 were called up, the rest in September as mobilisation for war against the Turks got under way.[61] In the same month the balance between the land and sea militias was radically changed and conscription for the latter carried further.[62] The militia of arquebusiers was to be reduced to 15,000. From the 9,000 men discharged and the 6,000 already enrolled in the sea militia, 12,000 of the most suitable were to be enrolled in an enlarged sea militia. The burden was to be spread equally among all communities on the *terra ferma* (Venice had inherited the feudal right to exact labour and military service from the territories it had conquered piecemeal in the preceding centuries), though no community could be called on twice until all the others had already sent men to galley service. The men would have the tax exemptions of 1522 and the right to bear arms from call-up until six months after discharge. Among those enrolled, men who volunteered on call-up would be paid two ducats a month (by their communities), the rest would be chosen by lot. In this way the manning of sixty-six galleys should be assured.

Again, however, the government's hopes were disappointed by the negligence of provincial governors, by the disinclination of local communities to pay the two ducats to volunteers, and by the draft-dodging ingenuity of individuals. When a general mobilisation of the whole sea militia was put in motion in the war scare year 1545, it was found that there were still only 6,000 men enrolled. The Collegio was then ordered to increase it to 8,000 and in 1561 — population growth having led the arquebus militia to be increased from 15,000 to 20,000 — to 10,000:[63] 30,000 in both militias at a time when the total number of adult males fit for active service on the *terra ferma* was reckoned at around 200,000.[64]

The Turkish war of 1537-40 put such a strain on the recruitment of of oarsmen, that on 20 June 1539, the *scuole* (fraternities), craft associations and guilds of Venice and the islands and coastal villages of the lagoon were called on to enroll 4,000 potential oarsmen. The perquisites offered were these: on their return oarsmen could be accepted for full membership of their occupational organisation without paying the usual fee; they would have priority in filling vacant places in the city's numerous ferry services (*traghetti*) and for certain jobs such as watchmen, customs guards and warehousemen; each period of naval service would gain them the right to go on a merchant voyage, with its attendant freight- and custom-free allowance.[65] By 1594 a bonus of ten ducats had been added as an additional incentive.[66] In 1595 the regulations of 1539 were to be printed and distributed to the organisations concerned, with a number of additions.[67] To raise crews of 160 for fifty light galleys, plus an on-board reserve of 1,000 between them, the enrolment of 4,000 was to be increased to 9,000. To this end names were to be submitted (they came to 23,095)[68] from which the 9,000 would be chosen either as volunteers, or as the result of choices made or lots cast by individual organisations or, as a last resort, by lots cast by the presidents of the College of the *Milizia da Mar*, the age limits being 18-45. The cash incentive was increased to twenty-five ducats in addition to normal pay (provided by the organisations, not by the government), and during their time of service and for six months afterwards, oarsmen could not 'save in grave circumstances' be taken to law.[69]

Nevertheless, neither the *terra ferma* nor the city system proved adequate to provide oarsmen in sufficient numbers or of adequate quality in times of war. Faulty administration, legal quibbles concerning exemption, the possibility of using, or faking, substitutes, simple draft-dodging — these were among the reasons which had caused the Senate in 1539 to invite petitions from outlaws and prisoners to have their sentences remitted if they volunteered to row in war galleys,[70] and which led the government in 1570-1 to seek 2-3,000 oarsmen among the Swiss,[71] to ask the permission of the Duke of Ferrara to recruit among his subjects,[72] and to debate the propriety of contracting for 600 and upward from the Swiss canton of Graubünden.[73]

Lepanto, the greatest Mediterranean naval victory of the century, was not regarded by the Venetians as conclusive. The following two years saw larger fleets aimed for and achieved amidst a flurry of expedients. The goverment's proposal in 1572 to winter galleys crewed by oarsmen from the *terra ferma* abroad was challenged as illegal and unwise within the Senate, but was passed nevertheless — fear of the delays caused by assembling new crews for the spring junction with the Spanish and Papal fleets over-riding the dismay with which this decision would be greeted.[74]

The government's optimistic view that additional oarsmen would be lured from Dalmatia by the prospect of loot in the continuing action against the Turk, who could at last be represented as on the defensive,[75] was not, as it turned out, shared by men on the spot and in February 1572 the Senate authorised negotiations with a Swiss entrepreneur for the supply of at least 600 oarsmen from Graubünden 'or others, as long as they are Catholic [this was meant to be an orthodox holy war] and live "catholicamente" and are not our own subjects'. They were to be paid the inflated 'Mantuan' rate of fifteen lire a month plus basic rations.[76] In August a more radical note was struck. All those who had been using Turkish captives as slaves after Lepanto and the coastal skirmishes that followed it, were to send them, for a compensation of twenty ducats or more, depending on their quality, to be chained oarsmen.[77] In November the fleet commanders were ordered to recruit Turkish subjects, voluntarily if possible, or by force, though still paying them as though they were volunteers.[78] And the accounts kept by Captain General Giacomo Foscarini record purchases of slaves at sums varying between ten and twenty-five ducats (for Mustafa da Constantinopoli, among others).[79]

For the mobilisation of 1573 recourse was again had to the Duke of Mantua, with the promise that his subjects would be discharged without fail in October.[80] Another Swiss entrepreneur, Colonel Mechior Lusi, with a long-standing contract to supply troops to Venice, was now asked to supply 1,200 oarsmen — at a price that had crept up to sixteen lire a month plus travel allowance and on his condition that the bargain should include the same number of infantry;[81] when Venice, disillusioned as to the militancy of its allies, edged its way out of the Christian League in March, the oarsmen were dismissed with a *douceur* of two ducats each while the troops, lesss amenable to summary dismissal, were apportioned among the *terra ferma* garrisons.[82] More revealing still of Venice's shortage of manpower was the response in the following year to rumours from Constantinople that yet another Turkish fleet was fitting out. Lusi was asked to raise another 1,200 oarsmen from his canton, Unterwalden — where few, if any, men had been in a boat let alone seen the sea. The rumour was denied within a few days, and a courier sent to overtake the contract,[83] but the episode reveals the disadvantages of a dependence on oared warships.

Apart from the years immediately following Lepanto, the Venetians did not use slaves as oarsmen. Nor do slave raids at other times appear to have been adopted as a deliberate means of filling the benches, and what have been taken to be such raids[84] were probably the result of bribes, promises of pardon for offences[85] or of exemption from militia or pioneer services, pressures just inside the letter of the law. However, some thirty years before, in 1542, the difficulty of obtaining volunteers was thought to justify the use of chained criminals, men who would otherwise have been imprisoned. From 1545 *galee de condannati* were regularly sent to sea and by 1579 vessels manned in this way were referred to by the Council of Ten as 'the chief sinew (*il principal nervo*) of our fleet'.[86] In 1615 an offer from the Duke of Bavaria to export criminals from his gaols to serve as oarsmen was gratefully accepted.[87] In 1616 orders were given to the commissioners with the army in Friuli to send archducal prisoners of war to the galleys,[88] but the decision was reversed in the following year as counter to Christian duty and to the charitable nature of the republic.[89] Perhaps it had not been put into effect. Certainly it would have compromised ransom settlements and exchanges of prisoners of war at the end of hostilities.

Chained oarsmen received no wage. They were given the oarsman's basic ration: soup made from vegetables or rice, or from stale bread or crushed biscuit with a little oil, plus ship's biscuit on its own.[90] Like the free oarsmen they were charged for clothing, paliasses and medical services and if they could not raise cash they had to row on past the conclusion of their sentences until they were judged to have paid for them.[91] The free oarsman's 'monthly' wage of twelve lire for the first four months and nine thereafter[92] was changed in 1524 to a flat ten lire a month,[93] and, as our crew list shows, so it remained throughout the century. What the government thought about the conditions of service at the oar is clear from a law of 1548 which pronounced transfer to the sea militia as the sentence for breaches of certain regulations concerning the arquebus militia.[94] All the same, motley as their origin and grim as their lives on board might have been, thanks to the poverty and hardships that for many were the alternatives ashore, to the wide disciplinary powers granted to commanders and the group discipline imposed by the three, four or five men to an oar system which gradually gained ground from the 1570s,[95] there were few complaints about oarsmen being unable to propel galleys adequately in combat.

Oarsmen, moreover, both chained and free, were issued with weapons and were expected to use them. From December, 1518, the Council of Ten's order that arquebuses were to replace crossbows on galleys[96] was quickly taken up in Senate equipment orders. In addition to the firearms issued to marines, A.B.s and craftsmen, it was ordered in 1528 that each light galley should take fifty for use by rowers. Each craft was to have enough ammunition to allow for six practice shots a month and the men were to be encouraged by three prizes worth ten ducats each.[97] When the Arsenal's experimental quinquereme was being fitted out in the following year, 100 arquebuses were to be provided for its oarsmen.[98] Cristoforo da Canal claimed, however, to have been the first to have trained oarsmen to use the arquebus; he had borrowed weapons from the Arsenal and had fifty of them trained by a professional soldier ('whom I called the "captain of the oarsmen-arquebusiers" ' and who received an extra ducat per pay) whenever the vessel touched land. The aim was not so much to produce accurate marksmen as men who could fire, reload and blaze away again at short range, while archers filled in the reloading periods. He had had, he claimed, as many as 500 of these oarsmen-arquebusiers in his squadron. Unlike the marines, whose weapons were stored in a central magazine, they kept their weapons in chests fastened down between the benches. But, aside from the arquebus, he went on, oarsmen should be fully involved both in attack and defence. The inboard member of each bench should have a short pike; the middleman a 'long bow of the sort used by our country folk' which he should stand on the bench to use, the outboard oarsmen, hampered between his fellows and the portable defences (the *pavesata* of wooden shuttering mounted on the gunwale), could at least throw stones and lumps of lead from the pile under his bench. And, he concluded, chained prisoners were as useful as free oarsmen. The most trustworthy could be released in combat and promised liberty in exchange for gallant service, the others could handle weapons in self-defence as far as their chains allowed and, unlike free men, could not jump overboard when the odds against them seemed too threatening.[99] In the mid-1570s an ex-chained oarsman with long experience in the galleys of Tuscany remarked that of all the Christian governments operating in the Mediterranean, the Venetians got the most fighting service out of their oarsmen.[100]

The arquebus did not displace the bow. The crossbow does appear to have dropped out of use apart from its largely symbolic role in the hands of a commander, but the longbow held its ground sturdily. We have seen them used to cover the arquebusiers' loading periods in da Canal's description. Galleys arming in Crete in 1538 were to take on 'good, reliable and skilled archers';[101] an inventory of 1556 lists twenty arquebuses firing half-ounce (*oncia*) balls, together with twenty of the older hand guns (*schioppi*) and fifty bows.[102] As the musket came to rival, though not supplant, the arquebus on land, it was employed increasingly at sea, partly because its weight could be steadied on top of, or in, the ambrasures of the temporary combat defences built up at prow and poop and (unlike the practice in Turkish or Spanish vessels) along the sides. The Venetian war galley in action was like a self-propelled fortress and could use the weapons appropriate to curtain and bastion. Each great galley in 1617 was to have 100 muskets.[103] Even so it was as late as this year that the Senate still found it necessary to inveigh against the continuing use of 'bows and arrows, which are useless and superfluous weapons'.[104] For defence against missiles and handstrokes, oarsmen wore helmets and flexible jacks (*corrazzine, curazine*), which allowed freedom of movement, while marines and other crewmen-combatants used the stouter cuirass (*corsaletto*) of plate. Armour for thighs, legs and arms is seldom mentioned, presumably because, as Pantero Pantera remarked, at sea it was necessary 'to fly, as it were, from one vessel to another', full armour only being appropriate for the commander and the captain of *soldati* who remained exposed while giving orders throughout an engagement.[105]

With *soldati* we come to the last and most purely military element in a galley's complement, the soldiers recruited to reinforce the marines in time of threatened or actual war. Their numbers were not simply determined by the needs of large-scale sea battles. These were few and undertaken with reluctance. Numbers were also conditioned by the potentially amphibious nature of naval operations. During the Apulian campaign of 1528-9, the bombardment of ports from the sea, the landing of raiding parties or of the entire military component of a fleet to reinforce land armies, had all played an important part in Venetian strategy.[106] During that campaign, as in the Turkish war of 1537-40, warships were on occasion used straightforwardly as troop transports, to land an army and then sail away, But troops might at any time be needed to distract the enemy's recruiting activities, relieve a siege, strengthen a threatened garrison or take back a captured port. In 1570-3 Venice's vessels had to match the military component in Turkish fleets manned for the conquest and occupation of her Adriatic bases as well as for the domination of her trade and military supply routes. And, as Sebastiano Venier wrote with reference to an attempt to destroy the fort built by the Turks in 1572 to block the entrance to the Venetian base at Cattaro (Kotor), guns were not enough. Galleys, he pointed out, are at a disadvantage when engaged in an artillery duel with a fortress, 'because, being in movement, they shoot awry, and when they do score a hit it is on a stone bastion or a thick and stout earthwork, whereas shots from the land strike thin, vulnerable wood or human flesh'.[107] He says nothing of the difficulties confronting the land gunner: the problem of aiming consistently at small, thin, moving targets at a level below his own platform; but the moral, that galleys needed landing parties as well as guns, was in any case established doctrine. Nor was it shaken by the war of 1615-17, when not only formal combined operations but the temporary borrowing of naval troops by land forces were constant themes.[108]

During March and April 1570, Venice contracted for 11,600 infantry to join the fleet,[109] enough to guarantee the bare minimum of eighty fighting men per light galley quickly, and to build towards the number thought necessary — 100.[110] In 1572 12,000 fighting men (the distinction between marines and soldiers tended to be ignored in wartime) was fixed as Venice's contribution to the Christian League's fleet, and efforts were made to select from newly enrolled men, and from those serving in garrisons, those who would best stand the conditions of sea service[111] – in the winter of 1570-71 the wastage, primarily due to privation, had amounted to some 5,000.[112] Possession of the full complement of marines and soldiers was considered of paramount importance; Marc' Antonio Colonna justified his inaction against the Turkish fleet in 1570, which led to the fall of Nicosia, by saying that, with fewer troops per vessel, the Venetians would have been unlikely to have won.[113]

Soldati for the fleet were raised, as for the land forces, by contract with mercenary captains. There were almost always gaps in their numbers when mustered before embarkation, always losses thereafter from sickness and desertion. The difficulty of keeping numbers up is reflected in the measures taken in 1570-72: peasant volunteers from the *terra ferma* were offered four years of exemption from personal taxation from the end of their service, outlaws (*banditi*) were offered amnesties, patrician volunteers were not to be inhibited by any legal proceedings in which they were involved, naval commanders were allowed to recruit members of the militias of Dalmatia and Albania.[114] By means such as these, any means short – legally, at least – of actual conscription or the press gang, Venice accumulated a floating army. Paruta later stigmatised it as composed of 'men for the most part unused to military service'.[115] This was an exaggeration. The floating army at Lepanto was probably not much less experienced, taken as a whole, than land armies of the period, and its inexperienced elements were to some extent compensated for by the restricted need for tactical discipline on shipboard, the impossibility of flight, and the terror of falling captive to the Turk.

Terror was, indeed, the keynote of Pantero Pantera's graphic account of the special demands made on the morale of troops by naval service. First the soldier had to become accustomed to the vessel's constant movement, then to exposure to squalls of rain, finally to visual horrors: the flashing cannon,

> 'the havoc wrought among human limbs now by iron now by fire (which is not so terrifying in land battles), the sight of this man torn to shreds and in the same moment another burned up, another drowned, another pierced by an arquebus ball, yet another split into wretched pieces by the artillery. On top of this there is the terror caused by the sight of a vessel swallowed up by the sea with all hands without the remotest possibility of rescue, to see the crew, half alive, half burned, sink miserably to the bottom while the sea changes colour and turns red with human blood, covered the while with arms and with scraps and fragments of broken ships.'[116]

How far this passage, a recruiting officer's nightmare, represented the popular view of military service at sea, can only be guessed at. The normal hazards of land service, disease, food shortages, rough living, arrears of pay, harsh discipline, were well known. Among the voluminous series of petitions, often including *curricula vitarum*, addressed by soldiers to the government, there is no hint that service at sea gave rise to any special grievance or sense of alarm. Indeed, it is generally referred to (not, of course, necessarily sincerely) with pride. Venice paid no more for sea than for land service,[117] and the system of stoppages for food, armour and weapons and replacement clothing was roughly comparable. Certain contracts with military entrepreneurs specifically excluded service at sea, but these related exclusively to Swiss troops; men recruited *da mar* and the 'foreign' Italian troops on which Venice chiefly relied, as well as the *terra ferma* volunteers she increasingly came to rely on, were aware that they were signing on for service on land or at sea according to the orders given their captain. The difficulty Venice had in amassing troops for the War of Gradisca, which led to the amassing of the most cosmopolitan, desertion- and sickness-prone and fractious of all her armies, applied equally to land and sea service. It would be incorrect to suggest as a general rule that the quality or quantity of soldiers in galleys was such as seriously to impede the aims of those who had designed and armed them.

These aims were to build (as cheaply as possible, with the wage bills of large crews in mind) long, narrow, low, fast and, as necessary, self-propelled vessels, to equip them with a formidable variety of weapons, and to cram them with men trained in their use. In spite of the problems of firing from a moving platform, long and medium range artillery continued to be mounted in the hope of successful attack at a distance. As the range shortened, loopholed portable defences provided cover for men using firearms and bows, while temporary platforms gave vantage points for the most skilled marksmen. At contact, sword and pole-arms came into play, together with such incendiary materials as had not been affected by damp.[118] At each of the three stages the military potential of the ship's company was progressively augmented; first the gunners, then the marines and soldiers, finally all those mates, craftsmen, seamen and oarsmen who were not engaged in keeping the vessel locked to windward of the enemy in order to clear the decks of smoke and reduce the danger of fire.

And the commanders? There is no space here to discuss the effectiveness of the command structure of a fleet,[119] or to do more than note that though, numerically, the patriciate which supplied the commanders of individual ships and the captains of squadrons and fleets was becoming progressively more land- than sea-centred, the system of office-holding which switched men from naval commands to military responsibilities on land and *vice versa*,[120] continued to provide a leadership which soldiers, as well as sailors, appeared to respect.

Notes

N.B. In this, and following note sections, place of publication of books cited is London, unless otherwise stated.

*   This article owes much to the unstinted generosity with references and advice of Dr Marco Morin, and to the encouragement of Professor Frederic C. Lane, whose sequel to the article on seamen cited in note 1 will greatly supplement the information given here.

1.   Notably, Frederic C. Lane, *Navires et constructeurs à Venise pendant la Renaissance* (Paris, 1965), *Venice and history* (Baltimore, 1966) Nos. 11 and 12, and 'Venetian seamen in the nautical revolution of the middle ages', in *Venezia e il Levante fino al secolo XV* (Florence, 1973); Alberto Tenenti, *Cristoforo da Canal; la marine Vénitienne avant Lépante* (Paris, 1962) and *Piracy and the decline of Venice, 1580-1615* (Berkeley U.P., 1967); G. Giomo and F. Visentini, *Le grosse galere veneziane nel 1593* (Venice, 1895). More generally, R. G. Anderson, *Oared fighting ships* (1962); John Francis Guilmartin Jr., *Gunpowder and galleys* (1974); W. L. Rodgers, *Naval warfare under oars, 4th to 16th centuries* (Annapolis, 1939). For additional works, see the bibliographies to Lane's *Venice, a maritime republic* (Baltimore, 1973) and Tenenti's *Cristoforo da Canal*.
2.   S[enato], M[ar], D[eliberationi], R[egistro] 61, ff. 46-46[v]. All manuscript references are to Archivio di Stato, Venice, unless another source is given.
3.   Asterisks denote men who were given food above the basic ration of biscuit and soup.
4.   Council of Ten (henceforward Cl. X.) Misti, D.R. 31,2 f.23[v], 19 May.
5.   Even when the crossbow was replaced by the arquebus in 1518. These positions, for patricians between the ages of 12 and 30, increasingly became sinecures, bartered for cash, and in 1551 their numbers were limited to fifty in any one year (S.M.D.R. 31,ff.81-81[v]). From 1571 the 'nobeli di galea' who appear on crew lists were patricians who volunteered for military duties out of patriotism and for a wage. Eight were killed and five wounded at Lepanto (Archivi propri, Pinelli, 1-2, f.13[v]).
6.   'Homeni maritimi' who had served at Padua were to be offered priority places on the next merchant galleys going to Beirut and Alexandria, S.M.D.R. 17, f.64[v], 20 Oct. 1509. The same practice was observed, scare by scare. E.g. on 12 Nov. 1526 'homeni di le maistranze di l'arsenale' were sent to defend Padua; Marino Sanuto, *Diarii* (Venice, 1879-1903), xliii, col. 221.
7.   For Cristoforo da Canal, killed in action in 1552, see *Della milizia da mar* [c. 1540], ed. M. Nani Mocenigo (Rome, 1930) 12. The seventy-five-year-old Sebastiano Venier, at Lepanto, 'stava armata d'una corazza all'antica, in pianelle, con un balestra in mano'; P. Molmenti, 'Sebastiano Veniero dopo la battaglia di Lepanto', *Nuovo Archivio Veneto* (1915), 10-11.
8.   This, at least, is how I read a reference to 'i balestrieri de maestranze et tutte gl'altri tolti al bersaglio' in Pinelli, 1-2, n.p., 'da mandare galie in ponente', item 45. The reference is to merchant galleys.
9.   Arsenal inventory of 1544. Archivi propri, Secreta, G. Contarini, 25-6: 'Corazine et zellade et spade bone per galliotti' (9,000, 2,000 and 1,200 respectively) with a note that each [light] galley was to be issued with 150 jacks and

sallets, i.e. one of each per oarsmen, and thirty swords. This last figure had been amended to fifty by 1556, a figure confirmed by an issue in 1582. (da Canal, ed. cit., notes on pp. 102 and 107. Cl.X.C[omune].D. R. 36, f.121^v, 3 July.)
10. A late reference, but this is unlikely to be an innovation. S.M.D.R. 62,f.144.
11. E.g., 'Gente da remo, homini da spada et soldati'. S. S[ecreta] D.R. 78,f. 166^v, 3 Jan. 1573 [all dates in these notes are modernised]; 'cosi alli scapoli ordinarii come alli soldati estraordinarii' (pay regulations, S.M.D.R. 37,f.191^r, 23 Sept. 1566. And see below, pp. 15-16.
12. S.M.D.R. 31,f.66^r.
13. *Ibid.*, R.37,ff.22^v-25^r. All galley commanders (*sopracomiti* and *governatori*) raising crews in Venice or in Dalmatia, Albania or Crete, are to take two extra gunners from those enrolled for at least two years in an artillery company on the *terra ferma* or *da mar*.
14. At the turn of the century there was a proposal (unimplemented) to reduce this number to thirty-two in the interest of economy. Materie Miste Notabili, 29. Unpaginated proposal to the Doge from the Presidents of the Collegio della Milizia da Mar ('Prima scrittufa').
15. Especially, at mid-century, that of Dragut. E.g., twenty extra marines per galley; S.M.D.R. 30, 107-107^v. On smaller oared vessels, *fuste* and *brigantini*, figures for patrol and combat were respectively 8, 24; 4. 10. S.M.D.R. 23, f.168; *ibid.*, 27, ff.27^v-28; *ibid.*, 28, ff.117-18.
16. *Libro della repubblica di Veneziani* (Florence, 1850), ii, 161-2.
17. Ed. cit., 119-20. He gives a valuably specific account of the positions around the galley taken up by *scappoli* on guard duty, and their relief system.
18. Pantero Pantera, *L'armata navale* (Rome, 1614), 168.
19. Depending on whether it was calculated at ten lire per calendar month, or twelve lire an 'Arsenal' month (eleven to the year).
20. On 12 March 1587, a petition signed by twelve *sopracomiti* protested that these cheeseparing moves would rob the service of efficient and loyal marines. Materie Miste Notabili, 29, n.p., endorsed 'in lettere del Prov.^{e} dell'Armada, 27 Aprile'.
21. S.S. Filze, 24 Jan. 1573.
22. Materie Miste Notabili 29, *parte* of 12 Mar. 1587.
23. S.S.D.R. 78, ff.173^v-174.
24. S.M.D.R. 74, f.80^v-81. The offence was to be punishable with death.
25. The *Collegio* was authorised to call up 10,000 men, however, in 1520 and 1566; Sanuto, xxviii, 559 and S.M.D.R. 37, 174^v. In each case the war scare passed before more than a proportion of the men (1,500 in 1566) had been mobilised.
26. E.g., S.M.D.R. 21, f.154, 22 Sept. 1529.
27. S.M.D.R. 33, f.169; *ibid.*, 42 ff.63^v, 105.
28. Cl.X.C.D.R. 13, 10 Oct., F.216.
29. Artillery was calibrated according to the weight of the proving shot in pounds. From 12 lb. down, however, the proof ball was of lead, whereas iron balls, a third lighter, were used in action. Perriers were proved with stone balls, and used them in action.
30. Bronze light artillery, not to be confused with the portable *moschetto*. The musket 'da zuogo' (380-400 lb.) was bedded in a heavy wooden base; the musket 'da braga' (80-120 lb.) had an iron stirrup welded into a bronze barrel and was charged through removable chambers fitting into the stirrup.
31. C.X.C.D.R. 30, f.49^v.
32. Tenenti, *Piracy*, 188, where 'mortars' are misleadingly given for perriers.

In 1558 the following armament was given as 'customary' for light galleys: 1 cannon of 50; 1 falcon of 6; 3 falconets of 3; 2 perriers of 6; 4 perriers of 3. Materie Miste Notabili, 13, f.16.^{v}.
33. Proveditori all'Artiglieria, 36, no. 4. A typical example from 11; the other totals were 28, 26, 23, 42, 37, 33, 22, 40, 40, 35.
34. *Ibid.*
35. Given because the weight of individual guns issued to a galley is seldom found and can make it easier to appreciate a vessel's firepower. I do not know whether the 'heavy' Venetian lb. (= 1.05 English lb.) or the 'light' Venetian lb. (= 0.66 English lb.) is meant; most probably the former.
36. S.M.D.R. 75, f.45^v.
37. S.S.R.R. 87, f.26^v and Collegio, Secreta, Relazioni, 52, 17 July 1590.
38. Materie Miste Notabili, 22, 6 Apr. 1589 and S.M.D.R. 51, f.101. S.M.D.R. 61, f.8, 7 Apr. 1601, for adoption of breech-loaders.
39. Alessandro Capobianco, *Corona e palma militari di artiglieria* (Venice, c. 1598), 34. His ranges square with trials described in e.g. Archivi Propri Contarini, 25, 1 Sept. 1544.
40. The Venetian *passo* = 5.5 English feet.
41. Cl.X.C.D.R. 12, 7 June, f.35-35^v.
42. *Ibid.*, 13 Sept. 1537, f.37^v.
43. Collegio, *doc. cit.*
44. Savio alla Scrittura, 193, 3 Feb.
45. Tests of a new type of breech-loader on the Lido range in 1590 were attended not only by the *proveditori* of artillery, the *patroni* of the Arsenal and the professional superintendent of fortifications, but all 'li nobili nostri che si trovano al presente in città che hanno fin hora portato fanò' — i.e. served as galley commanders. S.M.D.R. 51, f.101.
46. S.M.D.R. 61, f.8.
47. While there are references to 'prepackaged' fustian cartridges (*scartozzi*) — e.g., Cl.X.C.D.R. 21 Mar. 1566, f.93^v — it seems unlikely that sufficient quantities were made up in advance, given the damp conditions of naval gunnery.
48. Scuole Piccole, 257, Capitolare, 20 Oct.
49. *Ibid.*, 20 June.
50. Cl.X.C.D.R. 13, f.13^v.
51. S.M.D.R. 22, f.58 (a useful crew list for a 'galion grande'), confirmed by the crew list for a great galley in 1538, S.M.D.R. 24, f.103^v-104.
52. E.g., Savio alla Scritture, 193, 8 Aug. 1607.
53. S.S.D.R. 78, ff.187-8^v. Venice had agreed to raise her contribution to 130, 'computate le grosse a una per due sottili'. 160 is the number of oarsmen for a light galley that appears most frequently.
54. S.M.D.R. 20, ff.7-8^v.
55. Padua 800, Vicenza 800, Verona (and Colognese) 800. Brescia (and Salò and Riviera) 1,200, Crema 200, Bergamo 600, Udine (and Friuli as a whole) 700, Treviso 800, Rovigo and the Polesine 200.
56. 'da ogni gravezze, sì personale come real per quello pagano sopra li estimi della persona sua, a le qual gravezze mai in alcun caso possuno essere astretti etiam che fosse statuito ed ordinato che exempti havessero a contribuire'.
57. The Council of Ten, responsible for public order, subsequently cut this down to the times when men were actually going to join, or were returning from their vessels.
58. 'exceptuanda li debiti de afficti et livelli che stimo de lire 50 de pizoli in suso'.
59. S.M.D.R. 23, ff.39^v-40.
60. S. T[erra] D.R. 28, ff.94^v-95^v.

61. S.M.D.R. 23, ff. 182^v-183; S.T.D.R. 29, f.158.
62. S.M.D.R. 24, ff.53-54.
63. *Ibid.*, 35, ff.65-69^v, 22 March.
64. Marciana Library, Venice, MSS, It. VII, 1213 (8656) f.62^v. On f.65^r there is a 'Carrata de Terra ferma per homini 8,000 per armar galie 50 a 160 per galia' which itemises the men enrolled in each territory. The exact total is 8,026. The manuscript is undated but appears to be c.1550.
65. Provisions listed on ff.203-205 of the *doc. cit.* in n. 67.
66. S.M.D.R. 55, ff.62-62^v. Eight were to be given along with pay on board, two witheld until debts incurred on board (e.g. treatment from *barbiero*) had been settled.
67. S.M.D.R. 55, ff.200-202^v.
68. Mentioned in S.M.D.R. 65, ff.4-4^v.
69. A complete list (126 items) of the organisations and lagunar communities subject to these provisions is given in S.M.D.R. 61, ff.44-46.
70. Cl.X.C.D.R. 13, f.3.
71. S.S.D.R. 77, ff.31^v.
72. S.M.D.R. 39, ff.295-295^v. Pointing out to the Duke that the fleet would be operating to the advantage of Christianity as a whole.
73. S.S.D.R. 77, f.7^v. Voting on this proposal dragged on irresolutely from February to April 1571.
74. S.S.D.R. 78, ff.56^v-57.
75. *Ibid.*, ff.56^v-57.
76. S.S.D.R. 78, ff.63^v-64.
77. *Ibid.*, ff.123-123^v. Some Lepanto captives were still at the oar in 1616, when a merciful government released them to almshouses — because they had become Christians. S.M.D.R. 74, f.20^v.
78. *Ibid.*, f.140.
79. Procuratori di S Marco, 190, e.g. ff.3^v and 12. I owe this reference to Dr R. Muller.
80. S.S.D.R. 78, ff.168^v-169^v.
81. *Ibid.*, ff. 171^v-172 and 186^v.
82. S.S.D.R. 79, 4 Apr.
83. *Ibid.*, ff.100^v-102^v.
84. E.g., when R. C. Anderson, *Naval wars in the Levant 1559-1853* (Princeton, 1952), 31, speaks with reference to 1570 of 'the time-honoured method of sending a division of galleys to raid the Archipelago . . . and a good haul of slaves secured'.
85. E.g., in 1532 the *capitano general del mar* was allowed to accept volunteer *banditi* from Corfu, Dalmatia, Albania and Istria, and to determine when their sentences should be cancelled. S.M.D.R. 22, f.116.
86. Cl.X.C.D., 8 Feb. 1579, ff.54-54^v.
87. S.S.D.R. 105, ff.177-177^v.
88. *Ibid.*, 106, ff.244-244^v.
89. S.T.D.R. 87, ff.117-117^v. To these pious reasons was added the belief that 'ne conferire finalemente al nostro servitio'.
90. S.S. Filze, 24 Jan. 1573.
91. These debts were sometimes paid by the state, e.g. S.M.D.R. 33, f.70^r, more frequently by relatives, but in times when oarsmen were desperately in short supply, as during the War of Gradisca, the right to pay their debts in cash was suspended, and they were forced to row them off; S.M.D.R. 74, ff.55^v-56.
92. S.M.D.R. 20, f.7^v. This provision of the sea militia ordinance of 18 March 1522 contradicts a decison of 1519 that the wage should be reduced to eight lire for the first four months and six thereafter.

93. Lane, *Venice, a maritime republic*, 366.
94. S.T.D.R. 35, ff.179bis-182.
95. One man per oar was probably the rule in the first half of the century, as the terms trireme, and quadrireme suggest. Writing in 1593 Francesco Duodo, noting that one oar per bench had proved more effective for light galleys, urged the adoption of the same principle for great galleys. Archivi propri, Contarini, 25, no. 1. For the adoption of this suggestion, S.M.D.R. 74, ff.85^V-86^V.
96. Cl.X.Misti D.R. 42, f.143. The word used is 'schiopeto', but the terminology used for firearms in this period was not yet standardised.
97. S.M.D.R. 21, ff.121^V-122.
98. *Ibid.*, 24, f.141^V.
99. *Ed. cit.*, 125-149.
100. 'Le memorie di un uomo da remo' [Aurelio Scetti], *Rivista Marittima* (1884), 217.
101. 'Buoni et sufficienti et periti arcierii'. S.M.D.R. 24, f.89^V.
102. Da Canal, *ed. cit.*, 177, note. 50 bows were recorded, again in a light galley inventory, in 1574. S.M.D.R. 42, f.3-3^V.
103. *Ibid.*, 75, f.29.
104. *Ibid.*, f.87; 'archi et frezzie, quale sono armi inutili et superflue'. Great galleys in 1570 had been issued with sixty arquebuses, twenty-five *archibusoni* and 100 bows – double stringed, so that two arrows could be discharged at once, saturation compensating for reduced accuracy. *Ibid.*, 39, f.165^V
105. *Op. cit.* (Rome, 1614), 166-7.
106. V. Vitale, 'L'impresa di Puglio degli anni 1528-9', *Nuovo Archivo Veneto* (1907). See especially 162-3 for the capture of Molfetta.
107. Molmenti, 25.
108. E.g., S.S.D.R. 107, f.57.
109. Summarised in S.M.D.R. 37, f.149^V.
110. S.S.D.R. 76, ff. 65-65^V; *ibid.*, 78, f.1.
111. *Ibid.*, 78, ff.91^V-92 and 85^V.
112. S.M.D.R. 39, f.228, 12 Sept. 1570, on the effects of cold and rain on men unhardened to service in open galleys. Five thousand additional troops were raised, but could not get past the Turkish fleet blockading the mouth of the Adriatic to join the Venetian fleet off Messina in July-August 1571. Venice was forced, humiliatingly, to bring numbers up to 100 fighting men per galley by borrowing troops from Don Giovanni, thus giving a most unwelcome extra weight to his influence on strategic decisons.
113. Capi di Guerra, 1. 29 Sept. 1570.
114. Paolo Paruta, *Dell. historia venetiana 'ella guerra di Cipro* (Venice, 1645), 104-5; Collegio, Notatorio, R.38, ff.199^V, 200^V, 223^V-224; Molmenti, *op. cit.*, 84.
115. Paruta, *op. cit.*, 148-9.
116. *Op. cit.*, 154-5.
117. Soldiers in galleys in 1570 got three ducats per 'month' (eleven per year), of which one third was stopped against loans and expenses over and above the basic ration; S.S.D.R. 76, f.66. At this time troops serving in garrisons *da mar* were being paid three ducats per calendar month; sea pay was brought into line with this in 1572; S.S.D.R. 78, f.154. By 1605, soldiers 'chi siano di questa citta, o Albanesi, Crovati, Greci, Dalmatini et de subditi dello stato nostro' were to get four ducats a calendar month; S.M.D.R. 65, f.24^V. Four ducats (twenty-eight lire) was still the monthly rate in 1617; S.M.D.R. 75, ff.32^V-33. I have not been able to find what effect these rates had on marines' pay in wartime.
118. Most commonly: *trombe* and *pignate*, i.e. wooden-cased iron tubes using an explosive charge to project flaming material, and fire bombs. E.g., S.M.D.R. 42,

ff.3-3^v, for eight *trombe* and sixty *pignate da fuoco* on a light galley.
119. S.S.D.R. 76, ff.78-80 for a careful spelling out of the relations between naval commanders (*proveditori*, captain general, captains of the great galley and Gulf squadrons) and the military governor general of the troops in the galleys; 15 April 1570.
120. As when Giacomo Foscarini, *Proveditore Generale* in Dalmatia (responsible for infantry, cavalry and fortifications), was switched in January 1572 to being captain general of the fleet (in association with Sebastiano Venier, the victor of Lepanto). S.S.D.R. 78, f.60^v.

III

CONTEMPORARY REACTIONS TO WAR

SIXTEENTH-CENTURY EXPLANATIONS OF WAR AND VIOLENCE

WIDESPREAD AND CONTINUOUS INTEREST IN WAR AS AN OBJECT OF study, rather than simply as a phenomenon to glorify, deplore, justify or chronicle, began in the sixteenth century. Wars between individual states and between coalitions of states, civil wars, wars of intervention, wars against deliberate unbelievers: these familiar forms of conflict came to be waged on a larger scale than ever before, and they were joined by two others, novel and perturbing. Catholic against Protestant, wars were fought in the name of religion within Christendom itself and against peoples so far beyond its limits that the greatest ingenuity was required to show that they were occupying lands to which any European could advance any demonstrable claim. On the battlefield new tactics were introduced, a hitherto scarce-proven class of weapon — pistol, musket, cannon — became ubiquitous, the appearance of towns changed dramatically as new methods of fortification replaced those which had served the middle ages. Wars became more expensive, touched more pockets, induced more radical changes in administrative institutions and in constitutional practice. More important still in prompting thought about the nature of warfare was the printing press, with book, broadsheet and woodcut all both disseminating news and — for this was also the founding century of modern propaganda methods — interpreting it. A new invention, the atlas, enabled political events to be located in space with some accuracy, and war, together with the individual's relationship to it, was brought into still clearer focus by more demanding notions of citizenship and nationhood.

> I think there is no man so far estranged from civil humanity [wrote Thomas Becon in 1543] which knoweth not how much every one of us is indebted to our native country ... but also allured unto the love and desire of the same even by a certain inspiration both of God and nature. For how glad is an Englishman, being in France, Germany or Italy or elsewhere, to know by the transmission of mutual letters what is done in England, in what case the public weal consisteth, how it prospereth .... The love of our country must needs be great, seeing that the grave, prudent, sage and wise governors of the public weal heretofore in all their acts sought nothing so much as the prosperity and wealth thereof. What goodly sweet sentences did they instill into the breasts of their younglings, even from the cradles, to encourage them unto the love of their country? As there are; *Pugna pro patria. Mortem oppete pro patria. Dulce et decorum est pro patria mori* ....[1]

---

[1] "The policy of war" in *Early Works* ed. J. Ayre (Parker society, London, 1843), pp. 232-5. Spelling and punctuation have been modernized in all quotations.

Finally, a moral focus was added by Erasmian and Anabaptist pacifism, both of which acted as a creative irritant to those who wrote about war throughout the century.

War acquired a new prominence in writings on politics from Machiavelli and Seyssel to Mariana, Bodin, Botero and Althusius, and among moralists as different in temperament and nationality as More, Vives, Montaigne and Romei. It produced a novel touchiness among theologians, a Calvin, a Bellarmine, a Suarez, and opened a vein never mined before with such vigour by preachers of all shades of belief. Through the work of Matthei, Vittoria, Belli, Ayala and Gentili, war forced maturity on the study of international law to such an extent that it emerged as virtually a new discipline. It is also worth remembering that war had become more truly an international form of culture than it had been even in the age of chivalry. Tactics, weaponry, methods of fortifying were eagerly copied, mercenaries and technical experts were transferred from one theatre of operations to another, books dealing with military affairs were produced by the hundred and there was a brisk traffic in translations. Again, all writers on military affairs and most educated soldiers shared a common respect for the military prowess and skill of antiquity, and nearly all subscribed to a common ideal, that of the learned soldier, to whom the pen was almost as manageable as the sword. It was this culture, together with the news of war from Peru to the Celebes that enabled Alberico Gentili not only to justify his subject on the grounds that "military science and the law of war are not confined within the bounds of communities, but on the contrary always look outward and have special reference to foreigners", but to claim that "this philosophy of war belongs to that great community formed by the entire world and the whole human race".[2]

As far as the rights and wrongs of international conflicts are concerned, this philosophy has been explored with considerable thoroughness.[3] But little has been done to investigate another of its components: the attempt to explain war and to account as well for other forms of violence. This attempt was one aspect of a widespread preoccupation, almost an obsession with human behaviour and its

---

[2] *De jure belli libri tres*, trans. John C. Rolfe (Oxford, 1933), p. 3.
[3] From a large literature, the following general works are particularly useful and have good bibliographies: William Ballis, *The Legal Position of War: Changes in its Practice and Theory from Plato to Vattel* (The Hague, 1937); R. H. Bainton, "Congregationalism: from the Just War to the Crusade in the Puritan Revolution", *Andover Newton Theological School Bulletin* (April, 1943); Robert P. Adams, *The Better Part of Valor: More, Erasmus, Colet and Vives on Humanism, War and Peace 1496-1535* (Seattle, 1962).

secular motivation. One aspect of this, and perhaps the best known, was the concern with social behaviour, with good manners, the various accomplishments suited to the gentleman. This involved above all the study of oneself. More important was the study of the behaviour of others in order to determine what attitude a man should adopt towards the spectacle of life in general, and what conclusions he should draw from it.

The increase in what could be known about other people in the sixteenth century was spectacular. Taking western Europe as a whole, this was the really invasive age of humanism. Information about the Greeks and Romans and the larger world they had known and written about was spread not only by complete texts and translations but by popular compendia and by absorption into works written for circles of readership far wider than the nucleus of scholars: books on the art and on the law of war are only two examples. Alongside this opening of sepulchres, this continual listening to Europe's ancestors, contemporary histories, news pamphlets, the writings of travellers and topographers enabled men for the first time to have a reasonably clear idea about the customs of their contemporaries from Ireland to Lapland and Muscovy. And some of these contemporary cultures challenged particular attention because, like Venice, they had emerged as sane and successful political models, or, like the Ottoman empire, were modern Utopias where matters were better arranged than in countries that had had the presumed advantage of centuries of Christian teaching. Ethnology now appeared beside history as a moral guide. Johannes Boemus explained that he had described the peoples of Africa and Asia "that using them as present examples and patterns of life thou mayest with all thine endeavour follow the virtuous and godly and with as much awareness eschew the vicious and ungodly".[4] For together with the ancient and the new Europe appeared the lineaments of other civilizations, the most challenging of which was that of China. By the end of the century, Joseph Hall could transport himself imaginatively to the orient and ask

> Who ever expected such wit, such government in China? Such arts, such practice of all cunning? We thought learning had dwelled in our part of the world; they laugh at us for it, and well may, avouching that they of all the earth are two-eyed men, the Egyptians the one-eyed, and all the world else, stark blind.[5]

[4] *The fardell of facions*..., orig. edn. Augsburg, 1520, trans. William Watreman (London, 1555); repr. in *A Selection of Curious, Rare and Early Voyages* (London, 1812), p. 277.
[5] *The discovery of a new world*..., orig. edn. London 1605, trans. John Healey (London, 1608), p. 13.

And the habit of comparing life in an observer's own city with life in other earthly cities rather than with the city of God was still further strengthened by the information that came flooding in about peoples who did not live in cities at all, but in caves or huts or who slept in hammocks slung under the stars, peoples who had not simply been guessed at by Herodotus or Pliny or Solinus or Mandeville, but actually seen, chaffered with and shot at by contemporaries of those who read about them.

Of all these sources, information about antiquity was most pervasive but least influential; it served chiefly to give prestige to opinions already held. Knowledge about other European peoples aroused curiosity but in the main flattered pre-existing prejudices against foreigners. Information about the virtues and achievements of Turks and Chinese was welcomed partly because it fed the vein of masochism deeply implanted by the Christian moral code, but it also led to a real extension of understanding. Potentially most challenging was information about the "ethnicks" of the Americas, peoples without the advantages either of Christianity or civilization, whose customs had a special, though delayed, power to jolt Europeans into taking fresh stock of themselves and their institutions.[6]

Whatever the gradations of stimulus, the sum of all this new information about human behaviour (for it is the quantity, not the absolute novelty that differentiates the sixteenth from earlier centuries) stimulated two mental processes of the greatest importance for the future: thinking comparatively rather than by analogy, and looking to general principles in a secular rather than a theological sense. Above all, it forced those who chose to learn how to live and think from the world rather than from the Bible to seek guidelines through the increasingly unmanageable accumulation of information about human behaviour, and in finding their way about this information and drawing conclusions from it, writers were led to anticipate, to some extent in method but chiefly in direction of inquiry, some of the characteristic concerns of the modern social or behavioural sciences. These anticipations have to be discerned in a far more miscellaneous body of writings than the historian of pure or applied science looks to for his sources, and evidence appropriate to several of them frequently jostle one another within the covers of a single book. There was no orderly succession of arguments relating to explanations of violence, no systematic citing of other authors, no work of synthesis; the best

---

[6] See J. R. Hale, "Geographical and Mental Horizons", in *The Age of the Renaissance,* ed. Denys Hay (London, 1967) and J. H. Elliott, *The Old World and the New* (Cambridge, 1970), esp. ch. 1.

that can be done (as I shall attempt in this essay) is to state the explanations and impose some order on them by relating them to areas of inquiry which became more or less self-sufficient. For even a cursory searching and sorting reveals the rudiments of what were much later to be labelled social and medical psychology, the relationship between animal and human behaviour, human geography, sociology, demography, anthropology and ethnology — in fact pretty well the full range of disciplines which contribute today to an understanding of aggression, violence and conflict at all levels from the smashed rattle to global war.[7]

Let us, then, return to the international lawyers as a point of entry to an account of sixteenth-century attempts to explain the nature of the various manifestations of human aggressiveness. While by no means a closed, let alone a mutually admiring circle, they shared certain major assumptions. All agreed that the motive for war must be just, that it should only be waged at the command of a legitimate sovereign superior, and that the means used, and the nature of the peace settlement, should be as moderate as possible. All, moreover, agreed that war was a continuation of justice by other means and should only be undertaken when all possibilities of peaceful arbitration had been exhausted. That is, war was seen as an essentially secular phenomenon, begun, conducted and ended voluntarily by men. "War was first brought in by necessity", William Fulbecke summed up, "for that decisions of courts of law and the determining of controversies by their ruler could not be betwixt two strange princes of equal power, unless they should willingly agree to such an order, because they have no superior nor

[7] The modern literature on the causes of violence is enormous. I restrict myself to a few titles of a general nature for the reader who is interested in seeing how many contemporary explanations were anticipated in the sixteenth century. The most satisfying general appraisal of violence on a large scale is no longer the still valuable study by Philip Quincy Wright, *A Study of War*, 2 vols. (Chicago, 1942), but Gaston Bouthoul, *Les guerres* (Paris, 1951). Other synoptic works or symposia include: E. F. M. Durbin and John Bowlby (eds.), *Personal Aggressiveness and War* (London, 1939); E. B. McNeil (ed.), *The Nature of Human Conflict* (Englewood Cliffs, 1945); Stanislaw Andrzejewski, *Military Organization and Society* (London, 1954); J. D. Carthy and F. J. Ebling (eds.), *The Natural History of Aggression* (London, 1954); A. de Rueck and Julie Knight (eds.), *Conflict in Society* (Ciba Foundation, London, 9166); M. Harris, M. Fried and R. Murphy (eds.), *The Anthropology of Armed Conflict and Aggression* (New York, 1968). If the reader of this essay is tempted to feel some impatience with the explanations of violence put forward in the sixteenth century, he might consider the remarks of E. B. McNeil (*op. cit.*, pp. 27-8) to the effect that "the paradox which aggression presents is that in all its abundance and despite the massive scrutiny it has endured since the beginning of time, it remains as enigmatic as if its presence had not yet been detected by man". This situation has not significantly changed since 1945.

ordinary judge, but are supreme and public persons".[8] That individual wars were not part of a divine plan for punishing the sinful but were undertaken by individual rulers for specific political purposes — to hamstring a rival, support an ally or enforce a legal claim to territory — was, of course, taken for granted in proclamations, formal defiances and the preambles of alliances, and this personal or political motivation was accepted by subjects, at least at the start of a campaign. It was when war dragged on, bringing increasing desolation, or when one war was followed by another, that men were tempted to revert to non-secular explanations of international conflict and see it as the painful working out of God's inscrutable purpose.

Religious conviction apart, the theological explanation of war was the natural answer given by the common man's despair or incomprehension at a time when political decisions were exclusive, when reassuring governmental propaganda reached only a minority and when standing armies, with regimental pride supplementing political indoctrination, were small and exceptional. But the thesis that war was punishment for sin, the work of the devil, also retained its hold on a sizeable, if decreasing number of intellectuals.

> Even before the world itself was fashioned by the supreme Artificer [wrote Pietrino Belli], we read that there was war in heaven.... It is no occasion for surprise, therefore, that in all ages since the world began, peoples, kings and other rulers have persisted in war even down to our time,... and that there will be no end to this evil until the world itself shall pass away we are warned by divine utterance.[9]

Others, seeking as an explanation for war a prototype of personal aggressiveness, saw its origins in Cain's murder of Abel. It was even proposed that, as wars are fought with stratagems as well as force, the origin could be pushed back to Adam himself, because, being tricked into becoming subject to sin, and therefore to death, he could (just) be seen as having been slain in battle by the serpent.[10] More representative was the Jesuit Juan de Mariana's suggestion that violence was part of God's plan to turn man from an individual into a social or political being. Created without fang or claw or protective hide, man first joined with groups of his fellows to protect himself from the beasts. Then, as men themselves become predators on their own kind,

> those who were pressed by the more powerful, began to draw themselves together with others in a mutual compact of society and to look for someone

---

[8] *The pandectes of the law of nations* ... (London, 1602), p. 34v.

[9] *De re militari et bello tractatus*, orig. edn. Hanau 1598, trans. H. C. Nutting (Oxford, 1936), p. 3.

[10] See F. R. Bryson, *The Sixteenth Century Italian Duel: A Study in Renaissance Social History* (Chicago, 1938), p. 150.

outstanding in justice and trustworthiness.... In this manner, from fear and the realization of frailty, the consideration for each other ... and the civil society by which we live well and happily were born.[11]

Yet throughout the century the theological explanation steadily lost ground. It was not just that international law, generalizing from individual wars to warfare as a phenomenon, broadened political motivation into a rule. Wars undertaken in the name of religion, which had been hitherto seen as blameless co-operations with God's will, were now seen in a more cynical light. The crusading appeals of such popes as Alexander VI, Leo X and Clement VII were appraised by the princes of Europe and their councillors in terms of secular profit and loss. The legitimacy of converting the infidels in the New World by force of arms was challenged with reference to their physical well-being and the economic and political motives that underlay forcible conversion. Military operations against the Turks, from the Venetian campaign of 1499-1503 to the battle of Lepanto in 1571 and beyond, were conducted on the same lines, and with the same aims as wars between Christian powers. To purely secular causes of war, Emeric Crucé was to say, "one could add religion, if experience had not made known that this serves most often as a pretext".[12] And similar remarks had been made of the rival sides in the French "wars of religion".

The theological explanation was also weakened by extending the consideration of war to include all forms of violence. Grotius was only summing up a good deal of earlier discussion when he remarked "when arms have once been taken up there is no longer any respect for law, divine or human; it is as if, in accordance with a general decree, frenzy had openly been let loose for the committing of all crimes".[13] Person to person violence (murder, rape, assault), person to property violence (arson, theft), or group violence in the forms of banditry and piracy, riot, revolt or rebellion: these forms of violence were all too familiar, as were those used by the law to counter them. What was new was a growing tendency to link them all to war and to see war as infecting society with them. Medieval society had been alive to the problem of re-absorbing disbanded troops but had seen it primarily in administrative terms. The sixteenth century learned to associate personal aggressiveness with war partly through the image

[11] *De rege*, orig. edn. Toledo 1599, trans. G. A. Moore (Washington, 1948), p. 113.
[12] *The new Cyneas*, orig. edn. Paris 1623, trans. T. W. Balch (Philadelphia, 1909), p. 20.
[13] *De jure belli ac pacis*, orig. edn. Paris 1625, trans. F. W. Kelsey et. al. (Oxford, 1913-27), ii, p. 20.

of the mercenary, a sexual swashbuckler, killing for cash and indifferent to the justice of any cause, an image created by artist-mercenaries like Urs Graf and Nicolas Manuel and given wide currency in woodcuts, stained glass, literature and song. It also made the association through a proliferation of writings about civil obedience which, in their discussion of the powers of magistrates and the duties of subjects, brought crime and war under one conceptual roof, as it were.

Both secular and clerical writers continued to stress the moral dangers that beset the man who joined an army, the temptations to gamble, drink, fornicate, blaspheme and forget God that awaited him there. But to this was now added the fear that he would become habituated to violence. "Can someone be even minutely sensitive about killing one person when mass murder is his profession"? asked Erasmus.[14] Prolonged exposure to war, said François de la Noue, himself an experienced soldier, made a man incapable of returning to the peace of a home and the tenderness of a family. Instead, he became conditioned to think that

> La guerre est ma patrie,
> Mon harnois ma maison;
> Et en toute saison
> Combattre, c'est ma vie.

And even if they did return, he continued, they brought the violence they had learned in the wars home with them.[15] One of Henri IV's motives for concluding the Peace of Vervins in 1598 was, as his ambassador explained in Venice, to try to bring to an end what he called "the inhumanity and cruelty which, after wars of so long duration, have passed into custom and become a habit".[16] And the danger was not merely that ex-soldiers might become criminals. They might also become rebels. "In Flanders and France", Botero pointed out, "long wars have so accustomed the people to warfare and bloodshed that when peace had been made with their enemies they turned their weapons against their own country".[17] Pierre de la Primaudaye agreed that "the Frenchmen, who were inferior to no nation whatsoever in courtesy and humanity, are greatly changed

---

[14] *The complaint of peace*, orig. edn. Basel 1517, in *The essential Erasmus*, ed. J. P. Dolan (Mentor Books, N.Y., 1964), p. 198.

[15] "War is my country, my armour my home; all the year round I live but to fight": *Discours politiques et militaires*, orig. edn. Basel 1587, ed. F. E. Sutcliffe (Paris, 1967), p. 211.

[16] See Albert Desjardins, *Les sentiments moraux au XVIe siècle* (Paris, 1887), p. 291.

[17] *The reason of state*, orig. edn. Venice 1589, trans. P. J. and D. P. Waley (London, 1956), p. 171.

from their natural disposition and become savage since the civil wars began", but he also ran through the degrees of violence the other way, pointing to individual "quarrels and dissentions amongst men, from whence seditions and private murders proceed, and in the end civil and open wars".[18]

This conning of the whole spectrum of violence started off so many explanations, from Thomas More's essay in sociological criminology[19] to the numerous explanations of sedition and revolt on class and economic lines, that the theological explanation of war itself was weakened by analogy. But it is a mark of the times — and important to note in a survey of printed sources, necessarily reflecting the views of an educated minority — that the most thoughtfully discussed of all forms of violence, apart from war itself, was not common assault, or rape or conspiracy or even rebellion, but the duel.[20] The custom grew to such an extent throughout the sixteenth century that towards its end a writer could say that most of the discord among men arose from questions concerning honour. Francis Bacon spoke for legal-minded England when he looked back in 1614 on a practice which he saw as "a kind of satanical illusion and apparition of honour; against religion, against law, against moral virtue ... as if there were two laws, one a kind of gown-law, and the other a law of reputation".[21]

The debate pro and con the duel, and the literature of honour as a whole, faced the problem of human aggressiveness with a combination of highmindedness and slyness. It expressed the dilemma of a class that needed firm central government for protection and occupation but had not yet been emotionally integrated into it, that was threatened economically and therefore socially, that was coming to share, both for profit and intellectual delight, the educational norms of the progressive bourgeoisie and sought means for differentiating its status from theirs. Defenders of the duel rummaged for justification among anti-pacifist arguments and attempted to apply the arguments for just causes of war — ignoring the fact that both the church and the civil courts were open to those who believed themselves to have been dishonoured. It pulled down the often quoted remark of Demosthenes, that "an honourable war is ever to be

---

[18] *The French academie*, orig. edn. Paris 1577, trans. T. B[owes], Richard Dolman and W. P. (London, 1618), pp. 308 and 285.

[19] *Utopia*, orig. edn. 1516, book i.

[20] Apart from Bryson's work cited in n. 10, see also his *The Point of Honor in Sixteenth Century Italy* (Chicago, 1935) and Fredson T. Bowers, *Elizabethan Revenge Tragedy* (Princeton, 1940).

[21] Quoted Ruth Kelso, *The Doctrine of the English Gentleman in the Sixteenth Century* (Urbana, 1929), p. 102.

preferred to a disgraceful peace", to its own intra-personal level. Not all writers on honour approved of the duel. We do not know who read which specific works. But the implication of this literature was that somewhere, beyond a law suited only to saints, and laws invented to suit the problems set by majorities, there was an ideal, a really true law that existed for the man who saw himself as exceptional. This was a law that would permit him to give rein to his aggressiveness but at the same time protect him from its full consequences by a ritualization of the preliminaries to and the actual forms of combat — the result of a punctilio sufficiently ridiculed by Shakespeare. It was the law of a class which protected its exclusiveness while conserving its numbers, and which offered only one justification in the public interest: that it was better for revenge that might set families and clans at one another's throats to be settled by their representatives.

By taking the individual's latent aggressiveness for granted and justifying its controlled release in defiance of society's search for order, the duel stimulated attempts to explain the causes of violence in the individual. The common medical explanation was that "savagery comes ... from a lack of proportion in the mixing of humours"[22] due primarily to celestial influences and that it was susceptible to correction by drugs, regimen and charms. That there was a link between physiology and behaviour was widely taken for granted. Moralists spoke of the physiological basis of passion — was "anger" seated in the heart, or the liver, or somewhere between the two?[23] Acceptance that the mind influenced the body led to psychologically valid explanations of, for instance, male impotence.[24] But medical psychology was gravely inhibited by the doctrine of the witch hunters that abnormal behaviour was due solely to the working, welcomed or involuntary, of the devil. The insight that comes from treatment was banned by theology, and one of the saddest aspects of the sixteenth century was its lack of sympathy for the mentally ill.[25]

Non-medical psychology continued among philosophers who discussed the working of the mind in terms of cognition, memory and perception. The shift from analysing human motivation in terms of a balance of virtues and vices to investigating the working of qualities

---

[22] Jean Bodin, *Method for the easy comprehension of history*, orig. edn. Paris 1566, trans. Beatrice Reynolds (New York, 1966), p. 102.

[23] See Anthony Levi, *French Moralists. The Theory of the Passions, 1585-1649* (Oxford, 1964).

[24] E.g. Montaigne, *Essays*, bk. i, ch. 20, "of the force of imagination". Quotations that follow are from the London, 1908 edn. in 2 vols. of the Florio translation. The essays cited date from the 1570s.

[25] Gregory Zilboorg, *A History of Medical Psychology* (New York, 1941), ch. 6.

like ambition, greed and fear enabled biographical case studies to enhance the objective study of human behaviour. Educationalists endeavoured to give "no precept unaccompanied by some remarkable examples",[26] even if the examples were commonly drawn from Plutarch's *Lives*. Historians stressed the dependence of events on human drives. The century that produced Guicciardini's portrait of Pope Clement VII and Shakespeare's of Iago was certainly not psychologically naïve in the description of behaviour or the explanation of it in the light of the individual's life experience. Explanation stopped short of actually connecting a specific experience that led to vengefulness or lust for conquest to the nature of the emotional processes themselves, yet within that explanation there was a psychological theory, and a theory couched in terms of conflict. More alluded to the conservative view of it when he described a game "rather like chess" played by the Utopians: "a pitched battle between virtues and vices, which illustrates most ingeniously how vices tend to conflict with one another, but to combine against virtues".[27] At about the same time, Erasmus expressed the more advanced view, "I failed", says Peace, "to discover even one who did not fight within himself. Reason wars with inclinations; inclination struggles with inclination; piety goes one way, cupidity another; lust desires one thing, anger another; ambition wants this, covertousness that".[28] All psychological theory took interior strife for granted, whether it was couched in terms of good *versus* evil, reason *versus* appetite, or animus *versus* anima.[29] All but the most theologically orthodox accepted that no single element should or could be banished and told the individual that personal happiness and sound social behaviour depended on the "well ordering and composing of thy mind". Compose the conflict in the mind and there would be no more war: thus Erasmus and Postel. A map of the mind; an analysis of the passions; a meticulous portraiture of behaviour: these elements of a psychological explanation of violence co-existed without fusing.

The passion most frequently analysed with reference to violence was anger. There was a large measure of agreement about its nature: imagination sensed a potential injury to self-respect or self-interest, the blood began to heat up in the heart and when some of this heated blood ascended to the brain violent behaviour followed unless the individual was on his guard. There was less agreement

[26] C. B. Watson, *op. cit.*, p. 61.
[27] *Utopia*, trans. Paul Turner (London, 1965), p. 76.
[28] *Op. cit.*, p. 182.
[29] W. J. Bouwsma, *Concordia Mundi: the Career and Thought of Guillaume Postel, 1510-1581* (Cambridge, Mass., 1957), pp. 111-12 and 115.

about the value of anger, those who followed Aristotle seeing it — if suitably restrained — as a phenomenon "which serveth for a prick to provoke and stir up fortitude and genorosity", those who followed the Stoic line of thought claiming that "virtue never proceeded by vice".[30]

The chief classical stimulus to the discussion of anger was Seneca's *De Ira*, which listed all its evil consequences, from murder to war, and which dealt with one of the most perturbing elements in any discussion of the passions: the connection between instinct in animals and behaviour in man. He admitted that certain initial reactions in men were involuntary, yawning, for instance, flinching from danger, blinking when startled. But then reason intervened. Animals flare up in what looks like anger, but it is unpremeditated, its cause not understood, it is quickly over and leaves no aftermath in the mind. Lacking reason "brute beasts ... know no more to be angry than how to pardon".[31] This refusal to see the human organism in terms of an inherited animal nature was strengthened by Christian theology. The doctrine of salvation required that man, though he appeared later than the animals, should be thought of as different in kind and in no sense an evolution from them. Yet through bestiary lore and the use of symbols, some sort of kinship of behaviour had been established. Animals provided lessons in fidelity, charity, industry or chastity to man because they experienced impulses similar to his. The rabbit, the bee, the ermine, the elephant stood for qualities man had been encouraged by the discipline of confession to recognize in himself. In addition to the near-man, or wild man, the mermaid and the dog-headed man of the Middle Ages, the sixteenth century inherited, and dwelt on with increasing delight, the satyr, the faun and the centaur. The centaur, from Machiavelli onwards, became indeed a familiar symbol of statesmanship, half beast, half man "as if to show", Baltasar Ayala noted, "that a good prince ought not only to be endowed with wisdom and judgement and other mental gifts, but also to be trained to feats of strength and arms".[32] But these hybrids, like the sluggard-reproaching ant, preached a moral, not a biological lesson. Belief in the separate creation of man, reinforced by a terrified fascination with monstrous births that confused man with animal, led to a steady reiteration of

---

[30] La Primaudaye, *op. cit.*, pp. 496 seq.
[31] *The workes of L. A. Seneca both morall a. naturall*, trans. T. Lodge (London, 1614), p. 513.
[32] *De iure et officiis bellicis et disciplina militari*, orig. edn. Douai 1582, trans. J. P. Bate, ed. John Westlake (Washington, 1912), p. 7.

the qualities that distinguished man from brute: an urge towards the social life, "the faculty of knowing and acting in accordance with general principles",[33] the power of foresight, intelligence and reason. Montaigne, indeed, with his usual patient lack of prejudice or, rather, with his prejudice against prejudice, deduced the operation of reason, foresight and logic in what he saw and read about animal behaviour and concluded by asking "wherefore do we attribute the works [of animals], which excel whatever we can perform, either by nature or by art, unto a kind of unknown, natural [innate] and servile inclination"?[34] But he was not led by this parallel to see man as necessarily sharing the aggressiveness of animals because of his similar biological make-up.

In discussions of violence the ferocity of beasts was emphasized in order to criticize man for perverting it, not inheriting it. Animals, it was repeated over and over again, do not indulge in intra-specific slaughter. When they kill it is for food, or in the defence of territory or of their young. Only man is greedy beyond his day-to-day needs, only man covets more land than he requires for survival, only man chooses to make a career of fighting, "a tragic and servile life ... which is so austere and rigorous that the brute beasts hold it in horror".[35] Denying any parallel with animals, let alone any inheritance from them, Gentili concluded that

> if man's desires are boundless and there is not sufficient glory and power to satisfy them, that is not a law of nature but a defect.... Men are not the foes of one another by nature. But our acts and our customs, whether these be like or unlike, cause harmony or discord among us.[36]

Only through being nursed on animal milk was there any chance of man containing an animal nature.[37] He was potentially better, he was often worse, but he was entirely different from the beasts.

The hunting of animals (defended chiefly because it provided a training in the qualities needed in war) had produced a literature which discussed the breeding of horses, dogs and birds of prey. There was some discussion of eugenics on parallel lines: marriage partners should be chosen with an eye to eliminating inherited physical defects, and it was also noted that "men have vices" —

---

[33] Grotius, *op. cit.*, p. 12.
[34] "An apologie of Raymond Sebond", bk. ii, ch. 12, p. 177.
[35] Pierre Boaistuau, *Le théatre du Monde* (Paris, 1572), f. 38-9, quoted F. E. Sutcliffe, *Le réalisme de Charles Sorel* (Paris, 1965), p. 117.
[36] *Op. cit.*, p. 54. Antonio Brucioli had argued that man's inherent peaceableness was part of God's plan to force him to develop the power of reason: *Dialogi* (Venice, 1526), sig. iiii^r.
[37] E.g. *The Civile Conversation of M. Steeven Guazzo,* orig. edn. Brescia 1574, trans. G. Pettie and B. Young (London, 1925), ii, p. 47.

including cruelty and a tendency to violence — "because they come of poor stock". Attention should be paid, therefore, to character as well as physique and age, and, "besides, who ever sought the advice of the doctors with respect to the season and hour of mating, which is so important"?[38] But neither eugenics nor the common belief that a mother's imagination could imprint an embryo with the impression made on her by some shocking experience led to any serious attempt to explain aggressiveness in terms of inheritance or embryology. All the same, the irritant that nagged many writers towards generalization was doubt about what did determine the predispositions of the human organism at birth. "Man's debased nature"; "natural disposition, or habit converted into nature"; "the natural disposition of men": such phrases haunt the inquiry into conflict. No matter how much new information turned up, the origin of the tendency towards good or bad, peaceableness or violence, remained a void. On one side lay the already socialized human being. On the other lay — original sin? Hereditary degradation from a Golden Age? Was violence determined or conditioned? Was war an inheritance or an invention, and if the latter, who invented it? A particular man, as Polydore Virgil suggested; the devil, as Richard Pace believed; or values evolved by society, as Vives thought?[39] In this nature *versus* nurture controversy, we move among the emotional and spiritual flashpoints of the century. Those who conducted it were either self-educators or the would-be educators of others; so they wanted to say: *nurture*. But they were Christians by conditioning if not by belief; so they also wanted to say: *nature*. Behind "nature" lay the idea of a God-given natural law, but this was itself a concept challenged by what the sixteenth century was discovering about the variety of human behaviour. The observation of simple societies could not solve this problem though, as we shall see, it could strengthen preconceived ideas; and in spite of some intermittent interest in young infants (the mother's breast as against that of a wet-nurse, for instance), the lack of interest in childhood as a separate stage in identity worthy of specific study was another barrier. Infancy was used as an image, an analogy to a stage in the development of society or of the arts, but it did not lead to anything resembling child psychology or the study of the aggressions of childhood.

Doctrinally safer and in any case more congenial than the study of

[38] Mariana, *op. cit.*, p. 185.
[39] For Polydore, see *An abridgement ... conteygnyng the devisers and first finders out aswell of artes ... as of rites & ceremonies ...* , orig. edn. Venice 1499 (London, 1546), sig. xlviii^v. For Pace and Vives, see Adams, *op. cit.*, pp. 177 and 289-91.

what a child brought with him into the world was the study of where he was born in terms of physical and social geography. Habits, laws, institutions:

> About these [wrote Bodin] no generalizations can be made, because they vary infinitely and change within a brief period through natural growth or at the will of a prince. Since that is so, let us seek characteristics drawn, not from the institutions of men, but from nature, which are stable and are never changed unless by great force or long training, and even if they have altered, nevertheless they return to their pristine character.[40]

By "nature" here Bodin means site and climate. Launching himself from the passage in the *Politics* in which Aristotle discussed the influence of geography on political institutions, he showed that the overall character of a given people was determined by latitude, temperature, prevailing wind and exposure to or shelter from it, altitude and drainage. Botero agreed that the fiercest and boldest men are those from northern (but not circumpolar) regions, or from the mountainous districts of temperate zones, "whereas those of the south are thin and dry and more ready to evade than to oppose". This could be material for observations that were merely curious: "a Spaniard doubles his energy and his appetite when he goes into France, while a Frenchman in Spain becomes languid and dainty".[41] But essentially it was the stuff of universal history. This, Bodin asserted, was why

> the greatest empires always have spread southward — rarely from the south towards the north.... The French often suffered serious defeat at the hands of the English in France itself and almost lost their territory; they could never have penetrated into England had they not been invited by the inhabitants. The English, on the other hand, were frequently overwhelmed by the Scots.... Unless I err, this is what Ezekiel, Jeremiah, Isiah and the remaining prophets threaten so many times: wars from the north, soldiers, horsemen, and the coming downfall of empires.'[42]

Elsewhere he checked an otherwise headlong enthusiasm for this theme with the caution that "this compulsion is not of the order of necessity".[43] But it was a theme for which readers were well prepared.

> There is no help in it [observed one of the protagonists in Guazzo's *Civil Conversations*] but you must settle yourself ... to think that every nation, land and country, by the nature of the place, the climate of the heaven and the influence of the stars, hath certain virtues and certain vices which are proper,

---

[40] *Method, op. cit.*, opening of ch. 5.
[41] Botero, *op. cit.*, pp. 38, 147.
[42] *Op. cit.*, p. 93.
[43] *Six Books of the Commonwealth*, orig. edn. Paris 1576, ed. M. J. Tooley (Oxford, 1955), p. 157.

natural and perpetual, unto it. [As a result] there are ... people who by natural virtue are given to the industry and discipline of war.⁴⁴

This geographical determinism was attractive because it appeared to give added seriousness to the traditional attribution of overriding characteristics to men of different nations, but while these attributions were still commonly taken for granted as having acquired almost the status of folklore, they were increasingly criticized by those who preferred to see character in terms of nurture.

> The French are commonly called rash [wrote Hall] the Spaniard proud, the Dutch drunken, the English the busy-hands, the Italian effeminate, the Swethens timorous, the Bohemians inhuman, the Irish barbarous and superstitious. But is any man so sottish as to think that France hath no staid man at all in it, Spain no meacock or Germany none that lives soberly? They are fools (believe it) that will tie men's manners so firm unto the stars that they will leave nothing to a man's own power, nothing to the parents' natures, nothing to nurture and education.⁴⁵

Sir Thomas More had explained that senseless pursuits like gambling and hunting were, in the eyes of the Utopians, simply bad habits which appeared pleasurable because of "a subjective reaction",⁴⁶ and both Montaigne and Bodin pointed to customs overseas, like eating the dead or distorting the body for aesthetic purposes, which proved that "the influence of custom and training is so great ... that gradually they develop into *mores* and take on the force of nature".⁴⁷ And behind this line of thought was knowledge of the Pavlovian experiment of Lycurgus. As Mariana reminded his readers, he had taken two puppies,

> born of the same parents and at the same time. He accustomed one to the chase, the other to be fed with flour balls. Then he put them together and threw them some food. The latter eagerly went for it; the other ignored it because he was preoccupied with giving chase to a hare that had been liberated at the same time. In this way he showed the citizens how strong habit was if formed in childhood, and he taught that it generally was more powerful than nature.⁴⁸

A gentle education could not by itself shield a youth from growing up to be aggressive. Justice could also be responsible; "cruel laws and customs make men cruel".⁴⁹ Cruel occupations, like the slaughtering of animals, let alone military service, could develop aggressive tendencies. So could cruel pastimes. Doni banished the

---

⁴⁴ *Ed. cit.*, vol. i, p. 64. Military writers had long taken this for granted. Petrus de Montis, for instance, had given brief accounts of the suitability to warfare of the various peoples of Europe in terms of skill, courage and savagery in ... *artis militaris collectanea* ... (Milan, 1509), bk. I, *caps.* lxxxi-cviii.
⁴⁵ *Op. cit.*, pp. 10-11.
⁴⁶ *Ed. cit.*, p. 95.
⁴⁷ Bodin, *Method, op. cit.*, p. 146.
⁴⁸ *Op. cit.*, pp. 184-5.
⁴⁹ Botero, *op. cit.*, p. 85.

tournament from his ideal city for the reason also given by Botero that "men who constantly see wounds, blood and death in their diversions will necessarily become fierce, cruel and sanguinary, and fighting, murder and other disturbances will more readily occur in their city".[50] It was also widely believed that just as reading erotic literature and looking at suggestive paintings tempted men to fornicate, so tales of glorious bloodshed tempted them to war. The Utopian genre as a whole, with its ideal cities and states, was largely stimulated by the desire to portray an environment, a form of nurture, which would discourage violence; it expressed a strong belief in the ability of a culture to determine character. Thus for Campanella, as for More, greed and ambition would be neutered if private property were abolished. Others would to all intents and purposes dismantle the formal structure that produced social and political tensions. Yet others, seeing the family as the original source of tension and violence, would have children reared communally, and allow free love.[51]

Utopianism looked above all to cultural and sociological explanations of violence and paid particular attention to conflicts arising from class jealousy and the allocation of political privilege and power. This tendency was encouraged by the century's preoccupation with sedition. Among the causes of revolt, La Primaudaye encyclopaedized, was "the natural disposition of places where men are born, which maketh them more inclined to commotions and seditions", but this genuflection to geographical determinism came at the end of a string of other explanations: the thwarting of legitimate political ambition; the insolence of superiors; too great an imbalance between classes, "extreme poverty and excess of wealth".[52] The means of allaying the violence that arose from class conflict had preoccupied Machiavelli and Seyssel (who had clearly stated the safety-valve theory of social mobility)[53] at the beginning of the century, and Utopian writers clearly learned much from the formal political theorist's growing concern with sedition, while enriching that concern through their own interest in cradle to grave acculturalization. They

---

[50] See Paul F. Grendler, *Critics of the Italian World, 1530-1560: Anton Francesco Doni, Nicolò Franco and Ortensio Lando* (U. of Wisconsin, 1969), p. 490.

[51] See, e.g., Francesco Patrizi, *La città felice* (orig. edn. Venice 1553) and A. F. Doni, *Il mondo savio e pazzo* (orig. edn. Venice, 1552), both in Bruno Widmar (ed.), *Scrittori politici del '500 e '600* (Milan, 1964) which also contains Campanella's *La città del sole*.

[52] *Op. cit.*, p. 293. For a similar list, see Frederick Carney, trans. '*The politics*' *of Johannes Althusius* (London, 1965) 176-7; orig. edn. Herborn, 1603.

[53] *La monarchie de France*, composed 1515, ed. J. Poujol (Paris, 1961), p. 41.

were chiefly preoccupied with domestic violence, but it is at least tempting to see an impulse to think in wide sociological terms that arose from war itself. Preoccupation with the morale as well as the skill of the soldier had grown in *quattrocento* Italy, chiefly as the result of comparing native with mercenary troops. In the sixteenth century the theme was developed throughout western Europe into a topic which, had it been collected from the sources among which it was scattered, would be considered even today a by no means negligible contribution to the social psychology of the soldier. The individual's morale was considered in the light of his home background, his attachment to his family, his pay, diet, sickness provision and pension, his sex life (should there be or should there not be prostitutes with the army?), his technical training, his political indoctrination, his religious feelings, his degree of education (too much as bad as too little) and his relationships to his officers and to his fellows. This was a range of inquiry applied to no other occupation group in the century, whether courtier, cardinal or prince.

Up to now we have been dealing with explanations of personal or group violence. Unlike assault and revolt, war was constantly argued about, justified or abused, but seldom examined with a view to explaining it as a phenomenon (individual wars were of course explained in terms of immediate political, religious or economic threats or grievances). Armed robbery in the streets, riot in the market square, insurrection against the rich or the powerful: these were the most immediate issues, and the urge to explain war was to some extent neutered by the conviction that it was the only solution to them.

However explained, violence existed, in the individual and in society. Lottini's suggestion that all excessively violent men should be banished was clearly out of the question.[54] The problem was how to divert them, how to provide a "moral equivalent", as William James was to put it. Bodin saw litigation as one harmless channel for violence. Hunting, the tournament, police work against brigands were advocated as substitutes. Thomas Nashe even saw the theatre as playing a therapeutic rôle.

> There is a certain waste of the people for whom there is no use but war ... if the affairs of the state be such as cannot exhale all these corrupt excrements, it is very expedient they have some light toys to busy their heads withal, cast before them as bones to gnaw upon ... [Plays] show the ill success of treason, the fall of hasty climbers, the wretched end of usurpers, the misery of civil dissention, and how just God is evermore in punishing of murder.[55]

[54] *Avvertimenti civili*, orig. edn. Florence, 1574, in Widmar, *op. cit.*, p. 601.
[55] *Pierce Penilesse his supplication to the divill*, orig. edn. London 1592, in *Works*, ed. R. B. McKerrow (Oxford, 1958), i, p. 213.

But commonly the solution to the problem of domestic violence was seen in war, the "foul refiner of the state", as the poet Daniel put it. A warlike people, Machiavelli's adversary Innocent Gentillet pointed out, "must be employed in that wherein is their natural disposition, or else they will move war against themselves".[56]

The psychology of mobilization was well expressed by Botero.

> Military enterprises are the most effective means of keeping a people occupied, for nothing arouses their interest so much as an important war.... Everyone who is able is ready to play his part either in council or in action, and all discontent is vented on the common enemy. The rest of the people either follow the camp to bring supplies and to perform similar necessary services, or remain at home to offer prayers and vows to God for ultimate victory, or at least are so stirred by expectation and by news of the progress of the war that there is no place for thoughts of revolt in their minds: either in thought or deed everyone is preoccupied by the war.[57]

Machiavelli, Gasparo Contarini,[58] Mariana and Bodin were among those who recommended war against a foreign enemy as a bloodletting of violent humours in the body politic. "There are divers nowadays", noted Montaigne, "which will speak thus, wishing this violent and burning emotion we see and feel amongst us might be derived [diverted] to some neighbour war".[59] And there were rulers who agreed with the theorists. Henri II justified the war of 1551 partly on these grounds; Coligny used them in urging war against Spain; the Venetian ambassador Giovan Michiel reported in 1575 that Henri III's entourage were talking about the need for a foreign war to divert peasants who had been trained to wars, from pillage and possible revolt.[60]

A less "foul" refiner of individual nations was the diversion of internal violence against the Turk. Erasmus, the Spanish poet Juan de Mena[61] and the Frenchman Guillaume Postel were among those who saw a crusade as the solution, and the peace plans of Emeric Crucé and Sully were to consider this form of diversion as the only

---

[56] *A discourse upon the meanes of wel governing ... against Nicholas Machiavel the Florentine,* orig. edn. n.p. 1577, trans. Simon Patericke (London, 1608), p. 152.

[57] *Op. cit.,* pp. 76-7.

[58] See Myron Gilmore, "Myth and reality in the Venetian state", in *Venetian Studies,* ed. J. R. Hale (London, 1972).

[59] "Of bad meanes emploied to a good end", bk. ii, ch. 23, pp. 511-12.

[60] See Dejardins, *op. cit.,* p. 308. It is not surprising that the authors of military books stressed the need to divert the potentially violent elements in a country into foreign wars "so that they will not be the cause of sedition or revolt there": Michel d'Amboise, *Le guidon des gens de guerre,* orig. edn. Paris 1543 (reprint, Paris, c. 1880), p. 104. Again, "idle men corrupt a populace as polluted places corrupt the air; the idleness of peace leads to sedition": Girolamo Garimberto, *Il capitano generale* (Venice, 1556), p. 80.

[61] Quoted Eugène Baret, *De L'Amadis de Gaule et de son influence ...* (Paris, 1853), p. 75.

guarantee for tranquillity in Europe. And not necessarily a formal war: "it is an excellent plan", wrote Botero, "to keep a fleet of galleys, so that those who are of a restless disposition can find an outlet for their youth and courage in fighting the true enemies".[62] To the same end de la Noue recommended enrolment with the Knights of Malta.

Explanations of war were further inhibited by the realistic (as opposed to the Utopian) strain in political thought. The origin of society itself in violence was increasingly taken for granted, as was the repressive rôle of government, "that rod of Circe's which tameth both men and beasts that are touched therewith".[63] Wider historical views revealed the character thrust upon states by their adjustment to conquests and defeats. It was assumed that princes needed to be skilled as war leaders and that all states had to be prepared to fight for survival because of jealous neighbours and, more loosely, because of a continuing belief in cycles, either fatalistic (peace was simply too good to last) or moralizing (peace brought luxurious degeneracy which had to be expiated and purged by war). Economic was subordinated to political rivalry as a cause of war. Such demographic thinking as there was, was primarily concerned with problems of taxation and productivity, but the association of crime with poverty was a further impulse to discuss population figures. In the main, however, war only entered the demographic picture as a convenient dumping ground for rogues, vagabonds and others who threatened law and order or the standard of living. "War is necessary so that youth can leave and the population diminish", warned Ulrich von Hutten in 1518, and twenty years later Sebastian Franck complained that "if war and death do not come to our aid it will be necessary to leave our country and wander abroad like the gypsies".[64]

While welcoming, this argument did not try to explain war. Indeed, the assumption that social and economic causes set maxima to population figures, the vagueness about what these figures actually were, and the realization that unemployment was due to changing agricultural practices and displacement to towns rather than to any notable overall increase, discouraged any attempt to see war in terms of population pressure. Thanks to peaceful migration and to a lack of concern for poverty unless it threatened revolt, no European nation thought in terms of a desire for *Lebensraum* as a cause of war,

---

[62] *Op. cit.*, pp. 172-3.
[63] Justus Lipsius, *Six bookes of politickes* ... orig. edn. Leiden 1589, trans. William Jones (London, 1594), p. 17.
[64] Both quoted Bouthoul, *op. cit.*, pp. 278-9.

expecially as world maps showed so many spaces empty of all but "ethnicks".

What, then, was to be learned about the causes of violence from observing the peoples revealed by the great wave of discoveries and re-discoveries in the sixteenth century? Partly because Africans were long-familiar figures in the slave ports of southern Europe, partly because few Europeans actually settled overseas, and partly, again, because of the government's policy of secrecy, little fresh information got into circulation as a result of the Portuguese exploration of the West African coast during the fifteenth century. But almost as soon as contact was made with the Americas a steady stream of information about the peoples discovered there, first by the Spaniards and then by the Portuguese, French and English, began to find its way into encyclopaedias of customs, the works of cosmographers, and the writings of political theorists and moralists. Early in the century Peter Martyr's *De orbe novo* provided a model for reporting on American cultures in some depth. In the second half of the century, the Jesuit newsletters began to fill out the background to earlier travellers' accounts of the peoples who inhabited the land masses and islands of the Far East. There was thus an abundance of anthropological and ethnological material and traces, at least, of modern approaches to it. Thus José de Acosta proposed a classification of non-European peoples. First, those who have the knowledge and use of letters and hence possess a high degree of civility, like the Chinese and Japanese; second, those who lack writing but have an organized government and religion and live in stable settlements, like the Mexicans and Peruvians; and third, those whom he classified as savages, like the Caribs and the Brazilians. Within the third class he made a distinction between savages like wild beasts who have no sort of organization, and somewhat superior ones who have the rudiments of political organization and are more peaceably inclined.[65] Again, Louis LeRoy distinguished between the vertical (social heritage) and horizontal diffusion of customs.[66] More significantly still, Montaigne, commenting on the Canadian Indians encountered by the French, sounded the point of view that was to become fundamental to the study of "primitive" peoples: "I find, as far as I have been informed, that there is nothing in that nation that is either barbarous or savage, unless men call that barbarism which is not common to them".[67]

[65] See John H. Rowe, "Ethnography and Ethnology in the Sixteenth Century", *Kroeber Anthropological Soc. Papers* (1964), p. 8.
[66] See J. W. Bennett, *American Anthropologist*, lxviii (1966), p. 218.
[67] "Of the caniballes", bk. i, ch. 30, p. 257.

Accurate observation, however, especially in the Americas, was hampered by a frame of mind in which voyagers, from Columbus to Raleigh, "saw" or at least said they heard about the marvels and monsters they were conditioned to expect from their reading of Pliny, Solinus and Mandeville. Accurate observation was hampered, too, by the vision of a simple, peaceful society, redolent of the Golden Age, which men carried as a mental prophylactic against brooding overmuch on the violence in their own society. There was a tendency for observers to see, and writers at home to interpret the cultures in Acosta's third category as lacking the laws and institutions that complicated the attempt to live peacefully and virtuously in Europe. Vespucci reported on the Tupinamba in Golden Age terms while a century later Ludovico Zuccolo couched his panegyric on his native country, San Marino, in terms of a life so simple that there was no strife between classes, banditry, or wars of aggression because this mountain eyrie had not been corrupted by princes and bankers and sellers of luxuries, nor had its health been invaded by doctors.[68] Bodin, tough-minded as always, tried to destroy the myth by historicizing the Golden Age and its successor, concluding his sombre picture:

> these were the golden and silver ages, in which men were scattered like beasts in the fields and the woods and had as much as they could keep by means of force and crime, until gradually they were reclaimed from that ferocity and barbarity to the refinement of customs and the law-abiding society which we see about us.[69]

He wrote, however, at a fortunate moment. For most of the century men could not see a law-abiding society about them, and fed by painting, the masque, and the pastoral *genre* in literature, men continued to look to ethnological evidence for reassurance that a peaceable kingdom was attainable, even if not for themselves.

Besides this nostalgic appetite, information about non-European societies was sought for many other reasons. For a scholar, like Henri Estienne, news from the New World was important to his attempt to reinstate the veracity of Herodotus — if such strange customs obtain over there, why should we scoff at the strangest of Herodotus's anecdotes?[70] After the multiple backslidings among those baptized during the first wave of missionary activity in Africa and the Americas, the religious orders, especially the Dominicans and the Jesuits, recognized that it was only practical to learn the languages, understand the reasoning behind the institutions, and try to grasp the

---

[68] *La città felice*, in Widmar, *op. cit.*, pp. 848-9; orig. edn. Venice 1625.
[69] *Method*, *op. cit.*, p. 298.
[70] *Apologie pour Hérodote* (Geneva, 1566).

existing supernatural beliefs of the men they wished to convert. For the moralist, as Guillaume du Bellay put it, "one of the chief means of acquiring prudence [in the sense of *prudentia*, a reasonable philosophy of life] is not merely to learn about the customs, manners and traits of all peoples but to concentrate on the actions of virtuous men in order to imitate them and of vicious ones in order to avoid and flee them".[71] For Guillaume Postel, such information was an essential preliminary to the realization of his vision of a world without war, "since it is impossible, because of the diversity of customs, languages, opinions and religions, that men should unite together in one community until they first come to know each other".[72]

But, once more, anthropological and ethnological information did not lead to any really important insights into the causes of personal aggressiveness or of war. More attention was paid to marriage and funeral customs, religious beliefs, diet and clothing.[73] Contrasts between "ethnick" and European behaviour were used rather as the middle ages had used comparisons between men and animals: if beasts could be patient, faithful or industrious, then it was shameful for man, with the advantages of reason and a soul, not to surpass them. Similarly the virtuous savage was held up as a reproach to the vices of civilized man. But certain conclusions were reached, particularly with regard to the Americas. The simpler a society appeared to be, the less crime it produced and its wars were fought either in self-defence or to exercise and prove the valour of the individual. Trickery — the sleights and stratagems that so fascinated European writers on military affairs — was not resorted to. Summing up the information available to him, Montaigne concluded that "their wars are noble and generous and have as much excuse and beauty as this human infirmity can admit; they aim at nought so much, and have no other foundation amongst them, but the mere jealousy of virtue".[74] Challenged by increasing knowledge, the belief that man can live without violence — a view which at first appeared to have some colour from Columbus's account of the Tainos and Vespucci's of the Tupinamba — gave way to the view that society can at least restrict the violent potential in human nature to tests of virility with limited repercussions on society at large.

In general, then, men found no new explanation of violence in the

[71] See Pierre Villey, *Les sources de l'Evolution des Essais de Montaigne* (Paris, 1908), ii, p. 190. The quotation dates from 1548.
[72] Bouwsma, *op. cit.*, p. 130.
[73] See in general Margaret T. Hodgen, *Early Anthropology in the Sixteenth and Seventeenth Centuries* (Philadelphia, 1964).
[74] "Of the caniballes", bk. i, ch. 30, p. 264.

New World, and information from the Americas served chiefly to reinforce the view that human nature was such that the more complex a society became the more opportunities for violent behaviour it offered. The more closely men looked at war the more it seemed that "in accordance with a general decree" it was inevitable. Even Erasmus conceded that it might be, in certain otherwise ideal circumstances, impossible to avoid. Even More's Utopians were prepared to fight not only in self-defence but to succour allies and to take over lands which others did not appear to be putting to productive use. The theological argument that war was an instrument for punishing sin which God had perforce to place now in the hand of one ruler now of another retained its appeal, but the search for secular explanations of personal and group violence and the notion that there was a link between individual aggressiveness and war: these deepening preoccupations set on foot the enduring search for a secular explanation of international violence as well.

13

WAR AND PUBLIC OPINION IN RENAISSANCE ITALY

Quatro nouanta quatro cento e mille
De l'anno che dio prese carne, essendo
Tutte le parte del mondo tranquille,
Le creature in gran pace viuendo,
Marte con turbulente suo fauille
Poner le volse insanguinoso mendo,
Mettendo in cuore a vn tramontan signore
De l'uniuerso farsi Imperatore.[1]

Contemporaries would not have been surprised by the significance with which the year 1494 was invested by later historians. Within a generation it was seen as marking the end of one period and the beginning of another. Before it lay a time of quiet prosperity, after it came an age of battle and disaster. As it became increasingly clear that the barbarians had come to stay, the contrast was painted in heightened colours; rueful self-criticism darkening the present, while nostalgia lightened the past. Before: a time of splendour and renown; after: an age in which Italian claims to prolong the glories of the Roman past had become a mockery. Of all these contrasts the most obvious was between a period of peace and one of war or, at least, between a period of mild wars that did little more than trace patterns on the surface of the waters of Italian civilization, and one of savage wars that raised great waves and littered the shores with wreckage. The fact that this

---

[1] *Guerre horrende d'Italia* . . . (Venice), 1535, canto 1, verse 2, punctuated, abbreviations resolved.

contrast did not involve the arts, which continued to flourish, was no consolation: the historians, the political theorists and the moralists who recorded this sad division took little interest in them. The fame of Italy, for them, was bound up with her independence: a freedom from foreign meddling that allowed the states of the peninsula to pursue private advantage to the common good. The arts, it is true, gilded the links binding New Rome to Old Rome, but the links themselves were independence and reputation, and the defeats that followed 1494 came near to breaking them.

In contrasting the periods that preceded 1494 and followed it there was much exaggeration. For Guicciardini, the youthful historian of Florence, Lorenzo de' Medici was a tricksy tyrant; the same historian, writing about Italy as a whole a generation of disappointments later, hailed him as the genius who had presided over the peninsula's golden age. Machiavelli deepened the contrast between the bloody wars of the *Cinquecento* and those which preceded it by making the latter seem such holiday flourishes that the blood he staunched in the military history of the *Quattrocento* has only been set flowing again in the present century.[1] The change that came over the nature of warfare after 1494 was overstressed by Machiavelli in the interest of proving a thesis about the relative merits of militiamen to *condottieri*, as it was by Guicciardini in the interest of turning the knife in the wound to Italy's self-esteem, but a change there certainly was, and it was greeted with widespread horror. This horror, however, was not directed against large-scale war as such, as opposed to earlier small-scale wars, nor even against a long period of such wars; nor was it directed to any important extent against the changed nature of war—more bloody, more total, more expensive. It was caused by the evidence provided by these wars of a failure of morale, a failure of the Italian character to meet their challenge.

Why were Italian armies beaten by barbarian ones? When every excuse on the score of technical inferiority, lack of training and divided command had been made the conclusion still remained:

[1] Notably by W. Block in his *Die Condottieri* (Berlin, 1913).

the Italian soldier was inferior to his rival. What had made him inferior, and what could be done to improve him? These questions could not be answered in straightforward military terms. A good soldier is the product of his whole environment, not just of a military academy. The failure of the Italian soldiers in war was due, it was felt, to their corrupt condition in peace. Faulty constitutions had not provided the setting needed for the development of responsible citizens capable of defending themselves. The practical problems—how to provide good native troops—intensified concern with constitutional reform. Interest in the individual's behaviour not only at the polls but on the battlefield led to a new and urgent preoccupation with all the forces that could condition him to do his best there: political, economic and religious.

The extent to which an interest in military affairs influenced political thought is best exemplified by Machiavelli. His political ideas were dominated by a scorn of modern armies and an admiration for the constitutional framework that had supported the finest army of all, that of the Roman republic, and his main concern—the transformation of the bad citizen into the good soldier—directed every aspect of his thought about the state and the individual's place in it, just as his overriding interest in war and war-like crisis directed his thinking about international relations.

Before showing, however, that the horror which followed 1494 —or, more properly, Fornovo, in 1495, the first full battle of the Italian Wars—was due to a revelation of the poor state of Italian morale, it must be stressed, and in some detail, that this horror was not a reaction against war as such, nor, primarily, against the nature of the warfare waged by the French and Spanish and their Swiss and German allies.

Despite nostalgic regrets for the 'peaceful' *Quattrocento*,[1] it was

---

[1] For an extreme example see Paolo Giovio, *Historie del suo tempo*, trans. Lodovico Domenichi (Venice, 1555), p. 2r: 'Questo anno, che fu dal parto della Vergine mccccxciiii, apportò a tutto il mondo una lietissima pace, quale doppo Augusto non si ricordava alcuna età de gli antichi. Ma questa pace, che nel primo aspetto sicura, e fiorita, havea empiuto gli huomini di buona speranza di

accepted that wars were inevitable. The cyclical theories of Machiavelli (valour brings peace, peace idleness, idleness disorder, disorder ruin, ruin good order, good order valour, etc.) and of Luigi da Porto (peace brings riches, riches pride, pride wrath, wrath war, war poverty, poverty mildness, mildness peace, peace riches, etc.) took war as a matter of course, as a red splash on Fortune's turning wheel.[1] Some Italian rulers were professionally bound to accept the inevitability of wars, for their prosperity depended on an ability to supplement tax and toll with the fees of war. The gift of Pollaiuolo's helmet from the city of Florence to Federigo of Urbino was entirely suitable: the duke's arms were as necessary to him as they might be on occasion to some less military neighbour state.[2] Nor did the practice of the papacy imply that war was undesirable in itself. It was, again, appropriate that the Duke of Modena should celebrate the news of Pius II's election by holding military manœuvres.[3] The 'bloody armour' for the wearing of which Julius II was so roundly swinged by Erasmus was only one of the more sensational symbols of the popes' dependence on war to hold their own in the hurly-burly of international rivalries.[4] Pasquino was robed as Mars for his festival in

tranquilità al mondo, subito sparse per tutte le provincie una molto crudele e lunghissima guerra.'

And Giovio sounds, too, the note of humiliation. He writes of Fornovo: 'Questo è quel notabil fatto d'arme del Taro, dove con alquanto maggior temerità, che dapocaggine noi perdemmo l'antica riputatione della militia Italiana: e con nostra inescusabil vergogna incomminciammo à essere in disprezzo alle nationi straniere....' Ibid., p. 101v.

For Ammirato, writing a generation later, the 'peaceful quattrocento' had been worn down to the status of a cliché. The 26th book of his *Dell' Istorie Fiorentine* refers to the years that preceded 1494: 'Questa è quella pace tanto celebrata per le memorie de' nostri scrittori....' Guicciardini had written as early as 1509, in the *Storie Fiorentine*, of 'quegli tempi lieti che erano innanzi al 94'. 1859, p. 255.

[1] *Lettere Storiche di Luigi da Porto*, ed. Bressan (Firenze, 1857), pp. 26 and 46. Machiavelli, *Istorie Fiorentine*, beginning of fifth book.

[2] Millard Meiss, *Andrea Mantegna as Illuminator* (Hamburg, 1957), p. 1.

[3] *Commentaries*, trans. F. A. Gragg, *Smith College Studies in History*, xxii, nos. 1–2, p. 106 (book 1).

[4] In the *Julius Exclusus*.

May 1512 by the Bishop of Camerino, and bellicose and jingoistic verses were attached to him, calling all faithful Italians to help the pope expel the French with fire and sword.[1]

The ideal of princely state-craft—a nice knowledge of when to achieve restraint and when to apply force—expressed, too, an unquestioning acceptance of war. The bombshell *impresa* of Duke Alfonso of Ferrara with its motto *Loco et Tempore* implied that the Duke was prepared at the right juncture to allow restraint to explode into violence.[2] Leonardo's mechanical lion with its breast full of lilies was a graceful acknowledgement that Louis XII also possessed this necessary combination of restraint and potential violence.[3] Similarly Federigo da Montefeltro chose an *impresa* which balanced a sword against an olive branch,[4] and Machiavelli impressed upon rulers the need for combining the lion's qualities with those of the fox.

And all these antitheses were but extensions into the realm of politics of special aspects of the many-sidedness expected of the good man, a many-sidedness which expected the same hand to be able to wield both the pen and the sword. For Cicero and Quintilian, the ideal orator—conversant with all subjects, fired by all causes, understanding the feelings of men of all ranks and all occupations—needed to be *homo universalis*. This ideal of many-sidedness appealed to the Renaissance partly because authors could still exploit an otherwise outmoded encyclopaedism and canalize reflections on every human quality into a portrait of an ideal type whether cardinal, soldier or courtier; partly because

---

[1] D. Gnoli, in 'Storia di Pasquino', *Nuova Antologia* (1890), pp. 280–3, gives some extracts. My attention was drawn to the relevant pasquinades in the Vittorio Emanuele Library in Rome by Mr. David Chambers.

[2] Illustrated in Paolo Giovio, *Imprese* . . . (Lyone, 1574), p. 80, who says that he wore the *impresa* at the battle of Ravenna, 1512. A medal of -1505 with a bust of Alfonso shows him wearing a cuirass with a flaming bomb on the breast. It is illustrated (plate 60) in Edgar Wind, *Pagan Mysteries of the Renaissance*, 1958, where there is a general discussion of this concept.

[3] This point is made by Professor E. Wind in the *Journal of the Warburg and Courtauld Institutes* (1943), p. 222.

[4] Hill, op. cit., no. 304.

it dignified dilettantism; partly because it solved—or shelved—the dilemma of how to harmonize the active with the contemplative life. The most striking conjunction was that which showed the same man as successful both on the battlefield and in the study,[1] and as, outside the Republics, the patron class was also the warrior class, it was stressed by soldiers and intellectuals alike.

Castiglione lauded the conjunction and was praised for it himself. Da Porto required it of his heroes and was possibly the most appealing of all its exemplifiers. Pius II recorded with pride that his forebears were not only among the oldest and noblest families in Siena but also were illustrious both in arms and in letters. Each state described in his *Commentaries* is given due praise for its prowess in war, and in the lists of prominent citizens, soldiers are given a conspicuous place among the rest. The question, which is preferable: arms or letters? with the invariable answer: both must be combined, was, of course, one of those weary clichés which, like the mock battle staged for Lucrezia d'Este's marriage to Annibale Bentivoglio between Wisdom and Fortune, was bound to end in a draw.[2] In the princely states, where the profession of arms was taken for granted, it was commonly up to Letters to prove a place beside Arms.

> *Nè mi par che convenga a gentilezza* [said
>   Boiardo's Agricane]
> *Star tutto il giorno ne' libri a pensare;*
> *Ma la forza del corpo e la destrezza*
> *Conviense al cavalliero esercitare.*
> *Dottrina al prete ed al dottor sta bene:*
> *Io tanto saccio quanto mi conviene.*

---

[1] Federigo of Urbino was shown in the famous portrait by Justus of Ghent as reading in his study while clad in full armour, and his successor, Guid' Ubaldo, was described by Polydore Vergil as 'principi saeculo nostro latinae linguae simul et graecae, ac militaris disciplinae peritissimo'. *Anglica Historia*, ed. Denys Hay, Camden Series (1950), p. 140.

[2] C. M. Ady, *Morals and Manners of the Quattrocento*, Annual Italian Lecture of the British Academy, 1942, p. 17.

> *Rispose Orlando:*—*Io tiro teco a un segno,*
> *Che l'arme son de l'omo il primo onore;*
> *Ma non già che il saper faccia men degno,*
> *Anzi lo adorna come un prato il fiore.*[1]

In republics, on the other hand, especially in Florence (for in Venice young noblemen often served on galleys as 'bowmen of the quarterdeck') it took special crisis and special spleading to persuade the citizens out of their conviction that though arms were all very well in their place, that place was in the hands of others. When the Florentine militia was instituted in 1506, special provision was made for church parades in the course of which the citizen troops were to be harangued on the importance of combining arms with trade or study. In the greatest crisis of all, the siege of the Last Republic, the theme was stated and restated with the greatest urgency. The political need for self-defence was obvious: what was needed was to persuade the citizen to stop despising the trade of arms. *Questa è la virtù della disciplina militare,* said Pandolfini in the course of his harangue to the militia in 1528, *la quale supera tutte le altre scienzie et virtù.*[2] Luigi Alamanni spoke to them of the *glorioso et salutevole campo delle armi.*[3] Bartolommeo Cavalcanti, in the most stirring of these harangues, charged his audience of amateur soldiers to remember the feats of the citizen-soldier of Athens, of Sparta and of Rome, and to compensate for generations of debilitating refinement by reacquiring a military frame of mind. *Scacciamo da noi ogni molle pensiero, spogliamoci d'ogni effeminato habito; non le donnesche delicatezze, ma piu tosto la militare antica rozzezza a noi giudichiamo convenirsi.* And lest this picture should be too dismaying to the more fastidious of his auditors, he brought in the cult of many-sidedness by loading his picture of the ideal soldier with so many qualities—firmness, temperance, obedience, devoutness, and so on—that he became hardly distinguishable from the ideal man.[4]

---

[1] *Orlando Innamorato* lib. I, canto 18, 43-4.
[2] *Archivio Storico Italiano*, ser. i, vol. xv, 351.
[3] Ibid., p. 346.
[4] His harangue is printed in F. Sansovino, *Diverse Orationi* . . . (Venetia, 1561).

The difficulty of persuading civilians to become soldiers had no connection with their views about war as such. Broadly speaking, the rulers of states like Rimini, Urbino, Mantua and Ferrara favoured wars because they made money out of them, while republics were dubious because of the cost involved in hiring mercenaries. But it would be quite wrong to push this into a contrast between militarism and pacifism. Florence indulged in loud sabre-rattling by proxy whenever her trading interests were threatened, and her citizens, no less than the inhabitants of other Italian states, were familiar with ideas and sights and sounds that helped them take war for granted and did much, indeed, to glorify it.

Just as the martial scene was thought to be the most fitting theme for the epic,[1] so it was for the pageant. For the stage-managers of processions and spectacles military life had much to offer. Jousts and mock battles for the piazza, parades of horsemen, magnificently accoutred, for the streets. Piero de' Medici diverted his fellow-citizens' attention from failure in real war by staging a mock battle and a mock siege so splendid that it would be difficult, Machiavelli remarked, to imagine anything finer.[2] For the designer of carnival costume and floats nothing was better suited than the military triumph, with its swaggering conquerors, its cowering prisoners, passing under arches modelled on those of Severus and Constantine. To amuse his people in peacetime, Lorenzo, hero of the golden age, staged such triumphs, and in jousts and mock battles encouraged them to play at war.

The legitimacy of settling differences by resorting to arms, even if only to allow divine justice to operate more swiftly than it could by diplomatic and legal means, was emphasized by the very altars where men prayed for peace. Saints in armour suggested a divine sanction of arms, and if the warlike character of St. Michael and St. George was allegorized away by their being pitted against evil beasts, warrior saints like St. Maurice (made protector of an order of chivalry—René of Anjou's Order of the

---

[1] See R. C. Williams, 'The purpose of poetry and particularly the Epic as discussed by critical writers of the sixteenth century in Italy', *Romanic Review* (1921), pp. 1–20.   [2] *Istorie Fiorentine* ed. Mazzoni and Casella, p. 579.

Crescent—as recently as 1448), St. Victor, St. Eustace and St. Proculus appeared as straightforward warriors with whom any soldier might identify himself—St. Proculus, indeed, being associated with specific acts of violence, for the head he is sometimes made to hold is, unconventionally for a martyr, not his own. The pacific aspect of the incarnation itself created no uneasy tensions in the soldier's conscience. On the breastplate of an Italian armour of the period of the Italian wars was etched a frieze showing the Virgin and Child between St. Paul and St. George. Below them was the inscription: CHRISTUS RES [REX] VENIT IN PACE ET DEUS HOMO FACTUS ES[T].[1]

The Church was quick to associate itself with artillery as well and thus to veil to some extent the increasing horrors involved in the use of gunpowder. Representations of St. Barbara, formerly rare, increased with the use of guns, for on account of the thunder and lightning that destroyed her treacherous father, she was connected with explosions, whether they were brought about harmlessly by firework makers or lethally by gunners. Her image was represented on cannon, and according to the rules issued by Charles V to the artillery school in Sicily, each gunner, as he put the ball into his piece, was to make the sign of the cross over its muzzle and call on the Saint's aid.[2] Palma Vecchio's altarpiece in S. Maria Formosa in Venice, which shows the saint standing among cannon, was painted for the Association of *Bombardieri*. And it appears that not only was she invoked by gunners to protect them from being blown up by their own pieces (an invocation which doubtless merged with a desire that their aim might be straight), but also by those who feared being shot at. A mid-*Quattrocento* broadsheet shows a man interceding with the saint on behalf of a figure at whose breast a cannon has just discharged its ball.[3]

---

[1] Sir James Mann, 'Notes on the armour of the Maximilian period and the Italian wars', *Archaeologia* (1929), p. 225.
[2] S. Peine, *St. Barbara die Schutzheilige der Bergleute und der Artillerie* (Freiberg, 1896), p. 10.
[3] Reproduced in P. Heitz, *Italienische Einblattdrucke*, Strassburg, 1933, pt. 1, no. 18.

The horrific nature of guns was veiled, too, in other ways. The festive value of detonations was quickly appreciated, and guns took their place with music and dancing on occasions of special rejoicing. After the capture of Francis I at Pavia in 1525 the allied ambassadors in Venice were supplied with gunpowder from the arsenal to use at their celebrations.[1] The arts, by prettifying and glamourizing guns, did much to make them seem less terrifying. The golden cannon made for Charles V was only one of the innumerable attempts to put guns into court dress.[2] Cannon appear in Agostino Busti's monument to Gaston de Foix among the corselets, the piled arms and the drums of heroic triumphs *à l'antique*. Intricately carved, on ornate carriages, appearing as they do in the company of putti, satyrs and Roman standards, Busti's guns are robbed of any unpleasant associations: they blend discreetly with the calmly triumphant mood of the monument as a whole. And when naked *amori* play at shooting one another with pistols, as they were made to do on a *Cinquecento* powder flask,[3] then crafts and arts can be said to have done their utmost to tint the lenses through which the Renaissance looked at war. Illuminated manuscripts and printed books, too, had done much to domesticate the gun, regardless of theme. Biblical scenes might contain guns; military books were on occasion supplied with woodcuts of religious subjects, and in an age which was beginning to take archaeology seriously, illustrations of Roman battles could show guns battering at city walls, and bullets filling the air as rival galleys came together on the ocean.[4]

There was, indeed, some notion that the ancients had used gun-

---

[1] *Calendar of State Papers, Venetian 1520–1526*, nos. 736 and 942.

[2] Ibid., no. 1021.

[3] Plate XV of H. J. Jackson and C. E. Whitelaw, *European Hand Firearms* (London, 1923).

[4] As in the Venetian edition, 1493, of Livy's *Decades*, and the subsequent editions of 1495 (Latin) and 1506 (Italian). The German edition (Mentz, 1505) had different illustrations, including some unusually clear and detailed drawings of firearms. These illustrations were taken over for the Spanish edition of 1520 (Çaragoça). Firearms occur, too, in the separately illustrated Paris edition of 1514.

powder, for descriptions of their sieges and battles involved the use of propellant engines and combustibles (like Greek fire) which could be used to give a noble ancestry to modern explosives. An important aspect of the lively interest in ancient history was a fascination with the wars of antiquity. Classical military writers like Vegetius, Frontinus, Onosander and Aelian were printed and reprinted. Contemporary authors like Valturio in his *De Re Militari*, printed at Verona in 1472, reflected this fascination, and larded their observations on modern war with lessons of dubious relevance taken from antiquity, and yielded, in their descriptions of weapons and gadgets, to the armchair warrior's delight in ingenuity at the expense, sometimes, of practicability. Certainly the complex grappling devices recommended by Valturio for siege-work could never have been mounted, nor could his telescopic or revolving gun-turrets have been brought to bear. His device for enabling men to swim under water for long periods is not dissimilar to Leonardo's, but that Valturio's device appealed to the ingenuity rather than the common sense of his readers is made clear when his submarine trooper is shown in full armour.

The more complex war becomes, the more veins of interest it taps.[1] Many of these are concerned more with technology than directly with killing. It is possible to study fortification and artillery without really being concerned with human beings at all. The latent mathematician, the vestigial engineer in many a man of letters, responds to these orderly and calculable elements in war. The Italian wars saw the beginnings of fortification as a science, and the reduction of ballistic observations to rule. A beautiful arquebus appealed not only to a craftsman like Cellini but to a

[1] Jacob Burckhardt, *Civilisation of the Renaissance in Italy* (Phaidon ed., 1944), p. 63: 'The Italian literature of the day is rich in descriptions of wars and strategic devices, written for the use of educated men in general as well as of specialists, while the contemporary narratives of northerns, such as the "Burgundian War" by Diebold Schilling, still retain the shapelessness and matter-of-fact dryness of a mere chronicle.' According to Joseph Schnitzer (*Savonarola*, Munich, 1924, i, 392 and 480) *Schlachtenbücher* were among the demoralizing influences sought out for burning by the friar.

princely collector, like Alessandro de' Medici.[1] The special features of modern war, the example of its serious and orderly treatment by the historians of antiquity, and the worship paid to men who had achieved greatness in arms as well as in letters, made it appropriate that a Renaissance bishop should write, as Paolo Giovo did, biographies of famous soldiers.

The *Quattrocento*, then, had been a time when wars were restricted in scope, when casualties had been moderate and the impact of war on civilians had been slight, and at the same time it had been a time when the appeal of war as something glamorous and intriguing had been made on a more complex and penetrating level than ever before. Italy, if less warlike at Lorenzo's death than she had been a hundred years before, was certainly not less war-minded. War may have receded from the public imagination to the extent to which its sombre association had dimmed, but this retreat was more than compensated for by the advance made in its heroic and decorative aspect.

Symbolic of these developments were changes in the person of Mars himself. The once terrifying god of war became tamed and dandyfied. To the Middle Ages, which looked on war as something which, though capable of being turned to good account, was potentially evil, the war god was a bloodthirsty warrior, tinged with the demoniacal. His aspect was rough and forbidding, his progress through the skies inspired terror and dismay.[2] His *Planetenkinder* were not only soldiers but robbers and murderers, and his chariot stormed impartially over pitched battles and lonely scenes of assassination and rape. Unless there were special circumstances, as at Florence and Rome, where ancient statues identified with Mars became something like secular patron saints,[3]

---

[1] See Cellini's account of his dealings with Alessandro in 1535. Vasari's portrait shows him seated in armour, holding a small culverin.

[2] See, for example, F. Saxl, *Der Islam* (1912), plate 12 and the accompanying description of Mars from the *Liber Introductorius* of Michael Scotus. For many references to the medieval Mars, see Jean Seznec, *La Survivance des Dieux Antiques* (London, 1940, Eng. trans. New York, 1953), *passim*.

[3] F. von Bezold, *Das Fortleben der antiken Götter im mittelalterlichen Humanismus* (Leipzig, 1922), p. 32.

Mars represented war at its most brutal. Then, in the late fourteenth and early fifteenth centuries, he began to change. He came increasingly to typify the chivalrous ideal of knighthood, and he was seen less as the warrior than as the lover of Venus. If he still rules the sky over battlefields, it was as the perfect knight looking down approvingly on an ordered combat in which no blood was seen to flow. In Cossa's decorations for the Palazzo Schifanoia he kneels in chains before his mistress, and a generation later Botticelli showed him naked and defenceless in the company of Venus. The theme was eagerly followed up by the painters of every school, and when they turned, as did Perugino, Schiavone, and Sodom, to portraying the surprising of the lovers by Vulcan, Mars appeared in not only an unmartial but a downright ridiculous light. The appeal of the Mars and Venus theme was, of course, a strong one. It enabled the artist to contrast the metallic and the soft, armour with flesh. It played with the familiar antithesis of force and tenderness, the fashionable image of beauty taming cruelty, mildness subduing ferocity. It was as suitable for a political allegory as for a marriage picture.[1]

In his paintings for the Palazzo Rucellai in Rome, Giacomo Zucchi, dismayed by the bloodshed of his own epoch, deliberately portrayed Mars once more as the bloodthirsty warrior, the personification of anger, dissension and violence.[2] This was a breach with the *Cinquecento* tradition whereby Mars, when he was portrayed as a personification of war—a tradition maintained alongside that of the victim of Venus and sport of Vulcan—appeared as a personification of the glorious, triumphant, heroic side of war. If a ruler was given the attributes of Mars it was not to indicate that he was bloodthirsty but valorous. Cellini designed a piece of sculpture for Francis I in which the god of war, some fifty-four feet high, was accompanied by four other figures, not wolves and furies, but the arts and sciences, Learning, Design, Music and Liberality. 'The

[1] This is suggested of Botticelli's painting by E. Gombrich in *Journal of the Warburg and Courtauld Institutes* (1945), pp. 49–50.

[2] As he explains in his *Discorso sopra li dei de' Gentili, e loro imprese* (Rome, 1602), reprinted by F. Saxl, *Antike Götter in der Spätrenaissance* (Leipzig, 1927). See p. 49.

great statue in the centre', Cellini explained to his patron, 'represents your Majesty himself, the god Mars, unique in valour: and you employ your valour justly and devoutly, in the defence of your glory.'[1] In fact as war became more depraved, the god of war became more respectable. It was only in illustrations designed for bourgeois consumption—for the classes, that is, who saw war in terms less of glory than of death and taxes—that Mars retained his seamier aspects. It was as the feral bringer of destruction that he drive his chariot in Florentine astrological broadsheets over scenes of carnage, abduction and looting.

This transformation of Mars meant that he was no longer appropriate as a personification of war as something brutal, something to be deplored. The artist or writer seeking for an image that would convey disapproval or horror or grief had to turn elsewhere. To associate Mars with gunpowder, for instance, would have been unthinkable. The need for a pejorative image led to the disinterment of Bellona. As the companion of Mars, sometimes his charioteer or harbinger, she had made tentative appearances before the *Cinquecento*, but it was the Italian wars that saw her reinstated as a war goddess in her own right. In 1523 and 1528 the same woodcut title-page was used for two books printed in Venice, the *Duello* of Paris de Puteo and the *Libro continente appertenentie ad Capitanii* of Battista della Valle. On either side of the page was a triumphal pile of arms. On one side a pile of *armes blanches*: swords and maces, bows and axes. Over this presided the figure of Mars. On the other side was a pile of firearms and explosives, bombs, mortars, arquebuses, cannon and kegs of powder. Presiding over this new-fangled arsenal was an image of Bellona. The cult of the Roman war goddess was well known at least since Boccaccio's *Genealogia Deorum*, and it was dwelt on in detail by Giraldi in 1548. In Cartari's account

---

[1] *Life*, translated by George Bull (Penguin Books, 1956), p. 271. The conceit was not new. When Louis XII had entered Milan in May 1507, he was met by a procession which included the chariot of Mars who sat on a throne surrounded by the cardinal virtues. J. Chartrou, *Les Entrées Solonnelles et Triomphales à la Renaissance* (Paris, 1928), p. 76.

of the gods of the ancients he dwelt on her bloodthirsty and ruinous nature.[1]

In the history of popular attitudes of war the gentling of Mars must take, of course, a very marginal place. The shot from a gilt and exquisitely chased cannon was as lethal as a shot from a plain iron one. No one believed that battles were as ordered and pageant-like as Uccello made them look, and no one was misled by the dearth of casualties in a carnival siege into thinking that real cities were taken without loss of life. But the arts played a part in keeping the idea of war familiar. With their power to prettify and dignify, they prevented the more appalling aspects of war from leading either to a conspiracy of silence or to a sense of dread. Wherever the glare of battle became too great for the eye to bear, the arts interposed a gauze which softened its intensity.

Because the *Quattrocento*—and especially the period following the convention of Lodi in 1454—had been dubbed a peaceful age, it must not be looked upon as an age when statesmen did not think about war, or whose population was not constantly kept in mind of it. When the French blow came, Italy was not psychologically unprepared for war, even if some of her inhabitants were reluctant to do any fighting themselves. There had been enough military activity[2] to make sure that as far as military technique was concerned, her armies contained units that were

---

[1] Like Mars, Bellona came to have a heroic aspect, but she continued to be associated with gunpowder, and not only in Italy. Miss Frances Yates drew my attention to François Billon, *Le Fort Inexpugnable de l'Honneur du Sexe Feminin* (Paris, 1555), where the woodcut borders at the beginning of each book show a female figure in the act of applying a match to cannon. Cf. Milton's description in *Paradise Lost*, ii, lines 920-4, of the Fiend looking back on the pit:

> ... *Nor was his eare less peal'd*
> *With noises loud and ruinous (to compare*
> *Great things with small) than when Bellona storms,*
> *With all her battering Engines bent to rase*
> *Som Capital City.*

[2] See Piero Pieri, *Il Rinascimento e la Crisi Militare Italiana* (1952), part two, especially ch. iii. See also E. W. Nelson, 'The origins of modern balance-of-power diplomacy' in *Medievalia et Humanistica* (1942), pp. 124-42.

not inferior to the French and their allies. Nothing was considered deplorable about war, or even the long continuance of war, apart from the losses it entailed. Even the comparatively unmilitaristic Florentine republic decorated its holy of holies, the Sala del Gran Consiglio, where the God-given constitution expressed itself most fully, with battle scenes, and Venice, in the peaceful year 1490, took great pains to obtain expert tuition for young men both in the city and on the mainland, in the use of a weapon which the government saw would become increasingly important in future wars—the arquebus.

Italy, like France, had recruitment problems. Men were reluctant to leave a certain livelihood for an uncertain and increasingly hazardous one. There must have been many like the unheroic hero of *Ruzzante Returns from the Wars*, who limps back home without leave, to lick his wounds and cure his pox in Venice: 'Canchero ai campi, alla guerra, ai soldati. Dico non mi accalappieranno piú in guerra. Ora non sentirò piú, come sentiva, quei rumori tamburini. E trombe e allarmi. Ormai non avrò piú paura. Quando sentivo l'allarme, sembravo un tordo che avesse ricevuto una botta. E schioppi, artiglieria. Ora so che non mi raggiungeranno. Semmai mi prenderanno in culo.'[1]

But there were others like da Porto for whom war was still a glamorous opportunity to show how the *cortegiano* should behave in action; brave, courteous, love-smitten, able to dash off a sonnet when there was a lull in the fighting and, with an eye cocked shrewdly at present promotion and future fame, indulging in self-advertisement. For his class, warfare presented a series of splendid and legitimate opportunities for the individual to shine and show his worth. Such men preferred small actions where their deeds could be noted to sprawling operations which would absorb and conceal them. Da Porto wrote that it was more praiseworthy to fight a hundred against a hundred than a thousand against a thousand, 'because in a small number everybody's *virtù* can be

[1] This is from the Italian version of Beolco's Venetian dialect given in *Teatro Italiano*, i, ed. Silvio d'Amico (Milan, 1955), p. 453. I owe this reference to Mrs. C. Roaf.

seen'. And he goes on to say, even more revealingly, that this cannot happen in a great battle, and so people simply do not take the trouble and risk to display *virtù*. This is the temperament of men who thought of the military life more in terms of the combat of Barletta in 1503 between thirteen Italian and thirteen French knights, than of campaigns and mêlées like that of the Garigliano in the same year, the temperament for which the printing presses catered with a flood of chivalrous romances full of single combats and deeds of individual derring do. It is a temperament whose ideal of fighting conflicted with the actual nature of war.

The Italian war effort was hampered in many ways: by political disunity, by the reluctance of governments to trust the troops they employed, by the tendency of some *condottiere* leaders to think of themselves rather than the cause they were paid to support, especially when their *condotta* was nearing the end of its term. But important, too, was this courtier-knight feeling among the officer class. The larger the scale on which wars were carried out, the more important it was that the individual should allow himself to serve the interests of an overall plan. How difficult he found it is made disturbingly clear by Castiglione. It must be understood, says Federico Fregoso in *Il Cortegiano*, 'that where the Courtier is at skirmish, or assault, or battaile upon the land, or in such other places of enterprise, he ought to worke the matter wisely in separating him selfe from the multitude, and undertake notable and bolde feates which hee hath to doe, with as litle company as he can, and in the sight of noble men that be of most estimation in the campe, and especially in the presence and (if it were possible) before the very eyes of his king or great personage he is in service withall: for in deede it is meete to set forth to the shew things wel done.'[1] Elsewhere in the book Castiglione's audience is reminded that 'in great matters and adventures in wars the true provocation is glory'—but it was the glory of the individual, not of the cause for which he was fighting.

Da Porto, with his affection for *bellissime scaramucce* and his romantic enthusiasm for individuals like the mysterious Hungarian

[1] Book 2, ch. 8, Hoby's trans.

knight who turned up in Gradisca 'like a true knight-errant', was dismayed to a quite unmilitary degree when he himself was wounded. From the way in which he described the episode to Bembo it might almost seem that there was a tacit agreement between the fates and the courtier-knight that if he obeyed the rules of chivalry he would not be cut off in the flower of his youth and in an unspectacular manner. He described his wound—'which out-does all other wounds and even death itself'—with aggrieved self-pity and concluded the letter, which pathetically he had to dictate *dalla mia debolissima voce*, by complaining of the chance that had struck him down when these *belle guerre* were at their peak.[1]

The Italian wars were not, alas, *belle guerre*, they were wars for survival. They involved unglamorous defensive campaigns and inconclusive battles, they required the subordination of the individual, they saw unprecedented loss of life. The courtier-knight, intent on his own glory, or anxious to shine in the eyes of a prince who, very probably, was accustomed to turning his coat to suit his own convenience and not that of Italy as a whole, was a less effective instrument than his French equivalent. But this dwelling on one of the weaknesses of Italian arms is simply a means of demonstrating how prepared Italy was for warfare—of a kind, and to prevent the complaints of authors such as Machiavelli that men have lost their military virtues and interests from being applied to Italy as a whole.[2] The sense of shock, the cries of dismay that singled out 1494 as *anno infelicissimo*, these were not caused by the bringing of war to a country set in the ways of peace.

Nor were they caused by the fact that war took a turn for the worse. There is no doubt that the hazards of war became abruptly more drastic with the arrival of the French. The alarm caused by their sack of Fivizzano on their advance into Tuscany was sustained by their behaviour on entering the kingdom of Naples,

---

[1] The letter describing his wound is no. 59. See also pp. 191 and 194.

[2] For some other reactions see V. Cian, 'La coscienza politica nazionale nel Rinascimento' in his *Scritti Minori*, ii, Torino, 1936, especially p. 155, a reference I owe to Professor Grayson.

where after taking Monte di San Giovanni they murdered the populace and set fire to the town. 'This way of making war, not having been practised in Italy for many centuries,' noted Guicciardini, 'filled the whole kingdom with the greatest terror.'[1] As in sieges so in battles. Of Fornovo, fought in the next year on the French withdrawal from the peninsula, he wrote that the effete Italians were amazed how much blood could be shed in the course of an hour's fighting. To the atrocities of the French and their Swiss allies[2] after 1494 and the Spaniards after 1503 were added those of the Germans after 1509, who behaved, in the opinion of the sober Venetian Priuli, worse than infidels, looting churches, violating women and assassinating the very children.[3] On the surrender of Vicenza, in spite of terms which guaranteed the safety of the inhabitants, the behaviour of the Germans was so violent that large numbers of men, and more women and children, took refuge in a system of caverns nearby. The Germans thereupon lit fires in the entrances until they were all dead.[4] And so it went on. The sack of Brescia by the French and Germans and the sack of Prato by the Spaniards in 1512 were the occasions for more lamentation at the unheard-of cruelty and callousness with which war was being waged.[5]

Most shocking was its spreading to non-combatants. With long lines of communications, which at times broke down entirely, the French were forced to live off the country. Erratic pay forced the Germans and Swiss to do the same. The Spaniards, isolated in

[1] *Storia d'Italia*, ed. C. Panigada, i (Bari, 1929), 106.
[2] Ibid., p. 171. Cf. Commines, *Mémoires*, ed. B. de Mandrot, ii (Paris, 1903), 251.
[3] Muratori, *Rerum Italicarum Scriptores*, 1928, xxiv, fasc. ii, parte iii, p. 184.
[4] Da Porto, op. cit., p. 203, Guicciardini, op. cit., iii, 15.
[5] See, for instance, *Il miserando sacco di Prato cantato in terza rima da Stefano Guizzalotti* in *Archivio Storico Italiano*, ser. i, vol. i, pp. 263-71, where the poet declares (p. 265):

>   Non tanta crudeltà Turchi infedeli
>   Usaron mai cotanto alli Cristiani,
>   Quanto ch'a Prato gli Spagnoi crudeli,

and goes on to particularize them.

Naples in 1504, were forced to supply themselves as best they could, a situation all the more deplorable, Guicciardini recorded, in that it was a novel one. 'For ever since the times of antiquity in which military discipline was severely exercised, the soldiery had been always licentious and burdensome to the people, yet they never gave themselves a loose to all manner of disorders, but lived for the most part on their pay, and their licentiousness was restrained within tolerable bounds. But the Spaniards in Italy were the first that presumed to maintain themselves wholly on the substance of the people.' And he dourly adds, 'This was the beginning of a corruption which soon spread.'[1]

When his narrative approaches the bloody consequences of the League of Cambrai, he again sounds the same note:

'Though many wars and revolutions had happened in Italy during the last fourteen years, yet the disputes being often terminated without blood, or mostly at the expense of the lives of the barbarians engaged in them, the people suffered less than their princes. But now a door being opened to new contentions, there followed a train of mischievous and cruel events which overspread the face of Italy, and affected the Italians themselves, who saw nothing but scenes of infinite slaughter, plunder and the destruction of multitudes of town and cities, attended with military licentiousness, no less destructive to friends than foes.'[2]

Even after making some allowance for Guicciardini's masochistic bias, it is clear that he is expressing generally what local records and popular printed laments and prophecies say in detail. Yet alongside complaints of the ruthlessness of the barbarians went positive admiration for it. If war were to be waged at all it should be waged whole-heartedly. Guicciardini praised the dash and the uncompromising will-to-win of the French soldier; Machiavelli did not swerve from his admiration for the Swiss after their devastation of Pontremoli, nor because of their reluctance to be burdened with prisoners. As the wars proceeded, the Turks themselves, the very symbols of ruthlessness, were increasingly held up to admiration at the expense of the ill-disciplined and

[1] Ibid., ii, 138.   [2] Ibid., ii, 245.

irresolute Italian soldiery.¹ If war were to be waged effectively, it must be waged *à l'outrance*, and the grief of the afflicted populace was deepened by the fact that their troops did not seem capable of replying in kind.

This, then, was the greatest shock provided by 1494 and the years that followed: the realization that the Italians, though prepared for war and equipped to wage it, were to become the abject prey of barbarian nations which had once bowed the knee at the name of Rome. Where were Caesar, Fabius and Scipio? Where was the *élan* that had made the legionaries so terrible? What had become of the military virtues, the morale without which the best-prepared, the best-equipped army is useless? Under conventional queries as to what had become of the glory, the fair name of Italy, lay a more searching concern with what had happened to the Italian character; among conventional explanations given in terms of the complainant's *bête noire*—luxury, it might be, or irreligion, or immorality—were others which depended on a scrutiny of recent history and a reassessment of the individual of the social and political organization in which he grows up. From technical books of military instruction to works of political theory, a novel concern with morale made itself felt, caused not by abstract twinges of millenarianism or reform but the humiliation of actual defeats.

The lines on which this heart-searching was to be conducted had been anticipated in Florence during the struggle against the Visconti in the early *Quattrocento*,² and traced again by Alberti in the *Della Famiglia*. The preservation and reputation of States, he wrote in the *proemio*, do not depend on providence but on *le buone e sancte discipline del vivere*. Looking back into the past in a way which must have seemed balefully prophetic to his readers after 1494, he pointed out that as long as *da noi furono le optime e sanctissime nostre vetustissime discipline observate*, the greatness of

---

¹ By Paolo Giovio, for instance, in his *Turcicarum Rerum Commentarius* (Paris, 1539), p. 83.

² Hans Baron, *The Crisis of the Early Italian Renaissance*, 2 vols. (Princeton, 1955).

Rome endured, and every nation, however barbarous and ferocious, feared and obeyed her. Among the qualities that made Rome great was *la iustitia di Torquato, qual per osservare la militare disciplina non perdonò al figliuolo*, and it was *colle quali virtù non meno che col ferro et colla forza* that her rule was buttressed. But once the good laws and *sanctissime consuete discipline* are lost, Italy is lost. *E le barbare nationi . . . quali soleano al tuo venerando nome, Italia, rimettere ogni suberbia, ogni ira, e tremare, subito queste tutte presoro audacia d'inrumpere in mezzo al tuo sanctissimo seno, Italia, sino ad incendere el nido e lla propria antica sedia dello imperio di tutti gli imperii*.[1]

1494 was to show how far *sancte discipline* had lapsed. In comparing the forces ranged on either side in that year, Guicciardini was not content to give names and numbers; he compared their morale. The French: intrepid and valorous; the Swiss, who by stern training and practice had *rinnovata la fama antica della ferocia*; and the Italians who *non aveano, nè per natura nè per accidente, stimolo estraordinario al bene servire*; poor material, and often poorly led. Speaking of Virginio Orsini's decision to let his sons serve on the French side while he himself fought for Naples, Guicciardini comments that this decision amazed the French, *non assueti a queste sottili distinzioni de' soldati d'Italia*. He speaks sarcastically of the *cautela italiana* with which the Duke of Ferrara, while himself professing neutrality on the formation of the League of 1495, allowed his son to fight for Milan against the French. And summing up the Italian resistance to the French conquest of Naples he concluded that it displayed *nè virtù nè animo nè consiglio, non cupidità d'onore non potenza non fede*, and that the whole sorry business ended *con sommo vituperio e derisione della milizia italiana e con gravissimo pericolo e ignominia di tutti*.[2] And this concern with morale was not felt only by Florentine writers with their tradition of concern for social ethics. Castiglione, referring in *The Courtier* to the fact that the Italians had not displayed of late much valour in arms, sought *la vera causa delle nostre ruine e della virtù prostrata, se non morta, negli animi nostri*, that moral failure as a result of which

---

[1] Ed. R. Spongano, Florence, 1946, pp. 7–8.
[2] The passages quoted are from op. cit., i, 73, 99, 140, 106 and 113.

il nome italiano è ridotto in obrobrio, nè si ritrovano se non pochi che osino non dirò morire, ma pur entrare in uno pericolo.[1]

For Castiglione these reflections did not lead to the consideration of any constitutional changes. Not that he was unconcerned with political theory: the fourth book is largely concerned with proving—to the great convenience of the courtier—that the best government is that of a prince. Urbino was already organized for war. What was needed was an improvement in morale through the private self-education of the courtier. But in Florence, where the state was not organized for war, concern with morale was firmly linked with concern for the constitution. What was wrong with a political organization that had left the state reliant on the arms of mercenaries, and the citizens devoid of military feeling? What measures should be taken to secure a civic militia, and, once having obtained it, what measures should be taken to make sure that it was used only against the enemies of the state, and not against the state itself? The experience of war, then, led to consideration of the formal structure of government: the sort of constitution that worked best in an emergency when crucial decisions had to be made quickly and definitely; and it led, too, to a consideration of the personal element: the way constitutional changes could improve the civic temper of the populace as a whole.[2]

No political thinker was more influenced by the spectacle of Italy's military defeats than Machiavelli. It is worth recalling the sheer bulk of references to specifically military matters in his work. About one-sixth of the *Prince*, about one-fifth of the *Discourses*, the whole of the *Art of War*. Of the rather few generalizations in the *Florentine History* a large number are concerned with military affairs, and Books 1 and 2 end, and Books 3, 5 and 6 begin, with discussions about war and valour. War, after all, was Machiavelli's hobby-horse. From his first months of office in 1498 he had showed an interest in the technicalities of war. On diplomatic

---

[1] Ed. Cian, 4th ed., Florence, 1947, pp. 109 and 411.
[2] For these points, see the political discourses of Guicciardini, especially the *Del Modo di Ordinare il Governo Popolare* and the *Dialogo del Reggimento di Firenze*, ed. Palmarocchi (Bari, 1932), pp. 65-7 and 90-2.

missions abroad he had seen armies in the process of formation and in the field. He had been made responsible for the organization of his darling project, the Florentine militia in 1506, and though dismayed, he was not daunted by its poor showing against the Spaniards at Prato in 1512. By temperament a keen armchair soldier, his diplomatic career had shown him that Florence would be despised until she had a strong army of her own, his knowledge of his city's history showed him why she had none, his study of Roman history showed him how one could be built up. As a student of the international scene he thought of the armies which foreign powers could put into the field. As a student of the Florentine constitution—as who could not be, in a period of experiment and crisis?—he thought of the citizen as a potential soldier. From the time he devoted to military matters—first the militia, then the city's fortifications—the space he gave them in his works, and the enthusiasm with which he wrote of them, it is probable that Machiavelli would have wished to be remembered, first and foremost, as a great writer on war. Certainly it is the topic on which he speaks to us with least reservation. Hobby-horses can be ridden over ground impracticable for real ones, and thus we learn more about the character of their riders. Any aspect of Machiavelli's work—his use of ancient history, his disturbing blend of sober observation and almost trancelike conjecture—can be studied best when Machiavelli has entered his *scrittoro* at San Cascino and, having passed into *le antique corti delli antiqui uomini*, talks to the great soldiers there.

He started from the contention that the Italian armies of his own day were despicable. He speaks of them as a 'blind chance rabble', 'the scorn of the world', the result of fighting having been 'reduced to a trade so vile that any peddling captain, in whom the mere ghost of ancient valour had reappeared, would have laughed them to scorn'.[1] The best armies, like those of Rome, were those that combined ardour with discipline. Next are those which had ardour without discipline, like the Gauls'. Last came those who

[1] In ed. Mazzoni and Casella: *Discorsi*, iii, c. 36, p. 251: *Arte della Guerra*, vii, 366; *Istorie Fiorentine*, i, 407.

'have neither natural courage nor discipline. Of this kind are the Italian armies of our time, which are of no use at all.'[1]

Machiavelli looked back on two ages with special nostalgia. One was that of the Roman Republic, the other was the Florentine *Trecento*. Both were periods when fresh territories and glory had been gained by citizens fighting for their own countries.[2] Since then Florence, like all Italy, had come to rely on mercenary troops, dangerous in peace, fickle in war, eating up the profits of victory and doubling the hazards of defeat. And the employment of mercenaries and auxiliaries was not the only way in which the citizen had burked the responsibility of taking arms himself. He put device after device between himself and each threat. He trusted first to diplomacy to win him allies, then he attempted to stop an opposing army with subsidies and treaties.[3] If these failed, he tried to turn it back at the borders of the state, and if their defence failed, to rely on fortresses, and on artillery as a last resort to prevent his having to come to blows himself. All mistaken, and all vain; 'it is the heart and vital parts of the body that should be protected', he wrote in the *Discourses*,[4] 'and not the extremities, for without the latter life is possible, but without the former death is certain.' The citizen must learn to fight. For hired troops must be substituted a militia. I venture to affirm that the first state in Italy that shall take up this suggestion, he concluded, 'fia . . . signore di questa provincia'.[5]

But the quality of a militia, as Machiavelli saw, depended on the quality of the citizens, and they had become corrupted by peace

---

[1] *Discorsi*, iii, c. 36.

[2] For a criticism of Machiavelli's interpretation, see P. Pieri, *Guerra e Politica negli Scrittori Italiani* (Milan, 1955), ch. 1.

[3] Luca Landucci comments sardonically when taxes were raised on one such occasion, in 1480, 'We Florentines have the wise custom of giving money in payment to everyone who does us an injury, and who destroys and pillages our territory . . . it will always be the same; anyone who wants money from the Florentines has only to do them an injury.' *A Florentine Diary*, ed. I. del Badia, Eng. ed. 1927, p. 30.

[4] iii, c. 30.

[5] *Arte della Guerra*, Mazzoni and Casella, p. 367.

and luxury. To pursue their own affairs the better, they had left the business of fighting to others, and had come to think, as Rome in her greatness had never thought, that the civilian and military aspects of life were quite discordant. Things had gone so far that if a young man elected to go to the wars, his reputation would actually suffer for it.[1] Machiavelli begins his *Art of War* by introducing into the city garden of Cosimo Rucellai a soldier, Fabrizio Colonna, who has come to Florence from the wars in Lombardy. Invited to admire it, he says bluntly that Cosimo's grandfather, who founded the garden, would have done better if he had lived actively and hardily like the ancients, rather than providing for leisure and luxurious ease. His host agrees, but adds that his grandfather, in fact, had 'found it impossible either for himself or his sons to practise what he most approved: for such was the corruption of the age he lived in, that if anyone had spirit enough to deviate ever so little from the common customs and manner of living of those times, he would have been universally ridiculed'. But Machiavelli was convinced that affairs could change, and declared in the preface 'that it is not even yet impossible to revive the discipline of our ancestors, and in some measure to retrieve the reputation of our soldiery'.

What was needed, he suggested, was the re-education of the citizen, and this could be achieved by means of a good military organization. Without such a training, riches, pride, dominion itself is empty. This was obvious simply from the example of Florence. And he pointed to the situation of the Venetians when they had lost their first battle against the French in 1509. 'Their miserable baseness of spirit, caused by a wretched military organization, made them lose at a single blow their courage and their state.' With a sound organization, morale can be improved, valour return and great deeds once more be possible.

More than this: in securing a good militia, a corrupt state will be made healthy. Just as poor military institutions or—in Florence's case—only vestigial ones can sap civic spirit, so good military institutions can restore it. Once get rid of the false notion that there

[1] Guicciardini, *Dialogo del Reggimento di Firenze*, ed. cit., p. 91.

is a fundamental split between the soldier and the citizen, and it will then be clear that as the ideal soldier is also the perfect citizen, to improve him in one capacity is to improve him in the other. The corrupt citizen, through the influence of good military institution, becomes a good soldier, and, at the same time, a better citizen. From a sound military organization follow good laws, and these too help in the re-education of the citizen. A corrupt state, in fact, can be reformed by the right military organization.

It follows from this that the political theorist who wants good laws should also be a military theorist intent on producing good soldiers. Army reform will produce the right citizen material for the best possible state, whereas 'without good military organization there can neither be good laws nor anything else good.' It follows too that the military theorist who wants good soldiers is planning something with necessary political consequences. A state's constitution is affected by the martial temper of the populace and the specific nature of the way in which they are organized for war.

He recognized that the bad citizen could only be made into a good soldier by strong persuasion. The Soderini republic could put men into uniform but it could not make real soldiers of them. One of the main tragedies of Italy was that her rulers had been too weak to introduce good military institutions. These can only be put into effect 'through the method I have described and with the co-operation of some powerful princes'.[1] Bad soldiers must, then, be made into good ones by a prince. This will involve their becoming reformed citizens, capable of governing themselves once more. The finest political type the world had seen was, for Machiavelli, the citizen of the Roman republic. The best way of rescuing a corrupt Florence was, by introducing Roman military institutions, to reanimate the citizens of Florence. But this was a time of crisis, and the process had to be carried out quickly, before it was too late.

At this point, however, the argument blurs. The neat solution would have been: let a prince, then, compel military reforms in

[1] Ed. cit., *Arte della Guerra*, p. 366.

Florence in the interest of an improved civic temper. Machiavelli advised the Medici, it is true, to foster the sense of political responsibility among the Florentines in preparation for a return to more broadly based republican institutions on the death of Cardinal Giulio and Leo X, but this was to be done through reviving the *Consiglio Grande*. Just as Machiavelli's plans for a militia were flawed by his distrust of armed city-dwellers as opposed to men from the contado, so his conviction that a prince could best produce (as Cesare Borgia had done) a resolute native soldiery failed at the point of applying the conclusion to Florence. His attitude both to the citizen and to the state was affected by his preoccupation with war, but his prejudice against the armed townsman and his inherited republican bias prevented him from thinking in terms even of a temporary military autocracy for his native city.

War, too, affected his attitude towards political morality, adding an infection from its own drama to his conviction that for a public figure in a time of crisis to luxuriate in a private conscience was irresponsible, for 'although deceit is detestable in all other things, yet in the conduct of war it is laudable and honourable', and he stresses the importance of 'those feints and stratagems which you employ against an enemy that distrusts you, and in the employment of which properly consists the art of war'.[1] What he has in mind are the tricks reported of Roman and Greek generals by ancient military writers, but it is difficult not to feel that the ruthlessness and deviousness necessary on the eve of battle, and sanctified by classical example, was considered appropriate by Machiavelli to any time of crisis and emergency in the intervals of battles, in the intervals even of wars, when peace itself was but an uneasy pause from combat. In the chapter from the *Discourses* quoted above, he makes it clear that he does not confuse these military stratagems 'with perfidy, which breaks pledged faith and treaties'. He distinguishes between placid peace which must not be broken by deceit, and a state of uneasy peace, continually on the verge of war, and which must therefore borrow the manners of war. And Machiavelli's whole active life was passed in a period of crisis, of war or warlike peace, when politicians and generals alike could plead necessity, and when political thinkers who were also students of war could find it easy to grant that plea.

If these wars affected political and constitutional ideas—and Machiavelli was exceptional only in the depth of his interest—they also affected historical thought. From time to time it was admitted that the Italians were more skilled or more resourceful than their adversaries, that individual Italians might be braver, but the dominant judgement was cynical and contributed to that note of disillusioned analysis which has been seen as a salient factor in the 'modern' tone of Renaissance historiography. The later Renaissance cannot be understood without taking into account the pessimism induced by defeats inflicted on a society which had no quarrel with war as an activity in itself. 'Misera Italia,' mourned an anonymous poet after the sack of Rome in 1527,

> *Misera Italia, a che condotta sei*
> *suggetta al nome che più fiate hai vinto;*
> *la gloria, el pregio e quel vigore è estinto,*
> *che già dato ti fu da' sommi Dei.*[1]

---

[1] *La Presa di Roma* (Sonetto), ed. F. Mango in *Scelta di Curiosità Letterarie*, Bologna, 1886. Punctuated.

14

GUNPOWDER AND THE RENAISSANCE: AN ESSAY IN THE HISTORY OF IDEAS.*

Few survivors remain from the spacious days of unchallenged historical generalizations, but from time to time The Influence of Gunpowder on Civilization can still be glimpsed, stalking through the careful husbandry of modern historical writing. "Gunpowder blasted the feudal strongholds and the ideals of their owners," a modern military historian has stated. "By changing the character of war, gunpowder changed the medieval way of life. The search for the perfection of firearms and of defence against them gave birth to a spirit of inquiry which soon embraced all things."[1]

The notion that gunpowder blasted feudalism at the behest of the centralized state can be found in Hume, Adam Smith, and Hallam. For Macaulay the invention of gunpowder was, with that

---

* I have included in this essay some material which has appeared in two much briefer treatments of this subject: "The Cruel Art," *The Listener*, April 19, 1956, pp. 454–6, and a paper read at a *Past and Present* conference on "War and Society 1300–1600," *Past and Present*, July, 1962, esp. pp. 28–32. I am grateful to the editors of these journals for their permission to do this.

of printing, one of the two greatest events which took place in the Middle Ages. For Carlyle it was one of the three great elements of modern civilization (the others were printing and the Protestant religion). In 1857 Buckle elaborated his thesis that firearms had led to the creation of a specialized military class: "The result was, that the European mind, instead of being, as heretofore, solely occupied either with war or with theology, now struck out into a middle path, and created these great branches of knowledge to which modern civilization owes its origin." From this it was a short step to the textbook quoted by Johan Huizinga which announced that "the rebirth of the human spirit dates from the discovery of firearms."

These claims are attractive, but the historian of Renaissance Europe will not find them easy to accept. An occasional rebellious baron may have been brought to heel by royal cannon, but the complex development of the feudal into the centralized state began before cannon became effective and can be explained without reference to firearms. The same is true of changes in the "European mind." The English bow and the Swiss and Spanish pike required as much training and discipline as the arquebus: the existence of a specialized military class in the non-feudal sense is the result not of a particular weapon but of the concept of a standing army and thus belongs to the seventeenth century.

The effects of firearms were specific and dramatic: they raised problems of tactics, equipment, and supply; wars cost more, new methods of fortification had to be devised, but they had little effect on the fortunes of campaigns as a whole or on the balance of political power. It is true that states which had guns were at an advantage over armies which as yet had none, or few: thus the Turks beat the Mamluks and the Spaniards found conquest easy in the New World. It is true that guns knocked down unreformed fortifications, and this gave the French an advantage over the English at the beginning of the fifteenth century and the Spaniards an edge on the Moors at the end of it. But by the second decade of the sixteenth century, when cannon and portable firearms first became really effective on the battlefield, they were owned by all the powers, and the rapid spread of the new fortifications meant that anything like a *blitzkrieg* was out of the question. Firearms may have decided the issue of a single battle, as at Ravenna in 1512, or the tactics of one—the Armada fight of 1588, so brilliantly described by Mattingly, is an example—but they cannot be said to have decided a war. Nor can they be said to have influenced the mounting diplomatic tension of the sixteenth century; for a surprise attack their striking power was neutralized by the cumbrous organization of their supply trains. Gunpowder, in short, revolutionized the conduct but not the outcome of wars.

If gunpowder did not hasten the "European mind" toward attitudes which we recognize as "modern," it did trouble that mind. Its use was accompanied, throughout the Renaissance, by considerable debate, *pro* and *contra,* and the purpose of this essay is to watch the conscience of Christendom adjusting itself to the use of a weapon of hitherto unprecedented destructive power and one commonly thought to have been brought into existence by the devil himself.

Firearms had been used in Europe from early in the fourteenth century, but when humanist historians discussed the origin of gunpowder, they attributed its invention to a mid-fourteenth-century German, and its first use to the Venetians in their war of Chioggia (1378–81) against the Genoese. The first *locus classicus* for this opinion, endlessly quoted and requoted for the next two hundred years, was Flavio Biondo's *Roma triumphans,* written between 1455 and 1463, in which he spoke of bombards, "*machinae omnium impetuosissimae, quam anno nondum centesimo inventam fuisse docuimus, teutonicū munus Venetis delatum, quando Genuenses in Clugia clausi a Venetis obsidebantur.*"[2] Platina made the same point in his history of the popes (1474), and in 1493 Antonio Cornazano identified the German as an alchemist,[3] an opinion shared in the most influential of all early accounts of the origin of gunpowder, a passage from Polydore Vergil's *De Inventoribus Rerum,* first published in 1499. In the words of the English translation of this work, the first gun

> was perceived by a certain Almain, whose name is not known, after this sort: it chanced that he had in a mortar powder of brimstone that he had heated for a medicine and covered it with a stone, and as he struck fire it fortuned a spark to fall in the powder. By and

by there rose a great flame out of the mortar, and lifted up the stone wherewith it was covered a great height. And after he had perceived that, he made a pipe of iron and tempered the powder, and so finished this deadly engine, and taught the Venetians the use of it when they warred against the Genoese, which was in the year of our Lord MCCCLXXX.[4]

Similar accounts occur in two contemporary works, the chronicle of Rafael of Volterra[5] and the *Rapsodiae Historiarum Enneadum*[6] of M. C. Sabellico, both of which were frequently quoted by later writers. Under the influence of these works it was generally taken for granted in the sixteenth century that guns were first used in 1380.

This theory ran counter to an earlier one, mentioned by Petrarch,[7] that gunpowder had been known to the ancients and invented by Archimedes. For those humanists who believed that the ancients had anticipated everything, it was easy to read accounts of ancient sieges, especially those employing some form of Greek fire, in terms of guns. Pius II told Duke Federigo of Urbino that "in Homer and Virgil could be found descriptions of every kind of weapon which our age used"[8]—a reference to the machine made by Salmoneus to counterfeit the thunder of Jupiter and described in the sixth book of the *Aeneid*. In 1472 Roberto Valturio, in his *De re militari*, named Archimedes as the inventor of the gun, but by the end of the century the military engineer Francesco di Giorgio expressed the majority view when he asked: If the ancients had guns, why don't we find any traces of gun-ports in their walls? Why did they go on using rams and catapults?[9]

Spanish historians, it is true, said that gunpowder had first been used by the Moors against Alfonso XI in 1343,[10] and a number of writers believed that it had been invented by the Chinese. Buonaiuto Lorini, for instance, said it had been brought into Europe via Turkey by German merchants.[11] Raleigh accepted the Chinese thesis in his *History of the World* (1614),[12] but in the same year Camden discounted it in his *Remaines concerning Britaine*. He opted for the German alchemist (by now named as Berthold Swart, or Schwarz, and identified as a monk or Franciscan friar) as the inventor of the gun, but pointed out that firearms had been used from the early fourteenth century.

Nearly all the writers we have mentioned deplored the introduction of the new weapon. The Chinese and Moorish theories had the advantage of placing the responsibility on infidels, who could not be expected to know better, but preference was given to the most picturesque and shocking story. Men like to think that great inventions are the work of an individual whom they can imagine at work; this, the popular distrust of alchemists, and the Protestant dislike of monks, made the image of Swartz, pursuing his secret labors at the devil's prompting into one of the most compelling figures in the folklore of technology.

In the paper debate which accompanied the actual use of guns the bulk of the argument was provided by the opposition. The supporters of firearms were few. They lacked, of course, the spur of moral indignation, and in an age almost innocent of pacifism, war was thought to be necessary to the state and good for the individual, even when it included cannon. "Musk and civet have too long stifled us," says the captain in Shirley's *The Doubtful Heir*,[14] "there's no recovery without the smell of gunpowder." Guns were necessary for the defense of one's country, so Roger Ascham, an academic scholar with a passion for the longbow, could encourage men to practice with them,[14] and so could a cleric like Daneau.[15] In the right hands, guns were a guarantee of order. For Jean Taisnier they protected the individual and his household;[16] Sebastian Münster pointed out that by destroying the strongholds of brigands, cannon served the merchant and allowed trade to prosper.[17] On a bombard cast in 1404 for Sigismond of Austria is the motto, I AM NAMED KATRIN, BEWARE OF WHAT I HOLD; I PUNISH INJUSTICE;[18] and two hundred years later the English antiquarian historian Sir Henry Spelman could describe the gun as *"machina ad stabilienda Humana Imperia, potius quam ad delendum humanum genus. Execrantur pacis invidi hanc machinam: mihi autem semper visa est non sine Dei opt. max. providentia revelata."*[19] Some authors claimed that the introduction of firearms had reduced casualties in battle, and Camden produced some dubious statistics in support. He contrasted the losses at the battle of Hastings (47,944 English killed) and Crécy (30,000 French killed) with those of battles where guns were used—Flodden, 8,000, Musselburgh, 4,000—and drew a drastically *post hoc, propter hoc* conclusion.[20] The commonest argument in defense of the gun, however, was that God had not armed man with fangs and claws like animals, but that He had given him the intelligence to invent weapons of his own; to render himself defenseless, especially unilaterally, against an enemy armed with guns would be an insult to the Creator and a neglect of His gifts. This argument occurs from the middle of the sixteenth century[21] and was used both by secular writers like Sir Walter Raleigh[22] and clerics; the Rev. J. Davenport defended the making of guns by saying—it is true, in a sermon to the Artillery Company of London—that man "can take . . . from within the bowels of the earth, what may serve for his use and benefit."[23]

Among the arguments against the use of firearms the least cogent was that they were less effective than the old familiar weapons. Very few men went so far as Montaigne in his opinion of the gun: "Except the astonishment and frighting of the ear, which nowadays is grown so familiar amongst men, that none doth greatly fear it, I think it to be a weapon of small effect, and hope to see the use of it abolished."[24] Some, like Sir John Smythe, complained that the effects of firearms were exaggerated, and that the bow should be retained as the most reliable and efficient missile weapon;[25] others, like the French soldier François de la Noue,[26] distrusted the more complicated firearms, especially the pistol. According to Du Bartas, when Henry IV of France was confronted by an enemy cavalryman:

> Le courageux Henri lui porte tout à coup
> Le pistolet au front, il fait feu, non pas coup,
> Lors d'une voix colère: "O tromperesses armes,
> Je vous quitte" (dit-il); l'épée est des gendarmes
> La gloire plus insigne.[27]

Most arguments, however, were based on the assumption that firearms were devilish and their use blasphemous, that they were unchivalrous and that they caused too much suffering.

From John Mirfield's mention in c.1390 of *"instrumento illo bellico sive diabolico quod vulgariter dicitur gonne,"*[28] the idea that gunpowder was a malicious patent of the devil became a commonplace. The title page of the 1489 Basel edition of Augustine's *De Civitate Dei* shows two walled towns—one manned by angels, the other by devils, one of whom is armed with a gun. Francesco di Giorgio, himself a designer of cannon, wrote that this weapon "*non senza qualche ragione da alcuni non umana ma diabolica invenzione è chiamata,*"[29] and the practical and sophisticated Francesco Guicciardini referred to guns in his *History of Italy* as "diabolical rather than human."[30] Erasmus made Peace exclaim: "O God immortal! With what weapons doth anger arm a man? Christians do invade Christian men with the engines of hell. Who can believe that guns were the invention of man?"[31]

Even a man like Vanuccio Biringuccio, who wrote the first detailed treatise on the making and use of cannon, could remark that "a great and incomparable speculation is whether the discovery of compounding the powder used for guns came to its first inventor from the demons or by chance."[32] An illustration in Munster's *Chronicle* did not share this doubt; it showed a devil leading the monk Schwarz toward a cannon,[33] and the point was made even more dramatically by a woodcut in Johan Stumpf's *Schwyzer Chronik* (1554) which showed monks at work in a laboratory; a small monster with a long tube-like snout is mixing powder for them, while a demon shaped like a flying goat is helping one of them grind it in a mortar.[34] Ben Jonson was only rephrasing an old tradition when he referred to the friar "Who from the Divels-Arse did Guns beget."[35] The supreme example of the devil-gun identification in English literature, however, is in book six of Milton's *Paradise Lost,* where Raphael tells Adam how, after his initial rout on the first day of his battle with the hosts of heaven, Satan invented the gun, so that batteries of them confronted the heavenly army on the second day:

> at each behind
> A Seraph stood, and in his hand a Reed
> Stood waving tipt with fire.

Before the linstocks could be applied, the good angels buried the cannon under mountains, and there they remained. But Raphael warns Adam lest

> haply of thy Race
> In future dayes, if Malice should abound,
> Some one intent on mischief, or inspir'd
> With dev'lish machination might devise
> Like instrument to plague the Sons of men
> For sin, on warr and mutual slaughter bent.

Such a rediscovery would not only serve the devil's end, but it would be blasphemy. "*Non erat satis de coelo tonantis ira Dei immortalis,*" asked Petrarch, "*nisi homuncio (O crudelitas iuncta superbiae) de terra etiam tonuisset?*"[36] God showed his wrath in thunder and lightning; it was not for man to imitate it.

The chivalrous contempt for firearms as a coward's weapon had been anticipated by a scorn for missile weapons that went back to the Greeks. In Euripides' *Hercules Furens* Lycus says scornfully of Hercules that his reputation for bravery is based on his combats with wild beasts. With men "he never seized a shield on his left arm or came close to the spear point but had bow and arrows, the most cowardly of weapons." Each new missile contrivance met with similar opposition. The Emperor Napoleon III cited "the well-known exclamation of Archidamus, King of Sparta, at the sight of the first catapult: 'This is the tomb of bravery!' "[37] Anna Comnena referred to the crossbow as "a really devilish contrivance."[38] A few Renaissance authors reported anecdotes of a generalized anti-missile sort: "What said the Laconian when wounded by a dart?" asked Henry Salmuth. " 'I am not,' quoth he, 'concerned at my death, but at my fall by a wound from a feeble archer,' "[39] but mostly they concentrated their scorn on the gun. From Polydore Vergil onwards there was a running fire of attack on the new weapon, thanks to which "*vera virtus bellica corrupta, et fere sublata sit.*" All over Europe men were asking, with the anonymous eulogist of the French warrior Louis de la Tremouille, "*De quoy servira plus l'astuce des gensdarmes, leur prudence, leur force, leur hardiesse, leur preudhommie, leur discipline militaire, et leur desir d'honneur, puisqu'en guerre est permis user de telles invencions?*"[40] It is enough here to quote one example each from Italy, France, Germany, Spain, and England.

The most famous and influential of all attacks on gunpowder as unchivalrous came from Ariosto, in cantos nine and eleven of the *Orlando Furioso*. The poet tells how Orlando is begged by the daughter of the Count of Holland to avenge the death of her family, butchered by the King of Friesland, a vengeance all the more urgent in that they were not killed in fair fight but struck down at a distance by that cowardly new invention, the gun. Orlando accepts the charge and after defeating the evil king and his army, takes the cannon, together with its powder and ball, and sails away until his ship stands over the ocean's profoundest depths. There he has the accursed engines dropped overboard and sails away, thinking that the chivalrous virtues have been saved. But the respite is short. Two cantos later the grapnels go down:

> More than a hundred fathom buried so,
> Where hidden it had lain a mighty space,
> The infernal tool by magic from below
> Was fished and born amid the German race.[41]

And thence it spread from country to country, until the poet breaks out,

> How, foul and pestilent discovery,
> Did'st thou find place within the human heart?
> Through thee is martial glory lost, through thee
> The trade of arms becomes a worthless art:
> And at such ebb are worth and chivalry
> That the base often plays the better part.
> Through thee no more shall gallantry, no more
> Shall valour prove their prowess as of yore.[42]

Henry IV of France called the *Commentaries* of Blaise de Monluc "the soldier's Bible," and in them the fiery marshal, a veteran of nearly sixty years of war in Italy and France, said of guns: "Would to heaven that this accursed engine had never been invented. I had not then receiv'd those wounds which I now languish under [he had been shot in the face by an arquebus in 1562], neither had so many valiant men been slain for the most part by the most pitiful fellows, and the greatest cowards; Poltrons that had not dar'd to look those men in the face at hand, which at distance they laid dead with their confounded bullets."[43] In Germany, the most important and most frequently reprinted military book of the sixteenth century was the *Kriegs Ordnung und Regiment* of Leonhard Fronsberger, and he too was of the opinion that "many a time and oft it happens that a brave and manly hero is killed by a shot from a craven who would not dare look him in the face."[44]

Even more widely read were the words of a Spaniard who was tempted to give up knight-errantry altogether, because the gun prevented the battlefield from functioning as the finishing school for personal valor. "Blessed were the times," complained Don Quixote in his Curious Discourse on Arms and Letters, "which lacked the dreadful fury of those diabolical engines, the artillery, whose inventor I firmly believe is now receiving the reward for his devilish invention in hell; an invention which allows a base and cowardly hand to take the life of a brave knight, in such a way that, without his knowing how or why, when his valiant heart is full of furious courage, there comes some random shot—discharged perhaps by a man who fled in terror from the flash the accursed machine made in firing—and puts an end in a moment to the consciousness of one who deserved to enjoy life for many an age."[45]

English pride in her missile troops, the archers, meant that while Englishmen could condemn guns as being devilish or deride them as inefficient, few thought of them as cowardly. An exception was Samuel Daniel, who castigated men's use of guns in his poem *The Civil Wars* (1595):

> For, by this stratagem, they shall confound
> All th' ancient forme and discipline of Warre:
> Alter their Camps, alter their fights, their ground,
> Daunt mightie spirits, prowesse and manhood marre:
> For, basest cowardes from a far shall wound
> The most couragious, forc't to fight afarre;
> Valour, wrapt up in smoake (as in the night)
> Shall perish without witnesse, without sight.[46]

The suffering which firearms—the "crudel arte" of Ariosto—inflicted was also fairly widely deplored. After discussing the weapons used by the ancients, Pedro Mexia remarked that "*à todo esto vence en crueldad la invencion de la polvora y artilleria,*"[47] and the French surgeon Ambroise Paré, who devoted much of his career to treating gunshot wounds, made the same point and added that cannon are properly called basilisks and serpents, for they are as cruel among weapons as these among beasts.[48] For Biringuccio, too, guns were "horrible and fearful," so horrible, in fact, that he burned the manuscript of his treatise on artillery. But—and the force of all these anti-gunpowder arguments was reduced by a "but"—when in 1537 the rumor spread that Suleiman was preparing to move west, he wrote it out again and sent it to the printer: Christians must not be left at a disadvantage. And Paré, for all his protestations, was unable to resist having a gun turned on a party of "fourescore whores and wenches" waiting to draw water at a well outside the besieged Hesdin; "and at that shot fifteene or sixteene were kild, and many hurt."[49]

Similarly, the knightly class did not take a united stand against the use of guns. Froissart revised his account of Crécy by removing references to the English guns lest they should be offensive to the taste of his English readers,[50] but in thinking that the relish of victory would be soured by associating it with artillery he was showing an unusual deference to chivalrous ideals. The gap between these ideals and the actual conduct of war in the late Middle Ages needs no laboring.[51] The pageantry became more gorgeous, the values more cynical. At the end of the fourteenth century Eustache Deschamps portrayed a gathering of knights and squires at the Burgundian court. Were they discussing love or valor? No; on every lip was the question, *Et quant venra le Trésorier?* [When does the paymaster come?].[52] And a few years later his English contemporary Hoccleve admitted that "experience and art" were worth more in a battle than "hardinesse or force,"[53] a sentiment repeated in *Le Jouvencel,* the mid-fifteenth-century Burgundian romance in which Jean de Bueil described his ideal of the perfect knight: "One should take every advantage in war, for faults are always dearly paid for. And one should always accomplish one's purpose, if not by force, then by cleverness."[54]

One advantage was to make use of the new weapon. Christine de Pisan's translation (1408-9) of Vegetius' *Art of War* was written for knights and courtiers, but she interpolated a long section on the use of guns in siege-craft with no suggestion that this gave a mean or unchivalrous advantage. The use of guns is taken for granted in

Le Jouvencel. From the 1330s French nobles had been providing themselves with cannon,[55] and by the middle of the next century the artillery of chivalrous Burgundy was second to none in Europe for efficiency and inventiveness.[56] Aristocrats coveted the office of master of the ordnance for the prestige and the powers of patronage it offered. Princes took a growing interest in the techniques of gun casting. The illustrations to Maximilian I's *Weisskunig* make it clear that to this most self-consciously chivalrous of rulers a training in the manufacture and use of cannon was, with hunt and tilt, part of the routine training of the Christian knight.

It is true that much has been made of certain instances in which chivalrous complaint led to action being taken against the users of firearms. The most quoted instance is that of the late-fifteenth-century *condottiere,* Paolo Vitelli. "We read that Paolo Vitelli," wrote Burckhardt, "while recognizing and himself adopting the cannon, put out the eyes and cut off the hands of the captured *schioppettieri* of the enemy, because he held it unworthy that a gallant, and it might be a noble knight, should be wounded and laid low by a common, despised foot soldier."[57] Burckhardt is here following the *Elogia virorum bellica virtute illustrium* (1548) of Paolo Giovio. Now Giovio, historian and ecclesiastic, was a man with a romantic and antiquarian interest in knights and chivalrous deeds. It is from the same work that we get the assertion that Bartolommeo Colleoni was the first military leader to use guns in the field, instead of merely in siege operations, which is palpably false, and that when one of Colleoni's shot wounded Ercole d'Este the duke protested that Colleoni "had behaved evilly and barbarously, trying to kill with a novel and horrible storm of shot valiant men who fought with lance and sword in the name of honour and glory."[58] The duke's wound is mentioned by one of his contemporaries, the Florentine Vespasiano da Bisticci, without any comment at all.[59] And in the same way, Vitelli's conduct at Buti in 1498 was noticed *at the time* in two sources, one Pisan, the other Florentine, neither of which make any reference to Vitelli's attitude to firearms.[60] Nor did Guicciardini make any such reference when he dealt with the capture of Buti in his *History of Italy.* Not only do the sources before Giovio give no hint that gunners were discriminated against because of their weapon, but there were other considerations involved in Vitelli's action: the gunners were German mercenaries—his cruelty may have been a warning against employing more of them; the cruelty on this occasion was general—"yesterday," says the Pisan source, "our enemies took the Castello of Buti by force, employing their usual inhuman cruelty, taking prisoner and tormenting with divers tortures the men of the place, ejecting the women and violating some, and cutting all the bombardiers' hands off with such inhumanity that the barbarians and Turks could hardly use more." Giovio's facts are right, but it is very possible that his interpretation of them owes something to what he hoped, rather than knew, Vitelli's attitude to be. Certainly the practice current in Italy at the time of Buti was for captured *schioppettieri* to be pardoned or exchanged on the same terms as were other soldiers.[61] Monluc, it might be noted, used arquebusiers throughout his campaigning life and complained of firearms only when he had been wounded by one.

Gunpowder might well be a grievance for the horseman who had invested his fortune in his equipment and for the individual fighting for personal glory (rather than for a state or a cause), but it was accepted, however reluctantly, by the overwhelming majority of knightly soldiers. Guns were invented by the devil, de la Noue agreed, "howbeit, mans malice hath made them so necessarie that they cannot be spared. To the end therefore to profite by them...," and he goes on to describe how they can be best put to use.[62] As Robert de Balsac, Sieur d'Entragues, had pointed out in his *Nef des Princes et des Batailles* (1502), a prince, before undertaking a war, must be satisfied that his cause is a just one; after that he must make sure that he has enough artillery. A good cause is God's cause, and "what can more encourage and strengthen soldiers who shall fight the battailes of God and our Prince," asked the English printer of an Italian treatise on artillery in his dedicatory epistle to the Earl of Leicester, "than skilfull shooting in great and small peeces of artillerie?"[63] Or as a clergyman told a soldier audience in the English Midlands, "As S. Paul gives a Christian in his welfare, the whole armour of God; a Sword to offend, a Shield to defend; so in this kind of Warre, we must improve all things whatsoever the bowels or face of the earth can affoord for our defence ... [including] such an invention that many a brave spirit dies by the hand of a Boy, or as ignoblie as Abimelech, by the hand of a Woman. But seeing the fierie disposition of our enemies, use this as all others to our annoyance, why may we not snatch those weapons out of madde mens hands, and turne them into their own bosome?"[64]

This was not the first time that Christian society had been threatened by a new and cruel weapon. When the crossbow first inflicted its jagged tearing wounds, the Church condemned its use. But this did nothing to stop the acceptance of the crossbow, or its evolution into an ever more precise and powerful killing machine. Why should the Church now deprive herself, at a time when she was fighting her own wars to regain prestige and power in Italy, of a weapon already in her enemies' hands? Why should she emasculate the efforts of archbishops to maintain the integrity of their sees?[65] Why should she try to deprive Christians of a weapon that was in the hands of the common enemy? The Infidels had guns, they battered down the walls of Constantinople with them; why should not Christians have them too? Necessity coated the speck of grit in Christendom's conscience, and the Church eased the process by supplying gunners with a patron saint of their own, Saint Barbara.[66] Because her father, who had denounced her as a Christian, was struck down by thunder and lightning at the moment of her execution, she was connected with explosions, and by the time Palma Vecchio painted her standing over the muzzles of cannon for the Venetian association of *bombardieri,* she was popularly invoked both by gunners (according to the rules issued by Charles V to the artillery school in Burgos, the artilleryman was to call on the aid of Saint Barbara as he put the ball into his weapon) and by soldiers praying for protection against such missiles. Her image is thus found both on guns and on armor.[67] As the popularity of her cult grew with the increased use of firearms, her powers were commemorated in cheap woodcuts and ceramics as well as in paintings[68] to such an extent that Erasmus could scoff at "the foolish but gratifying belief that . . . whoever salutes an image of Barbara will come through a battle unscathed."[69]

The acceptance of firearms did not, of course, depend on the issue of a debate. Fundamentally, guns came to stay because they worked; they won battles, they demolished walls. But they were accepted, too, because of their appeal at a less rational level. They appealed because of their noise and violence, because they were modern and ingenious, because they enlisted both national and professional pride.

A fascination with their violence can be traced throughout the battle descriptions and poems with military themes of the period. From an anonymous English cleric of the mid-fifteenth century comes this description of a battle at sea:

> The canonys, the bumbard and the gunne,
>   Thei bloweth out the voys and stonys grete,
> Thorgh maste and side and other be thei runne,
>   In goth the serpentyne after his mete;
> The colveryne is besy for to gete
>   An hole into the top, and the crappaude
> Wil in; the fouler eek will have his laude.[70]

Sir Thomas Coningsby recorded his reaction at seeing a cannon ball discharged against Rouen in 1591, "where we might heare such ratling of houses, and see it fly through one house and grace upon the other, as were yt not for charytie it were pleasure to behold."[71] And typical of the frank pleasure found by a violent age in its most violent machine are these lines from *The Scottish Souldier* (1629): Away with silks and womanish conceits, cries the author, George Lawder,

> Let me still heare the Cannons thundring voice,
> In teror threaten ruin: that sweet noyse
> Rings in my eares more pleasing than the sound
> of any Musickes consort can be found. . . .
> Then to see leggs and armes torne ragged flie,
> And bodyes gasping all dismembered lie,
> One head beate off another, while the hand
> Sheaths in his neighbour's breast his bloodie brand,
> A Cannon bullet take a Ranke away,
> A Volley of small shot eclypse the day
> With smoke of sulphure, which no sooner cleares,
> Than death and honour everie where appeares.[72]

On the Elizabethan stage, the cannon—"Alarum, and chambers go off"—joined the drum in providing the atmosphere, frightening, yet thrilling, of war,[73] and patriotic poets called men to arms and to the music of Mars, "the roring Cannon, and the brasen Trumpe."[74] This same double music became part of the routine of celebration and salute. The announcement of the anti-French league of 1523 in Venice was accompanied by music and gunfire, and after the resulting victory at Pavia in 1525 the victorious ambassadors were allowed to draw gunpowder from the Venetian arsenal to commemorate it.[75] During the festivities in 1532, when Francis I—now free after his capture at Pavia—and Henry VIII came to Calais they "were saluted with great melody what with guns and all other instruments. . . . And at Boulogne, by estimation, it past not 200 shot but they were great pieces."[76] For the Moor it was not blasphemy that was in his mind but a consciousness of the thrill and terror of war when he bade farewell to its pride, pomp, and circumstance,

> And, O you mortal engines, whose rude throats
> Th'immortal Jove's dread clamours counterfeit,
> Farewell! Othello's occupation's gone!

And at a more trivially endearing level, fireworks, including set pieces showing mock battles, became a popular spectacle from the late sixteenth century.

From the fifteenth century, when men were only beginning to take sides in the Ancients *versus* Moderns controversy, the success of the new weapon was a key argument for those who felt that man could discover things unknown to the ancients, and that his intelligence should not be directed only to the rediscovery of ancient wisdom but to advancing, increment by increment, on what he could find out for himself about the physical world. The author of *Knighthode and Battaile* listed all the ancient siege weapons which could now be blown to bits.[77] The cult of the military methods of the ancients, which lasted well into the seventeenth century, after first attempting, with Machiavelli, to play down the effectiveness of firearms, contented itself with accepting the importance of the new weapon, but emphasizing that the really crucial lessons of ancient warfare, which above all concerned organization, discipline, and morale, were as relevant as ever. "I could heartily wish," Robert Barret made a captain say in 1598, "that, as neere as possible we might, we should reduce our selves with such armes as we now use, unto the forme, manner, and course of the aunciant Romanes in their Militia and discipline of warre, although ages, seasons and inventions, have altered much and many weapons by them used."[78]

The growing scientific interests of the moderns welcomed the gun for what it revealed about ballistics and the laws of motion, and what its technology taught about metallurgy and the chemistry of explosives. Gunpowder manufacture was one of the industries that Francis Bacon recommended for study,[79] and it is no accident that on the title page of Bishop Thomas Sprat's *History of the Royal Society* Bacon, "Artium Instaurator," is portrayed pointing to a gun.

Another instinct the gun tapped was a love of ingenious devices and technical expertise. From the late fourteenth century men had toyed with the idea of putting the paddle boat and military machines described in the late classical manuscript *De rebus bellicis* into practice;[80] the illustrations to Valturio and, early in the sixteenth century, to editions of Vegetius, and the drawings of Renaissance artists like Francesco di Giorgio and Leonardo, to mention only the most famous, show elaborate and mostly impracticable devices: revolving turret guns, multibarrelled guns (a version of these was actually used), combination cannon and mortar and the like.[81] The taste for these inventions was satirized by Rabelais' description of the assault vehicle, "the great sow,"[82] and by Jonson in the *Staple of News*, where among other inventions, like submarines and the cork shoes which would enable Spinola's army to cross the Channel dry-foot, he mentions the Rosicrucians' notable discovery of "the art of drawing farts out of dead bodies."[83] Ingenious firearms, like the little gun carried at his girdle by Erasmus' friend Peter Falk, who was "curious about novelties in arts and machinery,"[84] appealed to collectors, and gunsmiths produced a wide range of combination weapons in which guns were combined with shields, war hammers, swords, daggers, even crossbows.[85] Though the simple matchlock proved the most practical military weapon, experiments were made with double- and triple-barrelled firearms, and the workmanship lavished on the locks and mountings of pistols and sporting guns put them among the most cherished of personal possessions.

The professional pride of the gunfounder comes out clearly from Biringuccio's remarks that he is not going to discuss mortars—the earliest guns were frequently of this type—"because they are not esteemed by us moderns,"[86] and Tartaglia boasts that he is dealing with

> ... *nuove invenzioni*
> *non tolte da Platon né Plotino,*
> *né d'alcun altro greco ovver latino,*
> *ma sol da l'arte, misura e ragione.*[87]

Theorists of gunnery put their art on a par with that of music, medicine, astronomy, and mathematics,[88] and Captain Macmorris' outburst when he is not allowed to blow up the town of Harfleur splendidly expresses the involvement of the professional with his craft. "By Chrish, la, tish ill done; the work ish give over, the trompet sound the retreat. By my hand, I swear, and my father's soul, the work ish ill done; it ish give over: I would have blow'd up the town, so Chrish save me, la, in an hour: O, tish ill done, tish ill done; by my hand, tish ill done!"[89] Dekker's "Praise of the Shotte" in *The Artillery Garden* is a stirring eulogy of gunpowder and the deeds that are done with it:

> Some say the Pouder is the Meale of hell. . . .
> O shallow empty sculls, that under foote
> Tread such a Mine, out of which growes the root,
> Of all new warlike Discipline!

And he goes on to celebrate the gun as the bulwark of kingdoms, preserver of the world (for he too believes that battles had been more bloody in the Middle Ages), mother of inventions, the soldier's choicest music.[90] This pride in man's achievement was allied, in the case of Germans, to national pride. Smarting from the contempt shown them as barbarians by the sophisticates of Italy, the German retort was: "You may have studied the ancients longer than we have, but it took us to invent the most potent instrument in modern war." Toward the end of Jacob Wimpheling's *Rerum Germanicarum Epitome* (1505), where he explains why the Germans are such an admirable people, after chapters "On the Courage of the Germans," "On the Noblemindedness of the Germans," "On the Generosity of the Germans," there is one "On the offensive weapon, popularly called the Bombard, invented by the Germans." But the possession of an extensive park of artillery was a source of pride to all nations, and cities were proud of the guns which armed their new, bastioned fortifications. The cannon, in terms of national and civic politics, was one of the foremost status symbols of the Renaissance.

The appeal of guns was so strong, and they slipped into men's consciousness by so many insidious routes, that opposition was partly disarmed by familiarity. Early-fifteenth-century manuscript illuminations showed the armies of Alexander the Great and of the Crusaders conducting sieges with cannon. Cannon and handguns figure in the earliest illustrated printed editions of Livy: battles seemed unthinkable without gunpowder.[91] Guns were given names, and this helped to domesticate their terror. Pius II named two of his cannon Enea and Silvia after his own name, Eneas Silvius Piccolomini, and another after his mother, Vittoria.[92] They were named after birds and girls and animals, and both Charles V and Henry VIII had batteries known as the Twelve Apostles. From the time when Pisanello designed guns for Alfonso I of Aragon the menace of cannon was veiled by their beauty. Francesco di Giorgio's designs for large guns have an elaborate charm that diverts attention from their purpose; Biringuccio always added urns or heads of men or animals "to make the gun beautiful."[93]

Increasingly, wherever a man looked, he saw guns. The chivalrous battle scenes carved in 1489 for the choir stalls of Toledo cathedral showed cannon in action, or being hauled in oxcarts;[94] the elaborate marble monument sculpted before 1520 for Gaston de Foix by Agostino Busti (and now broken up) had panels where guns were introduced into piles of trophies *à l'antique*.[95] Guns appeared as trophies on the title pages of books from at least 1528.[96] Henry Peacham's *Minerva Britanna* (1612) illustrates the tag "*Quae pondere maior*" with a hand holdng a balance; in one pan are a pen and a laurel wreath, in the other a cannon; the gun had taken over from the sword as "Symbole of th'art Militar." And on the title page of the French translation (Rouen, 1627) of Giorgio Basta's *Il governo della cavalleria leggiera,* the figure of Bellum himself, though in one hand he flourishes a sword, in the other he holds a gun. Kings and princes exchanged cannon as tokens of respect—Charles V received one of "gold, silver and metal"—even as wedding presents.[97] Battle scenes showing artillery in action were embossed on armor from the middle of the sixteenth century.[98] Duke Federigo of Urbino, though he would not allow a printed book in his famous library, used a bomb as one of his *imprese*,[99] and Ariosto's own patron, Alfonso d'Este, bore the emblem of a flaming bombshell on his cuirass at the battle of Ravenna in 1512.[100] In this device the projectile symbolized not the horror of war but a praiseworthy moral quality, energy held in check until the critical moment, vigor tempered by a wise restraint. When Alfonso was painted by Titian he chose to be portrayed with his hand resting on the muzzle of a cannon: here I stand, he implies, a man of prudence, but capable, should the occasion demand it, of lethal activity.[101]

While guns were quietly taking their place among the iconographical clichés of statecraft, they were becoming still further domesticated by common use and usage. They were used as signals that processions or ceremonies were starting;[102] "gunshot" was used as a matter of course as a measurement of length in 1548;[103] and from the beginning of the seventeenth century the phrases "as sure as a gun," "right as a gun" appear.[104] When Isabella's brother vainly warns Bracciano to keep away from Vittoria in Webster's *The White Devil*, he warns him not with "We'll settle this by the sword" but "Wee'le end this with the Cannon."[105] The Spanish dramatist Veléz de Guevara wrote *La Serrana de la Vera* in 1613 in order that the most famous actress of her time could swagger about in it, shouldering an arquebus.[106] In early Stuart England gunpowder was used to cure toothache,[107] and the London bookseller Grismond disposed of his wares "at the signe of the Gun in Pauls Alley." Humor, too, helped to take some of the sting out of the lethal nature of artillery. Cannon balls were likened to tennis balls in Tudor ballads,[108] and when the tobacco controversy got under way at the goading of James I, Thomas Pestell defended it as the cheapest form of artillery with which to puff an enemy into subjection, and Joshua Sylvester attacked it as even worse than the gun,

> For Guns shoot from-ward, onely at their Foen;
> Tobacco-pipes, home-ward into their Owne
> (When, for the Touch-hole, firing the wrong end,
> Into our Selves the Poyson's force wee send).[109]

By 1620 water was spouting from the stone cannon of a fountain shaped like a galleon in the gardens of the Vatican,[110] and at about the same time the first miracle concerning small arms was recorded when a Dominican missionary turned a pistol with which he was being threatened into a crucifix.[111] From the middle of the sixteenth century, moreover, guns began to take their place in the symbolism of love. Naked *amori* shoot pistols at one another on an ivory powder flask,[112] a cupid is carved on the arm which sparks the flint and fires the pistol[113]—and in the Boar's Head tavern, Eastcheap, "Pistol's cock is up, And flashing fire will follow."[114]

English Renaissance drama shows that the gun took over from the sword as a virility symbol[115] at about the same time that it became a symbol of war itself, "Here, Pistol, I charge you with a cup of sack," says Falstaff. "Do you discharge upon mine hostess." "I will discharge upon her, Sir John, with two bullets."[116] In Beaumont and Fletcher's *The Honest Man's Fortune* the servants are discussing their mistress's new lover: "Ay, marry, boys! There will be sport indeed! There will be grappling! She has a murderer [a type of culverin] lies in her prow, I am afraid will fright his main-mast, Robin."[117] The medieval convention of describing love in terms of an attack by desire on the castle of chastity was revitalized by the use of guns and the elaborate outworks of the new bastioned fortification: ravelins, redoubts, half moons, horn works, and the rest. Modern siege imagery—used tenderly, as in Thomas, Lord Vaux' "The assault of Cupid upon the fort where the lovers hart lay wounded" (1585),[118] or crudely, as in Stephen Gosson's attack on corsets[119]—came to be used extensively in the drama, as in the scene in Beaumont and Fletcher's *The Woman's Prize* in which the heroine locks herself in her room, or the act in Shakerley Marmion's *Hollands leaguer* (1632) which passes in front of the "fort," a brothel.

This working of gunpowder imagery into the language of sex is a symptom of its acceptance by society at large, and literary men seized gratefully on the further opportunities it offered of freshening images concerned with speed, violence, and accuracy. Romeo begs for a poison that will spread through the body "As violently as hasty powder fired Doth hurry from the fatal cannon's mouth"; Falstaff is "afraid of this gunpowder Percy though he be dead"; Sir William Lucy expresses his anguish at the news of Talbot's death with "O, were mine eye-balls into bullets turn'd, that I in rage might shoot them at your faces!"; and when Juliet calls out for Romeo she weeps "as if that name, Shot from the deadly level of a gun, Did murder her."[120] Images were drawn from the whole range of artillery training and technology, from Friar Lawrence's attempt to dissuade Romeo from suicide, "Thy wit . . . Like powder in a skilless soldier's flask, Is set a-fire by thine own ignorance, And thou dismember'd with thine own defence," to Henry V's reference to the effect of ricochet, "Mark then abounding valour in our English, That being dead, like to the bullet's grazing, Break out into a second course of mischief," and Webster's "My friend and I, Like two chaine-bullets, side by side, will fly Thorow the jawes of death."[121] With "Invention flye in Fire, clap sulphery winges, Whilst every line like a ramde Bullet singes," Dekker likened gunpowder to literary inspiration itself.[122]

This service of gunpowder to imagery, and its heightening of atmosphere in the interest either of terror, as in Patten's description of the battle of Pinkie, [123] or of pathos, as in Drayton's poem on Agincourt[124] (an instructive contrast to Froissart's treatment of Crécy), meant that men met the gun in language as familiarly as in painting and sculpture, and this helped to reconcile them to meeting it in real life. And from the pulpit as from the stage: in his sermon for Trinity Sunday, 1535, Latimer warned his congregation that the devil "hath great peeces of ordinaunce, as mighty kinges and Emperours to shoote against Gods people. . . . He hath yet lesse ordinaunce, for he hath of all sortes to shoote at good christen men. . . . These be Accusars, Promoters, and slaunderers, they be evill Ordinaunce, shrewd handguns."[125] In a sermon at Paul's Cross in 1598 Gosson said that preaching itself :"is haile-shot; we send it among the thickest of you, desirous to hitte you all."[126]

With the intellectual debate *pro* and *contra* the use of gunpowder being, as we have seen, so inconclusive, and taking into account the powerful appeal of the new weapons both to the practical needs and the imagination of contemporaries, we must, I think, be careful not to give too much weight to the effect of the chorus of disapproval which accompanied the use of guns. It has recently been suggested that the effect of gunpowder might have been more terrible and destructive had it not been for the restraint imposed by moral and intellectual values and the diversion of inventive energy into decoration and display. Professor A. R. Hall has remarked that "the design of artillery remained essentially unchanged, less on account of the inability of science and industry to produce better weapons than of the absence of pressure to this end. Military opinion was happy in a surviving tradition of chivalry that close combat was more honourable than a long range bombardment between invisible foes."[127] And Professor Nef has referred to "the moral and intellectual scruples and the love of beauty which were still characteristic of Europeans in the early seventeenth century, and which bound them—scientists, artists, craftsmen, governors and statesmen alike—by a kind of voluntary servitude to make choices which seemed to them pre-eminently rational,"[128] *i.e.,* to restrict the effects of gunpowder.

When there were so many ways in which men could accommodate their consciences to the use of gunpowder it is, I think, very unlikely that in fact "the Christian sense of responsibility" moderated the use of firearms, or that the "concern of builders and craftsmen with beauty blunted the force of bullets, shot, balls and explosives."[129] Professor Nef takes the horror felt at the slaying by a cannon ball of Salisbury in *Henry VI, Part One*,[130] as an expression of contemporary anti-gunpowder feeling. The only support for this view, however, is Talbot's reference to "the treacherous manner of his mournful death," and this refers much more probably to the fact that Salisbury was killed not in combat but by a ruse—the covering by a gun of a vantage point in a tower used for observation purposes by the English. "Treacherous" in this situation would have suited a bowshot equally well. Here was a flower of English chivalry shot nastily to death ("One of thy eyes and thy cheek's side shot off," as Talbot observes) from a distance, and not even by a gunner but by a gunner's *boy,* and yet Shakespeare does not make any overt anti-gunpowder point. More revealing of contemporary opinion is Hotspur's contemptuous description of a gun-shy courtier:

> ... he made me mad
> To see him shine so brisk, and smell so sweet,
> And talk so like a waiting-gentlewoman
> Of guns, and drums, and wounds—God save the mark!
> And telling me the sovereign'st thing on earth
> Was parmaceti for an inward bruise;
> And that it was great pity, so it was,
> This villainous saltpetre should be digg'd

> Out of the bowels of the harmless earth,
> Which many a good tall fellow had destroy'd
> So cowardly; and but for these vile guns
> He would himself have been a soldier.[131]

Certainly some inventors claimed to have discovered means of destruction so horrible that they suppressed them. Leonardo would not reveal his secret for destroying ships from under water (though he was prepared to cannonade and asphyxiate their crews from the surface);[132] Tartaglia would not reveal the composition of his noiseless powder;[133] John Napier said he had torn up the formula of a new explosive of terrifying power.[134] But we have no way of knowing if these things would have worked; the notion of silent gunpowder was pooh-poohed in 1601 by the English gunnery expert, Thomas Smith.[135] Moreover, other horrors were actually used: explosive shells, various forms of liquid fire, gasbombs, with which the Venetians were experimenting as early as 1482.[136] When Giambelli's explosive-packed infernal machine killed some five hundred of the besiegers of Antwerp in 1585, the European reaction was one not of outraged sensibility but rather of grudging admiration.[137] Nor was there any suggestion from the development of sporting guns—a competitive industry, unhampered by ethical considerations—that military weapons could have been made more lethal. Biringuccio's concern to beautify his cannon did not impede his desire to make them as effective as possible. There were alternative types of missile that caused more destruction than the spherical ball, but "because things cannot always be made according to desire, they often fail in operation."[138] The barrier to advance was not moral or esthetic, it was technological. More accurate guns had to wait until the use of machine tools in the nineteenth century; longer ranges awaited improvements in metallurgy; better explosives depended on advances in chemistry, a science still in its infancy in the Renaissance.

It is natural for modern historians, sickened by the arms race of their own day, to look back in nostalgia to an age when there is literary evidence to suggest that the race could be slowed by an appeal to men's better nature. This nostalgia, alas, is misplaced. By the early seventeenth century, ideals had given ground to the arguments of fact. Opposition to gunpowder retreated to one form of one weapon: the rifled musket, which, as a sharpshooter's weapon to pick off officers, was deplored as violating the code of war. But it was used, nevertheless.[139] Optimistic students of human nature can take little comfort from the reactions of their Renaissance ancestors to the greatest challenge to Europe's conscience offered by military technology before the atom bomb.

NOTES

1. J. F. C. Fuller, *Decisive Battles of the Western World and their Influence upon History* (2 vols, London, 1954–5) I, p. 470.
2. (Basel, 1531), p. 132.
3. *Opera bellissima del arte militar* (Venice), book II, chap. 2.
4. Modernized from the translation by Langley, *An abridgement of the notable woorke of P. Vergile* (London, 1546), f. lxix[v].
5. *Commentariorum* (Paris, 1526), f. cccxxii[r].
6. (Lyons, 1535), Vol. II, p. 429.
7. In the *De remediis utriusque fortunae*, c. 1366. Quoted by H. Delbrück, *Geschichte der Kriegskunst im Rahmen der politischen Geschichte* (4 vols, Berlin, 1900–20) IV, p. 37.
8. *Commentaries*, book 5, F. A. Gragg and L. C. Gabel, eds., *Smith College Studies in History* (1947), p. 393.
9. *Trattato di architettura civile e militare*, Cesare Saluzzo, ed. (Turin, 1841), pp. 249–50.
10. For example, Pedro Mexia, *The Forest, or Collection of Histories*, trans. T. Fortescue (London, 1571), f. 15[r].
11. *Le Fortificationi* (Venice, 1609), p. 152.
12. Book I, chap. vii, note i.
13. Ed. 1629, pp. 202–4. There is no mention of artillery in the first edition of 1605.

14. *The Scholemaster* (London, 1570), ff. 19ᵛ–20ʳ.
15. L. Daneau, *Brieve Remonstrance sur les Ieux de sort* (n. p., 1574), pp. 18–19.
16. His *Astrologiae . . . encomia* (1559) is described in Lynn Thorndike, *History of Magic and Experimental Science* (New York, 1923–58), Vol. V, p. 585.
17. *La Cosmographie universelle* (Basle, 1552), p. 545.
18. Musée de l'Arsenal, Paris.
19. Quoted by J. S. D. Scott, *The British Army: its Origin, Progress, and Equipment* (2 vols, London, 1868), II, p. 193.
20. *Remaines, ed. cit.*, pp. 202–3.
21. Vallo [Battista della Valle], *Du faict de la guerre et art militaire* (Lyon, 1554), ff. 5ᵛ–6ʳ. This section does not occur in the earlier Italian editions.
22. "A discourse of . . . War," *Works* (8 vols, Oxford, 1829), VIII, p. 253:
    "it is needful that against the wit and subtelty of man we oppose, not only the brute force of our bodies, (wherein many beasts exceed us) but, helping our strength with art and wisdom, strive to excel our enemies in those points wherein man is excellent over other creatures."
23. *A royall edict . . .* (London, 1629), p. 9.
24. *Essays* (trans. Florio), "Of steeds, called in French destriers."
25. The bow-*versus*-gun controversy is discussed in my edition of Smythe's *Certain Discourses Military* (1590), Folger Documents of Tudor and Stuart Civilization (Cornell, 1964).
26. *The Politicke and Militarie Discourses* (Eng. trans. London, 1587), p. 202.
27. *The Works of Guillaume de Salluste, Sieur Du Bartas* (Chapel Hill, 1940), p. 496.
28. Quoted from British Museum MS. Harleian 3,261, in C. Ffoulkes, *The Gun-founders of England* (Cambridge, England, 1937), p. 3 n.
29. *Trattato . . . , ed. cit.*, p. 245.
30. *History of Italy,* book I, chap. 3: "piuttosto diabolico che umano."
31. *Complaint of Peace,* W. J. Hirten, ed. (New York, 1946), p. 32.

32. *De la Pirotechnia* (Venice, 1540) trans. Smith and Gnudi (New York, 1943), book X, chap. 2.
33. (Basle, 1552), p. 544.
34. Reproduced in O. Guttmann, *Monumenta Pulveris Pyrii* (London, 1906), fig. 14.
35. "An execration upon Vulcan."
36. Quoted from *De remediis utriusque fortunae*, in Delbrück, *op. cit.*, IV, p. 37. Translated in *Phisicke against Fortune* (London, 1579), f. 126ᵛ.
37. *Political and Historical Works* (London, 1852), Vol. II, p. 246.
38. Quoted by A. Toynbee, *A Study of History* (10 vols, Oxford, 1934–54) III, p. 386.
39. Guido Camerarius *Nova Reperta*, with Salmuth's commentary (1602), (trans. 1715), p. 389.
40. *La Panegyric du chevalier sans reproche* (1527), quoted in Gladys Dickinson, The *Instructions sur le Faict de la Guerre of Raymond de Beccarie de Pavie Sieur de Fourquevaux* (London, 1954), p. xliv.
41. Trans. W. S. Rose (2 vols, London, 1858) I, canto xi, verse 23.
42. *Ibid.*, verse 26.
43. C. Cotton's English translation (London, 1674), p. 9.
44. Quoted by Delbrück, *op cit.*, IV, p. 39.
45. English trans. by J. M. Cohen (London, 1950), p. 344.
46. *Complete Works*, A. B. Grosart, ed. (n. p., 5 vols, 1885–96), II, book 6, stanza 40.
47. *Silva de varia lecion* (Valladolid[?], 1543), p. 41.
48. *La Methode de Traicter les Playes faictes par Harcquebutes* . . . (1545), English translation (1634) reprinted in *The Apologie and Treatise of Ambroise Paré . . . with many of his writings upon Surgery*, Geoffrey Keynes, ed. (London, 1951), p. 132.
49. *Ibid.*, p. 50.
50. H. W. L. Hime, *The Origin of Artillery* (London, 1915), p. 132.
51. For example, M. A. Gist, *Love and War in the Middle English Romance* (Philadelphia, 1947).

52. *Oeuvres Complètes,* Saint Hilaire, ed. (Paris, 1884), Vol. IV, p. 289.
53. *Regiment of Princes,* F. J. Furnival, ed. (E.E.T.S., London, 1897), p. 144.
54. Quoted in R. L. Kilgour, *The Decline of Chivalry* (Harvard, 1937), p. 325.
55. Napoleon III, *op. cit.,* p. 7.
56. C. Brusten, *L'armée bourguignonne de 1465 à 1468* (Bruxelles, 1953), p. 7.
57. *The Civilization of the Renaissance* (London, 1944), p. 62.
58. *Elogia,* Italian translation by Lodovico Dominichi (Florence, 1554), p. 173.
59. *The Vespasiano Memoirs,* translated by William George and Emily Waters (London, 1926), pp. 89–90.
60. *A Florentine Diary from 1450 to 1516 by Luca Landucci,* I. del Badia, ed. (London, 1927), p. 147 and 147n.
61. G. Canestrini, *Scritti Inediti di Niccolò Machiavelli risguardanti la Storia e la Milizia (1499–1512)* (Florence, 1857), pp. xxvi–xxvii.
62. *Op. cit.,* p. 199.
63. Niccolò Tartaglia, *Three bookes of Colloquies concerning the arte of shooting in great and small peeces of artillerie* . . . (London, 1588), f. 3^r.
64. Samuel Buggs, *The Midland Souldier* (London, 1622), pp. 26–27.
65. On the breech of a cannon cast near Coblenz, the residence of the Archbishop of Trèves, there is an inscription: "I am called the Griffon. I serve my gracious Lord of Trèves; where he bids me force my way, I cast down gates and walls." The gun is in the Musée de l'Arsenal, Paris.
66. S. Peine, *St. Barbara, die Schutzheilige der Bergleute und der Artillerie* (Freiberg, 1896).
67. For example, a superb cannon of Ferdinand II of Tuscany in the arsenal at Venice; horse armor in the Tower of London presented by Maxmilian I to the young Henry VIII in 1509.
68. For example, the broadsheet reproduced in P. Heitz, *Italienische Einblattdrucke* (Strassburg, 1933), Part I, No. 18; plaque in the

Museo Civico, Turin, which shows her standing above what looks like model cannon; a painting attributed to Jan or Hubert van Eyck which shows her in front of a tower (her usual attribute) in which is a statue of Mars, reproduced in Reinach, *Repertoire des peintures* (6 vols, Paris, 1905–23), Vol. II, p. 364.

69. *Praise of Folly*, trans. H. H. Hudson (Princeton, 1941), p. 56.
70. *Knyghthode and Battaile*, R. Dyboski and Z. M. Arend, eds. (London, E. E. T. S., 1935), p. 104.
71. *Journal of the Siege of Rouen*, J. G. Nichols, ed. (Camden Miscellany I, 1847), p. 40.
72. George Lawder, *The Scottish Souldier* (Edinburgh, 1629), f. A4^t.
73. See Paul A. Jorgensen, *Shakespeare's Military World* (University of California, 1956), pp. 15–17.
74. *A farewell, Entituled to the famous generalls of our English forces: Sir J. Norris & Syr F. Drake* (London, 1589), in D. H. Horne *The Life and Minor Works of George Peele* (2 vols, New Haven, 1952), I, p. 221.
75. *Calendar of State Papers, Venetian, 1520–1526*, nos. 736 and 942.
76. *The maner of the tryumphe at Caleys and Bulleyn* (London, 1532), modernized in E. Arber, *An English Garner* (8 vols, London, 1877–96) II, pp. 38–9.
77. *Ed. cit.* in note 70 above, p. 93. For examples of gunpowder being cited as a triumph of Modern over Ancient learning, see A. F. Jones, *Ancients and Moderns* (St. Louis, 1961), p. 12 and *passim*, and J. B. Bury, *The Idea of Progress* (London, 1920), p. 54.
78. *The Theoricke and Practike of Moderne Warres* (London, 1598), p. 32.
79. See Christopher Hill, *The Century of Revolution 1603–1714* (London, 1961), p. 94.
80. *A Roman Reformer and Inventor; being a new Text of the Treatise De Rebus Bellicis, with a Translation and Introduction by E. A. Thompson* (Cambridge, England, 1952), pp. 18 ff.
81. See, for example, G. Canestrini, *Arte militare meccanica medievale* (Milan, 1940).
82. *Gargantua and Pantagruel*, book 4, chap. 40.
83. III, ii.

84. F. M. Nichols, *The Epistles of Erasmus* (3 vols, London, 1907–17), II, pp. 335–56.
85. Specimens of all these varieties can be seen in the Metropolitan Museum of Art, New York.
86. *Pirotechnia, ed. cit.*, p. 227.
87. Quoted from *Quesiti e Invenzioni Diverse* (1546), by U. Forti, *Storia della Technica Italiana* (Florence, 1940), p. 294.
88. That is, Richard Rotheruppe's prefatory poem to Thomas Smith's *The Art of Gunnery* (London, 1600). On the use made of classical mythology to justify the use of gunpowder on the title pages of books on gunnery and fortification, see my "The argument of some military title pages of the Renaissance," *Newberry Library Bulletin* (March, 1964), pp. 61–102.
89. *Henry V*, III, ij.
90. f.D i^{r-v}.
91. For example, British Museum MSS., *Conqueste de Jerusalem* (15. E.1.ff.241^r and 357^r), *Roman de la Rose* (Harleian 4425, f. 139^r), *Quintus Curtius* (Burn. 169, ff. 69^r and 127^r) and Livy: Venice, 1493, 1495, 1506; Mentz, 1505; Saragossa, 1506; Paris, 1514.
92. *Commentaries, ed. cit.*, p. 388.
93. On Pisanello's designs, see Canestrini, *op. cit.*, p. 232; Francesco di Giorgio's are in the manuscript of his *Trattato* in the National Library of Florence, MS. II. I. 141, f. 48^r; Biringuccio, *ed. cit.*, pp. 243–44.
94. Preface by Walter Starkie to Ramón Menéndez Pidal, *The Spaniards in their History* (London, 1950), p. 43.
95. Giorgio Nicodemi, *Agostino Busti* (Milan, 1945), esp. pl. 20.
96. Battista della Valle, *Libro continente Appartenentie ad Capitanii* (Venice.)
97. Charles's cannon is referred to in *C. S. P. Venetian, 1520–1526*, no. 1021; Bashford Dean, *The Metropolitan Museum of Art. Handbook of Arms and Armor* (New York, 1930), p. 83.
98. Examples are: gauntlets of the Duke of Guise (1565) in the Metropolitan Museum, New York; gorget of Philip II in the Armory at Madrid.

99. G. F. Hill, *A Corpus of Italian Medals* (2 vols, London, 1930) I, p. 76.
100. Its significance is explained in Paolo Giovio, *Imprese* ... (Lyons, 1574), p. 80. The motto that accompanied this device was *Loco et tempore*.
101. On this concept, see E. Wind, *Pagan Mysteries of the Renaissance* (London, 1958), pp. 95 ff.
102. As at the Field of Cloth of Gold in 1520. *C. S. P. Venetian, 1520–1526*, no. 67.
103. In Sir William Patten, *The Expedicion into Scotlande*.
104. In "Of Catesby, Faux, and Garnet," printed in Hyder Rollins, *Old English Ballads, 1553–1625* (Cambridge, 1920), p. 361, and John Fletcher, *The Prophetess*, I,iii.
105. II,i.
106. Starkie, *op. cit.*, p. 69.
107. *Duchess of Malfi*, III,ii, 17–19.
108. G. G. Langsam, *Martial Books and Tudor Verse* (New York, 1951), pp. 124 and 130.
109. *Complete Works*, A. B. Grosart, ed. (2 vols, London, 1880) II, p. 265. For Pestell, see *Poems*, H. Buchan, ed. (Oxford, 1940), p. 32, "On Tobacco."
110. Cesare d'Onofrio, *Le Fontane di Roma* (Rome, 1951), p. 147.
111. E. Mâle, *L'Art religieux après le Concile de Trent* (Second edition, Paris, 1951), p. 101.
112. H. J. Jackson and C. E. Whitelaw, *European Hand Firearms* (London, 1923), p. xv.
113. Pistol in Metropolitan Museum of Art, New York.
114. *Henry V*, II,i.
115. For the sword as a symbol of a swaggering kind of virility, see the overtly phallic treatment of hilts in engravings, painted glass, etc., especially German portrayals of *Landsknechte* in the early sixteenth century.
116. *Henry IV, Part Two*, II,iv.
117. V,iii.
118. *Poems*, ed. A. B. Grosart (Blackburn, 1872), pp. 39–40.

119. *Quippes for upstart newfangled gentlewomen* (London, 1595), p. 9.
120. *Romeo and Juliet*, V,i; *Henry IV, Part One*, V,iv; *Henry VI, Part One*, IV,vii, III,iii.
121. III,iii; IV,iii; *Challenge for Beauty*, quoted in Webster, *Works*, F. L. Lucas, ed. (4 vols, London, 1927), II, p. 189.
122. *The Artillery Garden, a poem* (Oxford, 1952), f. Bi^v.
123. Patten, *op. cit.*, esp. ff. G v^{r-v}.
124. *The battaile of Agincourt, Works*, J. William Hebel, ed. (five vols, Oxford, 1961) III, pp. 28–29.
125. *Fruitfull Sermons* (London, 1571), f. 2^r.
126. *The Trumpet of Warre* (London, n.d), f. G vi^r.
127. A. R. Hall, *Ballistics in the Seventeenth Century* (Cambridge, 1952), p. 9.
128. J. U. Nef, *War and Human Progress* (London, 1950), pp. 132–33.
129. *Ibid.*, p. 129.
130. II,iii.
131. *Henry IV, Part One*, I,iii.
132. Bern Dibner, "Leonardo da Vinci; military engineer," in *Essays in the History of Science and Learning offered . . . to George Sarton*, M. F. Ashley Montagu, ed. (New York, 1944), p. 104.
133. T. M. Spaulding in *Adams Memorial Studies*, J. G. McManaway, G. E. Dawson, E. E. Willoughby, eds. (Washington, 1948), p. 497.
134. Nef, *op. cit.*, pp. 121–22.
135. *Certain Additions to the Booke of Gunnery* (London, 1601), f. A2^r.
136. L. Simeoni, *Le Signorie* (2 vols, Milan, 1950), I, pp. 551 and 570.
137. L. Van der Essen, *Alexandre Farnèse* (5 vols, Brussels, 1933–37), IV, pp. 55 ff.
138. *Ed. cit.*, pp. 430–31.
139. For example, by Gustavus Adolphus' ally, the Landgrave William of Hesse-Cassel; Michael Roberts, *Gustavus Adolphus, A History of Sweden 1611–1632* (2 vols, London, 1953–58), II, p. 227.

The True Shakespearian Blank*

Claudius. Come, Gertrude, we'll call up our wisest friends
And let them know, both what we mean to do,
And what's untimely done [so haply slander,]
Whose whisper o'er the world's diameter,
As level as the cannon to his *blank*
Transports his poison'd shot, may miss our name,
And hit the woundless air.
Hamlet IV. i. 38 ff.

Desdemona [to Cassio]. . . . I have spoken for you all my best
And stood within the *blank* of his displeasure
For my free speech! you must awhile be patient.
Othello III. iv. 127-129

Lear.   Out of my sight!
Kent. See better, Lear; and let me still remain
The true *blank* of thine eye.
King Lear I. i. 159-161

Leontes.   . . . the harlot king
Is quite beyond mine arm, out of the *blank*
And level of my brain, plot proof.
Winter's Tale II. iii. 4-6[1]

IN each of these four passages the force of the imagery depends on the meaning of the word "blank". Editors have followed the *O.E.D.* definition of *blank* as "the white spot in the centre of a target", or the "white spot in the centre of a target; fig. anything aimed at, range of such aim", suggested by Onions in *A Shakespeare Glossary*.[2] Most editors have chosen "white spot in the centre of a target" to explain "blank" in these passages,[3] or included "range" only as a secondary element in the image. It is the purpose of this note to suggest that "range" is the more important element, and that "blank" is forcefully precise, having the full implications of the term *point-blank*.

* This paper owes much to the generous interest taken in it at all stages by Professor Eric Dobson, and to the scrutiny by my colleague Professor George Hunter of the final draft.
[1] Line references are throughout to *The Complete Works of Shakespeare*, ed. Hardin Craig.
[2] And cf. A. Schmidt, *Shakespeare-Lexicon* (1902) "the white mark in the centre of a butt, the aim"; R. J. Cunliffe, *A New Shakespearian Dictionary* (1910), "The white spot in the centre of a target, anything aimed at . . . the range of the aim."
[3] E.g. J. Dover Wilson (*Othello*, glossary): "The white spot in the centre of the target."
J. H. P. Pafford (*Winter's Tale*, note): "The white bull's-eye of the target."
E. Dowden (*Hamlet*, note): "the white spot in the centre of a target."
Kenneth Muir (*King Lear*, note): "the white spot in the centre of the target, the white. . . . There may be a quibble on the white of the eye in the ordinary sense of the word."

It is important to note in the first place that the word *blank* is never used in the sense of "target" in the printed technical literature of the Elizabethan age, and only once, to my knowledge, in an unpublished work.

As far as archery is concerned, from Ascham's *Toxophilus* (1545) to Gervase Markham's *The Art of Archery* (1634), the word used for target[4] in its broadest sense of anything aimed at was *mark,* and in more specialized senses *prick* and *butt,* the butt being the turf background against which marks of different shapes and sizes were placed, the prick being a card which might be so placed but could be secured against any standing object or in the ground. Ascham speaks of "shooting . . . at buttes and prickes", of "hitting of the pricke", of those who "shote . . . and never care for any marke at al".[5] The language of the statutes regulating archery used the same terminology. Thus in 33 Henry VIII c. 9. we find "Be it further enacted by authoritie aforesaid, that no man under the age of twenty foure yeeres, shall shoot at any standing Prick, except it be at a Rover, wherat he shal change at every shoot his marke."[6] The ballads tell the same story.

> There was not shoote these yeomen [the king's archers] shot,
>   That any pricke might stand.
> Then spake *William of Cloudesle,*
>   by him that for me dyed
> I hold him never a good Archer,
>   that shooteth at Buts so wide.[7]

And, in a more sophisticated passage, Drayton, while discharging a capacious volley of technical terms, makes no mention of blank. With reference to Robin Hood and his men, he says that

> Of Archery they had the very perfect craft,
> With Broad-arrow, or But, or Prick, or Roving Shaft,
> At Markes full fortie score, they us'd to Pricke, and Rove,
> Yet higher than the breast, for Compasse never strove;
> Yet at the farthest marke a foot could hardlie win:
> At Long-buts, short, and Hoyles, each one could cleave the pin.[8]

Shakespeare himself used the conventional equivalents when he wished to convey the sense of target in its modern meaning. York cries out,

> Come bloody Clifford, rough Northumberland,
> I dare your quenchless fury to more rage:
> I am your butt, and I abide your shot.
>   (3 *Henry VI,* I. iv. 26-29)

---

[4] It would be as well to make the point at once that the word target did not acquire its modern sense until the 18th century. One of the marks shot at in the archery grounds at Finsbury Fields was called, it is true, "Target Tree", (James Partridge, *Ayme for Finsburie Archers* (1628), *passim*), but there is no reason to doubt that "target" here = shield, the conventional contemporary sense.

[5] In the *English Works,* ed. William Aldis Wright (1904), pp. 56, 63, 57.

[6] The government believed that shooting regularly at a fixed distance undermined the versatility needed on the battlefield; hence the exhortation to shoot at roving, or variable marks.

[7] *Adam Bell, Clim of the Clough, and William of Cloudesle* (1605), c2ʳ.

[8] *Poly-Olbion,* ed. J. William Hebel (1933), Song XXVI, p. 529, ll. 329 ff. The second line refers to arrows of different designs, the last line to different ways of approaching the marks. The pin held the mark in place. To shoot compass was to raise the arrow well above the line of level flight and thus obtain greater range (but more doubtful accuracy) with less effort.

And in *Othello,* when the Moor draws his sword and is about to kill himself, he says

> Here is my journey's end, here is my butt,
> And very sea-mark of my utmost sail.
> (V. ii. 267-268)

Shakespeare refers to an informal sort of mark when he makes Shallow say of Double, "Dead! a' would have clapped i' the clout at twelve score",[9] and the play made with the formal *prick*—as in *Love's Labour's Lost* IV. i. 134ff.—has presented a long-familiar problem to editors. Moreover, as the marks, whether of card, or peeled wood, or cloth, were usually white, to attract the archer's eye, a popular expression, "to hit the white", had evolved. The phrase had a vigorous literary career, from the strained reference of Joshua Sylvester to

> Phoebus, to whose arrows bright
> Our Globy Grandame serves for But and White,[10]

to Shakespeare's straightforward use of the phrase in Petruchio's words to Lucentio, "Twas I won the wager, though you hit the white."[11]

The first technical reference to *white* = "target" I know comes from a Northamptonshire directive about the training of arquebusiers (1586):

> That for every corporall theyr maye be a butt: of xx^{tie} foote broade and sixteene foote highe erected in some convenient place remote from the highe waye or other common frequented place and in the middest therof to sett a rundell of borde of a yard and a halfe broade with certaine blacke rundells and a white in the middest against which the soldior is to levell his peece for his better ayme and reddye discha[r]ginge.[12]

And among the *errata* in Sir John Smythe's *Instructions, Observations and Orders Mylitarie* (1595) occurs this: "for, at a great But discharge, read, at a great white in the midst of a great But".

The "blank" passage from *Hamlet* makes it clear that the literature of gunnery, as well as that of archery, must be explored. In these books the word *blank* appears, and frequently, but always in the sense of point-blank range, i.e. either the distance a bullet or cannon ball flies more or less level with the bore of the gun before curving down towards the earth, or any point within that distance. It is never used in the sense of "target". The word for target is always *mark*.[13] The following extracts from the works on gunnery published in English during Shakespeare's lifetime will make the distinction clear.

From William Bourne, *The Art of Shooting in Great Ordnaunce* (1587), p. 24:

> Repaire unto a very levell ground, as a plain marish, that is iust water levell, and then to finde the right line or *point blanke,* rayse a butte or banke in that plain grounde and then sette uppe a marke the iust height of the peece.

[9] *2 Henry IV,* III. ii. 51. The clout, apparently a mark of cloth stretched over a frame, is nowhere mentioned as an orthodox mark, but there must have been many such improvised marks. None was known as a blank.

[10] Quoted by M. Rösler in her edition of *Nebuchadnezzars Fierie Furnace* (1936), p. 47.

[11] *Taming of the Shrew* V. ii. 186. There is a pun here, of course, on "Bianca".

[12] J. Wake, ed., *Papers relating to musters ... in the country of Northampton, 1586-1623,* Northants. Record Society (1926), p. 7.

[13] Small arms were sometimes spoken of as being fired "at buts" or "at banke"—i.e. where the mark was placed.

From the title page of Cyprian Lucar's translation of Niccolò Tartaglia's *Colloquies Concerning the Arte of Shooting* (1588):

> to teach him ... to shoote well at any marke within *pointe blanke*

From Sir John Smythe, *Certaine Discourses ... Concerning the Formes and Effects of Divers Sorts of Weapons* (1590), f. 17^v:

> If Harquebuziers also or Mosquettiers in taking their sights, doo faile butt the length of a wheate corne in the heighth of their *point* and *blancke*, they worke none effect at the marks that they shoote at.

From Leonard and Thomas Digges, *A Geometricall Practise, Named Pantometria*, 2nd (extended) edition (1591), p. 177:

> Any peece is saide to lye *Pointe blanke* with any marke, when the Axis of her Soule [i.e. bore] directeth perfectly to the very middel or Center of that marke.

From Humphrey Barwick, *A Briefe Discourse, Concerning the Force of All Manuall Weapons of Fire* (c. 1594), f. 11^v:

> There is not so simple a souldier that cannot make an estimation how farre his marke is without his levell, that is without *pointe blanck*.

From Thomas Smith, *The Art of Gunnery* (1600), p. 53:

> In Shooting without disparting your peece at any marke within *point blanke*, to know how far the bullet will flie over the marke by knowing the distance to the marke.

From the same author's *Certaine Additions to the Booke of Gunnery* (1601), p. 10.

> A *point blank* or level line is that which by supposition extendeth itself from the center of the peece through the centre of the Marke unto the true horizon.

Shakespeare's use of gunnery images apart from *blank* shows that he was familiar enough with the technicalities of the craft not to employ them arbitrarily,[14] and of all the technical terms *point blank* was most freely discussed in the military literature of Elizabeth's reign, for the study of ballistics, tapping the interests of soldiers, mathematicians, and students of the movements of bodies, was carried on in an atmosphere of lively controversy. Was the point-blank line exactly level when a gun was not fired perpendicularly up or down; should the movement of a projectile beyond the point-blank line be divided into five distinct modes of behavior, as Bourne suggested, or only three, as Digges preferred? These and allied questions were asked and illustrated with diagrams showing the difference between the level or direct line of flight, the "Helicall or Conicall Arke" (Digges), and the declining line—or, to quote the continental jargon on which much of the Tudor debate was based, *Motus Violentus, Mixtus et Naturalis*. Shakespearian references are perfectly explicit.

---

[14] From many examples: the reference to ricochet fire in *Othello* IV. i. 279 (it should be compared with the more explicit *Henry V*, IV. iii. 104-107); the reference in *Hamlet* to a project that might "blast in proof" IV. vii. 155.

"Bring me within the level of your frown", pleads the lover in Sonnet CXVII, "But shoot not at me in your waken'd hate". Ford remarks of Falstaff's page, "Why, this boy will carry a letter twenty mile, as easy as a cannon will shoot point-blank twelve score".[15] "Ah, thou say," Cade addresses Lord Say, "thou serge, nay, thou buckram lord! now art thou within point-blank of our jurisdiction regal" (2 *Henry IV,* IV. vii. 28). And if it should be pleaded that as the technical works always use the phrase point-blank,[16] and Shakespeare sometimes uses it, his use of *blank* on its own could mean something different, attention might be drawn to two passages in Fletcher's *The Woman's Prize.* Speaking of the room where Petruchio's new bride has barricaded herself, Sophocles says

> The chamber's nothing but a mere Ostend ...
> And all the lower works lined sure with small shot,
> Long tongues with firelocks, that at twelve-score blank
> Hit to the heart.[17]

And when Petruchio is about to flee abroad from her, his servant Jacques urges on the preparations with

> By your leave,
> We'll get us up to Paris with all speed;
> For, on my soul, as far as Amiens
> She'll carry blank.[18]

In these instances *blank* = *point-blank*. I have found but one instance to the contrary. In Sir John Smythe's unpublished *An Answer to Contrary Opinions Military* (British Museum, MS. Harleian 135, f. 19; the date is probably 1591)[19] occurs this passage: "a skillfull soldiour with a good harquebuze or with a currier may from a steadye rest discharge his piece from sighte pointe, at blanke or obiecte marke above 30. or 40. paces distant, and hit the said blanke being not above the bredthe of a Dollar, with great contentment and perfection of hittinge so small a marke."

With so much evidence to show that *blank* = "point-blank range" and only one example, and that unprinted, to show that it = "target", how is it that editors have so regularly found that blank = "the white spot in the centre of the target"? Some have shown themselves uncomfortable, and admitted that the use of the word in this sense is "rare outside Shakespeare",[20] but most have had no doubts, basing their definitions on the *O.E.D.* and on Cotgrave's *A Dictionarie of the French and English Tongues* (1611).

The *O.E.D.* illustrated its definition of blank as "the white spot in the centre of a target" by two quotations. The first must be given in an expanded

---

[15] *Merry Wives of Windsor* III. ii. 34.
[16] Smythe was mocked by Barwick for using 'point-and-blank'.
[17] I. iii, in *Works* (1812), ed. Henry Weber, V, 282.
[18] V. ii, *ed. cit.*, p. 389. Weber explains that "this allusion is to the white mark, or blank, at which archers take aim."
[19] On this MS., see pp. lxv-lxxv of my edition of Sir John Smythe's *Certain Discoveries Military* (Folger Documents of Tudor and Stuart Civilization), Cornell U. P., 1964.
[20] So H. C. Hart, *Othello,* notes, and W. J. Craig, *King Lear,* notes. Referring to the *Othello* passage M. R. Ridley, while equating blank with target, is led to the bizarre elaboration that "the *within* implies, I suppose, as the strict meaning 'within the limits of "scatter" of his (grape) shot' ".

form. It is from the anonymous *Enterlude of Youth,* at the point where Youthe has decided to ignore the appeals of Charite, and to allow his life to be guided by Pryde and Ryot. Ryot comments as follows:

> Sir than shall ye do well
> For we be true as stele
> Syr I can teache you to play at the dice
> At the quenes game and at the Iryshe
> The Treygobet and the hasarde also
> And many games mo
> Also at the cardes I can teche you to play
> At the triunph and on and thirtye
> Post, pinion, and also aumsase
> And at on other they call dewsace
> Yet I can tel you mor & ye wyll con me thanke
> Pinke and drinke and also at the blanke
> And mane sportes mo.[21]

There is much here that is obscure, but one thing seems plain: whatever it means, "blanke" is unlikely to have anything to do with archery. This is a list of deplorable games, all fit for the corruption of youth and virtue, and so far as they are identifiable they are, down to the last three lines, gambling games involving dice or cards. Under "pink" *O.E.D.* cites J. Heywood, *Four P.P.* (c. 1540), "And upon drinkyng, myne eyes wyll be pinkynge." "Pinke and drinke" may be some form of drinking competition. "At the blanke" may refer to a sort of lottery (*Coriolanus* V. ii. 10: ". . . lots to blanks"), or a gambling game with cards (cf. "he that hath a *Blank*, his *Blank* [hand without court cards] shall hinder the other *Picy* and *Repicy,* although he hath nothing to shew but his *Blank*"; Charles Cotton, *The Compleat Gamester* . . . (1674), in describing piquet).

Either of these alternatives seems preferable to the idea that archery is referred to. Archery at this time was *par excellence* the sport of health and virtue. "Even so shulde the teaching of youth to shote", wrote Ascham, "not only make them shote well, but also plucke awaye by the rootes all other desyr to noughtie pastymes, as disyng, carding, and boouling",[22] and in the contemporary "Act for the maintenance of Artillerie, debarring unlawfull games"[23] the government endorsed, nay, compelled men under sixty to "use and exercise shooting in long bows" and prohibited most of them from playing "at the Tables, Tennis, Dice, Cards, Bowles" and other games that were demoralizing and led to riot. For Ryot, then, to tempt Youthe with archery, would be as if Gluttony tried to corrupt his appetitie with a bowl of wheaties.

Neither is the *O.E.D.*'s second illustration entirely conclusive. It is a passage dealing with the training of musketeers and caliver men from Robert Barret's *Theoricke and Practike of Moderne Warres* (1598) p. 35: ". . . having a great but erected to that purpose (the which ought to be in every hundred or Bailywicke) to cause them to levell, and discharge, at the blancke there of". The use of the definite article before "blanke" introduces an ambiguity here, but if we

---

[21] From the edition of Copland (c. 1560), c. iii^r.
[22] *Toxophilus,* ed. cit., 59.
[23] 33 *Henry VIII,* c 9, quoted above. "Artillery" included archery at this time.

set the passage beside one on page three, comparing the merits of bows and guns, it appears possible that the "blanke" of the first = the "point-blank" of the second: "A good Calliver charged with good powder and bullet, and discharged at point blank by any reasonable shot, will, at that distance, performe a far better execution". The *O.E.D.* then adds the "blank" passages from *Othello* and *Hamlet*.

We may turn now to Cotgrave, who renders *toucher au blanc* as "to strike the white; to hit the nail on the head"; moreover, the second meaning he gives for *blanc*, as a substantive, is "the white, or marke of a paire of buts".

In French, *blanc* certainly could mean "target", and if we had not seen that there is only one certain instance in English (leaving Barret open to some doubt) in which *blank* = "target" we might assume that *blanc* = *blank* = "target" or the white part of a target. However, whether *white* came from *blanc* or was used independently, it was available as a common word for "target" when Shakespeare came to write. His *blank* came, I would suggest, from the most copious military literature of his time, that of Italy, where *bianco* in the phrase *di punto in bianco* meant not "white" but "zero".

The *O.E.D.* under "point-blank" says that "the phrase appears exclusively of English origin and use.... The probability ... is that *blank* is here the sb. and *point* the vb. referring to the pointing of the arrow or gun at the 'blank' or 'white'". This is in the same tradition as Dr. Johnson's explanation in his *Dictionary:* "Pointblank: directly: as, an arrow is shot to the *point blank* or white mark."

Another difficulty in accepting a French origin for the term *point-blank* is the fact that in France two phrases were used indifferently, *de but en blanc* and *de pointe en blanc* (Huguet, Littré). On the other hand no other term than *di punto in bianco, di punto bianco*, was used in Italian. The method of aiming a cannon by means of a gunner's quadrant marked with angles (*punti*) of elevation from zero (horizontal fire) to a point near the vertical had been made by Niccolò Tartaglia in his *Nova Scientia* of 1537 and elaborated in his *Quesiti, ut inventioni diverse*, dedicated in 1546 to Henry VIII. Tartaglia did not use the phrase *di punto in bianco*, but this occurs in Girolamo Ruscelli's *Precetti della militia moderna* (1568) on f. 3^r; and Luys Collado, in his *Pratica manuale di Arteglieria* (1586) refers on f. 59^r to level fire, "il quale comunemente è domandato tirar di punto in bianco". Later in the century Galileo defined the term: "quel tiro, che non ha elevazione alcuna, vien detto tiro *di punto bianco,* cioè di punto nessuno, di punto zero."[24] With the quotations from *Hamlet* and *The Winter's Tale* in mind it is perhaps worth mentioning that a gun aimed for point-blank fire was said to be "a livello".

It would seem likely, then, that in the early seventeenth century *blank* did not normally signify "white" and therefore did not mean "target". By association, however, the *blank* from *point-blank* could be used, as in Smythe's manuscript (not, significantly, in either of his printed works) as the thing aimed at as well as the aim. Smythe was concerned to emphasize the shortness of the effective range of guns, and was preoccupied with targets set within the point-blank range, the only distance over which their accuracy compared with that of the bow.

[24] *Trattato di fortificazione* (Florence, 1932), p. 93.

What then are the consequences of this possibly ponderous demonstration? If the actual drift of the few "blank" passages is not significantly changed, our knowledge of the mental picture which produced the imagery on which the meaning depends is clearer; there is, after all, a considerable difference between a target with a white spot in its centre, an object to be hit, and the passage of a shot over the most lethal part of its course—a passage visually familiar from the ballistic diagrams in Elizabethan gunnery books.

With this in mind let us look again at the Shakespearian *blank*:

"As level as the cannon to his blank" = "As level as the cannon sends its ball within the limit of its point-blank range".

"And stood within the blank of his displeasure" = "And stood within the lethal range of his displeasure".

"Let me still remain the true blank of thine eye" = "Let me still remain the one who represents a true and undeviating line in your affection".

"Out of the blank and level" = "Out of the point-blank, effective range".

"Target" and "range" are implied in all these cases; but it is a specific line of fire that predominates in images depending on the true Shakespearian blank.

16
Printing and Military Culture of Renaissance Venice

Between 1492 and 1570 there were printed in Venice 145 works devoted to military affairs or dealing with them to a significant degree (see Appendix 1). Of these, 53 were titles (by 46 different authors) originally printed in Venice, 32 were editions of works first printed elsewhere, 48 were new editions or issues of works first published in Venice, 4 were translations of books already first published in Venice, 4 were works originally published elsewhere, and 4 were new editions of translated works. If we disregard new editions and reissues, Venetian printers produced 67 titles that were fresh to the local public (Table 1).

Comparing this number, 67, with similarly but less thoroughly based figures for whole *countries*, we get Italy (excluding Venice), 22-plus; England, 14-plus; France, 10-plus; Spain, 3-plus. Thus, not only did the production of military books in Venice vastly exceed that of any other individual printing centre, but Venice's 67 was close to the comparable

Table 1. *Books of military interest printed in Venice*

Category	Original titles	Titles first published elsewhere	Translations of works first published elsewhere	Total
Art of war	13	3	1	17
The military character	2	0	0	2
Laws of war and chivalry	15	1	1	17
Horses and riding	5	2	2	9
Fencing and gymnastics	2	2	0	4
Fortification	9	0	0	9
Artillery	4	0	0	4
Military medicine	0	2	0	2
Miscellaneous	3	0	0	3
Total	53	10	4	67

figure for the rest of Europe as a whole: 64-plus. Imperfect as these figures must be,[1] Venice's leadership in this field is startlingly apparent. It is too startling to be explained simply by remembering that Venetian printers accounted for something like half the total number of books produced in Italy during this period.[2] As Table 2 shows, only 1 author was himself a Venetian, and only 5 lived in the Veneto. Did the other 40 choose Venice because its printing industry offered authors better conditions than they could find elsewhere, or because they could anticipate a wider readership in the republic's dominions than elsewhere in Italy? If the latter reason predominated, as this article will suggest, then the maritime and commercial image that Renaissance Venice is commonly made to present will have to be revised to take account of the evidence of Table 1: that is, the absence of any work dealing with war at sea and the presence of many dealing with chivalrous interests.

Certainly the uniquely high proportion of military books did not reflect the presence of any dominating student of the subject – as the presence of Regiomontanus made Nuremberg the European centre for the publication of original contributions to mathematics. Nor was there any single publisher or printer (a not unmeaningful but uneasy distinction at this period) who built up a demand, as Aldo Manuzio did for reasonably priced classical texts. The 145 military books were produced over no fewer than 66 imprints; thirty-one different printers were responsible for the first editions of the 53 original titles. Again, works dealing with fortification, artillery and tactics, as well as a number of those concerned more generally with the art of war, required illustrations and diagrams, as, indeed, did those on fencing and one or two of the riding manuals. But taking all the books together, the level of production is competent, rather than distinguished or even particularly attractive. Only two deserve to be called "fine": the 1493 folio edition by Cristoforo da Mandello of Antonio Cornazano's *Opera belissima del arte militar* and the anonymous 1570 edition of Galasso Alghisi's *Delle fortificationi*, also a folio. Between these dates, which almost define our period, lie a mass of workmanlike, readable quarto and octavo volumes distinguishable from other Italian products by neither the aesthetic quality of the type-faces and the quality of the paper, nor the accuracy of type-setting.

The comparative (if sometimes exaggerated) indulgence of the Venetian censorship may have encouraged authors whose political or religious views or whose general scurrility might have intimidated printers elsewhere, but military books were uncontroversial. They dealt with tactics and weapons, siegecraft and fortification: Methods of warfare were broadly uniform throughout Western Europe, and the mercenary system, together with the employment of foreign engineers and artillerists, kept them so.

If censorship is irrelevant to our subject, a glance at another aspect of

Table 2. *Place of origin of authors (chronological order of publication)*

Author	Place of origin	Author	Place of origin
Ruffo	Calabria	Attendolo	Bagnacavallo
Cornazano	Piacenza	Ferretti (Giulio)	Ravenna
Brucioli	Florence	Centorio	Milan
Columbre	Santo Severo	Belli	Asti
Porcia	Pordenone	Memmo	Venice
Tortaglia	Brescia	Maggi	Anghiari
Biringuccio	Siena	Castriotto	Milan
Alciatus	Milan	Montemellino	Perugia
Socinus	Siena	Coniano	Coniano
Rusius	?	Rocca	Piacenza
Muzio	Padua	Caracciolo	?
Fausto	Longiano Forlivese	Cicuta (recte for Adriano)	?
Possevino	Mantua	Urrea	Spain
Zanchi	Pesaro	Sansovino	Rome
Cataneo	Siena	Mora	Bologna
Pigna	Ferrara	Cicogna	Verona
Garimberto	Parma	Ferretti (Francesco)	Ancona
Farra	? Pavia	Ruscelli	Viterbo
Lanteri	Brescia	Mercurialis	Forlì or Bologna
Nannini	Florence	Ballino	Unknown. In Venice from c.1530 on.
Susio	Mirandola	Grassi	Modena
Cyllenius	? Greece	Alghisi	Carpi

governmental contact with the book trade, the granting of exclusive sales privileges to authors, printers and publishers, might seem more promising. Yet, out of the fifty-three first editions of the original titles, only sixteen carried Venetian privileges. Twenty-five bore the unspecific formulae "con gratia e privilegio" or "con privilegio," and nine mentioned none at all. The use of the general formula increased over the years, a tendency reflected in later editions of the earlier works: Venetian privileges become general, and general ones are dropped altogether. Of the twenty-eight titles published between 1560 and 1570 only three carry Venetian privileges. Moreover, half of the works bearing Venetian privileges support them with privileges granted by other governments. But without knowing more about the enforcement of privileges it is safest to see them as conveying an aura of protection generally considered more useful than not. What can be concluded with some confidence is that there is no indication that the nature of the Venetian privilege was a factor inclining our authors to send their works for publication there.

Not enough is known about the comparative sizes of print orders for it to be guessed whether Venetian printers promised a wider numerical distribution than their rivals elsewhere. The 1,000 copies which were printed in 1547 of Niccolò Tartaglia's first pamphlet answer to criticisms of his *Quesiti, e inventioni diverse* (1546) possibly reflected a norm. Still less is known about the profitability to authors of the sale of books. Probably, it was small everywhere. Certainly, the frail (because self-interested) evidence contained in petitions to the Senate for grants of sole publication rights, which stress the heavy labour that goes into writing and printing a book, the difficulty of realizing even the capital investment, does not point to Venice as offering the inducement of greater profits than did other printing centres.

Authors, in any case, were only interested in privileges if they were underwriting the costs of printing themselves. There were, after all, no royalties, and the notion of purely literary copyright did not exist. It is doubtful whether authors received even an outright fee for the use of their manuscripts unless they were *poligrafi* writing to publishers' demands and providing editorial services for vocational reasons. What the great majority of military authors wanted from the press was fame, a reputation for expertise and support in the form of a job, a stipend or a present of cash. The printer thought in terms of the market, the author in terms of a patron. It was important, therefore, for an author to feel free to dedicate his work to the individual most likely to help him or, at least, to add lustre to his name by association.

Only two of the original titles carried no dedication, the anonymous *Libro della natura delli cavalli* . . . (1537) and *Libro de' marchi de cavalli* . . . (1569). Only four are addressed to Venetians, only two to men who were natives of the Venetian *terra ferma*. Six were dedicated to condottieri or members of well known military families outside the Veneto. Most aimed higher still: Three works were dedicated to the Grand Duke of Tuscany, Cosimo I; two were dedicated to Alfonso, the heir of Duke Ercole II of Ferrara. Giacomo Lanteri, in his *Del modo di fare le fortificationi di terra* . . . of 1559, said that he wanted to have his name associated with so famous and warlike a prince as Alfonso, and he wished him all the children he could possibly want from his Medici bride. He dedicated the Latin translation of 1563, however, to Maximilian II of Hapsburg. Of the ducal family of Mantua, only one member, Ferrando Gonzaga, received a dedication.

The Farnese were more popular. In 1556 Girolamo Garimberto, himself a native of Parma, addressed his *Il capitano generale* to its duke, Ottavio Farnese, with the hope that it would help his son Alessandro match the degree of military glory attained by his ancestors. Ottavio also received dedications from the Bolognese Domenico Mora, a professional soldier who wrote that he was sending the book, *Il soldato*, "accioche vedutolo, posse giudicare quello, che io voglio per servirla," and from Giovan Matteo Cicogna, the Veronese author of *Il primo libro del trattato militare* . . . (1567), who described him as the "idea et vero essempio di capitano perfettissima" and expressed the wish "di tutto core servirla . . . come da Signor mio unico, et singolare." In addition, Bernardino Rocca dedicated the third part (1570) of his *Del governo della militia* . . . , and Ascanio Centorio the second discourse (1558) of his *Sopra l'ufficio d'un capitano generale di essercito*, to him. The second part of Rocca's work was addressed to Alessandro Farnese, who had already, in 1568, been the dedicatee of Girolamo Ruscelli's *Precetti della militia moderna*. . . . Girolamo Muzio dedicated his *Il duello* . . . in 1550 to Emanuele Filiberto of Savoy, as did Domenicus Cyllenius his *De vetere et recentiore scientia militari* . . . in 1559. Lesser Italian princes included Jacopo Appiano, Lord of Piombino, to whom Sebastiano Fausto dedicated the *Duello* . . . (1552), which he had finished while "sotto gli honoratissimi tetti di V.S.," but they were outnumbered by monarchs.

It was natural enough for Lorenzo Suarez de Figueroa, the Spanish translator of Cornazano in 1558 to dedicate the work to Philip II, and Pietrino Belli, who addressed his *De re militari et bello tractatus* to him in 1563 had acted as a military auditor under Charles V and had been promoted by Philip to the Spanish war council. Girolamo Maggi, however, simply gave as his reason for dedicating his *Della fortificatione delle citta* . . . to him in 1564, that Philip, being "il più potente Re che sia fra Christiani," was concerned about fortifications "massimamente per essere alla sacra corona di V. Maiestà sottoposti molti di quei paesi, che hoggi sono come una trincea contra e' potentissimi nemici del nome Christiano." Maximilian II also had works on fortification dedicated to him, Giovanni

Battista Zanchi's *Del Modo di fortificar le città* . . . in 1556 and Alghisi's splendid *Delle fortificationi* . . . of 1570, while the brothers Giovanni Battista and Giulio Fontana dedicated both their newly illustrated editions of Marozzo's fencing manual and the first Venetian edition of Camillo Agrippa's *Trattato di scientia d'arme* (both 1568) to a prominent member of Maximilian's court, Don Giovanni Manriche. An earlier Hapsburg dedication had been Jacopo di Porcia's offering of his *De re militari* to the Archduke Ferdinand in 1530.

In contrast, only two works were dedicated to the Valois, Andreas Alciatus's *De singulari certamene* of 1544, which was addressed to Francis I, and Giovanni Battista Susio's *I tre libri della ingiustitia del duello* . . . offered in 1558 to Henry II; and only one was dedicated to a King of England, Tartaglia's *Quesiti e inventioni diverse* of 1546, a dedication to Henry VIII prompted by his friend and pupil in Venice, Richard Wentworth.

Dedications may, indeed, reveal more about the attractiveness of Venice to our authors than colophons. The republic's relations with its Hapsburg neighbours, and with the papacy and its satellite families and states, were often strained. Yet the dedications reveal a complete indifference to the reputation of foreign rulers and military leaders in the government's eyes. Ironically, it looks as though one factor that made Venice the leading producer of military books was her proclaimed intention of remaining neutral, with ill-will towards no-one, save the infidel.

A few authors, it is true, might be styled honorary Venetians. As a lecturer and teacher, Tartaglia, though from Brescia (which had a fairly lively printing industry of its own) was a frequent visitor and occasional resident: His *Nova scientia* . . . was published "Ad instantia di Nicolò Tartalea brisciano il qual habita a San Salvador." There were a few others who, from circumstance, visited the city for long enough, or regularly enough, to make them turn naturally to its printers. There were yet others, again few, who were honorary Venetians in a second sense: As writers on other subjects they had already associated themselves with the city's presses, had become "Venetian" authors. Before Muzio's *Il duello* appeared in 1551, Giolito had already published his edition of Tullia d'Aragona's *Dialogo della infinita di amore*, his *Operette morali* and *Egloghe*. The year 1551 also saw the publication by Giolito of his *Rime diverse*, *Lettere* and *Le mentite ochiniane*. Fausto was another author whose support from Venice's printers made it natural that his *Duello* . . . should appear there. Before its publication in 1552 he had already produced works on geography, meteorology and the art of translation, and editions of Petrarch, Erasmus, Dioscorides, Marcus Aurelius and Cicero through at least four (some works have no printer's name) different firms. Two other authors who had been drawn to Venice before writing on military affairs were Garimberto, who started authorship with a concern for religious and moral issues, and Maggi, the classical scholar whose lively interest in warfare exemplified an attitude we shall have to examine in some detail. In the same year, 1564, that Rutilio Borgominiero printed his *Della fortificatione* . . . , Giordano Ziletti issued his *Variarum lectionum seu miscellaneorum libri IIII*, a patchwork of mainly classical materials which, nevertheless, included the most thorough account yet printed of the origin and development of gunpowder.

All the same, the "Venetian" authors were but a small minority of those who sent works to be published in Venice, many of them authors of only one book. Some sent their manuscripts because they were in contact with the *poligrafi* who, in addition to writing and editing, acted in a role which in some respects anticipated that of the literary agent. It was Ruscelli who persuaded Zanchi, during a visit to Venice, to leave his manuscript with him when he left and who arranged its publication. It was Dolce who urged Susio to send his treatise on the duel to Giolito. And it was the presence in Venice of the Spanish *poligrafo* Alfonso de Ulloa that led Ximenez de Urrea, who had previously used the presses of Antwerp, to send the manuscript of his *Dialogo* (1566) from Naples. Contacts could be fortuitous. In a letter dated from Venice on 15 July, 1566, Captain Giovanni Spinelli urged Cicogna to publish the manuscript of *Il primo libro del trattato militare* . . . (1567) which he had shown him and not "far torto di tenirla come intatta verginella più lungamente appo voi celata, et custodita."

There are other references to contacts in Venice that encouraged publishers and authors alike to believe that there was a market for their wares. Among the interlocutors of Tartaglia's *Quesiti* . . . the author names the Venetian commander-in-chief, the Duke of Urbino, and two members of the outstanding military families of the *terra ferma*, Gabriel Martinengo and Giulio Savorgnan, men whose employment by the Republic brought them frequently to Venice. He names the patricians Bernardo Sagredo, Giovanni Battista Memmo and Marc'Antonio Moro; the famous gun-founder, Alberghetto de' Alberghetti, member of a clan who had for generations been identified with the cannon cast in the Arsenal; and the Spanish ambassador, Don Diego Hurtado di Mendoza.

Another ambassador who acted as a focus for the discussion of military affairs was Giangiacopo Leonardi, the Duke of Urbino's resident representative and author of a much talked-about manuscript treatise on fortification. Lanteri, indeed, warned his readers that his own book might not treat the subject as it deserved, but "vi goderete questo fin tanto che lo Ill. S. Gio. Giacomo Leonardi vi farà vedere in questa materia un volume . . . piu tosto miracoloso che altrimenti." It was thanks to Leonardi that Daniele Barbaro inserted a section on modern fortifications in his superb Venetian edition (F. Marcolini, 1556) of Vitruvius, which also contained the chapter headings of Leonardi's own work – still unprinted. Something of the tone in which warfare was discussed in patrician circles can be caught in a letter appended to Zanchi's book by Ruscelli. We have been bewailing the fact, he told his correspondent, Nicola Manuali, that Roberto Valturio "in quel belissimo libro" (the, indeed, most beautiful 1472 Verona edition of the *De re militari*) had not dealt with fortification. He went on to describe a conversation with Domenico Venier, who was ill in bed, and his doctor Fedele Fedeli (who was to write an unpublished history of the War of Cyprus) about the extent to which civilians knew more about the theory of fortification than did many professional soldiers. If only a true balance could be struck, he went on, between the experience of captains and the knowledge of scholars, the controversy over the precedence of Arms or Letters would be at an end. Ruscelli's own discussion about fortification in his *Precetti* . . . of 1568 contains, he acknowledges, "cose narrate da M. Gio. Tomasso da Venetia, ingegniero eccellentissimo."

In this atmosphere, where patricians, foreign ambassadors, educated non-patrician Venetians, *poligrafi* and publishers, professional soldiers and engineers discussed military affairs, there was, as the interests of Maggi have already suggested, a common ground: the relevance of the experience of classical antiquity. "Letters" stressed it, "Arms" admitted it, the press capitalized on it.

Brucioli's dedication to the Duke of Urbino referred to "lo alto valore della peritia militare, non essendo stato mai alcuna antica, o nuova arte di guerra incognita à vostra eccelentia." In 1555 Muzio wrote a prefatory letter to Lauro Gorgieri's *Trattato della guerra* . . . , which was published at Pesaro and was entirely based on classical sources. The letter was addressed to the ducal secretary of Urbino, Paolo Mario. "Veramente ha bisogno il nostro secolo di un libro tale," Muzio claimed,

Percioche tanto è guasta la militia, che ella ha mestieri di una totale riformatione. Hoggi senza haver consideratione alla qualità, et alla conditione delle persone, si danno danari à quelli che prima corrono al suono del tamburo: i gradi si distribuiscono non à chi piu ne è degno, ma à chi piu è caro, o à chi piu ha da spendere. . . . I tradamenti si procurano: le fedi delle trègue non si mantengono: et in somma nella militia di vera militia non ci rimane altro che il nome. [To correct these abuses it is necessary to study] **la forma della antica vera, et regolata militar disciplina.**

The need for the reform of the Italian military system had been stressed by another of our authors, Jacopo di Porcia, as early as 1492, in his *De liberorum educatione* (Gerardus de Flandria, Treviso). He recommended that boys should prepare themselves for a military career by hunting and learning to handle weapons before serving their apprenticeship under some famous commander. But when he came to deal with such men in his chapter "De militum ducibus" his tone was one of deep bitterness.

> Nam in Italia omnes iam artis bellicae peritia penitus extincta est, tum ob Italorum principum avariciā, qui militiae pecuniā anteponunt, tum etiam quia ad plebeios tantum et agricolas (heu dedecus ingēs) res militaris deducta est, nobiles autem qui haereditario quodam iure in strenuissimos quodem milites, optimosque imperatores evadere possent, sine gratia, sine auctoritate, sine ulla denicque existimatione, apud principes suos hebescunt, hinc nostrae culpae ascribendum est, si a barbaris quottidie vincimur, quottidie in servitutem redigimur.

This reformist zeal, anticipating by two years the invasion of Italy by Charles VIII of France, was developed in his *De reipublicae Venetae administratione* (Gerardus de Lisa, Treviso, 1495?), a short work entirely devoted to Venice's need to prepare in peace for war, to choose good leaders and to be willing to pay them and their men enough, and in time.

Accusations and advice on these lines remained constant in the following generations, but gradually, and after the virtual adoption by Venice of Machiavelli's heavily classicizing *Arte della Guerra* (six editions between 1537 and 1554), with increasing consistency, the discussion of military reform became identified with the example of "la antica vera et regolata militar disciplina." It was conceded, for example, by Ruscelli in his letter accompanying Zanchi's *Del modo di fortificar* . . . , that gunpowder had necessitated such changes in fortifications that "si vede di gran lunga avanzar l'antiche de' Romani, de' Greci et d'ogn' altra famosissima natione." It was not accepted, however, that gunpowder weapons had destroyed the relevance of ancient tactical procedures. Indeed, the superiority of Roman and Macedonian battle formations became so familiar a theme that in 1562 Cicogna could take it for granted that "si loda la triplice ordinanza de' Romani . . . , si conosce la utilità della Falange Macedonica." Garimberto coupled a defence of ancient formations with another popular theme, the superior morale of those days; "i soldati Romani attendevano solamente à vincere, dove pel contrario i nostri attendono più al predare, spogliar, et far prigioni, che all' acquisto della vittoria." He saw this as increasing the need for modern commanders to be well read,

> perchè con nissun altro mezzo più facilmente, che con quel dell' eloquenza si possono regolar le passioni dell'anima: lequali, per l'ordinario sogliono abondar nella moltitudine, massimamente quando ella è composta d'huomini per natura incontinenti, come si potrebbe dir de i soldati.

It was a belief which had already led Nannini to urge the relevance of his *Orationi militari* (1557), a collection of (mainly classical) harangues whose largest section was headed "Per esortar soldati a combattere."

The relevance of ancient to modern warfare became axiomatic. It was *the* bridge between Arms and Letters. Four of our military authors were primarily concerned with classical warfare and military training: Cyllenius,

Rocca (in his *Imprese* . . .), Cicuta and Mercurialis. One of the arches of the bridge was Porcia's insistence on preparation in peace for war, a preparation seen increasingly in terms of study, of reading. The Machiavelli, not only of the *Arte della guerra* but of *Il Principe*, chapter XIV, helped to support this arch: "Non si dovria per tanto non solo mai levare il pensiero dall' essercitio delle armi, ma nella pace non meno essercitarle che nella guerra." The soldier should hunt, for exercise and in order to imagine how to fight over different terrains; but

Si aggiunge anchora à cotali essercitij la diligente et assidue lettione de gli scittori dell' arte militare, et dell' historie, et in quelle considerare i gloriosi et degni fatti di gli huomini grandi et eccellenti, et vedere come si sono governati nelle guerre . . . et parimente fare come han fatto per l'adietro molti huomini rari et singolari, che han preso ad imitare se alcuno è stato innanzi à loro lodato et valoroso.

Up to now we have been examining almost exclusively the Venetian books dealing overtly with military matters. This quotation, however, prompts us to take notice of another category of works: editions, especially in translation, of classical historians and tactical authors, which also demonstrate a concern for the subject of war. It comes from the translation by Nicolo Mutoni of Polyaenus' *Strategemi dell' arte della guerra* (V. Valgrisi, 1552). Another translation of Polyaenus, by Lelio Carani, was published in the same year, by Giolito, and the same point is made briefly in its title: *Gli stratagemi di Polieno, di grandissimo utile a i capitani nelle diverse occasioni della guerra.*

Mutoni emphasized that his Polyaenus, based on manuscripts "delle più honorate librarie di Venetia," should be read in conjunction with the works "de' tempi nostri" of Valturio, Machiavelli and Jacopo di Porcia, of Alciato, Soncino, Fausto and Muzio. And he, too, referred to Giovan Giacopo Leonardi "il qual fra non molto tempo si spera che arrichirà il mondo con un miracoloso trattato suo." Among the ancients he cited "Heliano anchora novellamente ridotto al l'antico suo splendore con le vive et miracolose figure del raro et dottissimo nell' una e l'altra lingua il S. Francesco Robortello."

Robortello, whose works as a scholar included the first commentary on the *Poetics* of Aristotle, and who was a friend of Girolamo Maggi, had, in fact, published his Greek and Latin editions of Aelianus Tacticus, carefully illustrated with diagrams, earlier in that same year, 1552. They were printed in the same volume by Andrea and Jacopo Spinello, a small firm which took great pains over its appearance. Robortello based the Greek text on a manuscript (c. 1330) which was part of the collection left to the city by Cardinal Bessarion, and he dedicated it to one of Venice's most trusted *condottieri* and military advisers, Mario Savorgnan – "qui artis militandi veterum tum Graecorum, tum Romanorum peritissimus es" – in a letter saying how important it was for modern armies to understand the practice of ancient ones and to adopt those that could improve their efficacy. The Latin text was addressed to another *condottiere*, the Istrian cavalry captain Antonio Sergio, with a message to the same effect. And, lest this emphasis on the relevance of what is, after all, a somewhat obscure and confused work seem due solely to Robortello's personal enthusiasm for it, it may be noted that Francesco Ferrosi had made the same point in his Italian translation of Aelian, which had been printed in the previous year – and again in Venice – by Giolito. In his dedication "Al valoroso capitano Nicolo Passerini" Ferrosi wrote of Greek formations:

et quantunque generalmente elle sieno differenti da quelle, c'hoggi di s' usano dei moderni soldati italiani, nondimeno egli non è dubbio alcuno, che s'uno esperto et giudicioso spirto consideratamente le vorra leggere, ne potrà trarre un grandissimo frutto, scegliendone tutte quelle miglior parti, che sono piu accommodate al moderno uso.

The relevance of Polybius to the contemporary military reformer had been clear from Machiavelli's use of the Greek historian. The anonymous translator of *Libro della militia de Romani et del modo dell' accampare tratto dell' historia di Polibio* (s.l., 1536) dedicated it to the Duke of Urbino. Translating the *Undici libri di Polibio nuovamente trovati* (Giolito, 1553), Lodovico Domenichi, who dedicated his work to another soldier, Captain Camillo Caula, wrote that Polybius was an historian "di quella grandezza, che voi stesso sapete, et piu volte ancho havete udito celebrare da qual rarissimo et perfetto giudicio che Sig. Giovan Iacopo Lionardi ... ch'è da me nominato qui per cagion d'honore." In 1546 Giolito himself had dedicated Fabio Cotta's translation, *Onosandro Platonico dell'ottimo capitano generale*, to Leonardi in terms which suggest, more clearly than we have yet been able to see, the almost salon-like liaison between scholars, soldiers and publishers which helps to explain Venice's prominence as a centre for the printing of military books. I have dedicated it to you, Giolito wrote, because

Tiene V.S. tale notitia dell' arte della guerra, cosi intorno a i costumi de gli antichi, come alle usanze dei nostri tempi; che di piu non se ne potrebbe desiderare a volersi chiamare perfetto in si fatta disciplina. Della qual cosa non pure a tutto 'l mondo ne fa chiarissimo testimonio l'universal concorso, che ogni di si fa a lei da gli huomini piu intendenti, ed piu valorosi; ma si spera anco, che i celebratissimi scritti suoi in cotal materia, quand' appariranno in publico, ne debbano dare intiera contezza, et por silentio a tutti gli altri, che dopo voi vorranno.

These last were words which, had Giolito obtained the manuscript, he would have had to swallow, for military books, and classical translations aimed at an audience interested in military affairs, played a growing part in his list of publications.

Giolito's belief in the audience for translations of classical works with military applications can be seen from the first full translation of the *Guerre esterne* and the *Guerre civili* of Appian (1554-9). Lodovico Dolce, the editor and partial translator, dedicated the first part "al chiarissimo e valoroso S. Christoforo Canale" perhaps the most imaginative and pugnacious of contemporary Venetian naval commanders; like Leonardi, he had written a treatise (but on naval warfare) which was widely admired but never given to the press. The third and last part was addressed to the Marquis of Pescara, the great Spanish soldier-administrator.

It would be wearisome to continue demonstrating the relevance felt to exist between ancient and modern military experience. In the range of authors and the numbers of editions, especially of translations, Venice led not only Italy but the rest of Europe, and the number of military dedicatees, and the theme of relevance, establish Venice as – from this point of view – the centre of the utilitarian humanism of the Cinquecento.

The connection between an interest in classical history, on the one hand, and, on the other, in the art of war was most strikingly illustrated by a hitherto unprecedented publishing venture: the issuing, in uniform format, of a series comprising translations of thirteen Greek historians, together with a parallel library of military books. The publisher was Gabriel Giolito, his editor the Tuscan *poligrafo* Tomaso Porcacchi, and the component volumes spanned the years 1557–70, though the idea of the series, as such, only took hold from 1564.[3] From that date Porcacchi and Giolito deliberately planned the continuation of some previous Giolito titles into a *Collana Historica*, a collection of translations, each called on its title page an *Anello*, to be decorated with *Gioie*, interpretative compendia and original works supporting the assumption that ancient history was chiefly important to those who plotted, organized and waged wars in the present.

The Greek historians were, in chronological order: Dictys Cretensis and Dares Phrygius (in one volume), Herodotus, Thucydides, Xenophon, Polybius, Diodorus Siculus, Dionysus of Halicarnassus, Josephus, Plutarch, Appian, Arrian and Dion Cassius. Some of the translations were reprints; others were, in whole or in part, the work of Porcacchi and his fellow *poligrafi* Nannini, Lodovico Dolce and Lodovico Domenichi. A comparable *Collana* of Latin historians was envisaged briefly but was dropped – probably for copyright, or, at least, inter-press reasons. The *Collana* had a message:

Deve principalmente avertire di tutte l'operationi che si leggono nell' historie i qual sia maggiore, et di piu importanza: et essendo senza dubbio la guerra, perche da essa dependono gli stati et gli imperi, ha da considerare il giudicioso lettore, in che modo sono stato da gli antichi maneggiati le guerre, et paragonatele con le moderne, valersi a tempo [the military lessons that could be learned from the past.]

But the lessons were buried in the flow of narrative. It was necessary to extract and collect them in a series of supplementary volumes: This, affirmed Porcacchi, "è la mia concatenatione, che in effetto desidero fare all'historia." No-one, moreover, could remember everything an historian said. For the busy, practical man what was needed was "una raccolta di quasi tutte l'historie, fruttuosamente ordinata per beneficio di chi essercita la militia." Hence, the *Gioie*.

Before looking briefly at the items in this remarkably methodical prospectus (Appendix 2), it is worth emphasizing that the collection – the *Collana* and its *Gioie* – was conceived as a whole, as a complete library for the student of warfare, lacking only works on the duel and on fortification which were already freely available. Title pages carried the announcement that the volume constituted such and such an *anello* or *gioia*, and there were frequent prefatory references from Giolito or Porcacchi to the scope of the collection as it grew. The last volume of the historians contained a biographical appendix relating to the authors as a whole. Each book was indexed with unusual fullness, though, as was common in the period, the haphazard use of keywords reduced their practicability: "Errori de Carthaginesi," or "Guerra sanguinosa," for example. All the volumes were printed in italic and in the same quarto format – "tutti in una giusta et convenevol forma, et con equali, ma però sempre belli et sempre vaghi ornamenti," as Porcacchi put it in one prefatory letter. In another, Giolito reminded his readers that with this collection "potrete poi adornare le vostre stanze." And that readers did build up the complete collection is confirmed by the sale of one in 1773 from the library of Joseph Smith, the famous British Consul in Venice.

The first of the military *Gioie* referred to was *Le cagioni delle guerre antiche* (1564), in which Porcacchi produced an anthology of (mostly condensed) passages from the Greek historians which dealt primarily with the causes of war. Against these he noted the moral, or general principle, each appeared to illustrate, so that the reader could consider not only why wars came to be waged but under what circumstances they had the greatest likelihood of success. It was, in fact, a thematic key to the *Collana*: "A beneficio," or, as the title put it, "di chi vol' adornarsi l'animo delle Gioie dell' historie." Porcacchi did not produce, as the prospectus implies, a companion volume.

The second was Centorio's *Il primo discorso . . . sopra l' ufficio d' un capitano generale di essertio* (1558), the first part of the five-part work we have treated as one volume in our list of Venetian military books, as they appear to have been issued together in 1568, although each has a separate title page. The third was Centorio's *Il terzo discorso di guerra . . . nel qual si tratta della qualità, ufficio, et autorità d' un mastro di campo generale* (also 1558). The fourth was another on our list, Mora's *Il soldato . . . nel qual si tratta di tutto quello, che ad un vero soldato, et nobil cavalliere si conviene sapere ad essercitare nel mestiere dell' arme*, first printed by Giovanni Griffo in 1569 but taken over by Giolito in 1570. The fifth was Centorio's *Il quinto et ultimo discorso* (1562), the sixth, another on our list, was Rocca's *La seconda parte del governo della militia . . . nella qual si tratta con discorsi e con essempi de' più eccellenti historici, come s'ha da provedere ne' fatti d'arme, ne gli assalti delle fortezze, ne' ripari di tutti i pericoli di guerra, e nella conservatione de gli stati* (1570). This is normally bound with *La terza parte . . .* (also Giolito, 1570; separate pagination and title page), though there is no reference to its status as a *Gioia*.

The seventh was another of Porcacchi's "keys" to the *Collana, Paralleli o essempi simili . . . cavati da gl' historici, accioche si vegga, come in ogni tempo le cose del mondo hanno riscontro, o fra loro, o con quelli de' tempi antichi* (1567). On its title page it was denominated "la seconda Gioia," but this was before the publishing team had decided to intersperse the theme of the military relevance of antiquity with works concentrating on contemporary warfare. In the dedication to the patrician cleric Luigi Diedo, Porcacchi pays tribute "al Magnifico S. Gabriel Giolito de' Ferrari, primo padre et fautor di cosi honorato assunto" and describes his own role as the provider of reference works that will extract the military pith from the historians and cut down the time which the reader might otherwise have spent, in spite of the indices, locating passages which would bring light from the ancient world to bear upon the military problems of the present. The work lives up to its title: It quotes illustrations from the past, along with comparable actions and consequences in modern times; it is based on the assumption that the present can learn from the past.

The eighth work, the treatise on castrametation, was not published. The ninth was Bernardino Rocca's *Imprese, stratagemi et errori militari . . . ne' quali discorrendosi con esempi, tratti dall' historie de' Greci, et de' Romani, s'ha piena cognition de' termini, che si possono usar nelle guerre, cosi di terra, come di mare,* announced as "la quarto gioia" when it was published in 1566. This is another work that may be considered to be a military book, though its general resemblance to Porcacchi's *Paralleli . . .* is a warning as to how indeterminate the definition of a "military book" can be. Rocca does, at least, draw on personal experience in his comments on the feints and other devices employed by commanders in antiquity. The tenth work was another of our titles, Nannini's *Orationi militari. Raccolte . . . da tutti gli historici greci e latini, antichi e moderni . . .* , published by Giolito in 1557, two years before Porcacchi's arrival in Venice, and not improbably the work that suggested the premise of the whole collection. The publisher had been encouraged enough by its reception to bring out a second, enlarged edition in 1560. The demand, however, was not sufficiently great to call for an edition which would identify the book as a *Gioia*.

Giolito did publish Rusconi's edition of Vitruvius, but not until 1590, and with no reference then to the *Collana* and its *Gioie*. On the other hand, another *Gioia* was published but then dropped from the prospectus: Oratio Toscanella's *Gioie historiche, aggiunte alla prima parte della vite di Plutarco* . . . , which Giunta published in 1567; a companion volume to the "seconda parte" appeared in 1568. This was planned as a "key" to a new edition of a translation by various hands of Plutarch's *Lives*. In a letter to his readers prefaced to the 1566 edition of Dion Cassius, Giolito announced this, "ch' è un Anello nella nostra Collana Historica de' Greci; con l'aggiunta di tutte le Gioie piu preciose, che vi son dentro, scelte da M. Horatio Toscanello, per dimostrar l' utilità che si trahe da quella lettione." The *Vite di Plutarco Cheroneo* duly appeared in two parts in 1567 (part two) and 1568 (part one), and a letter to the reader drew attention to Toscanello's *Gioia*, which gathered together, as in a vast subject index, "tutti i frutti che si possono cavar dalla lettion di questo famoso auttore." The work itself, however, carried no reference to the *Collana* or to the other *Gioie*, which suggests that the decision had already been taken not to include it in the collection. Whatever the reason, it was not, in thematic terms, a logical one, for among the *Gioie historiche* was a rich assortment of articles, resembling those in an encyclopedia, dealing with the history and development of weapons and armour, with warfare in general and, in particular, with the ranks, training and tactics of the infantry and cavalry of the Romans.

Among contemporary architects, Palladio showed an unusual lack of interest in fortifications, neither designing them nor writing about them. He explained this in the Introduction to his richly illustrated edition of *I commentari di C. Giulio Cesare*, pointing out that no fortification can be made strong enough to resist a really determined enemy in the long run: Not walls and bastions but properly organized armies were a country's best defence. Though its publication (Pietro de' Franceschi, 1575) lies beyond the chronological scope of this survey, the edition splendidly sums up the connection between the study of ancient history and that of modern warfare. Moreover, its Introduction allows us to see how the literary culture of Venice and its *terra ferma* encouraged authors to write about war, and the book trade to print their works with confidence in the buoyancy of the home market. For, however good a printing house's colportage system was, an estimated profit margin depended in the first instance on the probability of local sales.[4]

Palladio's interest in the training and organization of ancient armies and the lessons to be derived from studying them had, he said, been aroused by his early patron and intellectual guide, Count Giangiorgio Trissino. Trissino's long epic poem, *Italia liberata da Gotthi* (3 vols., Rome and Venice, 1547–8) had been written to underline this lesson, as the author pointed out in his dedication of the work to Charles V. Encouraged by Trissino, Palladio set himself to read widely (in translation) in the historical and technological literature of antiquity. He was encouraged by other contacts he made through his patron with Mario Savorgnano, Robortello, Filippo Pigafetta, author of an unpublished translation of the Emperor Leo VI's treatise on tactics, Francesco Patrizi, author of two works comparing ancient and modern military practice, and, perhaps above all, the Vicentine professional soldier Valerio Chieregato, who wrote an original treatise (again, unpublished) on Roman and Macedonian troop formations. Palladio dismissed the argument that firearms had negated the relevance of classical battles; method and discipline were more important than any weapons. He rebutted, as well, the suggestion that modern soldiers were too clumsy and ignorant to be tought the drills and formations that had brought victory to ancient armies. Patrizi and Chieregato were both present when Palladio proved his point by actually putting an ad hoc collection of pioneers and galley oarsmen recruits through a training session *all 'antico*. That an architect of villas and churches could take to barking orders on an impromptu parade ground is an index, just as suggestive as is the presence of erudite soldiers like Savorgnan and Chieregato, of a fairly calculable body of readers for military books; the Venetian press, and the authors who used it, could reckon on an audience comprising both practising and armchair students of the art of war.

For a wider appraisal of that audience it is necessary to take some note of the military system of the Venetian republic. Though based on the employment of mercenary troops it was not merely peripheral to the consciousness and experience of the reading public in Venice itself or the *terra ferma*. Among the permanent army, garrisoned among Venice's subject towns and cities, of from four thousand to eight thousand men, depending on the international situation, were many representatives of families who served the republic generation after generation. While never anything like in a majority, there was an increasing tendency to employ natives of the Veneto as officers in the army's permanent core and to rely on native volunteers in time of peace. And, while the presence of troops in garrison was a familiar feature of citizen life, a peasant militia of some twenty thousand men was organised among the villages and hamlets of the countryside and assembled for regular training periods on a regional basis. Every large town had its locally-recruited, part-time *scuola* of bombardiers and was the scene of periodic marksmanship contests where it was open to all who could handle an arquebus to compete for prizes. Finally, the Veneto was the seat of an important arms industry; from heavy cannon to bits and bridles, it was a net exporter of military equipment.

Nor was Venice itself isolated from the sights and sounds of military life. As street names like Spaderia and Frezzaria suggest, it was a centre for the production of small arms, and the whole of the republic's bronze guns were cast in the Arsenal. The armoury in the Arsenal was supposed to be capable of outfitting ten thousand soldiers and, together with the smaller but more select armoury of the Council of Ten in the Ducal Palace, was a coveted attraction for important visitors. The shooting competitions on the Lido could attract over eight hundred entrants from all classes. Suggesting the reorganization of a civic militia of six thousand in Venice, Adriano met the argument that it could be dangerous to arm the *popolo minuto* by saying "che ad ogni modo il popolo di Venetia ha l'arme in mano: percioche non vi è artista, nè piu minimo meccanico, che non habbia in bottega, et in case arme d'asta, di fuoco et di ferro, per offendere et difendere." And, in fact, throughout its domains, Venice was probably of all governments the one most willing to trust its subjects to possess arms. It was an attitude supported by the lack of mutinies on vessels in which every man, from oarsman to patrician commander, was armed against the possibility of combat at sea or while watering and taking in stores.

Few patricians fought as professional soldiers – about thirty in 1509–30, perhaps a dozen thereafter. Several hundreds went as temporary volunteers to Padua and Treviso in the years immediately following the disaster of Agnadello. Thereafter, small numbers were sent, again for short periods, to raise morale and command the companies defending city gates. The practice was revived in the Turkish war of 1537–40 and in 1570 twenty-two patricians were sent for gate duty at Zara, Sibenico, Traù, Spalato and Cattaro. From 1509 and 1515 to 1542 there were sporadic moves to pass legislation encouraging young patricians to train as army officers, but all evaporated in debate.

Yet it is probably not an exaggeration to suggest that no other governing class had so informed an interest in military affairs as did the Venetian patriciate. Experience at sea accounted for much, but at any given time more patricians were occupying posts involving some military duties by land than on shipboard. Patricians acted as *castellani* of forts; *rettori*, primarily the *capitano*, but also the *podestà*, were responsible for town garrisons and the country militia in their jurisdiction. In wartime special military *proveditori* were appointed to command key cities and to accompany the army and its chief detachments, and these were men whose opinions on military planning were taken seriously by professional officers and who frequently rode into action with them; the image of the military proveditor as simply a political watchdog is a quite misleading one.

Moreover, thanks to the principle of rotation, men with military experience by sea and land were constantly drawn into the chief councils and magistracies where military policies were discussed and implemented: the Senate, the Council of Ten and the College. Add to these the permanent magistracies responsible for artillery, the arming of galleys and the planning and construction of fortifications, the responsibility of itinerant *inquisitori* to report on garrisons and fortresses, the constant coming and going of professional commanders to discuss army affairs with the doge and College, plus the hundreds of secretaries and accountants from the citizen class who accompanied *rettori* and proveditors and sat on councils and magistracies – and the resultant picture is of a large group of men likely to be interested in military books. Add, again, the military families of the *terra ferma* and their retainers, and the home market may be imagined as a potentially broad one. And this is without taking into account the more scholarly or purely recreational or predominantly legal interest in the subject.

This interest, as far as the somewhat loose category (see Table 3), the Art of War, is concerned, was satisfied chiefly in the fifties and sixties; that is, after the conclusion of the war period 1494–1529 and the Turkish War of 1537–40. Partly, this reflects the increasing productivity of the printing industry as a whole, but it also reflects the common experience that more military books are written and printed in periods of peace than when fighting is imminent or actually going on. The tag, "in peace prepare for war," was much bandied about. Reformers urged that changes be made before the outbreak of hostilities meant that there was time to do nothing but reimplement the old methods, faults and all. In 1542, in a confidential *Discorso sopra la sicurezza di Venetia*[5] (one of many such pieces

Table 3. *Works by category (numbers refer to Appendix I)*

Category	Original titles	Title first printed elsewhere	Translations of works first printed elsewhere
Art of War	2,14,66,68,85,100, 109,116,118,125, 128,134,140.	3,7,24	48
The military character	9,102		
Laws of war and chivalry	31,32,42,49,52,54, 62,72,87,88,89,97, 101,119,120	5	65
Horses and riding	1,18,19,117,138	51,96	35,36
Fencing and gymnastics	135,141	44,132	
Fortification	58,61,69,86,106,107, 108,124,142.		
Artillery	22,26,39,129		
Military medicine		114,123	
Miscellaneous	70,136,143		

of advice), Alvise Gritti, illegitimate son of the great wartime doge Andrea Gritti, stressed that "è tempo che questa Republica si faccia più gelosa assai del solito a questo poco stato che gli è rimasto," that the militia should be improved, defences strengthened, control over the permanent army tightened; and he made another unsuccessful plea that young patricians should be trained for war on land. It was among the first of a flood of memoranda submitted to the government by *rettori*, *proveditori* and commanders-in-chief, all appealing for changes to be made before it was too late. These arose from tours of inspection, from parades, from discussions between *rettori* and municipal councils, all of which served to sustain public interest in the role of the military among them.

Before 1550, the only original publications in this category were the books of Cornazano (1493) and di Porcia (1530), both strong on exhortation and weak on information. More solid fare was provided by works reprinted in Venice. First printed in Augsburg in 1473, Egidio Colonna's *De regimine principum* was brought out in 1498 and 1502. Though written around 1285, the last twenty-three chapters, which dealt with war, provided the clearest summary of classical thinking about the subject then available. More specific in the practical advice they had to offer were two imports which Venetian printers made practically their own. First published in Naples in 1521, Battista della Valle's *Vallo: libro continente appertenentie ad capitani* . . . appeared in Venetian editions or reissues no fewer than thirteen times between 1524 and 1569 (elsewhere, only in French, at Lyons in 1529 and 1554). Also first published in 1521 (in Florence; second edition 1529), Machiavelli's *Arte della guerra* became "Venetian" with editions in 1537, 1540, 1541, 1546, 1550 and 1554. For all their discursiveness and lack, at times, of a sense of practicability, these two works nevertheless set new standards for Europe as a whole, new with regard to their relevance to current practice and with respect to the use of elaborate and accurate diagrams. The quality and popularity of these "imports" may well have encouraged the publication of original works in the fifties and sixties.

That the first work published in these decades (within the same category) was a translation is none the less appropriate, for Raimond de Fourquevaux's *Instructions sur le faict de la guerre* (Paris, 1548) drew heavily on Machiavelli. Translated by Mambrino Roseo as *Tre libri della disciplina militare* (1550), it was ascribed in the privilege to "Monsignor di Lange"; that is, to Guillaume de Bellay, Sieur de Langey, with whom the work was regularly associated in all its sixteenth-century editions and translations. The works originally printed in Venice then appeared in a cluster: Garimberto and Farra (1556), Cyllenius (1559), Centorio (1558–62), Giovacchino da Coniano (1564), Rocca (1566), Adriano (1566), Cicogna (1567), Ferretti (1568), Moro (1568), Rocca again (1570).

Most of these works touch with more or less emphasis on the qualities required of the soldier, especially of senior officers. It is appropriate, then, to associate with the Art of War category the works by Brucioli (1526) and Memmo (1563), which, though not treatises on war, contain sustained discussions of the military character. It was, of course, a topic of deep concern to the civilian employers of mercenary captains and to the natives of the *terra ferma* who suffered from the indiscipline of their men. The Venetian literary tradition hardly encouraged a trust in the military: Ruzzante's cowardly peasant volunteer, Aretino's young officers, "schiave da la desperazione e figliastre di quella porca fortuna che non si stracca mai di crocifiggerci per tutti i versi," the braggart of classical comedy brought back to the stage in such works as Lodovico Dolce's *Il capitano* of 1545 (new editions, 1547, 1560). The cowardly (partly because ill-trained) peasant was a cause of concern to those who ran or wished to reform the militia, but, while his inefficiency was deplored, he was not seen as a potential danger to the state. The long-service troops who formed the peacetime garrisons were, again, often licentious and idle, but this was, in the main, shrugged off as inevitable. The real tensions arose when debating the potential loyalty of commanders-in-chief – debates which could drag on for months – and when considering the dangers to be anticipated when recruiting in time of war very large numbers of men who had had no previous connection with Venice: tensions, painfully irresolvable, between need and trust.

In theory, wrote Memmo in his *Dialogo nel quale . . . si forma un perfetto principe ed una perfetta republica, e parimente un senatore, un cittadino, un soldato e un mercatante*, war was an "illustre et eccellente arte . . . senza la quale . . . niuna Republica si può conservare et illustrare." But this is not demonstrated by men who serve "solo per un vil stipendio et mercede. Divenuti lupi sitibondi del sangue humano, non attendono ad altro, che a rubbare et far ogni male, abbrucciando insino le case de i poveri contadini . . . et in vece di esser forti contra gli inimici questi sono crudeli et superbi contra gli amici." The patrician class has always served at sea. "Ma all' incontro nella Terra ferma, dove sempre ha adoperato le arme mercenarie et forestiere ha fatto poco progresso, et il tutto con suo grandissimo disavantaggio et ruina. Che se havessero i nostri padri adoperato le arme proprie cosi in terra, come in mare havevano fatto essercitando in quelle i suoi Cittadini, havrebbono superato lo Imperio Romano." He then fends off the suggestion that such arms might be turned against the state (could not naval commanders have done that if they wished?) and proceeds to advocate military training for "tutti i giovani della Città . . . et de' luoghi soggetti a quella." The interest of this discussion does not lie in its originality, for it has none, but in the evidence it provides for the long-prevailing nervousness about the republic's military system, a nervousness that provided another incentive to read about the conduct of wars, actual or ideal.

Given the popular image of Venice as a marine and mercantile capital, it may seem strange that the second largest category is that of books dealing with the laws or war and of chivalry, backed up by subordinate categories dealing with horsemanship and personal combat. Does the argument that printers first considered the home market apply here too?

To give an added resonance to the question it may be asked why one Venetian printer, Domenico Nicolini, was so quick to publish, in a translation from the French, the herald Sicile's *Trattato de i colori nelle arme, nelle livree, et nelle divise* (1565) or why another, Giordano Ziletti, produced an edition of Paolo Giovio's *Ragionamenti sopra i motti et disegni d'arme et d'amore* only a year after its appearance in 1555 in Rome. (Giolito printed a Spanish translation, by Alfonso de Ulloa, in 1558.) Indeed, why was it Venice which took over such authors as Pulci, Boiardo and Ariosto and became *the* publishing centre for those who wished to read about the chivalric adventures of (among others) Amadis, Altobello, Mambriano, Sir Bevis, Il Cavallier del Sole, Drusiano dal Leone, Falchonetto, Fioravante, Ganelon, Il Cavaliere de l'Orsa, Palmerin, Perceforest, Platir, Primaleon of Greece and Rinaldo de Montalbano?

The connection between the Art and the Law of War had always been close, because writers on the former were seldom able to resist justifying the existence of warfare and defining the just use of it, while writers on the latter were forced to specify the situations to which the laws applied. In Venetian experience the laws were particularly relevant in their applicability to capitulation terms (the campaigns of 1509-29 had come to centre on the siege and defence of towns) and to declarations of war and truces. Adequate defence and instantly mobilizable military self-sufficiency were all the more necessary, "non procedendo più la maggior parte dei principi con l'antiqua e buon costume solito di mandar li araldi a nuntiar la guerra", as Alvise Gritti wrote. "Taccio che si fanno le guerre non per giustitia, ma per appetito," Muzio wrote deploringly in his introduction to Gorgieri's *Trattato della guerra* . . . in 1555, "nelle taglie et ne' prigioni le giuste regole non si servano: i tradimenti si procurano: le fedi delle tregue non si mantengono: et in somma nella militia di vera militia non si rimane altro che il nome."

There was, similarly, a connection between the law of war and the conventions of the duel; the lawyers saw war as a duel between nations, and writers on the honour code applied to the motives and conduct of the duel something like the concept of the just war. The mixture can be seen in the reprint which stands earliest in the category Laws of War and Chivalry. First published about 1471 in Naples, the Venetian titlepage (1521) of the work by "il generoso misser Paris de Puteo" reads: *Duello, libro de re, imperatori, principi, signori, gentil' homini, et de tutte armigeri, continente disfide, concordie, pace, casi accadenti, et iudicii con ragione, exempli, et authoritate de poeti, hystoriographi, philosofi, legisti, canonisti et ecclesiastici*. Five editions followed, each produced by a different firm, in 1523, 1525, 1530, 1536, and 1540. Elsewhere, the work appeared in collections which now stressed the duel, now the general law of war; in Venice it was printed together with Belli's *De re militari et bello* (Venice, 1563) in the collection *Tractatus universi juris* of 1584. The editions of original works dealing more or less exclusively with the duel and the honour code start with Alciatus and Socinus (printed together in 1544 and translated together in the following year in two separate editions by Vincenzo Vaugris and by Alvise de Tortis). In the 1550s came an impressive cluster: Muzio, two different works in 1550 and 1551; Fausto da Longiano in 1552; Possevino in 1553; Pigna in 1554; Susio in 1558; another work by Muzio in 1559; Attendolo and new works by Fausto in 1560. The two works that conclude this category deal with more general chivalric themes: the *Dialogo de la verdadera honrra militar, que tracta como se ha de conformar la honrra con la conscientia* (the nub of the duelling issue!) of Geronymo Ximenez de Urrea and Francesco Sansovino's *Origine de cavalieri*, both of which appeared in 1566.

The only "cavalieri" created by Venice were those of San Marco. It was a non-hereditary title, and though it was granted to soldiers, especially to stradiot captains from the empire *da mar*, it was not primarily a military one, nor were its members (as with the Tuscan Knights of San Stefano, for instance) part of a formally constituted order. On the face of it, indeed, a purely legally defined upper class, as was that of Venice, was difficult to accommodate to the chivalrous overtones of other aristocracies, though the legal definition gave ample scope for genealogists and heralds. Muzio himself faced the question of what sort of nobility was represented by the patriciate in *Il gentilhuomo* (1571). Venice, he wrote, is "città nobilissima per antichità, per Signoria, et per gloria d'arme, et di lettere, piene di Signori, et di cavalieri. . . . Oltra che essi sono Signori del mare. . . . Si che se per nascimento, et virtù sono nobili, per istato etiando sono Signori. Di che ne seguita, che dir si dee di loro, che sono nobilissimi."

Muzio's *Lettere* (Giolito, 1551), containing an epistle to the Marchese del Vasto in which he sums up his attitude to knighthood and the duel, was dedicated to the patrician military proveditor and ambassador Vicenzo Fedeli, whom he represents as "tra gli armati eserciti . . . sostenendo la persona della Eccellentissima Vinitiana Republica." But references to Venetians in a chivalrous context are rare. Susio, exceptional as an opponent of the duel, said in his *I tre libri della ingiustitia del duello* . . . (1558) that "io gia più di dieci anni sono, tenni, et difesi il mio parere in Venetia." Together with Porcacchi's remark in a letter to Mario Cardoini, prefacing Rocco's *Imprese* . . . of 1566, to the effect that in a discussion he had had about "un perfetto Cavaliero" with Pietro Bizarro and the diplomat and Knight of Malta Sir Richard Shelley, Cardoini had been named as an ideal example, this suggests that chivalrous topics were not uninteresting to Venetians and their friends, though it was doubtless among readers outside the lagoon that the market envisaged by the printers lay.

That this market was wide is shown by Sir Christopher Hatton's copy of the second edition (Giolito, 1558) of Possevino's *Dialogo dell' honore* in the Bodleian Library at Oxford; but, as with works on the art of war, the chivalrous category was probably aimed in the first place at Venice's aristocratic subjects in the castles and cities of the *terra ferma*, cities like Vicenza, "la qual è stata sempre florida per studio di lettere, e d'arme," as Fausto put it in the dedication to the "Signori Academici Costanti, nobilissimi Vicentini" of his *Dialogo del modo de la tradurre* . . . (Giovanni Griffio, 1556), or Brescia, where Porcacchi was entertained with "giostre e torneamenti" by Count Alfonso Cavriolo, according to a letter in one of his *Gioie*, Rocca's *La seconda parte del governo della militia* (1570). Apart from absorbing the values of the influential military dynasties, Avogaro, Martinengo, Collalto, da Porto, Savorgnan and many others, and of the "foreign" captains in garrison, the *terra ferma* remained open to the example of knightly pastimes and the cult of duelling in its neighbour states, Milan, Austria and the Tyrol, Ferrara and Mantua. Venice also recognized the value of the honour code, and the skills in riding and fencing it called for, as a means of keeping the energies and ambitions of the young nobles of the *terra ferma* within reasonable bounds. The deliberate encouragement of these potentially useful occupations came later, with the formal creation of military academies between 1608 and 1610 in Padua, Verona, Udine and Treviso. In our period only one attempt was made to harness the energies associated with "honour," the setting-up in 1566 of a riding academy in Verona. Among its regulations was one requiring members to serve the government for four months, at their own expense, in time of war. It lasted until 1607, and it was the example of its beneficial effect on formalising violence that might otherwise have been politically dangerous, that prompted the Senate to support the more formal institutions that took its place.

The social habits of the *terra ferma*, then, provide ample explanation for the publication of books in this "aristocratic" category and in the more technical categories that depend on it: Horses and Riding, Fencing and Gymnastics. Some of these, it should be acknowledged, have but a tenuous connection with the actual practice of war. The *Libro de marchi de cavalli* . . . of 1569, for instance, is simply a guide to the identification of thoroughbreds through their brands. Fieschi has illustrations of numerous types of bits and horseshoes, and his illustrations of riding techniques (some with bars of music for the rider to hum as a guide to the rhythm of the exercise) are aimed at the *manège*, not the battlefield. Ruffo wrote for the *marescalco*, rather than his employer. Only one chapter in Mercurialis's *Artis gymnasticae libri sex* . . . refers directly to the military relevance of physical exercise. The fencing manuals are often coy about the applicability of their art to combat in the field. Yet at a time when horsemanship and swordsmanship were virtually the only attainments required of a potential army officer it is perhaps pedantic to omit the books which illustrate the degree of interest taken in these skills, especially when they underline the extent to which the Venetian printing industry was conditioned by the taste of the *terra ferma*. For, at least as far as military culture is concerned, it is artificial to think of the lagoon as a sealed world – a point every *rettore*, proveditor, inquisitor or ambassador, forced to spend much of his time in the saddle, with a sword at his side, would have taken for granted.

The most impressive category among Venetian military books was the group devoted to fortification. Among the earlier works reprinted there were some (those by Colonna, della Valle, Machiavelli) which treated the subject as an ingredient of the Art of War, in general. But with the publication in 1554 of *Del modo di fortificar le città* . . . , by Giovanni Battista Zanchi, a military engineer in the republic's employ, there began a series of specialized works, all printed for the first time in Venice. The only book devoted to fortification which had appeared in Europe before Zanchi's treatise was Albrecht Dürer's *Etliche underricht, zu befestigung der Stett, Schloss, und flecken* (Nuremberg, 1527). Between 1554 and 1570 only two other works on fortification were published anywhere else than in Venice: Girolamo Cataneo's *Opera nuova di fortificare* . . . (Brescia, 1564) and the *Discorsi di fortificationi* of Carlo Theti (Rome, 1569). Zanchi's book was published in French as *La manière de fortifier villes, chasteaux, et faire autres lieux forts* (Lyons, 1556) by a translator, François de la Treille, who posed as the author. Three years later, via what was basically a translation of la Treille's text, it passed into English as Robert Corneweyle's *The maner of fortification*. . . . This version remained unpublished, but when the first printed English work dealing with fortification, Peter Whitehorne's *Certain waies* . . . (London, 1562), appeared, much of it was translated more or less exactly from the Italian edition of Zanchi.

That this sort of diffusion through piracy should have happened to Zanchi, rather than to Pietro Cateneo, whose *I quattro primi libri di architettura* was also published in 1554, is understandable; the latter was much longer, and only one of its four books dealt principally with fortification. It was, indeed, the last treatise to deal with both civil and military architecture, for, as fortifications became more complex, their design was increasingly seen as the province of specialists. Giacomo Lanteri's *Due dialoghi* . . . (1553) are rigorously concerned with the geometrical basis of fortress design and with surveying and model-making – that essential means of communication between engineers on the site and the government and their advisers in the capital. Equally technical is his treatise on earthen fortifications of 1559 (translated into Latin in 1563). Girolamo Maggi's *Della fortificatione delle citta* of 1564 was, for all the author's humanistic and literary bent, a practical work made all the more useful by the clearest illustrations of fortification methods yet produced and by his including edited versions of two supporting texts: the posthumous treatise of Jacopo Castriotto on the fortifications he had come to know when working as Superintendent of Fortresses in France and Francesco Montemellino's *Discorso sopra la fortificatione del Borgo di Roma*. Fortification occupied only one of the *Tre quesiti* ... (1567) of Domenio Mora, but our period ends with the thoroughly technical and splendidly illustrated *Delle fortificationi libri tre*, by Galasso Alghisi. So specialized, indeed, had military engineering become that Alghisi, or his anonymous publisher, commissioned an engraved title-page showing a Roman triumphal arch peopled with statues representing the Quadrivium and the Virtues associated with a sturdily defended polity: fortitude, prudence, justice and temperance. It was to provide a model for a host of later title-pages whose imagery was devoted to pleading that, though military engineering relied on brute strength, it was nevertheless a liberal art and required the exercise of *ingegno*.

That Venetian printers should have produced a near-monopoly of works dealing with the new art of fortification that had been forced into being by the use of effective siege artillery is not surprising if we think, again, in terms of the potential market. Other states, in Italy and beyond, were building new fortresses and bringing town *enceintes* up to date, replacing walls and tall towers with squat curtains and pointed bastions. It is doubtful that any state, however, had a larger re-building programme in this period than Venice, nor one that was so widely discussed. In 1517 Andrea Gritti, the most respected military proveditor of his time, and a future doge, recommended what was to remain the republic's defence strategy. It was unwise, he wrote, to trust to frontier fortresses, for, once broken through, they left the republic's armies nowhere to shelter. Certain places should be strengthened because of their strategic value, such as Asola, Peschiera and Legnago, but the chief care should be to refortify the large centres of population, not only so that they could resist siege but also to turn them into cities of refuge for retreating or assembling armies. Brescia, Bergamo, Crema, Verona, Padua, Treviso, Udine: The fortification of all were to undergo changes which were the subject of intense interest to their populations – if only because they had to bear one-third of the costs. On these grounds, indeed, coupled with an outcry against the losses to property that followed the modification of walls and the clearing of a deep glacis, Vicenza managed to defeat a whole series of proposals and remained the only city on the *terra ferma* whose walls were more or less unaltered from pre-gunpowder days.

The need for up-to-date fortifications was not only a strategic but a political necessity, to give credibility to the policy of armed neutrality adopted by the republic after 1529. And the constant menace of raids by, and the possibility of war with, the Turks meant that the process of modernization had to be carried on in the ports down the Dalmatian coast and in Cyprus and Crete. The patriciate thus came to contain a large number of men who, as rectors, proveditors, inquisitors and castellans, had been forced to acquaint themselves with the principles of modern military engineering. In addition, there were constant interviews in the College with engineers, Senate debates during which models and plans were explained, the appointment of special proveditors to supervise changes once they had been decided on or to confer with experts on the spot and report back to Venice. From 1542 the pressure of building-work was so great that a new magistracy was created, that of the *proveditori alle fortezze*. When we add the arm-chair experts in Venice, like Leonardi and the men Ruscelli mentions in his letter accompanying Zanchi's book, the senior officers of the permanent army who were concerned in every new project, and the self-constituted experts in the *terra ferma* who showered gratuitous advice on the government, we can assume that printers could think reasonably safely of an adequate market within Venice and its own dominions.

To connect books on artillery with those on fortification is an obvious step. Here, too, Venice took the lead and remained without the need to reprint works first published elsewhere. The *Nova scientia* of Niccolò Tartaglia (1537) was aptly named. It was the first work devoted to the subject of artillery to be printed and the pioneer contribution to the new science of ballistics. Biringuccio's *Pirotechnia* (1540) was the first printed book on metallurgy, the casting of cannon and the manufacture of explosives and incendiary compounds. Gabriello Busca's *Istrutione de' bombardieri* . . . (1545), the next work on artillery to be published in Europe, was the first practical guide to the handling of guns. In 1546 Tartaglia published his *Quesiti, et inventioni diverse*, a work which extended his ballistic theories, as well as containing important sections on fortification, surveying and troop formations. Between this work and the publication in 1568 of Ruscelli's posthumous *Precetti . . . ne' quali si contiene tutta l'arte del bombardiero* only two works dealing with artillery had appeared outside Venice, Walter Ryff's *Der furnembsten, notwendigsten der ganzen Architectur angehörigen mathematischen und mechanischen kunst* . . . (Nuremberg, 1547) and Girolamo Cataneo's *Un trattato de gli esamini de' bombardieri* . . . (Brescia, 1564). The subject had also been touched on in a few works on the art of war published elsewhere, but for books exclusively or weightily concerned with artillery Venice's lead was as striking as in the field of fortification.

To describe the gunfounding industry, the organisation of the *scuole di bombardieri*, the duties of munitioneers and the responsibility of patrician councillors and office-holders to keep abreast of changes in the making and use of artillery by land and at sea would serve only to labour a now-familiar point, that Venetian leadership in the production of military books depended on a capacious and widely recognized industry which could reckon on an interested local market. There is, all the same, one further point to make about that market. Fortification, ballistics, troop evolutions and formations: All came to assume a knowledge of mathematics. Tartaglia had lectured on Euclid in Venice before the publication of his *Nova scientia*. On its title-page the author is shown standing between maidens labelled "Aritmetica" and "Geometria" while he watches the trajectories of a cannon and a mortar; in the background philosophy sits enthroned in an enclosure, the entrance to which is guarded by Plato, who flourishes a scroll inscribed "Nemo huc geometrie expers ingrediatur." Zanchi pointed out that "son necessarie la geometria, l'aritmetica, per numerare et dividere le misure delle fortezze." Pietro Cataneo's *Le pratiche delle due prime matematiche* . . . was published in Venice in 1559. One of Lanteri's *Due dialoghi* was "del modo di disegnare le piante delle fortezze secondo Euclide," and in his treatise on earthen fortifications he emphasized the prime importance of "la cognitione delle forme, la quale non si puo in vero perfettamente possedere, senza la geometria," and in 1569 Mora told his readers that nowadays the Sargente Generale, the officer responsible for brigading an army, "deve essere buon arithmetico et abbachista."

An interest in mathematics was widespread in Italy, but it is particularly appropriate that it was in Venice that science in this form came to affect the nature of books about the art of war. The foundation had been laid, well before the setting up there of a public lectureship in mathematics in 1530, by the instruction given at the Scuola di Rialto in the mid-fifteenth century and in the first publication of works like Fra Luca Pacioli's *Summa* . . . (1494) and the first Latin translation of Euclid (1505). The original holder of that lectureship was the patrician Giovanni-Battista Memmo, a friend of Tartaglia's. When the latter was attacked in a pamphlet of 1547 by a rival mathematician, Ludovico Ferrari, fifty copies were addressed personally to influential men in different parts of Italy; by far, the largest group, twenty, were natives or residents of Venice. The activities of the Accademia Venetiana, set up in 1557, were to have a strongly mathematical bias. When Curtio Troiano published Tartaglia's formidable posthumous work, *Il general tratato di numeri et misure* in six parts in 1556, three of the parts were dedicated to military men: Camillo Martinengo, not only a soldier but a man drawn to learning "et massime alla divina scienza di Matematica"; Venice's commander-in-chief, Sforza Pallavicino; and the influential condottiere Girolamo Martinengo, "essendo Ella un de' primi lumi, che in questi nostri tempi si trovino, della militia, et dilettandosi sommamente delle cose delle fortificationi, et delle ordinanze, le quali cose non si possono perfettamente intendere, senza l'aiuto delle Mathematiche."

Of the nine European works printed in this period that dealt specifically with military medicine, especially with the treatment of gunshot wounds, four were reprinted at Venice, though only two of these had not already been reprinted elsewhere: Leonardo Botallo's *De curandis vulneribus sclopettiorum* (1564; original edition, Lyons, 1560) and Giovanni Rota's *De tormentariorum vulnerum natura* (1566; original edition, Bologna, 1555). More initiative was shown in the two works, first published in Venice, that comprise (in addition to Nannini's *Orationi militari . . .*) the admittedly vague and subjective category "Miscellaneous." Giulio Ballino's *De' disegni delle piu illustre città et fortezze del mondo*, which Bolognino Zaltieri produced in two separate editions in 1565, was the first topographical work aimed at an audience primarily interested in war, with its engraved views of forts and battle sites in Italy, France, Hungary and Transylvania. The *Informatione a soldati christiani et a tutti coloro che sono su la potentissima armata . . .* of 1570 was the shrewdest piece of propaganda that had yet been issued to a military force. Francesco Sansovino opened it in the traditional vein of the eve-of-battle harangue that had been represented in Nannini's *Orationi militari*. "La Maestà di Dio, o soldati, vi apparecchia una bella et honorata vittoria, la quale continouando voi nell'ardente dispositione dell'animo vostro, vi sarà facile ad ottenere." God will humble the pride of the Turks. What is more, "il nemico si trova per mare inferiore alle nostre forze, tanto per legni, quanto per capitani et soldati." The Turks are legally in the wrong, for they, not the Venetians, have broken the truce. Their morale has been sapped by years of peace. Their vessels are outmoded, over-weighted with rigging, their oarsmen are not trusted to carry arms. Sansovino then breaks with tradition by introducing a series of woodcuts illustrating the various types of troops the Venetians are about to encounter. All of them, including the dreaded Janissaries, are made to look remarkably harmless. Here they are, he emphasizes, men of flesh and blood, no nobler nor more valourous than other men; indeed, easier to defeat because they are "infami et privi d'ogni ordine di militia." And he ends with a reassuring reminder of the Turkish failure in Malta in 1565.

The vast proportion of writings about war in this period that exist in Venice were not, of course, intended for publication: reports, surveys, projects and suggestions submitted to or requested by the government. The majority were, in any case, too topical, or too narrow in subject matter to have repaid publication. A very few were too confidential, an example being Maggi's compilation of fortification devices and secret weapons (including poisons) designed to help Famagusta, were it to be besieged by the Turks; "il qual libro," as the endorsement to the Council of Ten's minute of 23 February, 1570, reads, "fo salvato, dal mg.co concellier grande nel suo leto."[6] But while it is hazardous to generalize about military culture on the evidence of published works alone (even in a century when the press was so active), two things can be said with some confidence: the archival material supports the interest in military affairs already claimed for the Venetian patriciate and the citizens of the *terra ferma*, and the manuscript treatises that remain in libraries would not, had they been printed, affect the impression given by the published works, either in range or quality – with one most notable exception.

The first book printed anywhere in Italy that dealt exclusively, or even at length, with naval warfare was Pantero Pantera's *L'armata navale* (Rome, 1614), a fact that makes the silence of the Venetian presses less surprising. Yet some surprise must remain, given the numbers of Venetians who had had ship-board experience, the continuity of combat or anti-corsair activity, the experimentation with new craft and the means of arming and manning them and the recognition of naval warfare as a subject: Underneath the armoured busts of Alessandro Contarini and Girolamo Michiel in the church of San Antonio in Padua the inscriptions read "totius maritimae disciplinae simulacrum" and "rei navali scientia . . . praestanti." In 1558 Vincenzo Valgrisi printed the *Elogia venetorum navali pugna illustrium* of the Venetian cleric Antonio Stella, a collection of forty-seven brief biographies of patrician sea captains designed to stimulate a patriotic ardour among the young. But no battles are described, no interest in naval warfare evinced. The materials for Mario Savorgnan's *Arte militare terrestre e maritima . . .* (1599) were accumulated, as we have seen, before his death in 1574; yet, in spite of the title, naval affairs amount to little more than a description of Lepanto.

The silence is not to be explained in terms of secrecy. Huge numbers of men were constantly being recruited from the *terra ferma* and the empire *da mar* and then being redistributed there. The trials of new warships were conducted publicly. Naval tactics were more or less common to all the Mediterranean naval powers. Continual piracy meant that the vessels of one state were constantly falling into the hands of others. Three reasons explain the silence. One is familiarity; naval powers are less interested in writing or reading about navies than about armies. Another is sameness; naval tactics were extremely simple and changed very little during the period we are considering. The last and possibly most important reason is that there was no classical precedent for the independent, or even reasonably detailed, treatment of naval warfare. Cyllenius's title (1559) recalls that of Savorgnan, *De vetere et recentiore scientia militari, omnium bellorum genera, terrestria perinde ac navalia . . . complectente*, and its treatment of war at sea, which is exclusivly classical, is just as brief as his. What is surprising, then, is not that no work on naval warfare was published but that one – Cristoforo da Canal's *Della milizia marittima* – was actually intended for the press.

Da Canal was born in 1510 and died of wounds received in combat at sea in 1562. He exemplified those poor patricians whose lives were entirely dedicated to government service. In his case, apart from a term of office as proveditor of Marano, this was spent entirely at sea: "I quali tutti carichi, et honori non sarebbono stati a vostra Magnificenza," wrote Lodovico Dolce, dedicating his edition of Appian to him in 1559 (though the colophon has 1554), "cosi spesso, e con tanto favore conceduti, se non si fosse in lei veduto trovarsi tutte o la maggior parte di quelli conditioni, che convengono a vero e perfetto capitano." He continued,

Taccio che come che'l suo proprio e principale esercitio, sia stato sempre quello delle arme, in quello della penna riesce lodevolissimamente: come ne rende chiara fede il Dialogo da lei gia gran tempo fatto della militia maritima; ove tratta pienamente e leggiadramente di tutto quello, che appartiene a condurre un' armata, alle battaglie, et alle cose di mare, formando un legno, et un capitano a perfettione.

That this manuscript had a status comparable to that of Leonardi's is suggested by a reference in Porcacchi's *L'isole piu famose* . . . (1572) to

Christoforo Canale, oltra che in mare fece molte prove; fu ancho tanto prattico in quei governi, che pare c' hoggi tutti gli altri siano per imitar la disciplina di lui, trovandosi per le mani de' nobili un libro, ch' io ho veduto, composto da esso Canale: il quale insegna con giudicio et con ordine tutta la disciplina navale.

The manuscript is not dated, nor, on internal evidence, is it easy to date. Influenced by Dolce's "gia gran tempo," M. Nani Mocenigo, who first printed it (Rome, 1930), put its composition at around 1540. Alberto Tenenti, whose *Cristoforo da Canal: la marine Vénitienne avant Lépante* (Paris, 1962) renders prolonged description of the work here superfluous, prefers a later date, 1553–4. It is not uninteresting, however, that P. A. Zeno, whose *Memoria di scrittori veneti patritii* (Venice, 1662) cites Canal's work as the first of a military nature to be produced by a Venetian patrician before Pietro Maria Contarini's work on land war, *Corso di guerra* . . . (Venice, 1601), dates it 1538.

The dialogue form (one of the interlocutors is the Alessandro Contarini whose tomb commemorates him as "totius maritimae disciplinae simulacrum"), the references to Rome and Carthage, the emphasis on the usefulness of writing about, as well as practising military affairs, are aspects of the work, as well as a strong if cumbrous attempt at a literary style, which make it clear that Canal had publication in mind. He was, moreover, a friend of Dolce, one of the most prolific writers of the age, and da Canal took it upon himself to get the work of another friend ("anchora che senza il consentimento di lui") into print: Antonio Pellegrini's *I segni de la natura ne l' huomo* (Giovanni Farri for J. Gryphius, 1545) – a topic interesting to Canal for its bearing on the choice of men to crew galleys. *Della milizia marittima* is a mine, indeed *the* mine, of detailed information about the design, armament, crewing and handling of war galleys and their deployment on patrol or in war. Yet that the writer was also a reader is made clear, time after time. Discussing the theme that "l'arte della guerra non si aprende nei libri," one of his characters goes on to say:

ricordomi haver udito raccontare [the story was told by Bandello] che Nicolò Macchiavelli, il quale così ben ragionò et scrisse delle cose che appartengono a un capitano et soldato da terra, essendo messo dal sig. Giovanni de' Medici alla cura delle genti delle quali esso era capitano pose ogni cosa in disordine.

It is certainly not unlikely that Canal, at the end of a life increasingly heavily committed to naval service, left the manuscript unfinished and unprinted because of his conscious rivalry with the literary form (also a dialogue) of such a work as Machiavelli's *Arte della guerra*.

The work also suggests a more general reason for the lack of books on naval warfare – the degree to which the subject overlapped that of war on land. Naval tactical formations for the highly manoeuvrable, fore-and-aft firing galleys comprised little more than variations on the advance guard, main body and rearguard of contemporary armies. Battle at sea was avoided as much as possible; apart from convoy escort, coastal patrol and deterrent shows of strength, the warship's characteristic function was that of a troop-carrier supporting amphibious or purely terrestrial operations. With its *scapoli* and *soldati*, a galley carried a company of infantrymen whose armament, training and organization are treated by Canal with frequent reference to the companies garrisoning the fortresses of the *terra ferma*. Whether it concerned the character of a commander or the preliminary bombardment followed by grappling and boarding which made naval engagements resemble sieges, the *arte militare maritima* – especially in the absence of an independent, classically based tradition – was difficult to imagine as a subject in its own right, and Canal was able to make it one only by reconsidering naval affairs, from ship design to strategy, with the verve of an anecdotalist and the zeal of a reformer.

What, then, can be concluded from this survey? Hopefully, it suggests that neither what is known about the functioning of the printing industry nor what might be conjectural about the existence of an international market can explain Venice's unique role in the production of books dealing with military, or quasi-military subjects. The explanation lies mainly in the existence of an informed and interested local market for such works, both in Venice and its territories. If this is so, then a larger place than has hitherto been acknowledged must be accorded to the role of military culture in the *forma mentis* of Renaissance Venetians and their subjects.

NOTES

This article is a revised version of a study which is to appear in the volume devoted to Renaissance Venice in the *Storia della Cultura Veneta*, to be published by Neri Pozza of Vicenza. I am most grateful to Signor Pozza for permission to publish in this form. I am indebted to Dr. Dennis E. Rhodes, and Professor Conor Fahy, whose scrupulous reading of the draft of this study saved me from many errors. It has also benefited from the vigilance of the editorial board of *Medievalia et Humanistica*.

1. In the absence of a short-title catalogue of Italian books printed in the fifteenth and sixteenth centuries, they are based on: Maurice J. D. Cockle, *A Bibliography of English Military Books up to 1642 and of Contemporary Foreign Works* (London, 1900; reprinted 1957); M. d'Ayala, *Bibliografia militare italiana* (Torino, 1954); *Short-title catalogue of books printed in Italian and of Italian books printed in other countries from 1465 to 1600 now in the British Museum* (London, 1958). *Short-title catalog of books printed in Italy . . . 1501–1600 held in selected North American Libraries* 3 vols. (Boston, Mass., 1970). Also useful were: Horst de la Croix "The literature on fortification in Renaissance Italy," *Technology and Culture* (1963), 30–50; T. M. Spaulding, "Early military books in the Folger Library," *Journal of the American Military History Foundation* (1937), 91–100; J. R. Hale, "A Newberry Library Supplement to 'Cockle,'" *Papers of the Bibliographical Society of America* (1961), 137–9; T. M. Spaulding and L. C. Karpinski, *Early Military Books in the University of Michigan Library* (Michigan, 1941).
2. Horatio Brown, *The Venetian Printing Press* (London, 1891) is still useful. Apart from Salvatore Bongi's *Annali di Gabriel Giolito de' Ferrari*, 2 vols. (Roma, 1890–5), there is very little discussion of post-Aldine Venetian printing; see the excellent bibliography in Ruth Mortimer, *Italian Sixteenth century books* (Cambridge, Mass., 1974), vol. 1.
3. See Paul F. Grendler, "Francesco Sansovino and Italian popular history," *Italian Renaissance Studies* XVI (1969), 158–61.
4. Rudolf Hirsch surely exaggerates the effectiveness of Venice's distribution system north of the Alps, especially for works in Italian in his *Printing, selling and reading, 1450–1500* (Wiesbaden, 1967), 58–9.
5. Marciana Library, Venice, Mss. Misc. c.3504.
6. Archivio di Stato, Venice, Consiglio dei dieci, Secreta Deliberationi, Registro 9.f.57.

APPENDIX 1

A check list of books of military interest printed in Venice, 1492–1570

Check no.	Year	Status	Author	Short title[a]	Printer[b]
1	[1492]	A	Ruffo, Giordano	. . . arte del congnoscere la natura de cavael . . .	Piero Bergamasco
2	1493	A	Cornazano, Antonio	Opera belissima delarte militar . . .	Christophorus de Pensis [Mādello] for Piero Benalio
3	1498	C	Colonna, Egidio	De regimine principum (orig. Augsburg, 1473)	Simon Bevilaqua
4	1502	C		New ed. of no. 3.	Bernardinus Vercellensis
	1517[o]				
5	1521	C	Puteo, Paris de [= Pozzo, Paride dal]	Duello . . . (orig. Naples, 1471)	[Gregorio de Gregoriis for Melchiorre Sessa and Pietro dei Ravani]
6	1523	C		New ed. of no. 5	Gregorio de Gregoriis
7	1524	C	Della Valle, Battista	Vallo . . . (orig. Naples, 1521)	[Gregorio de Gregoriis]
8	1525	C		New ed. of no. 5	[Gregorio de Gregoriis] for M. Sessa and P. dela Serena
9	1526	A	Brucioli, Antonio	Dialogi	Gregorio de Gregoriis
10		B[d]		New ed. of no. 2	Melchiorre Sessa
11		C		New ed. of no. 7	?
12	1528	C		New ed. of no. 7	Pietro dei Ravani
13	1529	C		New ed. of no. 7	Nicolò d'Aristotile Zoppino
14	1530	A	Porcia, Jacopo di	. . . de re militari . . .	Joannes Tacuinus
15		C		New ed. of no. 5	Aurelio Pincio
16	1531	C		New ed. of no. 7	Vittore dei Ravani & Co.
17	1535	C		New ed. of no. 7	Vittore dei Ravani & Co.

461

APPENDIX 1. Continued

Check no.	Year	Status	Author	Short title[a]	Printer[b]
18	1536[e]	A	Columbre [or Colombre], Agostino	Libro . . . dedicato al . . . re Ferdinando . . .	Piero dei Nicolini da Sabbio for Pietro Facolo
19		A	Anon	. . . natura delli cavalli . . .	Francesco Bindoni and Mapheo Pasini
20		B		New ed of no. 2	Piero dei Nicolini da Sabbio
21		C		New ed. of no. 5	Piero dei Nicolini da Sabbio
22	1537	A	Tartaglia, Niccolò	Nova scientia . . .	Stefano dei Nicolini da Sabbio for N. Tartaglia
23		B		New ed. of no. 9	Bartholomeo Zanetti
24		C	Machiavelli, Niccolò	Arte della guerra (orig. Florence, 1521)	No printer.
25	1539	C		New ed. of no. 7	Vittore dei Ravani & Co.
26	1540	A	Biringuccio, Vanuccio	De la pirotechnia	Venturino Ruffinelli for Curtio Navò
27		C		New ed. of no. 24	Sons of Aldus
28	1541	C		New ed. of no. 5	Comin da Trino
29		C		New ed. of no. 24	Comin da Trino
30	1543	C		New ed. of no. 7	Heirs of Pietro dei Ravani
31[f]	1544	A	Alciatus, Andreas	. . . de singulare certamine	Vincenzo Valgrisi
32[f]		A	Socinus, Mariano	Consilia . . . in materia duelli	Vincenzo Valgrisi
33		B		New ed. of no. 19	Francesco Bindoni and Mapheo Pasini
34		B		New ed. of no. 9	Francesco Brucioli & Bros.
35		D	Rusius, Laurentius	. . . de l'arte del malscalcio (orig. Latin, s.n.)	?
36		D	Vegetius Renatus, Publius	. . . dell'arte di manescalchi . . . (orig. Latin, Basel, 1528)	Michele Tramezzino
37	1545[g]	D		Duello, Italian tr. of no. 31	Vincenzo Valgrisi
38		D		Another setting of no. 37	Alvise de Tortis
39	1546	A	Tartaglia, Niccolò	Quesiti et inventioni . . .	Venturino Ruffinello for N. Tartaglia
40		C		New ed. of no. 24	Aldus

462

41	1548	D	Muzio, Girolamo	New ed. of no. 35	Michele Tramezzino
42	1550	A		Il duello . . .	Gabriel Giolito & Bros.
43		B		New ed. of no. 22	No printer, for N. Tartaglia
44		C	Marozzo, Achille	Opera nova . . . (orig. Modena, 1536)	Giovanni Padovano for Melchiorre Sessa
45		B		New ed. of no. 26	Giovanni Padovano for Curtio Navò
46		C		New ed. of no. 24	Gabriel Giolito & Bros.
47		C	Fourquevaux, Raymond de[h]	New ed. of no. 7	Heirs of Pietro dei Ravani & Co.
48		D	Muzio, Girolamo	. . . della disciplina militare . . . (orig. Paris, 1548)	Michele Tramezzino
49	1551	A	Grisone, Federigo	Le risposte cavalleresche	Gabriel Giolito & Bros.
50		B		New ed. of no. 42	Gabriel Giolito & Bros.
51		C		Gli ordini di cavalcare (orig. Naples, 1550)	?
52	1552	A	Fausto da Longiano, Sebastiano	Duello . . .	Vincenzo Valgrisi
53	1553	D		New ed. of no. 37	Comin da Trino
54		A	Possevino, Giovanni Battista	Dialogo dell'honore . . .?	Gabriel Giolito & Bros.
55		B		New ed. of no. 42	Gabriel Giolito & Bros.
56		B		New ed. of no. 49	Gabriel Giolito & Bros.
57		C		New ed. of no. 51	?
58	1554	A	Zanchi, Giovanni Battista	Del modo di fortificar le citta	Plinio Pietrasanta
59		B		New ed. of no. 39	Niccolò de Bascarini for N. Tartaglia
60		C		New ed. of no. 24	Domenico Giglio
61		A	Cataneo, Pietro	. . . libri di architettura . . .	Sons of Aldus
62		A	Pigna, Giovanni Battista	Il duello	Vincenzo Valgrisi
63		B		New ed. of no. 1	Heirs of Giovanni Padovano
64		B		New ed. of no. 42	Gabriel Giolito [and Bros.?]

APPENDIX 1. *Continued*

Check no.	Year	Status	Author	Short title[a]	Printer[b]
65	1555	D	Massa, Antonio	Contra l'uso del duello (orig. Latin, Rome, 1556)	Michele Tramezzino
66	1556	A	Garimberto, Girolamo	Il capitano generale . . . [j]	Giordano Ziletti
67		B		New ed. of no. 58	?
68		A	Farra, Alessandro	. . . dell'ufficio del capitano[k]	A. della Paglia
69	1557	A	Lanteri, Giacomo	Due dialoghi . . .	Vincenzo Valgrisi and Baldassar Costantini
70		A	Nannini, Remigio	Orationi militari . . .	Gabriel Giolito
71		B		New ed. of no. 66	Giordano Ziletti
72	1558	A	Susio, Giovanni Battista	. . . della ingiustitia del duello . . .	Gabriel Giolito
73		B		New ed. of no. 22	No printer
74		B		New ed. of no. 42[l]	Gabriel Giolito
75		B		New ed. of no. 49[l]	Gabriel Giolito
76		B		New ed. of no. 54	Gabriel Giolito
77		B		New ed. of no. 26[m]	Comin da Trino for Curtio Navò
78		C		New ed. of no. 7	Giovanni Guarisco & Co.
79		D		Las reglas militares. . . . Spanish tr. of no. 2	Giovanni Rossi
80	1559	B		New ed. of no. 26	Girolamo Giglio & Co.
81		D		New ed. of no. 35	Girolamo Cavalcalupo
82		B		New ed. of no. 52	Rutilio Borgominieri
83		B		New ed. of no. 26	Girolamo Giglio & Co.
84		B		New ed. of no. 54	Gabriel Giolito
85		A	Cyllenius, Domenicus	. . . de vetere et recentiore scientia militari . . .	Comin da Trino for F. da Portonari
86		A	Lanteri, Giacomo	. . . fare le fortificationi di terra . . .	Bolognino Zaltieri for Francesco Marcolini
87	1560	A	Muzio, Girolamo	Le faustina . . . delle arme . . .	Vincenzo Valgrisi

88		A	Attendolo, Dario	Il duello	Francesco Lorenzini
89		A	Fausto da Longiano, Sebastiano	Duello ... con un discorso e con due risposte ...[n]	Rutilio Borgominieri
90		B		New ed. of no. 58	D. and C. de' Nicolini da Sabio
91		B		New ed. of no. 42	Gabriel Giolito
92		B		New ed. of no. 62	?
93		B		New ed. of no. 52	Rutilio Borgominieri
94	1561	B		New ed. of no. 1	Rutilio Borgominieri
95		B		New ed. of no. 18	Francesco Fasani
96		C		... del modo dell'imbrigliare ... (orig. Bologna, 1556)	Domenico Nicolini
97		A	Fiaschi, Cesare	Consilia et tractatus ...	Lodovico degli Avanzi
98	1562	B	Ferretti, Giulio	New ed. of no. 22[o]	Curtio Navò
99		B		New ed. of no. 39[o]	Curtio Navò
100	1558–62	A	Centorio, Ascanio de Hortensii	... sopra l'ufficio d'un capitano generale	Gabriel Giolito[p]
101		A	Belli, Pietrino	De re militari	Francesco Portonari
102	1563	A	Memmo, Giovanni Maria	Dialogo	Gabriel Giolito
103		B		New ed. of no. 42[q]	Gabriel Giolito
104		B		New ed. of no. 49[q]	Gabriel Giolito
105		D		De modo substriendi terrena .... (Latin tr. of no. 86)	Vincenzo Valgrisi
106	1564	A	Maggi, Girolamo	Della fortificatione delle citta ...[r]	Rutilio Borgominieri
107		A	Castriotto, Giacomo Fusto	Della fortificatione delle citta[r]	Rutilio Borgominieri
108		A	Montemellino, Francesco	La fortificatione del Borgo di Roma[r]	Rutilio Borgominieri
109		A	Coniano, Giovacchino da	Trattato dell'ordinanze ...[r]	Rutilio Borgominieri
110		B		New ed. of no. 42[s]	Gabriel Giolito
111		B		New ed. of no. 49[s]	Gabriel Giolito
112		B		New ed. of no. 54	Gabriel Giolito

APPENDIX 1. *Continued*

Check no.	Year	Status	Author	Short title[a]	Printer[b]
113		B		New ed. of no. 88	Gabriel Giolito
114		C	Botallus, Leonardo	De curandis vulneribus scloppetorum (orig. Lyon, 1560)	Francesco Rampazetto
115	1565	B		New ed. of no. 88	Gabriel Giolito
116	1566	A	Rocca, Bernardino	Imprese, stratagemi et errori . . .	Gabriel Giolito
117		A	Caracciolo, Pasquale	La gloria del cavallo . . .	Gabriel Giolito
118		A	Adriano, Alfonso[t]	Della disciplina militare . . .	Lodovico degli Avanzi
119		A	Ximenez de Urrea, Geronymo	. . . de la verdadera honrra militar . . .	Giovanni Griffio
120		A	Sansovino, Francesco	Origine de cavalieri	C. and R. Borgominieri
121		B		New ed. of no. 66	Giordano Ziletti
122		B		New ed. of no. 42	Gabriel Giolito
123		C	Maggius, Bartholomeus	De vulnerum sclopetorum (orig. Bologna, 1552)	Gratioso Perchacino[u]
124	1567	A	Mora, Domenico	Tre quesiti . . .	Giovanni Varisco & co.
125		A	Cicogna, Giovan Mattheo	Il primo libro del trattato militare . . .	Giovanni Bariletto
126		B		New ed. of no. 100	Gabriel Giolito
127		B		New ed. of no. 61	Paolo Manuzio
128	1568	A	Ferretti, Francesco	Della osservanza militare . . .	C. and R. Borgominieri
129		A	Ruscelli, Girolamo	Precetti della militia . . .	Heirs of Melchiorre Sessa
130		B		New ed. of no. 54	Francesco Sansovino
131		C		New ed. of no. 44	Antonio Pinargenti
132		C	Agrippa, Camillo	Trattato di scientia d'arme . . . (orig. Rome, 1553)	Antonio Pinargenti
133		B		New ed. of no. 100	Gabriel Giolito
134	1569	A	Mora, Domenico	Il soldato . . .	Giovanni Griffio
135		A	Mercurialis, Hieronymus	Artis gymnasticae . . .	Giunta[v]

136		A	Ballino, M. Giulio	De disegni delle . . . citta et fortezze . . .	Bolognino Zaltieri
137		B		New ed. of no. 136	Bolognino Zaltieri
138		A	Anon.	Libro de marchi de cavalli	Niccolò Nelli
139		D		Del vero honore militare (Italian tr. of no. 119)	Heirs of Melchiorre Sessa
140	1570	A	Rocca, Bernardino	La seconda [e terza] parte del governo della militia . . .	Gabriel Giolito
141		A	Grassi, Giacomo di	Ragione di adoprar . . . l'arme . . .	Giordano Ziletti & Co.
142		A	Alghisi, Galasso	Delle fortificationi	No printer
143		A	Sansovino, Francesco	Informatione a soldati . . .	No printer
144		B		New ed. of no. 134	Gabriel Giolito[w]
145		B		New ed. of no. 120	Heirs of Melchiorre Sessa

Key: A = Work first printed in Venice.
B = Later edition of works first printed in Venice.
C = Venetian editions of works printed elsewhere.
D = Translation.
? = Unseen by compiler.

[a] Excluding classical works, histories, campaign reports and biographies of military figures.

[b] Printer's names given as in British Library *Catalogue of Italian books . . . 1465–1600.*

[c] Cockle follows Ayala (see text note 1) in attributing a misdated copy of no. 44 (ed. of 1568) to this year, thus making it a work first printed in Venice. See Mortimer (see text note 2) Vol. II, p. 423.

[d] As the interest of this Appendix is primarily statistical, no distinction is made between new editions and new issues; some of the latter, for example, nos. 71, 115 and 133, are issues of existing page stock redated on the old title page.

[e] Doubtful, but earliest edition known to me.

[f] Published together.

[g] Cockle follows Ayala in attributing the first edition of Gabriel Busca, *Instruttione de' bombardieri* to this year. As Busca was born around 1540 and refers to a work of Domenico Mora's which must be our no. 124 of 1567, this cannot be right, nor can Ayala's Venetian editions of 1554 and 1559. The first is almost certainly Carmagnola, 1584.

[h] Attributed in 1548 and 1550 to Guillaume du Bellay. The common attribution since the last century to Fourquevaux is still unproven.

APPENDIX 1. *Continued*

i "Di nuovo stampato" on title page; but in sense of "for the first time."
j "Nuovamente mandato in luce" on title page; but again in sense of "for the first time."
k Date from, Ayala, followed by Cockle, who nevertheless gives Pavia, 1564, as the *princeps*. I have not found a copy of the 1556 edition. The dedication of the Pavia edition to Hestorre Visconte" is dated Pavia, April 1, 1564, which casts further doubt on the 1556 edition.
l Published together.
m Colophon 1559.
n Treated as an original work because of the amount of new material.
o Published together.
p Five parts, separate title pages, published together.
q Published together.
r Published together.
s Published together.
t Actually by Cicuta, Aurelio.
u T.p.: "Venetiis Apud Gulielmum Valgrisum et Io. Alexium Socios et bibliopolas Bononie." Colophon: "Venetiis apud Gratiosum Perchacinum."
v T.p.: "Venetiis, apud Iuntas"; colophon: "Venetiis in officina Iuntarum."
w Re-issue retains colophon "Per Giovan Griffio."

APPENDIX 2

It is printed in the last of the Greek historians to appear, *Ditte Candiotto et Darete Frigio della guerra troiana* . . . (1570).

Essendo la guerra la piu importante attion, che si legga nell'historie, poiche da essa dependono gli stati; et essendo certo che la guerra non si fa senza cagione esplicita, o implicita; però la prima Gioia congiunta all'Annello della mia Collana historica; sarà

Il libro delle cagioni delle Guerre, diviso in piu volumi, che tutti sono sotto Il prima Gioia. Et di queste fin' hora Thomaso Porcacchi da Castiglione Arretino n' ha publicato il primo volume. Et perche trovata la Cagion della Guerra; è necessario volendola fare; proveder primieramente d'un buon Capitano; però sarà

Il libro del Capitan Generale dell'essercito. Et questo è stato fin' hora composto, et descritto dal S. Ascanio Centorio de gli Hortensij nel suo primo Discorso. Et perche il Capitano Generale, subito ch' è creato, deve proveder d'altri ministri, et particolarmente del Maestro di campo: però sarà

Il libro che tratta della qualità del Maestro di Campo. Di che s'ha pienamente nel terzo discorso di detto S. Ascanio Centorio. Et perche trovato et eletto il Maestro di Campo, è necessario proveder soldati per poter far la guerra; però sarà

Il libro del Soldato: nel quale si tratta di quanto è necessario a un vero soldato, et a un nobil Cavalliero. Et questo fin hora è stato publicato dal S. Domenico Mora Bolognese, et gentil' huomo Grigione. Et perche trovato il soldato; si discorre del modo di far la guerra, però sarà

Il libro dell'arte della militia, che è il quinto discorso del S. Ascanio Centorio. Et perche trovato il modo del far la guerra; bisogna ancho saperla governare, et maneggiare, però sarà

Il libro del governo della Militia: il quale essendo stato composto dal S. Bernardino Rocca Piacentino; fra pochi giorni sarà posto in luce. Et perche in questo discorso del maneggiar l'imprese della guerra, molto utili son quelli argomenti che si deducono da' casi seguiti, o da gli Essempi simili, però sarà

Il libro de' Paralleli, o Essempi simili di Thomaso Porcacchi, gia publicato. Et perche trovato il modo di maneggiar dette imprese, si tratta del modo dell'accampare; però sarà

Il libro della Castrametatione: nel qual saranno posti insieme tutti quelli Auttori antichi et moderni, che del modo dell'accampare habbiano scritto. Et perche dopo questo debbe venirsi al far l'impresa della guerra: nella quale succedono stratagemi et Errori: però sarà

Il libro dell' imprese, de gli stratagemi, et de gli Errori militari;che fin' hora è stato descritto dal S. Bernardino Rocca Piacentino, et dato in luce. Et perche nell' Imprese intervengono spesse volte parlamenti di Capitani a' soldati; però sarà

Il libro dell' Oratori militari, raccolte et publicate da M. Remigio Fiorentino. Et cosi con queste consideratroni puo accrescersi quest'ordine di nuovi concetti, et pensieri: i quali secondo che alla giornata soverranno, o saran publicati; cosi vi saranno inserti, avisando che in questo ordine medesimo vanno inclusi i libri scritti in materia di Duello: ma non se n'ha fatto mentione; percioche sono stati molti gli scrittori di questo soggetto, et per esser l'opere loro state stampate da diversi; non s'ha voluto co'l nominare i SS. Girolamo Mutio, Gio. Battista Possevino, et Dario Attendolo; far pregiudicio a gli altri. Havremmo anchora adornata questa Collana di quella preciosa Gioia et traduttione, che fa il S. Gio. Antonio Rusconi del Vitruvio; in modo che tosto si spera con molte belle et utili figure darlo alla stampa; se quest' opera non appartenesso piu all' Architettura et elegantia del fabricare, che alla fortificatione de' luoghi, necessaria nelle guerre; et se da molti altri non fusse stato scritto in questo soggetto di fortificar terre et luoghi abbondantemente.

ANDREA PALLADIO, POLYBIUS AND JULIUS CAESAR

In 1575, five years before his death, Andrea Palladio, the most famous and among the busiest of Italian architects, produced an edition of Julius Caesar's *Commentaries*.[1] This apparently discrepant event, which has been treated with some impatience by Palladian scholars,[2] is all the more tantalizing because from 1617, when Paolo Gualdo published a brief biography of Palladio (of whom in all probability he had been a close acquaintance) it has been known that Palladio also

> produced in the same vein some splendid studies [nobilissime fatiche] devoted to Polybius, dedicating them to Francesco, Grand Duke of Tuscany, who held him in the warmest esteem.[3]

Of these studies there was still no trace when Count Francesco Algarotti, who around 1760 devoted one of his 'military discourses' to an enthusiastic account of the edition of Caesar, concluded that

> it is much to be desired, however, that the discovery could be made of Palladio's work on Polybius, which, in conjunction with his introduction to Julius Caesar, would perhaps provide us with a fine treatise on warfare composed by an excellent architect.[4]

The first concrete evidence, however, that such a work had existed was provided in 1845 by Antonio Magrini. He printed a document which Carlo Promis, the pioneer historian of Renaissance military engineering, had found in the Medicean archive in Florence. Addressed to the Grand Duke of Tuscany, and dated from Venice on 18 January 1579, it was not the draft of a dedication, as it has consistently been described, but a progress report from Palladio, the obsequiousness of whose language (unusual even for those days and at odds with the tone of his actual dedications) reflects the embarrassment of an author who has as yet nothing to offer 'but the promise and shadow' of 'my studies of Polybius [mie fatiche fatte intorno Polibio].'[5] Magrini also printed a document of 29 April 1588, from the notarial archive of Vicenza, which records the attempt of Palladio's son Silla to secure his financial rights over the copperplates 'drawn and executed [figurata et composita] by the aforesaid deceased Andrea in connection with the History of Polybius.' And he deplores the loss of these works, 'of which no knowledge of any kind has

---

[1] *I commentari di C. Giulio Cesare, con le figure in rame de gli alloggiamenti, de' fatti d'arme, delle circonvallationi delle città, et di moltre altre cose notabili descritte in essi. Fatte da Andrea Palladio per facilitare a chi legge, la cognition dell'historia*, Venice, Pietro de' Franceschi, MDLXXV. The colophon has MDLXXIIII. See R. Mortimer, *Harvard College Library, Department of Printing and Graphic Arts, Catalogue of Italian 16th-C. Books*, 1974, no. 97.

[2] Though Lionello Puppi has gone some way to naturalize it among the military interests of Vicentine society; *Scrittori vicentini d'architettura del secolo XVI*, Vicenza 1973, pp. 71 seq.

[3] I quote from the reprint in Giovanni Montenari, *Del teatro olimpico di Andrea Palladio*, Padua, 2nd. ed. 1749, ix-x.

[4] *Opere*, vol. 5, Venice 1791, p. 217. He says nothing about the illustrations to Caesar.

[5] *Memorie intorno la vita e le opere di Andrea Palladio*, Padua 1845. Appendices, 16. The document is dated 1569. Magrini (text pp. 119–20) convincingly shows that this was a slip for 1579.

reached us.'[6] More recently the loss has been confirmed by Wittkower[7] and Puppi.[8]

It is the purpose of this article to suggest that these works have been rediscovered; but before doing so it would be useful to take a closer look than has been afforded up to now at the studies that preceded them: the introductory matter and the illustrations to Palladio's edition of Caesar.

On 5 March 1575 the Venetian Senate granted him a printing privilege for fifteen years in answer to a petition in which Palladio explained that he had

> with great expense and application illustrated [ridotto in figure] all the military dispositions [ordini] of the Romans as extracted from the *Commentaries* of Julius Caesar

and wished to print them along with an introduction, or *proemio*, dealing with Roman military methods, the whole designed 'to facilitate the interpretation of the *Commentaries*.'[9] By this time the book, to judge from the colophon, was already set up, and later in the year it was duly published with 'con privilegio' on the title page.

The text used was a re-set and enlarged (from octavo to quarto) version of the Italian translation by Francesco Baldelli which Gabriel Giolito had first published in Venice in 1554 and followed up with a new edition in 1557 and a reissue in 1558. To this text, now out of copyright, Palladio prefixed a dedication and his introduction. The book was dedicated to Jacopo Boncompagno (1548–1612), the natural son of Gregory XIII, who in 1572 had appointed him Prefect of Castel S. Angelo and in the following year captain general of the papal armies. From 1 August 1575 he was appointed captain general of cavalry in Milan by Philip II of Spain, a fact that suggests a publication date before that appointment, for Palladio describes him simply as 'generale di Santa Chiesa'. Palladio is not known to have had any contact with Boncompagni, but as a prominent soldier and a political figure of some note he was an appropriate choice to appreciate and defend the book against the detraction of 'malign persons'; and the dedication of books to men of note who were unknown personally to the author was in no way unusual. There just may, however, have been something more behind the choice. It was Palladio's belief, as we shall see, that modern armies would be improved if they were trained and brigaded on the model of ancient armies. In 1594 Francesco Patrizi, dedicating his *Paralleli militari* to the same Boncompagno, says that Palladio, 'illustrating the deeds of Caesar', had

> dedicated his labours to your glory, thinking that a prince of political weight, entrusted with leading the splendid armies of the Church and the Catholic King, could organize them in such a way that they would be capable not only of defending Italy but in addition a great part of Christendom from the attacks [insulti] of heretics and infidels.[10]

[6] *Ibid.*, li–lii (notes) and p. 100 (text).
[7] *Architectural Principles in the Age of Humanism*, London 1949, p. 57.
[8] *Andrea Palladio*, Eng. tr., London 1975, p. 25, n. 123. Puppi says, without further reference, 'I believe, however, that I know one of these plates.'
[9] Magrini, *op. cit.*; petition in App., p. 31, privilege (forbidding others to reproduce or sell in Venetian territories) in Notes, p. xlix.
[10] Sig. 4ʳ.

This does not tell us that Palladio knew Boncompagno, but it does suggest that he was aware that Boncompagno, unlike the great majority of commanders, was prepared to do what armchair soldiers had been urging from Machiavelli onwards: reform the conservative tactical formations of the present by going back to the radical past.

Palladio's dedication refers to

> my efforts, made unceasingly from my youth, to bring into the light many of the noblest records [memorie] of antiquity.

And speaking of the effect he hopes his illustrations will have, he writes that it should be to reinforce the intellect with the aid of the senses, to clarify an understanding of the text, and to encourage the imitation of Caesar's achievements. These remarks call to mind the opening words of a work which he devoted to bringing other ancient records to the eye as well as the mind, *I quattro libri dell'architettura* of 1570.

> Guided by a natural inclination I gave myself in my earliest years to the study of architecture, and because I was always of the opinion that in building well, as in many other ways, the ancient Romans had gone far beyond all those who came after them

—and he goes on to explain that the basis of his study will be Vitruvius. There is no mention of war as one of the 'other ways'. Indeed, though he ends the preface by promising to conclude the work by discussing 'the method of fortifying cities', he does not do so. Yet that war was in his mind is clear from his dedication of the third and fourth books of the *Quattro libri* to one of the outstanding warrior princes of the time, Emmanuel Filibert of Savoy, and from the terms in which he addresses him. He is

> the only prince in our days whose prudence and valour resemble those ancient Roman heroes whose most potent activities [virtuosissime operationi] one reads about in history books and sees in part in the ruins of antiquity.

Again, the prince represents all the personal qualities and the active talents summed up in the notion of 'ancient Roman knighthood' [l'antica Romana milizia]. It is tempting, at least, to see Palladio as already convinced that ancient Rome offered the supreme example of both monuments and men, of architecture, which was his profession, and the leadership of armies, which was his hobby. Perhaps he had already been so convinced when he included in his *L'antichita di Roma* (which he published as his first work in 1554) a section— which was by no means essential—on the size and composition of Roman armies.[11]

The autobiographical element in the first of the two sections into which the Introduction to the edition of Caesar is divided confirms this. Headed '*Proemio* of Andrea Palladio, concerning the illustrations and the studies carried out by him to facilitate an understanding of C. Julius Caesar's *Commentaries*', it has been unduly neglected as a source of information about Palladio's interest in

---

[11] 'De l'essercito Romano di terra, et da mare, et loro insegne'. It is only a few lines long. He cites Appian, available in Alessandro Braccio's Italian translation from 1519.

military affairs. Although the days were passing in which architects, as had been the case from Brunelleschi, Francesco di Giorgio and Giuliano da Sangallo to Michele Sanmicheli and Michelangelo, could be expected to turn with equal interest from civil to military work, the scant attention paid by Palladio to fortifications arouses a surprise emphasized by his failure to treat the subject in the *Four Books*. Apart from taking part in a survey of Monte Berico in 1545, in connection with one of the numerous schemes to provide Vicenza with up-to-date fortifications, and a visit with the Proveditors of Fortifications to Chioggia in 1574,[12] the only sign of interest comes from his collaboration in the early 1550s in Daniele Barbaro's magnificent edition of Vitruvius. Though this is the first edition to pay any attention to modern methods of fortification, the inspiration behind the discussion is clearly Giangiacopo Leonardi, the Duke of Urbino's resident representative in Venice and the author of a widely talked about but unpublished treatise on the subject. Of the two illustrations representing fortifications, neither has any innovational or specifically 'Palladian' features save one: the plan of a bastion has a hinged flap to enable the reader to visualize its construction more clearly—the first example of this device in a book, and a visual aid in keeping with Palladio's desire 'to reinforce the intellect with the aid of the senses.'[13] This meagre evidence for an interest in fortification is, however, explained at the outset of the Introduction to Caesar. No place, Palladio writes, wherever situated, can be made strong enough to resist an enemy in the long term. For purposes of defence, then, 'nothing is as effective as to have an excellent and admirably organized [ordinatissimo] army which will be suited to combat any other, even if superior in numbers; and I take the example of Julius Caesar in confirmation of my opinion.' Having declared his stand with reference to one current debate[14] he turns to another and settles into his stride as a confirmed neo-classical military reformer. Individual soldiers and captains are as brave today as in antiquity, yet our armies are miserably inefficient, badly trained and badly organized. Military leaders give two reasons why they cannot be reformed according to the models of antiquity. One is the introduction of firearms and artillery. But they are greatly deceived; discipline is more important than any weapon. The other is the impossibility of training the sort of men who compose armies today in the drills expected of ancient armies. But why?

[12] See references in Puppi, *Andrea Palladio*, cit., pp. 260–1. G. G. Zorzi, however, is probably indicating a false trail by making more of Palladio's role as a fortifications consultant than can be substantiated, and by suggesting that his concern with 'ordinamenti militari doveva servire al Palladio in modo speciale come preparazione a quello dell' architetto militare, con speciale risguardo alle fortificazioni.' 'Un disegno di Andrea Palladio per la Rochetta di Vicenza', in *Studi in onore di A. Bardella*, Vicenza 1964, p. 189.

[13] *I dieci libri dell' architettura di M. Vitruvio tradutti et commentati da Monsignor Barbaro*, Venice 1556, pp. 30–31, 39–40, 39 bis–40 bis. Leonardi is mentioned on 31 and 39 bis. 40 bis contains the chapter headings of his treatise. The bastion is on 39. Palladio may also have been responsible for the superimposed discs, rotating on an anchor of string, used in the section on theatres in book 4, but no such devices are employed in the *Quattro Libri*.

[14] See J. R. Hale. 'To fortify or not to fortify? Machiavelli's contribution to a Renaissance controversy', in *Essays in honour of John Humphreys Whitfield*, ed. H. C. Davis et al., London 1975, pp. 99–119.

The soldiers of antiquity were peasants and craftsmen, rough and ignorant men nor were their captains demi-gods, but men like ourselves, and their evolutions are clear and simple to anyone who understands their principles, as, indeed, I do. In fact, being with some gentlemen experienced in military affairs, to satisfy them I took certain galley oarsmen and pioneers[15] who were on the spot and put them through every possible drill and military exercise without producing the least stumbling or confusion. So it would be far easier to introduce the practices and regulations of the ancients than many think.

Francesco Patrizi, who claimed to have been an eye-witness of this event, put the number of men drilled at 500 and said that Palladio, though without any military experience, had managed it from his knowledge of 'the books of Aelian, Leo and Caesar', and he reinforced Palladio's argument that this proved that the ancient art of warfare could be effectively revived.[16]

Palladio goes on to say that his 'desire to communicate to the world the training and organization of ancient armies' was first aroused by his early patron and intellectual guide, Count Giangiorgio Trissino, 'who had a perfect understanding of this subject, as can be clearly seen from his *Italia liberata*.' Prompted by him

I set myself to read all the historians and other authors of antiquity who had dealt with the topic, and studied them continuously for many, many years.

Trissino's epic poem *Italia liberata da Gotthi*[17] is, indeed, only bearable today if read as an evocation of late Graeco-Roman military practice. It even came provided with a meticulously calculated folding plan of one of Belisarius's military camps, and the dedication to Charles V suggests that if, among his many cares of state, the Emperor does have time to read it, he will find

besides the tactical formations, the methods of encampment and the training procedures employed by the ancients, many battles, the storming of many cities and many matters beside which will beyond doubt be relevant to future wars as well as to other aspects of human activity.

As well as Caesar, it can with some confidence be assumed that among the authors Trissino commended to Palladio was another of the authorities referred to by Patrizi: Aelianus Tacticus. Puppi has reproduced a tactical diagram drawn by Trissino[18] whose symbols derive from a fourteenth-century manuscript in the Marciana which was part of Cardinal Bessarion's gift to the city.[19] This manuscript was also used by the Udinese classical scholar Francesco Robortello for his attractively illustrated bilingual edition of 1552 (Francesco Ferrosi's Italian translation was also published in Venice in the same year). Robortello stressed the relevance of Aelian to current military needs and dedicated the Greek part of his edition to the Friulian *condottiere*

---

[15] 'galeotti e guastadori'. i.e., peasants enrolled for galley service and for earth shifting work on drainage or fortification projects.

[16] *Op. cit.*, p. 149.
[17] Rome and Venice, 3 vols., 1547–8.
[18] *Scrittori vicentini, cit.*, pl. 4.
[19] Marciana MS Venetus 516, now 904.

Mario Savorgnan, 'qui artis militandi veterum tum Graecorum, tum Romanorum peritissimus es', and whose own writings, cobbled together by Cesare Campana after his death, reveal him as a propagandist in the same cause.[20] Savorgnan was an associate of the Vicentine circle of gentlemen scholars to which Trissino introduced Palladio. So was Filippo Pigafetta, the translator of the third authority mentioned by Patrizi, the ninth-century Emperor Leo VI.[21] In fact, without pursuing a bio-bibliographical inquiry to the point of tedium, it can be affirmed that in his middle years Palladio was exposed to a body of opinion, usually associated with the Netherlands at the end of the century,[22] which employed the period of peace that settled on the Veneto after 1529 to reflect on the lessons that could have been, and now must be learned from antiquity. Looking back on the humiliations of the Wars of Italy, it was a generation which read ancient history primarily as a guide to the art of war (for Venetians, including the mainland citizens, believed they had nothing to learn from ancient politics) and to the traits of character exemplified by ancient military leaders, and which rummaged copiously in the technical military literature of the ancient world. Both preoccupations were catered for by Venetian publishing houses on a scale unmatched in any other printing centre, and both emphasized the relevance of ancient military experience as earnestly as previous generations had stressed the relevance of ancient moral philosophy. Palladio shared the enthusiasm of what has been termed the utilitarian humanism of his age and endorsed the opinion of Baldelli, the translator he used, that Caesar

> is, as it were, the mirror for our lives as far as military affairs are concerned, in which we can see images of how we should conduct ourselves both publicly and privately.[23]

There is, however, one more member of his Vicentine acquaintance whom we must take into account, Valerio Chieregato. Palladio, in his introduction, praises him as 'antico esempio de l'antico valore', and Patrizi said that he also was present when Palladio drilled his amateur soldiers.

Created 'cavaliere' by Venice in 1533, Chieregato was a practising soldier, serving the French during the war of Siena and Paul IV in his campaign against the Colonna before entering Venetian service. He was the author of an unprinted, scholarly and somewhat higgledy-piggledy manuscript in the Correr Library in Venice which contains detailed descriptions of Roman and Macedonian troop formations, sets to right previous misinterpretations of them including 'the false opinion of Machiavelli regarding the ordering of his army on the Roman model',[24] and commends their adaptation to modern usage. The work was highly praised by Pigafetta,[25] and in general Chieregato seems,

[20] *Arte militare terrestre, e maritime; secondo la ragione, è l'uso de piu valorosi capitani antichi e moderni . . . ridotta . . . da Cesare Campana.* Venice 1599.

[21] MS Ambrosiana, Milan 5. 77. Sup.

[22] Michael Roberts, 'The military revolution, 1560–1660' in *Essays in Swedish history*, Minneapolis 1967; Werner Hahlweg, *Die Heeresreform der Oranier und die Antike*, Berlin 1941, and *id.*, ed., *Das Kriegsbuch des Grafen Johann von Nassau-Siegen*, Wiesbaden 1973.

[23] Dedication, dated 1553.

[24] MS Cicogna, 883, chap. 68.

[25] In the printed edition of his Leo, Venice 1586, fol. 2ʳ⁻ᵛ.

in Veneto society, to have stood as authoritatively in relation to tactics as Leonardi did to fortification.

In his position as colonel of militia Chieregato was able to carry out the sort of experiment described by Palladio on a far larger scale. In May 1573 he was sent by the Senate to drill and muster the peasant militias of Friuli, the Trevisano and the Feltrino, altogether an enrolment of 6,600 men.[26] In his report to the Doge[27] he said that when he met them 'they could more readily be called a mere inventory of men and weapons than an army'. However, after teaching 'my own evolutions' to small groups for three or four hours, the whole force had learned enough to carry out their drill to the satisfaction of the professional officers and of the men themselves. And all this, he adds, 'without all the shouts, curses, threats and blows and other untoward excesses that are customarily used today.' What is more

> if your Serenity had seen it you would agree that by using such evolutions and training methods one could introduce in your domains in a short time a brave and trustworthy militia very much on the lines of the armies with which the Macedonians and the Roman republic defeated nearly every other nation in the world.

Whereas if things continue in the old way, he concludes, the militia forces will crumple before an enemy as they did at Agnadello (1509) and at the battle of Vicenza (1513). In August 1574 Chieregato was sent to reorganize and train the militia in Crete[28] and according to Andrea Cornaro's contemporary history of the island

> he was the first to introduce into modern warfare the very ancient phalanx of the Macedonians; and in training all the units in the island in this manner

he overstrained himself and died in Candia in the following year.[29] Writing before he had news of his death, Palladio expressed the hope that the local authorities in Crete would support him in introducing 'the ancient disciplines of war, perhaps to a greater state of perfection than ever before.' For if architecture could improve upon the models it followed, could not the art of war as well?

The second section of the Introduction to Caesar is headed 'On the legions, the arms and the military institutions of the Romans' and contains the description of ancient military methods so highly praised by Algarotti. Brief, assured and lucid, it is historically sophisticated in that it allows for changes within the Roman system itself. The sources he refers to apart from Caesar—Polybius, Vegetius and Josephus (all available well before 1575 in Italian translation)—have clearly been studied. The controversy as to whether Roman units combined into a continuous front or remained separated from one another is fairly acknowledged; in the interest of clarity, he notes, 'I have drawn them with gaps . . . so that the reader [with reference to the text]

---

[26] Venice, State Archives, Senato Terra, Registro 49, fol. 119^r.
[27] *Ibid.*, Lettere, Capi di Guerra, 25 May.
[28] *Ibid.*, Senato, Mar, Registro 42, fol. 57^r.

[29] Cicogna's notes at the back of Chieregato's treatise, quoting a MS of Cornaro's *Istoria Candiana*.

can make up his own mind.' The sections ends with a renewed plea for the re-introduction 'by the captains of our own times' of the practices described by Caesar.

An interest in the training of ancient armies, in the size of the units which composed them and in their fighting procedures; a belief that modern armies should be reformed along these lines: the Dedication and the Introduction have been dwelt on not for their originality but for what is learned about Palladio from tracing his connection with the military reform movement in late Renaissance Italy. His originality and his contribution to that movement consists in his providing it, through the illustrations of Caesar's campaigns, with a series of unprecedently lucid visual aids.

Apart from two folding maps, one of France, one of Spain, the book contains thirty-nine double-page etchings. Thirty-four of these show military activity of various sorts: armies facing one another in line of battle, actual combats, sieges, marches. Five are of 'static' subjects: the plan of a Roman encampment; a view for demonstration purposes of a legion and a phalanx facing one another; a plate explaining the construction of Caesar's wooden bridge across the Rhine; a depiction of the method by which defensive walls were built in France; and the portrayal of a defensive zone outside a town, strewn with caltrops and other anti-personnel and anti-horse devices.

The maps, the bridge and the last two illustrations were adapted from woodcuts in the Giolito editions of the same text of 1554 and 1557.[30] One of these, the bridge, which was the only illustration singled out for mention by Gualdo ('the famous bridge built by the Emperor over the river Rhine'), had a longer pedigree. Like boats propelled by paddle-wheels, and scythed chariots, it was one of the ancient feats of technology that caught the imagination of men in the Renaissance. Editions from 1523 of Agostino Ortica's earlier translation of Caesar had contained primitive, half-page wood-cuts labelled 'Ponte de Cesare',[31] that in the edition of 1539 being redrawn in a somewhat more sophisticated manner. After 1554 the next version is Palladio's own—in the 1570 *Quattro Libri*[32]—and the etched version in the *Commentaries* of 1575 is identical, save that drawings of details of the construction have been moved to allow for the change of format from a single folio page to a quarto double-spread. Of the remaining two 'static' representations, the castramentation plan resembles earlier plans in its convention but differs from them in layout,[33] while the legion-phalanx view is apparently an original composition.

The edition's most remarkable feature, however, was the long series of etchings illustrating military actions (Pl. 11a, b). None of the conventions employed in these bird's-eye views was novel. Technically even finer work in the genre had been produced elsewhere. The first semi-diagrammatic representation of an actual, as opposed to an imaginary battle had been

---

[30] All were etched to the enlarged scale from octavo to quarto. The maps are copied. The others are derived from 1554 but much altered. Palladio omits two illustrations, 'Cadenac' and 'Marsiglia' that were in 1554. None is signed.

[31] Venice. Other editions 1528, 1531, 1539. The only other illustrations were three examples of decorative battering rams in the Valturio tradition.

[32] Book 3, p. 14.

[33] Machiavelli *Arte della Guerra*, Florence 1521; Trissino, *op. cit.*, 1544; Guillaume du Choul, *Discorso sopra la castrametatione*, Bologna 1558; Pietro Cataneo, *L'architettura* . . ., Venice 1567. There were a number of MS

published in 1548.³⁴ But this was the first book to present a whole series of visual reconstructions of historical campaigns with the aim of combining topographical verisimilitude with diagrammatic clarity. And it is doubtful whether the joint appeal of this combination, to the analytical faculty and to the imagination, has been surpassed. Blocks of troops, readily identifiable as infantry or cavalry, are helped to convey a sense of real activity in actual terrain by scattered homunculi—fugitives, scouring horsemen, prone casualties. The tactical formations, their size, composition and spatial relationships, are based on a careful reading of the relevant pages of Caesar, supplemented, when these are inadequate, by general principles derived from the military information given in the work as a whole. And Palladio's determination to provide an accurate and convincing set of visual aids is supported by a quite unusual degree of care in their placing. Each illustration carries not only the number of the page it follows, but a letter which recurs in the margin at the point in the text at which the action portrayed begins. What is more, the type is so spaced that a smaller version of the letter (or letters, as when at the end of the alphabet double letters are used) occurs in the most relevant line, exactly as in a modern footnote reference.

In the small compass of part two of the Introduction Palladio cites passages in Polybius four times. The Greek historian's account of the extension of Roman rule from the first Punic War to the final destruction of Carthage, containing as it did graphic descriptions of campaigns and many first-hand descriptions of the terrain over which they had been fought as well as theoretical remarks about the organization of the conquering armies, had appealed to military reformers from Machiavelli's *Art of War* onwards.³⁵ It had been in Venice, in 1529, that Janus Lascaris published his partial Latin translation of book six, dealing largely with military affairs; in Venice, in 1545, that Lodovico Domenichi's Italian translation of the first five full books appeared. 'The human mind desires nothing more,' he reminded his dedicatee, the Marchese Girolamo Pallavicino, member of a famous military family, 'than to have an understanding of past actions in order that by this it

---

³⁴ The blocks of troops had evolved from low bird's-eye views showing receding rows of helmets or lances behind a first rank (or file) of more-or-less fully realized figures. For an example of c. 1515, see C. Santoro, *Libri illustrati milanesi*, Milan 1956, p. 230. Dürer's 'Great Siege' woodcut of 1527, though showing an imaginary event, has a naturalistic setting and uses animated homunculi; the plans in his treatise on fortification (1527) use letters and numbers to identify details referred to in the text. The finest battle scenes of the period are some of the large folding plates in Leonhart Fronsperger, *Von Kayserlichem Kriegsrechten*, Frankfurt-am-Main 1571–3, while three diagrams showing phases of the battle of Pinkie in Sir William Patten, *The expedicion into Scotlande* . . ., London 1548, are very early examples of printed diagrams of a real campaign. castrametation diagrams in circulation. Bartolommeo Cavalcanti sent one in 1545 to get Stefano Colonna's comments on it, for instance; *Calcolo della castrametatione*, Florence 1552, pp. 42–47. In his *La militia Romana*, Ferrara 1583, Francesco Patrizi reproduces this and also previously unpublished versions by the Duke of Urbino, Francesco Maria della Rovere (d. 1538) and by Robortello, together with his own. None is identical to, or very much like Palladio's. Different again are Serlio's drawings of c. 1546, repro. as figs. 14 and 15 in W. B. Dinsmoor, 'The literary remains of Sebastiano Serlio', *Art Bulletin*, 1942.

³⁵ For a brief but masterly survey of the 'fortuna' of Polybius, see A. Momigliano, 'Polybius' reappearance in Western Europe', *Polybe: Entretiens sur l'antiquité classique*, vol. 20, Geneva 1974, pp. 347–72.

can control the present and provide against the future.' In 1553, dedicating his translation (again published in Venice) of eleven newly discovered, but fragmentary, books to Captain Camillo Caula, he reminded him that he had many times heard Polybius praised by 'the most rare and perfect judgement of Sig. Giovan Iacopo Lionardi'—thus leading us to the circle who advised Barbaro, around this time, on his edition of Vitruvius, while the Polybian interests of Chieregato, Mario Savorgnan and Robortello were referred to later in another work by Patrizi.[36] Ten years later, in 1563, the whole translation was brought out in an enlarged, quarto format by the publisher of the earlier editions, Gabriel Giolitho,[37] and reissued in 1564.[38] With the misleading obviousness of the hiding place in Edgar Allan Poe's *The purloined letter*, it is in one of the British Library's copies of this reissue that Palladio's 'nobilissime fatiche' devoted to Polybius are to be found.[39]

Bound in before the title page are three unnumbered leaves covered on both sides in a clear late-sixteenth-century Italian handwriting (Pl. 10c).[40]

> Having dealt fully in the *Commentaries* of Caesar [it begins] with the Roman method of training soldiers and how they placed and organized their armies in battle array and in action, showing, moreover, in illustrations all the circumvallations, formations, armies and all the military operations carried out and then described by Caesar, it occurring to me now that it would not be superfluous to repeat such things, I will turn to another [author], showing how these formations differ greatly from these of our own times. This is certainly a mistake of no little importance, with battalions of six or eight thousand infantry being brought together today with more than a hundred being placed in file with no concern at all for the flanks being left unprotected, the ends of the front unguarded, and the great majority of the troops rendered completely useless because they can never, or very rarely, get themselves in a position to fight. It is not to be wondered at if formations of this sort, opposed by a large cavalry force, such as the Turks or others have, make so deplorable a showing, and will go on doing so unless a change is made by imitating the ancients and

---

[36] *La militia, cit., passim.* e.g. fol. 34ᵛ.

[37] *Polibio historico greco dell' imprese de' Greci, de gli Asiatici, de' Romani, et d'altri . . . con gli undici libri ritrovati di nuovo, tradotti per M. Lodovico Domenichi, et dal medesimo riformati et corretti. . . .* Though the title-page bears the date 1563, the colophon has 1562.

[38] Still with the 1562 colophon.

[39] Press mark 293.g.20. The catalogue remarks: 'Copious ms. notes. Numerous plates have been inserted in this copy.' The copy came to the British Library from the Library of George III where, as Dr. D. E. Rhodes pointed out to me, it is catalogued correctly: 'In questo Esemplare vi sono molte figure disegnate da *Palladio*; con uno discorso Ms. sopra la milizia, e le figure.' *Bibliothecae Regiae Catalogus*, London 1820, pp. 499–50.

It had been bought in 1762–3 along with the greatest part of the library of Joseph Smith, the famous British consul in Venice. In his catalogue it was described simply as follows: 'E in questo vi è un discorso ms. sopra la milizia, e le figure, che la descrivono.' *Bibliotheca Smithiana* . . ., Venice 1755, ccclxxxii. There is no annotation on the copy used as a receipt for the sale (B.L. 823.h.26), so the attribution to Palladio must have been made (presumably by comparison with Caesar, a copy of which was part of Smith's collection) between the purchase date and the publication of the King's catalogue in 1820 by the royal librarian, Frederick Auguste Barnard.

[40] For a full transcription, see Appendix.

putting only sixteen soldiers in file, as you see here in Polybius, where he talks of the Macedonian phalanx and the Roman legions.

The advantage of the ancients' use of long, shallow lines of battle can be seen, the writer goes on,

> in many engagements described by our Polybius, all of which I have decided to illustrate, even if inadequately, as I have also done with Caesar's, and similarly doing my best to preserve [i.e. take into account] all the words and phrases used by this divine historian in describing every battle and the situation of every city, mountain and river.

He goes on to regret that modern princes, 'as I have said on other occasions', care nothing for the example of the past, and singles out as a model Valerio Chieregato who, as governor general of the foot militia in Crete would, had death not intervened, have introduced the methods of the ancients on lines not inferior to those of antiquity itself. He then says that 'as I have sufficiently dealt with the whole subject of the infantry among the ancients in two chapters in the *Commentaries* of Caesar', he will now discuss their handling of cavalry; and this he does, with reference to four diagrams placed at the end of the manuscript (Pl. 10d). Just before the manuscript ends, however, comes an unexpected bonus.

> Moreover, because it seems that up to now the nature of the ancients' quinquereme has not been demonstrated, I have in the same way wanted to illustrate it here, at least according to my own opinion, though ready to defer to a better one on the part of anyone who wants to make good any error of mine, so that in this way a true understanding can be reached.

There follows, as in the Caesar edition, a group of four double-page etchings. One is the identical castramentation plan that had figured in that work. The others comprise an animated version of the manuscript cavalry diagrams, the idiom very closely modelled on an illustration in Robortello's edition of Aelian[41] (Pl. 12c) and a profile and plan of the reconstructed ancient quinquereme (Pl. 12a, b). These reflect the debate in Venice in the mid-1520s about the practical value of quinqueremes and the surprise which greeted the successful trials in 1529 of a vessel built to the designs of the republic's official lecturer in Greek, Vittor Fausto.[42] It is not surprising that the disillusionment with the quinquereme's performance which set in afterwards led the neo-Greek military reforming circle of the Veneto to take an interest in naval archaeology as well, but this, I think, is the first concrete evidence of it.

Lastly, interspersed through the text, there is a series of thirty-nine 'action' etchings illustrating armies, battles, marches and sieges described by Polybius (Pls. 12d, 14a–d). While somewhat more summary in technique (mainly in the

[41] *Op. cit.*, Latin translation p. 25. The purely conventional MS diagrams also derive from this work, p. 29. The two sets of diagrams in the Polybius edition do not exactly correspond to one another. In the etching, B has 6 instead of 7 horses in file, D has 8 instead of 12, and there is an extra 'D'.

[42] Frederic C. Lane, *Navires et constructeurs à Venise pendant la Renaissance*, Paris 1965, pp. 59 seq.

number of dots signifying the tips of weapons in each block of troops) they are identical in convention and style to the majority of the Caesar illustrations—'majority' because these reflect two draughtsmen's versions of the same conventions (Pl. 11a, b).[43] Moreover, though handwritten, the keys on the reverse sides of the double-page etchings differ in only one respect: they are followed by a brief summary of the engagement's significance (Pl. 13a,b). At the top of most of the illustrations the page reference has been written in. There is no identifying letter engraved as yet on the plate, nor is there any such reference added to the margins or lines of the text. Again, three of the 'action' etchings have neither page numbers nor key written on them (though they are inserted at the correct points in the text); similarly the group of four 'static' prints lack keys, though the plates are etched with letters for them. Finally, some of the illustrations are clumsily registered on the page and one or two have been pulled off the plate with a carelessness that has left gaps or smears.

What, then, is the status of this work? The handwriting is not Palladio's[44] but the thoughts expressed, the references to the Caesar edition (where, indeed, there is only a bare mention of the role of cavalry) and to Chieregato, the nature and placing of the illustrations: these surely represent the studies that Palladio, in his letter to the Grand Duke Francesco, said that he would devote his whole mind to carrying forward. That letter was dated 18 January 1579.[45] Given the inconsistency with which Venetian subjects used the conventions affecting the dating of a new year, the letter may have been written on 18 January 1580. In any case, when Palladio died on 19 August 1580 his studies were not quite completed. What we have is a mock-up which, though lacking a few keys and a dedication, is sufficiently advanced to enable a printer to envisage the overall appearance of the edition and calculate the cost of re-setting the text. What form the dedication would have taken we cannot tell. It would most probably have been directed, as was the letter, to the Grand Duke. Authors and editors using Venetian presses felt no inhibitions about dedicating works, even those dealing with advanced military ideas, to foreign princes.[46] The translation used by Palladio had itself been dedicated to Francesco's predecessor, Cosimo, and in 1566 Palladio had been elected a member of the Florentine Accademia del Disegno.[47] With this probability in mind it seems worth re-printing the letter here.[48]

Whether the mock-up was prepared by Palladio or, as is more likely, by Silla, it failed to find a printer. Pietro dei Franceschi, who printed Caesar in 1575, appears to have gone out of business two years later. Giolito found no demand for Polybius after the reissue of 1564, and this remained the last

---

[43] Pls. A, B, X, Y, LL and MM are in a somewhat more slapdash style than the rest.
[44] Introduction and keys (allowing for the somewhat looser forms used in these) are in the same hand, save for the keys to six of the illustrations which are in a more upright and print-like hand and a lighter ink (Pl. 13b). These do not have 'carta' written over the print, as all the others do.
[45] Accepting, again, Magrini's argument that MDLXIX was a slip of the pen.
[46] As Domenico Mora's *Tre quesiti sopra il fare batterie* . . . and Francesco Ferretti's *Della osservanza militare* . . . had been dedicated in 1567 and 1568 to the Grand Duke Cosimo I.
[47] G. Vasari, *Le vite* . . ., ed. G. Milanesi, vol. 7, Florence 1881, pp. 513 and 621.
[48] Appendix 2.

edition printed in Italy during the sixteenth century. Moreover, by outliving Trissino, Leonardi, Robortello, Savorgnan and Chieregato, Palladio had outlived the Italian phase of neo-classical military reform and the utilitarian humanism that saw ancient history as above all a treasury of military wisdom. Its epitaph was pronounced in the sub-title to the *La militia romana* (1583) of Palladio's acquaintance, Patrizi: 'which, when fully understood ... will make clear, by contrast, how far modern armies are defective and imperfect' Its future was to lie, as we have seen, beyond the Alps. Silla litigated for a property devalued by a shift in taste and representing an interest which he, in any case, may not have shared with his father and brothers.

This leads to a concluding query. The most striking features about the Caesar and the Polybius editions are the illustrations, which achieve, as in no previous Italian books, a perfect compromise between the purely schematic and the fully pictorial conventions.[49] The problem of giving a true account of a military engagement was a matter of real concern at the time.[50] Palladio's share in this concern, conveyed in the dedication to Caesar's *Commentaries*, may reflect discussions with Mario Savorgnan, whose work, when it finally got into print in 1599, contained the largest series of illustrations of historical battles since Palladio's books. Their crudity suggests that they may have been prepared early enough to have been known to him and influence the refined version of their conventions used in his books. Certainly his concern parallels Savorgnan's; 'as words on their own are not suitable or powerful enough to make an impression on our minds that leaves events fixed and, as it were, engraved there', it is useful, Savorgnan wrote, to have recourse 'to the sense of sight, so that the eye, through signs and pictures which become almost part of bodily sensation, can send them with greater impact to the mind and intelligence.'[51] In their turn, the Caesar illustrations were to become models to others.[52]

But what was Palladio's share in them and in the similar Polybius etchings? In the Introduction to Caesar, Palladio says that he had devoted himself to the study of authors who had recorded the wars of antiquity 'for many, many years

> When I felt that I had acquired the knowledge I required, I began to want to introduce my dearest sons Leonida and Horatio to it as well, young men, if I may say so, most worthily endowed with manners and learning.

They followed his lead so enthusiastically that

> they conceived the wish to represent all the armed camps, circumvallations of cities, battles and everything else that Caesar had described in his *Commentaries*.

---

[49] They may be compared with the semi-pictorial siege scenes in Giulio Ballino, *De disegni delle piu illustri citta* ..., Venice 1569, or the wholly schematic diagrams of Pompey's and Caesar's armies at Pharsalia in Domenico Mora, *Il soldato* ..., Venice 1570, pp. 132 and 135.

[50] Girolamo Diedo dwelt on the difficulty of portraying the battle of Lepanto in words.

G. Ruscelli, *Lettere di principi*, Venice 1575, fol. 240^{r-v}.

[51] *Op. cit.*, Proemio, last page. There are two castramentation, and twenty engagement woodcuts.

[52] G. Patrizi, *La militia, cit.*, and C. Agrippa, *Dialogo del modo di mettere in battaglia* ..., Rome 1585.

But death intervened to cut them both down within two months,

> and as, after their death, there came into my hands certain sheets [fogli] on which they had begun their work very well with words and drawings I decided, [Palladio continues] to carry out the project I had formed long before [il disegno assai prima da me fatto] . . . giving some elucidation to the part I found done by them and adding as much as I thought necessary for its completion.

And this he has done, as 'an afflicted and inconsolable father', to provide a memorial to his sons. And in the dedication he writes that

> as by chance there came into my hands during the past months a good part of the illustrations [buona parte delle figure] of the battles and other feats of arms of C. Giulio Cesare, already drawn [dessegnati] in conformity with the remainder [conforme al resto] of his *Commentaries* by my two sons . . . I wanted at once to honour their memory by publishing their work and to be of service to others.

On this evidence scholars have assumed that the etchings were 'certainly the work of his sons.'[53] Two sons, two styles; it seems to fit. But the evidence is not quite straightforward. Little is known about Leonida, save that he studied architecture, or about Horatio, save that he studied law. Yet the etchings display a very high degree of professional expertise. And not even when he is most moved by parental pride and grief does Palladio suggest that on their deaths the requisite number of illustrations was completed.

The title-page says simply that the edition contains 'copperplates . . . made by Andrea Palladio.' Gualdo similarly attributes them firmly to him, with no mention of the sons. Yet Palladio, as far as is known, neither etched nor engraved and did not even execute the woodcuts in the *Four Books*. Both sources surely point to Palladio as the authority for, not the authorship of the etchings. It seems most likely that the sons, encouraged by their father, made sketches of many of the actions described by Caesar and provided keys to them, and that on their death in 1572 Palladio completed the work and handed over his and their sketches to professional printmakers. Even discounting his 'during the past months', the time was short—the printing, according to the colophon, which unfortunately omits day and month, was finished in 1574, and the text includes references to every illustration—but not so unreasonably short as to preclude a sizeable contribution from Palladio himself. And can we still believe in the sons as etchers when confronted by the later series of Polybius illustrations?[54] Silla's petition of 1588 refers to them as 'designa in ramo figurata et composita per dictum q.^m Excellentem Dominum Andream super Historia Polibii.'[55] But again, these are Palladio's in the sense that he was the master-mind behind them. They were his because he had sketched, annotated, commissioned and paid for them. Whose they were in the artistic sense has still to be established.

---

[53] Zorzi, *op. cit.*, p. 189.
[54] Theoretically they could have been done together with those for Caesar. But against this there is silence, no mention by Palladio in the Introduction to Polybius, and signs of a later, because economizing style.
[55] Magrini, *op. cit.*, li–lii.

What then does the British Library's copy of Polybius tell us about Palladio? Little more (apart from satisfying a long-standing curiosity) than this: from it, and from the encouragement its discovery gives to take a closer look at his work on Caesar, we obtain a clearer view of his *alter ego* as a military reformer with a strong concern for bringing to life the relevance of the warrior heroes and military methods of antiquity. And this, perhaps, adds resonance to the humanism of an architecture antiquarian in bias, but adapted for men capable of living with the ancients' awareness of how far the enjoyment of domesticity, labour and prayer depended on the protection of well-led and well-organized armies.

APPENDIX I

Havendosi à pieno discorso nelli Comentarij di Cesare del modo di essercitar li soldati appresso de Romani, et come si ponevano, et ordinavano gli esserciti in battaglia, et al fatto d'arme, tuttavia rappresentando in disegni tutte quelle circonvallationi, ordini, esserciti, et tutte quelle imprese esseguite, et poscia descritte da esso Cesare: parendomi hora, che sarebbe se non superfluo il replicare simili cose me ne passerò ad altro, con dimostrare quanto quegli ordini sijno molto differenti da questi de' nostri tempi, errore certo di non poca importanza, ordinandosi hora battaglioni di sei, overo otto mila fanti, per il che si viene à ponere piu di cento soldati per verso non curandosi punto il lasciar li fianchi aperti, et le spalle senza alcuna diffesa, et che la più parte di questi soldati resti affatto inutile; poiche non mai, ò rarissime volte ponno quelli ridursi al combatere; onde poscia non è maraviglia se simili ordini contra una cavalleria numerosa, come è la Turchesca, ò altra, fanno cosi trista prova, e faranno fin à tanto, che non si mutino, imitando pur quelli antichi col metter solo sedici soldati per verso, come si può vedere qui in Polibio, dove egli disputa della Falange Macedonica, et delle legioni Romane, et per darne qualch' essempio, per far pur conoscer quanto il numero di sedici per verso sia utile. Alessandro Magno venendo à giornata con Dario in Cilicia, in modo ordinò il suo essercito, che si distendeva dalli monti fino sopra la marina, ch' era una distantia di quasi tre miglia, et non erano piu di sedici per verso occupando tutti quei luochi, imperoche havendo Dario un essercito infinito, et Cavalleria numerosissima, ogni volta che l' havesse circonvenuto, Alessandro perdeva la giornata. Questo ordine certo mirabilmente usavano tutti quelli antichi distendendo sempre la fronte in quella maggior lunghezza, che fusse stata loro possibile, et secondo che la occasione gli si prestava, come chiaramente si può vedere in molti fatti di arme descritti da esso Polibio, li quali tutti mi è parso se non bene rappresentare in disegni, come ho anco fatto quelli di Cesare, medesimamente sforzandomi di salvare tutti i detti, e parole di questo divino Historico mirabile in descrivere tutte le battaglie, et tutti i siti delle Città, de'Monti, et de' Fiumi, havendo voluto egli in persona, come lui medesimo afferma, veder tutti quei luoghi, e parlarne anco con quelli huomini, ch'erano presenti al passaggio d'Annibale in Italia. Et tornando al proposito nostro, certo à non piccola infelicità si può ascrivere la conditione di questi nostri secoli, che non si trovi alcuno Prencipe (come altre volte s'è detto) che vogli ponere in uso questi eccellenti ordini, se forse non si danno à credere di meglio intendere le cose della guerra, che non facevano quelli antichi: ma à loro doveria questo solo bastare, che tanto colui è tenuto più de gli altri eccellente in qual si vogli scienza, ò arte, che più à gli antichi si è accostato, come ne habbiamo l'essempio à giorni nostri dell' Ill^e. Cavalliero il S^r. Valerio Chieregatto Colonello della Sereniss. Repub. di Venetia, il qual mandato in Candia Governatore Generale delle ordinanze da piedi di quel Regno, ne riportò il nome del maggior Capitano de' nostri tempi, poiche con l'assidua essercitatione di quei soldati, secondo gli ordini antichi, et se morte non si fusse interposta riduceva in breve tratta quella militia all'antica non inferiore. Ma lasciando hora di ragionar di lui, et de' meriti suoi, poiche non è mio proposito, havendo io nelli

Commentarij di Cesare in dui Capitoli descritto à bastanza tutta la militia da piedi degli antichi, et toccato si può dir à pena della Cavalleria; la quale quando è bene ordinata apporta giovamento grandissimo à gli esserciti. Hora sarà se non buono il referir anco quegli ordini, che osservavano nel ponere i suoi Cavallieri in battaglia, cosa in vero di non poca importanza, et bene lo dimostrano molti fatti di Annibale, il quale mediante la sua Cavalleria restò assai volte vittorioso, essendo pur' in questa parte insuperabile. Dico adunque che prima dividevano tutta la Cavalleria in Ale, et ogni Ala era di trenta dui Cavallieri oltre ciò li mettevano in battaglia, il che facevano in diversi modi, imperoche alcune volte si ordinavano in triangolo, altre volte in rombo, spesso in quadrangolo, et ancora in forma di ovo, et in tutti questi modi potevano detti Cavallieri giugare, et non versare, versare et non giugare, ne giugare, ne versare, et finalmente versare et giugare, non volendo per hora inferire altro questa parola, Giugare, che ponere un Cavalliere al fianco dell' altro; Versare poi, ponere un Cavalliere dietro all' altro: quando adunque giugavano, et non versavano, facevano à questo modo. Ponevano nella prima fila i Cavalli l'uno alli fianchi dell'altro il che facevano anco nella seconda, ma con uno cavallo di manco, et nella terza ancora co' un'altro Cavallo manco, et cosi di mano in mano, come si vede in questa figura A. Ma quando versavano et non giugavano, li ordinavano altrimenti, cio è ponendo l'uno dietro all'altro, facendo che nel secondo verso sia un cavallo manco, che nel primo, et nel terzo uno manco, che nel secondo et cosi ordinariamente come si vede in questa altra figura B. la qual manca di uno per ogni verso. Veniamo hora al non giugare, et non versare, il che si faceva ordinando li Cavalli in forma di Rombo in questo modo. Facendo il primo fianco di cinque senza il capo; ma che 'l primo Cavallo, et cosi ogn'altro giungeva con la testa alla sella di quello, ch'era avanti à lui, cio è il secondo al primo, il terzo al secondo, et cosi successivamente, e bene si può vedere per la presente figura C. Et ponendo finalmente in ordinanza quelli che giugavano et versavano facevano che tutte le file erano del medesimo numero, et questa ultima figura D. lo dimostra. Ne altrimenti gli antichi ponevano li loro Cavalli in battaglia, che in qual vogliamo di questi quattro ordini. Concludendo adunque dirò che li cavalli sono molto utili à chi sà servirsene bene, come in tanti fatti d'arme narrati da questo gravissimo Hijstorico si può conoscere, i quali tutti mi è parso di porre in disegni pur per giovare, non havendo certo altro intento; et perche anco fin hora pare che non sij venuta in luce la forma della Quinquereme secondo il modo de gli antichi, io ho voluto medesimamente porla qui in disegno, pur secondo la mia opinione, rimettendomi sempre à miglior giudicio, essortanto qualunque esser si voglia à voler supplire a quello, che io haverò mancato, che cosi facendo si venirà in cognitione della verità. [Contractions expanded.]

APPENDIX II

(From Magrini, cit., Appendice, p. 16)

Al Ser.mo Sig. Col.mo il signor Gran Duca di Toscana
Ser.mo Sig.

Quando io presentai a V. Altezza Ser.ma le mie fatiche fatte intorno Polibio, hebbi solamente intentione di offerirle in quel modo la mia devotione et la mia servitù: la qual perchè cominciasse di più ad apparire in effeto volsi per questo accompagnar quella mia offerta con dono di cosa estrinseca. Però hora l'alto benignità col quale l'Altezza V. Ser.ma ha voluto riconoscermi mi è di tanto maggior obbligo quanto io vedo riconosciuto in me per effetto di adempita servitù quello che è stato solamente segno et ombra di essa. Et tanto più adunque io ne rendo humilissime gratie a V. Altezza Ser.me et come suo devotissimo servo et per deditione et per debito, procurerò per l'avvenire con tutto lo spirito che le mie fatiche così benignamente favorite da i suoi auspicii s'avanzino ogn'ora di studio et di diligenza, et di meritar io per esse quanto comporta la mia bassezza l'alta protettione di V. Altezza Ser.ma alla quale humiliss.te io bacio la mano.

Di Venetia à xviii di Gen.ro MDLXIX
Di V. Altezza Ser.ma
Humiliss.mo Ser.re
Andrea Palladio

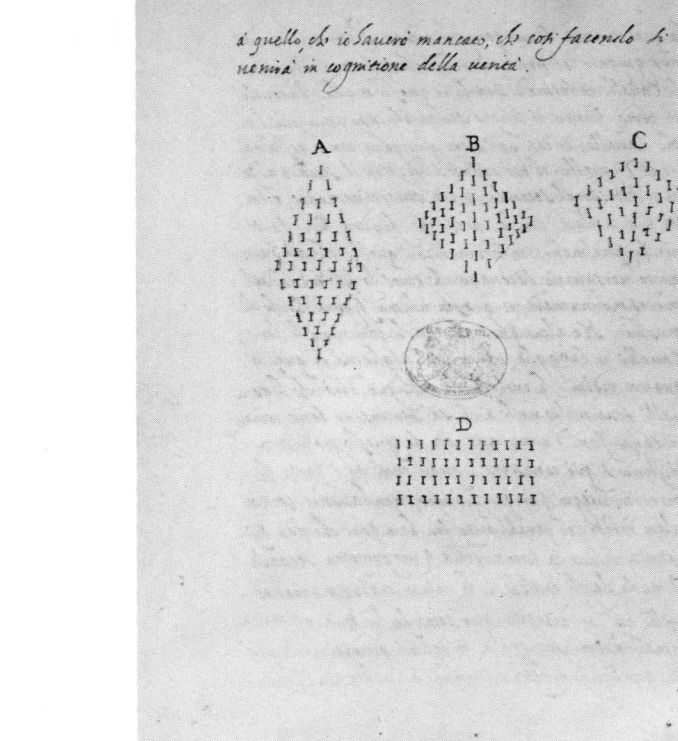

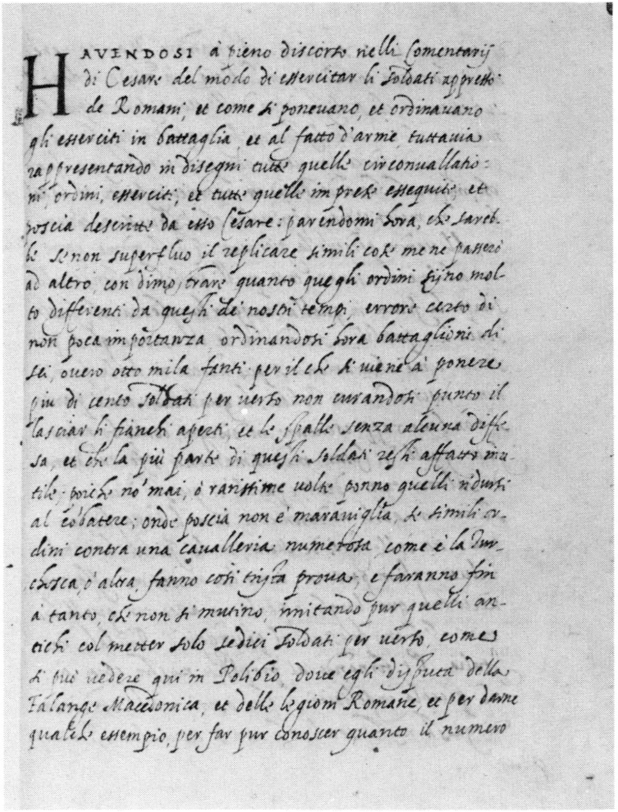

HAVENDOSI à tempo discorso nella Comenoni
di Cesare del modo di esercitare li Soldati appresso
di Romani, et come si pretiano, et ordinariano
sa essercati in Battaglia, et al fatto d'arme tuttaviia
rappresentando in disegni quelle ordinanze stabili-
mini, emendi, et tutte quelle in prese inguada, et
perche derivino da uso Cesare i servendom sene, che sapete
se stemen superfluo il replicare ambi ordi meno hauen-
dio altro con huomo brane quanto quelli ordini come mo-
to destino da quelli del nostri tempi, come cercò di
non fare impertanza ordinandoli sue Battaglioni di
sia ottava otto mila fanti per li li à venti li potrea
Falauni sfranchi appresso de la Spalla senza alcuna diff-
sa et la più parte di questi Soldati us li affatiii ma-
ti di picche ne mai, o rarissime volte vana quelli Soldati
all Battalha; onde perciò non è marauiglia, se similmente contro una Cauallerea numerosa come e la Sas-
aetica, o altra, finno certi cosa prevena e favorenor-
a tanto, et non si ma...ou... imitario per quelli or-
acis col nuoro solo Soldati per certo come
si sia veder ...... in Polibio docue desa disepor della
Falonga Macedonia, et delle legion Romanie, et per dare
quat ale essempio per fur conoscer quanto di numero

e quello, che si saremo marcate, et così facendo si
uennui in cognitione della uenita.

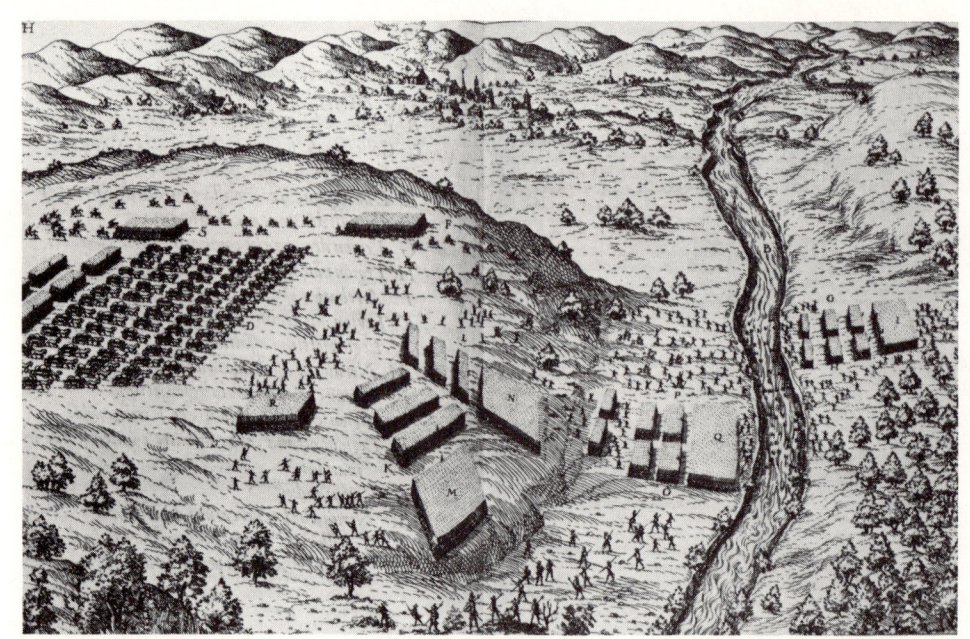

Courtesy British Library Board

11 a – CAESAR (DOMINANT STYLE) p. 44. CAESAR DEFEATS THE NERVII (pp. 478, 482)

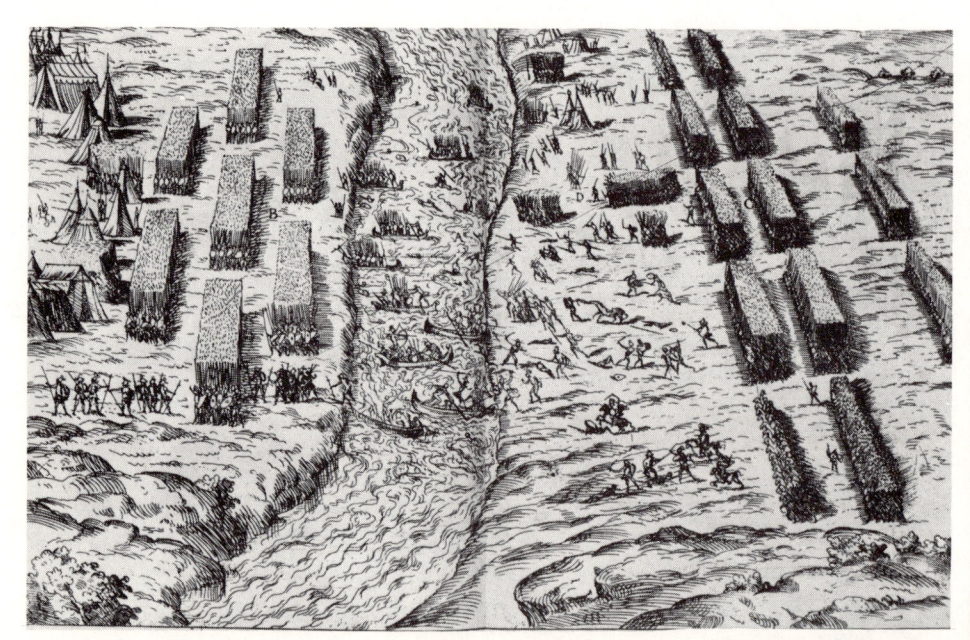

Courtesy British Library Board

11 b – CAESAR (SUBSIDIARY STYLE) p. 6. CAESAR ATTACKS THE HELVETII (pp. 478, 482)

PLATE 11

PLATE 12 a, b and c

12 a – QUINQUEREME, SIDE VIEW AND SECTION (p. 481)

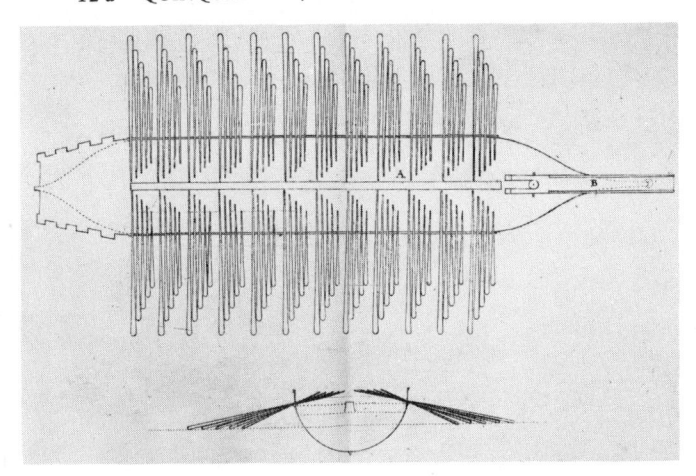

12 b – QUINQUEREME, PLAN AND ALTERNATIVE SECTION (p. 481)

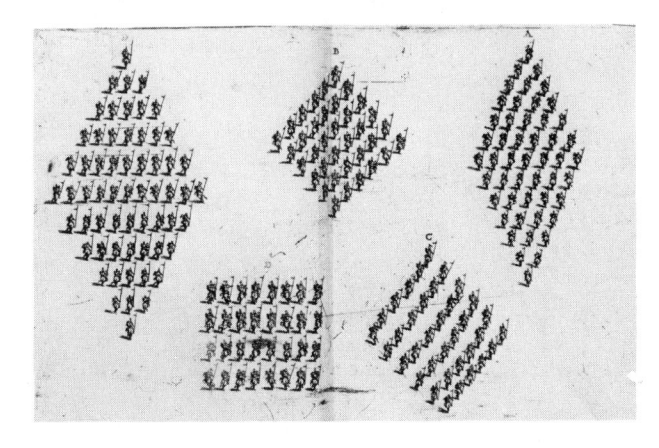

12 c – CAVALRY FORMATIONS (p. 481)

Courtesy British Library Board

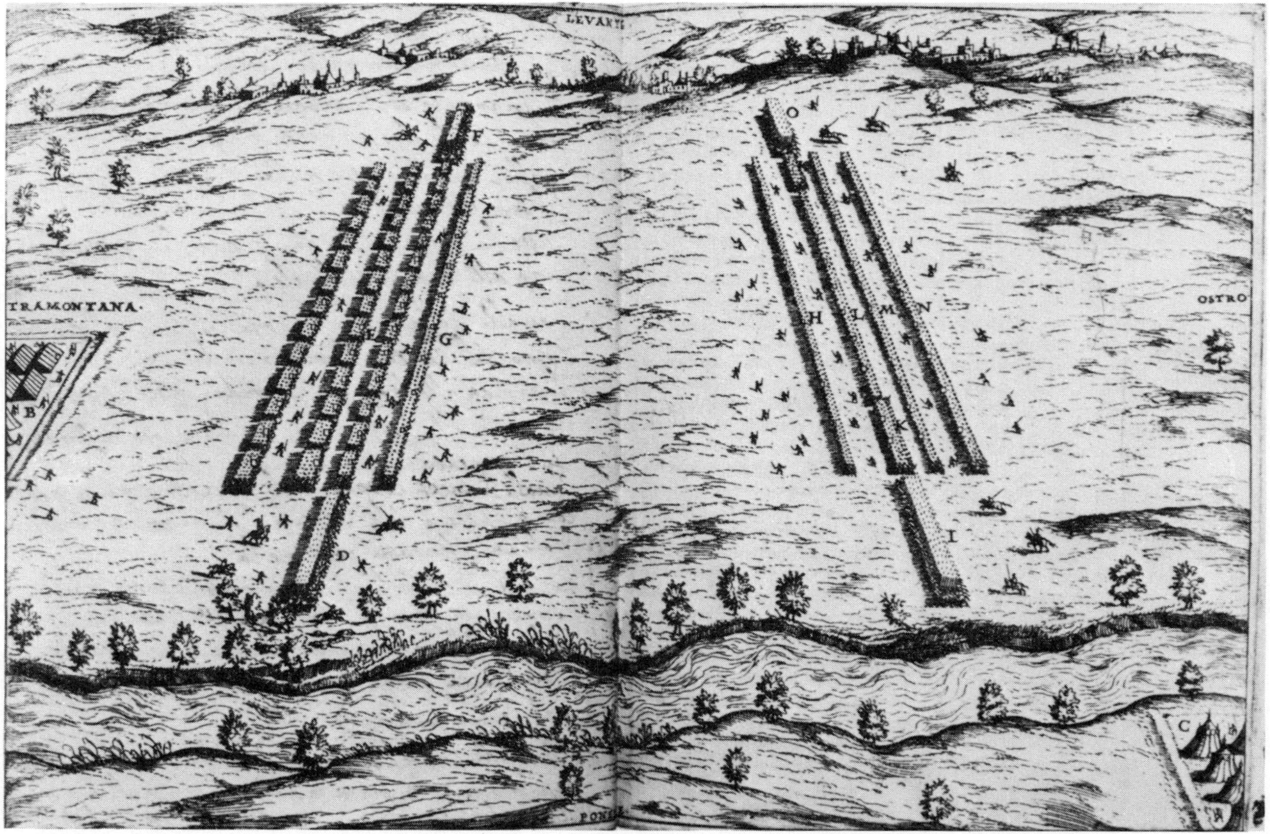

12 d – THE ARMIES AT CANNAE (pp. 481 f.)

13 a – KEY TO PLATE 12 d (p. 482)

A. Aufido fiume, el qual nasce nell'appennino, et corre nel mare Ionico.
B. Alloggiamento minore de Romani di là dal fiume.
C. Alloggiamento d'Annibale di qua dal fiume all'incontro de gl'alloggiamenti maggiori de Romani.
D. Cavalli Romani n.° 6 mila posti nel destro corno de suo esercito.
E. Tutte le legioni, ch'erano quattordici poste fra una alli fianchi dell'altra.
F. Cavalli Latini n.° tremila posti nel sinistro corno del esercito Romano.
G. Armati alla leggera de Romani, cioè à tutti l'esercito.
H. Armati alla leggera de Annibale, posti en fronte del suo esercito.
I. Cavalli Francesi et Spagnoli n.° cinque mila posti nel corno sinistro dell'esercito d'Annibale sopra il fiume.
K. Soldati Africani posti ne la [...]
L. Soldati in mezo li Africani messi a posta de sé.
M. Francesi, et Spagnoli, parimente detto.
N. Soldati Africani, ch'erano el nervo dell'esercito.
O. Cavalleria numidica n.° cinque milia posta ne l'altro corno dell'esercito.

Desi à vedere l'intelligenza d'Annibale el qual sa à nemici speza la mia in mano, per ne l'ordi[nare] l'esercito, l'hipponi [...] porto, de circonvenire li Romani, se bene ne è restato sconfitto.

13 b – KEY IN SUBSIDIARY HAND (p. 482 n. 44)

A. Alloggiamento de Romani.
B. Alloggiamento de Annibale.
C. Ircha fiume.
D. Luoco dell'imboscata de Cavalli e fanti.
E. Corno destro dove era diece milia fra Spagnoli, et Africani
F. Corno sinistro doue era altri diece milia de Spagnoli et Africani
G. Cavalli n. cinquemilia per ogni corno.
H. Elefanti n. 18. per adauon corno.
I. Armati alla leggiera de Romani.
K. Legion sacra fronte dell'Esercito de Romani, et ui era legion n.° 8.
L. Quadriera de Romani posta nelli Corni n.° 6000 diuisi la mittà per corno.
M. Battaglia di mezo dell'esercito di Annibale, et ui era 2000 fra Francesi, et Africani.
N. Armati alla leggera d'Annibale n. otto milla.

Non ui è cosa de maggior bene alli eserciti che quando sanno à combatere d'hauer mangiato, et beuuto, onde fece l'esercito d'Annibale il quale combattè con li Romani digiuni, et morti di freddo facendoli star l'esercito un imboscata di mille fanti, et mille cavalli, et così li uinse.

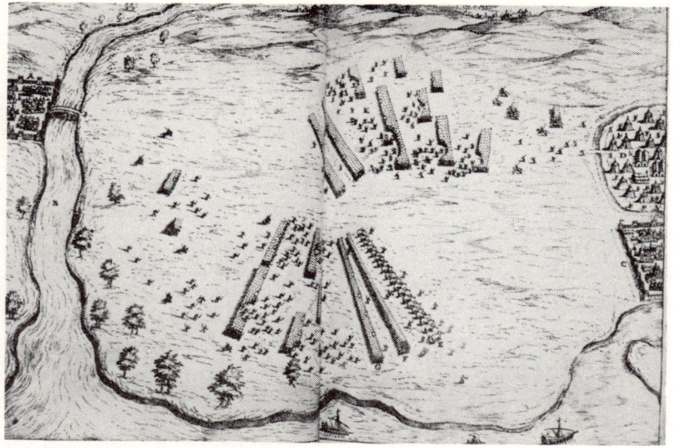

14 a – HAMILCAR'S VICTORY AT SEFIRA (AFTER p. 158) (pp. 481 f.)

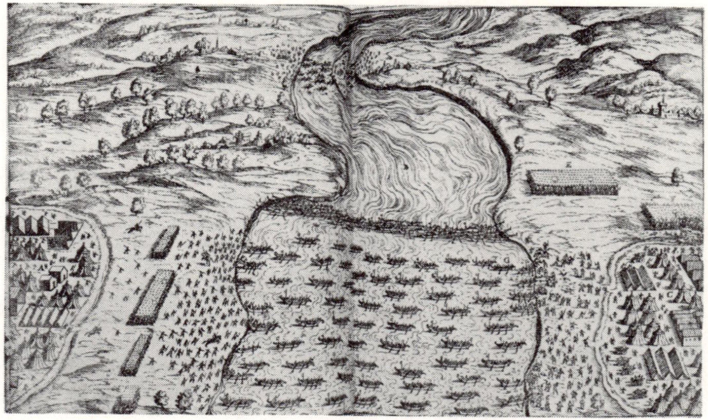

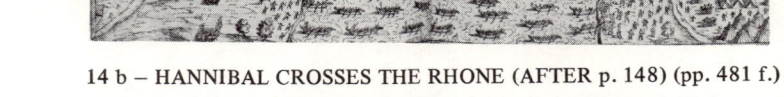

14 b – HANNIBAL CROSSES THE RHONE (AFTER p. 148) (pp. 481 f.)

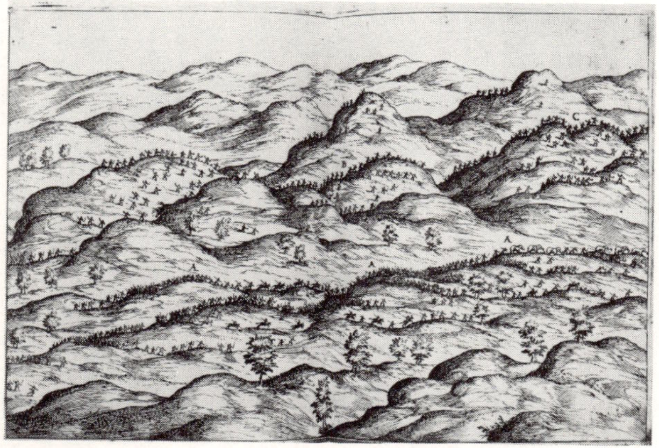

14 c – HANNIBAL CROSSES THE ALPS (AFTER p. 156) (pp. 481 f.)

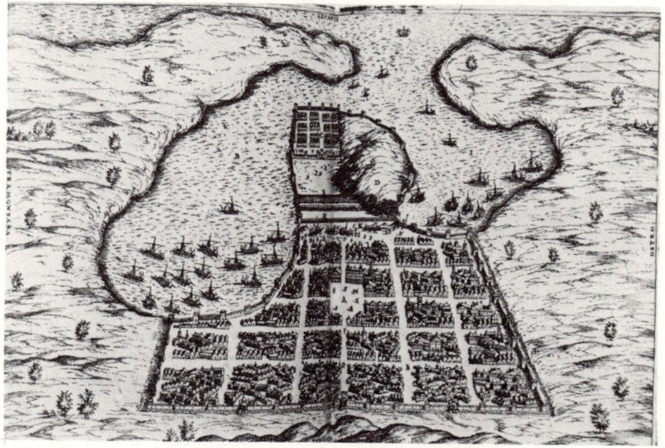

14 d – HANNIBAL BESIEGES TARANTO (AFTER p. 376) (pp. 481 f.)

a-d: *Courtesy British Library Board: Polybius*

INCITEMENT TO VIOLENCE?
ENGLISH DIVINES ON THE THEME OF WAR, 1578 to 1631

Elizabethan England was an unmilitaristic country where armies were raised with the greatest difficulty;[1] the civil wars, however, were fought by men who took up arms with a sharply contrasting, if not general, alacrity, and the pulpit, during this same period, had an enormous influence on public opinion.[2] This essay takes these two well-established generalizations and, through a survey of sermons and devotional works which concentrate on justifying war, suggests one possible link between them.[3] It attempts to do this first by considering this literature as a whole and showing how remarkably thorough and enthusiastic a defence of war it contained, and, secondly, by reviewing it chronologically, and drawing attention to the way in which puritanism, by its characteristic use of military imagery to describe the conflict between good and evil, could have encouraged individuals to see their cause as one justifying a recourse to arms.

We could not, of course, expect to hear pacifist views expressed from Elizabethan, Jacobean, or Caroline pulpits. Erasmian pacifism had faded away, leaving hardly more than the tag 'Dulce bellum inexpertis' behind it – and that was used to emphasize the seriousness, not the unchristian nature, of war;[4] anabaptist pacifism lingered only as a bogey; quaker pacifism was yet to come. All the strains which mingled in English theology supported the rightness of military service in a just cause. Catholic teaching, based on Aquinas, licensed the clergy to support a just war by every means in their power short of actually fighting;[5] Luther had pointed out that 'war is as necessary as eating, drinking or any other business' and that once war had been formally declared 'the hand that bears the sword is as such no longer man's, but God's, and not man it is, but God who hangs, breaks on the wheel, beheads, strangles';[6] Calvin 'repeatedly said that no consideration could be paid to humanity when the honour of God was at stake.'[7]

The English contributors to the secular literature of war which swelled so considerably from the mid-sixteenth century took it for granted that their subject-matter would be pleasing to God. 'For God,' wrote Roger Ascham in his treatise on archery, 'is well pleased with wyse and wittie feates of warre.'[8] Geoffrey Gates, an experienced soldier, begged his countrymen 'be wise ... and acquainte your selves with armes, both corporal and spiritual, that you may at all times and in all cases be compleate Iraelites ready for the fielde.'[9] It was God, William Neade, inventor of a combination bow and pike, pointed out, who first 'set his bow in the cloud' after the flood 'and afterward it pleased God to inspire men with such wisdom and policy to imitate and make materiall bowes.'[10] If preachers like Adams and Gouge used 'The Lord is a man of war' as their text, so did Edward Cooke in *The Character of Warre ... contayning many usefull directions for musters and armes* (1626) and William Barriffe placed a verse from psalm 144, 'Blessed be the Lord my strength which teacheth my hands to warre, and my fingers to fight,' on the title page of his *Military Discipline, or, the Young Artillery Man* (1635).

No convention suggested that laymen should keep clear of the theological aspects of war or that clerics should not dabble with the practical side of the subject. John Norden, the greatest topographer of his time and a surveyor of crown lands and forests, was also one of the most copious and popular devotional authors of his day: his *Pensive Man's Practice* (1584) went through more than forty impressions by 1627. His *Progress of Piety* (1596) was followed in the next year by *The Mirror of Honor*, in which he glorified the military profession to the extent of equating the good warrior with the good man and the bad man with the coward, who 'may be truly sayd to be an incarnate infernall spirit.'[11] Against the background of threatened Spanish revenge for the Cadiz expedition — and dedicated to its leader, the earl of Essex — the book warned 'every militarie man, to whom especially I bend my speech' that sinful behaviour would lead 'to the destruction and overthrowe of all godly discipline in warre' and put the country in peril.[12] In 1602 the discipline of God's own troops, the Hebrews, was described by Lodowick Lloyd, sergeant at arms to the queen and an author who hitherto had restricted himself to doggerel verse and jejeune historical compilations. Called *The Stratagems of Jerusalem*, it began with the uncompromising statement that 'the whole Bible is a book of the battles of the Lord.' If, to these works by a part-time devotional writer and an author whose interests were otherwise entirely secular, we add a purely practical guide to warfare written by a dean of Exeter and royal chaplain, the concern of the pulpit with war is robbed of its element of surprise. In his *The Practice, Proceedings and Lawes of Armes* (1593), Dean Matthew Sutcliffe swiftly dispersed any doubts about the morality of his topic. 'It is needeless (as I suppose) to dispute whether it be lawfull, either for Christian princes to make warres, or for Christians to serve in warres. Those that think it unlawfull, as men devoyd of iugement in religion and state, are declared long since to be both heretical and phrenetical persons.'

It should also perhaps be pointed out that there was nothing specifically English about the ready acceptance of war as part of God's plan. In

1574 Henry Grantham translated Girolamo Cataneo's *Most breif tables to knowe redily howe manye ranckes of footemen armed with corslettes, as unarmed, go to the making of a iust battayle*, in which, speaking of war, Cataneo says that 'whosoever behaveth himself honorablie in the exercise thereof, representeth nothing more than the true image of the most great and omnipotent God.' In the Armada year came a Huguenot view, *A short Apologie for Christian Souldiours*, translated from the French of Hubert Languet, and in 1591 John Eliot translated the Huguenot pastor Bertrand de Loque's *Deux Traitez, l'un de la Guerre, l'autre du Duel* (Lyon 1589), commending the book as 'setting downe the ancient rules of warre, grounded on God's holy word,' a description warranted by an elaborate introduction in which de Loque points out that men may fight not only 'because God hath so expressly commanded' but 'because Jesus Christ and his disciples have allowed the warre.'[13] As far as military literature was concerned, in English or in translation, the accordance of war to the word of God, in both the Old and New Testaments, was taken for granted – always subject to the caveat that 'warres are not to be taken in hand but in case of necessity.'[14]

The number of books on war and justifying war (again, both native works and translations) mounted steadily towards the civil wars[15] but, in a period when readers can rarely be identified, and the numbers of copies printed of each edition is, in almost all cases, unknown, the influence of books on public opinion is impossible to calculate. With sermons we are on firmer ground. This essay is based, it is true, on printed works, but each sermon had been delivered before a congregation, and, in the case of the Paul's Cross sermons[16] (Gosson, Hacket, Hampton, Stockwood, White), those preached in the key London parishes of St Stephen's Coleman Street (Davenport), St Andrew's Holborne (Everarde), St Anne's Blackfriars (Gouge), or before the monarch (Field) were assured of a large and, if John Manningham is at all representative, thoughtful auditory.[17] The sermon (the puritan sermon, at least) was intended not only as a crucial part of divine service but as the focus of a discussion in the homes of those who heard or read it. And, finally, it can be assumed that the subject-matter of printed sermons was representative of delivered, but unprinted, sermons in a sense far more meaningful than the suggestion that each printed book represents the drift of others mouldering in bottom drawers. Rejected (or suppressed) manuscripts are read by few: sermons, in a time when church attendance was compulsory, were heard by many. 360,000 has been suggested as the minimum number of sermons delivered between 1600 and 1640.[18] As the number of parishes remained unchanged in the period with which I am dealing (c1580–c1630) we can assume that of the minimum of 450,000 sermons delivered, a significant number, a *really* significant number, echoed the endorsement of military violence which is the common denominator of the works with which we are concerned.[19]

The fear of censorship or official disapproval hardly complicates this assumption. Peter Heylyn's comment in his *Cyprianus Anglicus* (1668) that Elizabeth 'used to tune the pulpits' was a fair one. From 1565 preaching was by licence only, and new incumbents had to swear 'I shall not preach, or publicly interpret, but only read that which is appointed by public authority, without special licence of the bishop under his seal.'[20] Licences were reviewed again in 1606, and by the articles of 1622 preachers were sternly warned against dealing with matters of state or with 'the deep points of predestination, election, reprobation or of the universality, efficacy, resistibility or irresistibility of God's grace.' They were to 'confine themselves to those two heads of faith and good life which are the subject of the ancient sermons and homilies.'[21] But war was one of the subjects of the ancient sermons and homilies; from Henry VIII's reign the state had sponsored appeals to Englishmen to take up arms against its enemies[22] and the chief non-doctrinal theme of the Elizabethan homilies was that of the subject's duty to defend the monarch against all threats, domestic and foreign.[23] Article 37 of the articles of religion stated clearly that 'it is lawful for Christian men, at the commandment of the magistrate, to wear weapons, and serve in the wars.' Provided that the impression was given that arms could only be borne against enemies of the state, the theme of war was safe from the tuning of pulpits or the censorship of the press. Five of the pro-war sermons discussed below were preached at Paul's Cross, where sermons 'were almost official Government pronouncements.'[24]

Lastly, the clergy were directly involved in the organization of military service. Armour, powder, and shot were stored in their churches, announcements about musters made from their pulpits, musters themselves were on occasion held in churchyards or even in the church itself. They were instructed to encourage their parishioners to contribute financially and in person to war and were themselves taxed for military purposes, being expected, according to the value of their livings, to provide money, men, or arms. When Whitgift called on the clergy through the bishops to contribute generously in the Armada year, Robert Wood, vicar of Shephall, went up to London and brought a caliver. 'I promise you,' he wrote, the demand 'could not have come to me in a worse time for I was bare of money, yet the Queen's Majesty must and shall be served.'[25] In general the clergy were grudging with their own contributions but willing to scold others into sacrifice. Roger Hacket, preaching at Paul's Cross on 14 February 1590 against the citizens' indifference to national defence, took his text from Judges 5:23: 'Curse ye Meroz, sayeth the Angel of the Lord, and in cursing curse the inhabitants thereof, because they come not to help the Lorde, to helpe the Lorde against the mighty.' We are dealing with a period when the feudal army had virtually disappeared, when mercenaries were, with good reason, distrusted, and when an effective permanent army was not yet in being. The clergy were needed, as never before or since, to goad men to take arms and to combat pacifism as well as to fulfil their more enduring functions: to equate patriotic with just causes, to bless soldiers and their weapons,[26] and to give spiritual comfort in the field. Their works provide a telling conspectus of what Englishmen were told by their pastors, from Paul's Cross to country church, to think about war.

The first concern of the church was to identify the enemies of England with the enemies of the Lord. 'Concerning Gog,' said Edmond Harris, 'looke Ezekiel 38 and 39, and there you shall see that Gog is called the Prince of Mesech and Tuball: by which Tuball are understood the Italians and Spaniards ... by Mesech the Turke.'[27] These are the enemies of the true servants of the faith; after quoting Deuteronomy 32, 41, and 42, 'I will execute vengeaunce on myne enemies (saith the Lord) and will reward them that hate me. I will make myne arrowes dronke with their blood,' he points out that this last remark especially should 'not bee lightly overpassed by us, considering the bowe and the arrowe are weapons of defence wherewith the Lorde hath armed our nation above the rest.' Hampton warned about the horrors that would follow if men did not take up the bow. He reminded his congregation of the Spaniards' behaviour toward the unarmed natives of the new world: 'Yea, they did not only feed their doggs but also themselves with men's flesh.' 'Unlesse our soveraigne be supplied,' he pointed out, you will 'see your wives ravished before your faces, your friends slain, your children murdered, your infants dashed against the stones or broached on the picke, and all the land made nothing but the shambles of Castillian and Ignatian butchers.'

After identifying the enemy and cataloguing the atrocities which may be expected to follow if he is permitted to land, the church played the fife to the recruiting officer's drum. The enemy seeks our blood, said Hacket; it is useless to rely on allies or on mercenaries. When Saul called on the people, 'they came, they hired not other, but they came in person ... But nowe, my brethren, when your rulers do call and countrie require, do you come?' He put the constitutional issue squarely to his congregation. 'For as in a clocke or watch all the wheeles shoulde goe when the maister wheele doth moove, and if any stay the same putteth all out of frame and must be mended, even soe in publicke states and civill governements, if the prince doe moove as the cheefe commaunder and master wheele, the people shoulde followe, and if any stay and trouble the whole, the same is to bee mended, and forced to his due and timely order ... since the prince representeth here the person of God, and is his vicegerent upon earth, hee ought to teeach the people, if they will not learne, that he beareth not, as the Apostle speaketh, the sworde in vaine."

When volunteers did come forward, they must drill and exercise conscientiously. 'Have we practised anie feats of armes whereby we may be ennabled to meete a Spaniard in the field?' asked E.R. 'Let us exercise the same daily, and continue in this forewardnes of service ... For although the Lord watcheth for his Israel, yet must not Israel snort securely.' The preachers roundly condemned any civil commotions that might blunt the war effort. 'The Lord knit the knot of peace,' said Thomas White, 'and make it fast from slypping and breaking, that being at quiet in our bowelles from sedition at home, we maye be stronger in body to resyst all forraigne powers abroad.' Mutiny, too, was soundly thrashed. One of the most chronic grievances among the troops was the irregular appearance of their pay. Be content, don't grumble about these delays, warned the author of *A Spiritual Chaine*. Don't let it be said that 'no longer plentie, no longer dutie; no longer pay, no longer Prince.' He went on, somewhat optimistically: 'A holy souldier will say thus in time of his governours disabilitie to pay wages: I serve a good Lord, even the Lord Jesus Christ, who hath promised not to leave us nor forsake us. He will pay you and me our wages, good captaine.' Nor must the soldier listen to subversive suggestions that the monarch's cause is not such as to justify a war. They must 'iudge lovingly of ther Prince ... and rest fully persuaded that the cause is good ... and then our gracious God, who seeth his holy purpose, will take this good hope conceived of his deputie in good part ... Beware then of false whisperings, which many times bring disobedient murmurings. Gods Vice-regent must not be denied aide, no, nor so much as grudged at, upon surmises and rumors.' Or, as Bachiler put it more crisply in a sermon to troops on active service, 'Another wicked thing is murmuring and mutining in the campe – see this taken notice of in those rebels (Numbers, 16, 1, 2, 3, 11), which was to be punished with death (Joshua, 1, 18).' And to support these armies in the field, and to provide for defence at home, the pulpit co-operated with the government by asking their congregations for cash contributions, as in E.R.'s 'Wee must forget our old vaine of sparing and begin to open our bags ... Shall we reserve in our coffers as it were swords to cut our owne throats?' 'There is a thing called *nervus Belli*,' William Hampton declared, 'without which warre cannot subsist ... for unless our soveraigne be supplied, that some course may speedily be taken for our defence, wee shall have neither lands, nor rents, nor money, nor corne, nor wives, nor children, nor anything else in safety, but all will fall into our enemies' hands.' The same message was forcibly put in 1626 by Thomas Barnes. 'Never had Chaldean greater cause to fight with Moab, than wee with Rome ... Fit purses for contribution must now stand open, fit persons for execution are now called upon ... Gird your swords therefore upon your thighes, O you valiant ones, and ride on with courage and renowne. Our Iehosophat summons against this Moab; what ranke, what degree amongst the gentry, amongst the commonalty of his dominions may not account it their glory to have an hand in this enterprise?'

The church could not preach war without feeling some tremors of unease, and commonly cleared its conscience by liberal abuse of the one recalcitrant sect. When threatened by war, said Thomas White, we must not 'tempt God in refusing lawfull meanes, as Anabaptistes that wyll weare no weapons.' Preaching at Paul's Cross, John Stockwood deplored 'the furie of the Anabaptistes, which, contrary to the scriptures, do teache that it is unlawfull for the magistrate to use the swords.' As late as 1626 Barnes set himself to combat 'that fantasticall conceit of the Anabaptisticall sect that it is not lawfull for true Christians to make warre.' Gouge spoke for clergy of all shades of opinion with his forthright declaration that 'warre is a kind of execution of publique justice and a means of maintaining right ... and though by their [soldiers'] valour much bloud may be shed, yet they need not be any more daunted thereat than iudges, iuries, executioners and other ministers of iustice for putting many malefactors to death.'

Moreover, the divines sought, in the words of one of them, 'to prove that warre was a blessing.' War, in the first place, could be a social good, a moral cleanser, God's scourge for vice. Peace led to laxity, to foul or at best indolent behaviour. War purified, energized. Peace corrupted, war restored. As Scott put it: 'All the beggerly nations of the world became rich and potent by raysing of warre, and were diminished and consumed to nothing by the corruption of peace and bewitching of pleasure.' In the second place, war brought a country fame and prestige while peace brought obscurity and scorn. What has made England 'famous and illustrious to forreigne Nations?': the warlike exploits of Cavendish, Drake, Essex, and Mountjoy. Show therefore, cried Hacket, 'That you carry in you the courage of the aunctient English, whose glory was to rule, not to be ruled.' Is war too risky? asked Scott. Why, look at the Dutch, and 'whether warre hath been a blessing unto them iudge for your selves, considering they have augmented their fame and renown abroad, and increased their wealth and territories at home.' War, again, was honourable, and warriors honourable men. As the author of *A Spiritual Chaine* pointed out, 'we perceive that all people of understanding despise a coward and respect a man of valour, whence it is that the name of a dastard is a base by-word of great reproach. And hence also it comes that they who are to be chosen to offices of any eminencie in the weale publike, one speciall qualitie regarded in them is (according to Ioshua's counsell) that they be men of courage.' In the third place, war was justified by God's action and teaching. In *The Bible-Battells* Bernard neatly brought together the most frequently quoted Old Testament examples.

> Some, as the Anabaptists, hold it not lawfull for Christians under the Gospell to make warre, but such are but dreamers, for God is pleased to be called a man of Warre (Exodus 15, 3). He hath given commandment to his people sometimes to fight (Numbers 31, 3; 1 Samuel 15, 3; Deuteronomy 2, 24). Hee made lawes for direction to them when they went to warre (Deuteronomy 20, 10, 15). Holy men of eminent place and graces have made warre, as did Abraham, Ioshua, David and others (Genesis 14). God would send his spirit upon them to encourage them to the warre, as he did upon Gideon, Ehud, Sampson, as wee may read in the book of Iudges. God raised up some prophets to comfort and set forward his people to warre (Judges 4, 2; Chronicles 14, 15). God taught David to play the part of a valiant captaine and souldier (Psalms 144, 1 and 18, 39, 40). In batell, when his people rested upon him and cryed to him, he did help them and made them conquerors (1 Chronicles 5, 20).

Most clerical authors were content to justify war out of the Old Testament, using these and comparable passages. But a few asked with Barnes, 'how stands this with that counsell of our Saviour: Love your enemies, bless them that curse you, pray for them that persecute you?' Bernard was one of those who accepted the challenge and, again, brought together the most frequently quoted texts.

> Our Prince of peace telleth us of warrs, and is pleased to be set out as a captaine of an host riding on horse back and subduing his enemies, and making a slaughter of them. Hereby shewing that his Church shall have warrs, and he will take their part and helpe to subdue their enemies, as he hath often done and yet will doe (Matthew 24; Revelations 19 and 17). When the souldiers asked Iohn Baptist what they should doe? Hee did not will them to forsake their calling, but to be content with their wages, as allowing the calling but reforming the abuse (Luke 3, 14). We find religious soldiers in the New Testament; the religious centurion, Cornelius, a Captain and a soldier fearing God that waited on him (Matthew 8, 8, 10; Acts 10, 1, 2, 3, 4, 7). Saint Paul maketh it a fruit of faith to be valiant in battle. If the lawfulness of warre had been out of date under the gospell, the Apostle would have left that out, as now no fruit of faith (Hebrews 11, 34). God hath now appointed kings to use the sword, not only to punish offenders under them, but also to defend their subjects from violence and wrong at home and abroad (Romans 13, 4). The Lord in calling the Gentiles to the gospell made choice in the first place to begin with one of this calling before another: even a Captaine called Cornelius.

And Bernard added another point which was common to the European pro-war literature: 'We must know that the gospell taketh not away the law of nature to defend ourselves by forcible meanes against violent enemies.' Furthering the case for a militant New Testament, Barnes commented on Isaiah's prophecy 'of the times of the gospell in the New Testament that when he said "They shall beate their swords into plow-shears": the Anabaptists allege that "therefore Christians may not make warre now under the gospell." I answer, the scope of the prophet there is not to forbid magistrates a necessary warre against the enemies of their lives, and Gods cause, but to shew what peace should be betwixt the Iewes and the Gentiles by the preaching of the gospell.' And the case was clinched by the author of *A Spiritual Chaine* with the syllogism: Christ took man's nature upon him; man is a warrior; therefore Christ is a man of war. 'As He took mens nature upon him, so taketh He mens' names unto him; they men of warre, He a man of warre.'

Indifference, let alone pacifism, was treachery. Harward took up his pen in defence of the military profession 'for that England hath (I doubt) many seditious malcontents which, being wearie of their own welfare, doe repine against those meanes whereby our prosperity is preserved.' So strong, indeed, was the defence of war that the eulogists of peace were few and cautious. It is with a characteristically tentative remark that Thomas Adams opened his *Eirenopolis: the Citie of Peace* (1622) : 'Peace take it with all its faults, is better then warre.' He hazarded a full-scale portrait. 'Peace is a fair virgin ... she hath a smiling looke ... snowy armes, soft as downe, and whiter than the swannes feathers ... her bowels are full of pitty,' etc., but later in the book he was at pains to point out that 'I am no Anabaptist, nor Libertine, to deny the magistracie or lawfulness of authoritie ... The Lord himself hath appoynted tribunals, and no law, no love.'

Like their secular counterparts, religious writers pointed out that fighting could only be approved if it were in a just war, that is, a war waged in a just cause, with righteous intent, and at the command of a lawful authority. It must be 'necessary' in the sense of defending oneself or succouring an ally or co-religionist. Religious writers, however, with the help of holy writ, could extend the scope of the just war concept beyond its use by secular writers, who were bound by a narrower legalistic approach. Besides, as Sutcliffe noted, 'if the unjustice of the warres be not notorious, the subject is bound to pay and serve, and the guilt shall be laide to his charge that commandeth him to serve.' The Old Testament illustrated specific points such as the notion that a neutral can be attacked if he hinders an army crossing his territory; Gosson pointed out that 'when Amelec had vexed the Israelites as they went out of Egypt, and smote the hindmost of them, God commanded them to revenge it, and to roote out the remembrance of Amelec from under heaven.' It also provided a general sanction for foreign conquest, for 'warres have beene justly made by Israel, God's people, at God's command to subdue nations and to possesse their kingdomes as they did the kingdomes of Canaan and inherited them.' Every aggressor could persuade himself that his cause was just, and it is not surprising that the pulpit devoted itself to reassurances like Gosson's 'you shall find the warres of the enemie in the Indies, in Portingale, in Grenada, in the Low Countries, in France, and against us to be uncharitable and uniust ... Looke upon your owne warres another while, you shal find them to be very charitable and iust.'

The Bible also provided precedents for most of the implements and customs of war. Practice with the bow and arrow was recommended from the pulpit usually by reference to King David's worthies. Gunpowder appeared too late to be mentioned in the Bible, but more than one preacher pointed out that, 'as St. Paul gives a Christian in his welfare the whole armour of God; a sword to offend, a shield to defend, so in this kind of [modern] Warre, we must improve all things whatsoever the bowels or face of the earth can affoord for our defence.' Thus, though gunpowder was invented with the Devil's aid, 'seeing the fierie disposition of our enemies use this as all others to our annoyance, why may wee not snatch these weapons out of madde mens hands, and turn them into their owne bosomes?' As for the employment of subterfuge and terrorism, why, in a good cause, the Christian might follow his instincts. So long as the issue of a war was in doubt, said Gosson, 'al the meanes are lawful that are requisite to the attaining of the victory; sleights, shifts, stratagems, burning, wasting, spoiling, undermining, battery, blows and bloud. I will give you one example in Scripture for al, Ioshua 8. In the taking of Ai there is a stratageme, an ambush laide behind the cittie, an assault given before it, semblance of flight by retiring to draw the enemy out, the city fierd, the enemy enclosed and then slaughtered before and behind.' As for loot, so long again as the cause is just, soldiers, Bernard comforted, may take what they find, for 'God allowed Israel to take what they did win in thier iust wars.'

There was considerable difference of opinion about how far the presence of evil-living soldiers spoiled an army's chances of success. Preachers were agreed that soldiers should behave in an orderly and Christian way. 'It is thought of some wicked person,' Harris told his congregation of recruits, 'that to have a payre of dice in the one hand and a whore in the other, this is souldierlike, but wo unto such.' And it was pointed out that such behaviour not only imperilled the immortal soul of the individual but, by undermining the discipline of the army, lessened its chances of victory. In real life, however, the good man was likely to be the snug, prosperous man who had no intention of trusting his fortune to the wars. Precept and practice were neatly bridged by Thomas Barnes' thesis that God can use unworthy instruments to good ends. 'It is as lawfull a thing to presse the bad for military service in times of warre,' he claimed, 'as to employ the good, yea, in the ordinary service of common souldiers. I doubt not it may stand as well with true piety as state-policy to spend the worst first, and spare the best to the last extremity ... Warre in it self is a punishment for sinne ... who better to taste it, than the lewdest men, that most deserve it?' He went on to suggest that war can frighten a bad man into a more virtuous state of mind. This being so, 'it were a thousand pities he should not see the pikes, nor be sent to the field. I speake this the rather that I may incite such as have the office of pressing in these needfull times committed unto them to be careful to cleanse the city and rid the country as much as may be of those straggling vagrants, loytering fellowes and lewd livers (so they be fit for service) which doe so swarme amongst us.'

As far as the use of prayer was concerned, the attitude was one of trusting God and keeping the powder dry. In the pulpit's opinion victories were won in heaven but prepared on earth. The Armada had been scattered by the protestant wind. 'Not an angell, but God himselfe had a favourable eye towards us, and an holy hand over us,' John Prime told an Oxford congregation, and 'hee was as much with us as ever with any nation, when, notwithstanding all their crakes and famous Dons and doutie adventeres, huge shippes all to be-swathed with gables and printed vauntes, we lost by them, who are now sent home a wrong way, neither man, nor ship, nor boat, nor mast of ship.' In 1626, however, the official *Forme of prayer, necessary to be used in these dangerous times of Warre*, issued by the king's printer, while it acknowledged that 'victory is absolutely in the will and power of God,' and that an essential prelude to victory was fasting, prayer, and repentance, went on to ask 'but are men spirits onely? Are they to fight their battels onely with spirituall armour? No; for were not that to tempt God, in neglecting the good meanes ordained by him for that end? Verely, politique preparations are God's ordinance, and have ever beene used by his good servants.' Thomas Scott reported a good practical prayer from the Low Countries in 1624. God's aid should be begged against the enemy, that He should 'lay open their plots, discover their devises, weaken their armes and overthrow their inventions, confound their councells, and consume their numbers.' Lest prayers of this sort, addressed to the God whose son had said 'Love your enemies ... pray for them which despitefully use you' should puzzle the conscience, the matter was cleared up by Bachiler. 'We are to know then,' he pointed out, 'that we must pray for *our* enemies, but against *God's* enemies ... We may lawfully pray against their designes though not against their persons ... or we may pray against their persons indefinitely, though not particularly ... or lastly, we may pray against their persons in particular, conditionally, though not absolutely; first, we are to pray for their conversion, and then if maliciously and wilfully they persist in their obstinacy, in the second place for their confusion. This was David's method.' As with the weapons and customs of war, the pulpit was able to justify the warrior's darker instincts with only the most general of qualifications; if the cause were just, in fact, then no holds need be barred – providing, that is, that discipline did not suffer. Christian and heathen were at one on this point; the priest at the provost marshal's elbow. 'There is nothing displeasing to God, but sinne,' Bernard wrote. 'As Moses exhorted Israel and as Aurelianus the Emperor said to his Generall in a military epistle of his, if thou be a tribune, yea, if thou wilt live, keepe back the souldiers hands from doing evill.'

Bernard's book was designed to support a biblical example with a classical one, to show that the Bible was comparable in value as a source of military information to the popular classical texts of, for example, Vegetius, Frontinus, and Caesar. 'Most that delight to reade, or almost all so delighted, do spend their time in perusing over humane stories, and do highly extoll the histories of the warres of heathen commanders ... but doe lightly price the scriptures' historie of warres, the right art militarie indeed, which was commanded to bee penned by that great man of warre (as Moses stileth him) the only cheife and highest commander, whose name is the Lord of Hosts.' The idea of using the Bible as a military handbook, lessons reflecting the ideas of a greater warrior than any the Greeks or Romans could name, was not original to Bernard. His book had been preceded by Alexander Leighton's *Speculum Belli Sacri* (1624), in which he said, 'I have applied the generall rules warranted by the Word to the particular necessity of our present times.' Though he gave more information of a practical kind in chapters like 'The oppugnation of a hold,' 'The ordering of the Battell,' 'The fight itself,' Leighton brought the Bible alongside the classical literature on war without suggesting that it could replace it. Bernard, however, was at pains to rebut the view that biblical wars were no longer relevant in the modern world. Basic considerations like the choice and training of soldiers, their discipline and morale, were unaffected by changing fashions in armament. The problem of supply, the ordering of a march, or a camp – all matters to which he devoted a chapter – were subject to little change through the ages. He too did not suggest that the Bible should take the place of Vegetius, but that it should be added to the shelf of classical texts as a work of equal practical value and higher authority. Though his points were all buttressed by biblical illustrations he drew on a wide range of ancient and contemporary authors as well; his remarks on discipline, for instance, were supported by references to Moses, Alexander, Severus, and the Turks who, thanks to their superior discipline, 'have mightily prevailed against us Christians, who may be ashamed of our over-much loosenes herein.'

It was not only in formal treatises that attention was drawn to the value of the Bible as a military text. Preaching in 1618, John Everarde said that some misguided persons had tried to explain away those passages in holy writ which referred to God as the lord of hosts, Christ as the captain of the lord's army, angels as soldiers, by suggesting that 'similitudes in the book of God be sometime drawne *a rebus non amandis,* from evill things, and applyed unto those that are good.' But, he went on in a characteristically puritan style, 'what neede wee strive so much to expresse and wring iuyce from symbolicall divinitie, which seldom concludes, when waters sufficient to quench our greatest thirst of knowledge do so plenteously gush from the rocke of the Word?' Are the scriptures not as exact 'in the affaires of the army as in the businesse of the sanctuary? Will you see *modum indicendi bellum,* a prescript form of denouncing warre? ... see Deuteronomy 20, 10; will you see *delectum militis,* the choice of souldiers? see Exodus 17, 9; will you see *sacramentum militare,* the oath of obedience from a souldiour to his captaine? see Ioshua 1, 16, 17; will you see colonells and captaines? looke Numbers 31, 14.' And so he proceeds, for 'the sounding of an all'arme, Numbers 10, 5, 6; the order of a camp, Numbers 2; a march, who have the van and who the riere, Numbers 10, 14 etc; a councell of warre, ib. 4; a city besieged, Ioshua 6; a city releeved, Ioshua 10, 9; an ambush, Ioshua 8, 9; a prey taken, 1 Samuel 30; the spoile divided, Numbers 31, 27. But what, should I stand wearying you with repetition of watches, spies, battels, skirmishes, defeats, supplies, strategems and six hundred things of like nature, whereunto the blessed spirit hath every where in scripture given not only approbation, but direction?'

The preachers who, like Everarde, were invited to speak to the military associations, identified themselves openly, almost ardently, with the military interests of their auditors, and it is in their sermons that the church's attitude to war appears most explicitly martial. 'I doe openly acknowledge and publickely professe,' cried William Gouge, preaching to the Artillery company of London, 'that my heart is set upon your Artillery company. I love it, I admire it, I honour it, I praise God for it.'

Samuel Buggs, addressing the company who practised arms in the Military garden at Coventry, explained his martial tone by pointing out that his intention was to 'imitate a son of the prophet Azaziah the sonne of Obed, who encouraged the valiant Asa, and gave him some directions how to fight the Lord's battailes,' while Leech was clearly tempted to jump down from the pulpit and shoulder a pike himself among the members of the London Artillery garden who formed his congregation. 'I wish I could add reall encouragements to those verball that I give you,' he mourned, and returning to the theme towards the end of his sermon, he said that 'we for our parts, we that are of poore Levie's tribe, we will helpe you what we can too ... If you fight for us, we will pray for you.' In these perilous times, he said, how could a man resist a longing to take arms? 'Shall he live like a luskish Sidonian, or like an effeminated Sybarite, languishing in ease and raveling out his time in courtship and dalliance? Shall he doe nothing but sit singing and sonnetting among ladies and gentlewomen, or perhaps stretch his armes now and then at shittlecock or billiards?' It is in keeping with the stirring tone and militant imagery of these sermons that Buggs announced the end of his with the words 'But now time compels me to sound a retreat.'

'In peace prepare for war.' This was an obvious theme for these sermons, and it was given vigorous treatment. 'I know prayers are good weapons,' admitted Thomas Adams, who was also addressing the members of the London Artillery garden, 'and Exodus 17 — there was more speed made to victorie by lifting up of Moses' hands than of Ioshua's sword ... But is it enough to bend the knee, without stirring the hand? Shall warre march against us with thundering steps and shall we only assemble our selves in the temples, lie prostrate on the pavements, lift up our hands and eyes to heaven, and not our weapons against our enemies? Shal we beat the aire with our voices, and not their bosomes with our swords? Only knock our own breasts, and not knock their heads? Sure, a religious conscience never taught a man to neglect his life, his libertie, his estate, his peace.' The sermons praised Solomon, the ideal ruler: a lover of peace but the supervisor of formidable preparation for war. They held up as a dread example the fate of the inhabitants of Laish, 'a people that were quiet and secure' and were exterminated for their indolence by the Danites. John Davenport took as his text 2 Samuel 1: 18 'Also he bade them teach the children of Iudah the use of the Bow,' and commented 'It is a care well beseeming kings, to provide that their subiects be instructed and trained up in military exercises.'

The preachers to the military companies took especial pains in tackling the texts which would seem to imply a condemnation of warlike activity. As Everarde said, recurring to a familiar stumbling block, 'Tis true, it was once prophesied of the dayes that were then to come ... They shall breake their swords into plough-shares, and their speares into sithes. But take away ... the cover of the letter, and you shall finde there no prohibition of the use of weapons and lawful war, much lesse of the due preparation there unto, but onely a sweet and gracious promise of unity and spiritual concord between them who are ... of the household of faith, and know themselves to be brethren by grace.' And, turning to the New Testament, Davenport explained that 'though the end of Christ his coming was to reconcile things in heaven and things on earth ... yet so long as Satan workes in the children of disobedience, and so long as any remnant of sinne is in the heart of any, there will be a necessity and lawfulnesse of war, and of this care to prepare for it.' It is not to be expected that, speaking to such an audience, a divine would hesitate to commend the use of guns and gunpowder. God gave animals horns and tusks to defend themselves, said Davenport, 'but unto Man, God hath given reason and understanding, which is in stead of all these, whereby he is able not only to espie meanes of escape from dangers, but he can take from every creature upon earth, yea from within the bowels of the earth, what may serve for his use and benefit.'

Whatever the danger and drudgery involved, whatever the weapons that had to be handled, the military career was a glorious one, and glorious too was the preparation for it. Buggs told his congregation 'You have entered now one of the two professions which are the onely life and lustre of true gentrie.' Go on, then! 'Tread all oppositions and encumbrances under your feete, and spurne with the heeles of contempt the base and faeculent vulgar, whose muddie braines and dull spirits neither can conceive nor dare attempt to high designs.' Go on, urged Gouge, 'The time would faile mee to speake in particular of Ioshua, Gedeon, Ieptha, David, Iehosophat, Hezekiah, Iosiah and other like worthies, royall persons, that were trained up in the artillery profession.' It was no easy thing to be a soldier, the demands of the calling were high. 'Many honourable parts and endowments are requisite to make a man expert in the artillery profession,' Gouge flattered his audience by going on to say, 'as soundnesse of iudgement, sharpenesse of wit, quicknesse of conceit, stoutnesse and courage of mind, undauntednesse in danger, discretion mixed with passion, prudence, patience, ability and agility of body, and of the severall parts thereof, with the like; all which doe demonstrate that the function whereunto they are required is an honourable function.' On him everything depends, however important, however trivial. Without him who would protect the monarch, the church? Without him, asked Adams, 'who should keepe the foggie epicure in his soft chaire after a full meale fast asleepe? Who should maintaine the nice ladie in her caroch, whirling through the popular streets?'

The military sermons were ceremonial occasions, attended by important civic dignitaries, and the frequency with which the preachers request money suggests that the officials of the companies put a word in their ear beforehand. 'Oh, you Londoners!' cried Adams reproachfully. 'You researve one bagge for pride, another for belly-cheare, another for lust, yet another for contention and sutes in law ... You then, that have the places of government in this honourable citie, offer willingly your hands, your purses, your selves to this noble exercise.' Leech acknowledged that some of the city worthies before him would not cut very likely figures on the parade ground themselves, but they should at least enable others to shoulder pike and musket there. 'You therefore that cannot be souldiers, make souldiers!'

From this kaleidoscopic treatment of our sources we can see how rich and how various was the defence of war offered by the church. If we now look more analytically, one point stands out very clearly: the preponderance of puritans among these militant divines, especially in the seventeenth century. Thomas White (?1550-1624), vicar of St Dunstan-in-the-West, London, when he preached at Paul's Cross, was to become successively canon of Christ Church, Oxford, and of Windsor; orthodox in the main, his outcry against superstitious observances, delicate living, Sabbath-breaking, and the theatres has led him to be labelled as a puritan.[28] John Stockwood (d. 1610), minister of Battle in Sussex and headmaster of Tonbridge grammar school at the time of his sermon, has also been called a puritan.[29] John Prime (1550-96), rector of Adderbury, Oxfordshire, appears to have been orthodox; about 'E.R.' and Edmond Harris I have no information. Roger Hacket (1559-1621), rector of North Crawley in Buckingham, was orthodox and so, in all probability, was Simon Harward (fl. 1572-1614), chaplain of New College, Oxford, and later vicar of Banstead. I can see nothing of the puritan in the work of Matthew Sutcliffe (c.1550-1629) who in 1593 was dean of Exeter and one of the queen's chaplains. Stephen Gosson, who as vicar of Sandridge in Hertfordshire had come forward with a caliver in the Armada year, held the living of Great Wigborough in Essex when he preached *The Trumpet of Warre*. Puritanical in his onslaught on the theatres (*The Schoole of Abuse*, 1579) and women's indecent fashions, in theology and politics he was a thoroughly establishment figure.[30]

From 1617, the date of *The Souldiours Honor*, the balance changes. Thomas Adams (c.1580 – c.1660) held the preachership of St Gregory's under St Paul's Cathedral; one of the best known from a literary point of view, of seventeenth-century divines, 'almost any sermon exhibits Adams' mastery of all the popular resources of the City and Puritan preacher.'[31] John Everarde (1575?-1650?), reader from about 1618 at St Martin's-in-the-Fields, was so often in and out of prison for meddling with state affairs that James I is reported to have said 'What is this Dr. Ever-out? His name shall be Never-out.' Strongly influenced by Tauler and the *Theologia Germanica*,[32] his highly individual puritanism led to a charge of heresy in 1636 and three years later he was deprived of his benefice. I know nothing about John Leech, but his being chosen as preacher by the Artillery company suggests (for reasons we shall see shortly) that he was a puritan. Samuel Buggs, 'minister of the word of God in Coventrie' was a puritan.[33] *A Spiritual Chaine* is a puritan work. Alexander Leighton (1568-1649), critic of the queen and rabid antiepiscopalian, has been described as a puritan 'of the narrowest type.' In 1630 he was convicted of sedition, degraded from orders, had his nose slit and was imprisoned for ten years. Thomas Scott (1580?-1626), appointed a chaplain to James I in 1616, left England after publishing a tract against the projected marriage of Prince Charles with the Spanish infanta and became preacher to the English garrison at Utrecht. A puritan. According to the life prefixed to his commentary on Hebrews,[34] William Gouge was counted as 'an Arch-Puritan' while a fellow of Kings. Rector of St Anne's Blackfriars from 1608, he was a member of the puritan society of the Feofees of Impropriations.[35] One of the best known of moderate puritans, 'it was said of him that "when the godly Christians of those times came out of the Country into London, they thought not their businesse done unlesse they had been at Blackfriars lecture." '[36] Thomas Barnes, 'preacher of God's word at Much-Waltham in Essex' was a puritan.[37] I am not sure about William Hampton. In 1628 Theophilus Field (1574-1636) was bishop of St Davids and moved without a breath of theological scandal to the see of Hereford in 1635. John Davenport (1597-

1670) was, like Gouge, a member of the society of Feofees and (again, like Gouge) a member of the group of London clergymen who created a fund for the relief of the distressed protestants of the Palatinate. Vicar of St Stephens, Coleman Street, from 1624 till 1633 when he resigned his living and emigrated to New England, Davenport was one of the most prominent puritan divines in London. Samuel Bachiler is known to me only through this sermon; from this he appears to have been chaplain to the English forces at Gorcum in the Netherlands and, as his *Campe Royall* is prefaced by lines from Thomas Scott, he was probably a puritan. About Richard Bernard's puritanism there is no doubt. Bernard (1568-1641) was suspended from his living at Worksop in Nottinghamshire (where he wrote his treatise on preaching, *The Faithfull Shepheard* [1607]) for his separatist ideas, but settled down under an indulgent diocesan as vicar of Batcombe to produce a long array of writings, the best known being his *Isle of Man or Proceedings in Manshire* (1627), an allegory faintly anticipating Bunyan's *Pilgrim's Progress*.

With this subject matter, and these men in mind, it is worth looking again, I think, at some familiar royalist comments on the outbreak of civil war. 'There are monuments enough,' wrote Clarendon, 'in the seditious sermons at that time printed and, in the memories of men, of others not printed, of such wresting and perverting scripture to the odious purposes of the preacher, that pious men will not look over without trembling ... There was one who, from the 48th chap. of the Prophet Jeremiah and the 10th verse, "Cursed be he that keepeth back his sword from bloud," reproved those who gave any quarter to the King's soldiers.'[38] John Hacket was of the opinion that the country had been 'preach't into disorder by Presbyterian divines' and that 'church-men are the most dangerous instruments to turn male-contents into sword-men.[39] According to Clement Walker it was the divines on both sides who 'inflamed the people to the rage of battell, as the elephant is inraged at the sight of red.[40] Finally, writing at closer quarters to the early stages of the conflagration, 'Mercurius Civicus' declared that 'the truth is, brother Rusticus, these military preparations had affected little, had not the fire been given from the pulpit.'[41]

Now these are biased opinions, and they refer with especial force to the period 1641-2. Before the breakdown of the censorship, printed works by divines had not preached rebellion; they did no more, I am suggesting, than habituate their auditors to the use of violence in a cause they believed just, a cause which, even within the tuning of pulpits and censorship of the press, could let 'Spaniards' blur into 'Antichrist' and 'Antichrist' become the forces inhibiting the practice of right worship.[42]

Mercurius Civicus does, however, reach back in another passage to the period of conditioning with which we are dealing. 'You may well remember,' he points out to his friend in the country, 'when the Puritans here did as much abominate the Military Yard or Artillery Garden as Paris Garden itself; they would not mingle with the prophane. But, at last, when it was instilled into them that the blessed reformation intended could not be effected save by the sword, these places were instantly filled with few or none but men of that faction ... so that when any prime commanders dyed, new men were elected wholly devoted to that faction.'[43]

The members of the Artillery company who practised in the Artillery garden were not all puritans; some became prominent on the royalist side in the civil wars.[44] But, on the evidence of the works under discussion here, the puritan connection was very strong. The puritan author of *A Spiritual Chaine* dedicated his book 'to those patterne captaines (so I call them who are leaders by their godly example) of the Artillery and Militarie in the Citie of London,' and he is unstinting in his approbation of 'the training up of the citie's valiant men, yea, youths, nay very children in feates of armes (being first taught to feare their God, and to be armed against, and fight against, Satan).'[45] This is a puritan addressing fellow spirits. Thomas Scott, referring to the Artillery company, would hardly have used this prayer before men to whose doctrine he was unsympathetic: 'Blesse, O Lord, we intreat, their new inventions of warre, and make them skilfull and full of knowledge, that all the world may know that Thou conductest our armies.'[46] Gouge was surely speaking to a significant number of co-religionists among his congregation of amateur soldiers: 'I say vacant houres cannot better be spent than in the Artillery Garden, and in the practise of martial discipline there exercised.'[47] The company, of course, chose their own preachers: Adams, Everarde, Gouge, and Davenport were all prominent puritans. Leech was possibly one. When Captain Henry Waller died in 1631 another well-known puritan, George Hughes, lecturer at All Hallows, Bread Street, was invited to preach at his funeral.[48] Following the example of Leech, who had told his congregation that he was 'your fellow-souldier in the battailes of our Lord Iesu,' Hughes referred to himself as 'your hearty orator and fellow-souldier in Christ's artillery.' Judging from the evidence of printed sermons, the Artillery company was told that the practice of arms was pleasing to the Lord and that the interest of lay worshipper and minister were identical – and it was told these things in tones of uncommon fervour. It is not without interest that Gouge said 'me thinkes that it is more then meete that everie citie and corporation, if not every towne and village throughout the land should have an Artillery Garden, and that the great populous cities, especially London, should have as many Artillery Gardens as it hath wards, and that publique allowances should bee afforded to such as willingly offer themselves to these military exercises.'[49] It is intriguing that Davenport referred approvingly to the example given by his congregation for 'as Paul speaks to the Romanes, "Your zeal hath provoked many" – as may be seene in Coventry, Chester, Bristow, Norwich, besides other places, who not only have raised up like companies in imitation of yours, but also have been guided therein by some of your followers and instructed by some of your schollers.'[50] But we cannot assume that there was a militant puritan plot to reach out from the Artillery garden in order to preach the country into disorder.

We must bear in mind an old strain in pulpit oratory: the praise of healthy open-air occupations (especially if they could be of service to the country) as against the tavern recreations – dice, cards, and so forth. Latimer regretted in a sermon of 1549 that 'now we have taken up whoring in taverns instead of shooting in the fields.'[51] A good proportion of our divines not only praised war but scourged vain pleasures and pastimes. To give examples merely from the extremes of our period, Stockwood asked a Paul's Cross congregation 'Wyll not a fylthie playe wyth the blast of a trumpette sooner call thyther a thousand than an houres tolling of a bell bring to the sermon a hundred?'[52] and Davenport, speaking of the activities of the Artillery garden, begged his audience 'abandon your caroling, dicing, chambring, wantonnesse, dalliance, scurrilous discoursing and vaine revelling out of time, to frequent these exercises.'[53] A petition to the privy council from Derby to have an artillery ground of its own referred, indeed, to 'some able persons of the younger sort who are willing for exercise sake and to avoid resorts to tavernes and ale houses and other improfitable employments ... to bestow that time to trayning, which by many of them is spent in idleness.'[54]

And yet, surely there is more in the enthusiasm, the military glee we have been watching than a 'puritanical' hand-clapping at the thought of men being kept away from vain shows and idle temptations? There is no need to emphasize the importance of preaching to puritans of all degrees of rigour, nor to stress the opportunities given by the lectureship system, the tolerance of certain bishops, and the protection of powerful men to the expression of their views. It is, however, worth emphasizing how frequently the puritan preacher likened himself to a military leader. 'The generall that for his proper gains,' wrote Richard Stock, a staunch puritan, and George Hughes' predecessor at All Hallows, 'or private respects shall admit captains and colonels and marshals for the leading of severall bands, which have no skill in war and martiall affaires, are not able to lead their bands and to go in and out before them, can never answer it to their prince if it be known that this is the cause why the battel succeeds so badly.'[55] All Christians are soldiers, wrote John Downame, 'but especially this courage and care is required of God's ministers, unto which is required not onely that they be valorous in fighting the Lord's battails, but also prudent and skilfull in the militarie discipline, that they may be able to teach and traine others in these feates of armes and how to use their valure, strength and weapons to their best advantage, seeing that they are called of God not to be common souldiers but captaines and leaders of his holy armies.'[56]

Every puritan would have agreed with John Traske that 'the maine or chiefe practice of preaching is to wrestle and fight with, yea, to overcome all opposition.'[57] Every puritan would have nodded agreement with Broade when, after pointing out that the scriptures likened Christians to soldiers and the resistance to evil to a battle, he went on 'this then being an usuall allegorie in the scriptures, if I shall continue it in handling of this text [Ephes. 6: 11: "Put on the whole armour of God ..."] it will not I hope seeme strange to any – unless happily themselves be strangers to God's word.'[58] But he might have been unaware how far, as the seventeenth century proceeded, the preachers were going to introduce the terminology of contemporary wars. 'Even children as soone as they be borne,' said Leech, 'they have presently their names put into the check-rowle and receive from their captain their press-money in their baptism.'[59] Watch your tongues, admonished Field, for 'the portcullis of the teeth and the counter-scarfe of the lips are not sufficient to keep in this unruly member.'[60] It was, of course, a time of wars, and of wars which were, or could be regarded as, wars of religion, with 'the proud race of Ottoman, now advancing his moony standards in Polonia'[61] and, more pertinently, with protestants being oppressed in the Palatinate, in France, and in the Low Countries, a time when puritan divines were agitated by the crown's flirtations with the Spanish-catholic bogey.

But the alertness to real wars on the continent, the experience of men like Bachiler and Scott who served as chaplains to the forces overseas, the relationship of ministers to the mock or trial wars of the Artillery garden were important, I would suggest, largely because these things enriched and made more strident a vocabulary of militancy that was, in any case, a part of puritan devotion, and had been so under Elizabeth. The wayfaring-warfaring theme in puritan literature has been described with great force, and delicacy, by Haller.[62] Man fared on his way toward God, and he needed God's armour to protect him from Satan's assaults and stratagems on his road. The difference between real war and allegorical war, the combat of the soul with sin, was clear, or should have been clear. 'In all our affayres of our outward warfare, Lord grant us grace especially to be zealous in our inward combate against sinne and wickedness,' ran part of the prayer[63] Harward wrote for seamen on active service. But already, in this prayer, there is what must have seemed to the ordinary man a confusing identity of terms between the nature of the inward and the outward battle.

In Downame's *The Christian Warfare* the emphasis is all the time on spiritual combat with spiritual weapons, but the language is so concrete that the image of real warfare is present with a modish insistence that runs the risk of occluding the image of spiritual warfare. The secular military literature was full of references to soldiers who found shotproof armour too heavy. Speaking of God's armour, Downame says that it is not enough 'that we put on one piece of the armour and, like young soldiers, leave off the next for ligh[t]nes sake.' Another secular theme was the difficulty of preventing troops from scattering in search of food or loot. 'We must keep us in God's armie and campe, the Church militant,' Downame wrote. 'For as those stragling souldiers who depart from the armie and range abroad to forraige or get some bootie are easily vanquished by their enemies, so those who depart and make an apostasie from God's Church ... are easily overthrowne, falling into Satan's ambushments.' He goes to unusual lengths to give his allegorical images a realistic cladding. Speaking of the girdle of virtue, he points out that 'the word here signifieth a broad studded belt used in wars in ancient times, wherewith the ioints of the breast-plate and that armor which defended the belly, loines and thighes were covered.' Practice was needed in the use of the sword of the spirit, for 'if a man have this two edged sword of God's word and have no skill to rule it, he will strike flat-long and not cut.'[64]

The divines were not unaware of the possibility of confusion. *A Spiritual Chaine* covers two themes: it urges upon the reader the legitimacy of fighting in just wars in thoroughly down-to-earth terms (there is a woodcut of an infantryman on the title-page),[65] and it encourages him to meditate on the purpose of his spiritual armour: Truth the girdle, Righteousness the breastplate, Peace the shoes, Faith the shield, Salvation the helmet, the Word the sword. Attempting to make the distinction clear between these themes, the author explains that:

> the heavenly armour of a soldier was in truth and substance before the earthly (howsoever for our weake capacitie the spiritual armour was afterwards made plaine to us by the corporall), so as according to a supernaturall sence, the bodily armour may be said to take dominion of the armour of the spirit, and the corporall combat dominion also of that spirituall combat which the children of God have with Satan and his children. For why? The armour of armours belonging to this combate (even the armour of God) was before any corporall combat could be used.[66]

This somewhat cloudy explanation was the more necessary for the turning away by puritan divines from the 'four senses' explanation of the significance of Holy Writ and their concentration at once on seeking a literal meaning and on writing and speaking in a style which was as graphic and immediate as possible. In urging warfaring wayfarers 'to repaire the breaches which Satan made, to fortifie their holds where they are weake, to trie their weapons in better manner'[67] the temptation of the style was to introduce contemporary military jargon, to keep abreast, as it were, of the news, and the consequence of the method was a playing up of the militancy of the Bible, because the battles recorded there lent themselves to literal interpretation, and a playing down of the 'pacifist' passages because they did not. Thus Gouge, faced by Isaiah's prophecy about swords being beaten into ploughshares and spears into pruning hooks – after a deluge of texts justifying war – comments: 'these and such-like propheticall phrases are somewhat hyperbolicall. They express that intire amity that should be betwixt true Christians and the alteration of their nature by the spirit of Grace ... to which purpose tend those other high transcendent hyperbolicall phrases of the prophet Isay.'[68] This is from a commentary on Exodus dedicated to the earl of Warwick because 'your lordship is known to be a man of warre,' written by the author of a work on spiritual warfare,[69] an author who justified torture in a case of 'requiting like for like: as the Israelites dealt with Adonibezek, whose thumbs and great toes they cut off, for so had he done to threescore and ten kings before' with the caution: 'what thou doest against thine enemies do in love. Love their persons though thou hate their practices.'[70] The borderline between inner and outward warfare was there, but it must have been increasingly difficult for puritan congregations to keep it in mind.

Alongside the 'orthodox' endorsement of war (typified towards the end of our period by Field) there was, then, a growing volume of puritan writing and preaching which not only justified war with increasing urgency, but which spoke of the soul's struggle against evil in terms which appeared to endorse the notion of fighting against the forces of Antichrist in real earnest. Against this background there is nothing surprising about a minister who, like Edmund Calamy, could urge parliament to bring in a Scottish army and (in the same year, 1643) publish a booklet justifying military service by describing the nature of the 'inner man that is a fit souldier to fight the Lord's battles.'[71] Nor is it surprising that parliamentary leaders should come to justify their militancy in terms not of a constitutional struggle but of a crusade.[72] And it has been the purpose of this essay to suggest that, if it was uncharacteristic that a generation of Englishmen fell to settling their differences by violence, a study of the theme of war in the age's only mass medium goes some way to reducing the element of surprise in the greatest anomaly in English history.

APPENDIX

SERMONS AND OTHER WORKS BY CLERICS LARGELY OR ENTIRELY DEVOTED TO JUSTIFYING WAR

1578 T[homas] W[hite]
A Sermon preached at Pawles Crosse on Sunday the ninth of December 1576
[1578] John Stockwood
A Sermon preached at Paules Crosse on Bartholmew day, being the 24. of August 1578
1588 John Prime
The Consolations of David, breefly applied to Queene Elizabeth, in a Sermon preached in Oxford the 17. of November (Oxford) 1588 E.R.

Two Fruitfull Exercises: a Christian Discourse upon the 16. and 17. verses of the 16. chapter of Judges ...
1588 Edmond Harris
A Sermon preached at Brocket Hall before the Right Worshipfull Sir John Brocket and other Gentlemen there assembled for the Trayning of Souldiers
1591 R[oger] H[acket]
A Sermon needful for these times ... Preached at Paules Crosse the 14. of Feb. 1590
1592 Simon Harward
The Solace for the Souldier and Saylour ...
[1598] Stephen Gosson
The Trumpet of Warre. A Sermon preached at Paules Crosse the seventh of Maie 1598
1617 Thomas Adams
The Souldiours Honour. Wherein by divers inferences and gradations it is evinced that the profession is iust, necessarie and honourable; to be practised of some men, praised of all men ... Preached to the worthy Companie of Gentlemen that exercise in the Artillerie Garden
1618 John Everarde
The Arriereban. A Sermon preached to the company of the Military Yarde, at St. Andrewes Church in Holborne on St. Iames his day last
1619 John Leech
The Trayne Souldier. A Sermon preached before the worthy Society of the Captaynes and Gentlemen that exercise Armes in the Artillery Garden, at Saint Andrew-Undershaft in London, April 20. 1619
1622 Samuel Buggs
Miles Mediterraneus. The Mid-land Souldier. A Sermon preached in the audience (and published at the request) of the worthie Company of Practizers in the Military Garden in the well governed City of Coventry
1622 Anon.
A Spiritual Chaine and Armour of choice for Sion Souldiers
1624 [Alexander Leighton]
Speculum belli sacri: or the lookingglasse of the holy war, wherein is discovered the evil of war, the good of war, the guide of war. In the last of these I give a scantling of the Christian tackticks, from the levying of the Souldier to the sounding of the Retrait ...
1624 [Thomas Scott]
The Belgick Souldier ... or, Warre was a Blessing [Dort]
1626 William Gouge

The Dignitie of Chivalrie; set forth in a Sermon preached before the Artillery Company of London, Iune xiij, 1626
1626 [Thomas Barnes]
Vox Belli, or an Alarum to Warre
1627 William Hampton
A Proclamation of Warre from the Lord of Hosts, or England's warning by Israel's ruin ... Delivered in a Sermon at Paul's Cross Iuly the 23. 1626
1628 T[heophilus] F[ield]
A Watch-Word, or the Allarme, or a good Take Heed. A Sermon preached at White-Hall in the open preaching place the last Lent before King Charles
1629 John Davenport
A Royall Edict for military Exercises, published in a Sermon preached to the Captaines and Gentlemen that exercise Armes in the Artillery Garden at their General Meeting
1629 Samuel Bachiler
The Campe Royall ... preached in the Army at the Leaguer
1629 Richard Bernard
The Bible-Battells, or the Sacred Art Military. For the rightly waging of Warre according to Holy Writ
1631 William Gouge
The Churches Conquest over the Sword: set out on Exod. Chap. XVII verse VIII &c. to the end
(This is the separate title-page of the last section of the three-part work, *Gods three Arrowes: Plague, Famine, Sword, in three Treatises,* to which a new edition of *The Dignitie of Chivalrie* is appended with continuous pagination.)

NOTES

* I am grateful to Mr Christopher Hill for reading the manuscript of this article. Arguments and inferences and any errors that may remain are, of course, my own responsibility.
1 Lindsay Boynton, *The Elizabethan Militia* (London 1967) and C.G. Cruickshank, *Elizabeth's Army* (2nd ed. London 1966) *passim*
2 'It is hardly possible to exaggerate the importance of the sermon in the seventeenth-century world.' D. Bush, *English Literature in the earlier Seventeenth Century* (Oxford 1945), p. 296. 'Surely the time has come for historians to turn their attention to the pulpits, which, as Macaulay said

long ago, were "to a large proportion of the population what the periodical press now is".' G. Davies, 'English political sermons (1600-1640),' *Huntington Library Quarterly* (Oct. 1939), p. 2. (The analogy today would be with television – and the inconclusive debate about the connection between violent programmes and violent behaviour warns us to caution when dealing with a period beyond the reach of sociological investigation.) Also, Christopher Hill, *Puritanism and Revolution* (London 1962), p. 269.

3 See appendix, pp. 511-2. As the purpose of this essay is no more than to raise an issue, I have not moved into the most crucial decade of all, 1631-41, which demands a far more thorough analysis than I can attempt here. When I wrote this essay I had not seen Michael Walzer's *The Revolution of the Saints* (Harvard 1965). He anticipates (pp. 277-8 and 290-1) two of the points developed in the following pages: the increasingly concrete nature of the imagery used in puritan sermons, which might have led to a blurring of the distinction between spiritual and physical warfare, and the suggestion that there can have been a connection between militant imagery and militant behaviour. I can only hope that my treatment of these themes appears in the guise of substantiation rather than of supererogation.

4 As in Adams, pp. 24-5. (Citation by author only is a reference to the works listed in the appendix.)

5 *Summa, q.* XL, *a.* II

6 *Ob Kriegsleute auch in seligem Stande sein können* (1526). H. Bender, 'The pacifism of the sixteenth-century Anabaptists,' *Mennonite Quarterly Review* XXX (1959), 7-8

7 Roland H. Bainton, *Christian Attitudes to War and Peace* (London 1961), p. 145

8 *Toxophilus* (1545), ed. E. Arber (London 1868), p. 70. (In quotations, original spelling is retained, but capitalization and punctuation is modernized.)

9 *The Defence of Militarie Profession* (London 1579), p. 62

10 *The Double-armed Man* (1625), f. B3^r

11 John Norden, *The Mirror of Honor* (1597), p. 48

12 *Ibid.*, p. 69

13 *Discourses of War and Single Combat*, f. A2^{r-v} and 1-2

14 John Denison, *Beati pacifici: The Blessednes of Peace-makers* (1620), p. 11

15 M.J.D. Cockle, *A Bibliography of English Military Books up to 1642* (London 1900). The supplements of T.M. Spaulding, *Proceedings of the Bibliographical Society of America* (1940), 186 ff., and J.R. Hale, *ibid.*, 137 ff., are but respectful flourishes on this admirable work.

16 For their importance, see M. Maclure, *The Paul's Cross Sermons, 1534-1642* (Toronto 1958)

17 *The Diary of John Manningham,* ed. J. Bruce, *Camden Society,* XCIX (1868) contains careful notes on sermons attended in 1602-3

18 This is a 'meagre allowance'; G. Davies. 'English political sermons,' 1. Meagre indeed; London clergymen commonly preached twice on Sundays

and on Wednesdays as well. Davies' figure is based on one sermon per parish per *year*.
19 A computerized theme-check of sermons, 1550-1642, would be of great value to the study of public opinion, especially if coupled with an analysis of the texts cited and of imagery.
20 Christopher Hill, *Society and Puritanism* (London 1964), p. 34
21 Henry Gee and W.J. Hardy, *Documents Illustrative of English Church History* (London 1896), pp. 516-17. According to Thomas Fuller, James was 'informed that it was high time to apply some cure to the pulpits, as sick of a sermon-surfeit' and that the effect of the articles was to 'cut off half the preaching in England ... at one blow.' *The Church History of Britain*, ed. James Nichols (London 1868), III, pp. 355, 358.
22 E.g., Richard Morison, *An Exhortation to styr all Englyshe Men to the Defence of theyr Contreye* (1538)
23 *Certayne Sermons appoynted by the Queenes Maiestie, to be declared and read, by all Parsons, Vicars and Curates, every Sunday and Holyday in theyr Churches* (1559)
24 Hill, *Society and Puritanism*, p. 35
25 This quotation, and the preceding facts are taken from Boynton, *The Elizabethan Militia*, p. 36, and *passim*.
26 As Davenport did with a prayer printed at the end of his sermon.
27 To avoid a surfeit of footnotes, references are not given in this section. All quotations are from works listed in the appendix, unless a new reference is made in the text.
28 J.W. Blench, *Preaching in England in the late Fifteenth and Sixteenth Centuries* (Oxford 1964), p. 170. Unless references are given, biographical information is from DNB.
29 Blench, *Preaching in England*, p. 169
30 W. Ringler, *Stephen Gosson: A Biographical and Critical Study* (Princeton 1942), *passim*. C.S. Lewis pointed out that 'in his sermon, *The Trumpet of Warre*, he quotes Aquinas and Cajetan.' *English Literature in the Sixteenth Century* (Oxford 1954), p. 395.
31 Bush, *English Literature in the earlier Seventeenth Century*, p. 398
32 Rufus M. Jones, *Spiritual Reformers in the Sixteenth and Seventeenth Centuries* (London 1914), pp. 207 ff.
33 Not so much on the evidence of *Miles Mediterraneus* as on that of another sermon, *Davids Strait. A sermon preached at Pauls-Cross July 8, 1621* (1622); e.g., p. 7, 'Indeed, in God's eternal predestination and election, no man ought to enquire; as why Iacob is loved and Esau hated, because the potter may doe with the clay as he listeth.'
34 Published posthumously, in 1655, three parts in one volume. On Hebrews 7: 1, Gouge comments: 'This giveth a plain proof both of the lawfulnesse of war and also of slaying enemies in war.' A similar point is made *à propos* 11: 33.
35 Valerie Pearl, *London and the Outbreak of the Puritan Revolution* (London 1961); see her index for Gouge and Davenport
36 W. Haller, *The Rise of Puritanism* (New York 1938), p. 68

37 To judge mainly from his *The Gales of Grace; or the Spiritual Wind: Wherein the Mysterie of Sanctification is opened and handled* (1622)
38 *The History of the Rebellion and Civil Wars in England, begun in the year 1641* (Oxford 1720), II, pt. i, 22-3
39 *Scrinia Reserata: a memorial offer'd to the great deservings of John Williams, D.D.* (1692), II, p. 139
40 Theodorus Verax [Clement Walker], *The Mysterie of the two Iuntos, Presbyterian and Independent* (1647), p. 3. My attention was directed to these three passages by E.W. Kirby, 'Sermons before the Commons, 1640-42,' *American Historical Review*, XLIV (1938-9), 528n.
41 *A Letter from Mercurius Civicus to Mercurius Rusticus* (1643), ed. Walter Scott, *Somers Tracts*, IV (1965), 583
42 E.g., Harward's 'Antichristian Catholics,' meaning Spaniards, *The Solace for the Souldier and Saylour*, f. C2^v
43 *A Letter*, 582
44 Pearl, *London and the Outbreak of the Puritan Revolution*, pp. 170-3
45 *A Spiritual Chaine*, f. A2^r
46 Scott, *The Belgick Souldier*, f. F2^r
47 Gouge, *The Dignitie of Chivalrie*, p. 19
48 *The Saints Losse and Lamentation* (1632)
49 P. 46
50 Davenport, *A Royall Edict*, pp. 14-15
51 For this reference, and a development of this theme, see Sir John Smythe, *Certain Discourses Military*, ed. J.R. Hale (Cornell 1964), pp. xlii ff.
52 *A Sermon preached at Paules Crosse on Bartholomew Day*; Blench, *Preaching in England*, p. 306
53 Davenport, *A Royall Edict*, p. 18
54 *Acts of the Privy Council*, 14 September 1622, p. 30
55 *A learned and very useful Commentary upon the whole Prophecy of Malachy*. This was published posthumously in 1642, in 2 parts, edited by Samuel Torshell. Stock died in 1626 (II, p. 49). The work was dedicated to (among others) Captain John Venn of the Artillery company.
56 *The Conflict between the Flesh and the Spirit. Or the last part of the Christian Warfare* (1618) f.2^v (the dedication to Francis Bacon)
57 *The Power of Preaching* (1623)
58 T. Broade, *A Christians Warre* (1613), p. 2. Referring to its publication, Broade said that his 'sermon ... is pressed forth to war, as thou seest. God grant it may stoutly fight the Lord's battles' (f. H5^v)
59 Leech, *The Trayne Souldier*, p. 41-2
60 Field, *A Watch-Word*, p. 20
61 Buggs, *Davids Strait*, p. 5. Dedicating *Vox Belli* to Sir Horatio Vere, Barnes says that he hopes 'what I have written may prevaile to provoke them whom it concernes to a readinesse to succour the distressed church in forreine parts.' And Scott, after running through a list of religious wars – Hus, Zizka, Luther, 'then stood Geneva on their guard, then Denmark, Norway, Sweden, England, Scotland' – asks 'if it be thus, was not warre a

blessing, and hath not religion beene propagated by that meanes?' (f. B2ᵛ – 3ʳ).
62 Haller, *The Rise of Puritanism*, in the chapter 'The Rhetoric of the Spirit'
63 Harward, *The Solace for the Souldier and Saylour*, f. G3ʳ
64 First printed 1604, I used the edition of 1612, pp. 47, 49, 51, 64
65 All the more down-to-earth for not being shown in allegorical company, as was the soldier on the 1634 title-page of Downame's *The Christian Warfare*
66 *A Spiritual Chaine*, pp. 4-5
67 William Jemmatt, *A Spirituall Trumpet exciting and preparing to the Christian Warfare* (1624), p. 195. The first edition is 1623. The work is dedicated 'To all the Lord's captains and souldiers.' Jemmatt, a puritan, was at that time 'preacher of God's word at Lechlade in Gloucestershire.'
68 *The Churches Conquest*, p. 211
69 *The Whole-Armour of God: or the Spirituall Furniture which God hath provided to keepe safe every Christian Souldier from all the Assaults of Satan* (1616)
70 Tonge, *The Churches Conquest*, p. 296
71 *The Souldiers Pocket Bible, containing the most (if not all) those places contained in Holy Scripture which doe shew the qualifications of his inner man that is a fit souldier to fight the Lords battels both before the fight, in the fight and after the fight*; see Harold Willoughby, *Soldiers' Bibles through three Centuries* (Chicago 1944), esp. pp. 3 ff.
72 R.H. Bainton, 'Congregationalism: from the Just War to the Crusade in the Puritan Revolution,' *Andover Newton Theological School Bulletin* (April 1943)

INDEX

Adams, Thomas 488, 496, 501, 503-4, 506, 512
Adriano, Alfonso 431, 466
Aelianus Tacticus 232, 261, 266-7, 438-9, 475
Agrippa, Camillo 434, 466
Alamanni, Luigi 365
Alberti, Leon Battista 7, 12, 20, 192, 379
Alciatus, Andreas 431, 434, 438, 462
Alessio, Giovanni (Nanni Unghero) 44, 46, 53-4, 58
Alexander VI, Pope 18
Alghisi, Galasso 218, 430-1, 434, 453, 467
Alnwick 67
Alviano, Bartolomeo d' 25, 100, 226
Ambleteuse 87, 90, 93
Ammirato, Scipione 201-2, 238, 362n.
Ancona 44
Antonio da Bergamo 88-9
Antonio da Castello 82-4, 164
Antwerp 82, 196
Arcano, Archangelo 74, 85, 88, 94
Ardres 79
Aretino, Pietro 226
Arezzo 23, 38, 58
Ariosto, Lodovico 397
Aristotle 193
Arles 80-1
Arnolfo di Cambio 7
Ascham, Roger 213, 235, 487
Assisi 27, 78
Attendolo, Dario 431, 465
Audley, Thomas 248, 261-4, 266-7, 269
Avezzano 16
Avignon, fortified camp near 81
Azzale, Baldassare 82

Bachiler, Samuel 493, 498, 505, 509, 513
Bacon, Sir Nicholas 237
Baglione, Astorre 288
Baif, Jean Antoine de 238
Ballino, Giulio 431, 456, 467
Bamborough 67
Bandinelli, Baccio 38
Barbaro, Daniele 435, 474, 480
Bari 24
Barkhede, Richard 248, 262
Barletta 24
Barnes, Thomas 493, 495, 497, 504, 513

Barret, Robert 426
Barrett, Henry 247 seq.
Barriffe, William 488
Barwick, Humphrey 424
Bayard (Pierre Terrail) 231
'Beato', engineer 104, 125
Becon, Thomas 335n.
Beddingfield, Thomas 235
Bellarmato, Girolamo 83
Belli, Pietrino 431, 433, 465
Bellona 220-1, 372, 373n.
Benedetto da Maiano 8
Benese, Richard 75
Bernard, Richard 494, 497, 499, 505, 513
Berwick 67, 70, 71n., 73, 80, 85, 92, 96
Billingsley, H. 219
Bingham, John 230
Biondo, Flavio 391
Biringuccio, Vanucci 6, 395, 399, 405, 412, 431, 454, 462
Bodin, Jean 199, 349, 352, 356
Boiardo, Matteo 364
Boncompagno, Jacopo 472-3
Bonhomo, Giovan Battista 182
Borgia, Cesare 7, 18, 21
Borgo San Sepolcro 23
Botallus, Leonardo 466
Botero, Giovanni 200, 349, 353-4
Boulogne 83-4, 87, 90
Bracciano 14-16
Bramante (Donato di Angelo) 23
Brancaccio, [?] Lelio 143, 145-6, 150
Brende, John 89
Brescia 305
Bresciano, Zenese 183
Broade, Thomas 508
Brolio 17
Broughty 93-4
Brownsea 69n.
Brucioli, Antonio 431, 436, 448, 461
Brunelleschi, Filippo 7
Buc, Sir George 231
Buggs, Samuel 501-2, 504, 512
Busca, Gabriello 454

Cagli 20
Calamy, Edmund 511
Calais 66, 69, 71-3, 75, 79, 93
Calshot 66-7, 71, 73

Camber 65, 67, 71n., 73-4, 77, 80
Canal, Cristoforo da 312, 321, 323, 327n., 440, 457-9
Canal, Marcantonio 104, 106, 109, 111, 114-5, 117-8, 123-4
Candido, Niccolò 103, 125, 146, 149-50
Caprarola 216
Carani, Lelio 438
Carey, Sir George 270
Carignano 81-2
Carlisle 67, 71, 74, 85
Carracciolo, Pasquale 431, 466
Cartari, Vincenzo 220n.
Castel S. Angelo 18
Castel d'Emilio 14
Castiglione, Baldassare 7, 212, 231, 245n., 375, 380
Castriotto, Jacopo 431, 453, 465
Cataneo, Girolamo 265, 489
Cataneo, Pietro 431, 452, 463
Cavendish, Richard 76, 88
Cellini, Benvenuto 7, 38, 372
Centorio, Ascanio de Hortensii 198, 431, 433, 441, 465
Certaldo 14
Cervantes, Miguel de 398
Cervia 9n.
Cesena 9n., 14
Charles V, Emperor 42, 52, 56-7, 63, 80
Chesnel, Jean 215, 240
Chieregato, Valerio 444, 476-7, 480-1
Christine de Pisan 280
Cicogna, Giovan Matteo 265, 431, 433, 435, 437, 466
Cipriani, Sebastian 149
Civitacastellana 18
Civitavecchia 9, 23, 25, 44
Clayton, Giles 270
Cleland, John 233-4, 239
Clement VII, Pope 9, 39, 41-2, 50, 53, 195
Colle Val d'Elsa 15
Colonna, Egidio 447, 461
Colonna, Stefano 81-2
Columbre, Agostino 431, 462
Coniano, Giovacchino da 266-7, 431, 465
Corfu 160
Corinaldo 13
Cornazano, Antonio 192, 391, 430-1, 433, 461
Corsini, Bertoldo 58
Cortona 78
Cosimo I, Duke 7, 17-18
Cotrone 27
Cotta, Fabio 439
Cowes 66-7, 72

Cromwell, Thomas 63-4, 66, 69, 73-4
Cyllenius, Domenicus 431, 433, 464

da Monte, Ludovico 288
Daniel, Samuel 398
da Porto, Luigi 100, 362, 374-5
Dartmouth 67, 77
Davenport, Rev. J. 394, 501-2, 504, 506-7, 513
Deal 65, 73, 75
De Conti, Ingolfo 299, 300
Dee, John 212, 214, 265
Dekker, Thomas 406, 410
della Rovere, Francesco Maria 101, 164, 177
della Valle, Battista 189, 260, 266, 372, 447, 461
del Monte, Cosimo 105, 143, 145-6
de Ville, Antoine 106, 114, 125, 140, 149-50, 219-20
Digges, Thomas 206, 214, 424
Dögen, Matthias 211, 221
Dolce, Lodovico 435, 439-40, 448
Domenichi, Lodovico 439-40
Dover 66, 69n., 77
Downame, John 508-9
Dunglass 93
Duodo, Pietro 290-1, 300
Dürer, Albrecht 78-9

Edmonds, Clement 174
Edward VI 91, 94
Erasmus 342, 345, 358
Erizzo, Francesco 103-11, 129 seq.
Este, Alfonso I, d' 25, 408
Este, Alvise d' 103
Este, Ercole I, d' 24
Euclid 214, 219, 300, 455
Everarde, John 500, 502, 504, 506, 512
Eyemouth 80, 93

Faenza 9n.
'Fagion, Ant. Sicilian' 74
Falmouth 67, 85
Fano 14
Farra, Alessandro 431, 464
Fausto da Longiano, Sebastiano 431, 433-4, 438, 463, 465
Feliciano da Lazesio, Francesco 213n.
Ferrara 24-6
Ferretti, Francesco 431, 466
Ferretti, Giulio 431, 465
Ferrosi, Francesco 439
Fiaschi, Cesare 451, 465
Field, Theophilus 504, 508, 511, 513

521

Filarete, Antonio 11-12, 20, 192, 216
Fiorentino, Antonio 25
Fiorenzuoli da Viterbo, Pierfrancesco 9
Florence 7, 24, 26-7; Fortezza da Basso 27, 31 *seq.*, 195; Citadella Vecchia 36-7, 44; S. Miniato (fortifications) 195
Flurance Rivault, David de 240
Foligno 13
Folkestone 66
Fontana, Giovanni Battista and Giulio 434
Fossano 82
Forli, 9n., 14
Forlimpopoli 14-15
Fourquevaux, Raymond de 59, 260, 447, 463
Francesco I, Duke of Savoy 81
Francesco di Giorgio 3, 8-9, 19, 192, 392, 395, 405
Francis I, King 80, 82-3
Frontinus 232

Galileo 215, 299-301, 427
Gap 81
Gariberto, Girolamo 431, 433-4, 437, 464
Garrard, William 270
Gates, Geoffrey 487
Gentili, Alberico 336, 347
Gentillet, Innocent 198, 353
Gilbert, Sir Humphrey 214, 227
Giocondo, Fra Giovanni 8-9, 24-5
Giolito, Gabriel 434-5, 439-42, 472, 480
Giovio, Paolo 361n., 362n., 400
Girolamo da Treviso 74, 88
Giuliano da Maiano 8
Giustiniani, Giovanni 123 *seq.*
Goldman, Nicholas 218
Gorgieri, Lauro 436
Gosson, Stephen 496-7, 503, 512
Gouge, William 458, 493, 500, 504, 506-7, 510, 512-3
Gower, Thomas 96
Grassi, Giacomo di 431, 467
Gravesend 65, 67
Grisone, Federigo 463
Gritti, Andrea 453
Grottaferrata 15
Grimsby 67
Guicciardini, Francesco 3, 6, 40-1, 197, 360, 377-8, 380, 395
Guicciardini, Luigi 39-41
Guines 66, 72-3, 76, 79, 86, 93

Hacket, Roger 491-2, 494, 503, 505, 512
Haddington 93
Hammes 66

Hampton, William 491, 493, 513
Hare, Robert 263
Harris, Edmond 491, 497, 512
Hartlepool 77
Harward, Simon 496, 503, 512
Harwich 66
Haschenperg, Stephen von 74, 76
Henry IV, King of France 239
Henry VIII, King of England 63 *seq.*
Henry, Prince of Wales 239
Hercules 218, 221
Hesse, Maurice of 238
Hollanda, Francesco de 7, 24, 61
Holy Island 85, 93
Hood, Thomas 243n.
Hull 71-3, 79
Hurst 66, 73, 79

Imola 9n., 14, 15
Ingolstadt 78

Johnson, Rowland 97
Jonson, Ben 395, 405
Julius II, Pope 6n.
Julius Caesar 471 *seq.*
Juno 221
Jupiter 221

Kelso 85, 88
Kingston upon Hull 67
Knyvet, Sir Anthony 90

Landrecy 71, 80
Langers Point 67
La Noue, François de 233, 238, 342, 354, 394
Lanteri, Giacomo 431, 433, 435, 452, 455, 464
Laparelli, Francesco 215
L'Aquila 29
Lauder 93
Lecce 27
Lee, Richard 72, 74, 85, 87, 89, 90, 94, 96
Leech, John 501, 504, 506, 508, 512
Leghorn 24, 38
Legnago 160, 167, 179
Le Havre 83
Leighton, Alexander 499, 504
Leonardi, Gian Giacomo 3, 435, 438-9, 474, 480
Leonardo da Vinci 7, 8, 11, 21, 363, 369, 405
Lido (Venice), fortifications 164, 172, 178
Livorno 24, 38
Lloyd, Lodowick 234, 488

Lorde, Robert 75
Lorenzo dalla Golpaia 49
Loreto 9, 25
Lorini, Bonaiuto 182n.,
Lorrain, Hanzelet 217
Lowestoft 67, 85
Lucca 7
Lynne 67

Machiavelli, Niccolò 3, 12, 78, 189 *seq.*, 247, 260n., 266, 351, 360-1, 381-7, 437-8, 447, 459, 462
Maggi, Girolamo 3, 266, 431, 433, 435, 438, 453, 456, 465
Maggius, Bartholomeus 466
Malacreda, Francesco 183, 301
Malatesta, A. Massari 289
Malthus, Francis 217
Marchese, Giovanni Giacomo 104, 121, 125, 128, 235
Marchesi da Settignano, Antonio 8
Marchi, Francesco de 17, 23-4, 36, 52, 60, 197-8
Mariani, Bernadino 103
Marini, Girolamo 82-3, 85, 87
Marozzo, Achille 463
Mars 217, 221, 370
Marseilles 80-1
Martinengo, Camillo 455
Martinengo, Giorgio 103, 105, 108, 117-8, 125, 455
Marzi, Angelo, Bishop of Assisi 48, 50, 55, 57
Massa, Antonio 464
Maximilian I, Emperor 71, 231, 400
Medici, Alessandro dei 32 *seq.*
Medici, Giovanni dei 226
Medici, Giulio dei 45
Medici, Lorenzo dei 17
Medici, Ottaviano dei 45
Melloni, Antonio 83
Memmo, Giovanni Maria 238, 431, 448, 465
Mercurialis, Hieronymus 431, 451, 466
Mercury 219
Michelangelo Buonarroti 7, 12, 23, 26-7, 36, 42, 195
Michele dei Leoni 25
Milan 196; Castello Sforzesco 22
Milton 65
Minerva 217, 219, 221
Mocenigo, Zuan 294-5
Moncalieri 81-2
Mondavio 20
Monluc, Blaise de 226, 233, 397, 401
Montaigne, Michel de 353, 357, 394

Montmorency, Anne de 80-2
Montefiascone 44
Montemellino, Francesco 431, 465
Montreuil 84
Mont. St. Michel 77
Mora, Domenico 431, 433, 466
More, Sir Thomas 343, 345, 350, 358
Morris, Sir Christopher 65
Morrison, Richard 66
Morro d'Alba 13
'Murmori', engineer 104
Mutoni, Niccolò 438
Muzio, Girolamo 431, 433-4, 436, 438, 449-50, 463-4

Nannini, Remigio 431, 437, 440, 442, 464
Naples 8, 14; Castel Nuovo 25
Nassau, John of 229, 232, 241
Neade, William 240, 487
Nepi 15
Nettuno 23
Nifo, Agostino 196-7
Norden, John 488
Nuti, Matteo 14

Offida 16
Orwell 67
Osima 16
Ostia 6n., 9, 16
Ostra 13

Pacioli, Luca 213
Padua 8, 24-5, 163, 167, 196, 228, 286 *seq.*
Palladio, Andrea 443, 471 *seq.*
Palma (Palmanova) 120, 185, 194, 196, 216
Palmer, Sir Thomas 88, 96
Pantera, Pantero 324-5, 457
Paruta, Paolo 202
Patrizi, Francesco 444, 472, 475, 480
Patten, Sir William 212, 233, 259, 267
Paul III, Pope 27
Paolantonio da Parma 55, 57-8
Pellezuoli, Donato Boni 82
Pendennis 67, 73, 95
Pesaro 7, 14, 25
Petit, Thomas 93-4
Pierfrancesco da Viterbo 45
Pigafetta, Filippo 44, 476
Pigna, Giovanni Battista 431, 463
Pinerolo 81-2
Pisa 7, 23
Pistoia 38
Pius IV, Pope 18
Plato 213

Pluvinel, Antoine de 235-6, 241
Plymouth 67, 85
Poggio Imperiale 17
Polyaenus 438
Polybius 83, 439-40, 471 *seq.*
Pontassieve 38
Pontefract 67
Pontelli, Baccio 9, 15-17
Porcacchi, Tomaso 440-2, 450
Porcia, Jacopo di 431, 434, 436-8, 461
Portinari, Giovanni 90, 96
Portland 67, 73, 95
Portsmouth 66-7, 77, 80, 90, 92, 94
Possevino, Giovanni Battista 431, 451, 463
Prato 46
Prime, John 498, 511
Priuli, Antonio 289, 290
Priuli, Michiel 105, 108-10, 128
Puteo, Paris de 449, 461

Queenborough 85

Rabelais, François 81, 216, 231, 405
Raffaello da Montelupo 58
Ramus, Petrus 213n.
Rangone, Guido 82
Ravenna 9n.
Recanati 9
Record, Robert 213n.
Revese, Ottavio Bruto 116, 127
Richelieu, Cardinal 241
Ridgeway, William 94, 96
Rimini 9n.
Ripa, Cesare 220n., 221
Robortello, Francesco 438, 444, 475, 480-1
Rocca, Bernardino 431, 433, 442, 466-7
Roccatagliata, Girolamo 111, 117-8
Rogers, John 72, 74, 79, 87-9, 96
Rohan, Henri, Duc de 142, 144-6
Rome, Bastione Ardeatino 61; Borgo 27
Rosetti, Giovanni di 89, 94
Rosetti, Biagio 24
Rossi, Ferrante dei 294
Rovigo 287-8
Ruffo, Giordano 431, 451, 461
Ruscelli, Girolamo 431, 433, 435-7, 466
Rusius, Laurentius 431, 462
Rye 85

Sabbioneta 216
Sagredo, Zaccaria 103, 111, 125, 128-9
St. Barbara 367, 402
Saint-Malo 77
St. Mary's (Scilly Isles) 95
St. Mawes 67, 73, 95

S. Arcangelo di Roma 13
S. Leo 20
Sandgate 66-7, 71n., 73-4, 79n.
Sandown 65, 73, 75, 80, 89
Sandsfoot 67, 95
San Gallo, Antonio da 8-9, 17-18, 24, 26, 36 *seq.*
San Gallo, Bastiano (Aristotile) da 45, 53
San Gallo, Giuliano da 8, 17-18, 23, 25, 207n.
Sanmicheli, Michele 3, 9, 25, 29, 101, 164, 173n., 182
Sansovino, Francesco 431, 456, 466-7
Sardi, Pietro 220
Sarti, Antonio 104, 125
Sarzana 8, 16
Sarzanello 19
Sassocorvaro 20
Savigliano 81-2
Savorgnan, Federico 293
Savorgnan, Giulio 185, 225
Savorgnan, Mario 438, 444, 457, 476, 480, 483
Scala, Gian Tomasso 88, 94
Scarborough 67
Sciaban, Baron Louis de 130, 133, 138-46
Scott, Thomas 494, 498, 504, 506, 509, 512
Scotto, Ferdinando, Count 103
Segar, Sir William 214
Senigallia 14-15, 25
Serlio, Sebastiano 83
Seyssel, Claude de 351
Shakespeare, William 406, 409-11, 421 *seq.*
Sharpenode 80, 90
Shute, John 251, 260n., 261
Siegen 229
Silver, George 236
Sisteron 81
Sixtus IV, Pope 6n.
Smythe, Sir John 232, 394, 423-5
Socinus, Mariano 431, 462
Somerset, Duke of (Edward Seymour) 92, 94-5
Soncino 438
Southampton 67
Southsea 80, 90
Speckle, Daniel 218
Spinola, Benedetto 105, 108, 111-5, 117
Spiritual Chaine, A 492, 494-5, 506, 510
Starkey, Thomas 237
Stevin, Simon 215
Stock, Richard 508
Stockwood, John 493, 503, 507, 511
Strozzi, Filippo 39, 41

Styward, Thomas 268
Suarez de Figueroa, Lorenzo 433
Susa 81
Susio, Giovanni Battista 431, 434-5, 450, 464
Sutcliffe, Matthew 488, 496, 503
Sydney, Sir Philip

Tàccola (Mariano di Jacopo) 4
Tarascon 81
Targone, Pompeo 104
Tartaglia, Niccolò 81, 217, 261, 405, 412, 431-2, 434-5, 454-5, 462
Tavannes, Jean de 239
Tensini, Francesco 99 seq., 221
Tilbury 65, 67
Tivoli 14
Tomaso da Venetia, Giovanni 436
Torbay 67
Toscanella, Oratio 443
Tournai 71, 75-6
Treviso 8, 24-5, 228, 286 seq.
Tribolo (Nicolò Pericoli) 58
Trissino, Giangiorgio 443, 475
Tron, Giacomo 289n., 290
Turin 81
Tynemouth 80, 85, 89

Udine 228, 286 seq.
Ulloa, Alfonso de 435
Unghero, Nanni v. Alessio, Giovanni
Upnor Castle 96
Urbino 25
Urrea, Ximenes de 431, 435, 466

Valle, Camillo 117-8
Valturio, Roberto 8, 192, 213, 369, 392, 405, 436, 538
Vasari, Giorgio 3, 7, 24, 32-3, 44, 55, 61

Vegetius, Renatus Publius 232, 236, 259, 263, 399, 405, 462
Venice, riding academy 307; military books 429 seq.
Vercelli 81
Verdala 216
Vergil, Polydore 391
Verona 25, 78, 167, 228, 286 seq.
Vettori, Francesco 40
Vicenza, fortifications 99 seq.
Villefranche-sur-Meuse 83, 87
Vitelli, Alessandro 40-1, 43, 45, 55, 57-8, 60
Vitelli, Paolo 400
Vitruvius 77, 435, 442, 473-4, 480
Vitry-le-François 83
Volterra 14-15
Vulcan 217

Wallop, Sir John 72, 84
Walmer 65, 73, 75
Wark 67, 85, 88-9
Wawan, William 89
Weymouth 67
White, Thomas 492-3, 503, 511
Whitehorn(e), Peter 247-8, 260-1, 267, 452
Williams, Sir Roger 226, 230
Wotton, Sir Henry 287
Wyatt, Sir Thomas 87

Yarmouth 67, 80, 85, 92
Yarmouth Castle (Isle of Wight) 91

Zabarella, Giulio, Conte 299, 304
Zanchi, Giovanni Battista 197-8, 431, 434, 452, 463
Zara 166
Zorzi, Alvise 143, 145-50